MANAGERIAL FINANCE

MANAGERIAL FINANCE

PRINCIPLES AND PRACTICE

STEVEN E. BOLTEN *University of Houston*

HOUGHTON MIFFLIN COMPANY BOSTON

Atlanta   Dallas   Geneva, Illinois   Hopewell, New Jersey
Palo Alto   London

Library of Congress Catalog Card Number: 75-31036
ISBN: 0-395-20462-3

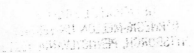

To Marjorie and Brian Andrew

Contents

Preface

MANAGERIAL FINANCE has been described as that blend of art and science through which firms make the important decisions of *what to invest in, how to finance it, and how to combine the two in order to maximize some appropriate objective*.[1]

"What to invest in" covers every item on the asset side of the balance sheet, from short-term cash to long-term capital projects lasting upwards of decades. In the aggregate, the resource allocation of the nation's private sector depends on these decisions, as does the operating integrity and success of the individual firm.

"How to finance that investment" covers every item on the liability side of the balance sheet, from short-term accounts payable to long-term equity capital with an infinite life expectancy. Again, in the aggregate, the nation's financial system depends on these decisions, as does the financial integrity of the individual firm.

"How to combine the investment and financing decisions in order to maximize some corporate objective" requires the individual's participation in many areas, from subjective soul-searching to defining a corporate identity and objective to communicating with stockholders, the public, and the governmental authorities; from daily supervision and control of the firm's operations to contemplation and implementation of large policy issues; and, finally, integrating the separate considerations and decisions into a unified whole.

The purpose of this text is to familiarize its readers with all basic organizational and functional aspects of financial management. The book was written primarily as a text but it is intended that people already involved in business as well as students will be able to benefit from it. Each financial function is identified and then discussed so that the reader moves through the organizational structure knowing where the function fits, how it interrelates with other functional areas, and what techniques to apply in order to perform appropriately when confronted with the tasks and problems of the function.

In Part One, the reader is introduced to managerial finance and prepared

[1] Solomon, Ezra, *The Theory of Financial Management* (New York: Columbia University Press, 1963), p. ix.

for the absorption of later material. Chapter 1 presents the concept of a firm and, particularly, the position, authority, and responsibility of the financial officer within the organization. It also introduces the reader to the various corporate operating philosophies. Chapter 2 describes the firm's operating environment, particularly its risks. Chapter 3 introduces the budgets, reports, and controls, emphasizing the internal, as opposed to the external, operating environment and giving the reader a comprehensive feel for the firm. Finally, Chapter 4 reviews the mathematics of finance, particularly compounding and present value. At the end of Part One, the reader has a comprehensive overview of the firm and the financial officer's position and is capable of seeing where the subsequent parts of the text fit. He or she is now in a position to see how the decisions on "what to invest in" and "how to finance the investments" can be combined into a package that will maximize the possible corporate objectives.

Part One provides a more comprehensive insight into the total environment in which the financial officer functions than most other texts. The intent is to demonstrate that financial decisions are not made in a vacuum, but are coordinated with other impacting considerations. The specific example of a disguised but actual nuclear power plant decision is used as a model for the general discussion, which shows the influence of the total operating environment on the financial decision. Part One also covers comprehensively the financial officer's use of budgets and accounting concepts. This is particularly valuable in the early years of a financial officer's career when he or she is first becoming directly familiar with the firm's operations. The internal control aspects as well as the external communications aspects are thoroughly covered so that the reader has the necessary background to supervise subordinates and report to superiors.

Part Two is devoted to capital budgeting. In Chapter 5 the reader is introduced to the decision criteria commonly found in capital budgeting. Chapter 6 expands the discussion of capital budgeting to include multiple project decisions, while Chapter 7 introduces risk into the decision-making process. The reader should now have a firm grasp on the specific procedures used in "what to invest in." Part Two devotes more discussion to the various applications of capital budgeting under different situations than most texts. The basic concepts are covered in depth, but the numerous situations in which those basic applications must be slightly adjusted are covered as well. This increased breadth of coverage allows the reader more opportunity to develop the skills needed in applying capital budgeting concepts in real-life situations.

Part Three introduces the reader to the cost of capital. Chapter 8 first acquaints the reader with the concept through both historical illustration and theoretical discussion. Chapter 9 explores the cost of capital for individual types of securities, while Chapter 10 discusses the overall cost of capital concepts and the capital structure. Chapter 11 discusses dividend policy. At the end of Part Three, the reader should have a firm grasp on "how to finance the investment."

Part Three gives the reader a clearer picture than any other text of how the financial officer should and does function in the financial markets. In this fund-raising capacity, the financial officer has to "read" the financial markets by being thoroughly familiar with their moods and potential changes. Part Three not only pinpoints what the reader should look for when assessing the financial markets and timing security offerings but also acquaints the reader with the historical lessons of past market fluctuations. The alert reader should grasp this opportunity to learn from experience before getting "burned" by an ill-timed or inappropriate security offering and should be able to avoid being whiplashed by market fluctuations. The reader also receives a more complete understanding of what makes the firm's security price fluctuate than in other texts. He or she can then recognize what factors are within the firm's control and can make a conscious effort to affect those factors in order to raise the firm's security prices and to neutralize, as much as possible, those factors beyond the firm's control.

Part Four discusses working capital management. Chapter 12 devotes itself to the management of cash and marketable securities, while Chapter 13 covers inventory management and Chapter 14 explores accounts receivable. At the end of Part Four the reader should have the knowledge to use each dollar of the firm's cash and liquid assets to its maximum profitability, trimming excesses and recognizing additional needs. The discussion of working capital management in Part Four is among the most complete of any basic finance text. The use of credit terms to promote sales must be constrained by the financial officer's analysis of the credit risks and collection policies. The financial officer's cash and inventory management functions are first discussed in basic, general terms, while the appendices demonstrate the more sophisticated models.

Part Five covers the short- and intermediate-term sources of funds, including trade credit, bank financing, and leasing. Part Six covers the long-term sources of funds, including their issuance, types of long-term debt, equity and quasi-equity instruments. At the end of Parts Five and Six the reader should know where to seek funds, not only what types of funds are appropriately needed, but also which lenders are most likely to provide those particular types of funds and how to negotiate the "best deal."

Part Five has a very useful discussion on how to deal with bankers, which is especially helpful to readers who intend to be small, independent business people and to readers who must negotiate their first loan on behalf of a firm. Knowing what the bank can and cannot reasonably do, how to talk the banker's language, and what supporting data to use in a loan application are very important lessons that should be learned before actually approaching loan negotiations. Part Six contains a highly current discussion of leasing.

Part Seven explores mergers and acquisitions, multinational financial management, and corporate failure and reorganization. The reader should be familiar with these topics, since they may be frequently encountered. Part Seven provides a ready basic reference to the major considerations. The ramifications of the international capital budgeting decision are more clearly covered than in other texts.

The text is designed for the basic managerial finance course where it is assumed the reader is heading for a middle or upper-middle management position of a relatively large corporation after a training period and a tenure in lower management. The text is self-contained and may be used in several different ways depending on the instructor's needs and constraints. Preliminary versions of the text have been used in one quarter and two quarter courses and in one semester courses by varying the use of the appendices included at the ends of certain chapters as well as at the end of the text. The longer courses generally use several of the appendices to gain a deeper insight into the topic under discussion. The shorter courses generally omit the appendices or assign them as outside reading.

The instructor may wish to vary the sequence of chapter assignments depending on the class level. The more basic, background material may be covered first by assigning Parts Four through Six prior to Parts Two and Three but after Part One. On the other hand, the instructor may choose to assign the chapters in a sequence similar to those in the text, covering the more analytical concepts of capital budgeting and cost of capital immediately after the background chapters in Part One.

I have also found that the basic courses at the University of Houston frequently have a substantial number of students with quantitative interests. I have had a very favorable response from these classes by assigning the more mathematically oriented appendices, such as Appendix 6A. However, there is no decrease in the course's effectiveness if these more quantitative approaches to the topics are omitted. If the readers have an active interest in the accounting aspects of finance, the instructor might assign the appendix at the end of Chapter 3.

Where a term paper is assigned, the appendices have often served as a springboard from which the learner can produce a better paper than he or she might otherwise have undertaken. The instructor may wish to coordinate term projects with the topics suggested in the Instructor's Manual. Frequently, the paper is presented to the class as a focal point for discussion of a more advanced topic. In that case, the instructor usually serves more as a guide than as discussion leader.

The use of the end-of-chapter problems and questions has been very effective in classroom instruction. The instructor may wish to assign problems and questions for discussion in class or may wish to use them as outside assignments, unannounced quizzes, or exams. The instructor may also want to use the exams provided in the Instructor's Manual.

The text is sufficiently flexible so that the instructor may progress sequentially through the chapters and be certain of covering the most important material within the limited time of the course or may assign the chapters and appendices to suit a particular course need. In either case, the instructor has the advantage of leading the learners through the material in a manner most conducive to his or her own style and thinking.

Throughout the text readers are asked to insert themselves into the role of the firm's financial officer. From this vantage point, they can then envision the entire panorama of the financial setting and the problems and considerations therein. All the material is tied together through the eyes of the financial officer. I have found that this approach works most successfully even when readers are not intending to concentrate in finance. They see the areas of concern most clearly and quickly develop a feel for the problems that the text brings to their attention and then shows how to handle through appropriate financial techniques, such as capital budgeting.

I wish to thank those who were so helpful during the writing of this text. Spearheaded by Professor Duane Kujawa of Georgia State University, the following have made this a much improved version of the material I provided them. My thanks are extended to: Professor Peter Bacon (Wright State University), Professor Glenn Henderson (Arizona State University), Professor Herbert Roth (Shippensburg State University), Professor William Scott (Memphis State University), Professor Robert Hutchins (San Diego State University), Professor Arthur A. Eubank, Jr. (University of Missouri at Columbia), Professor Philip Cooley (University of South Carolina), Professor Charles T. Rini (Cleveland State University), Professor David Springate (Southern Methodist University), Professor T. Gregory Morton (University of Connecticut), and Professor Stephen Claiborn (Wayne State University). Special thanks to Professor Robert "Charlie" Conn (Florida State University) for his efforts in the preparation of the end-of-chapter questions and problems and the Instructor's Manual.

I owe deep gratitude to Catherine Parker for her untiring efforts to meet my ridiculously short deadlines. This text would never have been completed without her support. My wife, Marjorie, aided in many ways, directly with the manuscript and otherwise. All her efforts are very much appreciated.

STEVEN E. BOLTEN

ONE

ORGANIZATIONS AND the FINANCIAL OFFICER

LET US LOOK AT SOME OF THE MAJOR QUESTIONS about finance that might be in your mind at the moment. When you read Part One, look for the answers to these questions:

1. What type of organization might I be working for?
2. How did it come into existence, who owns it, and for whom will I be working?
3. Can I form my own business?
4. Where would I fit in the organizational structure as a financial officer?
5. What are the typical goals of the organization, and are they compatible with my own?
6. What will be my duties and responsibilities if I become a financial officer?
7. What are the major considerations that I will face when representing my firm in its attempt to raise capital for its investment programs?
8. What do outside investors consider before committing their funds to a firm?
9. How do I go about advising my superiors of the best time to raise funds?
10. What are the typical operating risks I must consider before giving my advice?
11. How do I plan and control the use of the firm's funds?
12. How do I report my plans to my superiors and the results to outside investors?
13. How do I insure that I remain in control of the financial situation?

1
the CONCEpt of the firm

WHAT EXACTLY IS A FIRM? Webster's dictionary defines a firm as "the name, title, or style under which a company transacts business."[1] Yet, to the student of business, a firm is really much more than just a name, title, or even style. It is an independent entity consisting of one or more people capable of entering into legal arrangements that enable them to carry out all business functions from the initial purchase of raw materials and machinery to the manufacture of the product and its distribution and sale to the consumer. Obviously, in its larger sizes a firm is a rather complex organization with many internal relationships among the people who manage it and many external relationships between it and its suppliers, customers, and competitors.

The professional corporate manager must coordinate the efforts of those involved in the firm's profit-generating activities. To do this, the manager needs a carefully constructed plan from which he or she can supervise and control. Since we are dealing strictly with profit-oriented companies, the manager's plans and controls are always expressed in terms of money profits. All phases of the organization from production to marketing must be considered in light of their contribution to the whole and must be integrated into the profit plans of the entire firm. The manager must draw on the ideas of the operating officers concerning the profit picture in each area, taking only what is appropriate to the entire firm's profit picture and communicating the final, integrated plans to each of the operating officers for them to carry out. Finally, the corporate manager must see to it that the plans are implemented as intended. In general terms, then, we may say the corporate manager must plan, communicate, and control.

To formulate the profit plan, the manager turns to the company's financial officers, for it is they who must raise the funds for the projects proposed by the other departments. They also have the tools to analyze and select the most promising investments from the large number proposed, many of which are overly ambitious or ill-conceived. The major emphasis of the plan will be on what projects to invest in from among those available so that the firm can maximize its progress toward the corporate profit objective chosen during the planning period. In other words, the profit plan must tell the firm *what to invest in* and *how to finance those investments* in order *to maximize its corporate profit objective.* These are the general functions that comprise the financial officer's job.

[1] Webster's New Collegiate Dictionary.

2

Actually, these three phases of the financial officer's job simultaneously describe a firm itself. A firm faces the same tasks and decisions: what to invest in and how to finance its investments in order to maximize some corporate profit objective. We find that the financial officer is in many ways the embodiment of the entire firm, not just one section or operation. As a consequence he or she must view the firm as a whole and be able to integrate all its operations. To accomplish this job, the financial officer needs analytical tools which you will learn as we progress.

We now have a concept of the *firm*. It is a *legal entity* with an *organizational form* whose officers decide *what to invest in* and *how to finance those investments* in order to *maximize some corporate profit objective*. We will explore each of the major parts of this concept in more detail to give you a better idea of what you might face when you enter a business firm. First, we will examine some different legal structures that a firm may assume. Then we will discuss some of the organizational forms under which a firm may choose to operate. We will look at the possible goals a firm may select. Since the finance function is so heavily involved in profit planning, we will discuss the financial officer's position and duties as they relate to profit planning and control.

As a student using this finance text, you are required to put yourself in the position of the firm's financial officer, even if you are not majoring in finance. By playing the role of a financial officer, you can respond to the questions that will be posed throughout the text. Read each question as if you had to come up with the answer. Then see what financial techniques discussed in the text can be applied to answer the question effectively. You might even think of yourself as the senior financial officer. You are called upon to supervise first one area of the finance function and then another, directing assistants who are responsible for each area and have come to you, as head of the department, for guidance. They raise the question: How do I handle this problem? You have to answer it. The many areas of finance will fall into place as you see the diverse responsibilities that you, as financial officer, encounter.

TYPES OF ORGANIZATION—LEGAL IMPLICATIONS

What type of organization might I be working for as a student in finance? How did it come into existence, who owns it, and for whom am I working? Can I form my own business? Table 1-1 reveals that the proprietorship, the partnership, and the corporation are the three most common legal structures that a firm may assume.

Proprietorship

Requiring no formal procedures or notification for organization or entry, the *proprietorship* is the simplest form of legal enterprise. The very act of opening for business constitutes establishment of a proprietorship. Sole ownership and responsibility lie with the owner.

Proprietorships are commonly found among smaller businesses where the owner is directly involved in the daily operations of the firm, such as the corner grocery, candy store, or family-owned retail shop. Although the owners do not have to be involved at all if they choose to delegate the operating authority to others, they do remain personally responsible for all the actions of the firm. Even if operating under the title of Company (Professor Bolten and Company, Purveyors of Knowledge), the owners still remain responsible for the debts and actions of the firm. In

Table 1-1 Proprietorships, Partnerships, and Corporations—Number, Receipts, and Net Profit, by Industry and Size of Business Receipts: 1970

Number in thousands; money figures in millions of dollars.

Item	Proprietorships[1]			Active partnerships			Active corporations		
	Under $50,000[2]	$50,000–$99,999	$100,000 or more	Under $100,000[2]	$100,000–$499,999	$500,000 or more	Under $500,000	$500,000–$999,999	$1,000,000 or more
All industrial divisions:[3]									
Number	8,253	661	486	746	162	27	1,359	141	165
Business receipts	79,559	46,278	111,889	16,648	33,286	41,840	148,157	99,066	1,458,892
Net profit[4]	16,029	8,655	8,531	1,245	5,164	3,382	1,608	2,215	63,079
Agri., forestry, fisheries:									
Number	2,929	106	44	109	14	2	33	2	2
Business receipts	24,320	7,191	10,308	2,392	2,578	2,305	3,156	1,428	9,008
Mining:									
Number	45	2	3	13	1	(Z)	12	1	1
Business receipts	324	166	957	117	225	843	141	915	14,643
Construction:									
Number	588	54	43	39	10	2	106	16	17
Business receipts	6,336	3,847	9,916	1,232	1,932	4,439	15,158	11,526	62,261
Manufacturing:									
Number	151	17	16	20	7	2	128	28	42
Business receipts	1,681	1,165	3,856	604	1,433	3,170	19,618	19,687	660,785
Trans., comm., electric, gas, sanitary services:									
Number	272	14	10	14	2	(Z)	57	5	6
Business receipts	3,120	943	2,434	378	504	553	6,575	3,176	121,712

4

Wholesale and retail trade:								
Number	1,405	286	301	121	68	12	373	67	78
Business receipts	19,016	20,379	72,122	4,531	14,214	16,175	60,535	47,178	403,603
Finance, ins., real estate:								
Number	536	19	10	295	21	4	385	9	12
Business receipts[5]	4,499	1,313	2,533	3,922	4,462	6,781	18,241	6,533	152,546
Services:								
Number	2,287	162	58	132	39	5	261	13	8
Business receipts	20,033	11,193	9,644	3,396	7,871	7,523	23,650	8,594	34,216

Z Less than 500. [1] Individually owned business and firms. [2] Includes businesses without receipts. [3] Includes business not allocable to individual industries. [4] Less loss. [5] For partnerships and corporations, total receipts rather than business receipts were used as the size classifier.

SOURCE: U.S. Internal Revenue Service, *Statistics of Income, 1970, Business Income Tax Returns* as reported in *Statistical Abstract, 1973.*

fact, personal liability is unlimited: except in a few states with such specific exemptions as protection of the owners' homes, all personal assets may be confiscated to satisfy the debts of the firm. Of course, unless some profit-sharing arrangement with the managers exists, all the profits of the firm also belong to the owners.

Proprietorships are usually financed through the owner's personal savings, reinvestment of the firm's profits, and to a lesser extent government loans. These firms never issue shares or securities of any kind in their own name since they are no more than an extension of the owner's personal activities. It is to the owner that any loans are made, not to the firm.

The income of the proprietorship is included in the owner's personal income for tax purposes. The firm's income or loss is treated just like any other earned income, and it is taxed as such at the personal income tax rates under the personal income tax regulations. The self-employed also enjoy certain tax advantages such as the Keogh Plan, which entitle them to set aside annually 15 percent of their income up to a maximum of $7,500 tax-free for a retirement fund.

The proprietorship must, of course, comply with the regulations laid down by governments for the conduct of any business. These include compliance with local zoning ordinances, health codes, licensing provisions, labor and safety laws, and social security regulations, where applicable. However, it is not uncommon to find that these regulations specifically exclude very small firms on the grounds that they would overburden the owners and discourage free enterprise among small and new businesses.

The proprietorship does have disadvantages when the owner dies. The firm becomes part of the proprietor's estate and is subject to estate and inheritance taxes. In addition, the value of the proprietorship may be hard to assess for estate purposes and create difficulties for the family in settling the estate tax. Technically, the firm as such ceases to exist at the death of the owner until the heirs take control. This may disrupt operations of the firm, particularly if the heirs squabble among themselves, frustrating a smooth transition of ownership.

Partnership

A *partnership* is a legal association between two or more people, as co-owners, to carry on a business for profit. Unlike the proprietorship, the partnership is organized through somewhat more formal procedures, which usually involve a negotiated, contractual arrangement among the partners. However, a partnership may be legally recognized without a written agreement when the conduct of the firm and of one partner to another implies a partnership arrangement. (A simple letterhead listing the partners, for example, is evidence of implied partnership.) Most states have enacted the Uniform Partnership Act, under which partnership agreements can be filed with the secretary of that state and so be legally recognized. Law firms and accounting firms are typically organized as partnerships.

Since a partnership is a negotiated arrangement among the partners, its terms may vary greatly. However, there are several common types of partnerships that we should discuss. In the *general partnership* each partner is a general agent for the firm and may enter into any contractual obligation on its behalf. Further, each general partner is personally liable for the debts incurred in the firm's name by any other partner. (Since personal assets as well as the firm's assets may be attached and sold to satisfy the firm's debts, even if incurred by another partner, one should choose partners very carefully.)

The *limited partnership* represents a mixture of general partners with full and unlimited liability and limited partners whose liability is limited by contractual arrangement with the general partners. Usually the investment of the limited partner is also limited to a specific amount by the partnership agreement. A limited partnership agreement is often used to facilitate financing by silent partners who will not participate in the management of the firm but who are providing capital in expectation of a return on their money. The limited partnership arrangement is often used for the syndication of real estate ventures. Specific pieces of property are bought as a joint venture among the investors who have purchased limited partnerships from the syndicator, who is the general partner and the manager of the syndication and the property. The Empire State Building, at one time the tallest in the world, was syndicated under a limited partnership agreement.

The limited or general partnership is not taxed as a firm, but instead the firm's income or loss is divided among the partners according to the pro rata share they have contracted to receive, and then their personal income is taxed. If there are ten general partners all sharing equally, each would add 10 percent of the firm's income to his own taxable income. Then, the personal tax rate would apply just as in a proprietorship. The advantage of this tax status is that the firm's income is taxed only once at the personal tax rate, not both as the firm's income at the corporate tax rate and then as personal income when it is distributed to the individual owners. Of course, the pro rata share of the firm's loss may also be taken directly off against any other personal income the partner may have. If the firm's loss for tax purposes is more a bookkeeping loss than a real one, the tax savings for a partner in the high personal income tax brackets may be substantial. Sometimes partnerships are formed for just such purposes.

Partnerships, like proprietorships, must comply with applicable government regulations for the conduct of any business. Like the proprietorship, the partnership dissolves upon the death of one partner and must be reorganized. This can greatly hinder the continuity of the firm's operation, particularly if the heirs contest the evaluation put on the deceased partner's portion of the firm. This could interrupt the legal continuity of the firm for a considerable period. Further, the heirs of the deceased must be bought out. This requires the other partners or the firm to raise capital, which may put a financial burden on them. To avoid these problems, financial arrangements are frequently made prior to the death of any partner so that the transition will be smooth.

Corporation

The vast majority of the dollar volume of business in the United States today is carried on by firms that have selected the *corporation* as their legal form. Unlike the proprietorship and the partnership, which maintain a simultaneous legal identity with the owners, the corporation becomes a legal entity all its own with various rights and duties, such as the ability to enter into contractual obligations, and with the capacity of succession in its own name.

While the laws that govern the organization of a corporation vary from state to state, the same general procedures are usually followed. The organizers, who must number at least two or more, prepare a corporate charter (see Appendix 1-B for a sample charter), which they submit with a fee to the secretary of the state. The secretary checks to see that the charter contains all the necessary provisions and descriptions required by law and then certifies that the charter has been granted and that the firm is registered with the state as a corporation.

The charter contains such provisions as the nature of the firm's intended operations. In most cases the organizers have worded the charter so broadly that there is little the firm is not capable of doing within its charter. However, there are cases in which the organizers may intentionally limit the corporation's powers to specific areas or functions. For example, a firm that has been formed for the purpose of acquiring and liquidating the assets of another firm may be restricted to that one function by its charter. Legally, then, it can do nothing outside of the powers granted to it by the charter. If the managers of the firm act in the name of the firm to do something outside the powers granted in the charter, they may be personally liable for damages under the doctrine of *ultra vires,* operating outside the granted powers.

The charter must also provide information on the organizers such as their names, addresses, and positions in the firm. The interim board of directors who technically represent the shareholders of the firm during organization must be named, as well as the address of the firm and of the registered agent of the firm, so the state can reach him if necessary. The name of the corporation must also appear on the charter and not be confusingly similar to any other corporate name in the state. The procedures for electing the board of directors are frequently spelled out.

Capitalization of the firm must also be specified; that is, the number of shares the firm is authorized to issue and the number of shares that will be issued when the state grants the charter. The two do not have to be equal, but the number actually issued cannot exceed the authorized number. If in the future the firm decides to increase the number of shares issued to more than the number authorized, it must amend the charter by a vote of the shareholders and file the amendment with the secretary of the state. Further, the charter must specify the value of the shares to be issued, so that the total initial amount of investment in the firm is known, as some states have a minimum capital requirement.

Perhaps the most attractive and distinguishing feature of the corporate form is that it relieves the owners of personal liability for the contractual obligations incurred by the firm. In other words, the individual owner's assets cannot be attached by the courts and sold to satisfy the debts of the corporation. There are some rare exceptions such that the shareholders, as owners, can sue the managers and directors if they are negligent in their duties or perform *ultra vires,* outside the powers granted to them by the charter. In addition, there are infrequent cases where the initial capital specified in the charter is not provided. In those cases the shareholders may be asked to put up the remainder of the specified initial capital to satisfy the claims of the firm's creditors. However, for almost all purposes the personal liability of the owners is very limited; they are hardly ever forced to pay off the debts of the corporation, even if it goes out of business owing money.

The corporate form facilitates financing through the creation of readily transferable, standardized certificates of ownership known as shares, which may be sold to anyone. This ease of transfer and sale to the general public allows the corporation to tap vast reservoirs of capital on a regular and relatively simple basis. In addition, the corporate form facilitates the sale of different types of securities: the share represents ownership in the firm and the bond represents a loan to the firm. This ability to tailor the type of security to the needs of the investor makes fund raising easier. The fact that standardized shares are freely transferable usually means that a value can be readily established for them by their sale. This makes it much easier to establish a value for estate purposes.

Limited personal liability makes the corporation very attractive to persons who have capital to invest but are not interested in actively managing the firm. Since the most a shareholder can lose is the cost of the shares, risk is greatly reduced, and he or she is more willing to extend financing to the firm. This encourages capital investment and industry expansion.

Another by-product of the corporate form is that the firm's employees may be spurred to higher performance by the lure of stock ownership as part of their compensation. Employees may be granted a stock option which entitles them to purchase the firm's shares at an attractive price relative to the market price of the shares which may prevail at some future date. This vested interest may encourage loyalty and spur employees on to greater efficiency because they want the stock price to rise.

The corporate form does suffer from double federal—and sometimes state and local—income taxation. Not only does the firm pay taxes on its own income at the corporate tax rate, which in 1975 was 22 percent of the first $50,000 of income and 48 percent on all income over $50,000, but the individual shareholder must also pay income taxes at the personal income tax rate on all the dividends (that portion of the firm's income that is distributed to the shareholders) received.[2] Also, the corporation usually pays an annual state franchise tax in the state in which it is incorporated or in those states in which it conducts business.[3]

For regulatory purposes the corporation is treated just like a person. It must comply with all the prevailing laws and directives of governments. It can sue and also be sued, just as an individual can. The corporation has a life of its own and provides a continuity that is not found elsewhere. Owners and employees may leave, but the firm continues as a legal entity with no interruption of legal powers or responsibilities. We might say the corporation has an infinite life expectancy. This has led to the concept of the "on-going" firm, on which many accounting and security-evaluation principles are based. As a perpetuity, the corporation must have long-range financial policies as well as provide for daily operations. Acquired assets have life expectancies in excess of those who decide to buy them. Accounting records are kept in accordance with this principle of perpetuity.[4]

ORGANIZATIONAL STRUCTURES

Organization Charts

Where do I fit in the organizational structure as a financial officer? The organization chart in Figure 1-1 is typical of many firms.

Looking at its organization chart, we can see how one firm, Browning-Ferris Industries, Inc., is structured. Each functional area of responsibility is designated by a box bearing the name of the department, which is usually indicative of its function. In the case of Browning-Ferris, the box also includes the name of the individual re-

[2] The first $100 of dividends received by each person filing with the Internal Revenue Service is tax exempt. The dividends received by a "subchapter S corporation" are also entitled to the $100 exemption when declared on the income tax filings of the stockholders.
[3] See Appendix 2A for a further discussion of the tax environment.
[4] There are still other forms of the firm, including the business trust and the joint stock company. The trust is basically a device that places the title of the firm's property in the hands of a self-perpetuating board of trustees, who manage the firm for the holders of beneficial interest. The joint stock company is a combination of a corporation and a partnership. The stockholders' interests are represented by freely transferable stock certificates, but the stockholders' liability is unlimited as in a partnership. The property of the firm is usually held in trust by the board of directors. Neither of these two types of firms is common today.

Figure 1-1 Organization Chart of Browning-Ferris Industries, Inc. as of July 24, 1972

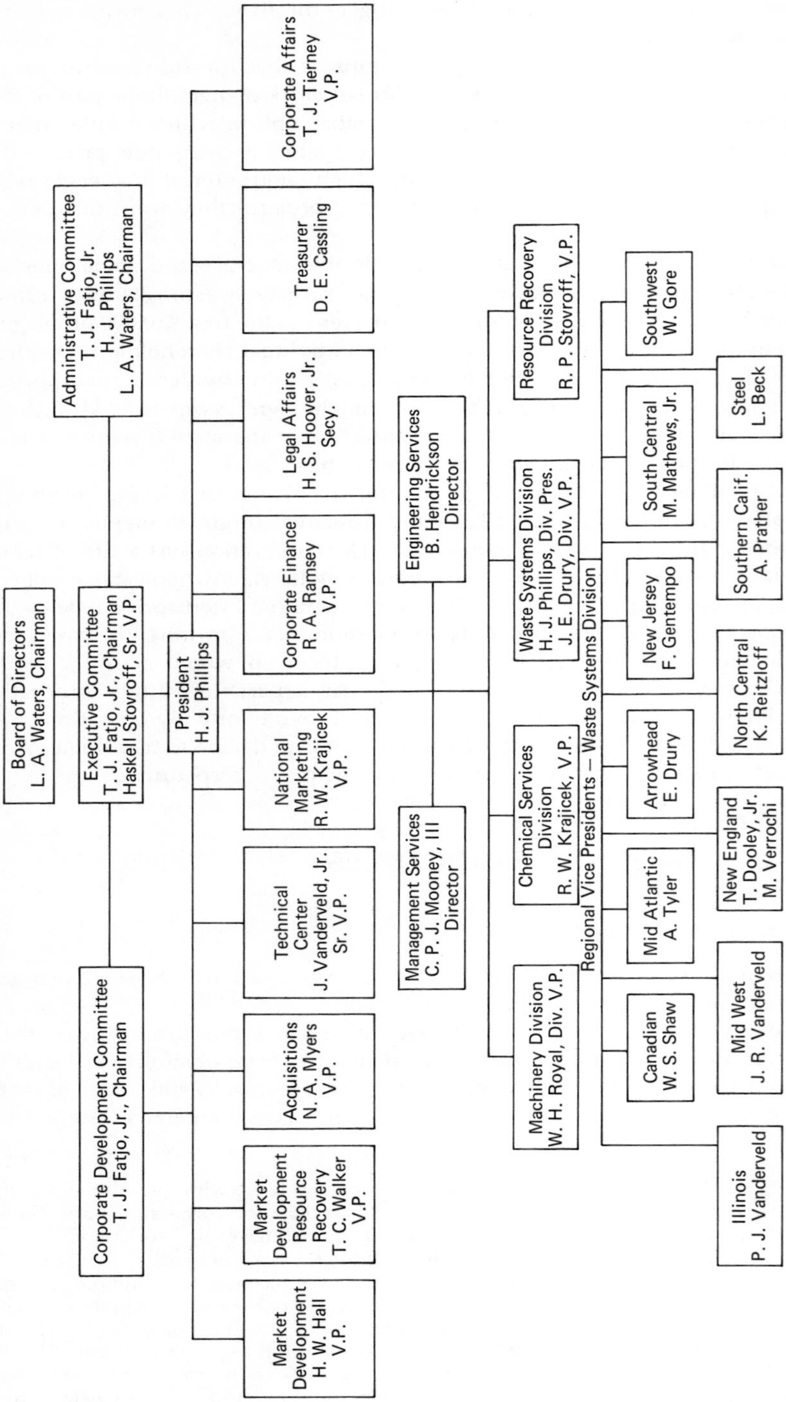

sponsible for the area and the job title. Each functional area is attached to a line that reveals who reports to whom, from the subordinate to the superior. For example, R. A. Ramsey is in charge of the corporation finance area, and reports directly to the administrative committee and to the president. As is typical, the various functions are grouped into areas of similar interests and assigned to a coordinator or coordinating committee. In this case the administrative committee is the coordinator for the financial, legal, treasury, and corporate affairs group of functions. As with all organization charts, the authority and the responsibility flow upward, the ultimate responsibility for the firm's daily operations resting with the president and the executive committee, and the ultimate responsibility to the owners, i.e., the stockholders, resting with the board of directors. In general, then, we can see from an organization chart the various functional areas of responsibility into which the firm is divided, who is responsible for each area, and the communication channels among the areas.

The Browning-Ferris organization chart reveals that the firm is divided into three basic groups: the corporate headquarters staff, the supervisory committees, and the operating services and divisions.

Corporate headquarters staff   The corporate headquarters staff consists of the president, the administrative committee with the associated group of functions that report to it, and the corporate development committee with its associated group of functions. From the nature of the functions assigned to it, the corporate development group appears to be oriented to penetration of new markets and expansion of old markets for the firm's services as well as to development of new products and services. The administrative group appears to be concerned with the firm's finances and external relationships.

As a financial officer you would probably be on the staff of R. A. Ramsey, vice-president in charge of corporation finance, so let us examine the organization of this staff. Figure 1-2 is a representative chart of what the staff of the vice-president in charge of corporate finance might look like. Reporting directly to this office would be the firm's economist, financial analyst, chief of the cash management division,

Figure 1-2 Organization Chart of the Corporate Finance Staff

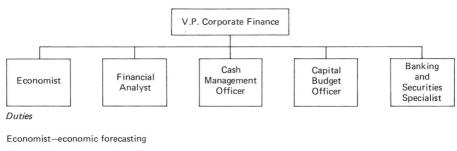

Duties

Economist—economic forecasting

Financial Analyst—internal audits

Cash Management Officer—cash inflow and outflow coordination, safe keeping of funds and securities

Capital Budget Officer—long-term investment project evaluation and implementation

Banking and Securities Specialist—arrangement of loans, credit, leases, and security sales chief of the capital budgeting division, and the banking and securities specialist. Of course, no two corporate finance staffs are organized exactly alike, so you can expect to find different titles and duties within your own corporate finance department. However, let us look at the duties the typical corporate finance staff may be required to perform.

The *economist* is concerned with economic forecasting and is responsible for communicating expectations on the future economic environment to the vice-president. The vice-president in turn channels that information to other staff members for use in their own calculations. If the economist forecasts a recession and highly restricted availability of funds during the next planning period, the other members of the staff should base their plans and actions accordingly.

As internal auditor for the firm, it is the job of the *financial analyst* to examine and analyze the performance of the firm's operating divisions and to report findings to the corporate staff so they can maintain control of the operations.

The *cash management* section coordinates the inflow and outflow of funds through its administration of the firm's cash budget. It usually has the safekeeping function of supervising the firm's temporary investments in liquid assets and of keeping careful track of their whereabouts.

The *capital budgeting* section is responsible for evaluation of the long-term investment projects proposed by others in the firm. Frequently this section is also responsible for overseeing the implementation of those projects that are accepted.

The *banking and securities specialist* is charged with maintaining a good working relationship with the firm's bankers and investment bankers (those who sell the company's securities to the public). This staff member is called upon to negotiate bank loans, establish lines of credit (sources of funds from banks), arrange the leasing of equipment, and supervise the flotation of new stock and bond issues.

It is important to recognize that these jobs are not necessarily as separate as Figure 1-2 might imply. Particularly in smaller firms, you may perform several of the jobs at the same or different times, depending on need. You must be prepared to handle all of these jobs and more, either by yourself or in conjunction with other members of the corporate finance staff or even the higher officers. For example, you could be the firm's banking and securities specialist, but when it came time to negotiate a big bank loan, you very likely would be working in conjunction with the president and the chairman of the board of directors.

Not surprisingly, the functions of the corporate finance staff cover the three considerations that figure in the firm's profit plan and very well capture the essence of the firm, itself. What to invest in is evaluated and implemented by the cash management section for short-term investments and by the capital budgeting section for long-term investment projects. How to finance those investments is coordinated through the banking and securities specialist with the economist's advice on financial market conditions. The final report, which should synthesize both the investment evaluation and the financing plan, is supervised and prepared by the vice-president of corporate finance for presentation to the president and the board of directors. While not particularly concerned with daily operations or the initiation of new ventures or products, the corporate finance department is in its way the very heart of the firm, taking in fresh ideas, evaluating them, and then sending the better ones out for implementation.

Supervisory committees The second major basic organizational group at Browning-Ferris is its supervisory committees, which it uses to coordinate the functional areas. The corporate development committee directs the forward thrust of the firm in such areas as marketing, acquisition of other firms, and new product development. The executive committee is responsible for the continuing control and guidance of the existing operations. The administrative committee is charged with coordinating the firm's financial planning, financial control, and legal services, as well as preparing the capital budget.[5]

One interesting feature of this particular organization is the attempt to integrate management from each area through an interchange of ideas and progress reports and a sharing of the control responsibility. The presence of T. J. Fatjo, Jr. on all three supervisory committees and in direct contact with the president promotes integration among the headquarters staff. Of course, should there be a breakdown or confusion in the communication channels, the whole corporate staff might be misled. Hopefully, the exchange among the firm's chief officers would prevent this from happening and also allow effective direction of all the firm's functions toward a common corporate goal.

Operating services and divisions The actual daily operations of producing and selling the product or performing the services that generate the firm's revenue are the responsibility of the chief operating officer, in this case the president, in conjunction with the executive committee. It is this officer's job to see, for example, that the waste systems division, which collects and disposes of garbage, does its job every day of the week. The same responsibility applies to the other operating units of the firm, down to the last garbage truck operating in the New Jersey region.

Lines of Communication

It may be helpful at this point to make a distinction between the *line* and the *staff* designation commonly given to different groups. Line functions are those involved in the daily operations of producing and distributing the product or service. They are so named because on the organization chart their channel of communication is a vertical line rising up through various supervisory levels to the chief operating officer. In Figure 1-1, the line functions all report directly to the president. The staff functions, on the other hand, may be recognized by the horizontal line of communication between them and the chief operating officer or committee. In Figure 1-1, the administrative group and the corporate development group are staff functions diagrammed to either side of the chief operating officer and reporting on horizontal lines of communication. The *line functions* carry out the orders of the chief operating officer, while the *staff functions* advise the chief operating officer.

As the staff and line functions indicate, most reporting is in an upward direction, with shared information at the president and executive committee levels, which in turn flows upward to the board of directors (the stockholders' representatives).

Communication is by no means exclusively upward. Guidance and control flow down the channels. For example, if the report from the New Jersey operation was off the targeted goal, the president's office would investigate to identify the problem and lend guidance in solving it. Suspicious of one area operation, the president might dispatch a financial analyst from the corporate finance department to audit the operating results of that area. As a result, the regional vice-president might be replaced. In addition to communicating control, the chief officers use the channels to inform everyone which projects they have approved for implementation in the

---

[5] *Waste Management,* July-August, 1972, 6.

regional vice-president's area, perhaps including instructions for their implementation.

In summary, budget information flows both up and down the channels. Project initiation and operating data flow up and are coordinated and shaped into corporate policy, which is communicated back down to the junior operating officers for implementation. Ideally there should be a constant flow of information and exchange of ideas, giving maximum exposure to any problem.

Decentralized versus Centralized Management

The degree of your authority and responsibility as a financial officer depends on the extent to which the chief operating officers centralize the decision-making power in their own offices. The degree of centralization frequently depends on the firm's management structure, on the attitude of the chief operating officers, and on the size of the firm.

Centralized authority in a large firm means that the junior officers, such as yourself, are employed more as advisors than as decision-makers. In fact, it is quite common among larger corporations to have a finance committee consisting of one member of the board of directors, the president of the firm, and the vice-president in charge of financial planning. In that case you might be called in from your position in the corporate finance department to give technical advice in your particular area of expertise. You would be a resource person to the finance committee, advising them, for example, on the environments for raising capital within the securities markets or from banks. In the larger company the chances are that you will be more specialized and more frequently consulted as a technical advisor.

Smaller firms, many with family-oriented management, tend to be centralized. Since they usually operate within a confined geographical region and are concerned with one product line, these firms are relatively easy to control from one central point. Furthermore, in smaller companies, the finance function is often handled by the treasurer or controller rather than a designated financial specialist. Generally, the controller will coordinate all the budgets and spending authorities—including a capital budgeting committee, which selects the firm's long-term investment projects.

Figure 1-3 Organization Chart of Controller Office with the Finance Function

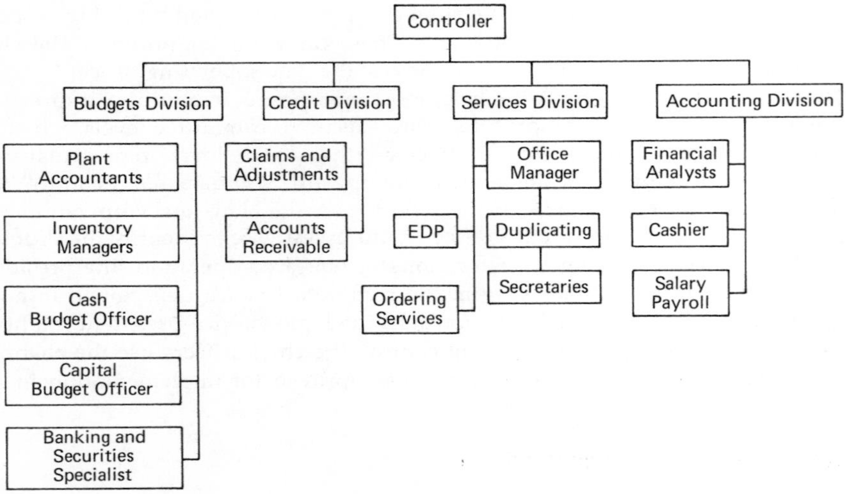

If the controller does administer the finance function, an organization chart of this area may be similar to Figure 1-3.

The decentralized firm tends to delegate to junior officers the authority to make decisions and implement them. Frequently, a firm's wide geographical interests or diverse product lines make it impossible for one person to handle all the decisions. In those instances, you would probably have the authority to enter into contractual agreements on behalf of the firm up to a specific dollar amount without prior authorization from the chief operating officers. Emphasis at the top level is more on control than on supervision, allowing the younger officers more decision-making power and more opportunity to demonstrate their managerial abilities. In the case of Browning-Ferris, Inc., the regional vice-president is relatively decentralized from the headquarters staff and acts independently when handling field operation problems. The chief operating officers control the situation by comparing the actual performance with the expected performance that was planned, budgeted, and communicated earlier.

CORPORATE GOALS

Will I be in tune with the management philosophy under which I will have to work? What are the typical goals of the organization and are they compatible with mine? If I work for a small business or for a nonprofit institution, must I also be aware of corporate goals and of business financial management? The answer is clearly "yes." The small business is a miniature large business; it has the same problems and many of the same objectives. By mastering the general procedures and techniques contained in the text, you can apply them to the small business. The small business person also has to know what to invest in, how to finance it, and how to attain the best combination of both. The same problems also face the nonprofit institution. It, too, must know how to raise funds and invest them so as to maximize the benefits for its invested dollar. The nonprofit institution must think of its service as a product that has a cost to provide and that generates benefits. The objective is to provide the most benefits for the least cost—the identical problem for the profit-making corporation or small business. The concepts and techniques are the same; the differences are in the measurement of those benefits.

Corporate goals are the pre-requisites that determine the firm's priorities, policies, and procedures.[6] The firm formulates its investment and financing decisions in terms of the corporate goals; they define its general direction and its specific strategies. Sometimes the goals are derived through collective soul-searching. Sometimes the goals are derived by one or a few individuals who force them on the firm. Of course, goals may differ greatly among firms. It is obvious that the nonprofit institution has a considerably different goal from the profit-oriented firm. But even within the profit sector, goals may differ.

Regardless of how they are derived or what they are, corporate goals serve as a point of reference for the planner and a device to coordinate the efforts of all involved. Without established goals, a firm tends to wander without direction, going first one way and then another. The corporate planners, such as the financial officers, must have a specific goal in mind as they plan. As long as the goal establishes and communicates where the energies of the firm should be directed, the efforts of all personnel can be coordinated. The goal does not have to be elaborate.

[6] Herbert G. Hicks, *The Management of Organizations: A Systems and Human Resources Approach*, 2d ed., McGraw-Hill, New York, 1972, p. 60.

It can be a relatively general target, such as a certain share of the market, making the *Fortune* 500, or an annual growth rate in earnings per share.

Corporate goals are usually targets against which the firm's operating performance can be measured. They depend on management's philosophy, attitudes, focus, and purpose, and we can categorize them into four major groups for our discussion: shareholder wealth maximization, profit maximization, behavioral objectives, and managerial utility maximization.

Shareholder Wealth Maximization

When operating under a *shareholder wealth maximization* objective, management has to coordinate its profit plan so that stockholders receive the highest combination of dividends (payments from the firm's income) and increase in share value or price for any given period. In order words, a shareholder's proportional ownership of the firm should be as valuable as possible.

To satisfy its commitments to its shareholders, the firm must allocate its resources efficiently in order to show a good return on its investments within the appropriate constraints of risk. If the firm wastes money foolishly on overly risky investments or fails to take advantage of profitable opportunities, the stockholders will sell the stock, thus depressing its price. If the firm chooses the wrong type of financing or overburdens the firm with debt, the stockholders will also sell out, even if the debt was used to finance profitable investments. Notice that this corporate goal directly affects the policy decisions of what to invest in and how to finance the investments. When this goal is in force, the objectives of the stockholders and management are compatible.

Notice also that the stockholder wealth maximization objective is highly compatible with the concept of the perpetual life of the firm. Since the present price of the stock reflects the future benefits to which stockholders are entitled because of their proportional ownership in the firm, management's decisions cannot emphasize short-term profits at the expense of the longer-term health of the firm.

Financial theorists favor the wealth maximization objective because it serves as a focal point for all the considerations in operating the firm and it is an easily observed measure. Theoretically, if the firm is not making the right investment or financial decisions, the stock price will sink. If it is making the right decisions, its stock price will rise.

There are problems with implementing this objective as a measure of performance. Foremost is the fact that share price is subject to outside influences beyond management's control. A slump in the economy could depress stock prices, yet management has no control over the economy in general. Daily fluctuations in stock prices sometimes draw too much attention from management and distract them, to the detriment of the firm's profit plan. Management may feel frustrated and disillusioned if the stock price performance does not seem to reflect what they consider to be a good effort. While it is a useful goal, shareholder wealth maximization may be something more to strive for than to achieve.

Profit Maximization

The maximization of total profits has been frequently considered an alternative goal to shareholder wealth maximization. The corporate goal in *profit maximization* is to increase dollar earnings to as large an amount as possible, usually in as short a time as possible.[7]

There are, however, several problems with using profit maximization as the exclusive corporate goal. First, profit maximization ignores the risk constraints, letting management undertake all profitable investments regardless of the associated risk which they might bring to the firm. For example, opening a copper mine in a politically unstable country that is threatening to expropriate your investment without compensation would add considerable risk to the firm's operations. It may not be worth that risk, despite its potential profitability. Second, management would ignore the risks associated with the financing of the investment. As long as the investment was profitable, management might borrow to excess, overburdening the firm, just to add another few dollars to the profit total. In terms of the shareholder wealth model, this would defeat the firm's purpose because stockholders would sell their shares and depress the stock price. On the other hand, management's improper use of too little debt, forcing the firm to sell many additional shares to finance the next dollar of total profit, would dilute the present stockholders' proportional wealth, not a desirable part of any corporate objective.

The profit maximization objective also tends to aggravate the existing separation between the shareholders and management. Since management is not relating its decisions to any measure of stockholder benefit, its investment and financing policies tend to become more self-centered and fail to satisfy the firm's commitment to its owners. This objective also tends to emphasize the short run, sometimes at the expense of the longer-run welfare of the firm. Management may undertake highly profitable short-run investments despite a slim chance of profitable reinvestment at their termination, while failing to take advantage of longer-term investments that may be less immediately—but more consistently—profitable.

Let us agree that profits are a necessary condition for the success of any firm, but that profits are only one ingredient in the total picture when formulating a corporate objective. Profit maximization, therefore, emphasizes only a partial condition for success. Shareholder wealth maximization is a total picture, although it is difficult to interpret because of its complexity.

A variant of the profit maximization objective is maximization of the percentage return on investment. Under this corporate objective, the firm attempts to employ its funds such that each dollar invested yields the most dollar profit. Management would undertake all those investment opportunities that had a percentage return in

---

[7] Paul A. Samuelson, *Economics*, 9th ed., McGraw-Hill, New York, 1973, Ch. 25. We have learned from economic theory that the firm maximizes its profits where its marginal cost (the cost attached to the next additional unit of production) equals its marginal revenue (the revenue generated from the next additional unit of sales). As long as the marginal unit generates more than it costs, the firm's total profits will rise. In the figure, the shaded area represents the firm's profits. The largest shaded area occurs when the marginal cost line crosses the marginal revenue line.

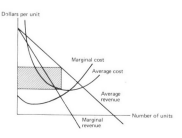

excess of the percentage cost of the financing. Return maximization suffers from the same drawbacks as profit maximization.

Behavioral Objectives

Contrasting with maximizing profit or shareholder wealth is a category of goals which are not oriented to maximizing any single objective whatsoever. This category emphasizes the reasonable level of achievement that suffices to satisfy stockholders and management alike. Management operating under this objective looks for the middle course that pacifies everyone but does not maximize anyone's position. Management theorists have called this type of operating goal *satisficing*. It gives stockholders a sufficient profit performance within a reasonable amount of risk, so that the stock price is not unduly depressed nor is management threatened with a loss of their jobs for unsatisfactory performance.

Satisficing is justified as the only operational corporate goal that can be used by management without exerting undue strain upon the organization and its ability to work as a cohesive team. As an operational device, satisficing tends to resolve the conflicts among the operating goals. This is particularly true of the conflicts among the internal goals of the firm. For example, the marketing department may want to increase sales at the expense of return on investment. A satisfactory compromise could restore harmony between the exponents of each objective, although it would sacrifice maximizing either one. Further justification is that satisficing is the best we can expect from managers who must make decisions within the constraints of risk. They cannot maximize in the face of uncertainty because the penalties for failure, such as being fired, are severe, whereas the penalty for a mediocre job is practically nonexistent. In fact, chief operating officers have frequently received salary increases in years in which the firm's performance was only mediocre.

The major problem with satisficing is that it partially ignores risk, return on investment, profit, dilution of earnings per share, correct financing, proper resource allocation, and the rest of the considerations associated with the maximization goals. Further, it is vulnerable to competing firms that do maximize when they enter the industry. For this reason, satisficing is more common among entrenched companies in industries where entry is difficult.

Satisficing firms tend to have vaguely stated corporate goals which emphasize the status quo and do not really serve as a focal point for all the considerations that should go into deciding what to invest in and how to finance it. Frequently the goals are expressed in terms of a market share, making the *Fortune* 500 list, or some other measure of size, rather than profitability, for it is important to a satisficing manager that there be no signs of deterioration in the firm's position of importance. Deterioration of importance means loss of prestige and increased vulnerability to attack. Provided there is a modicum of forward progress and no deterioration relative to other firms within the industry, inertia works in the satisficing manager's favor. Satisficing does not allow guidance from the stockholders; once their minimum requirements are pacified, they are forgotten. As a consequence, the stock price of the firm may suffer if stockholders find alternative shares that maximize their position.

A variant of this behavioral objective is to maximize revenues instead of profits or shareholder wealth.[8] Provided there is no deterioration below a satisfactory level of profits, managers frequently stress sales maximization as an appropriate goal. They

---

[8] William J. Baumol, *Business Behavior, Value, and Growth*, Macmillan, New York, 1959.

find it easier to relate to total revenues as an operating objective and to control the sales effort than other operating goals. However, sales maximization also suffers from the same problems as do the other behavioral goals.

Managerial Goals

A fourth major category of corporate goals applies when managers try to maximize their own welfare and benefits. These managers base their decisions on what would give them the largest salaries and expense accounts. Frequently, as in the case of revenue maximization, this means maximizing size so that there is slack in the operations above that which satisfies the stockholders, and which can then be drained off for the benefit of the managers themselves.

This can be done because stockholders usually exercise little control over the election of the managers. The shareholders suffer because much of what they should be receiving is drained off. The allocation of the firm's resources is also inefficient because the larger, perhaps less attractive, investments tend to have the most slack and are, therefore, frequently chosen over the more attractive, if smaller, projects.

This goal is hardly ever expressed publicly by management, but it may always be lurking in the back of their decisions. Like satisficing, it partially ignores risk, return on investment, dilution of earnings per share, and correct financing in its attempt to maximize the manager's own welfare.

Conflicts Among the Goals

Regardless of which goal a firm adopts, there will be conflicts that must be resolved. Internal operating target objectives often conflict with the objectives of the firm as a corporate entity. For example, the marketing department's attempt to maximize sales may conflict with the corporate goal of maximizing shareholder wealth. Conflict often occurs because management lives with the internal operating goals and develops a myopia that prevents them from seeing the larger general goals.

It is easy for management to feel that they are not being sufficiently rewarded, so they adopt managerial goals as their guiding objective. Management may feel that profit or sales revenue is all they can control, so they adopt a profit or revenue maximizing objective, letting the stock price fluctuate where it may on the assumption that there is a proportional and stable relationship between profits and stock prices. Sometimes management is forced to adopt less than maximizing postures because of external pressures brought to bear on the firm by government antitrust policies or other controls. Thus, large, very efficient firms may be frustrated from maximizing shareholder wealth by forces beyond their control.

There are also conflicts among the general corporate goals themselves which must be resolved. If management chooses to satisfice, maximize profits, or enlarge their own welfare, they cannot maximize shareholder wealth. Shareholder wealth maximization then becomes more of a normative goal towards which firms should, but do not always, strive. As a financial officer you must be prepared to encounter all the major types of general corporate goals and variations thereof. You will probably live with some internal operating targets as your objectives when you first enter the firm, but as you rise in the organization, the corporate entity goal, or what is best from an overall corporate viewpoint, becomes more important.

Today's corporation is usually run by a management group separate from the owners. Consequently, conflicting viewpoints arise concerning ownership versus control and the social responsibility of the corporation.

Ownership versus control When the stockholder is an absentee owner, the hired managers tend to become alienated from the objectives of the owners and begin to feel that they are the corporate entity and that the firm is theirs to run as they see fit. This situation obviously leads to conflicts in the goals of the firm, unless management adopts a shareholder wealth maximization objective. Further, the lines of authority and ultimate responsibility become blurred. Theoretically, the owners are ultimately responsible for the deeds of the firm, but they appear to have less and less influence on the firm's policies and actions as they become more dispersed and further removed from direct contact with the management.

This gap may interfere with the stockholders' willingness to provide additional capital. It also leaves disgruntled stockholders with little recourse except to sell their stock, which does not change the problem within the firm and may not satisfy the stockholder. The ramifications of this separation have led to the creation of stockholder relationship departments, as strange as it sounds, to let the owners know what their firm is doing and to the development of stock options and share ownership for the officers to make them feel part of the ownership objectives. As financial officer, you must bridge the gap between owner and manager if you attempt to maximize shareholder wealth.

Corporate social responsibility There is also a conflict between the corporation as an entity in society and as a device for maximizing shareholder wealth. The traditional view maintains that the corporation's sole responsibility is to maximize the stockholders' welfare, because the firm will then achieve the most efficient allocation of resources for society as a whole. The argument assumes in its more complete form that certain resources, such as air and water, are held in common ownership by all citizens and that society should therefore bear the cost of these resources when the firm uses them. In turn, the company contributes to the general welfare by producing goods and services in the most efficient manner. Corporations continue to expect that the state will provide roads and educate the labor force. They may expect the state to absorb such costs as the retraining of workers who have been displaced by the corporation's installation of laborsaving devices. They may expect help in controlling industrial pollution.

The opposing view sees the corporation as a grant or trust from the state designed to be a relatively efficient way of increasing productivity. As such, it has duties to fulfill to its employees, suppliers, consumers, stockholders, and the general public. Like any individual, it must be a good citizen. It must not dirty the air or foul the streams, and it must not injure the position of any of its constituencies. It must be forced to take on this social responsibility since the competitive system of free enterprise no longer forces corporations to adsorb the cost, but allows them to pass such expenses on to the society through oligopoly (a few firms who control their industry) and monopoly pricing.[9] In addition, it is sometimes argued that the corporation owes a debt to society and should bear the cost of some of the external resources it enjoys, such as the roads and the education of its employees.

Exactly how far the corporation's social responsibility should go is debatable.[10] It could range anywhere from self-regulation designed to avoid injuring the position of any of its constituencies to the championing of political and moral causes. It has

[9] James McGuigan and R. Charles Moyer, *Managerial Economics: Private and Public Sector Decision Analysis*, Dryden Press, Hinsdale, Ill., 1975, Ch. 20.

[10] John G. Simon, Charles W. Powers, and Jon P. Gunneman, *The Ethical Investor*, Yale University Press, New Haven, 1972, p. 26; and Gilbert Burch, "The Hazards of Corporate Responsibility," *Fortune*, June 1973, 114ff.

been suggested[11] that there exists at least a "moral minimum," which implies that the corporation must at least avoid consciously creating moral and social injury. Perhaps this includes taking affirmative action to correct that which is already present, but it certainly excludes the formulation and perpetration of any new social injury. Corporate social responsibility can also include refusing to cooperate with the government when its requests conflict with "moral righteousness" and making reforms within the corporation that alleviate social injury to one of the corporation's constituencies.

Regardless of what the corporation finally decides is its social responsibility, there will be a conflict among the goals. Any action which the corporation takes to alleviate social injury will cost the firm, for it will now bear the cost that society formerly bore for what the firm formerly used as a free resource. This cost conflicts with profit maximization, shareholder wealth maximization, managerial welfare maximization, *and* satisficing objectives. Yet, as a financial officer you will have to weigh social responsibility in your investment and financing decisions, if nowhere else but in deciding whether to buy pollution-control equipment or to participate in government programs. To the other major categories of possible corporate objectives, we now have to add social responsibility. You must be prepared to cope with any one or combination of objectives.

THE FINANCIAL OFFICER'S POSITION AND DUTIES

Now that I know what a firm is and what goals it may have, what will be my duties and responsibilities if I become a financial officer? Do they appeal to me as a career?

Titles

As we have seen, you will encounter a wide variation in the titles by which financial officers are known, depending on the way the firm is organized, its size, and the attitude of its management. The title and duties of even the chief financial officer vary somewhat. Frequently, the position is titled vice-president in charge of corporate finance, as in Browning-Ferris. Financial officers may also combine other duties and be titled treasurer or controller, implying not only responsibility for financing the firm but also the responsibilities of collecting and disbursing the firm's cash. The position is frequently associated with membership on the finance committee, sometimes as chairperson. Sometimes it is also synonymous with the chair of the capital budgeting committee or membership on that committee. But, whatever the title, the financial officer's duties are similar in all firms.

Functions

He or she is charged with determining what to invest in, how to finance these investments, and how to combine the first two functions to maximize the corporate goals or objectives.

What to invest in As financial officer, you will be in charge of coordinating, formulating, finalizing, and supervising the firm's profit plan, which indicates what real

[11] Ibid., p. 18.

assets (pieces of productive machinery, plants, and property) and what financial assets (the shares of other firms or the temporary holding of the liquid debt securities of others) the firm will acquire.

The real assets are handled by the capital budget officer. In this capacity, your functions would include gathering information and ideas on proposed projects into a standardized form that allows comparison among all the proposed projects so that the most profitable can be selected. These proposals might include such varied investments as the establishment of a new distribution system, the building of an overseas factory, the introduction of new products, and investment in research and development. Whatever the proposed investment, it is up to you to see that each proposal is properly evaluated so that unprofitable projects are not selected and the most profitable are.

The cash management officer manages the firm's cash assets, including investments in liquid, marketable securities in which temporarily idle cash balances are put to work earning interest for the firm. In this capacity, you will have to forecast the firm's cash flows so that you are never caught short of cash but are also never losing interest because the firm's cash is idle. Other financial asset acquisitions that you will have to evaluate are the shares of potential merger candidates. Specifically, what price should the firm pay to acquire another firm.

How to finance investments Once you have selected the projects for investment, you must raise the capital necessary to finance their implementation. Specifically, you must decide what proportion of these funds should be raised by reinvesting the profits of the firm and what proportion by raising capital from the public in the financial markets. This requires a careful analysis of the sources and techniques available so that the least expensive source may be tapped. You will have to decide what type of security you want to sell and by which of various methods you want to sell it. You might not even choose to sell a security; you might decide to borrow from a bank instead. All of this means that you must be in constant, close touch with the financial market.

You must also consider the important implications your financing has on the financial risk of the firm. Too much debt could seriously jeopardize the existence of the firm if it were to experience a temporary cash shortage and be unable to repay borrowings when due. You want to avoid financially embarrassing your firm. You are responsible not only for selecting the assets, but also for deciding what should be the firm's liabilities, its obligations, in other words, to its creditors and owners.

How to maximize the corporate goal The investment selection process must be coordinated with the raising of capital, for it does no good to have capital that cannot be profitably invested or to discover profitable investments that cannot be undertaken because of a lack of funds. Furthermore, investments must contribute to corporate goals, and as we have seen, several conflicts can arise in the process of maximizing—and reconciling—these objectives. Among the more common conflicts are those which involve: (1) profitability and control of the firm, (2) profitability and the riskiness of the investments, (3) differences in corporate goals among the persons involved, (4) profitability and social responsibility and (5) the difficulty of integrating all the conflicts into one effective analysis.

The conflict between profitability and control may arise when there exists an overabundance of profitable projects, all of which are very attractive but only a few of which may be financed. Resorting to outside financing so that all the projects may be undertaken has frequently entailed turning over control of certain aspects of the management, if not all the management, to the lender or new stockholders. It is not uncommon among the smaller firms to find lenders demanding majority or controlling stock ownership in return for the loan.[12]

There is always a conflict between the profitability of an investment and the risk it brings into the firm. As financial officer, you would have to weigh your stockholders' desire in the matter and try to determine how much risk they want you to take on their behalf. This, of course, is not easy to judge, but generally you can sense that certain firms attract stockholders who are more adverse to risk than others. Every proposed investment will involve a certain amount of risk. Generally, the return increases as the risk increases. If you were foolish enough to ignore the risk entirely in an effort to simply maximize profit, you might jeopardize the entire firm. We can think again of that fabulously rich vein of copper in a politically unstable country, which is threatening to expropriate your investment without compensation. To maximize the firm's objectives, then, you have to weigh return against risk in relation to the stockholders' aversion to risk.

The profitability-versus-risk conflict also arises in financing. Borrowing just to finance profitable projects without consideration for the firm's liquidity needs or solvency may impose a great financial risk. The financing of profitable projects has to be weighed against jeopardizing the ability of the firm to repay its lenders and provide a satisfactory per-share return to its stockholders. Inappropriate and excessive financing can lead, in the extreme, to the firm's going out of business. In less extreme cases it could lead to a lower than satisfactory dividend expectation by the stockholders and depress the price of the firm's stock below what it could have been.

There is also a fundamental conflict among the various parties involved as to what the appropriate goal is. The stockholders naturally want their stock to appreciate in value as well as pay high dividends, not necessarily compatible objectives. The management, who are probably separated from the stockholders, desire higher salaries, and the employees desire bigger wages and better working conditions and benefits. Again, the goals of these groups are not necessarily compatible; yet they must be welded into a workable corporate objective.

The corporation's profit objectives and its social responsibility may also conflict. Financial officers are often consulted in the evaluation of the alternatives, such as abandoning or refurbishing facilities to conform to government anti-pollution standards.

Maximizing the corporate goal encompasses the entire spectrum of the financial officer's functions. As financial officer, you must consider all aspects of the problem within the constraints imposed by the various interest groups in the firm and the conflicts which inevitably exist. The finance function is not simple.

The Scope of the Job

The finance function has developed to a point where it serves as the coordinator of input received by the chief operating officers from every department in the firm. Whenever one department proposes a project which looks attractive to it, the finance department must compare it to the projects proposed by other departments to find what is best for the firm as a whole, not just for that one department. Then, the finance department must coordinate all the selected projects through the financ-

---

[12] Many small business investment corporations will insist upon a controlling or majority interest in the firm as one condition for lending to under-capitalized firms.

ing of them. Obviously, the finance officer must be prepared to evaluate claims other departments make on behalf of their proposals and to understand the rudiments of their claims in order to be capable of the critical appraisal so necessary to the overall prosperity of the firm. Nevertheless, the finance department was not always looked upon as an interdisciplinary coordinator of the firm's investments and financing.

The traditional view   The traditional view of the finance function restricted it to raising funds to finance the projects proposed by others in the firm. In a sense it was viewed as an episodic function of minor importance, which every once in a while was called upon to perform the task of negotiating with a friendly banker or selling securities. It was an extremely passive department operating on the orders and requests for funds from other departments within the firm. The rest of the department's time was filled with the daily routine of firm cashier, collecting and disbursing funds. That is why today the finance function may be in the controller's department instead of having its own department, particularly in the more established firms.

This traditional view led to the feeling that the only training needed for a financial officer was a description of the financial markets, their institutions, and the securities that comprised them. A knowledge of the sources of funds—what securities to sell to whom and by what techniques to sell them—was all that was needed. Therefore, traditional managerial finance texts heaped page upon page of description about the financial markets and the types of securities. While knowledge of the institutions and securities of the financial markets is still necessary, the contemporary view has expanded the financial officer's function well beyond the mere descriptive into the analytical.

The contemporary view   The contemporary view gives the finance function a more active role, that of coordinating the firm's investments and financing. This change probably came about because of increased need for a better allocation of the firm's resources to meet the increasing competition of other firms and nations. Much less waste and inefficiency could be tolerated, so techniques to make the most of the firm's limited capital had to be developed. In addition, the expanding economy had presented so many alternative investment opportunities that methods had to be found to sift out the most profitable, since no firm could undertake them all. This also led to expanded competition for capital in the financial markets, necessitating a better understanding of the costs of each type of capital so that the firm could minimize its capital costs. Finally, the firms also became more responsive to the stockholders and to their objectives and attitudes toward risk as more firms went public and as government authorities encouraged fuller financial disclosure by the firms.

Techniques had to be developed to more efficiently allocate resources and minimize idle funds. Most firms turned to the finance function and its capital budgeting process for the answer. Now financial officers were more in demand. They were asked to tell management what to invest in and how to finance the most profitable projects at the least cost. Financial officers applied cost minimization techniques to their firm's cash management operations. But above all, they were the only members of the management teams in a position to coordinate their firms' expansion strategies and policies. It was up to them to see that the marketing and the production departments were working for the overall good of their firms and not against each other. And they still retained the cashier function in many cases.

The finance function of the future seems destined to be even more active and expanded. There is a continuing increase in capital investment opportunities but at even higher costs with stiffer competition and more limited availability of capital. These factors necessitate even more sophisticated techniques to weed out even marginally inefficient projects and to discover the least expensive method of raising funds. The future finance function is going to be a blend of the science and art of finance, mixing the precision of statistics and operations research techniques with the instinct and educated intuition of the trained businessman.

An example Let us go back to the Browning-Ferris organization chart (Figure 1-1) and trace what might be the typical path of an investment proposal, noting the role of the corporate finance department.

1. The idea for a new product might originate in the technical center (it could have originated anywhere, even in a suggestion box) and is reported to the vice-president of the technical center.

2. The vice-president of the technical center sends a memo to the president and to the corporate development committee informing them of the breakthrough.

3. The corporate development committee gets the national marketing vice-president to work up figures on the product's revenue potential and the technical center to estimate the cost of producing the product.

4. The president and the corporate development committee request the administrative committee to direct the vice-president in charge of corporate finance to evaluate the project's acceptability in light of the technical center's cost estimates, the national marketing department's revenue reports, and the corporation's financial situation and profit and risk objectives.

5. The corporation finance vice-president reports to the administrative committee and the president on the recommendation to accept or reject the proposed project.

6. The administrative committee acts on the recommendation and, if necessary, lets the executive committee submit it to the board of directors for approval.

Notice how the corporation finance vice-president coordinated all the information and had to consider all financing, marketing, and production factors as well as the firm's goals in the evaluation report. As a member of the corporation finance department, you would have been involved in the creation of that report.

THE ORGANIZATION OF THE BOOK

Now that I know what a financial officer's duties are, what can I expect the rest of the book to tell me about financial management?

Remember that you are to assume the role of the financial officer throughout the course. By playing that role, you will become acquainted with the problems, responsibilities, and skills associated with that position. Even if you are not majoring in finance, you will undoubtedly work with financial officers during your career. The financial officer controls the purse strings, and you will have to get his or her approval before you can spend any money to undertake a project or get something done. Obviously, financial officers will be more receptive to your suggestions if you approach them with a knowledgeable presentation, speak in their own terms, and demonstrate an understanding of their problems. You can acquire that insight here by assuming the financial officer's role as you take this course.

The book is divided into seven parts, each devoted to one segment of the finance function.

Organizations and the Financial Officer

Part One is designed to acquaint you with the concept of a firm and the functions of the financial officer. After reading this part, you should know not only how a firm is organized and structured but also where you, as a financial officer, fit into that structure and what you are expected to be able to do. Thus far you have explored such topics as the types of organization that the company may select, the organization chart, typical corporate goals you may be expected to work toward, and the finance department's duties.

This part will also acquaint you with the operating environment in which you will have to make your decisions on what to invest in and how to finance those investments. You are expected to learn how society and government can affect your decisions and to understand the major characteristics of the financial markets. You will be introduced to the general concept of operating risk associated with any investment.

You will learn the tools of analysis, which allow the financial officer to maintain control over the implementation and operations of the selected investments, and the language of the budget, which serves as a vehicle for communication among the officers. This section involves you in the use of ratio analysis and the preparation of financial statements. You will also learn the mathematics behind the terminology of finance, including the concepts of present discounted value and compounding.

Capital Budgeting

Part Two explains the techniques and tools the financial officer uses in deciding what to invest in. This whole procedure is known as capital budgeting. First, you will encounter the components and figures the financial officer isolates for use in capital budgeting. Then you will see how they are used in situations of certainty, capital rationing, and uncertainty.

Cost of Capital

Part Three will teach you how to finance investments; it is your introduction to the financial markets. Familiarity with financial markets will help you improve the timing of your firm's security offerings and enable you to determine which type of security to sell during which market. You will then learn to estimate the cost of capital for each type of security, so you can select the least expensive and consider the overall effect on the firm's cost of capital. You will also explore dividend policy and gain a working knowledge of the cost of capital policy issues, which are so frequently discussed among financial officers.

Working Capital Management

Part Four will acquaint you with the daily operations of the firm's cash flows. You will learn how to minimize the firm's investments in cash, accounts receivable, and inventory—desirable since excessive investment in these assets merely ties up money at an unprofitable rate of return.

Short-Term Sources of Funds

In Part Five you will become familiar with the various types of short-term securities that you might authorize for sale to raise money for the firm or to buy as temporary investments for the firm's idle cash balances. You should also become acquainted with the institutions to whom you can sell these short-term securities and from whom you can buy them.

Long-Term Sources of Funds

Part Six describes the long-term securities you must consider when trying to raise long-term funds for the corporation. This section includes a discussion of the legal requirements involved in complying with government regulations before you can sell long-term securities. You should be able to decide on the appropriate type of long-term financing for any given financial market environment once you have studied these chapters.

Other Areas in Managerial Finance

In your position as financial officer, you will be called upon to participate, if not lead the firm, in such areas as acquiring other firms, conducting multinational financial operations, and, if necessary, guiding the firm through bankruptcy and reorganization. These are not typical parts of the finance function, but the finance department is asked to participate in these matters more often than you would think. You should know what they entail.

SUMMARY

After having read Chapter 1, you should be able to answer these questions:

1. What is a firm?

A firm is an independent agent consisting of one or more people and capable of entering into legal arrangements which facilitate its performance of all business functions. These may include the purchase of raw materials, fabrication of a product or development of a service, advertising, and sale.

2. What type of organizational structure might I work for?

A firm may select any of several legal forms including the proprietorship, the partnership, and the corporation.

3. Where do I fit in the firm if I become a financial officer?

The corporate finance department of a typical organization is the major coordinator of the company's profit plan, including the decisions of *what to invest in* and *how to finance investments* in order to *maximize the firm's corporate objective.* We also saw that the corporate finance department is typically a headquarters staff function.

4. Will I be in tune with the management philosophy under which I have to work?

The major considerations involved in defining a firm's corporate goal are shareholder wealth maximization, profit maximization, satisficing, manager welfare maximization, and corporate social responsibility. The conflicts that arise among these different goals lead firms to adopt various combinations of goals at different times in their history.

5. What will be my duties if I do become a financial officer?

Your major function will be coordinating the firm's profit plan. The finance function typically entails managing the firm's cash position, maintaining working relationships with the firm's bankers and sellers of its securities, preparing the firm's internal audits, and handling the cash flows.

QUESTIONS

1-1 Compare the legal advantages and disadvantages of different types of organizational forms in which firms exist.

1-2 Distinguish between the "line" and "staff" functions of various groups in the firm.

1-3 Define briefly the duties of a firm's financial officer.

1-4 What are some of the difficulties or conflicts that may arise for the corporate officer in carrying out his or her duties?

1-5 The role of finance in the firm has been changing rapidly. Contrast the traditional view of the finance function with the more contemporary view.

1-6 (a) Delineate several groups of possible corporate objectives.

(b) Do any of these objectives appear mutually exclusive?

1-7 Do you think the firm has a social responsibility for the "external" effects of its operation? If so, to what extent should the firm bear the costs of these effects (both positive and negative)?

BIBLIOGRAPHY

Antony, Robert N. "The Trouble with Profit Maximization." *Harvard Business Review*, 38 (November–December 1960), 126–134.

Bacon, Jeremy, and Francis J. Walsh, Jr. *Duties and Problems of Chief Financial Executives.* Managing the Financial Function, Report No. 1. National Industrial Conference Board, Inc., New York, 1968.

Donaldson, Gordon. "Financial Goals: Management vs. Stockholders." *Harvard Business Review*, 41 (May–June 1963), 116–129.

Drucker, P. F. "Business Objectives and Survival Needs." *Journal of Business*, 31 (April 1958), 81–90.

Harkins, Edwin P. *Organizing and Managing the Corporate Financial Function.* Studies in Business Policy, No. 129. National Industrial Conference Board, Inc., New York, 1969.

Lewellen, Wilbur G. "Management and Ownership in the Large Firm." *Journal of Finance*, XXIV (May 1969), 299–322.

Moag, Joseph S., Willard T. Carleton, and Eugene M. Lerner. "Defining the Finance Function: A Model-Systems Approach." *Journal of Finance*, XXII (May 1966), 411–415.

Simon, Herbert A. "Theories of Decision Making in Economics and Behavioral Science." *American Economic Review*, XLIX (June 1959), 253–283.

Solomon, Ezra. *The Theory of Financial Management.* Columbia University Press, New York, 1963, Ch. 1 and 2.

Weston, J. Fred. *The Scope and Methodology of Finance.* Prentice-Hall, Englewood Cliffs, N.J., 1966.

Appendix 1A **Incorporation Procedure**

The procedure to be followed in obtaining a corporate charter will vary among the states since they are the ones with the power to grant these charters. Traditionally, the procedure has not been arduous, for the states do not like to prevent enterprise and they do collect revenue from both the incorporation procedure and from the firm, if it is successful. Delaware has been considered the most lenient state for incorporation because of its relatively few requirements.

The first step in obtaining a charter is to prepare the articles of incorporation (a sample of which appears in the following appendix). The articles should contain the following information: name of the corporation, location of its principal office, purpose or purposes of its business, the number of shares and consideration received for them, the initial capital, and the name and address of the firm's registered agent.

The second step is to petition the state for a charter. This usually entails paying a filing fee and presenting the secretary of the state with the prepared articles of incorporation bearing the notarized signatures and addresses of the incorporators.

Once the secretary of the state gives approval, he or she usually affixes the seal of the secretary of state and registers the name of the corporation in the book of approved charters.

The last step is for the chartered corporation to organize itself through the election of directors and the adoption of a set of by-laws governing such things as the firm's annual meetings and their conduct.[1]

Appendix 1B **Sample Articles of Incorporation**

In the name and by the authority of

THE STATE OF TEXAS

Office of the Secretary of State

Certificate of incorporation of

UNIVERSITY FINANCIAL COUNSELORS, INC.

The undersigned, as Secretary of State of the State of Texas, hereby certifies that duplicate originals of Articles of Incorporation for the above corporation duly signed and verified pursuant to the provisions of the Texas Business Corporation Act, have been received in this office and are found to conform to law.

[1] William H. Husband and James C. Dockeray, *Modern Corporate Finance*, Irwin, Homewood, Ill., 1972, p. 41ff.

ACCORDINGLY the undersigned, as such Secretary of State, and by virtue of the authority vested in him by law, hereby issues this Certificate of Incorporation and attaches hereto a duplicate original of the Articles of Incorporation.

Dated_____JULY 27_____, 19__71.

_____

Secretary of State

Articles of incorporation of
UNIVERSITY FINANCIAL COUNSELORS, INC.

We, the undersigned, natural persons of the age of twenty-one (21) years or more, at least two of whom are citizens of the State of Texas, acting as incorporators of a Corporation under the Texas Business Corporation Act, do hereby adopt the following Articles of Incorporation for such corporation.

I. The name of the corporation is UNIVERSITY FINANCIAL COUNSELORS, INC.

II. The period of its duration is to be perpetual.

III. The purpose or purposes for which the corporation is organized are:

To prepare, publish, formulate, promulgate, sell, or otherwise engage in the gathering and distributing of information, data, advice, suggestions, recommendations, and other management and advisory services pertaining to investments, financial instruments, portfolio management, securities of every class and description and other real and personal property of every class and description and to contract, sub-contract or otherwise make arrangements for the gathering and distribution of such information.

To manage, advise, service, or otherwise engage in the supervision and functioning of investments of every class and description and real and personal property of every class and description for its own account and for the accounts of others.

To manufacture, repair, remanufacture, purchase or otherwise acquire and to hold, own, mortgage or otherwise lien, pledge, lease, sell, assign, exchange, transfer or in any manner dispose of, and to invest, deal and trade in and with goods, wares, merchandise and personal property of any and every class and description, within or without the State of Texas.

To contract, sub-contract, or otherwise make arrangements for the manufacture, purchase or sale of goods, wares, merchandise and personal property of any and every character and description, within or without the State of Texas.

To purchase or otherwise acquire, apply for, register, hold, use, sell or in any manner dispose of and to grant licenses or other rights in and in any manner deal with patents, inventions, improvements, processes, formulas, trademarks, trade names, rights and licenses secured under Letters Patent, copyrights or otherwise.

To lease, rent, operate or own an office building or office space in a building.

To enter into, make and perform contracts of every kind for any lawful purpose, with any person, firm, or corporation, town, city, county, body politic, state, territory, government or colony or dependency thereof.

To have one or more offices and to conduct any or all of its operations and business and to promote its objects within or without the State of Texas, without restrictions as to place or amount.

To do any or all of the things herein lawfully set forth as principal, agent, or contractor.

Nothing herein shall be construed to give this corporation the power or authority to form partnerships.

The objects and purposes specified herein shall be regarded as independent objects and purposes and, except where otherwise expressed, shall be in no way limited or restricted by reference to or inference from the terms of any other clause or paragraph of this certificate of incorporation.

The foregoing shall be construed both as objects and powers and the enumeration thereof shall not be held to limit or restrict in any manner the general powers conferred on this corporation by the laws of the State of Texas.

IV. The aggregate number of shares which the corporation shall have authority to issue is one hundred thousand (100,000) without par value.

V. The corporation will not commence business until it has received for the issuance of its shares consideration of the value of One Thousand and No/100 ($1,000.00) Dollars, consisting of money, labor done or property actually received.

VI. The address of its initial registered office is 1617 Fannin, #2817, Houston, Texas 77002, and the name of its initial registered agent at such address is Kenneth G. McCoin.

VII. The number of Directors of this corporation shall be not less than three (3), and the names and addresses of the persons who are to serve as Directors until the first annual meeting of the shareholders or until their successors are elected and qualified are:

Names	Addresses
Kenneth G. McCoin	1617 Fannin, #2817, Houston, Texas 77002
Steven E. Bolten	10010 Memorial Drive, Houston, Texas 77024
Linda A. McCoin	1617 Fannin, #2817, Houston, Texas 77002

The names and addresses of the incorporators are:

Kenneth G. McCoin	1617 Fannin, #2817, Houston, Texas 77002
Steven E. Bolten	10010 Memorial Drive, Houston, Texas 77024
Linda A. McCoin	1617 Fannin, #2817, Houston, Texas 77002

IN WITNESS WHEREOF, we have hereunto set our hands as of this 26th day of July, 1971.

_____

Kenneth G. McCoin

_____

Steven E. Bolten

_____

Linda A. McCoin

State of Texas, County of Harris:

I, _____, a Notary Public, do hereby certify that on this 26th day of July, 1971, personally appeared before me KENNETH G. McCOIN, who, being by me first duly sworn, declared that he is the person who signed the foregoing document as an incorporator, and that the statements therein contained are true.

_____
Notary Public in and for
Harris County, Texas

State of Texas, County of Harris:

I, _____, a Notary Public, do hereby certify that on this 26th day of July, 1971, personally appeared before me STEVEN E. BOLTEN, who being by me first duly sworn, declared that he is the person who signed the foregoing document as an incorporator, and that the statements therein contained are true.

_____
Notary Public in and for
Harris County, Texas

State of Texas, County of Harris:

I, _____, a Notary Public, do hereby certify that on this 26th day of July, 1971, personally appeared before me LINDA A. Mc-COIN, who being by me first duly sworn, declared that she is the person who signed the foregoing document as an incorporator, and that the statements therein contained are true.

_____
Notary Public in and for
Harris County, Texas

2

the operating environment of the firm

WHAT IS THE ENVIRONMENT in which I, as a financial officer, will have to make decisions on what the firm should invest in and how it should finance those investments in order to maximize its corporate objective? No firm operates in a vacuum. Every decision and action affects relationships with other groups in society as well as within the firm. For example, if the financial officer of your local electric utility were to approve investment in a nuclear generating facility, many parts of society would be affected as a result. Local consumers would have a greater supply of electricity, which the utility assumes they want to purchase. The local government and property owners would have a new resident, which they may or may not want. Although the plant may increase the tax base and thereby increase the city's revenues, local residents may object to the location of the plant for environmental reasons or fear of nuclear power. The federal government would have to approve the plans through its Atomic Energy Commission. In addition, the firm would have to go to the capital markets and raise additional funds from new stockholders and lenders, which would alter the position of the present stockholders. The decision to use nuclear instead of conventional fuels would have to be made in light of the relative availability and cost of both. At the same time, effects throughout the operating environment of the firm must be considered.

Many more aspects than the mere operating efficiency of the project must figure in your decision on what to invest in. Together, they all make up what we will call the *operating environment* of the firm. Some are externally imposed upon the firm by other sectors of society. In the nuclear power plant decision, the federal government imposed regulations in the name of the authority and responsibility given to it by the public to provide for public safety and health. The plant's location and even its construction may be externally imposed by the local government and environmentalists. Law suits and other tactics have been known to delay or even cancel large investment projects, despite their profitability and operating efficiency.[1] The capital markets in which financing must be raised may or may not be receptive to the securities offered by the firm because of reasons well beyond the firm's control. Other companies, for example, with which the firm must compete in the capital markets for funds, may be willing to pay a higher rate of interest and force the elec-

---

[1] The delay in the Alaska oil pipeline, for example.

tric utility securities off the market. Many factors—from governmental policy restricting the availability of credit to international events that are draining off United States funds to overseas capital markets—could affect the financing of the nuclear plant.

In your evaluation, you must also consider internal aspects imposed by the operating characteristics of the industry and the firm itself. Foremost in our nuclear plant evaluation is the consumer's need for electricity. Is the demand for the product sufficient to warrant the additional generating capacity? For any investment a firm may consider, the financial officer must carefully scrutinize the revenue projections furnished by the marketing department to be sure the project is needed before including it in the capital budget.

Obviously the financial officer examines the costs of operating the nuclear plant. Does the plant operate efficiently? Even this is determined by the availability of fuel. Sometimes decisions to build nuclear plants are influenced more by the fear that alternative fuels will not be available to the industry than by comparison among the operating costs of various types of electric generating plants. The firm itself may impose a return on investment below which the project is unacceptable.

A large number of factors in the operating environment must be considered other than the project's profitability in deciding what the firm should invest in. These considerations fall into three broad categories:

1. Externally imposed by other sectors of society
2. Imposed by the operating characteristics of the industry
3. Internally imposed by the firm itself

Among the externally imposed considerations, financial officers ask themselves such questions as: What major groups in society do I have to consider in my evaluation? How can each of these groups affect my evaluation? What must I consider when I represent my firm in its attempts to raise capital? What financial risk considerations do outside investors examine before committing their funds to the purchase of the firm's securities? How do I time my firm's security offerings to the best opportunities in the financial markets?

Among the considerations imposed upon the firm by the operating characteristics of the industry, financial officers ask themselves such questions as: What are the pertinent operating characteristics I must consider in my evaluation of what the firm should invest in and how to finance it?

Among the internally imposed considerations, financial officers ask such questions as: How do I plan the use of the firm's funds? How do I report my plans and the results of those plans to my superiors and to the owners? How do I remain in control of the financing situation? We will study internal considerations in Chapter 3. This chapter addresses the considerations imposed by the industry and society.

SOCIETY AND GOVERNMENT

What major groups in society do I have to consider in my evaluation? How can each of these groups affect my evaluation?

Consumerism

Consumers, as a class, have recently exerted more influence on the firm's investment decisions because they have acted in a concerted and intentional manner to influence the actual processes of production. Not only are they consciously refraining from buying particular items on a formal and organized basis, but they are also demanding that resources be shifted to the production of other items which are more satisfying and suited to their needs. In some instances they are actually requesting that production of certain items be stopped and the production of other items be started by governmental edict.

How do we account for the advent of consumer activism? Certainly it is in sharp contrast to the former economic view of the consumer as a rather passive individual whose only recourse is not to buy the product—a recourse that many claim has been practically eliminated by the advent of created demand and monopoly power over the production processes of major industries.[2] In the days of fierce competition among many firms for the consumer's dollar, producers would seek out what consumers wanted and build the product to their desires. But as advertising and selling techniques were perfected, there were indications that the product was being developed first, after which the consumer was "educated" to buy it. Created demand endowed producers with the power to produce whatever they chose without the inconvenience and expense of consulting the customer. Further, as the number of firms producing a particular item dwindled to just a few, these few became less responsive to the customer's desires and needs, for the consumer had nowhere else to turn for many items that had become necessities of life.

The doctrine of *caveat emptor,* let the buyer beware, which implies that customers more or less pay their money and take their chances, has also fallen from favor as an assumption in selling. As new products have become more complex and less read-ily understood at first glance by consumers, they can no longer be expected to sat-isfy themselves that a particular product was in the condition warranted by the pro-ducer at the time of sale. Consumers now assume the right to return items that do not perform as specified. The firm has become liable for the performance of the item after, as well as before, the sale. As consumers have become more educated, they have become more aware of their rights under the law to the implied and written warranties which an item carries at sale. This has made them more aware of such problems as misrepresentation and shoddy manufacture and more vocal when they encounter them.

The consumer movement has manifested itself in many ways. There have been national boycotts of some products. Consumer-oriented groups have been more influential in getting legislation that makes the consumer's rights explicit and opens up broader avenues of consumer recourse, such as the laws that allow the return of the product for a cash refund within so many days of purchase and the class action suits brought by consumer groups' lawyers on behalf of all injured consumers. Divisions have been established in the various levels of government to handle consumer complaints; licensing departments have been instituted to assure quali-fied service.

A variant of the consumer movement is environmentalism. Environmentalists champion the preservation of ecological balance. In response to their organized protests, courts may issue injunctions against a firm's undertaking projects which in the past might have been considered simply in terms of the technological breakthroughs they represent.

The effect of these groups has been to increase the number of elements the finan-cial officer must consider in making investment decisions and to compound the un-certainty over the investment's profitability. The projected sales revenues on which

[2] Among the leading exponents of this thinking are Vance Packard and John Kenneth Galbraith.

the financial officer partly bases an evaluation may be unreliable; the consumer may not be as easily convinced of the merits of the product as before. The environmental considerations of pollution and plant site are more complex and must be incorporated into the financial officer's capital budget. Now as never before, the investment evaluation process requires that the operating environment be given careful attention before a project is approved.

Fiscal Policy

Fiscal policy is the federal government's effort to influence the level of economic activity through its spending, taxing, and wage and price control powers. Government policies in these areas affect the environment in which the firm's investment decisions take place.

Government spending plans can affect the investment environment in two direct ways. Those companies which are suppliers to the government, its agencies, and programs supported by government funding depend on how much the government decides to spend and what it decides to buy. For example, the shift away from the space program in the late 1960s and early 1970s caused many firms to call on their financial officers to initiate diversification plans. These firms had to get out of government business dependent on the space program and into nongovernment, consumer-oriented areas. Any potential shifts in the emphasis of the federal government budget must be taken into account by the financial officer when evaluating the firm's investment opportunities, if for no other reason than that these shifts tend to be very large, very dramatic, and very sudden.

The second effect of the federal government's budget on the firm's investment evaluation is through its impact on the general level of economic activity. Theoretically, the government uses its budget to stabilize the business cycle at full employment within acceptable limits of inflation. If the pace of the economy is too rapid for sustainable growth, the federal budget should decrease, going into a surplus to siphon off spending and cool the economy. In periods of economic recession, the government's budget should increase spending, going into a deficit to fuel business activity.

As a financial officer deciding on the firm's investment program, you will be affected by this attempt to stabilize the economy through the budget. Specifically, you will have to compete with the federal government for funds in the financial market when it is financing a deficit. This will raise interest rates and the cost of acquiring funds. You will also have to anticipate the effect that federal spending policies will have on the ability of the economy to absorb your product and satisfy your sales projections. Frequently the government's timing is not as good as it should be, and its spending pattern only aggravates a recession instead of relieving it. Restriction in federal spending during a recession may cause your sales to be way off your projection and turn what looked like a profitable investment into an unattractive one. On the other hand, an incorrect fiscal policy which caused excessive inflation could distort the estimated cost of the investment and, again, make it unprofitable.

The government's taxing policies are theoretically designed to be another stabilizing device. During recessionary periods, tax relief is supposed to be granted, increasing spending power and stimulating the economy. In unsustainable and inflationary booms, taxes are to be increased to absorb excessive purchasing power and to slow the economy. You, as the financial officer, must be prepared to include the federal taxing policy in your evaluation. The government may grant tax relief to new investment which directly increases the profitability of your investments. At other times, the imposition of higher taxes stifles the market potential of the product and turns a lucrative investment into an unprofitable one.

Wages and price controls are another tool of the federal government in its continuing effort to control the economy. During periods of "excessive inflation," the government actually comes directly to you and dictates what prices you can charge for your products. Obviously, government action forbidding you a price hike can instantly alter your opinion on the revenue potential and profitability of an investment project. It can also affect the willingness of investors to provide capital, for a deterioration in the firm's profitability which cannot be rectified by a needed price increase can, in the extreme, affect its solvency.

Regulatory Environment

Today's business environment includes many federal, state, and local agencies empowered to impose various regulations on the operations of a firm within their jurisdiction. These range anywhere from provision for employee safety to the setting of gas prices at the wellhead for interstate natural gas producers. Whatever these regulations, their potential effect on the profitability and feasibility of investments must be considered. We shall briefly note a few of the well-known regulatory areas. The Federal Power Commission (FPC) regulates prices and competition in the interstate energy industry. The Civil Aeronautics Board (CAB) regulates the rate and route structures of the airline industry. The Federal Aviation Agency (FAA) regulates the operations of the airline industry. The Interstate Commerce Commission (ICC) regulates the rate and route structures of the interstate transportation industry. The Environmental Protection Agency (EPA) enforces, along with state and local agencies, federal antipollution standards. The Department of Justice enforces the antitrust laws. The Department of Labor enforces the equal job opportunity laws. The Internal Revenue Service enforces the tax code. The Occupational Safety and Health Administration (OSHA) enforces employee safety regulations. Many more bureaus at the state and local level swell the ranks of the regulatory agencies you must take into account.

The financial officer should carefully consult the firm's lawyer before proceeding with any project which might be under the jurisdiction of one or more of these agencies. If even then it is not clear what the regulations are, you will have to operate under this uncertainty. For example, the FPC for many years has had conflicting and confusing regulations on the rate gas producers could charge. Natural gas producers simply had to assume certain interpretations of the regulation, while asking judicial clarification, in their investment evaluations.

The most direct regulation the financial officer will experience is that of the Securities and Exchange Commission (SEC), which regulates procedures for the sale of the firm's securities to the public investor. We will discuss these regulations in some detail in Chapter 20; for the time being it is sufficient to note that there are rather extensive regulations governing the sale of securities.

FINANCIAL MARKETS

What must I consider when I represent my firm in the financial markets and how do I time the sale of securities in such a way that my firm gets the best deal when raising funds? What are potential buyers of the firm's securities looking for? How can I make my securities attractive to them?

The financial market is actually comprised of several markets wherein sellers (corporations) and buyers of securities actively participate. The individual markets are usually distinguished either by the length of the security's life or by the type of security. Short-term securities, with life expectancies of less than one year (at which time the firm is expected to redeem them from the buyer), are offered in what is commonly referred to as the *money market.* Longer-term securities are offered by the firms in the *capital markets.* We have said that the markets are also frequently classified according to the type of security offered. Since we will cover the types of securities in Parts Five and Six, we will only mention in passing the examples of the *equity market,* in which a firm offers its stock, and the *corporate bond market,* in which a firm offers its long-term debt obligations.

Interest Rates

Interest rates are the price the financial officer negotiates for the firm to pay the purchaser of the security offered. Each separate time and for each type of security offered, the financial officer negotiates, either directly with the buyer or the buyer's representative, the rate of interest the firm will pay the buyer if he or she lends to or invests money in the firm. We can look upon the *rate of interest* as the price of the credit extended to the firm by the lender. Many different interest rates apply, depending on the relative bargaining strength of the firm and the potential buyer during negotiations, market conditions at the time (the supply and the demand for credit in the market), and the particular terms of the security being offered. Further, it is apparent that interest rates will fluctuate as the conditions of the market and the relative positions of the firm and the potential buyers change.

Interest rates are customarily expressed in annual percentage rates, such as 6 percent per annum. We have all seen savings and loan associations which advertise their interest rate as $5\frac{1}{4}$ percent. Even without any indication of the period over which the interest is paid, we automatically know that it is an annual rate. Loans to the corporation and the debt securities offered by the corporation also express their interest cost as an annual rate. If the ABC corporation borrows from the XYZ bank at 7 percent, it pays an interest rate of 7 percent a year over the life of the loan, even if the loan is for less or more than one year. We will explore the various interest rate calculations in Chapter 4.

Since interest rates fluctuate according to the conditions of the market and the relative negotiating powers of the firm and potential buyers, the financial officer's skill in timing the firm's securities offerings to fall in a period of low interest rates can save the firm substantial sums. In addition, a lower cost of funds may make marginal projects attractive investments and enhance the profits of the firm. Conversely, marginal projects may have to be dropped if the interest paid is too high. The daily cashflow operations of the financial officer are also affected by the interest rate. As interest rates increase, it becomes more expensive to be inefficient in cash management and to maintain idle cash balances. Cash management policies have to be changed to take advantage of increased interest rates.

Monetary Policy

Just as it uses the federal budget, the federal government uses its ability to control the supply of money and to influence interest rates in an attempt to stabilize the level of economic activity over the business cycle. During periods of inflation and unsustainable boom, the Federal Reserve System, an independent governmental agency which controls the money supply, restricts the rate of growth in the money supply, curtailing the spending ability of the consumer and the amount of money available to potential buyers of securities. This not only dampens the sales potential of the product but also makes it more expensive to finance, as interest rates rise.

The Federal Reserve System is actively engaged in buying and selling in the financial market devoted to the debt of the United States Treasury. When the Federal Reserve System sells these United States Treasury obligations to potential buyers of the firm's securities, it drains their funds, restricting the supply of credit and raising interest rates. Conversely when it buys Treasury obligations from potential buyers of the firm's securities, it provides them with funds, increasing the supply of credit and lowering interest rates. The Federal Reserve System can also directly allocate funds through its control over the banking system and its ability to regulate interest rates at banks. The financial officer who is concerned with interest rates must be aware of the Federal Reserve System and prevailing monetary policy.

Monetary policy affects the investment decisions, the financing decisions, and the cash management policies of financial officers. Since Federal Reserve System policy tends to be countercyclical, the availability and cost of funds tightens when the general corporate demand for funds is increasing. In the extreme, funds can become absolutely unavailable and lead to credit crunches such as occurred in early 1970 when the Penn Central railroad was unable to borrow funds and was forced into bankruptcy. Funds were so very tight during that credit crunch that many corporations had to curtail their investment program and others simply could not borrow at all just to finance their daily operations. What funds were available were very expensive.

This restriction on the availability of credit adds uncertainty to a firm's cash management operations, particularly its repayment or refinancing of maturing debt and its handling of accounts receivable and accounts payable. In the case of the maturing debt, it is imperative that financial officers *not* be caught in a credit crunch and be unable to arrange refinancing or repayment. This means they will have to anticipate periods of restricted credit availability and pre-arrange the refinancing. In the case of accounts receivable and accounts payable, financial officers can expect distortions in the timing of both. They will delay paying to use the funds more profitably elsewhere, and will expect delays in receiving payment, forcing them to raise additional funds to support the accounts receivable.

Inflation

Inflation is the rate of change in the price level. It is another element in the operating environment that affects the investment and financing decisions of the firm, and it must be included in the financial officer's evaluation. Inflation tends to disrupt the financial markets, frequently sending interest rates higher. Potential lenders demand higher interest rates for the use of their funds to protect themselves from the loss of purchasing power they experience from higher prices during the period for which they have given up the use of their money. Inflation usually prompts the Federal Reserve to tighten credit. These uncertainties make negotiations with lenders very difficult for the financial officer.

Inflation makes the investment evaluation procedure more difficult. Increased costs may turn profitable projects into unprofitable ones. This is particularly true of projects which may take several years to implement, such as the development of large ore bodies. Inflation increases the cost of the raw materials and labor involved in production, which may make the investment less profitable. Inflation can also force the firm to raise the selling price, possibly allowing foreign competition to capture a larger share of the market and thereby reducing profitability.

Financial Risks

Potential buyers of the firm's securities are always interested in the risk attached to those securities. They are particularly concerned that the firm can meet the interest payments and the repayment schedule of any borrowings, for as the amount borrowed increases, so does the risk that the firm may not meet its commitments to repay. It is very similar to your borrowing to finance a new car. You may be able to cope with a little bit of debt, although you could not repay a very large loan. Of course, if you bought the car for cash and did not borrow at all, you would have no risk. As we shall see in Chapter 10, this concept of borrowing to finance a portion of the firm's investments is known as *leverage*,[3] and it increases the volatility of the firm's earnings per share and the risk that investors attach to the firm's securities. As financial officer, you will have to use that amount of debt which best satisfies the potential purchasers of the firm's securities and maximizes the corporation goal. Most importantly you will have to decide whether to issue more shares or to incur more debt so as to make the securities most attractive to potential buyers.

All the factors in the operating environment which we have explored in this section bear on the financial officer's timing of the firm's borrowings and security sales. He or she must be aware of financial market conditions and design the terms and timing of any security offering to lower the cost of those funds while obtaining sufficient funds to support all selected projects and avoid being caught in a credit crunch. It is not an easy task.

OPERATING RISKS

What are the operating characteristics I must consider in my evaluation of what the firm should invest in and how to finance its investments?

In addition to the external influences of the society, the government, and the financial markets, the industry imposes its own characteristics upon the firm's operating environment in which financial officers have to make their investment and financing decisions. In fact, we can define *operating risks* as those factors peculiar to one industry or type of firm that introduce uncertainty into the investment and financing process because they increase the variability in the project's income and the chance that the profitability projections for any particular investment may not be realized.

Certain firms operate in industries with relatively stable patterns of performance. The sales and production costs of these firms are usually highly predictable. Investment projects by these firms are typically based on accurate estimates of profitability. We can see, for example, that the electric utility industry tends to have a high degree of stability and accuracy in its profitability projections because electricity sales tend to be stable and the rate of profit on each dollar of investment is guaranteed by the local government. At the other extreme are firms whose sales and production costs are erratic, lessening the potential accuracy of profitability projections for each investment project. The farm equipment manufacturer whose sales are highly dependent upon the income of farmers who buy the equipment faces un-

---

[3] For a more detailed discussion of this topic see Chapter 10.

certain sales prospects because farmers' income may vary considerably as growing conditions and the prices of farm commodities change. During periods of large crops and high commodity prices, farm equipment sales rise. During poor harvests and low prices, farm equipment sales fall. This hard-to-forecast variability in the sale of farm equipment makes it very difficult for the financial officer to decide what to invest in and how to finance it.

Since the operating risks are peculiar to individual industries and firms, there are too many to enumerate here. We will describe general categories of operating characteristics which seem to transcend industry lines. The farm equipment manufacturer's sales volatility results from fluctuations in the income of farmers; therefore, the general operating characteristic is the income volatility of the consumer. The same general factor applied to the automobile manufacturer would be the income of automobile purchasers.

We shall discuss operating risk in three general categories: (1) external operating risks which are, for the most part, beyond the control of management; (2) internal operating risks which are, for the most part, within the control of management; and (3) operating leverage.

External Operating Risks

External operating risks vary among industries and firms in both type and degree, but all are imposed upon the firm by industry forces outside its control.

The business cycle   The first major general external operating risk is the sensitivity of the investment project to the business cycle. Certain projects have sales revenues and incomes which fluctuate with the business cycle. While these projects are still highly profitable, they have a higher risk than projects which do not have cyclical profitability. Firms in cyclical industries must recognize the fact and plan their capital investments accordingly. For example, airline transportation companies tend to be very cyclical, with pronounced increases in revenues and profits when the economy is rising and pronounced slumps when the economy is slowing. The industry also requires rather large outlays for investment in very expensive jet aircraft. If the required outlays should coincide with a slump in profits, there would be a large financial strain on the company. It is the job of the financial officer to avoid such occurrences.[4]

Many other industries and firms are sensitive to the business cycle. Typically, durable items, which last several years and are relatively high priced, are sensitive to the business cycle. As the income of potential purchasers of these items rises, the sales and profits of firms producing them also rise. As the purchasers' income falls, they tend to postpone purchase, and the sales and profits of the producers fall. Common examples of such cyclically prone industries are the machine tool industry, automobile manufacturers, the expensive jewelry industry, and other industries whose sales are dependent on the personal income of the consumer.

Quality of sales   The second major category of external operating risk is the quality of sales, which may also lead to variation in expected sales and profits of investment projects. While certain projects may be highly profitable, they are more sensitive to sudden shifts in the desires of potential purchasers of the product. Typically, companies and industries dependent on one customer, one geographical region, one

[4] See for example "What Ails American Airlines," *Business Week*, May 12, 1973, 134–136.

product, or very select and highly transient styles and tastes have investment projects with poor quality of sales. For example, the space program companies whose sole revenue source was supplying space hardware to the national space program suffered severe setbacks when the government curtailed the space program in the early 1970s. Other obvious examples of poor quality of sales are industries that cater to fads and fleeting fashions. Frequently the toy industry experiences such fads as the hula-hoop, and the clothing industry experiences changing tastes. Several manufacturers of business suits went out of business during the shift to more informal attire among men. As a financial officer for a firm engaged in an industry with a typically poor quality of sales, your job will be to see that the return on the investment is sufficiently high and reliable within a sufficiently short period to warrant undertaking the risk of having the one customer or the fad fade away.

Cost and availability of materials The third major general category of external operating risks is the quality and quantity of inputs used in the project's production process. Certain investment projects depend on raw materials sources not controlled by the firm. The profitability of the entire project hinges on the ability of the firm to acquire these raw materials. Projects which were once profitable have become unprofitable because of the lack of raw materials. Industries have resorted to sources in less accessible or less politically stable environments, raising costs and increasing the risk that the project might not be operational, feasible, or profitable. The job of the financial officer is to incorporate these possibilities into the investment analysis so that the firm is prepared to handle restricted raw material supplies and rising raw material costs without financial embarrassment. Recognizing the existence of these uncertainties is a major part of the investment evaluation procedure.

Typical industries that might experience restricted and increasingly costly raw material supplies would include United States oil refiners who depend on foreign supplies of crude oil to manufacture gasoline and heating oil. Adverse political changes in those countries could curtail the raw material flow to United States refiners. Meat processors, who depend on the farmer to provide live hogs, cattle and other commodities, have wide fluctuations in their profits because the cost of those commodities tends to fluctuate substantially. Any fabricating firm which depends on outside sources of raw materials with large price volatility usually experiences volatility in its own operations. As financial officer, you want to be sure you arrange your financing such that large portions of debt do not come due during years in which the firm is suffering a temporary decline in profitability because of high commodity prices, and you do not want the firm to undertake ill-timed investments and cause an undue financial burden during a temporary slump.

Internal Operating Risks

In contrast to the external operating risks that are largely imposed upon the firm by outside forces, internal operating risks are largely under the control of management and can be minimized through good management. Of course, each management has its own particular internal operating risks to contend with, but certain general categories exist.

Asset utilization The evaluation of any investment project is less uncertain if management has the ability to utilize the project's assets more profitably than other firms within the industry. Traditionally some firms have a higher profit return per dollar of investment and less excess capacity than their competitors. These firms appear to have the ability to select those projects which consistently perform the best. Management of these firms never seems to be taken by surprise. They often find ways to use by-products, such as the lumber companies that pioneered the use of scraps for salable lumber items.

Diversification The management that diversifies properly without losing control of the operations or going beyond its expertise also lessens the operating risk. Tailoring several different products to several different customers in several geographical regions decreases the chances of a sudden and unexpected reversal in sales and profits, which, in turn, lessens the chances of financial embarrassment. Even if one product or one customer is no longer profitable, the other products and customers may offset the decline. Disappointing results in one area may be offset by results better than expected in another. Good management will also select diversified sources of supply, so that if one source is curtailed another can be counted on. Even the financial officer should diversify suppliers of funds, dealing, for instance, with several banks to avoid the possibility of being shut off from borrowing.

General operating skills Management's general operating skills play a significant part in reducing the operating risks in the financial officer's evaluation of investment opportunities. Any skill which increases the operating efficiency of the firm makes every investment project that much more potentially profitable. For example, the ability to maintain internal control is an important management skill which increases efficiency. The ability to retain valuable and competent employees, to keep abreast of technology, to patent properly the firm's products and processes, to instill consumer loyalty—all are examples of good operating skills. Before the best financial officers select an investment opportunity for implementation, they try to be sure management has the operating skills to realize the project's profitability. It takes only a little bad management to ruin a good idea.

Countercyclical response Management must also be able to respond quickly and correctly to the business cycle. A good countercyclical response can turn cyclically sensitive projects, which might otherwise be rejected because of the volatility in their sales and profits, into highly profitable investments. A good countercyclical response means that profits, which might normally slacken during business slowdowns, retreat little, if any, because the firm has managed to reduce expenditures as rapidly as the demand for its product has declined. This requires, among other things, that management have an accurate forecast of the economy and react quickly. The fact is, however, that most firms do not or cannot react quickly to the business environment and do experience cyclical variations in their profits.

   As a generalization, firms can be classified as those which do respond reasonably well to the business cycle and those which do not. Typically, those firms that require a large fixed investment to produce the product, have high, fixed operating costs, or have inflexible production methods do not respond well. For example, the automobile industry has large amounts of money invested in production facilities; during temporary lulls in business, it is common to find automobile assembly plants with idle capacity. Combining this with high operating costs that are incurred, regardless of the sales level, limits the ability of the automobile manufacturers to mount a good countercyclical response. On the other hand, there are firms which require relatively little fixed investment and have few fixed costs. These firms generally respond well to the business cycle. In either case management ability can improve or hamper the cyclical response.

The variability in profit attributable to the nature of a business and the ability of management to react to the business cycle is commonly referred to as operating leverage. As a good financial officer, you would have to incorporate your firm's operating leverage characteristics into your analysis of its investment opportunities to see that the resultant profit variability does not cause financial embarrassment to the firm or misguide you into selecting a project which appeared good because business was rising—only to fail during the downturn in the business cycle.

Operating Leverage

Operating leverage arises whenever a firm can expand output and sales without a proportionate increase in costs. Under those circumstances, operating profits, those directly related to the item's production and sale, increase proportionately more than sales increase. Of course if output decreases without an accompanying proportionate decrease in costs, the firm's operating profits shrink proportionately more than the decrease in sales.

High degrees of operating leverage usually occur among those firms with high fixed costs and low variable costs. Fixed costs are those which do not change as output changes. The dollar amount of fixed costs remains constant whether the firm produces 100,000 or 1,000,000 units. Obviously, the fixed cost per unit of output decreases as the number of units produced increases and the fixed cost is spread over the greater number of units. Examples of *fixed costs* include executive salaries which remain constant even if the output of the firm dips, security guards, rent on buildings, heating, lighting, and general maintenance; all are required costs and must be paid even if output and sales decline. *Variable costs,* on the other hand, vary directly with the number of units produced and sold. For example, the total cost of raw materials used in production will rise whenever one additional unit is produced and fall whenever one additional unit is not produced. There are also costs which are *semifixed:* their totals are constant until a certain number of units have been produced, and then the costs jump. Rent cost is fixed up to the point where a second building has to be rented, at which point it jumps to a new fixed level. Typical examples of firms with high fixed costs and low variable costs are automobile manufacturers, electrical utilities, railroads, airlines, trucking companies, steel manufacturers, and mining firms.

We can trace the effect on a firm of a high degree of operating leverage:

1. The firm encounters a large expenditure to acquire the means of production. Railroads have to lay a substantial amount of costly tract, airlines have to acquire large fleets of aircraft and many terminal buildings, and steel companies need enormous rolling mills and blast furnaces. Already the firm has large fixed costs. It must pay property taxes on the property, plant, and equipment it has purchased; it must maintain the plants and incur other expenses even before it starts production.

2. The firm buys the raw material, hires the labor force, and starts production. At very low levels of production, the firm buys limited amounts of raw materials and hires a small work force, but it still must maintain the plant and equipment.

3. The output accelerates. The firm buys more raw materials and enlarges the work force, but it does not expand the plant or the equipment. The firm still may not be covering the costs of maintaining the plant and equipment and may still be losing money because it is not covering all the fixed costs.

4. Output expands to a point where fixed and variable costs are exactly offset by revenues. The firm is said to have reached its *breakeven point.*

5. Output continues to accelerate without need for expansion in plant or equip-

ment, revenues more than cover both the fixed and variable costs, and the firm starts to show an operating profit.

6. Further increases in output lead to still further increases in operating profits.

7. A decline in output accompanying a business recession forces the firm to reduce its labor force and curtail purchase of raw materials, but it does not reduce the firm's plant and equipment or fixed costs, and operating profits fall.

8. The fluctuations in operating profits continue as output rises and falls. The magnitude of these fluctuations depends on the firm's degree of operating lever-age—which we can measure.

We have said that operating leverage will be higher for a firm with high fixed costs and low variable costs than for a firm with low fixed costs and high variable costs. The exact degree depends on the relative proportions of the two types of costs and on the firm's present level of output. Specifically, the degree of operating leverage is measured by the relationship of the percentage change in operating profits to the percentage change in output, as in Equation 2-1.

$$\text{Degree of operating leverage at } x \text{ units} = \frac{\text{Percentage change in operating profits}}{\text{Percentage change in output}} \quad (2\text{-}1)$$

For example, assume for the ABC Company the information shown in Table 2-1. The percentage change in operating profit (OP) is:

$$\frac{\text{OP}_{1977} - \text{OP}_{1976}}{\text{OP}_{1976}} \quad (2\text{-}2)$$

$$\frac{680{,}000 - 500{,}000}{500{,}000} = 36\%$$

The percentage change in output (Q) is:

$$\frac{Q_{1977} - Q_{1976}}{Q_{1976}} \quad (2\text{-}3)$$

$$\frac{120{,}000 - 100{,}000}{100{,}000} = 20\%$$

The degree of operating leverage (DOL) for the ABC Company at an output of 100,000 units is:

$$\text{DOL}_{100{,}000} = \frac{36\%}{20\%} = 1.8 \quad (2\text{-}4)$$

A DOL of 1.8 implies that the ABC Company has a combination of relatively high fixed costs and relatively low variable costs at its present level of output and can ex-

Table 2-1   Operating Statistics for the ABC Company

	1976		1977	
Units produced		100,000		120,000
Sales		$1,000,000		$1,200,000
Fixed costs	$400,000		$400,000	
Variable costs	100,000		120,000	
Total operating costs		$500,000		520,000
Operating profits		$500,000		$680,000

pand operating profits by a 1.8 factor of any increase in output. At a different level of output, the DOL could change, for the relationship between the variable and fixed costs might change.

We can also determine the DOL in terms of sales revenues (S) instead of units of output, although the answer remains the same,[5] if we use Equation 2-5.

$$DOL_x = \frac{S - VC}{S - VC - FC} \tag{2-5}$$

where

$\quad$ S = sales revenues at x units
$\quad$ VC = variable cost at x units
$\quad$ FC = fixed cost

For the ABC Company, the $DOL_{100,000}$ is:

$$\frac{1,000,000 - 100,000}{1,000,000 - 100,000 - 400,000} = 1.8$$

We can also graphically examine the degree of operating leverage through break-even analysis, which we will discuss in the next section.

The degree of operating leverage reveals important insight to the financial officer concerning the operating risks of the firm. A high DOL implies that there will be more fluctuation in operating earnings than a lower DOL. This alerts the financial officer to the necessity for faster and more accurate economic forecasts and the need to search for investment opportunities which might offset the operating risk. Large fixed investments in plant and equipment generate the need for huge amounts of borrowing to finance their purchase. The financial officer should be aware that to couple a high DOL with debt-heavy financing can lead to trouble because of the fluctuations in operating income of a high DOL firm. As the DOL increases, you should decrease your dependence on debt as a means of financing investment projects. The railroads with their historical record of numerous bankruptcies are ex-

---

[5] We can derive Equation 2-5 as follows:
$\quad$ The initial profit is $Q(P - V) - FC$, and the percentage change in profit is therefore:

$$\frac{\Delta Q(P - V)}{Q(P - V) - FC}$$

where:
$\quad$ P = price per unit
$\quad$ Q = number of units
$\quad$ S = P × Q
$\quad$ V = variable cost per unit
$\quad$ VC = V × Q
$\quad$ FC = total fixed cost

The percentage change in output is $\frac{\Delta Q}{Q}$, so the ratio between the two is:

$$\frac{\frac{\Delta Q(P - V)}{Q(P - V) - FC}}{\frac{\Delta Q}{Q}} = \frac{\Delta Q(P - V)}{Q(P - V) - FC} \times \frac{Q}{\Delta Q} = \frac{Q(P - V)}{Q(P - V) - FC}$$

Therefore:

$$\frac{S - VC}{S - VC - FC}$$

amples of high-DOL firms which used large amounts of debt, despite their high DOL, and collapsed under the financial burden.

BREAKEVEN ANALYSIS

Breakeven analysis is the graphic or mathematical representation of the degree of leverage, based on the relationship between the firm's total revenue and its total cost as the output changes. The breakeven point is that output at which the total revenue exactly offsets the total costs, which consist of fixed plus variable costs. In symbols the breakeven point is:

$$TR = TC \qquad (2\text{-}6)$$

where
   TR = total revenue
   TC = total cost

At that point the firm is neither losing money nor making any operating profit because:

$$TR = P(x) \qquad (2\text{-}7)$$

where
   P = selling price per unit of output
   x = the total number of units of output

and

$$TC = FC + VC(x) \qquad (2\text{-}8)$$

where
   FC = total fixed costs
   VC = variable cost per unit
   x = the total number of units of output

Substituting Equations (2-8) and (2-7) into Equation (2-6) yields the breakeven point (BEP) in units:

$$P(x) = FC + VC(x) \qquad (2\text{-}9)$$

$$BEP_x = \frac{FC}{P - VC}$$

For example, assume for the DEF Company the operating statistics shown in Table 2-2. The DEF Company breakeven point would be:

$$\$10(x) = \$1,000,000 + \$6(x)$$
$$4(x) = \$1,000,000$$
$$x = 250,000 \text{ units}$$

Table 2-2   Operating Statistics for the DEF Company

Selling price per unit	$10.00
Fixed cost	$1,000,000.00
Variable cost per unit	$6.00

Table 2-3 Tabular Calculation of Breakeven Point

Units sold	Fixed cost	Variable costs	Total cost	Total revenue	Operating profit (loss)
100,000	$1,000,000	$ 600,000	$1,600,000	$1,000,000	($600,000)
150,000	1,000,000	900,000	1,900,000	1,500,000	(400,000)
200,000	1,000,000	1,200,000	2,200,000	2,000,000	(200,000)
250,000	1,000,000	1,500,000	2,500,000	2,500,000	—
300,000	1,000,000	1,800,000	2,800,000	3,000,000	200,000
350,000	1,000,000	2,100,000	3,100,000	3,500,000	400,000
400,000	1,000,000	2,400,000	3,400,000	4,000,000	600,000
500,000	1,000,000	3,000,000	4,000,000	5,000,000	1,000,000

We could also find the breakeven point by the trial-and-error method shown in Table 2-3.

Both the mathematical and the trial-and-error methods indicate that the breakeven point for the DEF Company is 250,000 units. Below that output, the firm shows a loss in operating income; above that point, the firm shows an operating profit. Also note that the percentage increase in operating profits is proportionately more than the percentage increase in unit sales, indicating a high DOL. Operating profits doubled, for example, when unit sales rose only 16.67 percent from 300,000 to 350,000.

We can also graph this relationship among total revenue, total cost, and output as shown in Figure 2-1. The horizontal axis of the graph measures the output (x), or the number of units produced. Moving from left to right, the number of units increases. The vertical axis measures the operating revenues and costs in dollars, which increase as we move up the axis. Fixed costs, since they are constant regardless of the output, are represented by the flat line extending from the vertical axis at $1,000,000 (DEF Company's fixed costs). Notice that since there is no relationship between the fixed costs and the number of units produced, the dollar amount of fixed costs measured on the vertical axis remains the same regardless of how far to the right output extends on the vertical axis. Total costs, on the other

Figure 2-1 Breakeven Graph

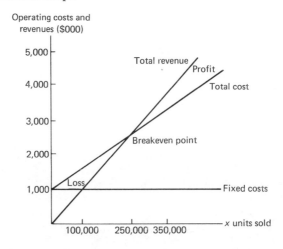

hand, rise in a direct relationship with the number of units because each additional unit costs another $6.00 in variable costs.

Since total costs are the sum of the fixed plus the variable costs, we plot the total-cost line starting at the $1,000,000 level of the fixed costs on the vertical axis. This corresponds to a position of no production and no variable costs for the firm. As the number of units increases moving out the horizontal axis, the total-cost line moves upward to the right by an amount of $6.00 measured on the vertical axis for each additional unit of production on the horizontal axis. Total revenues are also directly related to the number of units produced. In this example, total revenues increase $10.00 for every unit sold. We plot total revenues starting at zero on both axes, to represent a position of no sales and no revenue.

Where the total-cost and the total-revenue lines cross is the breakeven point. Reading off the graph, we can see this is 250,000 units, the same answer we derived through trial-and-error tabulating and mathematical calculations. To the left of and below the breakeven point, the firm is operating at a loss; to the right of and above the breakeven point, it is operating at a profit.

Notice how the financial officer can calculate the breakeven point for any project given the estimated selling price of the item and the variable and fixed costs projections. Once the breakeven point has been calculated, the financial officer can analyze the output needed to keep from operating at a loss and see if it is reasonably attainable. Further, the financial officer can use the breakeven concept to incorporate the operating environment into the analysis, for example, evaluating alternative production methods and the effect their different proportions of fixed to variable costs might have on operating profit. Assume that an alternative production method had fixed costs of only $100,000 (instead of the previous $1,000,000) yet retained the same variable cost per unit ($6) and the same selling price ($10). Then the breakeven point (BEP) would be:

$$\$10(x) = \$100,000 + \$6(x) \tag{2-10}$$
$$\$4(x) = \$100,000$$
$$\text{BEP} = 25,000 \text{ units}$$

only 25,000 units, considerably less than the 250,000 units that marked the breakeven point of the first production method. This concurs with our original intuition that lower fixed costs in relation to variable costs are indicative of a less volatile operating environment. Fixed-cost lines which are relatively low on the vertical axis and accompanied by relatively steeply rising total-cost lines are usually indicative of low operating risk, good countercyclical response, and limited fluctuations in operating profits.

The financial officer can also change the selling price or the variable cost per unit to determine the effect on the BEP. These changes can be examined for their effect on the BEP to help analyze the operating risk of the project.

Let us use breakeven analysis to examine the differences in operating performance between a firm with a combination of high fixed cost and low variable costs and a firm with a combination of low fixed costs and high variable costs. The breakeven graph in Figure 2-2 is typical of a high fixed-cost/low variable-costs firm, while Figure 2-3 is typical of a low fixed-cost/high variable-costs firm. Notice that the high fixed-cost/low variable-costs firm of Figure 2-2 does not reach the breakeven point until a considerably larger output has been achieved than is needed for the low fixed-cost/high variable-costs firm of Figure 2-3. However, once the firm in Figure 2-2 has increased its output past the breakeven point, its profits accelerate at a much more rapid rate than those of the other firm because each additional unit of output sold after the breakeven point has been surpassed adds a much larger mar-

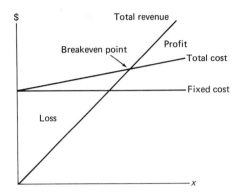

Figure 2-2 Breakeven Graph of a High Fixed-Cost Low Variable-Cost Firm

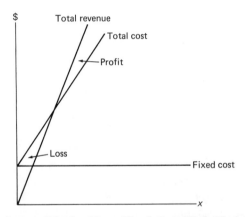

Figure 2-3 Breakeven Graph of Low Fixed-Cost High Variable-Cost Firm

ginal profit per unit. Conversely, when output declines, the firm with high fixed costs will experience a much more pronounced drop in operating profits.

We can also illustrate algebraically the effect of the two different combinations of fixed and variable costs. Assume the following operating statistics for companies A and B:

	A High fixed-cost firm	B Low fixed-cost firm
Selling price	$10.00/unit	$10.00/unit
Fixed cost	$1,000,000	$40,000
Variable costs	$2.00/unit	$6.00/unit
BEP	125,000 units	10,000 units

If sales increased above BEP by:	A's operating profits increase:	B's operating profits increase:
25,000 units	$200,000	$100,000
35,000 units	280,000	140,000
50,000 units	400,000	200,000
100,000 units	800,000	400,000

The high fixed-cost/low variable-costs firm A has a much higher breakeven point than firm B. A's operating profits also respond more dramatically to an increase in sales than do those of firm B. For the same 25,000-unit increase in output, firm A has a $200,000 jump in operating profits, double that of firm B. Consistently, firm A has twice the increase in operating profit than firm B for any given increase in sales, because A's profit on each additional unit sold ($8) is twice that of B ($4). On the other hand, firm A's operating profits would sink twice as fast as those of B for every given unit decrease in output.

We can also get the same illustration by measuring the degree of operating leverage for each firm at 150,000 units for A and 35,000 units for B,[6] assuming an increase of 10,000 units for each firm.

$$\text{DOL}_A = \frac{\dfrac{\$280{,}000 - \$200{,}000}{\$200{,}000}}{\dfrac{160{,}000 - 150{,}000}{150{,}000}} \tag{2-11}$$

$$= \frac{40\%}{6.6\%}$$

$$= 6.06$$

$$\text{DOL}_B = \frac{\dfrac{\$140{,}000 - \$10{,}000}{\$100{,}000}}{\dfrac{45{,}000 - 35{,}000}{35{,}000}}$$

$$= \frac{40\%}{28.57\%}$$

$$= 1.4$$

Firm A's degree of operating leverage of 6 is over 4 times that of B at 1.4 and is indicative of a very high operating risk. B's DOL is more in line with a firm of much lower operating risk.

All three methods of measuring operating risk (graphically, algebraically, and DOL) indicate that firms with a combination of high fixed costs and low variable costs have more potential for rapid upswings and declines in their operating profits than firms with low fixed costs and high variable costs. These large potential swings in operating profits make the financial officer's evaluation and financing of investment opportunities more difficult. Among other considerations, the financial officer will have to be more careful when borrowing to avoid having large repayments of the loan fall during a sharp decline in the operating profits. Negotiating loans and the sales of securities with investors will also be a harder job because of the greater operating risk. Investors will be more apt to demand a larger interest rate or pay a lower price for the stock of the firm with the greater operating risk, and the financial officer will have to try to offset that with shrewder negotiations.

Problems with Linear Breakeven Analysis

Up to this point we have been drawing the total-cost and the total-revenue lines as straight lines, implying that as output increased or decreased the cost and the revenues increased or decreased in direct proportion. For several reasons this does not

---

[6] The DOL formula does not work when the initial period's operating profit is zero.

have to be the case.[7] Variable costs per unit do not have to remain constant regardless of the number of units produced. It is possible that variable costs per unit will actually fall over a certain range of output and then begin to rise quite rapidly after that. The decline can come about because of quantity discounts on raw material purchases, more efficient utilization of the work force, or many other similar reasons. The rise in variable costs per unit begins to appear after a certain output as less efficient workers must be added to the work force, raw material quantity purchases become so large as to require expensive storage, or strains on the efficiency of production at high output appear, such as fixed costs which at the upper levels of output become partly variable.

Revenue per unit sold does not have to remain constant regardless of the output. In fact, it is common for firms to offer quantity discounts on larger orders or to lower the item's selling price to induce more purchases.

When more than one product is involved, application of breakeven analysis tends to be confusing. Unless the proportion of sales among the products remains constant, a single breakeven point or graph may mislead the financial officer. Several different breakeven graphs may have to be prepared, one for each product, when dealing with a multiple-product situation. For your evaluation of investment opportunities, it is a good idea to have separate breakeven graphs for each proposed project.

The breakeven graph also assumes a stability that may not be realizable. Basically, you use the breakeven graph to evaluate future operating risks. Generating the relationship lines between the total costs and revenues and the output on historical data may be misleading. You might have to build in some provision for possible changes in the relationships.[8] We can account for some of these problems by using nonlinear breakeven analysis.[9]

Nonlinear Breakeven Analysis

If there are reasons to suspect that the selling price per unit declines as the output increases, such that total revenue increases at a decreasing rather than a constant rate, we cannot represent the total revenue as a straight line, but must specify some other nonlinear relationship.

We might express the relationship between total revenues and output as in Figure 2-4. Notice how the total-revenue line curves inward to the right, reflecting a decreasing unit price as output rises. The total-cost line first curves inward to the right, reflecting the decreasing variable costs over that range of output, and then curves outward to the left, reflecting increasing variable costs per unit. The fixed-cost line remains flat since it does not change regardless of the volume.

---

[7] Donald L. Raun, "The Limitations of Profit Graphs, Breakeven Analysis, and Budgets," *Accounting Review*, October 1964, 927–945.

[8] It is possible to bound the breakeven relationships both above and below the expected relationship illustrated in the example to account for uncertainty and for a result higher or lower than expected. We will cover the concept and handling of uncertainty in greater detail in future chapters.

[9] Another fault of breakeven point analysis as usually employed is its failure to check on the solvency of the firm. Since the typical breakeven analysis includes the use of noncash expenses, that is those accounting expenses which do not require a cash outlay, it is possible that the firm may be breaking even on a cash basis although operating at a loss under the typical breakeven analysis. Since most firms will continue to operate for a relatively long period of time if they remain profitable on a cash basis, we might want to use the cash breakeven approach, which reflects the relationships between output and total cash expenses.

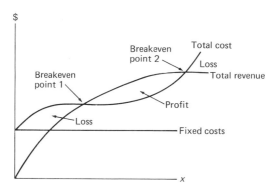

Figure 2-4 Nonlinear Breakeven Graph

Where the total-revenue and the total-cost curves intersect, we have a breakeven point. In Figure 2-4, we have two breakeven points. The lower breakeven point is where the firm first starts to show an operating profit, just as in the linear breakeven graph. To the right of that point the firm continues to operate at a profit, represented by the distance between the total-revenue and the total-cost lines. However, after a certain output level, the distance begins to narrow because each additional unit of output is bringing in less revenue than the one before, yet costing more to produce. Eventually, if fhe firm continues to expand output, total costs again catch up to total revenues and we encounter a second breakeven point, where the firm is just starting to *lose* money.

No firm will intentionally operate at a level of output which would bring it close to the second breakeven point. In fact, the firm will try to operate where the distance between the total-revenue and the total-cost curves is greatest. At that point on Figure 2-4, operating profits are maximized because the additional revenue from the last unit sold just equals the additional costs of producing that unit. If the firm sells one more unit, the additional cost of producing that unit will exceed the revenues generated, and the firm is on its way toward the second breakeven point.[10]

AN INTEGRATED VIEW OF THE FINANCE FUNCTION

As a member of the corporate financial staff, you must always look to the unified whole and not to the special interests of your department as a self-contained group. The concerted efforts of everyone in the firm must be focused upon remaining viable and hopefully excelling in the competitive world, moving the firm toward its goal, and assuring its continuity. It will be your responsibility to consider in some systematic fashion all the facets of investment opportunity evaluation and financing. These include:

1. Fostering a climate in which the initial idea may flourish
2. Gathering pertinent information on the project's sales potential, legality, government regulations, general economic activity, financial market conditions, and operating risks in the present and future business environments

---

[10] Remember that the firm is maximizing its profits in an economic sense when its MC = MR.

3. Screening the proposed projects for a go/no go decision (see Capital Budgeting, Chapters 5–7 for such systems)

4. Implementing the decision to go with particular emphasis on timing the production and financing to achieve the maximum profit position

5. Coordinating and controlling the ongoing operations, once started, and providing contingency planning if things are not working out as planned

Let us take a very brief and sketchy example of what might be involved in each of these steps. Assume we have a soap manufacturer with only one product, a very successful low suds, highly powerful detergent.

Step 1. The marketing research department initiates the idea of a low suds and milder detergent. It believes a large number of households will buy the product.

Step 2. We gather the following information:
  a. There is nothing illegal about the product. It is nontoxic, nondestructive, and has no side effects which could leave the company liable in a law suit.
  b. It meets all government regulations including a low phosphate content and other ecological considerations. It meets all prevailing health code restrictions and falls within government price guidelines.
  c. The potential market for the product has been estimated using test-market information, and consumer surveys indicate that homemakers do want a milder, less sudsy detergent. The selling price and quantity of the product is estimated. The expected costs for salespeople and advertising are established.
  d. The general economic conditions expected to prevail are favorable to the introduction of the new detergent, since the business cycle is in an up phase.
  e. The operating risks have been considered. There is a plentiful and inexpensive supply of the raw materials needed, the distribution channels are open to the firm since they are the same as those used for its high suds detergent, and the warehouse and production facilities are sufficient to handle the anticipated output.
  f. The financial markets have a sufficient supply of funds; the firm can easily and inexpensively raise the money to finance the project.

Step 3. The project meets the firm's criteria for profitability and is among the most potentially profitable of those the firm has available.

Step 4. The project is implemented such that initial production will coordinate with the demand for the product and the upswing in the economy. The financing is arranged so that it allows the company maximum flexibility while satisfying the lenders, thereby being as inexpensive as possible.

Step 5. The ongoing operations of the project are coordinated and controlled. Careful budgets are prepared for the project, and the results are watched to see that the project does not deviate from expected costs and estimated revenues. The low sudser flops because of new, unanticipated government regulations requiring a high suds level and because users develop a mysterious sneezing when they try the product. Contingency plans are implemented to liquidate the inventory and revamp production facilities for increased production of the high sudser.

While the details in each step will obviously vary with different circumstances, it is apparent that the financial officer must follow all the steps to be sure the firm as a whole is guided in the right direction at all times. (Rarely will such utter disaster befall the project that is carefully planned and monitored by an alert finance department.)

SUMMARY

After having read Chapter 2, you should be able to answer these questions:

1. Who are the other major groups in society which make up the operating environment of the firm?

The firm does not operate in a vacuum. It must weigh its investment and financing decisions with an eye toward the reaction of other groups in society. Prominent among these groups are the consumer, acting as a class, who in recent years has played a more active role in shaping the business environment; the government through fiscal policies which directly affect the economic climate; and the regulatory authorities which have control over specific aspects of particular industries.

2. What must I consider when I represent my firm in its attempt to raise capital?

We must consider interest rates, which represent the price of the capital you will be negotiating to borrow. Clever financial officers can negotiate lower interest rates for their firms if they time the offering of securities and the borrowing of funds to low points in interest rate fluctuations and if they tailor the terms of loans to the needs of the lenders without unduly restricting the flexibility of their own firms. Since monetary policy plays such an important role in determining interest rate fluctuations, you must constantly watch monetary policy and the rate of change in the level of prices.

3. What are the pertinent operating characteristics I must consider in my evaluation of what the firm should invest in and how to finance it?

You must consider those operating risks which are externally imposed upon the firm such as the business cycle, the quality of the firm's sales, and the quality and price of the firm's raw materials. We also examined internal business risks. These included management's ability to utilize the firm's assets, to diversify properly, and to mount an effective countercyclical effort—in addition to its general management skills. We saw how we could get some insight into the degree of operating risk by examining the firm's operating leverage and analyzing its position through break-even analysis.

QUESTIONS

2-1 (a) Define briefly what is meant by a financial market.
   (b) Distinguish between capital markets and money markets.
2-2 How might inflation affect the investment and financing decisions of the firm?
2-3 Discuss some of the factors that affect the external operating risks of firms. Identify specific industries and the specific external operating factors which affect them.
2-4 (a) Distinguish between the terms *operating leverage* and *degree of operating leverage* (DOL).
   (b) Most public utilities, such as electric and telephone companies, are felt to have a greater degree of operating leverage than most nonregulated firms. Why is this assertion generally true?
2-5 The financial managers of the Penn Central railroad are often accused of contributing to the railroad's bankrupt status due to the large amount of debt used

to finance investments (railroad and non-railroad related). What is the basis of this criticism, and do you agree?

2-6 What is (a) breakeven analysis and (b) the breakeven point?

2-7 If a firm divests itself of a portion of its fixed cost, but its variable cost per unit of output remains the same, what happens to (a) the firm's breakeven point and (b) the degree of operating leverage at any given output level?

2-8 Discuss some of the difficulties encountered in using linear breakeven analysis as opposed to nonlinear breakeven analysis.

PROBLEMS

2-1 AJAX Corporation produces and sells widgets in a highly competitive market. That is, the firm can sell as many widgets as it wants to at a price of $10 per widget. The firm has fixed costs of $10,000 regardless of the level of output produced, and a constant variable cost per widget of $2.

(a) What is the breakeven output level for the firm? Illustrate graphically.

(b) (1) If 1,800 widgets were sold in 1974, what was the firm's total operating profit? (2) If 2,000 widgets were sold in 1975, what was the firm's total operating profit?

(c) (1) What is the degree of operating leverage (DOL) at 1,800 units of output? (2) If 2,500 widgets had been sold in 1975 instead of 2,000, would the DOL for 1,800 widgets have changed? Explain precisely what your calculated answers mean. Use output, not dollar value of sales, in calculating DOL.

(d) Using sales revenues, calculate the DOL for 1974.

(e) If the price at which widgets can be sold increases to $12, what happens to the firm's breakeven point? Illustrate graphically.

(f) If the price of widgets increases to $12, does the DOL at 1,800 widgets change?

2-2 American Corporation sells United States flags in a highly competitive market at a price of $5. Its present fixed cost is $50,000 and its variable cost per flag is $3. Two plant modernization projects are being evaluated by the firm's management, but only one project will be selected. Project A will result in a thorough overhaul of the production facilities with fixed costs increasing to $150,000 and variable cost per flag falling to $2. Project B is a less ambitious undertaking that results in fixed costs increasing to $75,000 and variable cost per flag decreasing to $2.30. Currently about 55,000 flags are sold each year, but sales in the past have been unstable.

(a) Calculate the breakeven points for the existing facilities with no modernization, with project A, and with project B. Illustrate graphically.

(b) Calculate the degree of operating leverage (DOL) for sales of $275,000 (55,000 flags) for the existing plant with no modernization, with project A, and with project B.

(c) Which project seems the less risky? Why?

(d) Calculate the profits of the existing plant with no modernization, with project A, and with project B. Considering profits as well as risk, which project, if any, seems preferable?

BIBLIOGRAPHY

Crowningshield, Gerald R., and George J. Battista. "Cost-Volume-Profit Analysis in Planning and Control." *N.A.A. Bulletin,* XLV (July 1963), 3–15.

Eisner, Robert. "Factors Affecting the Level of Interest Rates." In *Savings and Residential Financing.* U.S. Savings and Loan League, Chicago, 1968.

Frazer, W. J., Jr. "Some Factors Affecting Business Financing." *Southern Economic Journal,* XXV (July 1958), 33–47.

Freund, William C. "The Dynamic Financial Markets." *Financial Executive,* XXXIII (May 1965), 11–26, 57–58.

Gaskill, William J. "What's Ahead for Corporations in Social Responsibility?" *Financial Executive,* XXXIX (July 1971), 10–18.

Haslem, John A. "Leverage Effects on Corporate Earnings." *Arizona Business Review,* March 1970, 7–11.

Hobbs, J. B. "Volume-Mix-Price Cost Budget Variance Budget Analysis: A Proper Approach." *Accounting Review,* XXXIX (October 1964), 905–913.

Hunt, Pearson. "A Proposal for Precise Definitions of 'Trading on Equity' and 'Leverage.'" *Journal of Finance,* XVI (September 1961), 377–386.

Jaedicke, Robert K., and Alexander A. Robicheck. "Cost-Volume-Profit Analysis under Conditions of Uncertainty." *Accounting Review,* XXXIX (October 1964).

Kelvie, William E., and John M. Sinclair. "New Techniques for Breakeven Charts." *Financial Executive,* XXXVI (June 1968), 31–43.

Morrison, Thomas A., and Eugene Kaczka. "A New Application of Calculus and Risk Analysis to Cost-Volume-Profit Changes." *Accounting Review,* XLIV (April 1969), 330–343.

Raun, D. L. "The Limitations of Profit Graphs, Break-even Analysis, and Budgets." *Accounting Review,* XXXIX (October 1964), 927–945.

Van Horne, James. "Interest-Rate Expectations, the Shape of the Yield Curve, and Monetary Policy." *Review of Economics and Statistics,* XLVIII (May 1966), 211–215.

Appendix 2A **Taxes in the Operating Environment**

Federal taxes on the income of corporations and individuals are part of the operating environment which you, as the financial officer, must consider in your evaluation of investment opportunities and their financing. Any money not paid out in taxes, which otherwise might have been, is a direct dollar benefit to the firm. Of course, you do not sacrifice profitable investment opportunities just to reduce the firm's tax liability, but you must always keep the tax effects in mind as another factor in your analysis.

Since federal tax codes are continually being changed, we will discuss only the major points in the present codes. As a financial officer, you would consult with your firm's tax attorneys regarding any question of the applicability of the codes to your particular circumstances. Basically, there are two sets of codes, one for corporations and the other for individuals.

CORPORATE INCOME TAX REGULATIONS

Corporations are taxed on their income, since they are independent entities separate from their owners. Only after the corporate taxes are paid do the shareholders have a claim on the residual income. Then, when they receive it from the corporation, another tax is levied on it as personal income.

There are several categories of corporate income which are taxed under different rates or regulations. These include: (1) ordinary income, (2) capital gains or losses, (3) net operating losses, (4) dividend income, (5) retained earnings, and (6) subchapter S corporation income.

Ordinary Income

The first $50,000 of income earned in the normal course of business (ordinary income) is taxed at a 22 percent rate by the federal government. All ordinary income above $50,000 is taxed at a 48 percent rate, which is technically a 22 percent base rate plus a 26 percent surcharge rate. The federal income taxes on $100,000 of ordinary corporate income would be:

$$22\% \times 50,000 = \$11,000$$
$$48\% \times 50,000 = \underline{24,000}$$
$$\$35,000$$

In addition, several states also tax the ordinary income of the corporation at various rates, although we will not discuss them here since there is such a large variation among the states.

Since the tax regulations changed in 1975, it is no longer possible to retain common ownership of several small corporations such that each has an income below $50,000 and is taxed at the lower rate. Presently, only one firm in the group will be taxed at the 22 percent base rate, while the others will be taxed at the 48 percent rate.

Capital Gains and Losses

Capital gains or losses arise from the sale of a capital asset at more (gain) or less (loss) than its current value on the company's books. For example, if a capital asset had a value on the company's books of $5,000 and was sold to another firm for $6,000, there would be a $1,000 capital gain to the seller. Obviously, this is not considered ordinary income, for it typically does not arise from the sale of the firm's product but from the sale of its machinery or plant used in the production of that product or from the sale of security investments.

Capital gains and losses are further classified according to the length of time the asset was owned before it was sold. Gains and losses on the sale of capital assets owned less than six months are considered short-term. For tax purposes, the short-term capital losses are subtracted from the short-term capital gains to derive the net short-term capital gains figure, which is included in the firm's ordinary income and taxed at the ordinary income tax rates. Gains and losses on the sale of capital assets owned more than six months are considered long-term. Net long-term gains, which are the difference between the long-term capital gains and the long-term capital losses, are subject to a maximum tax rate of 30 percent or 22 percent if the firm's income, including the net long-term gains, is less than $50,000.

Net capital losses, either short- or long-term, are not deductible from the firm's ordinary income and may only reduce the firm's tax liability against any future capital gains. However, there are specific exceptions to this rule, which allow such firms as banks to deduct capital losses on security investments directly from ordinary income, while paying a maximum of 30 percent on capital gains.

The capital gains tax regulations are also different when applied to assets which can be depreciated, their value being written down over the years. Federal tax regulations allow certain capital assets, such as machinery, to be depreciated at an accelerated rate in excess of the pro rata amount which would be proportional to the machine's expected number of years of life. The tax codes try to recapture the excess capital gain generated when a piece of equipment which had been rapidly written down in value on the company's books is sold. All proceeds of the sale in excess of what would have been the depreciated value of the machine under the straightline method of depreciation (the pro rata method) are taxed at ordinary income rates, while that portion of the proceeds which represents the difference between the straightline depreciation value and the sale price is taxed at the 30 percent maximum capital gains rate. For example, assume the following information on the sale of a machine:

Original cost	$100,000
Sale price	25,000
Book value using straightline depreciation	20,000
Value on books using accelerated depreciation	16,000
Portion of proceeds taxed as capital gain ($25,000 − $20,000)	5,000
Portion of proceeds taxed as ordinary income ($20,000 − $16,000)	4,000
Maximum tax on sale	30% × $5,000 = $1,500
	48% × 4,000 = 1,920
	$3,420

Notice how this taxing procedure allows the government to increase the tax liability on the sale to $3,420 from what otherwise would have been 30 percent of $9,000 or only $2,700. The idea is that since the government allowed the more rapid depreciation and gave up some tax revenues earlier, it should now recapture those lost revenues.

Capital losses may be carried backwards or forwards in the sense that they may be used to offset capital gains as far as three years back or five years into the future. To carry the capital loss backwards requires refiling the prior tax reports. A carryforward would be filed as recorded. For example, assume the firm had a capital loss this year of $50,000 and a capital gain of $75,000 next year. The firm would pay the capital gains rate on the $25,000 differential.

Net Operating Carryback and Carryforward

The net operating loss is distinguished from the capital gains loss because it arises from the ordinary operations of the firm. Such a loss can be deducted from ordinary income as far as three years back, if forms are refiled, and as far as five years forward. However, firms which purchase other firms exclusively to acquire their tax loss carryforwards and reduce the purchasing firm's tax liability are prohibited from using the tax losses unless they operate the acquired firm as an ongoing concern, not abandoning or selling any part of the acquired firm for two years.

Corporate Dividend Income

Corporate income which comes from the dividends on stock owned in other corporations is 85 percent exempt from federal income taxes. Thus, if firm A receives $10,000 in dividends from firm B, firm A's tax liability on that income is limited to its ordinary income tax rate on $1,500. If firm A were in the 48 percent income tax bracket, it would pay $720 in taxes on that $10,000 dividend, an effective rate of only 7.2 percent. The tax codes allow this exclusion on the grounds that taxing intercorporate dividend income would be triple taxation: once at firm B, once at firm A, and once again when received as dividend income by the stockholders of firm A.

Retained Earnings

Retained earnings are that portion of the firm's income which is not paid out to the stockholders as dividends. Many firms, in the past, have tried to avoid the double taxation effect by retaining all income and paying no dividends. This has been particularly true of closely held, family holding corporations. The federal tax codes, however, allow the government to make a determination of such intent and impose additional tax liabilities under Section 531 of the Internal Revenue Code. If the federal government can show that retained earnings were to avoid taxes and not for reinvestment in the operations of the firm, it may levy a 27.5 percent tax on the first $100,000 of retained earnings above $100,000 and 38.5 percent on additional amounts.

Subchapter S Corporate Tax

Subchapter S corporations are like any other corporation except in their federal tax liability. Upon filing with the Internal Revenue Service, a corporation of fewer than ten stockholders can qualify to be taxed as a partnership, avoiding the double taxation effect and allowing tax writeoffs against the stockholder's personal income while retaining the protection of the limited liability laws.

PERSONAL INCOME TAX REGULATIONS

The federal government levies taxes on the income of individuals as well as on the income of corporations. As in the case of the corporate tax regulations, personal tax regulations are always changing, subject to interpretation, and relatively complex in certain areas. Therefore, we will cover only the major points of the present regulations. As a financial officer or as an individual, you should always consult with your tax attorneys before taking any tax action which is subject to interpretation.

Ordinary Income

Table 2A-1 shows the 1972 tax rate schedules for individuals and for married taxpayers filing joint or separate returns. Notice that it is a graduated income schedule, such that you pay proportionately more of each additional dollar of ordinary income as your income rises. Thus, individuals with incomes over $200,000 will pay $.70 of each additional $1.00 to the federal government for taxes. Theoretically, it is easier for persons in the upper income brackets to stand the higher tax liability rate than for persons in the lower income brackets because each additional dollar of income has less utility to the persons with higher incomes.

This tax structure applies to the ordinary income of all individuals regardless of the source of that income. Income earned on the job, income earned in a sole proprietorship, income earned in a partnership, and income earned in a subchapter S corporation are all taxed at the same rate. Conversely, losses incurred in the ordinary course of business are deducted from the individual's taxable income.

There are, however, many deductions allowed the individual in calculating taxable income, which is gross income less all allowable deductions. First, one is allowed an immediate personal exemption of $750 for oneself and for each member of one's family. Then, one can deduct numerous specific items or take a standard deduction of 15 percent of one's income or $2,000, whichever is lower.

Among the specific allowable deductions are medical expenses, charitable donations, interest payments, and state and local property taxes. Political contributions may be directly credited against the tax liability itself up to $12.50 per person or 50 percent of the contribution, whichever is less. The first $100 of dividend income per person is exempted from reported taxable income. There are many more specific types of deductions which are available and which people use to reduce their tax liability. Many tax-shelter investments, designed to reduce taxes through the use of specific exclusions or deductions, are used by individuals in the upper income brackets who find that at marginal tax rates up to 70 percent, every dollar reduction in taxable income is very valuable.

Capital Gains and Losses

Individual capital gains are divided into long-term and short-term capital gains, just as they are for the corporation. Any profit from the sale of an asset owned less than six months is a short-term gain and is considered part of the individual's ordinary income. It is taxed at ordinary income rates.

The profit on the sale of any asset owned more than six months is a long-term gain and receives special tax treatment. Fifty percent of the net long-term gain may be added to the individual's taxable income and taxed at the ordinary income rates—up to a maximum rate of 25 percent. Thus, the effective tax rate on long-

Table 2A-1 1972 Tax Schedules

Schedule X—Single taxpayers not qualifying for rates in Schedule Y or Z.

If the amount on Form 1040, line 55, is: Enter on Form 1040, line 18:

Not over $500 — 14% of the amount on line 55.

Over—	But not over—		of excess over—
$500	$1,000	$70 + 15%	$500
$1,000	$1,500	$145 + 16%	$1,000
$1,500	$2,000	$225 + 17%	$1,500
$2,000	$4,000	$310 + 19%	$2,000
$4,000	$6,000	$690 + 21%	$4,000
$6,000	$8,000	$1,110 + 24%	$6,000
$8,000	$10,000	$1,590 + 25%	$8,000
$10,000	$12,000	$2,090 + 27%	$10,000
$12,000	$14,000	$2,630 + 29%	$12,000
$14,000	$16,000	$3,210 + 31%	$14,000
$16,000	$18,000	$3,830 + 34%	$16,000
$18,000	$20,000	$4,510 + 36%	$18,000
$20,000	$22,000	$5,230 + 38%	$20,000
$22,000	$26,000	$5,990 + 40%	$22,000
$26,000	$32,000	$7,590 + 45%	$26,000
$32,000	$38,000	$10,290 + 50%	$32,000
$38,000	$44,000	$13,290 + 55%	$38,000
$44,000	$50,000	$16,590 + 60%	$44,000
$50,000	$60,000	$20,190 + 62%	$50,000
$60,000	$70,000	$26,390 + 64%	$60,000
$70,000	$80,000	$32,790 + 66%	$70,000
$80,000	$90,000	$39,390 + 68%	$80,000
$90,000	$100,000	$46,190 + 69%	$90,000
$100,000	.....	$53,090 + 70%	$100,000

Schedule Y—Married taxpayers and certain widows and widowers

If you are a married person living apart from your wife (husband), see chapter 2 to see if you can be considered to be "unmarried" for purposes of using Schedule X or Z.

Filing joint returns and certain widows and widowers

If the amount on Form 1040, line 55, is: Enter on Form 1040, line 18:

Not over $1,000 — 14% of amount on line 55.

Over—	But not over—		of excess over—
$1,000	$2,000	$140 + 15%	$1,000
$2,000	$3,000	$290 + 16%	$2,000
$3,000	$4,000	$450 + 17%	$3,000
$4,000	$8,000	$620 + 19%	$4,000
$8,000	$12,000	$1,380 + 22%	$8,000
$12,000	$16,000	$2,260 + 25%	$12,000
$16,000	$20,000	$3,260 + 28%	$16,000
$20,000	$24,000	$4,380 + 32%	$20,000
$24,000	$28,000	$5,660 + 36%	$24,000
$28,000	$32,000	$7,100 + 39%	$28,000
$32,000	$36,000	$8,660 + 42%	$32,000
$36,000	$40,000	$10,340 + 45%	$36,000
$40,000	$44,000	$12,140 + 48%	$40,000
$44,000	$52,000	$14,060 + 50%	$44,000
$52,000	$64,000	$18,060 + 53%	$52,000
$64,000	$76,000	$24,420 + 55%	$64,000
$76,000	$88,000	$31,020 + 58%	$76,000
$88,000	$100,000	$37,980 + 60%	$88,000
$100,000	$120,000	$45,180 + 62%	$100,000
$120,000	$140,000	$57,580 + 64%	$120,000
$140,000	$160,000	$70,380 + 66%	$140,000
$160,000	$180,000	$83,580 + 68%	$160,000
$180,000	$200,000	$97,180 + 69%	$180,000
$200,000	.....	$110,980 + 70%	$200,000

Filing separate returns

If the amount on Form 1040, line 55, is: Enter on Form 1040, line 18:

Not over $500 — 14% of amount on line 55.

Over—	But not over—		of excess over—
$500	$1,000	$70 + 15%	$500
$1,000	$1,500	$145 + 16%	$1,000
$1,500	$2,000	$225 + 17%	$1,500
$2,000	$4,000	$310 + 19%	$2,000
$4,000	$6,000	$690 + 22%	$4,000
$6,000	$8,000	$1,130 + 25%	$6,000
$8,000	$10,000	$1,630 + 28%	$8,000
$10,000	$12,000	$2,190 + 32%	$10,000
$12,000	$14,000	$2,830 + 36%	$12,000
$14,000	$16,000	$3,550 + 39%	$14,000
$16,000	$18,000	$4,330 + 42%	$16,000
$18,000	$20,000	$5,170 + 45%	$18,000
$20,000	$22,000	$6,070 + 48%	$20,000
$22,000	$26,000	$7,030 + 50%	$22,000
$26,000	$32,000	$9,030 + 53%	$26,000
$32,000	$38,000	$12,210 + 55%	$32,000
$38,000	$44,000	$15,510 + 58%	$38,000
$44,000	$50,000	$18,990 + 60%	$44,000
$50,000	$60,000	$22,590 + 62%	$50,000
$60,000	$70,000	$28,790 + 64%	$60,000
$70,000	$80,000	$35,190 + 66%	$70,000
$80,000	$90,000	$41,790 + 68%	$80,000
$90,000	$100,000	$48,590 + 69%	$90,000
$100,000	.....	$55,490 + 70%	$100,000

SOURCE: *Your Federal Income Tax*, 1973 edition.

term capital gains is 50 percent of the individual's marginal tax bracket or 25 percent, whichever is less. However, after the individual's long-term capital gains exceed $50,000 in any one year, he or she must pay a surcharge of 10 percent on the amount in excess of $30,000, in addition to the regular income tax that is paid.

Unlike corporations, individuals can deduct net capital losses of up to $1,000 a year from ordinary income. Net short-term losses are deducted on a dollar-for-dollar basis, while it requires $2 of net long-term capital losses to reduce ordinary taxable income by $1. The net position is calculated by subtracting all capital losses from all capital gains, regardless of term. Deductions from ordinary income caused by capital losses and in excess of $1,000 must be applied to future capital gains, if any, and may then be deducted at the rate of $1,000 per year from ordinary income until exhausted. Capital losses may not be carried back by individuals. An exception to this rule is that capital losses from the sale of stock in a small business investment may be directly deducted from ordinary income.

Income Averaging

This is a procedure by which an exceptionally large income in one year may be averaged in with more normal income levels in the prior four years to reduce the tax liability. Income averaging lowers the marginal tax bracket for the individual in the year of the exceptionally high income.

3

FINANCIAL BUDGETS, REPORTS, AND CONTROLS

THE TWO PREVIOUS CHAPTERS DESCRIBED your functions and the external operating environment with which you have to contend as a financial executive. But what about the internal environment of the firm? As financial officer, you are responsible for the firm's funds. How do you plan their use and control their expenditure? How do you report your plans to your superiors and the results of those plans to your stockholders? How do you make sure you are not caught off guard, but always remain in control of the financial situation? This chapter explores some of the major accounting and financial tools which let you establish common terminology and concepts, command the situation through the development and coordination of the operating plans, and control actual expenditures to see that those plans are met. We will be concerned with both financial accounting and managerial accounting, particularly as the latter pertains to the preparation of budgets and the process of financial control.

Financial accounting concerns the preparation of reports on the firm's present financial condition (the balance sheet), the progress of the firm over the accounting period (the income statement), and the record of the flow of funds within the firm during the accounting period (the change in financial position statement). These reports are usually prepared by independent certified public accountants with the cooperation of the firm since they are extensively used to communicate with stockholders and interested outside parties such as bank loan officers, security analysts, and others who must be certain that the reports are accurate and truthful.

As a financial officer who has to deal with stockholders, bankers and other outside suppliers of capital to the firm, you must know the financial accounting principles that underlie the construction of these financial reports. You must understand what these outside parties are looking for in your financial statements and be prepared to provide satisfactory reports so that they continue to supply you with capital. For example, your banker will look for certain key financial ratios with which to judge whether or not to give you a loan. You must be sure that you have guided the firm during the accounting period so that your financial statements encourage the banker to provide the loan. When you are involved in considering a merger or the acquisition of another firm, you must be able to interpret the external financial statements of the other firm.

In general, we can say that financial accounting is externally oriented as it reports what the firm did during the accounting period and defines the firm's financial position at the end of the accounting period. It is more a record of what has taken place than a plan of things to come.

In contrast to financial accounting, *managerial accounting* is internally oriented, and it is largely a plan of present and future operations. It is basically concerned with internal management, particularly planning and control through the budget process, and is rarely seen outside the firm. Of course it is interrelated with financial accounting, since managerial accounting forms the basis of operations from which sales and income figures are generated.

In this chapter we explore the budgeting process and all the different types of operating budgets, including sales, production, and cash budgets. We will examine their construction and interpretation and see how budgets serve as internal communication to guide the firm's operations.

As financial officer, you will need to know about the budgets used in managerial accounting in order to communicate with the other departments and with your finance department personnel. For example, if you want to communicate to the marketing department that their proposed project has been trimmed from the budget, you will have to demonstrate in terms of the budget figures why the project is less attractive than the others which were selected. Rejection without an explanation based on the accepted budgeting procedures that apply to all departments in the firm will only undermine cooperation among the departments, and it may detract from your effort to achieve the corporate goal. You will also have to understand the budgets in order to properly participate in their construction, as you will be expected to do, since you will be coordinating them into one central budget and overseeing the firm's cash disbursements and receipts.

You must also know the rudiments of financial and managerial accounting in order to handle your duties of controlling the firm's financial flows. We will see later in this chapter how you can use financial accounting, partly in conjunction with ratio analysis, and managerial accounting, partly in conjunction with budget control and flexibility, to assure control over the firm's operations.

BUDGETING

What is budgeting? The term *budgeting* refers to the entire process of budget planning, preparation, control, reporting, utilizations, and related procedures.[1] In more specific terms, budgeting is a comprehensive operating plan which has been quantified so that it is easily communicated; it is the set of numbers with which you will work during the next operating period. Sometimes it is a highly formal presentation formulated by top management and including their quantitatively expressed goals, policies, objectives and plans for the concern as a whole and for each subdivision.[2] Each individual manager will be expected to achieve the goals expressed for him or her in the budget and to keep within the prescribed expenditures. Top management, if it is doing its job, has based the budget on accurate estimates of the future business environment and derived attainable targets for the managers.

---

[1] Glenn A. Welsch, *Budgeting: Profit Planning and Control,* 4th ed., Prentice-Hall, Englewood Cliffs, N.J., 1971.

[2] *Ibid.*

Budget Preparation

The operating budget for the entire firm is usually prepared by the budget committee or coordinated by the financial officer. This committee solicits pertinent information on expected revenues and expected expenses from the appropriate departments. For example, it would ask the marketing department to provide price and volume estimates, the economist to provide business environment forecasts, and the production department to provide unit production costs. All this information is digested by the budget committee or the financial officer who examines it for accuracy and then develops an overall operating budget that is both feasible and attuned to the firm's objectives.

Functions of the Budget

As a financial staff officer, you will find that budgets are very useful tools that help you fulfill your responsibilities. The budget forces planning at all levels of the organization. Having to put the numbers down on paper clarifies everyone's thinking and highlights points which may be troublesome or require more attention. Budget preparation also fosters a feeling of involvement in the operations of the firm, providing motivation for better performance and a basis for presenting one's own point of view in direct comparison to someone else's figures. The budget serves as a common focal point for communication among the firm's members, who may have varied backgrounds. Budgets serve as a means of communicating ideas and plans in a universally comprehensible fashion, since they are quantitative. Budgets afford management a systematic overview of the entire operation, replacing patchwork reports and intermittent communications. Without the master plan of the overall operating budget, there could be no coordination among departments or central guidance. Budgets also give management control over the operations. They allow evaluation of an individual subdivision's performance by revealing the deviations of each division from its budgeted figures and stimulating corrective action on the part of top management.

Budget Estimates

Since most budgets are forecasts of the future planning period, they are based on estimates and are only as good as the preparers who make those estimates. Incorrect information and unreasonable estimates will carry through the entire budget and result in unduly high or low performance targets and potentially harmful financing and investment decisions. Incorrect performance targets will frustrate the operating officers, and harmful financing and investment decisions can bankrupt the firm.

When you help prepare budgets you must develop reasonable standards for control. This means you will have to be sure the performance targets are attainable but sufficiently challenging to get the most out of each department. Sometimes this entails pruning down original budget requests and inputs that have been intentionally inflated or understated by the manager of a subdivision. The manager may be acting in expectation of some pruning by top management or to make individual performance targets low—and actual performance better by comparison. As a member of the budget committee, you must stop misleading inputs and convey an open and honest atmosphere about the budgeting process.

Implementation of the prepared budgets is also part of budgeting. Like preparation, budget implementation is only as good as the executives who carry it out.

Budget implementation requires constant supervision to see that junior officers are carrying out the plans as laid forth in the budget and will meet their performance targets. It is absolutely imperative that deviations from expected performance be reported as quickly as possible and corrective action taken. Since junior managers frequently try to bury their mistakes instead of reporting them for corrective action, constant surveillance and budget enforcement are necessary. It is also up to you to encourage junior managers not to bury their mistakes by pointing out how they pop up later as larger problems.

Finally, you must anticipate the possibility that the prepared budgets may be incorrect or unworkable for some reason, such as an unforeseen change in the business environment or unattainable performance targets. You need to prepare contingency budgets, backup plans that can be implemented quickly and with little confusion to adjust the operations to the new levels, be they higher or lower. It is important that contingency plans be prepared in advance and in an atmosphere of calm before the problem arises. The confusion and delay which result from hastily conceived stop-gap repairs to malfunctioning budgets are very costly. Equally damaging is an atmosphere of crisis-to-crisis top management which is very discouraging to the junior managers looking for leadership.

Types of Budgets

There are several types of budgets covering different areas of the firm's operations. We will mention them here and discuss them as we progress through the chapter. The primary operating budgets are concerned with the revenues and expenses of operations. Among the most important of these are the sales budget and such expense budgets as the production budget, the distribution expense budget, the administrative expense budget, the research and development expense budget, and others which detail the expenses of the various departments. When these sales and expense budgets are combined they form the *operating budget,* which is the master plan for the firm during the accounting period.

The *cash budget* coordinates the timing of the firm's cash receipts and disbursements. Since not all the firm's sales are made for cash but are accounted for on an accrual basis, a separate budget for the handling of cash must be prepared so that the firm is not caught short during periods of sluggish receipts and can temporarily invest excess cash holdings during periods of low disbursals.

The *capital budget* is the plan for the acquisition of capital assets, those, that is, with a life in excess of one year, such as machinery and equipment. Capital budgets are a major tool in determining the firm's future. We will discuss the preparation of the capital budget in greater detail in Chapters 5 through 7.

The *contingency budgets* are prepared separately as shadow budgets of all the other budgets. This does not mean that they do not deserve as much attention as their primary counterparts; they are reserve plans to correct the errors of judgment which inevitably arise.

OPERATING BUDGETS

How do you plan the use of the firm's funds?

Operating budgets are the plans for the conduct of business for the planning period. The major operating budgets are the sales budget and the various expense budgets. They combine to form the overall operating budget.

Sales Budget

The typical starting point for all the operating budgets is a realistic sales forecast for the planning period. This involves estimates of the unit sales and sales revenue for each subdivision and for each subperiod, particularly if there is a pronounced seasonality in sales. Frequently two sales budgets are forecast simultaneously. One covers the more immediate planning period sales, usually one year in advance; the other consists of a long-range forecast for each product and for products yet to be introduced, usually five to ten years ahead. The production budgets will be tied more directly to the short-range forecast and to existing demand, while the capital budget will be tied more directly to the longer-range forecasts that allow for the introduction of new products and for declines in the sales of existing items. The sales budget is also used to set the monthly sales quota for your salespeople and must be accurate enough to keep them motivated without frustrating them. A typical sales budget might look like Table 3-1.

The contingency sales budget, based on other selling prices and business conditions, would be prepared simultaneously and circulated as a reserve plan in case the original forecasts did not materialize. The forecasters' estimate of the probability that the original forecast will *not* actually occur is also circulated. Those preparing other budgets predicated on the sales forecast will have some idea of how they should make their own contingency plans.

Methods of forecasting sales The heart of any sales budget is obviously the sales forecast. There are several methods by which this forecast can be made. Some are intuitive, others are mechanical, and some are statistically sophisticated.

The first approach is *intuitive*, based on the forecaster's feelings and hunches, and not supported by hard evidence. Do not try to use this method without due regard

Table 3-1   Typical Short-Term Sales Budget for the Year Ending December 31, 19xx

Product A	Units ($10)	Revenue
January	100,000	$1,000,000
February	150,000	1,500,000
March	200,000	2,000,000
1st Quarter	450,000	4,500,000
2nd Quarter	500,000	5,000,000
3rd Quarter	1,000,000	10,000,000
4th Quarter	100,000	1,000,000
Total A	2,050,000	$20,500,000

Product B	Units ($1)	Revenue
January	1,000,000	$1,000,000
February	1,000,000	1,000,000
March	1,000,000	1,000,000
1st Quarter	3,000,000	3,000,000
2nd Quarter	3,000,000	3,000,000
3rd Quarter	3,000,000	3,000,000
4th Quarter	5,050,000	5,050,000
Total B	14,050,000	14,050,000
Total A and B	16,100,000	34,550,000

to the consequences. Experienced field personnel with a working knowledge of the industry and their firm's operating characteristics might appear to give these seat-of-the-pants forecasts, but they generally bring a lot of insight to bear on their estimates. And even the most experienced forecaster can become more accurate by looking at the problem from all sides and dwelling on it for a while. Seat-of-the-pants forecasts are frowned upon, not easily defended when incorrect, not easily communicated in written form when they have to be supported by the circumstances of the business environment, and usually not very reliable.

A second approach is simple *extrapolation* of past sales into the future planning period at some constant percentage increase or constant absolute unit increase. For example, if a company has had a sales increase of 10,000 units in each of the last five years, extrapolation would merely expect another increase of 10,000 units for next year's sales. Similarly, if sales had increased 10 percent in each of the last few years, extrapolation would forecast another 10 percent sales jump in the next period. This is hardly the best way to forecast, since the business environment, and particularly the competitive environment of a successful firm, will always be changing. Extrapolation assumes consistency in the operating environment from past to future periods and is, therefore, often incorrect in dynamic circumstances.

A third method of sales forecasting uses the *scatter diagram*, which is illustrated in Figure 3-1. This is a free-hand drawing relating the number of units sold to the level of some significantly important variable in each of the ten most recent past planning periods, represented by points 1 through 10. The variable to which sales are related must, of course, have some obvious bearing on the demand for the product. For example, if you are working for an automobile manufacturer, the disposable personal income of consumers would have that kind of impact on the sales of new cars. Obviously, as consumers' incomes increase, they can afford to purchase new cars. Conversely, when their incomes are down, consumers tend to postpone or forego altogether the purchase of a new car. Figure 3-1 reveals this relationship between car sales and consumer disposable income.

Figure 3-1 A Scatter Diagram of Automobile Sales in Relation to Consumer Disposable Income

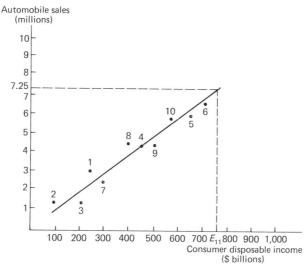

Notice in Figure 3-1 that automobile sales rise upward on the vertical axis as consumer income increases to the right on the horizontal axis, indicating the direct relationship between the two which we would expect to find. If we were to draw a free-hand straight line through the observations (dots) on the scatter diagram, we could estimate the typical relationship between consumer income and automobile sales. This is represented in Figure 3-1 by the upward sloping line. With a reliable estimate (E_{11}) of consumer disposable income during the next planning period from the staff economist, we can move up the dashed relationship line to its intersection with that estimate and then trace horizontally from there back to the intersection with the vertical axis, which reading will be the estimated sales. (We are assuming the typical past relationship holds for the next planning period.) If the firm's economist was estimating next period's consumer disposable income at $750 billion, our estimate of automobile sales in period 11 would be 7.25 million units.

While the scatter diagram is more reliable than extrapolation, it too must be used with caution. Inaccurate estimates from the economist, a change in the typical relationship that had previously prevailed, or a spurious relationship will lead to an inaccurate sales forecast.

A variant of the simple scatter diagram is the *multiple series diagram*, a graph of past sales and other variables over time. Figure 3-2 is a multiple series diagram. As a financial officer you can glance at such a graph and quickly see which factors tend to move with the fluctuations in your sales. It is quite possible that more than one economic or financial variable influences the demand for your product. For example, while consumer disposable income may be the most important variable influencing automobile sales, the price of gasoline may be another variable which you should consider, since as it rises automobile users may switch to other modes of transportation and not purchase so many cars. It is always advisable to look at all the factors which may influence the demand for your product. You should ask your

Figure 3-2 A Multiple Series Diagram

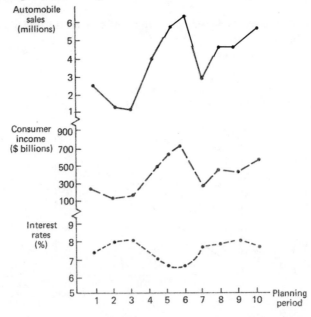

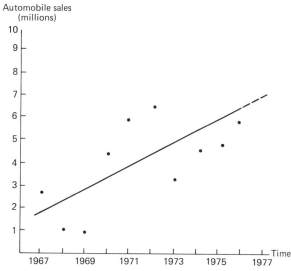

Figure 3-3 Trendline Graph

economists and others whom you respect for their forecasts of *each* of these variables so that all may be incorporated into the sales forecast. In the multiple series
diagram, your planning periods themselves become the horizontal axis. We can see
in Figure 3-2 that automobile sales are inversely proportional to interest rates
charged on car loans.

Again, caution must be exercised when interpreting multiple series diagrams.
Inaccurate estimates by the economist or a change in the relationship between any
of the variables and the demand for the product will lead to an inaccurate forecast.
However, these multiple series diagrams do make very good visual aids in your
presentation to others on the finance committee or your supervisors when you are
trying to illustrate the logic behind the forecast.

A fourth method of forecasting is the mechanically fitted *trendline*. This is merely
a statistical technique which can be performed on some electronic pocket calculators
in a matter of seconds. The trendline relates the demand for your product to the
progression of time by tracing sales growth or decline over time, as shown in Figure
3-3. Each dot in the figure represents the intersection of the year (on the horizontal
axis) with the actual sales for that year (on the vertical axis). A line through those
dots approximating their upward drift as closely as possible traces the trend of automobile sales, which is exactly what the trendline is.[3] Assuming that the typical
trend which prevailed in the past can be expected to prevail in the future, you can
forecast your sales by simply extending the line, like the dashed line in Figure 3-3.
By reading the vertical axis at the point which corresponds to the intersection of the
year 1977 and the trendline, we can see that the sales forecast for 1977 is 6.75 million.

In many ways the trendline resembles the extrapolation we have previously discussed in this section. Like extrapolation, the trendline assumes a constant proportional increase or decrease in sales for each additional year. If the business climate
or the firm's operating environment should change, the forecast will be wrong. A

---

[3] See Appendix 3B for computational procedures on trendline.

total reliance on trend analysis will *assuredly* be wrong sometimes, particularly if your sales are sensitive to the business cycle.

Simple and linear multiple regression are more statistically sophisticated and me-chanically computed[4] approaches to the scatter diagram. Instead of drawing the relationship line free hand, we statistically fit it by the mechanical method described in Appendix 3B. This method gives us a much closer fit of the line to the dots, which means a more precise measurement of the relationship between the vari-able(s) and the sales forecast. However, interpretation of the graph may still be mis-leading if the estimate(s) of the variable(s) are inaccurate or the relationship has changed.

Another method sometimes used to forecast a particular firm's sales for the next planning period is to estimate the total size of the market for your product and then to estimate your share of that market. This *share-of-market* approach is frequently used in industries where the products are homogeneous and the number of firms within the industry is relatively small, such as the automobile industry. In the au-tomobile industry, firms frequently formulate their plans on the percentage of the market they intend to capture. This requires an accurate estimate of the expected size of the market from your economist and a good marketing strategy for the firm.

Still other assorted techniques are used to derive estimates for particular markets and for individual firms. *Field surveys* are used in the industry producing capital goods equipment to judge the potential size of the market in the next planning period. Sometimes this is done by private services, such as the McGraw-Hill survey of capital investment intentions; sometimes it is done by the government, such as the Department of Commerce survey of capital investment intentions. Firms also use their *sales forces* to gather intelligence on potential demand for a product. Sales representatives are questioned as to the tone of the market, and buyers for large firms are surveyed to get their feel for the demand. *Test markets* are used for new products and services to estimate consumer receptivity.

Choosing the appropriate forecasting method There are numerous methods by which a sales forecast for the next planning period can be made. Choosing the correct method to achieve the greatest accuracy in any one situation is not always easy. Some methods may be inappropriate for certain situations, while a combination of methods may be best for other situations. There are many points to consider before making the choice. First, the cyclicality of the product must be weighed. If the demand for the product is sensitive to the business cycle, you want a method which reflects this. Since many of the more mechanical methods, which assume a steady progression in one direction, are not very flexible or sensitive to the business cycle, they may not be appropriate tools for a sales forecast. You must also weigh the ef-fect of competition, both domestic and foreign, particularly if you are using the share-of-market approach. You must pay attention to the price elasticity of demand for your product. If a change in the selling price causes a more than proportional change in the demand for the product, your sales forecast will have to reflect this; otherwise your estimate of unit demand and revenues will be incorrect. You will have to include discounts and returns, as well.

Remember too that each of the methods discussed in this section can be used to forecast other items in the budgeting process, and you should keep them in your tool kit for future reference when they seem appropriate.

---

[4] See Appendix 3B for computational procedures on regression analysis.

Table 3-2   Typical Production Budget for the Year Ending December 31, 19xx

	Product (units)	
	A	B
Unit sales forecasted	2,050,000	14,050,000
Desired inventory, Dec. 31	100,000	1,000,000
Total units required	2,150,000	15,050,000
Less present inventory, Jan. 1	200,000	50,000
Budgeted production	1,950,000	15,000,000

Production Budgets

Production budgets, such as those illustrated in Table 3-2, are concerned with all phases of producing and distributing the product or service. These budgets use the sales budget as a base from which to draw their projection of the number of units that must be produced during the next planning period. For example, if the sales budget calls for a sharp acceleration in demand for the product during the second quarter of the year, the production budget must call for stepped up production late in the first quarter to meet the sales forecast. If properly done, the production budgets allow you to schedule the setup of machinery at the appropriate time and the appropriate locations to coordinate assembly and minimize costs.

Notice how the production budget in Table 3-2 is coordinated with the sales budget in Table 3-1. In turn, the production budget forms the basis of the direct materials budget, which forecasts the necessary raw materials to meet the production budget, and of the direct labor budget, which forecasts the labor inputs needed to produce the required number of units. In addition, the production budget is coordinated with other budgets such as the purchases budget, which specifies the other materials besides the raw materials needed in the production; the maintenance budget, which specifies the required maintenance costs; and the manufacturing overhead budget, which allocates the manufacturing overhead costs such as plant expense to the various departments, essentially taking the common fixed costs and dividing them among departments.

Coordinating all these other production budgets is the budgeted cost of goods sold, which is the expected cost of the units produced and expected to be sold during the planning period. Table 3-3 illustrates a typical budgeted cost of goods

Table 3-3   Typical Budget Cost of Goods Sold for the Year Ending December 31, 19xx

Inventory, beginning of period		$1,845,000
Cost of inventory during period		
Raw materials	10,000,000	
Purchases	1,000,000	
Direct labor	5,000,000	
Manufacturing overhead	4,000,000	20,000,000
Inventory, end of period		21,845,000
Less inventory on hand, end of period		
Raw materials	800,000	
Work-in-process	425,000	
Finished goods	2,000,000	3,245,000
Cost of goods sold		$18,600,000

sold. This figure for cost of goods sold represents the budgeted cost of meeting the required production for the planning period as tied to the projected sales. Obviously, the lower you can keep the cost of goods sold for any given level of forecasted sales, the higher will be your operating profits.

Other Expense Budgets

There are still other budgets which you will help prepare or supervise for still other activities of the firm. Many of these other budgets are associated with the distribution and promotion of the product. For example, there is an advertising budget and a distribution budget to which the persons in charge of those activities should adhere. There is a research and development budget for that department and an administrative budget for the firm's administrative staff. Almost every department and function will have a budget, if for no other reason than financial control. You will have to be familiar with the entire budgeting process of your firm.

CASH BUDGET

As a financial officer, how do I control the firm's expenditures and coordinate them with the firm's inflow?

One of the major tools used by the financial officer to control the firm's expenditures is the cash budget. The cash budget is a schedule of cash receipts and cash disbursements to which the firm is committed or which it is expected to incur during the planning period. It operates much like your personal checkbook, where deposits are entered and checks written when the cash actually comes in and goes out. In essence, the cash budget is a projected cash record of income and expenditures and, as such, differs from the other budgets we have previously discussed in one important aspect. While the cash budgets deal only with actual cash, the other budgets deal with accruals. Thus the sales budget represents sales for which payment may not be received for several months in the normal course of business. Instead, the firm establishes accounts receivable in anticipation of payment at some future date. The accounts receivable and other accounts for which payment will be made or received at some future date are the accruals. You will not find an accrual in the cash budget.

Purpose of the Cash Budget

The major purpose of the cash budget is to coordinate the timing of the firm's cash needs. It pinpoints those times when the firm will be short of cash so arrangements to borrow can be made early and without undue pressure. The cash budget would pinpoint such seasonal or abnormally large cash requirements as repayment of a previous bank loan.

It also pinpoints those times when the firm will have a temporary excess of cash, so it can invest the funds in short-term securities and earn additional income. It is common to find corporate financial officers lending their excess funds for as short a time as overnight in order not to miss any interest. After all, when you are dealing with several million dollars, even one night's interest can amount to a relatively large sum in terms of earnings per share.

The cash budget also allows the firm to plan ahead so that it has sufficient cash on hand to take advantage of cash discounts on its accounts payable, to pay obligations when due, to formulate dividend policy, to plan financing of capital expansion, and to help unify the production schedule during the year so that the firm can smooth out costly seasonal fluctuations.

Construction of the Cash Budget

The first step in construction of the cash budget is to decide on the time span and the subperiods within that time span over which you want to project the firm's cash inflows and outflows. Typically, the cash budget covers relatively short periods within the time span of the other budgets. There may be weekly subperiods over the next year. In that case you might cast the cash budget in a format similar to the following:

Week	1	2	3	4	. . . .	51	52
Cash inflows							
a.							
b.							
.							
.							
.							
z.							
Total inflows							
Cash outflows							
a.							
b.							
.							
.							
.							
z.							
Total outflows							
Net cash needs or surplus							

You must also determine what operating factors will generate cash over the time span of the cash budget, making sure not to leave out any source or to include sources which will not materialize. Typically, the major sources of the firm's cash inflow are its cash sales and its collection on accounts receivable generated earlier when the sale was made. The lag between the creation of the accounts receivable and their collection depends on the terms of the credit the firm has extended and on the speed with which the firm's customers pay. You must judge the time distribution of the collection. You must also consider the discounts and allowances the firm grants its customers in return for early payment, returns of merchandise, and bad debts—all of which lower the cash inflows.

After you have established which operating factors bring in cash, you must determine which operating factors require a cash outflow during the time span of the cash budget. These typically include such items as cash purchases of materials and payments of the firm's accounts payable, estimates of which are taken from the purchase budget. The wages and salaries cash outflow estimate is taken from the direct labor budget, while the estimated cash outlays for direct factory overhead are taken from the manufacturing overhead and maintenance expense budgets. Estimated cash outflow for the administration and for the selling expenses are taken from those particular budgets.

Table 3-4   Recap of Sales and Production Budget Information Needed in Cash Budget

Budget	Month					
	1	2	3	4	5	6
Sales	$2,000,000	$2,500,000	$3,000,000	$3,000,000	$3,000,000	$2,000,000
Purchases	50,000	75,000	100,000	100,000	100,000	50,000
Direct labor	300,000	350,000	400,000	400,000	400,000	300,000
Mfg. overhead	650,000	675,000	700,000	700,000	700,000	650,000
Administrative	100,000	100,000	100,000	100,000	100,000	100,000
Distribution and advertising	100,000	150,000	200,000	200,000	200,000	100,000
Raw materials	700,000	750,000	800,000	800,000	200,000	750,000

You must then decide which financial factors, that is, those not directly associated with the operation of the firm, will generate cash inflows or require cash outflows during the time span of the cash budget. Typical inflows would include such items as the firm's borrowings at banks and other financial institutions, the sale of the firm's bonds to investors, interest and dividend income on the firm's investments, and the sale of the firm's stock. Typical financial outflows would include the repayment of previous borrowings, the redemption of the firm's bonds, interest and dividend payments to the firm's security holders, and repurchase of the firm's stock.

Once we have decided on the pertinent operating and financial factors, we are in a position to construct the cash budget. For convenience, let us first recap in Table 3-4 the information contained in the sales and productions budgets which we will need in constructing the cash budget. We will assume monthly subperiods over a six-month time span. Of course, budgets other than those used in this example may be pertinent, but for purposes of illustration let us use these. Let us also assume that 10 percent of each month's sales are for cash and that 90 percent are conducted on credit. The following statistics summarize the terms and credit experience of the firm:

a. No cash discounts
b. 1 percent of total credit sales are returned for credit by the customers
c. 1 percent of total accounts receivable is bad debt
d. 50 percent of all accounts that are going to pay, do pay within 30 days
e. 100 percent of all accounts who are going to pay, do so within 60 days

Thus the cash inflow from sales for this firm would be:

Month	1	2	3	4	5	6
Cash sales	$200,000	$250,000	$300,000	$300,000	$300,000	$200,000
Accounts receivable collection	—	882,000	1,984,500	2,425,500	2,646,000	2,646,000
Total cash inflow	200,000	1,132,000	2,284,500	2,725,500	2,946,000	2,846,000

Notice that the lag in collection of the accounts receivable has changed the timing of the cash inflow from sales. In fact it has pushed the collection of 50 percent of all the good accounts one month behind sales and the collection of the other 50 percent two months behind sales. Also notice that the allowance for bad debts and for returns has decreased the amount actually collected. For example, in month 2 we collect only half of the good accounts receivable created in month 1. It is not until month 3 that we collect the other half, along with half of the good accounts receivable created in month 2.

Let us assume that the following operating cash outflows are expected during the period from the production budgets:

Budget			Month			
	1	2	3	4	5	6
Purchases	$ 50,000	$ 75,000	$100,000	$100,000	$100,000	$ 50,000
Direct labor	300,000	350,000	400,000	400,000	400,000	300,000
Mfg. overhead	650,000	675,000	700,000	700,000	700,000	650,000
Administrative	100,000	100,000	100,000	100,000	100,000	100,000
Distribution and advertising	100,000	150,000	200,000	200,000	200,000	100,000
Raw materials	—	700,000	750,000	800,000	800,000	800,000
Total operating outflow	1,200,000	2,050,000	2,250,000	2,300,000	2,300,000	2,000,000

Notice that all the expected production expenses except raw materials are paid in the same month in which they occur, while raw materials are all bought on thirty days' credit, which creates a thirty-day accounts payable for the firm. Any expense accrued will create a lag from the date incurred until payment.

Let us assume the following financial cash inflows during the period:

Month	1	2	3	4	5	6
Interest received	$50,000	—	—	—	—	$ 50,000
Dividends received			$100,000			100,000
Stock sale	—	—	—	—	—	8,000,000
Total financial inflows	50,000	—	100,000	—	—	8,150,000

Notice that the inflows or outflows do not have to occur in consecutive subperiods. In this case, interest received is collected twice a year and dividends received are collected four times a year.

Let us assume the following financial cash outflows:

Month	1	2	3	4	5	6
Interest paid	$ 20,000	—	—	—	—	—
Dividend paid	100,000			$100,000		
Installment payments on machinery	—	—	—	—	—	$1,000,000
Long-term debt repayment	—	—	—	—	—	4,000,000
Total financial outflows	120,000	—	—	100,000		5,000,000

With this information, we can construct the total cash budget shown in Table 3-5.

Table 3-5   Cash Budget for the First Six Months of 19xx

Month	1	2	3	4	5	6
Cash receipts						
Cash sales	$200,000	$250,000	$300,000	$300,000	$300,000	$200,000
Accounts receivable collection	—	882,000	1,984,500	2,425,000	2,646,000	2,646,000
Interest received	50,000	—	—	—	—	50,000
Dividends received	—	—	100,000	—	—	100,000
Sale of stock	—	—	—	—	—	8,000,000
Total receipts	250,000	1,132,000	2,384,500	2,725,000	2,946,000	10,996,000
Cash disbursements						
Purchases	50,000	75,000	100,000	100,000	100,000	50,000
Direct labor	300,000	350,000	400,000	400,000	400,000	300,000
Mfg. overhead	650,000	675,000	700,000	700,000	700,000	650,000
Administrative	100,000	100,000	100,000	100,000	100,000	100,000
Distribution & advertising	100,000	150,000	200,000	200,000	200,000	100,000
Raw materials	—	700,000	750,000	800,000	800,000	800,000
Interest paid	20,000	—	—	—	—	—
Dividends paid	100,000	—	—	100,000	—	—
Installment payments on machinery	—	—	—	—	—	1,000,000
Long-term debt repayment	—	—	—	—	—	4,000,000
Total disbursements	1,320,000	2,050,000	2,250,000	2,400,000	2,300,000	7,000,000
Net receipts (Disbursements)	(1,070,000)	(918,000)	134,500	325,000	646,000	3,996,000
Cash on hand beginning of month	2,000,000	1,000,000	1,000,000	1,000,000	1,000,000	1,117,500
Cash on hand end of month	930,000	82,000	1,134,500	1,325,000	1,646,000	5,113,500
Minimum required balance	1,000,000	1,000,000	1,000,000	1,000,000	1,000,000	1,000,000
Short-term financing needs	70,000	918,000	—	—	—	—
Repayment of short-term financing	—	—	134,500	325,000	528,500	—
Short-term borrowing outstanding end of month	70,000	988,000	853,500	528,500	0	0

Analysis of the Illustrated Cash Budget

Notice how the cash budget allows you to reconcile the need for cash (particularly seasonal and predictable needs for cash) and the financing arrangements. In the first two months, this firm needs temporary financing, which it can pay back within months 3 and 4. The cash budget clearly highlights this and allows the financial officer the flexibility to negotiate a bank loan tailored to the firm's projected cash flows.

In months 5 and 6, the firm experiences an excess cash position, which the financial officer will have to make arrangement to invest temporarily until the funds are employed in the business. It is typical that after a stock sale, the firm will have a relatively large excess of funds until the projects for which the funds were raised are completed. The long-term debt to be repaid in month 6 and other debts are usually cleared up at that time. The cash budget is obviously a very helpful tool in planning the firm's finances.

The cash budget allows the financial officer to place in perspective the lag in cash collection of the accounts receivable, to schedule the dividends, to arrange the sale of the firm's securities, to meet installments on the loan and machinery on time, and to otherwise coordinate the firm's receipts and expenditures.

CAPITAL BUDGET

We will devote Chapters 5 through 7 to the capital budget. Briefly, it is a plan for implementing the capital projects which by definition have a life expectancy in excess of one year, such as plant and machinery. The summary capital budget which is submitted for approval by the financial officer may contain only the dates of implementation and completion and the estimated cost, but it actually represents and is supported by much deeper, more elaborate analysis.

The objective of the capital budget is to compile a list of potentially rewarding projects in terms of the corporate goal. Then this list is combined with a schedule of implementation to determine the timing of the project and the investment required for its completion. This is coordinated with the cash and operating budgets such that the project synchronizes with the rest of the firm's operations. For example, the sales budget is coordinated with the capital budget to determine what areas of production need additional capacity, and the operating budgets are coordinated to see if that area is a profitable one to expand. The capital budget analysis is conducted to determine if an expansion project in that area is among the most attractive in which the firm can invest. If so, the timing and financing of the project are undertaken. A typical summary capital budget might resemble Table 3-6.

Table 3-6   A Typical Summary Capital Budget for the Year Ending December 31, 1976

Project	Estimated starting date	Estimated completion date	Estimated cost	Required expenditures 1976	Required expenditures 1977
Machinery	Nov. 1976	Feb. 1977	$1,000,000	$1,000,000	—
Plant	Oct. 1976	Dec. 1977	5,000,000	3,000,000	2,000,000

PRO FORMA FINANCIAL STATEMENTS

How do I report this budget information to my superiors?

In addition to presenting the budgets themselves with all the attendant supportive thinking, the financial officer is frequently asked to submit a pro forma income statement and balance sheet compiled from the projections made in the sales and operating budgets. The *pro forma statements* represent what the income and balance sheet would look like at the end of the planning period if all the budget estimates

Table 3-7   Pro Forma Income Statement for the Year Ending December 31, 19xx

		From
Sales	$34,550,000	Sales budget (see Table 3-1)
Cost of goods sold	18,600,000	Cost of goods sold budget (see Table 3-3)
Gross profit	15,950,000	
Selling expense	3,000,000	Distribution & advertising budget
Administrative expense	1,000,000	Administrative expense budget
Operating profit	11,950,000	
Interest expense	1,000,000	Interest on bonds & loans
Profit before taxes	10,950,000	
Income taxes	5,475,000	50% tax rate
Net profit	5,475,000	
Dividends	400,000	Expected dividend policy
Transfer to retained earnings	5,075,000	

were exactly met. These pro forma statements bring all the budgeted revenues and expenses (accrued as well as cash, as distinguished from the cash budget) into a projected statement of results for the period. Table 3-7[5] illustrates a pro forma income statement. After we have constructed the pro forma income statement, we can construct a pro forma balance sheet, as shown in Table 3-8.[6]

The budget estimates are combined in this manner to create the pro forma statements. In the pro forma balance sheet, we can determine the accounts payable and the accrued liabilities by examining the expense budgets, seeing what we should have purchased, then looking at the cash budget, seeing what we should have paid on those purchases, and finding the difference between the two figures. This is what we still owe: our accrued liabilities. Other pro forma items are more directly read right off the budget estimates. Cost of goods sold comes directly from the cost-of-goods-sold budget; the cash balance comes directly from the cash budget estimates; and the interest payments can be read directly from the cash budget.

The advantages of a pro forma statement lie in its ability to communicate what the financial position of the firm may be expected to look like at the end of the period. It gives management a target to aim for, as it paints an ideal financial picture of the company. These pro forma statements can demonstrate the effect of growth on the firm's financial position. They may highlight financial strengths and weaknesses and pinpoint potential needs for funds to maintain a desired balance between debt and equity, for example. Pro forma statements also define future relationships among items in the income statement and the balance sheet, which can be compared to the standards set by management as an advance warning system to insure that the firm is meeting its operating and financial objectives.[7]

For all their usefulness, pro forma statements are no substitute for the cash budget, and they *can* be misleading. They are highly encompassing, sometimes hiding more than they reveal. They may obscure such changes in the company's financial position as may occur between balance sheet dates, and they do not isolate

[5] See, for example, Erich A. Helfert, *Techniques of Financial Analysis*, 3rd ed., Richard D. Irwin, 1972.
[6] *Ibid.*
[7] *Ibid.*

Table 3-8   Pro Forma Balance Sheet for the Year Ending December 31, 19xx

Assets		From
Cash	$1,000,000	Cash budget
Accounts receivable	4,500,000	Cash budget
Inventory	3,245,000	Cost of goods sold budget
Total current assets	8,745,000	
Plant, property & equipment	10,000,000	Capital budget
Accumulated depreciation	3,000,000	summary
Net plant, property & equipment	7,000,000	
Total assets	15,745,000	
Liabilities & stockholders' equity		
Accounts payable	1,500,000	Expense budgets
Accrued liabilities	3,000,000	Expense budgets
Total current liabilities	4,500,000	
Long-term debt	2,000,000	Cash budget
Common stock	4,000,000	Cash budget
Retained earnings	5,245,000	
Total liabilities & stockholders' equity	15,745,000	

the cash flows as cash budgeting does. These statements must be considered in conjunction with the rest of the budgets.

CONTINGENCY BUDGETING

How do I prepare for the possibility that my budget estimates are incorrect? Is there any way I can salvage the situation and demonstrate to my superiors that I am prepared to cope with the vicissitudes of the future?

Let's face it, nobody can predict the future with consistent accuracy. We must expect to be wrong sometimes when working with budget estimates. The idea is to be as little off the mark as possible and to be prepared to jump in with alternative courses of action more appropriate to the situation than the original estimates. The business climate and/or the operating environment of the firm can change in ways which you did not anticipate or which you dismissed as unlikely, but you must be prepared to cope with the unexpected. The firm that reacts fastest and in the most organized and effective manner to the unexpected is usually well rewarded. It is the job of the financial officer to see that the firm has contingency plans to fall back on.

The use of contingency budgets prepares you to react quickly and correctly to a changing business picture. When presented as an appendix to your primary budget estimates, they also demonstrate that you have thought about the less likely alternatives and are prepared to guide the firm through any change.

Contingency budgeting is the preparation of alternative plans or budgets and schedules to which your firm would retreat or expand in the event that the original estimates were off the mark. We know that budgets are only as good as the estimates and the estimators. When mistakes are made, you must have a planned retreat to avoid a confused rout. Contingency budgets will smooth out the bumps, ease the

Table 3-9 Contingency Cash Budget Presentation for Months 1 and 2

Month	1			2		
	Low	Expected	High	Low	Expected	High
Cash receipts						
Cash sales	$150,000	$200,000	$300,000	$200,000	$250,000	$350,000
Accounts receivable collection	—	—	—	700,000	882,000	1,000,000
Interest received	50,000	50,000	50,000	—	—	—
Dividends received	—	—	—	—	—	—
Sale of stock	—	—	—	—	—	—
Total receipts	200,000	250,000	350,000	900,000	1,132,000	1,350,000
Cash disbursements						
Purchases	40,000	50,000	75,000	60,000	75,000	100,000
Direct labor	250,000	350,000	400,000	300,000	350,000	500,000
Mfg. overhead	600,000	675,000	700,000	600,000	675,000	750,000
Administrative	100,000	100,000	100,000	100,000	100,000	125,000
Distribution & advertising	90,000	100,000	125,000	125,000	150,000	175,000
Raw materials	—	—	—	600,000	700,000	900,000
Interest paid	20,000	20,000	20,000			
Dividends paid	50,000	100,000	100,000	—	—	—
Installment payments on machinery	—	—	—	—	—	—
Long-term debt repayment	—	—	—	—	—	—
Total disbursements	1,150,000	1,320,000	1,520,000	1,785,000	2,050,000	2,550,000
Net receipts (disbursements)	(950,000)	(1,070,000)	(1,170,000)	(885,000)	(918,000)	(1,200,000)
Cash on hand beginning of month	2,000,000	2,000,000	2,000,000	1,000,000	1,000,000	1,000,000
Cash on hand end of month	1,050,000	930,000	830,000	115,000	82,000	(200,000)
Minimum required balance	1,000,000	1,000,000	1,000,000	1,000,000	1,000,000	1,000,000
Short-term financing needs	—	70,000	170,000	885,000	918,000	1,200,000
Repayment of short-term financing	—	—	—	—	—	—
Short-term borrowing outstanding end of month	—	70,000	170,000	885,000	988,000	1,370,000

shift from one level of operating activity to another, and, from a personal point of view, repair your professional reputation as a planner-manager. Contingency budgets will give you flexibility and save valuable time and dollars by stopping the forward momentum of the blunder. Without a contingency plan it may take months for a firm to shift gears, so to speak, because of that momentum.

Contingency budgeting applies to all the budgets including the sales, operating, and capital budgets. It may be presented in several different fashions, such as relating expenses to sales volume instead of absolute dollar amounts.[8] However, the simplest and most straightforward method of presentation is the three-tiered budget based on the expected business and operating environment, on a lower-than-expected level, and on a higher-than-expected level of business activity. Table 3-9 illustrates a contingency cash budget presentation.

Notice how the cash budget estimates change under the different circumstances. If in month 1 the actual is below the expected, there is no need for any financing during the first month. If there is a higher-than-expected operating level, the financing need increases, because there are now more sales and accounts receivables to be financed until collected. The financial officer can build sufficient flexibility into bank borrowings to take care of the higher- and the lower-than-expected contingencies. In the case of inventory budgeting, contingency planning allows you to organize an orderly liquidation of inventory if expected sales do not materialize.

The contingency budget shows you *where* to gear down. For example, in the cash budget of Table 3-9, you can see immediately that you could curtail the labor force, cut back on your advertising, and reduce your dividends, if sales are lower than expected. (Some of the cash budget estimates do not change even if the expected is not realized. These are items which you cannot gear down.) The contingency budgeting presentation also tells you exactly *how much* to decrease or increase in each area if sales are higher or lower than expected. There is no fumbling in the dark trying to regain the corporation's balance. The plans have been thought out in advance.

BALANCE SHEET

How do I report the results after the planning period is over?

Your stockholders, supervisors, management in general, and you yourself will want to know how well you actually did. You must now move from the internal managerial accounting concepts of the budget and pro forma financial statements to the financial accounting concepts of the financial statements.

The *balance sheet* is a financial statement reflecting the company's position at the end of the accounting period, a moment in time. It reveals the firm's accumulated assets (what it owns) and its accumulated liabilities (what it owes), as well as what remains to the account of the owners (stockholders' equity).

Table 3-10 is the balance sheet of American Brands, Inc. for the years ending

---

[8] Welsch, *Budgeting,* p. 197. We could use the variable-costs formula, which relates cost to actual output in the variable-budget concept such that expenses equal fixed costs plus variable costs per unit times the number of units produced. Such a formula is usually attached to the working budget as an appendix. In addition, this concept would allow us to more easily distinguish between fixed costs and semivariable costs. This concept differs from the contingency budget in that it assumes no specific plans to adjust to a higher or lower level of sales but calculates new expenses according to output as a means of control.

Table 3-10   American Brands, Inc. Balance Sheet for the Years Ending December 31, 1971 and December 31, 1972

Assets, December 31	1972	1971
	(In thousands)	
Cash	$ 32,196	$ 37,893
Accounts receivable, customers, less allowances for discounts and doubtful accounts, 1972, $5,561,000; 1971, $5,761,000	238,229	221,222
Inventories		
Leaf tobacco	535,923	505,894
Bulk whiskeys	55,677	55,907
Other raw materials, supplies and work in process	94,795	86,740
Finished products	155,696	178,573
	842,091	827,114
Other current assets	25,142	22,735
Total current assets	1,137,658	1,108,964
Property, plant and equipment, at cost		
Land, improvements to land and leaseholds	28,832	29,105
Buildings	203,598	186,938
Machinery and equipment	437,405	427,978
Construction in process	10,138	6,171
	679,973	650,192
Less accumulated depreciation and amortization	322,714	307,058
	357,259	343,134
Intangibles resulting from business acquisitions	434,625	438,915
Other assets	44,778	37,950
Total assets	$1,974,320	$1,928,963

Liabilities, December 31	1972	1971
	(In thousands)	
Notes payable	$ 167,721	$ 174,848
Accounts payable and accrued expenses	161,690	146,891
Accrued taxes, including current portion of deferred income taxes	115,711	123,800
Current portion of long-term debt	8,381	6,672
Total current liabilities	453,503	452,211
Long-term debt	441,171	437,972
Deferred income taxes and other deferred credits	25,667	35,430
Minority interest in consolidated subsidiaries	105,243	98,549
Total liabilities	1,025,584	1,024,162
Stockholders' equity		
Capital stock		
$6.00 Convertible Preferred stock, without par value, stated value $100 per share	75,000	75,000
Common stock, par value $6.25 per share	179,352	179,352
Additional paid-in capital	42,262	42,111
Retained earnings	752,843	694,170
	1,049,457	990,633
Less treasury stock, at cost	100,721	85,832
Total stockholders' equity	948,736	904,801
Total liabilities and stockholders' equity	$1,974,320	$1,928,963

December 31, 1972 and December 31, 1971. It is reasonably typical of an industrial company's balance sheet.

Assets on the Balance Sheet

The balance sheet is broken down into two major categories: assets, and liabilities and stockholders' equity. Assets consist of all that is owned by the firm. The assets themselves are broken down into further, more specific categories according to their *liquidity*, i.e., how readily they can be turned into cash. Current assets, which for American Brands consist mainly of cash, accounts receivable, and inventories, normally become cash, are consumed, or are sold within one year. The balance sheet records the amount of each of those items on hand at the end of the accounting period. American Brands had total current assets of $1,137,658,000 at the end of 1972.

The firm's accounts receivable were $238,229,000 at the end of 1972. These are the customer debts incurred in the normal course of trade, less any discounts for early payment and any allowances for doubtful accounts who may become nonpayers. The inventories in this example consist of raw materials (such as the bulk whiskeys and leaf tobacco used in the manufacture of the firm's cigars and cigarettes and liquor), supplies and work in progress, and finished goods.

The less liquid long-term assets consist of property, plant and equipment mainly in land holdings, improvements to land and leaseholds (rented land), buildings, machinery and equipment, and construction in progress. These assets are carried at an original cost of $679,973,000, less accumulated depreciation and amortization, i.e., the spreading of expenses for property, plant, and equipment assets over time. The other major long-term asset is the intangible goodwill resulting from business acquisitions. It represents the amount American Brands paid above the net worth of the assets it received when it acquired the other firms. Total assets for American Brands at the end of 1972 were $1,974,320,000.

Liabilities and Stockholders' Equity

The other side of the balance sheet reflects what the company owes to its creditors and what remains for the stockholders after those debts. Like the assets, the liabilities and the stockholders' equity are categorized by their liquidity. Current liabilities will be terminated within one year. American Brands' current liabilities of $453,503,000 consist of notes payable (short term borrowings usually from banks), accounts payable and accrued expenses (credit which has been extended to the company in the normal course of business), accrued taxes (the tax liability which has been incurred during the year but has not yet been paid), and the current portion of long-term debt.

American Brands' long-term liabilities consist of the firm's long-term debt, deferred income taxes and other deferred credits (debts incurred by the firm which are not payable for a period in excess of one year), and the minority interest in consolidated subsidiaries (that proportional amount of earnings which the firm owes other stockholders in companies controlled by American Brands).

Stockholders' equity represents the ownership interests in the company and reflects what was originally invested by them and what has since been earned on their behalf by the company and reinvested for them in the firm. American Brands has a total stockholders' equity of $948,736,000. The portion of the stockholders' equity represented by the preferred stock is $75,000,000, and holders of the preferred stock have a prior claim to that of the common stockholders on annual earnings up to $6.00 a year and on assets, in case of liquidation, up to $100 a share. The common stock account and the additional paid-in capital account of the stockholders' equity represent the amount paid for the common stock when first issued. The common stock account is that portion of the total paid which is specified in the corporation's charter (see Chapter 1) as stated or par value, while the additional paid-in capital is the amount paid in excess of that stated or par value. Retained earnings represent the income of previous years which has been reinvested in the firm instead of distributed to the common stockholders, while treasury stock represents common stock acquired by the company for its own account out of retained earnings.

The total assets of the company equal the total liabilities and stockholders' equity, as they must always do in double-entry accounting.

THE INCOME STATEMENT

The income statement reflects the earning power of the corporation over the accounting period. It shows the sources of revenues and the nature of the expenses and losses producing the net income.[9] Table 3-11 is the income statement for American Brands, Inc. for the accounting periods of 1971 and 1972.

American Brands had net sales of $2,998,869,000 in all of 1972. The cost of the goods that were sold was $2,335,306,000, leaving a gross profit of $663,563,000. After deducting operating expenses, particularly advertising, selling, and general administrative expenses,[10] the firm had income from operations (income not involved with the financing of the firm) of $310,454,000 in 1972.

The nonoperating income, mainly financial expenses and other income and deductions for 1972, includes the interest charges incurred on the firm's debt, the provision for taxes on income, and the proportionate income of subsidiary income due minority holders of companies controlled by American Brands. After all deductions and before dividends to preferred or common stockholders, American Brands had a net income of $123,300,000 for 1972.

Attached to this particular income statement is American Brands' statement of retained earnings, which shows that portion of net income for the year which was reinvested in the firm and that portion which was distributed to the stockholders in the form of cash dividends. In 1972, American Brands paid $4,500,000 in dividends to its preferred stockholders and $60,127,000 in dividends to its common stockholders. The remainder of the net income for the year was retained and reinvested in the company. Consequently the statement of retained earnings shows an increase in that account from $694,170,000 at the beginning of the year to $752,843,000 at the end of the year.

Finally, at the bottom of the income statement appears the earnings per share for the year, which is the net income divided by the number of shares outstanding, as taken from the balance sheet. The fully diluted earnings per share represents the earnings per share assuming that other securities of the firm, which can be converted into common shares, *had* been converted. (We will discuss these "convertibles" in Chapter 23.)

---

[9] J. A. Mauriello, *Accounting for the Financial Analyst,* C.F.A. Research Foundation, 1971, p. 45.

[10] The inclusion of depreciation in this account is a rather unusual treatment.

Table 3-11 Consolidated Statement of Income and Retained Earnings for American Brands, Inc. and Subsidiaries

For years ended December 31	1972	1971
	(In thousands)	
Net sales	$2,998,869	$2,827,771
Cost of sales	2,335,306	2,177,140
Gross profit	663,563	650,631
Advertising, selling and administrative expenses	353,109	345,121
Operating income	310,454	305,510
Other income	6,637	5,908
	317,091	311,418
Interest and related charges	39,421	44,633
Other deductions	5,743	6,794
	45,164	51,427
Income before provision for taxes on income and minority interest	271,927	259,991
Provision for taxes on income		
Federal income taxes currently payable	90,118	94,576
Foreign income taxes currently payable	29,371	22,578
Deferred income taxes	3,857	1,339
Other taxes based on income	10,737	10,116
	134,083	128,609
Income before minority interest	137,844	131,382
Minority interest in earnings of subsidiaries	14,544	11,966
Net income	123,300	119,416
Retained earnings at beginning of year	694,170	638,091
	817,470	757,507
Cash dividends		
Common stock: 1972, $2.288 per share; 1971, $2.20 per share	60,127	58,837
Preferred stock: 1972 and 1971, $6.00 per share	4,500	4,500
Retained earnings at end of year	$ 752,843	$ 694,170
Net income per Common share		
Without dilution	$4.52	$4.30
Fully diluted	4.37	4.15

CONSOLIDATED STATEMENT OF CHANGES IN FINANCIAL POSITION

The statement of changes in financial position, formerly called the statement of sources and uses (or applications) of funds, differs from the income statement and the balance sheet and resembles a cash budget for external reporting. The statement of changes in financial position reports the flows of cash through the firm during the year; it is an historical record of where the funds came from and how they were spent. Items accrued and not collected or paid for in cash during the period are not reported in this statement, and those cash items which are hidden in the balance sheet and income statement because they were commingled with accrued items are reported separately.

Generally, we can say that sources of funds derive from decreases in assets or increases in liabilities or stockholders' equity. Applications of funds (where they are spent) come from increases in assets or decreases in the liabilities or stockholders' equity. This is summarized below:

	Sources	Applications
Assets	−	+
Liabilities	+	−
Stockholders' equity	+	−

Any purchase of property, plant, or equipment represents a use of cash, as does the acquisition of all the other assets of the firm. Acquisitions of such items as the assets of other firms through a merger is also an application (use) of funds. When the firm buys back its own stock, retires some of its own debt, pays dividends from stockholders' equity, or in some fashion reduces its liabilities or stockholders' equity, it is using funds.

On the sources side, if the firm decreases its assets by selling them for cash, it has raised funds from the sale. Similarly, if the fund sells some new shares, borrows additional amounts at the bank, arranges other types of loans, or adds the net income for the year to retained earnings, it has raised funds.

Table 3-12 is the consolidated statement of changes in financial position for American Brands, Inc. during the years 1971 and 1972. We can see how the firm raised funds from net income, the issuance of long-term debt, disposition of property, plant, and equipment (sale of an asset), and the proceeds from stock sold to employees under a stock option plan. The firm also had an inflow of funds from items which did not require cash payment but which were recorded as expenses on an accrued basis for the balance sheet or income statement. The most common type of such noncash expenses is depreciation, which reflects the expensing of the asset over its lifetime, but which requires no cash outlay, since the machine which is being depreciated has already been paid for when it was first purchased. Since depreciation reduces net income yet requires no cash outlay, it must be recorded as a source of funds in addition to the net income reported on the income statement and as the first item in the statement of changes in financial position.

American Brands used the funds generated to acquire additions to property, plant, and equipment, to decrease its long-term debt, to pay dividends to its preferred and common shareholders and to purchase its own shares (a reduction in stockholders' equity). The $27,402,000 difference between the funds raised and the funds used was added to working capital, which consists of the firm's investment in current assets. For 1972, American Brands reduced its investment in cash while raising its investment in accounts receivable and inventory. The company used funds to reduce accounts payable and current portions of long-term debt (a reduction in the firm's liabilities), while raising funds through the increase in notes payable.

Notice how much more information external observers of the firm get from the statement of changes in financial position. We can tell where the funds came from and where they went—a very useful check on management's investment policies. The financial officer can make use of the statement in negotiations with potential lenders. The statement shows the amount of funds which flow through the firm and could be applied to meet interest and amortization charges on any borrowings. The statement also breaks out the depreciation and other noncash expenditures for easy analysis. A financial officer must be prepared to construct and interpret this statement.

Table 3-12 Consolidated Statement of Changes in Financial Position for American Brands, Inc. and Subsidiaries

For years ended December 31	1972	1971
	(In thousands)	
Source of working capital		
Net income	$123,300	$119,416
Charges to income not requiring use of working capital		
Depreciation and amortization	43,376	44,357
Minority interest in earnings of subsidiaries	14,544	11,966
Net provision for noncurrent deferred income taxes	4,393	1,094
Working capital provided from operations	185,613	176,833
Issuance of additional long-term debt	26,200	18,968
Unrealized (loss) gain from translation of foreign currencies		
(see note on Consolidated foreign subsidiaries)	(14,101)	14,101
Proceeds from stock options exercised and debentures converted	4,458	14,819
Disposition of property, plant and equipment	6,229	7,912
	208,399	232,633
Use of working capital		
Additions to property, plant and equipment	62,392	43,482
Net noncurrent assets of businesses purchased	—	8,320
Cost in excess of net assets of businesses acquired	—	8,751
Decrease in long-term debt (including transfer to current)	23,967	32,206
Dividends to stockholders	64,627	63,337
Dividends to minority stockholders of a subsidiary	7,818	7,713
Purchases of Common stock for treasury	20,071	37,851
Other, net	2,118	(7,751)
	180,997	193,909
Increase in working capital	$ 27,402	$ 38,724
Components increasing (decreasing) working capital		
Cash	$ (5,697)	$ (9,233)
Receivables, customers	17,007	5,899
Inventories	14,977	(51,012)
Other current assets	2,407	(8,620)
Notes payable	7,127	112,524
Accounts payable and accrued expenses	(6,710)	(15,993)
Current portion of long-term debt	(1,709)	5,159
Increase in working capital	$ 27,402	$ 38,724

FINANCIAL CONTROLS

Once I have helped lay the plans for the firm, how do I insure that they will be carried out? Can I constantly check for indications of unforeseen problems?

The answer to these questions lies in the financial control techniques available to the financial officer.[11] In addition to their use in planning and reporting, budgets and financial statements can help the financial officer control and oversee operations. The most common form of control involves ratio analysis to measure per-

---

[11] Mauriello, *Accounting*, p. 148.

formance in such general areas as the firm's liquidity and short-term solvency, profitability, long-term solvency (the ability to bear debt), and asset utilization (including ratios to measure physical as well as financial performance).

The ratios in each of these areas are computed according to the accepted method discussed below and compared to similar ratios for the firm in prior years to detect any progress or deterioration in the firm's position. They are further compared to an accepted industry standard derived from such sources as Dun and Bradstreet's *Key Ratios for 125 Industries*, Standard and Poor's *Industry Surveys*, The Federal Trade Commission Securities and Exchange Commission *Quarterly Financial Report for Manufacturing Corporations*, *Almanac of Financial Ratios*, Robert Morris Associates' *Statement Studies* (compiled from financial statements submitted as part of loan applications at major banks), Standard and Poor's *Analysts' Handbook*, and the various trade associations.

Deviations from industry standards are examined for both good and unfavorable indications. For example, if the industry standard for the debt/equity ratio is 1.0, a significantly higher figure for a particular company might indicate a greater-than-desirable use of debt, perhaps beyond the reasonable limits of long-term solvency. Of course every individual situation is different, and deviations should alert you to investigate further. There may be extenuating circumstances which make what at first appears to be an unreasonable deviation seem reasonable.

Common Ratios

We will use the 1972 American Brands, Inc. financial statements presented in Tables 3-10 and 3-11 to illustrate the more commonly used ratios with which you, as a financial officer, should be absolutely familiar.

Liquidity and short-term solvency Liquidity and short-term solvency ratios are used to judge the firm's ability to meet such current obligations as its accounts payable and the current portion of its long-term debt. By interpreting such ratios we can determine the degree to which assets which are quickly convertible to cash exceed the liabilities which require almost immediate cash payment.

　1. Current ratio

$$\frac{\text{Current assets}}{\text{Current liabilities}} = \frac{\$1,137,658,000}{\$453,503,000} = 2.51$$

The 2.51-to-1 ratio for American Brands, Inc. implies that it currently has a cushion of $2\frac{1}{2}$ times assets over liabilities in meeting its short-term obligations. Like all ratios, this is subject to interpretations. First, the 2.51 current ratio must be compared to an acceptable standard for companies operating in a similar environment to American Brands. Traditionally, for this industry, a ratio of 2.5 to 1 has been considered an acceptable level for proper liquidity. (In most other industrial firms, the acceptable level is 2.0 to 1.) The acceptable level will *vary* among industries, so it is absolutely necessary to compare the firm's ratio to the industry standard.

　2. Acid test ratio

The current ratio does not tell us about the liquidity of the individual components of the current assets and the firm's ability to turn them into cash for immediate payment of current liabilities. Inventory is singled out as the potentially most illiquid because it may become obsolete, unfashionable, or simply unsalable and not convertible to cash. To meet this objection, many bank loan officers use the acid test ratio.

$$\frac{\text{Current assets less inventories}}{\text{Current liabilities}} = \frac{\$1,137,658 - \$842,091,000}{\$453,503,000} = .65$$

American Brands' 0.65 acid test ratio reveals that without its inventories, it would not have sufficient funds to meet its current liabilities. Consequently the bank loan officer will have to examine American Brands' inventory to see if it really is sufficiently liquid to meet current liabilities as they arise. Since most of the inventory is tobacco, it *is* readily convertible to cash through sale in the open market, if necessary.

3. Average collection period ratio

To judge the liquidity of the accounts receivable component of the current assets, we use the average collection period ratio. This tells us how many days (using 360 days to a year) it takes the average account to be collected. A long collection period indicates low liquidity.

$$\frac{\text{Accounts receivable} \times 360}{\text{Annual credit sales}} = \frac{\$238,229,000 \times 360}{\$2,998,869,000} = 28.60 \text{ days}$$

American Brands' average collection period of 28.60 days is in line with its policy of extending 30-day credit to its customers in the regular course of trade. Since they are being paid on time, the accounts receivable are liquid.[12]

4. Accounts receivable turnover ratio

The accounts receivable turnover ratio also measures the liquidity of the firm's accounts receivable. As the number of times in a year that the accounts receivable turnover increases, their liquidity is assumed to increase.

$$\frac{\text{Annual credit sales}}{\text{Accounts receivable}} = \frac{\$2,998,869,000}{\$238,229,000} = 12.58$$

American Brands' accounts receivable turnover ratio of 12.58 indicates, as does the average collection period, that the liquidity of the accounts is relatively high, turning over more than 12 times a year. This is a good indication of liquidity since we know that American Brands extends 30-day credit to its customers, implying turnover 12 times a year if all accounts are collected on time. Of course, this is an average figure, and some accounts may pay sooner and others later than 30 days.

The turnover ratio can be converted into the average collection period ratio by simply dividing it into 360 days. Again, as in the average collection period, we used total sales instead of credit sales for this example, since the breakdown between cash and credit sales was not reported in the financial statements. However, as a financial officer, you would have such information.

It is also possible that too high a turnover ratio may expose poor management as well as highly liquid accounts receivable. A very high turnover ratio or very low collection period ratio might indicate an overly restrictive credit policy. Such a policy could limit profits by denying credit to potential customers who then go elsewhere. The trick is to set a credit policy that does not discourage customers from doing business with you, but tends to deny credit to bad risks who may not pay. Obviously, these ratios must be compared to acceptable industry standards and viewed in relation to the company's credit terms.

5. Inventory turnover ratio

The inventory turnover ratio measures the liquidity of the firm's inventories. We

[12] Since we do not have information on the portion of sales which were for cash and which were for credit, we will assume all the sales were for credit in our examples.

arrive at it by dividing the cost of goods sold by the average inventory for the period. The cost of goods sold is used instead of sales because the inventory is recorded on the firm's books at cost, and this makes the numerator and the denominator comparable. The average inventory (generally approximated by dividing the sum of the beginning and ending inventories by two) is used unless there is a strong seasonality in sales which might distort inventory levels. In that case, a more precise measure of average inventory must be computed.

$$\frac{\text{Cost of goods sold}}{\text{Average inventory}} = \frac{\$2,335,306,000}{(\$842,091,000 + \$827,114,000)/2} = 2.79$$

The general interpretation of the inventory turnover ratio is that as it increases, the liquidity of the inventory also increases, because the inventory is being more rapidly turned into accounts receivable through sales. But again, as in the case of the accounts receivable turnover ratio, an overly high inventory turnover ratio can mean bad management as well as high liquidity. A ratio too high in relation to acceptable industry standards may signal too many small orders and too high a cost for inventory management. If the ratio is too low in relation to an acceptable industry standard, inventories may be unsalable.

6. Basic defensive interval ratio[13]

$$\frac{\text{Total defensive assets}}{\text{Projected daily operating expenditures}} = \frac{\$270,425,000}{\$7,467,819} = 36.2 \text{ days}$$

This ratio measures the funds the firm can generate to meet immediate cash requirements without sales or other sources. Total defensive assets are cash, marketable securities, and accounts receivable, while the projected daily operating expenditures are the sum of the cost of goods sold, selling expenses, and general administrative expenses divided by the number of days in a year (360).

Asset utilization The next major group of ratios indicates the efficiency with which management utilizes the firm's assets to generate sales and profits. In general, as sales and profits increase for each dollar of assets, management is considered to be doing a better job. Of course each asset utilization ratio must be compared to an acceptable industry standard.

1. Asset turnover ratio

$$\frac{\text{Net sales}}{\text{Total tangible assets}} = \frac{\$2,998,869,000}{(\$1,974,320,000 - \$434,625,000)} = 1.94$$

This ratio measures the sales dollars generated per dollar of investment in tangible assets (physical assets such as machinery and equipment). To derive tangible assets we subtract intangible assets from total assets. As the ratio increases, there is more revenue generated per dollar of assets. American Brands' asset turnover ratio of 1.94 implies that it generated almost $2 of sales for each $1 of tangible assets.

Like most ratios, the asset turnover ratio might be misleading if used in isolation from other indications of management efficiency. Since we generally use the net value of the assets, depreciation has already been subtracted. Hence older equipment with a lower value on the firm's books may create a misleading impression of high asset turnover by giving the denominator of the ratio a low value. Further,

[13] George H. Sorter and George Benston, "Appraising the Defensive Position of a Firm: The Internal Measure," *Accounting Review,* October 1960, 633–640.

many firms depend heavily on such intangible assets as patents and copyrights to generate their sales, and if these are excluded because they are intangible, the turnover ratio may be distorted.

2. Earning power ratio

$$\frac{\text{Net profit after taxes}}{\text{Total assets}} = \frac{\$123,300,000}{\$1,974,320,000} = .06$$

The earning power ratio, also called the return on total assets ratio, reflects how effectively management employed every dollar of assets to generate that final dollar of net profit. This very important ratio provides a common measure of comparison between the firm's investment success and alternative investment opportunities. The 6 percent earning power ratio for American Brands is not overly attractive; many alternative assets in 1972 were yielding in excess of 6 percent, including government bonds. A continued low return would lead investors and the financial officer to look outside the firm for other investment opportunities. On the other hand, this may very well be a temporarily low return for the company.

3. Various physical ratios

In addition to the financial ratios which measure the firm's asset utilization, there are physical ratios which also measure in output terms how efficient management has been in its use of the firm's assets. Among retailing firms, for example, sales per square foot of floor space is a traditional measure of asset utilization. Since the rental of floor space is one of the retailers biggest expenses, efficient use of that floor space is a sign of good management. Similarly, airlines look to the load factor, which relates the number of passenger miles actually flown to the number that was available for sale. A high load factor is indicative of good asset management. Each industry has its own particular physical measures of asset utilization, which you will learn during your employment with the firm.

Profitability A third group of ratios measures the degree of profitability management achieved both in terms of how well it turned each dollar of sales into profit (measures of operational efficiency) and how well it used each dollar invested in the firm to produce those profits (measures of financial efficiency). Generally, as the profit produced per dollar of sales or invested capital increases, management efficiency is considered to increase.

1. Gross profit margin

$$\frac{\text{Sales less cost of goods sold}}{\text{Sales}} = \frac{\$2,998,869,000 - \$2,335,306,000}{\$2,998,869,000} = .22$$

The gross profit margin measures how efficiently management produced each unit of product. A high gross profit margin relative to an acceptable industry standard implies that it cost this particular firm less than average to produce the product. We could interpret the gross operating margin as a measure of manufacturing efficiency.

2. Operating profit margin

$$\frac{\text{Operating profit}}{\text{Sales}} = \frac{\$310,454,000}{\$2,998,869,000} = .10$$

The operating profit margin, which compares the firm's operating income to its sales, measures the efficiency with which management not only manufactured the product but also sold and distributed it, because operating income is after deductions for the cost of goods sold and for advertising, selling, and general administrative expense. By examining the operating profit margin in conjunction with the gross profit margin, the financial officer and external analysts can determine whether changes in the profitability of the firm were caused by changes in manufacturing efficiency or in selling and distributing. The financial officer would concentrate corrective actions in the area indicated by the ratio which declined more.

3. Net profit margin

$$\frac{\text{Net profit after taxes}}{\text{Sales}} = \frac{\$123,300,000}{\$2,998,869,000} = .04$$

The net profit margin reflects management's efficiency in manufacturing, selling, and financing. Deductions from operating income are generally financial in nature, primarily reflecting interest charges and taxes (as can be seen in Table 3-11, American Brands' income statement). It also reflects the financial officers' ability to hold down taxes, something which they may not be able to control. The net profit margin is the overall measure of management's ability to turn each dollar of sales into profit. When examined in conjunction with the gross profit margin and the operating profit margin, it affords insight into how efficiently the firm is being financed.

4. Return on invested capital ratio

$$\frac{\text{Net profit after taxes}}{\text{Long term debt plus stockholders' equity}} = \frac{\$123,300,000}{\$441,171,000 + \$948,736,000} = .08$$

The return on invested capital ratio reflects management's efficiency in using the dollars borrowed from creditors and invested by stockholders. As the return increases, management is considered increasingly efficient in selecting projects in which to invest the firm's capital.

5. Return on common stockholders' equity ratio

$$\frac{\text{Net profit after taxes less preferred stock dividends}}{\text{Stockholders' equity less par value of the preferred stock}}$$
$$= \frac{\$123,300,000 - 4,500,000}{\$948,736,000 - 75,000,000} = .13$$

The return on common stockholders' equity ratio reflects how effectively the firm has worked for its stockholders. An effective use of long-term debt, as we shall see in later chapters, means a higher return to stockholders' equity.

6. Return on total assets ratio

$$\frac{\text{Net profit after taxes}}{\text{Total tangible assets}} = \frac{\$123,300,000}{\$1,974,320,000 - 434,625,000} = .08$$

The return on total assets ratio reflects how effectively management has selected rewarding investments for the funds available to the firm. As such it serves as a check on the return on invested capital ratio.

7. Net operating profit rate of return

$$\frac{\text{Earnings before interest and taxes}}{\text{Total tangible assets}} = \frac{\$317,091,000}{\$1,974,320,000 - 434,625,000} = .20$$

The net operating profit rate of return meets the objections of some analysts and financial officers who feel that since the interest on the long-term debt is already deducted before net profit is calculated, the use of net profit in such ratios as the return on invested capital is misleading. Instead we use earnings before interest and taxes in relation to total tangible assets, because the interest charges used to support the long-term debt are included and the distortions in comparisons caused by uncontrollable tax laws are avoided.

Long-term solvency A firm's long-term solvency is a function of how it manages and maintains its debt. Essentially, can it support the amount of borrowing it has committed itself to repay over the long run? This depends on the size of the cushion provided by stockholders' equity, for if the stockholders are willing to put up the funds, the firm can keep borrowing. The ability to maintain the debt also depends on the firm's ability to generate sufficient funds to meet interest and repayment schedules.

1. Debt/equity ratio

$$\frac{\text{Total debt}}{\text{Stockholders' equity}} = \frac{\$441,171,000 + 453,503,000}{\$948,736,000} = .94 \text{ to } 1$$

The total debt includes the current liabilities. A rising debt/equity ratio is indicative of an increasing dependence on debt financing relative to equity financing. The firm is in a potentially riskier situation, since any increase in debt relative to the cushion available to maintain it exposes the firm to a greater chance of financial difficulty.

Interpretation of the debt/equity ratio, like all ratios, depends on the acceptable industry standard. A very low debt/equity ratio relative to the industry implies greater long-term solvency and less financial risk, but it also implies that the firm may not be taking proper advantage of less expensive financing, relying too heavily on the stockholders to provide new financing, and penalizing earnings per share and share prices.

2. Long-term debt/total capital ratio

$$\frac{\text{Long-term debt}}{\text{Total capital}} = \frac{\$441,171,000}{\$441,171,000 + 948,736,000} = .32 \text{ to } 1$$

Total capital is the sum of long-term debt and stockholders' equity. This ratio differs from the debt/equity ratio in that it excludes current liabilities from the denominator. Other than that the interpretation is similar. The current liabilities are excluded on the grounds that they are offset by the current assets and are, therefore, not really part of the firm's debt when we are concerned with long-term solvency.

3. Capital structure breakdown

It is also convenient to break down the capital structure into percentage form to see the firm's reliance on debt, preferred stock, and common equity. For example, American Brands' capital structure breakdown is:

Long term debt	$441,171,000	32%
Preferred stock	75,000,000	5%
Common equity	873,736,000	63%
	1,389,907,000	100%

Again, we compare this breakdown to some accepted industry standard for interpretation. Frequently, this breakdown is used by the public utility commissions to determine the type of financing to authorize.

4. Fixed charges earned ratio

$$\frac{\text{Earnings before interest and taxes}}{\text{Interest plus principal repayment } (1/1 - t)}$$

$$= \frac{\$317,091,000}{\$39,421,000 + \$23,967.000 \ (1/1 - .5)} = 3.63$$

where t equals tax rate. Earnings before interest and taxes are used because interest payments have prior claim on the earnings before taxes and because the interest payments themselves are available to meet the interest obligation; deducting them would be double counting. We can obtain the interest for the year from the income statement and the repayment of principal for the year from the changes in financial position statement. If there are other fixed charges such as lease payments on rented property, these are simply added to the denominator. Notice, however, that the principal repayment, since it is paid out of after-tax income, must be adjusted to a pre-tax basis to make it comparable with the other terms in the ratio.

5. Interest coverage ratio

$$\frac{\text{Earnings before interest and taxes}}{\text{Interest}} = \frac{\$317,091,000}{\$39,421,000} = 8.043$$

The interest coverage ratio merely measures the amount of funds available to pay the interest obligation during the year. It can be misleading if there are significant other fixed charges. As illustrated in the case of American Brands, the interest coverage ratio is an overall coverage ratio, measuring the coverage of all the interest on all the debt, because it uses the total interest obligation in the denominator.

There are other methods of computing the interest coverage ratio which are very misleading and should be avoided. The prior deduction method and the cumulative deduction methods are used to determine the coverage for individual bonds according to each bond's claim on the earnings of the firm. This is highly misleading because the failure to pay any debt obligation, no matter how junior, can force the entire firm into financial distress, dragging down all the bonds, no matter how senior. It is best to use the overall coverage ratio.[14]

6. Preferred dividend coverage ratio

$$\frac{\text{Net income after interest and taxes}}{\text{Annual preferred dividends}} = \frac{\$123,300,000}{\$4,500,000} = 27.4$$

[14] The prior deduction method reduces the amount available for payment of interest on all the bonds by the interest on the bonds prior in claim to the one for which the coverage ratio is being computed. For example, if there were $4,000,000 available for interest and a senior bond required $500,000 and the junior bond required $1,000,000, the coverage ratio for the junior bond would be:

$$\frac{\$3,500,000}{\$1,000,000} = 3.5$$

The cumulative deduction method accumulates interest payments on the bonds in descending order of seniority. Thus, the coverage ratio for the senior bonds would be:

$$\frac{\$4,000,000}{\$500,000} = 8.0$$

and the coverage ratio for the junior bonds would be:

$$\frac{\$4,000,000}{\$1,500,000} = 2.67$$

The preferred dividend coverage ratio is the preferred stock counterpart of the interest coverage ratio. It merely tells us how secure the preferred dividend is in relation to the earning power of the firm.

Common stock ratios Other ratios measure certain characteristics of the common stock itself, rather than the operating characteristics of the firm. These are of interest to the financial officer who wants to maximize shareholder wealth.

1. Book value per share

The book value, also known as the net worth, is the assets minus liabilities. In other words, net worth, book value, and stockholders' equity are all similar concepts.

$$\frac{\text{Stockholders' equity} - \text{preferred shares at par}}{\text{Number of shares outstanding}}$$

$$= \frac{\$948,736,000 - \$75,000,000}{\$179,352,000/6.25} = \$30.44$$

Book value per share may be of some consideration if the firm is to be liquidated, its assets sold, and the proceeds distributed to the shareholders, but it rarely reflects the actual market value of the shares or of the assets themselves at auction. Obviously, it has limited uses.

2. Payout ratio

$$\frac{\text{Dividends on common stock}}{\text{Net earnings after taxes}} = \frac{\$2.288}{\$4.37} = 52.35\%$$

The payout ratio reflects the proportion of earnings which are paid to shareholders. As the proportion increases, the amount retained for reinvestment in the firm decreases, theoretically diminishing the future asset base from which further earnings growth may come.

3. Price/earnings ratio

$$\frac{\text{Stock price}}{\text{Earnings per share}} = \frac{\$43.75}{\$4.37} = 10$$

The price/earnings ratio (p/e) reflects market price of the shares in relation to earnings. In the above example, if American Brands were selling at $43.75 a share, its price/earnings ratio would be 10. There are several schools of thought as to what determines the p/e, and we will discuss them later as they pertain to the firm's cost of capital.

Common-Size Financial Statements

Frequently the financial officer is asked to interpret financial statements between companies and over time. In order to get a comparability which may be hard to derive because of differences in firm sizes or between years, you can use the common-size financial statement. It expresses each category on the income statement or the balance sheet as a percentage of total sales or total assets or liabilities.

Common-size income statement American Brands' common-size income statement appears in Table 3-13. We can see that American Brands had a cost of sales in 1972 of 77.87 percent of total sales, an increase from 76.99 percent for 1971. Similarly, we can see exactly what percentage of total sales was expensed for any particular cate-

Table 3-13   American Brands' Common-Size Income Statement for the Years Ending December 31, 1971 and December 31, 1972

	1972	1971
Net sales	100%	100%
Cost of sales	77.87	76.99
Gross profit	22.12	23.00
Advertising, selling & general administrative expenses	11.17	12.20
Operating income	10.35	10.80
Other income	.22	.20
Interest and related charges	1.31	1.57
Other deductions	.19	.24
Income before provision for taxes on income and minority interest	9.06	9.19
Provision for taxes on income		
Federal income taxes currently payable	3.00	3.34
Foreign income taxes currently payable	.97	.79
Deferred income taxes	.12	.04
Other taxes based on income	.35	.35
Income before minority interest	4.59	4.64
Minority interest in earnings of subsidiaries	.48	.42
Net income	4.11	4.22

gory. This might be a very useful tool for the financial officer who has to keep track of any unusual increase in expenses and wants to concentrate corrective efforts in the area with the most deviation from what was expected.

Common-size balance sheet American Brands' common-size balance sheet appears in Table 3-14. Like the common-size income statement, the common-size balance sheet can be used by the financial officer to detect problem areas. Sudden shifts in percentages from one year to the next should alert you to problems. American Brands appears to have little movement in percentages between 1971 and 1972. If anything, the slight decline in total liabilities is a favorable change.

Trend analysis As the common-size balance sheets render financial statements of different size companies comparable, a careful analysis of trends in various ratios for one particular firm may also be revealing of deterioration or improvement in the financial position of that firm. A typical trend analysis is illustrated in Table 3-15. The trend analysis in Table 3-15 examines the progress of the firm over the last ten years with indicative ratios in the areas of liquidity, profitability, and long-term solvency. It is obvious that the firm's liquidity position, as indicated by the current ratio, has been declining in recent years relative to the industry. An alert financial officer would be concerned about this trend, as the firm has gone from a better-than-average current ratio to a worse-than-average current ratio.

The firm's profitability, as measured by the net profit margin and the return on total assets, has also deteriorated. Again, both of these ratios have gone from above industry average to below industry average with an almost consistent decline from year to year, if we smooth out the cycle in the industry for these ratios. The firm has

Table 3-14 American Brands' Common-Size Balance Sheet for the Years Ending December 31, 1971 and December 31, 1972

Assets	1972	1971
Cash	1.63%	1.96%
Accounts receivable	12.06	11.46
Inventories		
Leaf tobacco	27.14	26.22
Bulk whiskeys	2.82	2.89
Other raw materials, supplies		
and work in process	4.80	4.49
Finished products	7.88	9.25
Other current assets	1.27	1.17
Total current assets	57.62	57.49
Property, plant and equipment, at cost land,		
improvements to land and leaseholds	1.46	1.50
Buildings	10.31	9.69
Machinery and equipment	22.15	22.18
Construction in progress	.51	.31
Less accumulated depreciation and amortizations	16.34	15.91
Net property, plant, and equipment	18.09	17.78
Intangibles resulting from business acquisitions	22.01	22.75
Other assets	2.26	1.96
Total assets	100.00%	100.00%

Liabilities	1972	1971
Notes payable	8.49%	9.06
Accounts payable and accrued expenses	8.18	7.61
Accrued taxes, including current portion of		
deferred income taxes	5.86	6.41
Current portion of long-term debt	.42	.34
Total current liabilities	22.97	23.44
Long-term debt	22.34	22.70
Deferred income taxes and other deferred credits	1.30	1.83
Minority interest in consolidated subsidiaries	5.33	5.10
Total liabilities	51.94	53.09
Stockholders' equity		
Preferred stock	3.79	3.88
Common stock	9.08	9.29
Additional paid-in capital	2.14	2.18
Retained earnings	38.13	35.98
Less treasury stock, at cost	5.10	4.44
Total stockholders' equity	48.05	46.90
Total liabilities plus stockholders' equity	100.00%	100.00%

Table 3-15   A Typical Company   Trend Analysis

Year	Current ratio		Net profit margin		Debt equity		Return on total assets	
	Industry	Firm	Industry	Firm	Industry	Firm	Industry	Firm
1976	2.4	2.0	15%	12	1:1	1:1	10%	6%
1975	2.3	2.0	12	9	1:1	1:1	7	8
1974	2.1	2.1	13	11	1:1	1:1	15	14
1973	2.0	2.0	14	14	1:1	1:1	15	15
1972	2.0	2.0	10	12	1:1	1:1	14	13
1971	2.0	2.1	7	10	1:1	1:1	10	12
1970	2.1	2.2	10	16	1:1	1:1	13	15
1969	2.2	2.3	11	17	1:1	1:1	15	17
1968	2.1	2.4	14	18	1:1	1:1	12	15
1967	2.0	2.5	13	19	1:1	1:1	14	17

had no deterioration in its debt/equity ratio, and it appears intentionally to keep this debt/equity ratio at a constant level, as does the rest of the industry.

Problems with ratio analysis Certain problems arise when the financial officer uses ratio analysis for planning, control, or reporting purposes. There is the problem of accounting comparability between firms and accounting periods. Methods of recording and reporting various items in the financial statement of a single firm may have changed. And different firms and industries will surely have different accounting items in their financial statements because of the different nature of their operations.

The financial officer must be very careful not to rely upon just one or a few ratios in isolation or upon superficial investigation of any number of ratios. One ratio not up to the acceptable standard does not necessarily mean the firm is unsound. It is more of a warning signal requiring further investigation to either explain the deviation in terms of some temporary factor or uncover further signs of weakness. You must carefully examine an entire profile of ratios.

The use of ratios depends upon the validity of industry standards of comparison. But standard industrial classifications are vague. Many firms are active in more than one industry, and there is no real standard of comparison for them, since they operate in no one particular sector.

Ratios based on interim reports are highly misleading if there is any degree of seasonality in the firm's operations. A firm with a seasonal need for cash may have a very low acid test ratio at certain times and a very high acid test ratio at other times in the year and still be operating normally. If you do not recognize the seasonality, you may be misled. Further, the business cycle can make ratios misleading. In an exceptionally good year, the interest coverage ratio may look more than adequate, only to be much less than adequate in years in which earnings decline. As a precaution, particularly when using the long-term solvency ratios, it is important to examine a trend over time. Previous bad years will show just how vulnerable the firm is.

Finally, remember that ratios are based on historical data and may not be indicative of the future. If the operating environment of the firm should take an unexpected and dramatic turn, historical ratios will not help your analysis.

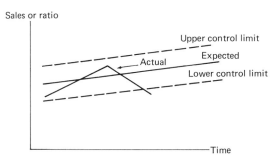

Figure 3-4 Control Interval

Budgetary Control

In addition to watching for deviations from acceptable standards for the ratios, the financial officer looks for deviations from each budget for early signs of problems. Deviations above or below the expected call for an investigation to determine if remedial action or implementation of a contingency budget is required.

One method by which you can keep track of deviations for control purposes is to use the *control interval* illustrated in Figure 3-4. If the middle line represents the expected budgeted amount and the upper and lower lines represent the limits of tolerable deviation from that expected figure, we can plot the actual figures as they occur and quickly detect worrisome deviations. For example, if actual sales dropped below the lower limit of the control interval on Figure 3-4, we would immediately investigate and perhaps initiate contingency plans.

For such a system to work, the actual results must be posted often and be forwarded to officers who can take the necessary action within a reasonable time. The control interval must also be sufficiently wide to prevent minor aberrations from needlessly triggering contingency or remedial action—yet sufficiently narrow for early signs of trouble not to be ignored or overlooked. You will have to be careful of such things as insignificant variation, reporting error, intentional deviations caused by management decision, and uncontrollable, temporary factors needing no response.[15] Proceed only after you have investigated and satisfied yourself that action is needed.

SUMMARY

After having read Chapter 3, you should be able to answer these questions:

1. How do I plan the use and control of the corporation's funds?

Planning is done mainly through the managerial accounting procedures of budgeting. Properly constructed budgets are an accurate estimate of the firm's operating revenues and expenditures for the coming accounting period. Budgeting requires a sales forecast, which can be derived in any of several ways ranging from rather subjective estimates to sophisticated statistical techniques. These methods

---

[15] Welsch, *Budgeting*, p. 383.

include regression analysis, scatter diagrams, trendline analysis, and share-of-market forecasts.

The other operating budgets, closely tied into the sales budget, estimate the firm's production and expenses. These include such budgets as the cost of goods sold, research and development expenses, selling and administrative expenses, and manufacturing overhead, among others.

2. How do I control the firm's expenditures so that they are coordinated with the firm's cash inflow?

The cash budget is a major tool in coordinating the firm's cash inflows and outflows. Unlike the other budgets, it deals only in cash accounts, allowing the financial officer to estimate financing needs and spot temporary investment strategy.

3. How do I report budget information to my superiors?

In addition to the budgets themselves, the financial officer frequently submits pro forma financial statements, which reflect the financial position of the firm over the accounting period, assuming the budgets were accurate.

4. How do I prepare for the possibility that my budget estimates are incorrect?

It is always wise to develop contingency budgets to fall back on in case the expected budget estimates are not met. Contingency budgeting gives an orderly plan which can be quickly and efficiently implemented to meet changing operating environments.

5. How do I report the results after the planning period is over?

The actual operating results for the company during the period are reported to your superiors and outside parties through the income statement. The financial position of the firm at the end of the accounting period is reported through the balance sheet. The changes in financial position statement reported the cash flows through the firm during the period.

6. Once I have helped lay the plans for the firm, how do I insure that they will be carried out and constantly check for indications of unforeseen problems?

The function of financial control is early detection of unanticipated problems, so that remedial action can be taken. Ratio analysis is one tool used to test the firm's liquidity, profitability, earning power, and long-term solvency. Ratio analysis must be used properly and its many pitfalls avoided. Common-size income statements and balance sheets, trend analysis, and presentations of control interval were also shown to be useful tools in financial control.

QUESTIONS

3-1 (a) From a financial officer's viewpoint, why is the cash budget important?
   (b) What is the principal difference between a cash budget and other budgets, such as a sales expense budget?

3-2 Distinguish between financial accounting and managerial accounting.

3-3 List some of the factors you need to consider in choosing the best method of forecasting sales for the next planning period.

3-4 Explain briefly what pro forma financial statements are and to what extent they are useful in financial planning.

3-5 Differentiate between an income statement and balance sheet.

3-6 Explain why the current ratio will always be higher than the acid test ratio.

3-7 Suppose your firm's inventory turnover ratio is about half the industry's average. Is this cause for concern?

3-8 Different industries have different values for their asset turnover ratios. Why is this so?

3-9 Explain how the various profitability ratios may be used to indicate the relative contributions to the firm's profitability of (a) the operational parts of the firm, (b) the advertising and administrative staffs, and (c) the type of financing.

3-10 What effect does the type of financing (debt versus equity) have on the following profitability ratios: (a) net profit margin, (b) return on invested capital, (c) return on stockholder's equity, and (d) return on total assets?

PROBLEMS

3-1 The following cash budget has been projected for Bloom Corporation for the first six months of next year. At the beginning of the year $1,000,000 in cash will be available. Similarly, the firm wishes to maintain a minimum cash balance each month of $1,000,000.

(a) Complete the cash budget in the space provided.

(b) Analyze the major short-term financing needs of the firm.

Cash Budget For Bloom Corporation
For First Six Months of 19xx

Month	1	2	3	4	5	6
Cash receipts						
Cash sales	$ 500,000	$600,000	$ 700,000	$ 750,000	$ 600,000	$ 500,000
Acct. rec's. collected		850,000	2,200,000	2,400,000	2,600,000	2,000,000
Interest received	—	200,000	—	200,000	—	200,000
Dividends received	—	—	50,000			50,000
Sale of stock	2,000,000	—	—	—	—	—
Total receipts	$2,500,000	$1,650,000	$2,950,000	$3,350,000	$3,200,000	$2,750,000
Cash disbursements						
Purchases	200,000	200,000	250,000	300,000	250,000	300,000
Direct labor	500,000	500,000	600,000	700,000	600,000	700,000
Mfg. overhead	150,000	50,000	200,000	100,000	100,000	200,000
Administration	300,000	200,000	300,000	250,000	250,000	300,000
Advertising	50,000	200,000	100,000	150,000	200,000	300,000
Raw materials	800,000	650,000	650,000	700,000	600,000	700,000
Interest paid	—	100,000	—	100,000		
Dividends paid	100,000	—	—	—		500,000
Long-term debt	500,000	—	200,000	—	2,600,000	—
Total disbursements	$2,600,000	$1,900,000	$2,300,000	$2,300,000	$4,600,000	$3,000,000

Net receipts (disbursements)						
Cash beginning of month						
Cash end of month						
Minimum required balance						
Short-term financing needs						
Repayment of short-term financing						
Short-term borrowing outstanding end of month						

3-2 The income statement and balance sheet for Bolcon, Inc., are given for the year
1975. Also given are the various financial ratios for the industry in which
Bolcon operates.
  (a) Compute the various ratios indicated for Bolcon Inc. The inventories were
      $13,600,500 for Bolcon at the beginning of the year.
  (b) Discuss the liquidity position of Bolcon in comparison to the industry.
  (c) How well does Bolcon seem to be utilizing its assets to generate sales, as
      compared to the industry?
  (d) How profitable is Bolcon as compared to the industry? Can you distinguish
      between profitability due to operational efficiencies versus that due to
      financial structure?
  (e) From a stockholder's viewpoint, how is Bolcon performing relative to the in-
      dustry?
  (f) Does Bolcon appear to be a growth-oriented company or a relatively conser-
      vative one?

Bolcon, Inc.
Consolidated Income Statement for Year Ending December 31, 1975

Net sales		$92,468,400
Cost of sales	(−)	66,334,006
Gross profit	(=)	26,134,394
Advertising and administrative expenses	(−)	19,175,620
Operating income	(=)	6,958,774
Interest charges	(−)	2,234,538
Other deductions	(−)	414,908
Net income before taxes	(=)	4,309,328
Federal income taxes	(−)	1,205,000
Net income	(=)	3,104,328
Previous retained earnings	(+)	33,589,977
Dividends, preferred stock	(−)	484,709
Dividends, common stock	(−)	1,422,927
Retained earnings	(=)	$34,786,669

Ratio name	Ratio equation	Bolcon	Industry
Current			4.02
Acid test			3.00
Inventory turnover			7.50
Asset turnover			2.30
Gross profit margin			0.26
Operating profit margin			0.06
Net profit margin			0.05
Return of stock- holders' equity			0.05
Debt/equity			0.40
Interest coverage			3.90
Preferred dividend coverage			7.50
Payout ratio			0.80

Bolcon, Inc.
Balance Sheet For Year Ending December 31, 1975

Assets

Cash	$ 461,335
Accounts receivables, net	18,756,847
Inventories	15,035,898
Total current assets	$ 34,254,080
Property, plant and equipment, net	68,244,561
Total assets	$102,498,641

Liabilities

Notes payable	$ 2,030,015
Accounts payable	7,085,013
Accrued taxes	448,666
Total current liabilities	$ 9,563,694
Long-term debt	36,073,532
Deferred income taxes	5,678,704
Total liabilities	$ 51,315,930
Preferred stock, par value	8,501,371
Common stock, par value	1,154,390
Capital surplus	7,392,297
Retained earnings	34,786,669
Less treasury stock	652,016
Stockholders' equity	$ 51,182,711
Total liabilities and stockholders' equity	$102,498,641

3-3 The acid test, net profit margin, and debt/equity ratios are compiled for Bolcon for the past six years, as are the corresponding industry ratios.
(a) Graph in three separate figures the trend in each ratio for Bolcon and the industry.
(b) Discuss briefly some of the major changes that have been occurring in the last six years in both the industry and Bolcon. Note particularly Bolcon's liquidity, profitability, and capital structure changes as compared to the industry's.

Year	Acid test ratio		Net profit margin (%)		Debt/equity ratio	
	Bolcon	Industry	Bolcon	Industry	Bolcon	Industry
1975	2.00	3.00	3.0	5.0	0.70	0.40
1974	2.40	3.10	4.0	5.0	0.60	0.40
1973	2.60	3.00	5.0	5.5	0.55	0.40
1972	2.60	3.20	6.5	6.0	0.40	0.40
1971	2.90	3.10	6.5	6.5	0.40	0.40
1970	2.95	2.98	7.0	6.5	0.40	0.40

BIBLIOGRAPHY

Ansoff, H. Igor. "Planning as a Practical Management Tool." *Financial Executive*, XXXII (June 1964), 34–37.
Anton, Hector R. *Accounting for the Flow of Funds.* Houghton Mifflin, Boston, 1962.
Bacon, Jeremy. *Managing the Budget Function.* Studies in Business Policy, Report No. 131. National Industrial Conference Board, Inc., New York, 1970.

Davidson, Sidney, George H. Sorter, and Hemu Kalle. "Measuring the Defensive Position of a Firm." *Financial Analysts Journal*, 20 (January-February 1964), 23–39.

Foulke, Roy A. *Practical Financial Statement Analysis*, 5th ed. McGraw-Hill, New York, 1961.

Henning, Dale A. *Non-Financial Controls in Smaller Enterprises*, University of Washington, College of Business Administration, Seattle, Wash., 1964.

Horrigan, James C. "A Short History of Financial Ratio Analysis." *Accounting Review*, XLIII (April 1968), 284–294.

Rappaport, Alfred. "A Capital Budgeting Approach to Divisional Planning and Control." *Financial Executive* (October 1968), 47–63.

Sorter, George H., and George Benston. "Appraising the Defensive Position of a Firm: The Internal Measure." *Accounting Review*, XXXV (October 1960), 633–640.

Trumbull, Wendel P. "Developing the Funds Statement as a Third Major Financial Statement." *N.A.A. Bulletin*, XLV (April 1963), 21–31.

Appendix 3A Commonly Encountered Financial Accounting Principles

From our discussion of financial statements and accounting, it is clear that the financial officer is frequently called upon to prepare, to examine, and to compare financial statements of interest to the firm. He or she may do this in conjunction with the firm's auditors, at the request of the president who wants to evaluate a potential merger candidate, or for internal purposes. Whatever the reason, the financial officer must understand the principles behind the statements in order to interpret their meaning and evaluate their comparability. To do this you need a working knowledge of the major accounting principles which cover how financial items are reported.

This appendix gives you a brief summary of frequently encountered financial accounting principles. Later chapters will elaborate on many of the accounting points raised here. And you will become more thoroughly acquainted with them in your accounting principles course. This appendix is intended to be an adjunct to financial statement analysis, particularly ratio analysis, to illustrate the necessity for comparability among the financial statements and to serve as a handy reference.

Finally, Table 3A-5 reflects the accounting principles used by American Brands, Inc. in its 1972 annual report.

THE INVESTMENT CREDIT

Periodically the federal government instates the investment tax credit, which allows a firm to reduce directly its tax liability up to 10 percent of the value of any new machinery or equipment purchased while the credit was in effect. This direct reduction in taxes increases the firm's net income after taxes. However, since the reduction is rather large in some instances and is also a temporary occurrence (because the credit can be suspended and is not a typical part of the firm's operations), accountants have questioned whether the reduction in taxes should be directly reflected in the first year the asset is acquired or amortized over the life of the asset. If the investment credit is recorded entirely in the first year, the firm may use the flow-through method; if amortized over the life of the asset, the firm may use the amortization method. The choice is up to the individual firm.

The differences in effect of the two methods are illustrated in the following example, which assumes that the firm purchases a $100,000 asset with a 10-year life expectancy, has a 50 percent tax rate, and is subject to a 7 percent investment tax credit. Using the flow-through method, the firm would derive its net income after taxes as follows:

Income before taxes		$200,000
Taxes (excluding investment credit)	$100,000	
Investment credit	7,000	
Taxes payable		93,000
Net income after taxes		107,000

If the firm chooses to amortize the investment credit over the life of the asset, the same firm would record the first year's data as follows:

Income before taxes		$200,000
Taxes (excluding investment credit)	$100,000	
Investment credit	700	
Taxes payable		99,300
Net income after taxes		100,700

The use of the amortization method has lowered the firm's reported earnings for at least that first year. If no further acquisitions are made or if the investment tax credit is repealed, the flow-through method will result in higher taxes and lower reported net income after taxes in subsequent years.

REPORTING OF LEASES IN THE FINANCIAL STATEMENTS OF LESSEE

The lessee should footnote all noncancelable leases which have not been recorded as assets or liabilities. Generally, the annual lease expense is disclosed in the footnotes because it is considered the right to use the property, somewhat analogous to rents. However, leases that are clearly installment purchases of property should be recognized as purchases, and accompanying liability, particularly if the terms of the lease result in a material equity in the property for the lessee.

The footnote should contain the following pertinent information:

1. The total annual rental expense
2. The minimum rental commitments in (a) each of the five succeeding fiscal years, (b) each of the next three five-year periods, and (c) the remainder as a single amount
3. Other information in general terms such as renewal options, restrictions on dividends, additional debt, and further leases in the lease, and any other information "necessary to assess the effect of the lease on the firm's financial position, results of operations, and changes in financial position"

The firm should also report the present value of the lease commitments calculated on the interest rates implicit in the leases at the time of signing or the weighted average interest rates in the leases.

ACCOUNTING FOR THE COST OF PENSION PLANS

General financial accounting principles support the practice of accruing the costs of the pension plan as they occur. These costs are generally calculated by an actuarial procedure which reflects the benefits earned during the accounting period by the firm's employees. The firm must recognize this potential liability, which, if vested, means that it is definitely owed to the employee. Otherwise, all or part of the benefits may be contingent upon the employee satisfying vesting requirements.

To meet the pension plan obligation, the firm usually funds all or part of the amount necessary to satisfy the liability when it comes due. The firm should pay interest on the unfunded portion and may amortize the past service costs over a 10- to 40-year period. If the vested benefits are actuarially underfunded, the firm is required to expense the benefits when they are paid out.

All financial statements are required to include the following:

1. A statement that a pension plan does exist, identifying the employee group
2. A statement of the firm's accounting and funding policies
3. The provision for the pension cost incurred in the period
4. The excess, if any, of the actuarially computed value of the vested benefits over the total of the pension fund and any balance sheet accruals, less any pension prepayments or deferred charges
5. The nature and the effect of significant matters affecting comparability among the accounting periods presented

ACCOUNTING FOR INCOME TAXES

The tax effects of loss carryforwards should not be recognized until the periods in which they are realized. The tax effects of loss carrybacks should be allocated to the period in which the loss occurred.

REPORTING THE RESULTS OF OPERATIONS

The firm is required to report separately and in a prescribed manner items which are extraordinary to the usual operations of the business. Extraordinary items are distinguished by their unusual nature and their infrequent occurrence. In other words, the event should "possess a high degree of abnormality" and should be unlikely to recur in the "foreseeable future." Each extraordinary item which materially affects the operating results should be reported in the following manner:

Income before extraordinary items	$xxx	
Extraordinary items (less applicable income taxes of $___)	xxx	
(note ___)		
Net income		$xxx

Material items which are either unusual in nature *or* infrequent in occurrence, but not both, should also be reported separately, but should not be aggregated with the extraordinary items.

If the operating results have been affected by certain of the firm's operations which have been discontinued according to a formal plan, then operating results should distinguish between the continuing and the discontinued portions of the business in the following prescribed manner:

Income from continuing operations before income taxes	$xxx	
Provision for income taxes	xxx	
Income from continuing operations		xxx
Discontinued operations (note ___):		
Income (loss) from operations discontinued (less applicable taxes of $xxx)	$xxx	
Loss on disposal of discontinued operations, including provision of $xxx for operating losses during the phase-out period (less applicable income taxes of $xxx)	xxx	
Net income		$xxx

When reporting the interim operating results, i.e., those for a period less than the full year, the firm must follow the same generally accepted accounting principles as it does in its annual report. If the firm has publicly held stock, the interim report must contain at least the following information:

1. Sales or gross revenues for the period
2. Primary and fully diluted earnings per share
3. Seasonal revenue statement
4. Significant changes in estimated income taxes
5. Disposal of business and extraordinary items
6. Contingent items
7. Changes in the accounting principles and their effect on operating results
8. Significant changes in the firm's financial position

ACCOUNTING FOR CONVERTIBLE DEBT AND DEBT ISSUED WITH STOCK PURCHASE WARRANTS

Convertible debt is debt which can be converted into the common stock of the firm. For the accountant's purposes, it must also bear a lower-than-typical interest rate, be initially convertible at a price higher than the market value of the stock, and have a conversion price which does not decrease except for antidilution protection. Financial accounting treats the entire amount raised with the convertible debt as debt, with no consideration for any potential value which may exist because of the conversion feature.

Debts sold with stock purchase warrants, however, are allocated to both the debt and the additional paid-in capital accounts. The proportions of the allocation should reflect the relative fair values of the two securities at the time of issue.

EARNINGS PER SHARE

Financial accounting requires a dual presentation of earnings per share. Companies with a simple capital structure, (less than a 3 percent dilution effect) use computed earnings per share based on the weighted average number of shares outstanding during the period.

Companies with complex capital structures (dilution in excess of 3 percent) have to report two different earnings per share. One is the *primary earnings per share:* the amount of earnings attributable to each share of issued common stock and common stock equivalent, where common stock equivalent is defined as any security which, because of its terms or the circumstances under which it was issued, was in substance equivalent to common stock. The most commonly encountered convertible security, the convertible debenture, is considered a common stock equivalent if its current yield at issue is less than 66⅔ percent of the prevailing bank prime interest rate.

Also required is the *fully diluted earnings per share:* the amount of current earnings per share reflecting the maximum dilution that would result from the conversion of convertible securities and exercise of warrants and options that individually would decrease earnings per share and in the aggregate would have a dilutive effect.

Frequently, primary earnings per share are reported as "earnings per common and common equivalent shares," while fully diluted earnings are reported as "earnings per common and common equivalent share, assuming full dilution."

BUSINESS COMBINATIONS

Two recognized methods may be used.

Purchasing

The assets of the acquired company are recorded at their fair market value on the books of the acquirer. Any payment in excess of the recorded costs and assumed liabilities is recorded as goodwill, an intangible asset which must be amortized over a maximum 40-year period. For example, assume A is acquiring B for 1,000 shares (par value $10) worth $30,000. The pro forma balance of the combined companies would be as shown in Table 3A-1. Notice that the effect of amortizing the goodwill is to reduce reported earnings.

Table 3A-1

	A	B	Debit	Credit	Pro Forma Balance sheet
Assets					
Current assets	$90,000	$5,000			$95,000
Net fixed assets	120,000	10,000			130,000
Goodwill			$23,000		23,000
Total assets	210,000	15,000			248 000
Liabilities and stockholders' equity					
Current liabilities	30,000	3,000			33,000
Long-term debt	20,000	5,000			25,000
Common stock	40,000	3,000	3,000	10,000	50,000
Additional paid-in capital	20,000	3,000	3,000	20,000	40,000
Retained earnings	100,000	1,000	1,000		100,000
	210,000	15,000			248,000

Consolidation of incomes is from the date of purchase only. To compute the earnings per share (EPS) of AB we would have:

	A	B	A + B
Net earnings	$10,000	$1,000	$11,000
Shares	4,000	300	5,000

AB's earnings per share = $11,000/5,000 = $2.20, providing the date of purchase was at the beginning of the accounting period. If the purchase was halfway through the year, the EPS would be:

$$\begin{array}{ccc} A & B & A + B \\ \$10,000 + 1/2(1,000) & = & \$10,500 \end{array}$$

AB's EPS = $10,500/5,000 = $2.10

Pooling

Pooling-of-interests is governed by the following rules:
1. Equity with identical rights must be exchanged.
2. The acquired firm's stockholders must retain an equity position (ownership interest continues).
3. At least 90 percent of the stock must be acquired.
4. The former accounting basis is retained.
5. No disposal of acquired assets is planned.
6. A single transaction is used.
7. Independent assets are combined.
8. Recorded assets and liabilities are carried forward at their recorded amounts.
9. Income is consolidated for the entire fiscal period in which combination occurs.

The pro forma statements in Table 3A-2 show what the combined financial statements would look like if the merger had taken place under a pooling arrangement. Assume Firm C exchanged 1½ shares of its stock for 1 share of firm D.

Table 3A-2

	C	D	Adjustments Debit	Adjustments Credit	C + D
Current assets	$100,000	$100,000			$200,000
Fixed assets	200,000	200,000			400,000
Total assets	300,000	300,000			600,000
Current liabilities	50,000	50,000			100,000
Long-term debt	60,000	60,000			120,000
Common stock ($10 par)	100,000	100,000		$50,000	250,000
Additional paid-in capital	60,000	60,000	$50,000		70,000
Retained earnings	30,000	30,000			60,000
Total liabilities and stockholders' equity	300,000	300,000			600,000

On a pooling-of-interest basis the two balances are merely added together, except for a shift of $50,000 from the additional paid-in capital to the common stock to reflect the increased number of C shares outstanding. The C + D earnings per share (EPS) would be:

	C	D		C+D
Net earnings	$10,000	$15,000	=	$25,000
Shares outstanding	10,000	10,000	=	25,000
C + D's EPS	=	$1 regardless of the date during the fiscal year on which the merger was consummated.		

INTANGIBLE ASSETS

Intangible assets are those that are not represented by a physical asset and are treated under their own financial accounting rules. If the intangible asset is purchased from another company, it should be recorded under the intangible asset account on the financial statements.

The costs of developing, maintaining, or restoring intangible assets which are not specifically identifiable, have indeterminant lives, or are inherent in a continuing business and related to the enterprise as a whole should be deducted from the firm's income as incurred. If these costs are capitalized or assigned a limited life, they should be amortized on a straightline basis not to exceed forty years.

THE EQUITY METHOD OF ACCOUNTING FOR INVESTMENTS IN COMMON STOCKS

The consolidated financial statements of the firm typically combine the assets, liabilities, revenues, and expenses of subsidiaries with the corresponding items for the parent company, after eliminating intercompany transactions.

The cost method of consolidation is used only if the subsidiary is less than 20 percent owned by the parent firm. The original price paid for the subsidiary is recorded on the parent's financial statements and remains unchanged. Any cash dividends from the subsidiary to the parent are recorded as income to the parent upon their receipt.

The equity method applies to subsidiary ownership in excess of 20 percent. This method records the original investment at cost, but the amount is increased (or decreased) by the parent's pro rata share of the subsidiary's additions to (or deductions from) its stockholders' equity account. The parent's pro rata share of the income is reported as other income (or loss) on its own income statement, while dividends received from the subsidiary reduce the parent's original investment.

INTEREST ON RECEIVABLES AND PAYABLES

If there is a difference between the market value of the receivable or the payable and its face value at the time of issue, the firm must recognize this difference and should treat it as a discount or premium to be amortized as interest expense or income over the life of the note.

EARLY EXTINGUISHMENT OF DEBT

If the firm redeems its debt obligation before the maturity of those obligations at a cost less or more than their face value, the difference between the acquisition price and the net carrying amount of the extinguished debt should be recognized in the income of the period of extinguishment as a loss or gain and identified as a separate item on the financial statements. This does not apply to gains or losses from cash purchases of debt to satisfy sinking fund requirements.

ACCOUNTING FOR INCOME TAXES: INVESTMENTS IN COMMON STOCK ACCOUNTED FOR BY THE EQUITY METHOD

There is a timing difference for tax purposes when a firm uses the equity method to account for income received from the ownership of common stock. The pro rata income of the company whose stock is owned is reported on the owner's financial statements when earned by the other company, but the owner does not pay taxes on that income until received as a dividend or in liquidation. If the income is eventually to be realized by the owner in the form of a dividend, the owning firm should recognize the tax in the current tax period. However, if the owner expects to realize the income through the eventual disposition of the owned firm, the owner should accrue the taxes at the appropriate rate. (These procedures do not apply to subsidiaries and corporate joint ventures.)

INVENTORY EVALUATION

The firm may select between the last-in, first-out (LIFO) or the first-in, first-out (FIFO) methods of evaluating its inventory. The LIFO method has the effect of including in the cost of goods sold the cost of the last units produced, while the FIFO method has the effect of including in the cost of goods sold the cost of the first units produced. In periods of rising prices, LIFO tends to give a higher cost of goods sold and consequently a lower net income before taxes, a lower tax liability, and a lower reported net income after taxes than FIFO for the same period. Conversely, during periods of falling prices, FIFO gives the lower reported net income.

The differing effects of LIFO and FIFO are illustrated in Tables 3A-3 and 3A-4. Notice the lower inventory and the higher cost of goods sold under the LIFO method. Because each unit sold has been more costly to produce, LIFO leads to a lower reported operating income for any given revenue level and lower tax liability and reported net income during periods of inflation.

The kicker is that the firm may choose to switch from one to the other to make a bad year look respectable through a reduction in cost of goods sold. As a financial officer, you must be prepared to evaluate the effect a switch will have on your own financial statements and those of other firms you may want to examine.

Table 3A-3   LIFO

Beginning inventory (1 mil units $10/unit)		$10,000,000
Purchases		
Raw material	$3,000,000	
Labor	4,000,000	
Manufacturing overhead	1,000,000	8,000,000
Cost of goods available for sale		$18,000,000
Ending inventory (500,000 units @ $10)		5,000,000
Cost of goods sold		13,000,000

Table 3A-4   FIFO

Assume cost of each unit rises to $12/unit.		
Beginning inventory (1 mil units @ $10/unit)		$10,000,000
Purchases		
Raw material	$3,000,000	
Labor	4,000,000	
Manufacturing overhead	1,000,000	8,000,000
Cost of goods available for sale		$18,000,000
Ending inventory (500,000 units @ $12)		6,000,000
Cost of goods sold		12,000,000

Table 3A-5   Summary of Significant Accounting Policies, 1972 and 1971 for American Brands, Inc.

Principles of consolidation   The consolidated financial statements include the accounts of the Company and all subsidiaries. Current assets and current liabilities of foreign subsidiaries are translated into U.S. dollars at the rates of exchange in effect at the balance sheet dates; other assets and liabilities and depreciation expense are translated at appropriate historical rates. Income and expenses, except for depreciation, are translated at the average rate for each year. In translating on this basis, unrealized gains in excess of current or prior years' unrealized losses are deferred as a reserve for future foreign exchange fluctuations; unrealized losses in excess of previously established reserves are charged to income.

Amortization of intangibles   Intangibles resulting from business acquisitions, comprised of brands and trademarks and cost in excess of net assets of businesses acquired, are considered to have a continuing value over an indefinite period and are not being amortized, except for intangibles acquired after 1970, which are being amortized over a period of 40 years.

Inventories   Inventories are priced at the lower of cost (average; first-in, first-out; and minor amounts at last-in, first-out) or market. It is a generally recognized trade practice to classify the total amount of leaf tobacco and bulk whiskey inventories as a current asset, although part of such inventories, due to the duration of aging processes, ordinarily will not be sold within one year.

The last-in, first-out inventory included in the consolidated balance sheet is $1,690,000 in excess of the valuation reported by a subsidiary for federal income tax purposes, resulting from a revaluation of this asset to fair value at the date the subsidiary was purchased.

Property, plant, and equipment   Depreciation and amortization are provided, principally on a straight-line basis, over the estimated useful lives of the assets. Profits or losses resulting from dispositions are, with minor exceptions, included in the statement of income. Betterments and renewals which improve and extend the life of an asset are capitalized; maintenance and repairs are charged to cost or expense.

Income taxes   Deferred income taxes relate to differences in the timing of recognition for book and tax purposes of certain items, principally depreciation. The investment tax credit, which was not material in 1972 or 1971, is accounted for as a reduction of taxes on income currently payable.

Deferred income taxes have not been provided on undistributed earnings, aggregating $1,537,000 at December 31, 1972, for three domestic international sales corporations, because it is intended that this amount will be permanently invested in these companies. Undistributed earnings of all other subsidiaries can be remitted to the parent Company without incurring any significant tax liability under existing tax laws.

Pension plans   Pension expense, which is being funded, is determined by independent actuaries and includes amortization of unfunded past service costs over periods ranging from 18 to 38 years.

Research and development costs   These costs are charged to income as incurred.

Table 3A-5 (Cont.)
Notes Accompanying Financial Statements,
1972 and 1971

Consolidated foreign subsidiaries The consolidated financial statements include the
following amounts related to operations outside the Western Hemisphere:

	December 31	
	1972	1971
	(In thousands)	
Total assets	$486,956	$466,304
Total liabilities (excluding minority interest)	199,859	199,048
Minority interest	105,243	98,549
Net income	27,371	22,291

Translation of the accounts of foreign operations into U.S. dollars resulted in a
$17,634,000 net unrealized loss, principally due to the decline of the British pound in
1972. After applying the $14,101,000 reserve created in 1971 from an unrealized gain
and deducting from the net loss $1,207,000 thereof applicable to minority interest,
$2,326,000 was charged to income in 1972.

Long-term debt

	Principal amounts at December 31, 1972
	(In thousands)
5⅞% debentures, due 1992 (a)	$ 87,050
5¼% convertible debentures, due 1988 (b)	17,289
Other debentures, 3¼% to 8%, due 1977 to 1990 (a)	33,519
8⅞% notes, due 1975	100,000
Eurodollar revolving credit notes, 6⅜% to 6¾% (c)	19,000
7½% Eurodollar borrowing, due 1980	25,000
7% German mark borrowings, due 1979	54,375
6% British sterling notes, due 1981 and 1985	43,200
Swiss franc borrowings, 6½% to 6¾%, due 1977 to 1986 (d)	34,860
Miscellaneous notes and mortgages	35,259
	449,552
Less current portion	8,381
Total	$441,171

(a) Amounts shown are net of debentures acquired by the Company through open
market purchases to cover sinking fund requirements.
(b) These debentures, sold by a subsidiary, are guaranteed by the Company and are
convertible into the Company's Common stock at $36 per share. At December 31,
1972, a total of 480,433 shares of Common stock costing $15,003,000 were held in the
treasury and reserved for such conversions.
(c) These lines of credit aggregating $25,000,000 expire on December 31, 1977; the
interest rate is fixed at the time of each borrowing.
(d) A Swiss franc borrowing of $11,628,000 which would have matured on De-
cember 30, 1973, was extended to mature on December 30, 1977.
Estimated payments for maturing debt and sinking fund requirements during the
next five years are as follows: 1973, $8,381,000; 1974, $16,244,000; 1975, $115,805,000;
1976, $23,869,000; 1977, $52,211,000.

Table 3A-5 (Cont.)

Stockholders' equity The Company has 15,000,000 shares of Preferred stock authorized, of which 750,000 shares of $6.00 Convertible Preferred stock are issued and
outstanding. The holders of this stock are entitled to cumulative dividends, to one
vote per share (in certain events, to the exclusion of the Common shares), to preference in liquidation of $100 per share plus accrued dividends, and to convert each
share of such stock on or after December 15, 1973 into two and two-ninths shares of
Common stock. The Company may redeem such Preferred stock on or after December 15, 1977 at prices beginning at $102 and declining to $100 per share on or
after December 15, 1979 plus accrued dividends.

The Company has 60,000,000 Common shares authorized. At December 31, 1972
and 1971, there were 28,696,253 shares issued, of which, respectively, 26,126,052
shares and 26,433,827 shares were outstanding and 2,570,201 shares and 2,262,426
shares were held in the treasury.

During 1972 the treasury shares increased through purchases of 454,600 shares at a
cost of $20,071,000 and decreased by 128,058 shares costing $4,414,000 as the result of
shares delivered upon conversion of debentures and exercise of stock options. Also,
18,767 shares costing $768,000 were delivered in connection with a business acquisi-
tion by a subsidiary.

During 1972 consolidated paid-in surplus increased by a net amount of $44,000 in
connection with the conversion of debentures and exercise of stock options, and by
$107,000 in connection with a business acquisition by a subsidiary.

Stock options Under the Company's qualified stock option plan, options may be
granted to key employees to purchase shares of the Company's Common stock at
fair market values at dates of grant. Options extend for a term of five years and may
not be exercised until one year from date of grant. Changes during 1972 in shares
under option were as follows:

	Shares
Under option, December 31, 1971	221,980
Options granted	41,250
Options exercised (at $32.25 to $44.1875 per share)	(44,550)
Options lapsed	(8,550)
Under option, December 31, 1972 (at prices ranging from $34.3125 to $49.25 per share)	210,130

At December 31, 1972 options for 169,380 shares were exercisable and 249,250
shares were available for future options under the Plan.

Treasury shares are delivered on exercise of options.

Pension plans The Company and its subsidiaries have a number of pension plans
covering substantially all employees. Total pension expense for the years 1972 and
1971 was $20,088,000 and $20,815,000, respectively, including provision for past service costs.

The actuarially computed value of vested benefits as of the latest valuation dates
exceeded the total of the pension funds at such dates by approximately $53,500,000.

Earnings per share Net income per share without dilution is based on the weighted
average number of shares of Common stock outstanding in each year, and after
Preferred stock dividend requirements.

Fully diluted net income per share assumes that the convertible debentures and
the Convertible Preferred shares outstanding at the beginning of each year were
converted at those dates with related interest (net of tax effect), Preferred stock divi-

Table 3A-5 (Cont.)

dend requirements and outstanding Common shares adjusted accordingly. It also assumes that outstanding Common shares were increased by shares issuable upon exercise of those options as to which market price exceeds exercise price, less shares which could have been purchased with the related proceeds.

Report of Independent Certified Public Accountants

To the Board of Directors and Stockholders of American Brands, Inc.:

We have examined the consolidated balance sheet of American Brands, Inc. and Subsidiaries as of December 31, 1972, and the related statements of income and retained earnings and changes in financial position for the year then ended. Our examination was made in accordance with generally accepted auditing standards, and accordingly included such tests of the accounting records and such other auditing procedures as we considered necessary in the circumstances. We previously examined and reported upon the consolidated financial statements of the Company for the year ended December 31, 1971.

In our opinion, the aforementioned financial statements present fairly the consolidated financial position of American Brands, Inc. and Subsidiaries at December 31, 1972 and 1971, and the consolidated results of their operations and changes in their financial position for the years then ended, in conformity with generally accepted accounting principles applied on a consistent basis.

Lybrand, Ross Bros. & Montgomery

1251 Avenue of the Americas
New York, N.Y.
February 1, 1973

FOREIGN CURRENCY TRANSLATION

If cash losses or gains have been realized from the translation of foreign-currency-denominated transactions, assets, or liabilities into the home currency of the firm, the amount of the loss or the gain must be charged or credited to the income statement. If there has been a decline in the translation of the current or working capital asset, even if it has not been realized, the losses must be charged against income, but unrealized gains are accumulated in a suspense account to offset any losses.

Current assets are translated at the now-prevailing rate of exchange. Fixed assets, on the other hand, are carried at the rate prevailing when they were acquired or constructed, unless shortly before that a substantial and permanent change in the exchange rate occurred.

Current liabilities are translated at the now-prevailing rate of exchange. Long-term liabilities are translated at the now-prevailing rate of exchange if issued shortly before a substantial and presumably permanent change in the exchange rate. However, under certain circumstances the accounting profession still recognizes the translation of long-term liabilities at the rate which prevailed when they were first sold.

The income statement is translated at the average monthly rate of exchange over the accounting period, unless change in the rate has been substantial. In that case, the new exchange rate is used.

The firm is required to disclose in the footnotes whether the current or the historical rate was used in the translation, the aggregate amount of the exchange adjustments originating in the period, the amount thereof reflected in the present income statement, and the amount thereof deferred. The footnotes must also disclose the amount the balance sheet would be affected if the long-term receivables and payables translated at the historic rate were translated at the current exchange rate instead, and the amount of unrealized gains and losses.

RESEARCH AND DEVELOPMENT COSTS

All research and development costs are generally charged to expenses when incurred.

ACCOUNTING FOR CONTINGENCIES

Estimated losses from contingencies are generally charged to income if both the following conditions exist: (1) it is probable that an asset held has been impaired or a liability has been incurred, and (2) the amount of the loss can be reasonably estimated. If there is only the possibility that a contingency loss may be incurred, the financial statements must disclose its nature and possible size. However, it does not have to be immediately charged against income.

Appendix 3B **Statistical Procedures for Trendline and Regression Analyses**

The trendline and regression analyses mentioned in Chapter 3 as possible methods for forecasting sales and other budget items are usually calculated by computer. However, you should understand the concept of the calculations behind them so that you can avoid pitfalls in their interpretation. This appendix covers the mechanics of calculating trendline and regression analyses.

TRENDLINE CALCULATIONS

The least-squares method of fitting the trendline to the observations over time very precisely finds the straightline that comes most closely to all the observations represented by the dots in Figure 3B-1. This is accomplished by minimizing the sum of the squared differences between the fitted line and the observations.

Figure 3B-1 Sales Over Time

The mathematical representation of the fitted line is:

$$\hat{Y}_X = a + bX \qquad\qquad (3B\text{-}1)$$

where
$\hat{Y}_X$ = estimated position of trendline in year X
a = the intercept of the trendline (where it crosses the vertical axis)
b = the slope of the trend line
X = number of years away from the base year

The standard formulae for determining the slope and the intercept are:

$$\text{slope } b = \frac{\Sigma XY - \Sigma X \Sigma Y/n}{\Sigma X^2 - (\Sigma X)^2/n} \qquad\qquad (3B\text{-}2)$$

$$\text{intercept } a = \frac{1}{n}\,[\Sigma Y - b\Sigma X] \qquad\qquad (3B\text{-}3)$$

We construct Table 3B-1 assuming Y represents actual sales in each year from 1967 to 1976, and X represents each year.[1] Then:

$$\Sigma(XY) = 105{,}000$$
$$\Sigma(X^2) = 285$$

$$b = \frac{105{,}000 - (45)(19{,}500)/10}{285 - (45)^2/10}$$

$$= 209.09$$
$$a = 1009.095$$

The fitted trendline is:

$$\hat{Y}_X = a + b(X)$$
$$= 1009.095 + 209.09(X)$$

___
[1] Among many references on trendline analysis see Taro Yamane, *Statistics: An Introductory Analysis*, Harper and Row, New York, 1967, pp. 368–430.

Table 3B-1   ABC Company   Historical Sales, 1967–1976

Year	X Year number	Y Sales (thousands)	XY	X²
1967	0	$ 1,000	0	0
1968	1	1,200	1,200	1
1969	2	1,500	3,000	4
1970	3	1,600	4,800	9
1971	4	1,700	6,800	16
1972	5	2,000	10,000	25
1973	6	2,500	15,000	36
1974	7	2,600	18,200	49
1975	8	2,600	20,800	64
1976	9	2,800	25,200	81
	45	19,500	105,000	285

For every unit increase in X (an additional year) $\hat{Y}_X$ increases by $209,090. Thus, the sales forecast would be:

$$\hat{Y} \ 1977 = \$3,099,995$$
$$\hat{Y} \ 1978 = \ \ 3,309,085$$
$$\hat{Y} \ 1979 = \ \ 3,518,175$$

REGRESSION ANALYSIS CALCULATIONS

The regression analysis calculations are very similar to the trendline calculations in that they also mechanically fit a line by using the least-squares method, which minimizes the sum of the squared deviations between that line and each of the observations. The major difference is that regression analysis relates the sales forecast (generally the dependent variable) to some casual variable (generally the independent variable), not the time progression of the trendline. For example, we might relate the firm's sales to the gross national product (GNP) or some other indicator of economic activity. If Y in Table 3B-2 were the firm's sales and X the GNP, we could construct the regression line through the observations using the formulae for the trendline:[2]

$$b = \frac{\Sigma XY - \Sigma X \Sigma Y / n}{\Sigma X^2 - (\Sigma X)^2 / n}$$

$$= \frac{14{,}017 - (6{,}740)(19.5)/10}{4{,}754{,}600 - (6{,}740)^2/10}$$

$$= .0041$$

$$a = \frac{1}{n} [\Sigma Y - b \Sigma X]$$

$$= -.8134$$

The fitted regression line is:

$$\hat{Y}_X = a + b(X)$$
$$= -.8134 + .0041(X)$$

[2] *Ibid.*

Table 3B-2

x GNP (Billions)	Y Sales (Billions)	XY	X²
$400.0	$ 1.0	400	160,000
480.0	1.2	576	230,400
600.0	1.5	900	360,000
620.0	1.6	992	384,400
650.0	1.7	1,105	422,500
700.0	2.0	1,400	490,000
800.0	2.5	2,000	640,000
820.0	2.6	2,132	672,400
820.0	2.6	2,132	672,400
850.0	2.8	2,380	722,500
6,740.0	19.5	14,017	4,754,600

such that for every unit increase in X ($1 billion in GNP), the firm's sales $(\hat{Y}_X)$ increase by a factor of $4,100,000. Thus, if the GNP is forecast to be $1,000 billion in the next planning period, sales are estimated at $3,286.6 million.

In addition, you should know how reliable that fitted regression line has been in the past. A loose fit could mean a very unreliable forecast using the regression line. Two common measures of reliability are the standard error of the estimate and the coefficient of determination.

Standard Error

The standard error (Syx) of the estimate measures the difference between the actual observation (Y) and the estimated value that lies on the regression line $(\hat{Y}_X)$. The standard error decreases as the distance between each estimate and the actual observation decreases. A very close and historically reliable regression estimate would have a very small standard error.

We can compute the standard error using the following formula:

$$Syx = \sqrt{\frac{\Sigma(Y - \hat{Y}_X)^2}{n}}$$ (3B-4)

$$= .1047$$

Table 3B-3   Worksheet for Standard Error of the Estimate

GNP X(Billions)	Estimated Sales $\hat{Y}_X$(Billions)	Actual Sales Y (Billions)	$\hat{Y}_X$-Y	$(\hat{Y}_X$-Y$)^2$
$400.0	.8266	$1.0	−0.1734	.0301
480.0	1.1546	1.2	−0.0454	.0020
600.0	1.6466	1.5	+0.1466	.0215
620.0	1.7286	1.6	+0.1286	.0165
650.0	1.8516	1.7	+0.1516	.0230
700.0	2.0566	2.0	+0.0566	.0032
800.0	2.4666	2.5	−0.0334	.0011
820.0	2.5486	2.6	−0.0514	.0026
820.0	2.5486	2.6	−0.0514	.0026
850.0	2.6716	2.8	−0.0840	.0071
				.1097

which utilizes the calculation contained in Table 3B-3. The Syx of 0.1047 is relatively low, indicating an historically close fit for the regression line.

Coefficient of Determination

The coefficient of determination (R^2) also measures the historical accuracy of the fitted regression line. A perfect fit would imply that the line passed through every observation and would have an R^2 equal to 1. As the R^2 decreases from 1 toward 0, the goodness of fit for the line also decreases. At 0 there is no relationship between the historically observed sales and the GNP. We have greater confidence in any sales estimate made from a regression analysis with a relatively high R^2.

Table 3B-4 Worksheet for R^2

$Y-\bar{Y}$	$\Sigma(Y-\bar{Y})^2$	$\hat{Y}_X-\bar{Y}$	$\Sigma(\hat{Y}_X-\bar{Y})^2$
−.95	.9025	−1.1234	1.2620
−.75	.5625	− .7954	.6327
−.45	.2025	− .3034	.0921
−.35	.1225	− .2214	.0490
−.25	.0625	− .0984	.0097
.05	.0025	− .1066	.0114
.55	.3025	.5166	.2669
.65	.4225	.5986	.3583
.65	.4255	.5986	.3583
.85	.7225	.7216	.5207
	3.725		3.561

We can compute the coefficient of determination using the following formula:

$$R^2 = \frac{\Sigma(\hat{Y}_X - \bar{Y})^2}{\Sigma(Y - \bar{Y})^2} = \frac{3.561}{3.725} = .956 \qquad (3B\text{-}5)$$

where
  $\bar{Y}$ = the mean of the observed sales and the worksheet calculations contained in Table 3B-4. The R^2 of .956 is very high, indicating that the regression line has explained over 95 percent of the past observations.

4

The Mathematics of Finance

Finance deals with capital (money) and its proper employment so that it can grow and maximize shareholder wealth. When all is said and done, capital value is the common demoninator with which the success of profit-oriented firms are measured. If you are going to be a financial officer you need to know exactly how capital works and be able to talk the language of the world of capital. Chapter 4 answers the question: How does capital work?

Properly invested capital can grow for you over time. Capital is often the lubricant which helps turn the wheels of the firm and move it toward its corporate goal. As such it may be invested in machinery, people (recruitment and training), legal commitments (pollution equipment), or other areas of the firm's operations.

Capital can be made to work for you. The mere presence of a positive rate of interest offers a choice between maintaining idle cash balances (unemployed capital) and investing, such that an *opportunity cost* is established. The savings deposit which offers 5 percent annual interest creates a 5 percent opportunity cost of maintaining idle balances, whether they are in a checking account which pays no interest or under the mattress.

In reality, a whole array of opportunities which bear positive rates of interest exist. By submitting them to systematic analysis, you can select those few which will most enhance the firm's progress toward its corporate goal. Remember that capital is a scarce resource, which in a market-price economy is allocated through its price, namely the interest rate. Like the other scarce resources of land and labor, capital has earning power. You must learn how that earning power comes about and make it work for your benefit.

SIMPLE INTEREST

How does the initial invested principal grow?

Simple interest is a percentage of the original principal, paid annually at the end of the year. Since all interest rates are typically quoted on an annual basis regardless of the investment period, we will observe that convention. A 5 percent interest rate will imply that the annual rate over the year is 5 percent, even if the investment is made for a period of less than or more than one year.

Let us assume we have a 5 percent simple interest rate and a $100 initial deposit at a savings and loan association. At the end of the first year for which those funds are on deposit, the account will have grown to $105; that is, the $100 initial deposit plus the $5 interest for the period.

The Formula for Simple Interest

The mathematical formula underlying this calculation is:

$$V = P(1 + i) \tag{4-1}$$

where

P = the principal at the beginning of the period
i = the annual simple interest rate
V = the value of the account at the end of the period

If we substitute $P = \$100$ and $i = 5$ percent in Equation 4-1, we see that the formula provides the obvious answer of $105, which we almost automatically infer from the information at the beginning of this section.

$$V = \$100(1 + .05) = \$105$$

As investors, we have done nothing but abstain from using the principal; the mere passage of time has seen our capital grow.

If, at the end of that first year, we withdrew the $5.00 in interest and spent it but left the original $100 on deposit, we could expect that, as long as the interest rate remained at 5 percent, the account would again be worth $105 at the end of the second year. With *simple interest*, there is no reinvestment of the interest earned during the period, and the interest rate is paid only on the initial principal deposit.

Simple Interest for Periods Other Than One Year

To calculate the interest for periods either less or more than one year, we must adjust the time dimension of Equation 4-1 to reflect the specific period in consideration. We can express the interest rate in terms of the proper time period by finding that rate which bears the same relationship to the annual rate as the time period in question bears to one year. For example, if the initial invested principal were deposited at a 5 percent annual rate for a period of 1 month, we would earn 1/12 of the annual interest. Even though the actual rate of interest does not change, it is convenient to adjust our formula at the point where i is entered. Accordingly:

$$V = \$100 \left(1 + \frac{.05}{12}\right) = \$100.42$$

If the initial $100 were deposited at a 5 percent annual interest rate for 2 years, we would earn twice the annual interest.

$$V = \$100(1 + 2(.05)) = \$110.00$$

Again the simple interest rate does not allow for reinvestment of the earned interest. It is calculated on the original principal in each year.

COMPOUND INTEREST

How does capital grow when the interest earned in preceding years is reinvested at the prevailing interest rate in succeeding years?

Compound interest is similar to receiving interest on interest. The interest earned by the invested capital in any period is accumulated so that simple interest in the next period is paid not only on the original principal but also on the accumulated interest of all the previous periods during which interest was paid.

Table 4-1 illustrates the effect of 5 percent compound interest over a 7-year period compared to 5 percent simple interest over the same period.

The gap between the value at simple interest and the value at compound interest becomes increasingly larger over the 7-year period, because the principal upon which interest is calculated is larger each year.

Formula for Compound Interest

The compounding formula is derived by using the simple interest formula over and over again. Let us use the same symbols as those found in the simple interest formula. And we will add a subscript to V to indicate that we are talking about the value at the end of the number of years shown in the subscript. Thus at the end of the first year:

$$V_1 = P(1+i)^1 \tag{4-2}$$

Since the exponent indicating a power of 1 does not change anything, this is just a more elaborate form of the simple interest formula. But in this form it can be adapted to compounding.

At the end of the second year, 1 year's simple interest is paid on the value of the capital at the end of the first year, which is V_1 (the initial principal plus the first year's earned interest) such that, at the end of the second year:

$$V_2 = V_1(1+i)^1 \tag{4-3}$$

At the end of the third year, simple interest is paid on the value of the capital at the end of the second year (V_2) such that:

$$V_3 = V_2(1+i)^1 \tag{4-4}$$

Now we can substitute the value of V_2 from Equation 4-3 into Equation 4-4 to derive:

$$V_3 = V_1(1+i)^1(1+i)^1$$

Table 4-1   Compound versus Simple Interest at 5%

Original capital	End of period	Capital at compound interest	Capital at simple interest
$100	1	$105.00	$105.00
100	2	110.25	110.00
100	3	115.76	115.00
100	4	121.55	120.00
100	5	127.63	125.00
100	6	134.01	130.00
100	7	140.17	135.00

And we can substitute the value of V_1 from Equation 4-2 to derive:

$$V_3 = P(1+i)^1(1+i)^1(1+i)^1 \qquad (4\text{-}5)$$

When we combine terms by adding the exponents, we get:

$$V_3 = P(1+i)^3 \qquad (4\text{-}6)$$

In more general terms to take into consideration any number of years:

$$V_n = P(1+i)^n \qquad (4\text{-}7)$$

where
  $n =$ the number of years over which the capital is invested
  $i =$ the simple interest rate
  $P =$ the initial invested capital
  $V =$ the value of the capital at the end of the investment period

Equation 4-7 is the compound interest formula. It was derived by repeating the simple interest over and over again on the original principal plus accumulated interest. If $i = 5$ percent, $P = \$1,000$, and $n = 3$, then $V_3 = \$1,000(1 + .05)^3 = \$1,157.60$.

Graphic Illustration of Compound Interest

Figure 4-1 illustrates the effect of compound interest on an initial investment of $1 over time. Notice how the compounding effect accelerates the increase in the capital value as time passes, particularly when compared to the effect of simple interest over the same interval.

Precalculated Compounding Tables

Since the compounding effect is mechanical given the formula of Equation 4-7, compounding tables have been compiled for varying combinations of i and n. One of these is illustrated in Table 4-2. (A more complete version of Table 4-2 appears, as

Figure 4-1 The Effect of $1 of Compounding Over Time

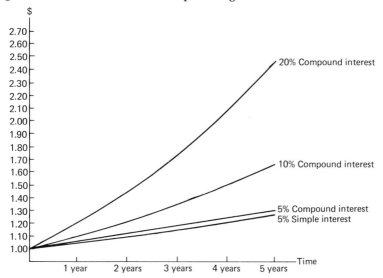

Table 4-2 Compound Sum of One Dollar

n	1%	2%	3%	4%	5%	6%	7%	8%	9%	10%	n
01	1.0100	1.0200	1.0300	1.0400	1.0500	1.0600	1.0700	1.0800	1.0900	1.1000	01
02	1.0201	1.0404	1.0609	1.0816	1.1025	1.1236	1.1449	1.1664	1.1881	1.2100	02
03	1.0303	1.0612	1.0927	1.1249	1.1576	1.1910	1.2250	1.2597	1.2950	1.3310	03
04	1.0406	1.0824	1.1255	1.1699	1.2155	1.2625	1.3108	1.3605	1.4116	1.4641	04
05	1.0510	1.1041	1.1593	1.2167	1.2763	1.3382	1.4026	1.4693	1.5386	1.6105	05
06	1.0615	1.1261	1.1941	1.2653	1.3401	1.4185	1.5007	1.5869	1.6771	1.7716	06
07	1.0721	1.1487	1.2299	1.3159	1.4071	1.5036	1.6058	1.7138	1.8280	1.9487	07
08	1.0829	1.1717	1.2668	1.3686	1.4775	1.5939	1.7182	1.8509	1.9926	2.1436	08
09	1.0937	1.1951	1.3048	1.4233	1.5513	1.6895	1.8385	1.9990	2.1719	2.3580	09
10	1.1046	1.2190	1.3439	1.4802	1.6289	1.7909	1.9672	2.1589	2.3674	2.5937	10
11	1.1157	1.2434	1.3842	1.5395	1.7103	1.8983	2.1049	2.3316	2.5804	2.8531	11
12	1.1268	1.2682	1.4258	1.6010	1.7959	2.0122	2.2522	2.5182	2.8127	3.1384	12
13	1.1381	1.2936	1.4685	1.6651	1.8857	2.1329	2.4098	2.7196	3.0658	3.4523	13
14	1.1495	1.3195	1.5126	1.7317	1.9799	2.2609	2.5785	2.9372	3.3417	3.7975	14
15	1.1610	1.3459	1.5580	1.8009	2.0789	2.3966	2.7590	3.1722	3.6425	4.1773	15
16	1.1726	1.3728	1.6047	1.8730	2.1829	2.5404	2.9522	3.4259	3.9703	4.5950	16
17	1.1843	1.4002	1.6529	1.9479	2.2920	2.6928	3.1588	3.7000	4.3276	5.0545	17
18	1.1962	1.4283	1.7024	2.0258	2.4066	2.8543	3.3799	3.9960	4.7171	5.5599	18
19	1.2081	1.4568	1.7535	2.1069	2.5270	3.0256	3.6165	4.3157	5.1417	6.1159	19
20	1.2202	1.4860	1.8061	2.1911	2.6533	3.2071	3.8697	4.6610	5.6044	6.7275	20
21	1.2324	1.5157	1.8603	2.2788	2.7860	3.3996	4.1406	5.0338	6.1088	7.4003	21
22	1.2447	1.5460	1.9161	2.3699	2.9253	3.6035	4.4304	5.4365	6.6586	8.1403	22
23	1.2572	1.5769	1.9736	2.4647	3.0715	3.8198	4.7405	5.8714	7.2579	8.9543	23
24	1.2697	1.6084	2.0328	2.5633	3.2251	4.0489	5.0724	6.3412	7.9111	9.8497	24
25	1.2824	1.6406	2.0938	2.6658	3.3864	4.2919	5.4274	6.8485	8.6231	10.835	25

Appendix A in the back of this book.) Simply by selecting values for n and i the user of Table 4-2 can read off the amount to which $1 will grow by the end of the specified time span. Assume we want to know the capital value of $1 invested at 5 percent interest at the end of 10 years. We would read down the first or last column to 10 years and across the top row to 5 percent and find the point of intersection between the row and the column in the body of the table. In this case the point of intersection would be 1.6289, showing that $1 will grow to $1.6289 at the end of 10 years at 5 percent annual compound interest.

We can compute the compound sum of any multiple of $1 from the table. For example, assume we have invested $10,000 at 5 percent for 10 years. Then the compound sum will be:

$$1.6289 \times \$10,000 = \$16,289.00$$

The compound sum is derived by taking the factor of 1.6289 and multiplying it by the original invested capital.

Compound Interest for Nonannual Periods

Frequently the compounding period is less than a year, as in the case of the savings and loan association which compounds quarterly, or four times a year. We have to adjust the compound interest formula to reflect the increased number of times the compounding will occur in the year, for the more frequently the interest is earned and begins, in turn, to earn further interest, the greater the effective annual compound rate of interest. We use the following formula for the value of an investment on which interest is compounded more often than annually:

$$V_n = P \left(1 + \frac{i}{m}\right)^{mn} \tag{4-8}$$

where
$\quad V_n$ = the capital value at the end of the investment period
$\quad P$ = the initial capital investment
$\quad i$ = the annual simple interest rate
$\quad m$ = the number of times the compounding occurs during the year
$\quad n$ = the termination year of the investment

For example, if we invested $1,000 for 2 years at the annual interest rate of 4 percent compounded quarterly, the value at the end of the second year becomes:

$$V_2 = \$1,000 \left(1 + \frac{.04}{4}\right)^{4 \cdot 2} = \$1,082.90$$

Notice that in addition to increasing the exponent of the compound interest formula to reflect the increased number of compounding periods, we also had to adjust the interest rate i to correspond to the shorter compounding periods. We did this by dividing the annual simple interest rate by the number of compounding periods in the year, deriving a pro rata interest rate for the shorter periods.

We can also read this answer from Table 4-2. In effect, we have quadrupled the periods and quartered the interest rate, so we read down the first column to 8 periods (instead of 2 periods) and over the top row to 1 percent (instead of 4 percent). The quarterly compound interest factor is then 1.0829, which tells us that $1,000 invested at 4 percent compounded quarterly will have a capital value of $1,082.90 at the end of 2 years. Significantly, the more frequent compounding has increased the interest factor to 1.0829 from the 1.0816 that would have applied had the interest been compounded annually.

PRESENT-VALUE DISCOUNTING

How much should I invest now to receive a given amount later?

Once we have a method of determining the future value of a present capital sum through the compounding process, we can ask the reverse question: What is the present worth of a guaranteed, no-risk, promised sum of money? This is a relatively common question which most people face without ever realizing it. For example, when we buy a United States savings bond which promises to pay us $25 in 10 years, the logical question is how much are we willing to pay for that bond now. As a financial officer you will face this question whenever you consider projects that promise a future reward but demand payment now. For example, the decision to invest in a new refinery for an oil company, in a new piece of equipment for an industrial manufacturer, or in a new computer for a bank all depend on whether you feel the expected future rewards from that project are worth your purchasing the equipment now. You must know how to evaluate such decisions, and present-value discounting is a primary tool in that evaluation process.

Let us look a little more closely at discounting as the reverse of compounding. When we compound we increase the principal because as we pass through time the positive rate of interest accrues to the investment. Now, if we have to forego that investment, we lose the opportunity to get the reward of that positive interest rate. This is a cost to us, and we must penalize the expected future rewards to compensate for the immediate loss. As the length of time we have to wait for future rewards increases, the penalty attached to the delay must increase to reflect the compounding value of the lost opportunity. For example, if we had to wait one year, we have lost 5 percent interest. If we had to wait another year, we have lost still another 5 percent interest plus the compounding effect of the earned interest foregone during the first year. This is equivalent to a compound two-year loss of 10.25 percent, read from Table 4-2.

The Mathematics of Discounting

We can express the concept of present-value discounting in a formula, just as we did for compounding. Remember that the compound interest formula was:

$$V_n = P(1+i)^n \tag{4-7}$$

We used it to find the future sum of an initial investment of P at an annual interest rate of i. The present-value discounting formula is:

$$P = \frac{V_n}{(1+i)^n} \tag{4-9}$$

where
  P = the initial capital investment
  V_n = the value of the capital at the end of n years
  i = the interest rate
  n = the number of years over which the capital is invested

You can see that the present-value discounting formula is derived by dividing both sides of the compounding formula by $(1 + i)^n$. We use Equation 4-9 to answer the question: For a given future value (P_n), what is its present value if I have to forego a positive rate of interest i for n years?

For example, let us take the $25 United States savings bond which promises to pay $25.00 at the end of 10 years from the date of purchase and assume we have a lost-opportunity interest rate of 5 percent. In terms of our formula:

$$V_n = \$25.00$$
$$i = 5\%$$
$$n = 10 \text{ years}$$

and:

$$P = \frac{\$25.00}{(1 + .05)^{10}} = \$15.35$$

In other words, after discounting each of the 10 years in the waiting period at a 5 percent annual compound rate, the present value of $25 received 10 years from now is only $15.35. As long as we are discounting at a positive rate of interest, the present value will always be less than the future expected sum.

Precalculated Discounting Tables

Since the discounting effect is mechanical given the formula of Equation 4-9, discount tables, such as illustrated in Table 4-3, have been precalculated. (A more complete version appears in Appendix B in the back of this book.) Simply by selecting values for i and n, the user of the table can read off the present value of $1 for any period in the future at any given discount factor. Assume we wanted to know the present value of $1 to be received 10 years from now if the lost-opportunity interest rate is 5 percent. We would look down the first or last column of Table 4-3 to 10 years and across the top row to 5 percent and locate the intersection of the row and column in the body of the table. We find that the present value of $1 10 years from now at 5 percent is $.61391. Applied to our savings bond example, the table reveals that each of the $25 to be received 10 years from now at an annual discount factor of 5 percent is worth only $.61391 and that the whole $25.00 bond is consequently worth only $15.35—the same answer we derived from the formula. Present-value tables solve $\left(\frac{1}{(1 + i)^n}\right)$, and compounding tables solve $(1 + i)^n$. They are limited only by the number of values for i and n that the compiler has chosen to list.

ANNUITIES

How do I handle compounding and present-value discounting if there are a series of cash flows over the life of the investment instead of a single future capital value or expected reward at the end of the investment period?

Frequently, investment opportunities consist of a stream of cash flows, such that you are required to invest a given amount annually until the time you want to withdraw the capital value. You might liken this to a periodic savings plan in which you invest a given dollar amount each period, allowing the funds to remain on deposit and earning interest until you are ready to withdraw them. For example,

Table 4-3 Present Value of One Dollar Due at the End of n Years

n	1%	2%	3%	4%	5%	6%	7%	8%	9%	10%	n
01	.99010	.98039	.97007	.96154	.95238	.94340	.93458	.92593	.91743	.90909	01
02	.98030	.96117	.94260	.92456	.90703	.89000	.87344	.85734	.84168	.82645	02
03	.97059	.94232	.91514	.88900	.86384	.83962	.81630	.79383	.77218	.75131	03
04	.96098	.92385	.88849	.85480	.82270	.79209	.76290	.73503	.70843	.68301	04
05	.95147	.90573	.86261	.82193	.78353	.74726	.71299	.68058	.64993	.62092	05
06	.94204	.88797	.83748	.79031	.74622	.70496	.66634	.63017	.59627	.56447	06
07	.93272	.87056	.81309	.75992	.71068	.66506	.62275	.58349	.54703	.51316	07
08	.92348	.85349	.78941	.73069	.67684	.62741	.58201	.54027	.50187	.46651	08
09	.91434	.83675	.76642	.70259	.64461	.59190	.54393	.50025	.46043	.42410	09
10	.90529	.82035	.74409	.67556	.61391	.55839	.50835	.46319	.42241	.38554	10
11	.89632	.80426	.72242	.64958	.58468	.52679	.47509	.42888	.38753	.35049	11
12	.88745	.78849	.70138	.62460	.55684	.49697	.44401	.39711	.35553	.31683	12
13	.87866	.77303	.68095	.60057	.53032	.46884	.41496	.36770	.32618	.28966	13
14	.86996	.75787	.66112	.57747	.50507	.44230	.38782	.34046	.29925	.26333	14
15	.86135	.74301	.64186	.55526	.48102	.41726	.36245	.31524	.27454	.23939	15
16	.85282	.72845	.62317	.53391	.45811	.39365	.33873	.29189	.25187	.21763	16
17	.84438	.71416	.60502	.51337	.43630	.37136	.31657	.27027	.23107	.19784	17
18	.83602	.70016	.58739	.49363	.41552	.35034	.29586	.25025	.21199	.17986	18
19	.82774	.68643	.57029	.47464	.39573	.33051	.27651	.23171	.19449	.16351	19
20	.81954	.67297	.55367	.45639	.37689	.31180	.25842	.21455	.17843	.14864	20
21	.81143	.65978	.53755	.43883	.35894	.29415	.24151	.19866	.16370	.13513	21
22	.80340	.64684	.52189	.42195	.34185	.27750	.22571	.18394	.15018	.12285	22
23	.79544	.63414	.50669	.40573	.32551	.26180	.21095	.17031	.13778	.11168	23
24	.78757	.62172	.49193	.39012	.31007	.24698	.19715	.15770	.12640	.10153	24
25	.77977	.60953	.47760	.37512	.29530	.23300	.18425	.14602	.11597	.09230	25

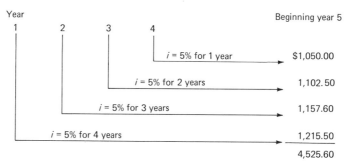

Figure 4-2 Compound Annuity

you might deposit $1,000 at the beginning of each year in an account which pays 5 percent per annum. At the end of the first year you would have $1,050. Then you would put in another $1,000 at the beginning of the second year and earn during the second year interest not only on that $1,000 but on the $1,050 capital value of the account at the end of the first year. Of course, the process could continue as long as you deposited $1,000 annually.

Compound Annuity

The process we have just described is known as a compound annuity. How do we determine the future capital value of a compound annuity? Figure 4-2 illustrates its growth. We can see that the $1,000 deposited at the beginning of year 1 at 5 percent earns interest for the entire period, in this case 4 years. The $1,000 deposited at the beginning of the second year earns interest at a compound annual rate of 5 percent for 3 years. The third $1,000 deposit earns interest for 2 years, while the fourth deposit, made at the beginning of year 4, earns interest for the last year in which the funds are invested. By adding the accumulated deposits with their earned interest together, we determine that $1,000 deposited at the beginning of each year for 4 years will grow to be $4,525.60 at the end of the fourth year.

Precalculated Compound Annuity Tables

As in the case of the compound interest tables, there are precalculated compound annuities like that illustrated in Table 4-4 (a more complete version is contained in Appendix C in the back of this book).[1] By selecting the interest rate and the number of periods for which the funds are invested, we can read off the amount to which $1 deposited annually for n periods will grow at the specified interest rate. Using our

[1] Table 4-4 and Appendix C were computed as an annuity due using the following formula:

$$V_n = P \left[\frac{(1 + i)^{n+1} - 1}{i} - 1 \right]$$

so as to conform with Tables 4-2, 4-3 and 4-5 and Appendixes A, B, and D. However, it should be recognized that the more commonly used regular annuity formula is:

$$V_n = P \left[\frac{(1 + i)^n - 1}{i} \right]$$

But, those tables do not conform precisely with the compound interest table in interpretation. Regular annuity tables assume that payments are made at the end of each year.

Table 4-4 Sum of an Annuity Due of One Dollar

n	1%	2%	3%	4%	5%	6%	7%	8%	9%	10%
00	1.0000	1.0000	1.0000	1.0000	1.0000	1.0000	1.0000	1.0000	1.0000	1.0000
01	1.0100	1.0200	1.0300	1.0400	1.0500	1.0600	1.0700	1.0800	1.0900	1.1000
02	2.0301	2.0604	2.0909	2.1216	2.1525	2.1833	2.2143	2.2463	2.2778	2.3100
03	3.0604	3.1216	3.1836	3.2426	3.3101	3.3750	3.4400	3.5063	3.5733	3.6410
04	4.1010	4.2040	4.3091	4.4163	4.5256	4.6367	4.7180	4.8663	4.9844	5.1050
05	5.1520	5.3081	5.4684	5.6330	5.8020	5.9750	6.1529	6.3363	6.5233	6.7160
06	6.2135	6.4343	6.6625	6.8983	7.1420	7.3933	7.6543	7.9225	8.2000	8.4870
07	7.2857	7.5830	7.8923	8.2142	8.5491	8.8983	9.260	9.637	10.028	10.436
08	8.3685	8.7546	9.159	9.583	10.027	10.491	10.978	11.488	12.021	12.579
09	9.462	9.950	10.464	11.006	11.578	12.181	12.816	13.487	14.193	14.937
10	10.567	11.169	11.808	12.486	13.207	13.972	14.784	15.645	16.560	17.531
11	11.683	12.412	13.192	14.026	14.917	15.870	16.888	17.977	19.141	20.384
12	12.809	13.680	14.618	15.627	16.713	17.882	19.141	20.495	21.953	23.523
13	13.947	14.974	16.086	17.292	18.599	20.051	21.550	23.215	25.019	26.975
14	15.097	16.293	17.599	19.024	20.579	22.276	24.129	26.152	28.361	30.772
15	16.258	17.639	19.157	20.825	22.657	24.673	26.888	29.324	32.003	34.950
16	17.430	19.012	20.762	22.698	24.840	27.213	29.840	32.750	35.973	39.545
17	18.015	20.412	22.414	24.645	27.132	29.906	32.999	36.450	40.301	44.599
18	19.811	21.841	24.117	25.671	29.539	32.760	36.379	40.446	46.019	50.159
19	21.019	23.297	25.870	28.778	32.066	35.786	39.995	44.762	51.160	56.275
20	22.239	24.783	27.676	30.969	34.719	38.993	43.865	49.423	56.764	63.002
21	23.472	26.299	29.537	33.248	37.505	41.392	48.006	54.457	61.873	70.403
22	24.716	27.845	31.453	35.618	40.430	45.996	52.436	59.893	68.532	78.543
23	25.973	29.422	33.426	38.083	43.502	49.816	57.177	65.765	75.790	87.497
24	27.243	31.030	35.459	40.646	46.727	53.865	62.249	72.106	82.701	97.347

example, $1,000 deposited annually at the beginning of each year for 4 years at an interest rate of 5 percent, we can read from Table 4-4 the factor of 4.5256, which implies:

$$\$1,000 \times 4.5256 = \$4,525.60$$

Notice that the compound annuity table sums the individual factors of the compound interest table (Table 4-2) to derive its factors. If you go back to Table 4-2 and add up the compound factors for $1 for 4 years, 3 years, 2 years, and 1 year at 5 percent, the sum will equal the compound annuity factor for 4 years at 5 percent.

The Mathematics of the Compound Annuity Due

We can express the concept of the compound annuity due in a formula, just as we expressed the concept of the compound interest. This formula is the basis for Table 4-4:

$$V_n = P \left[\frac{(1+i)^{n+1} - 1}{i} - 1 \right] \tag{4-10}$$

In our example:

$$V_n = \$1,000 \left[\frac{(1+.05)^{4+1} - 1}{i} - 1 \right] = \$4,525.60$$

Present Value of an Annuity

We can ask the reverse question of a compound annuity: How much should I pay for a series of equal annual receipts for a number of periods in the future if the present interest rate is i? As a financial officer you might encounter this concept in planning pension funds, buying the firm's insurance, or any other project which calls for a decision to purchase now but which will return funds over a series of equal future installments. Determining the present value of an annuity is illustrated in Figure 4-3.

Notice that as the length of the wait to receive the funds increases, the discount factor also increases, reflecting continuation of the lost opportunity to earn a positive rate of interest. Funds received at the end of the first year in Figure 4-3 are discounted at 5 percent for only one year, while the funds received in subsequent years are discounted for the additional waiting period at 5 percent.

Figure 4-3 Present Value of an Annuity

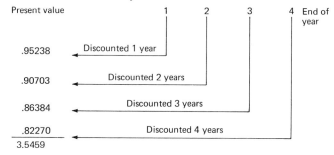

Table 4-5 Present Value of One Dollar per Year for n Years

n	1%	2%	3%	4%	5%	6%	7%	8%	9%	10%	n
01	.9901	.9804	.9709	.9615	.9524	.9434	.9346	.9259	.9174	.9091	01
02	1.9704	1.9416	1.9135	1.8861	1.8594	1.8334	1.8080	1.7833	1.7591	1.7355	02
03	2.9410	2.8839	2.8286	2.7751	2.7233	2.6730	2.6243	2.5771	2.5313	2.4868	03
04	3.9020	3.8077	3.7171	3.6299	3.5459	3.4651	3.3872	3.3121	3.2397	3.1699	04
05	4.8535	4.7134	4.5897	4.4518	4.3295	4.2123	4.1002	3.9927	3.8896	3.7908	05
06	5.7955	5.6014	5.4172	5.2421	5.0757	4.9173	4.7665	4.6229	4.4859	4.3553	06
07	6.7282	6.4720	6.2302	6.0020	5.7863	5.5824	5.3893	5.2064	5.0329	4.8684	07
08	7.6517	7.3254	7.0196	6.7327	6.4632	6.2098	5.9713	5.7466	5.5348	5.3349	08
09	8.5661	8.1622	7.7861	7.4353	7.1078	6.8017	6.5152	6.2469	5.9852	5.7590	09
10	9.4714	8.9825	8.7302	8.1109	7.7217	7.3601	7.0236	6.7101	6.4176	6.1446	10
11	10.3677	9.7868	9.2526	8.7604	8.3064	7.8868	7.4987	7.1389	6.8052	6.4951	11
12	11.2552	10.5753	9.9539	9.3850	8.8632	8.3838	7.9427	7.5361	7.1607	6.8137	12
13	12.1338	11.3483	10.6349	9.9856	9.3935	8.8527	8.3576	7.9038	7.4869	7.1034	13
14	13.0038	12.1062	11.2960	10.5631	9.8986	9.2950	8.7454	8.2442	7.7861	7.3667	14
15	13.8651	12.8492	11.9379	11.1183	10.3796	9.7122	9.1079	8.5595	8.0607	7.6061	15
16	14.7180	13.5777	12.5610	11.6522	10.8377	10.1059	9.4466	8.8514	8.3125	7.8237	16
17	15.5624	14.2918	13.1660	12.1656	11.2740	10.4772	9.7632	9.1216	8.5436	8.0215	17
18	16.3984	14.9920	13.7534	12.6592	11.6895	10.8276	10.0591	9.3719	8.7556	8.2014	18
19	17.2281	15.2684	14.3237	13.1339	12.0853	11.1581	10.3556	9.6036	8.9501	8.3649	19
20	18.0457	16.3514	14.8774	13.5903	12.4622	11.4699	10.5940	9.8181	9.1285	8.5136	20
21	18.8571	17.0111	15.4149	14.0291	12.8211	11.7640	10.3355	10.0168	9.2922	8.6487	21
22	19.6605	17.6581	15.9368	14.4511	13.1630	12.0416	11.0612	10.2007	9.4424	8.7715	22
23	20.4559	18.2921	16.4435	14.8568	13.4885	12.3033	11.2722	10.3710	9.5802	8.8832	23
24	21.2435	18.9139	16.9355	15.2469	13.7986	12.5503	11.4693	10.5287	9.7066	8.9847	24
25	22.0233	19.5234	17.4131	15.6220	14.9039	12.7833	11.6536	10.6748	9.8226	9.0770	25

Precalculated Present-Value-of-Annuity Tables

Table 4-5 illustrates a present-value-of-annuity table (a more completed version of Table 4-5 is found in Appendix D in the back of this book). Assume that in Figure 4-3 the inflow was $1,000 at the end of each year for 4 years and that the interest rate was 5 percent. By finding the intersection of 4 years and 5 percent on Table 4-5, we can read off the factor of 3.5459, which implies:

$$\$1,000 \times 3.5459 = \$3,545.90$$

The Mathematics of Present-Value Annuity

The present-value-of-annuity concept is based on a formula:

$$P = V \left[\frac{1 - \dfrac{1}{(1+i)^n}}{i} \right] \tag{4-11}$$

Using the same example of a 4-year annual inflow of $1,000 and a 5 percent interest rate we find that

$$P = \$1,000 \left[\frac{1 - \dfrac{1}{(1.05)^4}}{.05} \right] = \$3,545.90$$

This is the same answer obtained from Table 4-5.

CALCULATION OF UNEVEN STREAMS

How do I calculate the present value if the annual cash flows are not equal?

Not all projects to which you will apply present value discounting are of the annuity type with equal annual cash flows. In fact, most projects and investments have cash flows which will vary in dollar amount from year to year, as illustrated in Figure 4-4. In this case, the mathematics may be a little more complex, but the technique is the same. Each of the cash flows has to be discounted at the appropriate lost-interest rate for the number of years for which you have to wait to receive that particular cash flow. In Figure 4-4 we can see that at 5 percent, the $1,000 we are scheduled to receive 4 years from now is worth only $822.70, which we computed by reading the factor .82270 off Table 4-3 and multiplying it by $1,000. Similarly, the other inflows which we are scheduled to receive in 3 years, 2 years, and 1 year,

Figure 4-4 The Present Value of an Uneven Stream

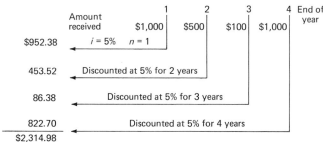

respectively, are also discounted by the appropriate factor read off Table 4-3. The present value of the cash flows illustrated in Figure 4-4 is $2,314.98.

When the cash flows describe a pattern combining annuity and uneven cash flow, we use a combination of Table 4-3 and Table 4-5. For example, assume we have a cash flow of $50 a year for each of 10 years and then a $1,000 lump-sum payment at the end of 10 years. We really have a combination of an annuity and a single sum. We consult Table 4-5 to find that the factor for the present value of an annuity at 5 percent for 10 years is 7.7217, which makes the present value of $50 a year for 10 years:

$$7.7217 \times \$50 = \$386.09$$

We consult Table 4-3 to find that the present value for a single $1,000 sum received 10 years from now at 5 percent is:

$$.61391 \times \$1,000 = \$613.91$$

The present value of the total stream of cash flows is therefore the sum of the two present values, or $1,000.

INSTALLMENT FINANCING

How much do I have to put aside annually to get a particular sum at the end of a given period at a given interest rate?

This question is frequently asked of the financial officer in connection with such projects and financing arrangements as installment funding on the mortgages and loans of the company, funding the company's pension, and other situations where equal annual fundings have to be made.

Assuming the payments are to be made at the beginning of each year, we can consult our Table 4-4 on compound annuity due in order to calculate the amount due each year.[2] We know that the Equation 4-10 is the formula for annuity due. It tells us the capital value (V_n) of equal annual deposits for any given interest rate i and for any number of years n.

$$V_n = P \left[\frac{(1+i)^{n+1} - 1}{i} - 1 \right] \qquad (4\text{-}10)$$

Installment financing asks the reverse question: How much do we have to deposit in equal annual installments to get the capital value V_n? We are looking for P (the amount of each installment in Equation 4-10). We can solve for P as follows:

$$P = \frac{V_n}{\dfrac{(1+i)^{n+1} - 1}{i} - 1} \qquad (4\text{-}12)$$

For example, assume we want a capital value at the end of 5 years of $10,000 and the interest rate is 5 percent. Then:

$$P = \frac{\$10,000}{\left[\dfrac{(1+.05)^6 - 1}{.05} - 1 \right]} = \$2,209.65$$

[2] Again, we have used the annuity due table instead of the regular table since the payment is as of the beginning of each year. If the payment had been at the end of each year, we would have used the regular annuity table.

We can use Table 4-4 to derive this answer and save ourselves the trouble of the complicated arithmetic. At the intersection of 5 percent and 5 years on Table 4-4, we find the factor 4.5256, which is the precalculated denominator in our example. Then, by dividing this factor into $10,000, we derive our answer of $2,209.65.

Conversely, the financial officer might want to know how much can be withdrawn annually from an account that is earning interest in order to have exactly nothing in that account at the end of n years. Frequently, the financial officer will encounter this type of calculation in dealing with pension funds, insurance schedules, and loan payments. The firm's repayment of a $10,000 loan in equal annual payments over the next 5 years is a typical case.

The financial officer in this case is really called upon to calculate the converse of the present value of an annuity (Equation 4-11) to find V_n. Knowing P, you can solve Equation 4-13 as follows:

$$V_n = \frac{P}{\left[\dfrac{1 - \dfrac{1}{(1+i)^n}}{i}\right]}$$ (4-13)

$$= \frac{\$10,000}{4.3295} = \$2,309.74$$

Rather than doing all the calculations, you can consult Table 4-5 at the intersection of 5 years and 5 percent for the factor 4.3295, which is the denominator of Equation 4-13.

DETERMINING INTEREST RATES

How does the financial officer use the mathematics of finance in an actual financing situation?

Direct application of the mathematics of finance will arise most frequently in the capital budgeting situations discussed in Chapters 5–7 and in the cost-of-capital calculations discussed in Chapters 8–12. Without repeating what we shall discuss in those chapters, let us illustrate the mathematics with a typical corporate bond.

A bond, when you think about it, is a combination of an annuity and single-sum payment. The annual interest payment for the life of the bond is the annuity and the redemption of the bond at maturity is the single lump-sum payment.

If we are thinking of buying a bond, we must evaluate it to determine how much we are willing to pay for it now. This price is the present value of the annuity and the single future sum combined. This is represented as follows:

$$P = \sum_{t=1}^{n} \frac{I_t}{(1+i)^t} + \frac{P_n}{(1+i)^n}$$ (4-14)

where
    P = the bond's price
    I_t = the annual interest payment
    P_n = the redemption price of the bond at maturity
    i = the interest rate
    n = the number of years until maturity
    Σ = the summation sign which, in this case, sums over the annual interest payments from the present until the bond's maturity

Assuming that the interest payment was $40.00 a year and that the bond would be redeemed for $1,000 in 10 years, the present value of the bond at the firm's opportunity interest rate of 5 percent would be:

$$P = \sum_{t=1}^{n} \frac{\$40_t}{(1 + .05)^t} + \frac{\$1,000}{(1 + .05)^{10}}$$

$$= \$308.87 + \$613.91$$

$$= \$922.78$$

In other words, we would be willing to pay $922.78 for this bond.

We can also compute the yield to maturity of this bond if we know the present selling price, which is typically recorded daily in the financial markets. In this case we are asking the reverse question from that above: Given that the bond is selling for $922.78 and that it pays $40 a year in interest and will be redeemed for $1,000 at the end of 10 years, what is the *bond yield* (i). Using Equation 4-14, we find that:

$$\$922.78 = \sum_{t=1}^{n} \frac{\$40_t}{(1 + i)^t} + \frac{\$1,000}{(1 + i)^{10}}$$

$$i = 5\%$$

We can use Tables 4-5 and 4-3 through a trial and error process to derive the 5 percent yield, or we can use precalculated bond tables by reading the intersection of the number of years until maturity and the prevailing price for any given annual interest payment.[3]

The implications of these calculations give the financial officer an idea of how much the firm's bonds will have to yield if new ones are issued as well as a feel for prevailing bond market conditions, which are so important in timing new financing. These particular calculations of bond price and yield are but a few of the many instances using techniques developed under the mathematics of finance concepts with which the financial executive must be very familiar.

SUMMARY

After having read Chapter 4, you should be able to answer these questions:

1. How does capital work?

Capital grows over time when invested at a positive rate of interest. We demonstrated this through the concept of simple interest, under which capital earns that positive rate of interest once a year on the principal.

2. How does capital grow with reinvestment?

With reinvestment capital grows a compound rate, which is really interest earned upon interest. The cumulative effect of compound interest over time can be dramatic, since there is an acceleration in the amount of interest earned as time passes.

3. How much should a financial officer allow his or her company to pay now for an expected amount later?

The technique of present-value discounting allows us to derive an appropriate answer to that question, given the opportunity interest rate and the number of years the firm has to wait to receive the expected amount.

[3] The bond tables are precalculated at almost all combinations of maturity and coupon rate by the Boston Financial Publishing Company.

4. How does the financial officer handle annuities?

Annuities are equal annual deposits or payments over a given time. We saw that the present value of an annuity deposit reflects the summation of the compound value of each year's deposit over the period. We also saw that the present value of the annuity payment is equal to the summation of the present value of each year's payment over the period. Both of these figures can be obtained easily from precalculated tables.

5. How does the financial officer handle uneven streams?

By summing the present value of each inflow or by summing the compound value of each deposit, the financial officer can handle uneven streams in much the same fashion as annuities.

6. How does the financial officer handle installment financing?

Typical installment financing considerations are variations of the present value of the annuity and the compound value of the annuity due. By using the appropriate tables, we can determine such figures as the equal annual payment needed to retire a debt.

QUESTIONS

4-1 Distinguish between simple interest and compound interest.

4-2 Bank A pays a simple annual interest rate of 4.5 percent on saving accounts, and Bank B pays 4.5 percent compounded quarterly. In which bank would you receive the greatest amount of interest for the year?

4-3 Illustrate that the compounding formula for annual periods is a special case of the compounding formula for nonannual periods.

4-4 Discuss briefly the statement that "discounting is the reverse of compounding." How are discounting and compounding related mathematically?

4-5 Define and give some examples of an annuity. Distinguish between the compound value of an annuity and the present value of an annuity.

4-6 How are bond yields determined using the discounting method?

PROBLEMS

4-1 Mrs. Smith is considering depositing $1,000 either in a commercial bank or a savings and loan association. The bank pays a simple annual interest rate of 5 percent and the savings and loan association pays 4 percent compounded quarterly. Mrs. Smith anticipates making no withdrawals for 3 years. Which financial institution will provide Mrs. Smith with the greater amount of money after 3 years?

4-2 If Bolcon, Inc. deposits $50,000 in a savings account at a commercial bank that pays a 4 percent interest rate compounded annually, how long will it take Bolcon to double the value of its deposit?

4-3 Twenty-five years ago Bolcon, Inc. purchased a tract of land in downtown Houston for $25,000. If this land grew in value at the rate of 9 percent per year, what is the current value of the land?

4-4 At the beginning of each year Tilex Corporation deposits $5,000 in a savings account that pays 5 percent interest per annum. At the end of 7 years, how much will the firm's savings account be worth?

4-5 Tilex Corporation wishes to set up a sinking fund to retire a $300,000 bond in 10 years. If the annual interest rate is 6 percent, what are the annual installments the firm must put in a savings account to accumulate sufficient funds to pay off the bond? Each deposit is made at the beginning of the year.

4-6 The Tilex Corporation had sales of $800,000 in 1958 and $4,000,000 in 1975. What is the annual compound rate of growth in sales for this 17-year period?

4-7 The Smith Company recently purchased a new building for $1,000,000 payable on terms of zero down payment and 25 equal annual installment payments to include interest at 8 percent per year. What is the size of the firm's annual payment? What is the dollar amount of interest paid during the 25-year period?

4-8 A firm has estimated the expected annual earnings from an investment project over the next 3 years as:

Year	Earnings
1	$10,000
2	$20,000
3	$15,000

What is the present value of the total-earnings stream for the investment project? Assume that the earnings accrue at the end of each period and that the firm has an opportunity return of 8 percent on projects of similar risk.

Appendix 4A Continuous Compounding and Discounting

If compounding takes place frequently enough over the course of a year, we approach what is called *continuous compounding:* an instantaneous process of interest earning interest, as there is instant reinvestment. While it may be hard to envision—and would certainly be impossible if a team of bookkeepers had to update accounts continuously—the concept can be expressed in terms of a formula. And the necessary calculations can be done on a computer with great ease.

Most of us have seen savings and loan associations which pay interest compounded continuously. The effect is to raise the simple interest rate for the year, because during the year the interest is earning interest. For example, 5 percent simple interest becomes 5.15 percent with continuous compounding.

CONTINUOUS COMPOUNDING

We saw in Chapter 4 that we could adjust the compound interest formula to account for more frequent compounding periods than once a year:

$$V_n = P\left(1 + \frac{i}{m}\right)^{nm} \tag{4A-1}$$

As we increase the number of periods during the year in which compounding takes place, m becomes larger and we approach continuous compounding. As m approaches an infinitely large number, then:

$$V_n = P \lim_{m \to \infty}\left(1 + \frac{i}{m}\right)^{nm} \tag{4A-2}$$

$$\lim_{m \to \infty}\left(1 + \frac{i}{m}\right)^{m} = 2.718 \tag{4A-3}$$

which is e, the natural log base, so that:

$$V_t = Pe^{it} \tag{4A-4}$$

and in more conventional symbols:

$$V_t = Pe^{gt} \tag{4A-5}$$

where
   g = the continuous growth rate counterpart of i
   t = the continuous growth rate time counterpart of n

CONTINUOUS DISCOUNTING

The converse of continuous compounding is continuous discounting. If:

$$V_t = Pe^{gt} \tag{4A-5}$$

then to find the present value:

$$P = \frac{V^t}{e^{gt}} \tag{4A-6}$$

or in the equivalent equation, but using the negative exponent to indicate division:

$$P = V_t e^{-kt} \tag{4A-7}$$

where
   k = the discounting counterpart of the compounding g.

CONTINUOUS DISCOUNTING OF A GROWTH STREAM

How do I apply the concept of continuing discounting to a stream of cash flows that are continually growing at a compound rate?

An example of the need for such a procedure is a stock price-model which grew at an annual rate g and was discounted to its present value at a rate k. We would have to combine Equations 4A-5 and 4A-7.

The series (annuity) is growing at e^{gt} over time, which is symbolized as:

$$V_t = F_0 \int_{t=0}^{n} e^{gt}dt \tag{4A-8}$$

where

F_0 = the initial annual cash flow

$\int_{t=0}^{n}$ = the calculus sign for integration over time from $t = 0$ to $t = n$

The present value of V_t is:

$$P = \int_{t=0}^{n} F_t e^{-kt}dt \tag{4A-9}$$

Notice that $F_t = F_0 e^{gt}$, so substituting we derive:

$$P = \int_{t=0}^{n} F_0 e^{gt} e^{-kt}dt \tag{4A-10}$$

and combining terms:

$$P = F_0 \int_{t=0}^{n} e^{(g-k)t}dt \tag{4A-11}$$

which simultaneously discounts at k and compounds at rate g over time $t = 0, n$, provided $k > g$ to insure that the effective discount rate $(g - k)$ is negative. If it is not negative, then Equation 4A-11 irrationally concludes that the receipt of funds is more valuable, instead of less valuable, the longer you have to wait.

We can solve Equation 4A-11 using the calculus if $n = \infty$ such that:

$$P = F_0 \int_{t=n}^{\infty} e^{(g-k)t}dt \tag{4A-12}$$

$$P = F_0 \int_{t=0}^{\infty} \frac{e^{(g-k)t}}{g-k} \tag{4A-13}$$

which, if $k > g$, is:

$$P = \frac{F_0}{k - g} \tag{4A-14}$$

This means that if $k > g$ and $n = \infty$, the present value of an initial sum F_0 is F_0 divided by $k - g$. Obviously as g increases, given that k and F_0 are constant, P rises too.

TWO

CAPITAL BUDGETING

LET US LOOK AT SOME OF THE MAJOR QUESTIONS which you, as the financial officer, must be able to answer in advising your firm on what to invest in. As you read Part Two look for the answers to the following questions:

1. What is the necessary information needed to form a capital budgeting decision?

2. What criteria apply in making a capital budgeting decision?

3. How are these criteria applied when more than one project is being considered?

4. How do these criteria apply when there is a limited amount of capital available for investment?

5. How are these criteria altered under a situation of risk?

5

iNVESTMENT ÐECiSiON CRiTERiA ASSUMiNG CERTAiNTY– SiNGLE PROJECTS

How DOES A FIRM'S MANAGEMENT DECIDE what to invest in? The firm's very survival depends on management's ability to conceive, analyze, and select investment opportunities that are profitable. Further, management's own survival may depend on selecting those projects which best maximize the firm's objectives under the constraint of the stockholders' wishes and governmental edicts. A less-than-satisfactory performance, even if profitable, often leads to changes in managers. Obviously, once management has decided on a corporate goal, it needs some general rules which can be applied to help make decisions on individual project proposals.

Since progress toward maximizing the chosen corporate goal is highly dependent upon the financial officer's decisions as to what investments the firm should undertake, he or she should be able to answer the question: How is the corporate goal related to successful investment selection? The relationship depends upon the goal which is chosen. In general, however, we can be certain that projects which make the firm more profitable or the shares of the company more attractive to investors should be undertaken, and any decision criterion we use should guide us to such projects from among the many proposed. If the project's return does not exceed its cost or increase the value of the firm such that each share is worth more than before, the project should not be undertaken.

CAPITAL BUDGETING DECISIONS

What is a capital budgeting decision criterion?

It is a rule or standard by which to judge the qualifications and desirability of a project. If the project does not measure up to the standard, it is rejected. Capital budgeting decision criteria are guidelines, expressed in terms of the firm's profitability or other measure of value, against which the profitability or other measure of value of potential projects is weighed.

To express the individual project's profitability or measure of value in order to compare it to the firm's standard, we must have certain information about the project. What data do we need? We need to know the project's net cashflow before interest and depreciation but after taxes. Net cashflow is dependent upon the project's cost, the subsequent cash inflows and outflows which accrue to it, the timing of these flows, the number of years in the life of the project, and its salvage value. The cost of the funds and the uncertainty of the net cashflows are other major factors, but their discussion is deferred until later chapters.

Once you have mastered the construction of these decision criteria, you can compare proposed projects in terms of a uniform set of criteria. Furthermore, those who conceived the proposal will have a standardized framework for presenting their case. And these criteria facilitate the selection process of the final decision-makers, who may be the firm's executive committee or board of directors.

What frequently applied criteria are there for you to use? The criteria fall into the two broad categories of *present discounted value techniques* and *rate of return techniques*. In the first category you have at your disposal approaches known as discounted cash flow (DCF), net present value (NPV), benefit/cost (BC), and terminal value (TV). In the second category you have available internal rate of return (IRR) and annual rate of return (ARR). There are also the payback and the plowback criteria, which do not fit into either of the categories and are more limited in their application.

Which of all these different decision criteria do you, as financial officer, select? The answer depends on the specific circumstances surrounding the capital budgeting process. In certain situations and for certain types of firms, one of the criteria may be preferred. The firm may find one decision criterion easier to relate to its chosen objective than another. The firm may even choose to use more than one of the decision criteria in its capital budget planning in order to view proposed projects from several different angles.

The Capital Project

Taken together, the decision criteria a company chooses to apply are referred to as capital budgeting or as a master plan for the funding of the selected capital projects during a given planning period. When a capital project is accepted under the appropriate decision rule, it is incorporated into the capital budget. A capital project is merely an investment opportunity requiring the commitment of capital and carrying an expectation of a cash return on that investment for a period in excess of one year. By definition, the capital budget deals exclusively with projects expected to last more than one year.

We can expect a typical capital project to involve an initial cash outlay to acquire the means of production. And we can expect to receive the benefits of that capital project in the form of a future stream of cash inflows over the life of the project. A new machine may cost $1 million, but it usually returns only a portion of that initial outlay in the first year, say $200,000. The remaining benefits of, say, $200,000 a year come in each of the remaining years in the 10-year life of the machinery. Any capital project with this particular sequence of an initial cash outflow (−) followed by cash inflows (+) is termed a *conventional capital project*. They may be schematically illustrated as follows:

Year	0	1	2	3	4	5	6	7	8	9	10
Project A	−	+	+	+	+	+	+	+	+	+	+

Any project which follows a different sequence of outflows and inflows, showing an irregularity or a reversal of the pattern sometime in its existence, is termed a *noncon-*

ventional capital project, as illustrated below:

Year	0	1	2	3	4	5	6	7	8	9	10
Project B	−	−	+	+	+	+	−	+	+	+	+
Project C	+	−	−	−	−	−	−	−	−	−	−
Project D	−	−	+	−	+	+	+	−	+	+	+

Projects B and D might require major renovations in years 6 and in years 3 and 7, respectively. Project C might be a loan to the company, which is an inflow only in the first year, after which the company repays a given sum each year.

A Typical Proposal

Before discussing the elements of information involved in the general decision rules, it may be helpful to follow a typical proposal from conception to acceptance. Figure 5-1 is a simplified schematic of the firm's organization chart (see Chapter 1). Let us assume that the marketing department, through its research division, conceives a new product which, for security purposes, they call product X. The marketing vice-president authorizes a preliminary marketing survey. An overwhelming majority of the potential customers who were surveyed say that they definitely feel there is a need for the product and that they would consider purchasing it. On the basis of these results, the marketing department decides to press the executive committee to approve the production and sale of product X.

As vice-president for financial planning, your boss is budget coordinator for the executive committee, so he receives the initial request from the marketing department. Since you are the financial analyst, your boss immediately throws the request on your desk, asks you to check it out, and have it ready by next week for presentation to the executive committee. Where do you turn first?

The first step is to check back with the marketing department to acquaint yourself with the concept and the product. You will want to determine such pertinent information as the marketing department's feel for product X's revenue-generating potential—specifically, how much of product X does the marketing department feel it can sell and at what price? You might also want to judge their feel for the product's revenue potential at various selling prices and for the degree of certainty which they assign their estimates. It is also necessary to get their estimate on the product's potential life expectancy, particularly if it is subject to rapid obsolesence or changes in consumer tastes. Of course, it would be impolite to accuse the marketing vice-

Figure 5-1 Simplified Diagram of a Firm's Organization

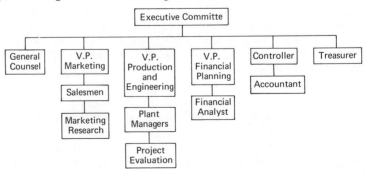

president of uncertainty and vacillation; tactfully penetrating questions will draw out the vice-president's thoughts on the subject. For example, a pet project may be too optimistically appraised, and your job is to discover the pessimistic possibilities as well.

You will certainly have to go to the production and engineering department to determine the feasibility and the cost of producing product X. Among the cost considerations you will have to assess are the initial costs of the machinery or "tooling up" necessary to start and maintain production of product X. There may be more than one production method to consider. Estimates of the cost per unit must be obtained and coordinated with the marketing department's estimates of revenue. Other pertinent information will include the expected life of the machinery and its salvage value at the end of that life. These facts obviously enter your calculations as they affect the amount of funds the firm will have to invest and the degree to which they are recoverable. As always, you will have to assess the certainty that the production department assigns these estimates and elicit the pessimistic as well as the optimistic possibilities.

Next, you will turn to your own finance department personnel to assess the feasibility of funding the production and marketing of product X, since neither of the other two departments has this financial expertise. You will need to know if the firm will have the funds available in its treasury at the time the project is undertaken. If it does not, what are the prospects for raising the necessary funds in the financial markets? You may require a subjective estimate of the receptibility of future financial markets to the sale of the firm's securities or to the firm's borrowing from its banks. You may also require a judgment as to the firm's overall financial strength, including the firm's ability not only to finance the original investment but also to maintain adequate working capital (cash, inventory, and accounts receivable) during the life of the project. Further, you must assess the cost of the funds to be employed. Obviously, if the funds are unavailable or too costly, the project may not be feasible.

In many instances you must ask the legal department to rule on the project's compliance with governmental regulations.

The big task still remains. You must now coordinate the information and opinions obtained in each department for your boss to present to the executive committee. You will have to summarize all the information and bring it all to some focal point on which the executive committee can reach a decision.

Techniques for doing just that are discussed in this chapter. After you have read this chapter you will know how to shape such information into a presentation based on the general rules of capital budgeting decisions.

ELEMENTS OF CAPITAL BUDGETING

What are the general pieces of information needed to make a capital budgeting decision for a particular project?

The essential elements to consider in formulating any rule by which to make a decision on a capital project are:

1. The project's cashflows
2. The uncertainty of the cashflows
3. The cost of capital to finance the project (including the value of money over time as discussed in Chapter 4)

Cashflows

Any project's cashflows involve:

1. The original cash outflow (including committed working capital)
2. The subsequent net cash inflows or net outflows (net earnings or loss, plus interest, and noncash expenditures such as depreciation, which is discussed in detail in Appendix 5A)
3. The timing of the subsequent net cashflows
4. The project's after-tax salvage value (including the release of the committed working capital)
5. The time of termination

We must distinguish among the various cashflows associated with the original outlay, the subsequent inflows or outflows, and the salvage value, because each is calculated in a slightly different manner. The *original outlay* is the typical gross cash outflow. It reflects the cash spent to acquire the asset.

The *salvage value* represents the typical after-tax cash inflow, which reflects the actual cash generated from the sale of the asset after any applicable taxes. If the sale generates cash over several periods, the salvage value cash inflow must be reflected over those periods as it is actually received.

A capital project's *subsequent net cash flow* is the revenue it generates (gross cash inflow) less all cash expenses, excluding interest paid on the capital raised to finance the project and the applicable tax savings because interest is a tax-deductible expense.

A typical subsequent net cash flow would be net sales attributable to the project less all cash nonoperating expenditures (excluding interest and applicable tax savings) and cash operating expenditures, such as cost of goods sold, selling and administrative expenses, and taxes paid (but excluding depreciation, a noncash expenditure). Examine the expected 1975 figures on the following proposed capital project Y:

Gross revenues	$500,000	
Less returns, discounts	25,000	
Net revenues		$475,000
Operating expenditures		
Cost of goods sold	200,000	
Selling and general administrative expenses	100,000	
Depreciation	50,000	
Total operating expenditures		350,000
Net income before interest and taxes		125,000
Interest		25,000
Net income before taxes		100,000
Taxes (50 percent tax rate)		50,000
Net income		50,000

The expected net cash inflow for 1975 would be:

Cash inflows		
Net revenues		$475,000

Cash outflows

Cost of goods sold	200,000	
Selling and general administrative expense	100,000	
Taxes paid	50,000	
		350,000
Net cashflow expected in 1975 (before tax savings)		$125,000
Tax savings applicable to interest deductibility		12,500
Net cash flow expected in 1975		$112,500

Notice that because the interest expense is tax-deductible, reflected in its position before taxes in the estimated 1975 income for project Y, the firm has saved $12,500 in taxes, or 50 percent of the $25,000 total interest. Since we cannot count interest in the calculations of the subsequent net cash flows, we must also exclude the tax savings from that interest. To do otherwise would be double counting, since interest and the associated tax savings are used in the computation of the cost of capital, discussed later in the text.[1]

We may alternatively compute the expected net cashflow for 1975 by adding all noncash expenditures[2] and interest to the project's net income. In our example, the expected 1975 net cashflow would be:

Net income	$50,000
Depreciation	50,000
Interest	25,000
Net cash flow expected in 1975 before tax saving	$125,000
Tax saving applicable to interest deductibility	12,500
Net cashflow expected in 1975	$112,500

The computed cash inflow in our example is only the expected net cash flow to the project *in 1975*. It is important to understand that in each year from the proposed project's inception until its termination, there will be an associated net cashflow, which will probably vary from year to year and which can be either positive (net cash inflow) or negative (net cash outflow). In all conventional projects, there will be a net cash outflow connected with the initial purchase and installation of equipment or undertaking of the project.

Original cash outflow Almost all capital projects require a sizable *initial cash outlay* before future benefits are realized. If our firm had decided to manufacture and sell soap powder, it would have had to invest in manufacturing facilities, raw materials, advertising, and numerous other items before it could begin generating revenues from the sale of soap powder. Our firm might have had to expend millions of dollars before ever realizing any revenue.

[1] See G. David Quirin, *The Capital Budgeting Decision*, Irwin, Homewood, Ill., 1967, pp. 84–85.
[2] Other noncash expenditures would have to be treated in the same fashion as depreciation. Among the more common is the amortization of intangibles such as patents and goodwill.

Even projects that do not need large amounts of machinery and equipment require initial capital outflows. For example, service-oriented companies such as collection agencies or computer facilities management organizations must first train their employees and promote their services before they can generate cash inflows. These start-up costs are frequently looked upon as the original cash outflow. In the schematics of negative cash flows (−) and positive cash flows (+), the expected pattern is an original outlay followed by a sequence of mostly positive cash flows, such that

Year	0	1	2	3	...	n
Cashflow	−	+	+	+	...	+

The necessary *working capital requirements* to support the operation of the project over its expected life are also included as part of the original outflow. These are the cash, accounts receivable, and inventory investments encountered in the daily operation of the project. There will be an increased need for all three working capital components as each additional capital project is undertaken, although the firm tries to keep its investment in each to the minimum required to support the project. We will explore the methods used to determine the minimum working capital requirements in Part 4. However, it should be obvious that with each new project undertaken, the firm will have to extend additional credit to its customers in the form of accounts receivable, carry additional inventory to fill customers' orders, and enlarge its cash balances to meet its enlarged transactions. All these additional asset requirements are treated as part of the initial investment.

Subsequent cash inflows and outflows   The original outflow expended to start the project is expected to generate cash inflows in subsequent periods. These inflows consist of the project's expected net earnings plus noncash expenditures and interest. It is important to realize that these cash inflows may vary in size from one inflow to the next. For example, the cashflows might resemble project A or project B. (Negative cashflows are enclosed in parentheses.)

Year	0	1	2	3	4	5
Project A	($1,000)	$700	$500	$1,000	$1,500	$300
Project B	(1,000)	400	400	400	400	400
Project C	(1,000)	800	(200)	500	1,000	(100)

Both are conventional capital projects, although B is an annuity type with equal annual inflows (see Chapter 4). Some of the cashflows can even be negative, as in project C.

Time of the subsequent flows   Just as the size of the cashflows may vary, so may the time when they are received. We will assume that the cash inflows are received once, at the end of each year, to conform with the compounding and present-value tables in the Appendices at the back of this book. But they may occur at any interval— semiannually, once in the middle of the year, quarterly, biennially, or even irregularly. It is important to recognize the time of occurrence, since, as we have seen in Chapter 4, there is a time value to money such that the more quickly it is received the more valuable it is to us.

Salvage value   The estimated realizable sale price of the project at its termination, typically called the salvage value, must be included in the cashflow. At the end of the project when it is disbanded, the leftover machinery, the scrap parts, even the land on which the project stood, or the resale value of the entire operation become cash inflows when sold. For example, assume a $1 million investment in a gas compressor substation (project E) with an expected 10-year life, an annual cash inflow of $200,000, and an estimated salvage value of $100,000 at termination. The cashflow pattern would be:

Year	0	1	2	3	4	5
Project E	($1,000,000)	200,000	200,000	200,000	200,000	200,000

6	7	8	9	10
200,000	200,000	200,000	200,000	300,000

In year 10, the cash inflow is $300,000, not $200,000 as in years 1–9 because the $100,000 salvage value is expected to be realized in year 10. Note that the salvage value, like all the other components of the cashflow, must be estimated at the beginning of the project's initial consideration and included in the decision criteria calculations.

At termination, the project's investment in working capital is no longer necessary and is released back to the company's general funds. When the project ceases to function, there is no need for inventory or accounts receivable to support sales. If, in our example, an additional $100,000 of working capital was required for the project, it would be released in year 10, and the salvage value of the project would be $400,000. It is important to note that the release of working capital is not considered part of the salvage value by the Internal Revenue Service and is not included in calculating depreciation.

Time of termination   The year in which the project is expected to terminate is the final component of cashflow. The expected life of the project influences its desirability: the longer it remains operational, the more total cash inflow it can generate. If our gas compressor substation (project E) were to have only a 5-year life expectancy instead of the 10 years we originally assumed, its cashflow would be:

Year	0	1	2	3	4	5
Project E	($1,000,000)	200,000	200,000	200,000	200,000	400,000

Total cash inflow over the 5-year period would be only $1,200,000—compared to $2,200,000 over the 10-year life. Sometimes as the life expectancy changes, the individual cash inflow will also change in size and create a new cashflow pattern.

The determination of life expectancy depends on many factors which are best considered by experts in the area. Among many possible considerations are the physical deterioration of the equipment, obsolesence due to the introduction of more efficient equipment, changing product demand, style changes, and other customer considerations. There are many other reasons for termination, but a termination date must be estimated at the project's initial consideration.

Uncertainty and the Cost of Capital

We will defer our discussion of uncertainty to Chapter 7 and the cost of capital to Part Three. For the moment we will assume that cashflows are known with certainty and that the cost of capital (k) is given as specified in each example. Under this situation of certainty, the cost of capital is equivalent to a risk-free or pure interest rate, since there is no chance of not realizing the expected cashflows. As we shall see in Chapter 7 and in Part Three, the cost of capital actually has to be adjusted for risk when there is a chance of not realizing the expected cashflows. For ease of exposition, we shall use the cost of capital as a general term for the cost of funds used to finance the projects under consideration.

CAPITAL BUDGETING DECISION CRITERIA

What frequently applied decision criteria are available to the financial officer?

We now examine the decision criteria most commonly used in evaluating a proposed capital project. Each criterion leads to an accept or reject decision for each single project.

Discounted Cashflow (DCF)

The discounted cashflow decision criterion, also frequently called the present-value approach, incorporates all the elements of the capital budgeting decision criteria into a consistent, one-figure guide by which to accept or reject the proposed project.

The general procedure behind the DCF is to determine if the present value (PV) of the expected future cash inflows is sufficiently large to warrant the original outlay (OO). *If the PV is greater than or equal to the OO, the proposed project is accepted.*[3] *If the PV is less than the OO, the proposed project is rejected.* In symbols, the DCF decision criterion is:

$$PV \geqslant OO \qquad \text{accept}$$
$$PV < OO \qquad \text{reject}$$

Let us examine the procedure more closely (see Chapter 4 for the mathematical derivation of PV). How do we determine the PV of the expected cash inflows? Let us assume that the expected cash inflows (CF) are $10,000 in each year of the project's life.

Second, we have to determine the timing of the inflows. Let us assume they are received at the end of each year.

Third, we have to determine the project's salvage value. Let us assume it is $20,000, including the release of committed working capital, and that it is received at the end of the last year.

Fourth, we have to determine the project's life expectancy. Let us assume it is five years.

We are assuming the cost of the funds (k) to be 10 percent, and we are assuming certainty.

The original outlay is known because we have received preliminary bids and prices on the project from suppliers and information on the working capital commitment from our own staff. Let us assume the original outlay is $60,000.

All the elements for a capital budgeting decision are present. The PV is then

$$PV = \frac{CF_1}{(1+k)^1} + \frac{CF_2}{(1+k)^2} + \frac{CF_3}{(1+k)^3} + \frac{CF_4}{(1+k)^4} + \frac{CF_5}{(1+k)^5} + \frac{S}{(1+k)^5}$$

[3] Even in the absence of any budget constraint, it is uncommon to find proposed projects accepted if their PV only equals their OO. Firms tend to leave leeway for error.

where
    PV = the project's present value
    CF_j = the project's cash inflow in year j
    S = the project's salvage value
    k = the cost of funds

Substituting our assumed value and consulting the present-value tables, we have:

$$PV = \$10{,}000 \left(\frac{1}{(1+.10)^1}\right) + \$10{,}000 \left(\frac{1}{(1+.10)^2}\right) + \$10{,}000 \left(\frac{1}{(1+.10)^3}\right)$$

$$+ \$10{,}000 \left(\frac{1}{(1+.10)^4}\right) + \$30{,}000 \left(\frac{1}{(1+.10)^5}\right)$$

or:

$$\$10{,}000 \times .909 + \$10{,}000 \times .8265 + \$10{,}000 \times .7513 + \$10{,}000 \times .6830$$
$$+ \$30{,}000 \times .6209 = \$9{,}090 + \$8{,}265 + \$7{,}513 + \$6{,}830 + \$18{,}627 = \$50{,}325$$

Notice that we must discount the individual cash inflows by a smaller factor from the present-value table as they become more distant, because of the time value of money (see Chapter 4). The PV is now stated in present time, since we have brought all the future cash inflows back to the present by discounting them for time. The PV can now be directly compared with the original outlay, which is also in present time. We compare the project's PV of $50,325 with its cost of $60,000, and the discounted cashflow criterion (DCF) tells us to reject the project. In other words, the original outlay buys less in terms of expected cash inflows adjusted for time than its cost. It would be an unattractive investment.

The annual cash inflow does not have to be uniform. For example, for a different project assume that $CF_1 = \$10{,}000$, $CF_2 = 20{,}000$, $CF_3 = 5{,}000$, $CF_4 = 10{,}000$, $CF_5 = 5{,}000$, $S = 20{,}000$, $k = 10\%$, and $OO = \$50{,}000$. Then PV = $51,728. Comparing PV to OO, we accept the project because PV is greater than OO. We can apply the identical procedure to any set of flows.[4]

Net Present Value (NPV)

Net present value is a variation of the DCF decision criterion. The difference between the two is that the NPV subtracts the original outlay from the present value of the future cash inflows, whereas the DCF does not. Thus, NPV = PV − OO. To compute the NPV of any particular project, we simply compute the present value of the future cash inflows at an appropriate cost of capital and subtract from that the original outlay.[5] For example, if the proposed project had a 5-year life expectancy with

[4] We can abbreviate the summation of this series of expected future cash inflows as follows:

$$PV = \sum_{i=1}^{n} \frac{CF_i}{(1+k)^i} + \frac{S_n}{(1+k)^n}$$

where
    Σ (the summation sign) = sum of
    $i = 1$ = the first period in the sum
    n = the last period in the sum
    S_n = salvage value

In our example, n would be 5 and the sum would be over years 1 through 5 inclusive.

[5] The formula for the NPV is:

$$NPV = \sum_{i=1}^{n} \frac{CF_i}{(1+k)^i} + \frac{S_n}{(1+k)^n} - OO$$

$CF_1 = \$10,000$, $CF_2 = 10,000$, $CF_3 = 10,000$, $CF_4 = 10,000$, $CF_5 = 10,000$, $S = 20,000$, $k = 10\%$, and $OO = 60,000$, its PV would be $50,325. Its NPV would be $50,325 − $60,000 = (9,675)$. The accept-reject criterion under the NPV is: *Accept if the proposed project's NPV is positive and reject if it is negative.* Symbolically, this is

$$NPV \geqslant 0 \qquad \text{accept}$$
$$NPV < 0 \qquad \text{reject}$$

In our example, we would reject: the NPV is less than 0.

The NPV approach distills the decision down to one figure, compared to the two figures (present value of the DCF and original outlay) needed in the DCF approach. Some financial officers find this more appealing for reporting their decision and communicating the analysis behind it, but they must still perform the comparison when subtracting the original outlay from the present value of the future cash inflows in order to derive the NPV. We shall see that the NPV has other advantages when you are comparing many projects (Chapter 6).

Internal Rate of Return (IRR)

The internal rate of return, or rate of return as it is sometimes more simply called, is the appropriate rate of discount which equates the future stream of cash inflows to the original outlay. In other words, it is that discount rate which gives the project a NPV of zero. In symbolic terms, the IRR would be r in the denominator of the equation below:

$$OO = \frac{CF_1}{(1+r)^1} + \frac{CF_2}{(1+r)^2} + \frac{CF_3}{(1+r)^3} + \frac{CF_4}{(1+r)^4} + \frac{CF_5}{(1+r)^5} + \frac{S}{(1+r)^5}$$

Let us take our DCF example, which had CF_1 through $CF_5 = \$10,000$, $S = \$20,000$, and $OO = \$60,000$, and see what the IRR criterion is. The IRR (r) of this project is

$$\$60,000 = \frac{\$10,000}{(1+r)^1} + \frac{\$10,000}{(1+r)^2} + \frac{\$10,000}{(1+r)^3} + \frac{\$10,000}{(1+r)^4} + \frac{\$30,000}{(1+r)^5}$$

$$r = 4.48\%$$

Notice how we have to compute the IRR by the trial-and-error procedure used to calculate the yield in Chapter 4. First, we had to approximate the appropriate r and then actually perform the calculations to see how close the discounted future stream of cash inflows comes to the original outlay. If the former were higher (lower) than the latter, we had to raise (lower) r until the two were equal. If we had used $r = 4.0$ percent, the present value of the cash inflows would have been higher than the original outlay:

$$= \frac{\$10,000}{(1+.04)^1} + \frac{\$10,000}{(1.04)^2} + \frac{\$10,000}{(1+.04)^3} + \frac{\$10,000}{(1+.04)^4} + \frac{\$30,000}{(1.04)^5}$$

$$= \$60,956$$

If we had used $r = 5.0$ percent, the present value of the cash inflows would have been lower than the original outlay:

$$= \frac{\$10,000}{(1+.05)^1} + \frac{\$10,000}{(1+.05)^2} + \frac{\$10,000}{(1+.05)^3} + \frac{\$10,000}{(1+.05)^4} + \frac{\$30,000}{(1+.05)^5}$$

$$= \$58,965$$

Interpolating, we find that the present value of the cash inflows equals the original outlay at $r = 4.48$ percent, as illustrated in the example. This degree of computational difficulty has discouraged many users, despite access to computers that can perform the arithmetic in seconds.

Notice too that the r is internal to the project itself, in contrast to the external nature of the given cost of capital k used in the DCF analysis. This gives us our decision rule: *Accept the proposed project if its IRR is greater than the firm's external cost of capital as determined in the financial markets. Reject the proposed project if its IRR is less than the firm's external cost of capital.* Thus,

$$\text{IRR } (r) \geq k \qquad \text{accept}$$
$$\text{IRR } (r) < k \qquad \text{reject}$$

In our example, if the external cost of capital k is given to be 10 percent, we would reject the project because it would return less than the funds used to undertake it.

The IRR criterion appeals to many firms because r is expressed as a percentage and is readily comparable to the firm's computed cost of capital k, which is also expressed as a percentage. Further, a few feel that the separation of the IRR calculation from the cost of capital presents a better position from which to judge the proposed project on its own operating merits, "independently" of the cost of capital, which appears to the few to fluctuate widely, frequently, and beyond their control.

Like the DCF and NPV, the IRR considers all the elements in the capital budgeting decision.

Benefit/Cost (BC)

The benefit/cost decision rule, frequently called the present-value index, compares in a ratio format the present value of the future cash inflows to the present value of the original and any future cash outlays, dividing the former by the latter. This is a slightly different presentation from the DCF and NPV approaches, but it is based on the same concepts. For example, continuing with the same proposed project as before:

$$\begin{aligned} BC &= \frac{PV}{OO} \\ &= \frac{\$50,325}{\$60,000} \\ &= .8388 \end{aligned}$$

The decision rule is: *If the benefit/cost ratio is greater than 1.0, accept the project. If the BC ratio is less than 1.0, reject it.* In symbols this is:

$$BC \geq 1.0 \qquad \text{accept}$$
$$BC < 1.0 \qquad \text{reject}$$

We would reject the project in our example.

Like the NPV and the IRR, the BC analysis reduces to a single, easily communicated figure upon which to base a decision. Further, it considers all the elements of capital budgeting. It also facilitates the handling of cash outflows which may occur among the future stream of cash inflows.

If there are further costs than the original outflow, these must be considered. The BC ratio specifically takes such outflows into account by comparing the present value of the cash inflows to the present value of all the cash outflows, regardless of the period in which they occur, such that

$$BC = \frac{PV \text{ of the cash inflows}}{PV \text{ of the cash outflows}}$$

For example, assume the following information on a proposed project: $CF_1 = \$5,000$, $CF_2 = 20,000$, $CF_3 = (10,000)$, $CF_4 = 10,000$, $S = 0$, $OO = \$20,000$, and $k = 10$ percent. The PV of the cash inflows is:

$$PV = \frac{\$5,000}{(1 + .10)^1} + \frac{\$20,000}{(1 + .10)^2} + \frac{\$10,000}{(1 + .10)^4}$$

$$= \$29,307$$

The PV of the cash outflows is:

$$PV = \frac{\$20,000}{(1 + .10)^0} + \frac{\$10,000}{(1 + .10)^3}$$

$$= \$27,131$$

And:

$$BC = \frac{\$29,307}{27,131}$$

$$= 1.08$$

We would accept this project under the BC criterion.

The BC approach to incorporating cash outflows allows them to be separated from the cash inflows, whereas in the DCF, NPV, and IRR methods the future cash outflows are lumped together with cash inflows of the same period, and only the net amount is incorporated into the analysis. Separate treatment sometimes brings the total timing and nature of the cash outflows into sharper focus, but in most instances the decision to accept or reject is not altered.

Terminal Value (TV)

The terminal value approach even more distinctly separates the timing of the cash inflows and outflows. Behind the TV approach is the assumption that each cash inflow is reinvested in another asset at the then-prevailing attainable rate of return from the moment it is received until the termination of the project. Assuming an original outlay of $20,000 and a 4-year project with annual year-end cash inflows of $10,000, we would reinvest each $10,000 when received at, say, 5 percent for the first 2 years and then at 7 percent per year until the end of the fourth year, in which the project terminated. This accounts for where the cash inflows go after they are received. The total sum of these compounded cash inflows is then discounted back to the present at k and compared to the present value of the cash outflows, the original cost in this case. Schematically, the TV approach looks like this:

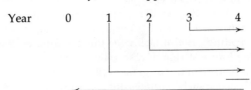

Year   0   1   2   3   4

If $k = 10$ percent in our assumed project, the present value of the terminal sum (PVTS) would be:

Year	0	1	2	3	4
Cashflows	($20,000)	$10,000	$10,000	$10,000	$10,000
				1 yr. @ 7%	10,700
			2 yrs. @ 5%		11,025
		3 yrs. @ 5%			11,576
					$43,301

$$\text{PVTS} = \frac{\$43,301}{(1.10)^4}$$

$$= \$29,576$$

If the present value of the summed total of the compounded reinvested cash inflows (PVTS) is greater than the present value of the outflows (PVO), the proposed project is accepted. In symbols:

$$\text{PVTS} \geqslant \text{PVO} \qquad \text{accept}$$
$$\text{PVTS} < \text{PVO} \qquad \text{reject}$$

Thus, since the PVTS of $29,576 exceeds the original outlay of $20,000, we would accept this assumed project under the TV criterion.

Note that the present value of the terminal sum differs from the present value of the future stream of cash inflows for the same project. This is because we have assumed varying reinvestment rates of return under the TV approach. (The reinvestment assumption is discussed in the next section.) If, for example, we had assumed the reinvestment rate of return to be equal to the cost of capital (10 percent) and constant over the life of the project, the present value of the terminal sum and the present value of the $10,000 annual cash inflows for 4 years would have been equal, as shown below:

$$PV = \frac{\$10,000}{(1+.10)^1} + \frac{\$10,000}{(1+.10)^2} + \frac{\$10,000}{(1+.10)^3} + \frac{\$10,000}{(1+.10)^4}$$

$$PV = \$31,699$$

$$\text{PVTS} = \frac{\$46,410}{(1+.10)^4}$$

$$= \$31,699$$

The advantage of the TV method is that it explicitly incorporates the assumption about how the cash inflows are reinvested once they are received and avoids any influence of the cost of capital on the inflow stream itself. A drawback is the difficulty of projecting what available rates of return will be in the future.

Average Rate of Return (ARR)

The average rate of return is an annualized expression of the net income earned on the average investment in the project. The idea is to derive a return, expressed in percentage form, which can be compared to the cost of capital. Specifically, the average annual net income (after taxes) attributable to the proposed project (NI) is divided by the average investment, including working capital requirements for the life of the proposed project. In symbols:

$$ARR = \frac{NI}{(OO + S)/2}$$

where the average investment is the original outlay plus salvage value all divided by 2, which approximates the average investment. The salvage value (S) is used to represent the project's value at the end of its life. Therefore, the average investment is the project's initial value (OO) and terminal value (S) divided by 2.

For example, assume NI = $1,000, OO = 10,000, and S = 2,000:

$$ARR = \frac{\$1,000}{\$6,000}$$

$$= 16.67\%$$

The decision rule is: *Accept the project if the ARR is greater than the cost of capital k and reject it if the ARR is less than the cost of capital.* In symbols:

$$ARR \geq k \qquad \text{accept}$$
$$ARR < k \qquad \text{reject}$$

While the ARR may be relatively simple to compute and easy to compare to the cost of capital, it has several drawbacks when used as a capital budgeting decision rule. First, it obviously ignores the time value of money by failing to discount the future cash inflows and outflows. Second, it does not consider the timing component of cash inflows, which may be very misleading. For example, both the following cash inflow streams have the same average annual net income, but stream 2 is obviously less desirable because most of its inflow occurs in the later part of its life, rather than in the early part as with the other project. Considering that money is less valuable the longer you have to wait for it, stream 1 is more desirable. The ARR would not reflect the superiority of the project offering inflow stream 1.

Year	0	1	2	3	4	5
Stream 1	(10,000)	$3,000	$3,000	$2,000	$1,000	$1,000
Stream 2	(10,000)	$1,000	$1,000	$2,000	$3,000	$3,000

Third, the life of the project is ignored. A project with a long life expectancy can have the same ARR as a project with a short life expectancy. For example, assume the following cash flow patterns:

Year	0	1	2	3	4	5	6	7
Project 1	($10,000)	$3,000	$3,000	$2,000	$1,000	$4,000	$2,000	$2,000
Project 2	($10,000)	$3,000	$3,000	$2,000	$1,000	$1,000		

The ARR for both projects is 20 percent, assuming no salvage value. The longer project is preferable because it offers a larger over-all stream of future cash inflows, but the ARR method could not distinguish between the two.[6]

[6] Sometimes the ARR is computed as a return on the original investment instead of the average investment:

$$ARR = \frac{NI}{OO}$$

Sometimes the ARR is computed as return on the weighted average investment:

$$ARR = \frac{NI}{\frac{(n+1)(OO - S - WC)}{2n} + S + WC}$$

Finally, the ARR does not consider depreciation (the return of the capital) as part of the cash inflow. This distorts the actual size of the cash inflows and is misleading in the analysis.

Payback (PB)

Payback is a measure of the rapidity with which the project will return the original capital outlay. The payback period is the number of years it takes the firm to recover the original outlay from the cash inflows of the project. *Projects offering a payback period less than some firm-determined number of years (N) are accepted and those projects with a payback period greater than that acceptable number of years are rejected.* In symbols:

$$PB \leq N \qquad \text{accept}$$
$$PB > N \qquad \text{reject}$$

For example, assume a project where $OO = \$100,000$, $CF_1 = 20,000$, $CF_2 = 30,000$, $CF_3 = 50,000$, $CF_4 = 25,000$, $S = 10,000$, and $N = 4$ years. The PB period is 3 years, and we would accept the proposed project.

There are several flaws in the payback method. First, it totally ignores many of the components of the cash inflows. All cash inflows beyond the payback period are ignored entirely. This could be very misleading in capital budgeting evaluations.

Payback also ignores the time value of money, since it does not discount the future cash inflows. It also ignores the entire question of the cost of capital.[7] Unless

---

where
$\qquad n$ = the asset's life expectancy
$\qquad$ WC = working capital commitment
$\qquad S$ = salvage value
$\qquad OO$ = original outlay
$\qquad$ NI = average annual after-tax net income

[7] Many socialist countries that do not recognize the existence of interest, (since all value springs from labor, and capital, according to their theories, is dormant), use payback to evaluate the relative attractiveness of projects.

This, in part, allows the yield (r) on the capital to enter the evaluation because the reciprocal of the payback for a perpetual life project is the yield, or the internal rate of return. We can demonstrate this as follows:

$$OO = \sum_{i=1}^{n} \frac{CF_i}{(1+k)^i} \tag{1}$$

which is equivalent to:

$$OO = \frac{CF}{k} - \frac{CF}{k}\left(\frac{1}{1+k}\right)^n \tag{2}$$

$$k = \frac{CF}{OO} - \frac{CF}{OO}\left(\frac{1}{1+k}\right)^n \tag{3}$$

The reciprocal of the payback is

$$k = \frac{CF}{OO} \tag{4}$$

As $n \to \infty$, Equation (3) $\to$ Equation (4).

See Myron J. Gordon, "The Payoff Period and the Rate of Profit," in *The Management of Corporate Capital,* ed. Ezra Solomon, University of Chicago Press, Chicago, 1959, pp. 48–55.

the acceptable number of years is directly related to the cost of capital, which in most instances it is not, a firm could be accepting projects on which they would pay more for their capital than the project would return, without even realizing it. Payback also ignores the project's salvage value and the life expectancy of the project. Projects with large cashflows in the later part of their lives may be rejected in favor of less profitable projects which happen to have a larger portion of their cash inflows in the earlier part of their lives.

The use of payback may be appropriate, despite its faults, under certain extenuating circumstances. Where the long-term outlook, say in excess of three years, is extremely hazy, payback may be useful. In a politically unstable country, for instance, a quick return to recover the investment is the primary goal, and subsequent profits are almost unexpected surprises.

In case of liquidity crises for the firm, payback may be appropriate. A firm with limited liquid assets and no ability to raise additional funds, which nevertheless wishes to consider capital projects in hopes of easing the crisis, might use payback as a selection criterion because it emphasizes quick recovery of the firm's original outlay and limited impairment of the already-critical liquidity situation.

Payback may also be of some use as a decision criterion if the firm insists upon emphasizing short-run earning performance over sound long-run budgeting procedures. A quick windfall may be management's objective, and shorter payback periods tend to provide those windfalls. Within a relatively short period of time, most of these shortsighted managements and their firms are usually in trouble. Furthermore, stockholders are seldom fooled into great confidence in a firm with very short-run, and obviously temporary, earnings gains.

Table 5-1   Summary of Capital Budgeting Decision Rules

1. Discounted cash flow (DCF)

$PV \geq 00$	accept
$PV < 00$	reject

2. Net present value (NPV)

$NPV \geq 0$	accept
$NPV < 0$	reject

3. Internal rate of return (IRR)

$r \geq k$	accept
$r < k$	reject

4 Benefit/cost (BC)

$BC \geq 1.0$	accept
$BC < 1.0$	reject

5. Terminal value (TV)

$PVTS \geq PVO$	accept
$PVTS < PVO$	reject

6. Average rate of return (ARR)

$ARR \geq k$	accept
$ARR < k$	reject

7. Payback (PB)

$PB \leq N$	accept
$PB > N$	reject

Plowback

Some firms, mostly in real estate development and usually privately owned, use the plowback method. That is, they simply reinvest indiscriminately in as many projects as their cash position, without borrowing, will allow. All profits from the firm's operation are reinvested in the firm. This obviously ignores all the elements of sound capital budgeting and should be discouraged.

THE APPROPRIATE DECISION CRITERION

With all these different decision criteria, which, as financial officer, do you use?

The choice of the appropriate decision criterion depends on the circumstances surrounding the decision and on the customary practices of the firm you join. You must have all the decision criteria in your repertory of techniques. Different firms have different acceptance standards which you must understand. Different decision-makers have different acceptance standards in terms of which you must be able to communicate. The same firm may want to consider more than one acceptance standard. Obviously, you must be prepared to use all or any of the decision criteria, but you must also be consistent in the use of whichever one you select. As the circumstances surrounding each situation can vary over a wide range, we are forced to limit our discussion to general terms, which you can relate to the specific situations you encounter. The DCF decision criterion typically works best for a firm that has a shareholder-wealth-maximization objective and that recognizes that the present value of the firm is enhanced by projects with DCFs in excess of the project's cost. This criterion is best applied in situations where the firm is looking for the absolute dollar amount of present value each project brings to the firm. A firm that wants the absolute size of the project to appear directly in the decision criterion should use DCF. It lends itself to situations in which there is little concern about ranking projects according to their relative attractiveness and little need to give specific consideration to cash outflows subsequent to the original capital outlay.

The NPV decision criterion is most appropriate for firms with shareholder-wealth-maximization objectives because, like the DCF, it communicates the dollar amount of the present value each project brings to the firm. In contrast to the DCF, however, the NPV is best suited for firms which are looking for the absolute amount of *additional* present value. This criterion is particularly appropriate for firms which wish to rank their projects by how much each adds to the firm's present value. It gives the clearest indication of the additional value of the project and is the most direct method of communicating this to others. It is best applied in situations where there is no concern with netting cash outflows and inflows in any one period and no need for an indication of the absolute dollar amount of the cost of each project.

The IRR decision criterion most readily relates to firms with profit-maximizing objectives because of its direct comparison of cost versus return. It is particularly appropriate for managements which use a return-acceptance criterion, and it easily compares with the cost of funds, which is traditionally expressed in percentage terms. It is readily compared to the externally derived cost of funds expressed as a percentage, such as interest rates on the firm's bonds. Sometimes this makes it much easier to communicate with the decision-makers. It is best applied in situations in which there is no need to worry specifically about the absolute size of the project or of cash outflows subsequent to the original outlay.

The BC decision criterion is hard to relate directly to either shareholders-wealth maximization or profit maximization, because there is no direct expression of cost-versus-return or of present value. This criterion is most appropriate for firms which are looking for a relative expression of the dollar benefits received per dollar of cost. It is also most appropriate when you want to evaluate the effect of cash outflows subsequent to the original outlay and when management wants a relative ranking of the projects. When used by itself, this criterion is exceptionally hard to relate to the absolute dollar amount of the cost of each project or to the additional present value each project brings to the firm.

The terminal value (TV) decision criterion works best for firms with shareholder-wealth-maximization objectives. It is most appropriate when you suspect that the interest rate at which you can reinvest the cash inflows you expect to receive or at which you have to finance future cash outlays is going to be distinctly different from the cost of funds you are presently experiencing. The added flexibility of the TV criterion makes it relatively easy to adjust for these anticipated changes and to communicate this to the firm's decision-makers. This criterion is not appropriate, however, if there is large concern for ranking the projects, because it gives only the absolute present value of each project and not the additional present value you would find in the NPV.

The payback criterion is hard to relate to any particular corporate objective, but it can be appropriately used for the firm with an overriding consideration for liquidity or a very short-term spurt in earnings. Since the criterion ignores the time value of money, the timing of the cashflows, the life expectancy of the project, and the value of the inflows beyond the acceptance year, it is not recommended in many situations.

The plowback is another criterion which is hard to relate to a corporate objective because it is so poorly conceived and ignores so many of the elements necessary for good capital budgeting. It should never be used.

The average annual rate of return (ARR) criterion is best applied by firms with profit-maximization objectives, but it is not a very effective criterion. Like the payback criterion, it ignores the life expectancy of the project, the cash generation of the depreciation, the time value of money, and the timing of the income stream. Only under those unusual circumstances in which the firm is looking for a net income return figure which approximates an average annual return might you use this criterion.

Obviously none of the criteria is applicable to all situations all the time. In fact, you will probably need to use more than one criterion in evaluating any set of proposed projects. For example, you might want to rank the projects by the additional net present value each brings to the firm, but you still want to communicate the project's cost in relation to its return and might find it necessary to consider expected shifts in the rate at which you reinvest the cash inflows or finance the additional future cash outflows. You would probably use a combination of the NPV, the IRR, and the TV decision criteria.

THE RELATION OF DECISION CRITERIA AND CORPORATE GOALS

Now that you are familiar with the typical corporate goals (Chapter 1) and the capital budgeting decision criteria, how does the successful use of the decision criteria relate to the chosen corporate goal?

Basically, the present-value group of decision criteria most readily enhance the shareholders-wealth-maximization objective, while the decision criteria based on rate of return most readily enhance the profit-maximization objective, although, as we shall see, all the criteria are interrelated when it comes to evaluating a single project.

The present-value-based decision criteria include the NPV, the DCF, the BC, and the TV approaches. The NPV decision criterion increases the present value of the firm as long as the projects undertaken have a positive net present value. Everything else considered, the value of the firm should increase as the firm continues to add further projects with positive net present values because then each additional project undertaken implies a further profitable employment of the firm's capital and encourages expectations of increased dividends and rising demand for the firm's shares. It is as if the pie had been enlarged and each share is now worth more. The firm should undertake as many projects with positive NPV's as possible.

The DCF criterion is similar to the NPV criterion in that if the present value of the project exceeds the original outlay, the present value of the entire package of projects known as the firm is also larger, and each share should be worth more.

The BC criterion is also similar to the NPV criterion for the same reason. As each additional project with a BC ratio greater than 1 is undertaken, the present value of the entire firm increases, and the firm's share price should also increase.

The terminal value criterion is also related to the shareholders' wealth maximization objective through the same mechanism as the other present value based decision criteria. As long as the firm continues to undertake projects with a present value of the terminal sum in excess of the present value of the outlays, the present value of the entire package of assets increases in value.

The rate of return based decision criteria, mainly the internal rate of return (IRR), is more clearly related to the profit-maximization objective. If the internal rate of return (r) is greater than the cost of funds (k) used to finance the project, the firm's profit increases and will continue to do so as long as additional projects whose return is greater than their cost are added. For example, assume we had a project which costs $1 million, is expected to have equal annual cashflows such that it would have an internal rate of return equal to 20 percent, and was financed with funds costing 15 percent. The annual dollar return would be $200,000, while the annual dollar cost of the funds would be $150,000. The project nets the firm $50,000 a year, and the firm's coffers grow. As long as the firm continues to undertake projects with an r greater than k, the firm's profit will continue to grow.

The relationship among the present-value and the return-based decision criteria is such that if *one* indicates acceptance of a particular project, *all* will indicate acceptance of that project. If the present value exceeds the original outlay, the NPV of that project will be positive, the BC ratio of that project will be greater than one, and the internal rate of return will exceed the cost of funds. In other words if:

$$PV > OO$$

then

$$NPV > 0$$
$$BC > 1$$
$$r > k$$

Thus all the capital budgeting decision criteria are related and we cannot derive conflicting results for a single project, although, as we shall see in the next chapter, we can get conflicting rankings.

SUMMARY

After having read Chapter 5, you should be able to answer these questions:

1. What is a capital budgeting decision criterion?

It is a standard or rule against which the financial officer measures a particular project's profitability or present value to determine whether to accept or reject the project. If the project's measure is within the standard's range of acceptability, it is undertaken.

2. What information is needed to construct the project's measure of profitability or present value?

In general, we must know the project's net cashflows before depreciation and interest but after taxes. These cashflows are dependent on the project's cost, the subsequent cash outflows and inflows which accrue to the project, the timing of the cashflows, the number of years in the project's life, and its salvage value. We must also know the cost of the funds and the uncertainty associated with the cashflows, although these topics were reserved for later chapters.

3. What frequently applied decision criteria are available to you as a financial officer?

Several decision criteria use the present discounted value as a basis for evaluation. Among these are the discounted cash flow (DCF), the net present value (NPV), the benefit/cost ratio (BC), and the terminal value (TV). The internal rate of return (IRR) and the average rate of return (ARR) are based on rate of return to the project rather than present value. In addition, there are the payback and the plowback approaches, which are less generally applicable but are still found in practice.

4. Which decision criterion should you use under what circumstances?

The present-value-based decision criteria lend themselves to corporations which adopt shareholder-wealth maximization as their objective, while the return-based criteria lend themselves more readily to profit-maximization objectives. The NPV approach is preferred in situations where the corporation wants a direct indication of the additional value added to the corporation by the project. However, the financial officer will favor the TV approach if specific consideration must be accorded to the future cash outflows of the project. The BC approach will furnish a direct indication of the relative benefits per dollar of cost. The DCF approach affords an indication of the size of the project. If the ability to express the criterion in percentage form is important, the IRR approach is indicated. The PB approach may be warranted if liquidity is of primary importance. The ARR method will provide a measure of the net-income-based return.

5. How does successful use of the capital budgeting decision criteria relate to the chosen corporate objective?

Since all the decision criteria are interrelated, a decision to accept a single project under one criterion is tantamount to acceptance under all criteria. As the additional number of acceptable projects undertaken increases, the firm's profits should increase and the value of the entire package of projects known as the firm should also increase. Investors' expectations of increased dividends and demand for the stock should boost share price, everything else considered, and the shareholders' wealth should be maximized.

QUESTIONS

5-1 Distinguish between conventional and nonconventional capital projects, giving examples of each.

5-2 Define the "net cash flow" of a capital project and indicate how it can be calculated.

5-3 Suppose a firm is contemplating construction of a plant facility in a nearby town and, after 10 years, plans to sell the facility at its estimated market price, $50,000. Should this $50,000 cash sale at the end of the life of the project be included in the capital budgeting decision?

5-4 Identify the similarities and differences between the discounted cash flow (DCF) and net present value (NPV) methods of capital budgeting.

5-5 How are future cash outflows handled in the benefit/cost method (BC) as compared to the discounted cash flow (DCF), net present value (NPV), and internal rate of return (IRR) methods?

5-6 Discuss the following statement. "The principal advantage of the terminal value (TV) method in capital budgeting over other methods (such as NPV, DCF, and IRR) is that it explicitly incorporates the assumption about how cash inflows are reinvested."

5-7 Evaluate the average rate of return (ARR) approach as a capital budgeting decision rule.

5-8 Some major United States petroleum companies are being advised to use the payback method (PB) in their capital budgeting decisions regarding the exploration and extraction of crude oil from foreign countries, especially in South America and the Middle East. Considering the deficiencies of the PB method, why do you suppose these companies are tempted to use it?

5-9 How might the method of calculating depreciation, for example the straightline method versus the double declining balance method, affect the capital budgeting decision in general? See Appendix 5A for a discussion of depreciation.

PROBLEMS

5-1 The AJAX Corporation is considering expansion of its investment budget to include project A—the building of a customer service facility in a nearby town. The facility has a life expectancy of 5 years and no salvage value. The only cost to AJAX is the original outlay of $10,000, and the estimated cash inflows for each of the 5 years following construction are as follows:

Year	Estimated cash inflow	Cash outflow
0	$0	$10,000
1	$2,500	
2	$2,500	
3	$2,500	
4	$2,500	
5	$2,500	

Assuming the cash inflows occur at the end of each year and the cost of capital to AJAX is 6 percent, indicate whether the project should be accepted or rejected if:

(a) The discounted cashflow (DCF) method is used.
(b) The net present value (NPV) method is used.
(c) The benefit/cost (BC) method is used.
(d) The internal rate of return (IRR) method is used.
(e) The payback (PB) method is used and the payback period is set at 3 years.

(f) The terminal value (TV) method, where the estimated cash inflows received the first 2 years can be reinvested at 9 percent per year, and the cash flows received in the last 3 years can be reinvested at 8 percent per year.

(g) Demonstrate that if the reinvestment rates of the TV method in (f) had been equal to the cost of capital, the DCF and TV methods would be identical.

5-2 Bolcon, Inc. is contemplating purchasing a new SUPER-X mass storage unit for its computer facility. The new mass storage unit being considered has an original cost of $100,000, plus a $10,000 maintenance cost each year of operation. Due to the high rate of technological development in the computer industry, Bolcon anticipates using SUPER-X for 5 years and then selling it and buying a newer model. The estimated market value of SUPER-X in 5 years is $25,000. Bolcon's cost of capital is presently 7 percent. The projected cash inflows that should accrue to Bolcon from its use of SUPER-X are as follows for each year of operation:

Year	Estimated cash inflows
0	$0
1	$30,000
2	$40,000
3	$50,000
4	$40,000
5	$30,000

Assuming the cashflows occur at the end of each year, indicate whether the project should be accepted or rejected if the following capital budget methods are used:

(a) The discounted cashflow (DCF) method.
(b) The net present value (NPV) method.
(c) The benefit/cost (BC) method.
(d) The internal rate of return (IRR) method.

5-3 The Bigbite Food Company is considering locating a ready-processed retail food outlet (a Bigbite Drive-Inn) in a nearby city. Estimates of sales, production costs, administrative costs, and the like have been calculated and an estimated income statement for the new facility drawn up. The income statement is thought to be representative of each of the 10 years of the expected life of the Bigbite Drive-Inn. The original outlay to build the facility is $100,000, and the firm's cost of capital is 8 percent. Here is the estimated income statement for the new Bigbite Drive-Inn for year 1.

Gross revenues	$100,000	
Less returns, discounts	5,000	
Net revenues		$95,000
Operating expenditures		
Cost of goods sold	40,000	
Administrative costs	20,000	
Depreciation	10,000	
Total operating expenditures		70,000
Net income before interest and taxes		25,000
Interest payments		5,000
Net income before taxes		20,000
Taxes (50% tax rate)		10,000
Net income after taxes		$10,000

(a) Estimate the annual net cashflow from the project.
(b) Using the net present value (NPV) method, indicate whether the project should be accepted or rejected.
(c) Appendix 5A explains several methods of calculating depreciation. If the double declining balance (DDB) method of depreciation is used, what will be the effect on the net cashflow of the project? Do you think the NPV of the project will be higher or lower if the DDB method of depreciation is used rather than a straightline depreciation (as shown above in the income statement)?

BIBLIOGRAPHY

Bailey, Martin J. "Formal Criteria for Investment Decisions," *Journal of Political Economy,* LXVII (October 1969).

Barrett, Edgard M. "Proposed Basis for Asset Valuation," *Financial Executive,* XLI (January 1973), 12–17.

Bierman, Harold, Jr. "ROI as a Measure of Management Performance," *Financial Executive,* XLI (March 1973), 40–46.

———, and Seymour Smidt. *The Capital Budgeting Decision,* 4th ed. Macmillan, New York, 1975.

Bodenhorn, Brian, "On the Problem of Capital Budgeting," *Journal of Finance,* XIV (December, 1959), 473–492.

Dean, Joel. *Capital Budgeting.* New York: Columbia University Press, 1951.

Haynes, W. Warren, and Martin B. Solomon, Jr. "A Misplaced Emphasis in Capital Budgeting," *Quarterly Review of Economics and Business* (February, 1962).

Jean, William H. *Capital Budgeting* (Scranton: International Textbook Company, 1969).

———. "On Multiple Rates of Return," *Journal of Finance,* XXIII, 1 (March, 1968), 187–192.

———. "Terminal Value or Present Value in Capital Budgeting Programs," *Journal of Financial and Quantitative Analysis,* VI (January, 1971), 649–652.

Jeynes, Paul H. "The Significance of Reinvestment Rate," *Engineering Economist,* XI (Fall, 1965), 1–9.

Mao, James C. T. "The Internal Race of Return as a Ranking Criterion," *Engineering Economist,* II (Winter, 1966), 1–13.

Masse, Pierre. *Optimal Investment Decisions.* Englewood Cliffs, N.J.: Prentice Hall, Inc., 1962.

Mendleson, Morris. "A Comment on Payback," *Journal of Financial and Quantitative Analysis,* VI (September, 1971), 1159–1160.

Merrett, A. J. and Allen Sykes. *Capital Budgeting and Company Finance.* London: Longmans, Green & Company, Ltd., 1966.

Solomon, Ezra. "Alternative Rate of Return Concepts and Their Implications for Utility Regulation." *Bell Journal of Economics and Management Science,* I (Spring 1970), 65–81.

———. "The Arithmetic of Capital Budgeting Decisions." *Journal of Business,* XXIX (April 1956).

———. *The Theory of Financial Management.* Columbia University Press, New York, 1963.

Teichroew, Daniel, Alexander A. Robichek, and Michael Montalbano. "An Analysis Criteria for Investment and Financing Decisions Under Certainty." *Management Science,* 12 (November 1965), 151–179.

Weingartner, H. Martin. "The Excess Present Value Index—A Theoretical Basis and Critique." *Journal of Accounting Research,* I (Autumn 1963), 213–224.

Appendix 5A **Depreciation**

Part of any cash inflow will consist of the return of the original capital outlay in the form of depreciation. Since in capital budgeting we invest most, if not all, of our capital (funds raised) at the original outlay, we expect to recover that amount in cash inflow over the life of the project (plus some profit as well). This is done through the formal accounting mechanism known as *depreciation*,[1] the major category into which a number of noncash expenditures fall.

A project's depreciable asset value (usually the original outlay for machinery, equipment, and buildings, but not the land or the investment in working capital) decreases over time through wear and tear. This decrease is charged against the project's earnings by some pro rata method over the project's life (we will discuss the commonly used methods shortly). Since the cash for the project has already been paid out when the asset was first acquired, these depreciation charges against earnings, which expense the asset's acquisition price over its lifetime, do not involve cash. They are *noncash expenses,* and they offset the project's reported earnings but do not diminish the project's cash generation. Depreciation is, therefore, part of the cash inflow attributable to the project.

Because depreciation is an expense against income it affects the firm's tax liability. As depreciation expense increases for any given revenue, the firm's taxable income decreases along with its tax liability, since the latter is a percentage of the former. If depreciation expenses were not regulated by the federal government, firms wishing to avoid taxes would increase depreciation expenses to a point where they would report no taxable income and pay no taxes. At the same time they would be receiving the entire cash inflow generated by the depreciation, since it is a noncash expense. For example, a firm with $100,000 in earnings before taxes and depreciation would have no taxable income and pay no taxes if it had $100,000 in depreciation expense. That same firm would pay $25,000 in taxes (assuming a 50 percent tax rate) if it had depreciation of only $50,000 and a taxable income, therefore, of $50,000.

Depreciation schedules are fixed by the Internal Revenue Service (IRS)[2] such that specific kinds of assets have specified lives over which they may be depreciated by the firm. These schedules prohibit too rapid depreciation and the avoidance of income taxes. They are available to all concerned parties from the IRS and must be observed as the minimum expected life, although for the firm's capital budgeting purposes a longer or shorter time of termination may be used, provided the tax savings from the depreciation do not exceed IRS guidelines.

Once the IRS schedule has been consulted, the firm may choose which method among those approved by the IRS it will use to compute depreciation expense. There are four basic approved methods which we will discuss here. They are:

1. Straightline
2. Double declining balance (DDB)
3. Sum-of-the-year digits (SOY)
4. Units of production (UOP)

---

[1] The same concept applied to intangible assets is called amortization. Applied to natural resource assets, it is called depletion.

[2] In the case of regulated companies such as railroads, depreciation schedules are often fixed by the regulatory authority rather than the IRS.

Table 5A-1   Straightline Depreciation

Year	Asset value beginning of year	Depreciation expense	Asset value end of year
1	$1,100,000	$100,000	$1,000,000
2	1,000,000	100,000	900,000
3	900,000	100,000	800,000
4	800,000	100,000	700,000
5	700,000	100,000	600,000
6	600,000	100,000	500,000
7	500,000	100 000	400,000
8	400,000	100,000	300,000
9	300,000	100,000	200,000
10	200,000	100,000	100,000

STRAIGHTLINE DEPRECIATION

The straightline method depreciates the asset's original purchase price minus the estimated salvage value (excluding the released working capital) in equal, yearly installments over the life of the asset. For example, a $1,100,000 piece of equipment
with a life expectancy of 10 years and an estimated $100,000 salvage value would be
depreciated $100,000 each year, as illustrated in Table 5A-1.

DOUBLE DECLINING BALANCE (DDB)

The DDB method reflects an intentional effort by the IRS to accelerate the rate of
depreciation for any single asset (project), by bringing forward the bulk of the
depreciation expense in the earlier years of the asset's life and decreasing the portion of the depreciation in the later years of its life. Note that DDB does not materially change the total depreciation expensed against any asset but merely shifts the
timing of that depreciation forward. The stated purpose of accelerated depreciation
is to provide firms with greater cash inflows sooner in order to increase capital expenditures. In addition, because maintenance and repair expenses on any equipment increase as the machinery ages, DDB, declining as the machinery ages, can
work as a balancing factor and keep the total expense associated with the machinery

Table 5A-2   Double Declining Balance Method

Year	Asset value beginning of year	Depreciation expense	Asset value end of year	Straightline depreciation
1	$1,100,000	$220,000	$880,000	$100,000
2	880,000	176,000	704,000	100,000
3	704,000	140,800	563,200	100,000
4	563,200	112,640	450,560	100,000
5	450,560	90,112	360,448	100,000
6	360,448	72,090	288,358	100,000
7	288,358	57,672	230,686	100,000
8	230,686	46,137	184,549	100,000
9	184,549	36,910	147,639	100 000
10	147,639	29,528	118,111	100,000

more uniform over its lifetime. Proponents claim this facilitates capital budgeting and economic stability.

The DDB method accelerates depreciation to twice the straightline percentage that would be charged on the value of the asset at the end of the year, but it does not deduct the asset's estimated salvage value. For example, if the straightline depreciation is 10 percent, the DDB method will each year depreciate 20 percent of the asset's undepreciated value. Using our $1.1 million project, DDB is illustrated in Table 5A-2. Notice that under DDB the depreciation is greater than the straightline method in the earlier years and less than the straightline method in the later years.[3] This reduces a project's reported taxable income and increases a project's cash inflow in the earlier years of its life.

SUM-OF-THE-YEAR DIGITS (SOY)

The SOY method does not increase the total amount of depreciation but merely shifts forward from the later years a large portion of the depreciation. Thus like the DDB method, SOY has the effect of reducing reported taxable income and income taxes paid, while increasing the project's cash flow in the earlier years.

In the SOY method, tne years in the asset's life are summed, and its total remaining years divided by the summed figure. This fraction is multiplied by the asset's original cost less any salvage value (excluding the released working capital). The product of that multiplication is the depreciation expense for the year. For example, assume we have a $1.5 million project with a 5-year life expectancy and no salvage value, as shown in Table 5A-3. The sum of the years' digits is $15(5 + 4 + 3 + 2 + 1)$, and the depreciation factor in the first year is $5/15$ of the asset's original cost (the salvage value is assumed to be zero). The first year's depreciation is $500,000 ($5/15 \times$ $1,500,000). The second year's depreciation is $400,000 ($4/15 \times$ 1,500,000) and so on.

UNITS OF PRODUCTION (UOP)

The units of production method (UOP) or as it is sometimes called, the service-life method, is based upon an estimated useful life in terms of units of output rather than chronological time, as in the previous methods. This method is frequently

Table 5A-3   Sum-of-the-Year Digits Method

Year	Asset value beginning of year	Depreciation factor	Depreciation expense	Straightline depreciation
1	$1,500,000	5/15	$500,000	$300,000
2	1,000,000	4/15	400,000	300,000
3	600,000	3/15	300,000	300,000
4	300,000	2/15	200,000	300,000
5	100,000	1/15	100,000	300,000

[3] Under an IRS ruling, a firm may switch its depreciation method on a particular asset once during the life of that asset. That gives the firm the advantage of switching from the accelerated method to the straightline method when the latter produces a larger depreciation expense. In our example (Table 5A-2), the firm would switch to straightline depreciation at the beginning of the seventh year, where the straightline charge to the remaining value of the asset would exceed the DDB charge.

used for those products in which the depreciation of the asset can be directly related to its production.

Using UOP, the estimated total number of units that the asset can produce is divided into the original cost less any salvage value (excluding the released working capital). The resultant rate is the depreciation expense per unit of production. As the number of units produced increases, so does the depreciation expense. For example, if the asset was expected to produce a total of 100,000 over its entire lifetime and cost $10,000 with a salvage value of $1,000, the depreciation rate per unit of production would be:

$$\frac{\$9,000}{100,000} = \$.09 \text{ per unit}$$

If in any accounting period production was 10,000 units, depreciation expense for that accounting period would be $900.

While the UOP method does directly tie the depreciation to production, it does not accelerate the depreciation or intentionally provide tax savings for the firm. Furthermore, it may be very costly to keep the additional production records necessary under this system.

INVESTMENT CREDITS

Investment credits are intermittently authorized by the federal government as credits against the firm's tax liabilities when the firm purchases new equipment. The idea is to encourage capital expenditures and stimulate the economy. Basically, when a firm purchases capital equipment during a period in which the investment credit is allowed, it can directly deduct a certain percentage of the purchase price (usually 7 percent to 10 percent) from its tax bill. This is a credit as distinguished from an expense against revenues, such as depreciation. The investment credit increases a project's cash inflow by a factor of the tax rate. Whereas depreciation would reduce the firm's tax bill $.50 for each $1.00 of taxable income, a $1.00 investment tax credit would reduce the firm's tax liability by $1.00.[1] The effect of the investment credit may be viewed in two fashions. It reduces the initial cost of the asset because of the immediate tax credit. Alternatively, it increases the first year's cash inflow by the amount of the credit. Either approach is acceptable for capital budgeting if consistently applied, but the two cannot be used together.

There are still other tax write-offs such as intangible drilling expenses in the oil and gas industry, depletion allowances in the extractive industries, amortization of patents, and amortization of other intangible assets. They all have the effect of reducing the firm's reported taxable income and increasing the project's cash inflows.

---

[1] For accounting purposes and for reporting to stockholders, the investment credit may be treated on a flow-through basis or deferred. The flow-through basis treats the investment credit as a direct reduction in taxes and reports it as such. This has the effect of increasing reported earnings in the year the credit is taken, but it has no effect in subsequent years. The tendency is to "bulge" earnings in that one year. To avoid this bulge, as well as to satisfy the critics of flow-through, some firms defer reporting the investment tax credit to their stockholders; instead they put the reduction in taxes as deferred income on the balance sheet and reflect it in income as a separate item as the asset is used and depreciated. See David F. Hawkins, *Financial Reporting Practices of Corporations*, Dow Jones-Irwin, Homewood, Ill., 1972, pp. 226–228.

Table 5A-4 Deferred Taxes

INCOME STATEMENT

	TAX BOOKS		STOCKHOLDERS' BOOKS	
Revenues		$10,000,000		$10,000,000
Cost of goods sold	5,000,000		5,000,000	
Selling and general administrative expenses	2,000,000		2,000,000	
Depreciation	2,000,000	9,000,000	1,000,000	8,000,000
Net income before taxes		1,000,000		2,000,000
Taxes (50% rate)		500,000		1,000,000
Net income		500,000		1,000,000

BALANCE SHEET

Assets

	TAX BOOKS		STOCKHOLDERS' BOOKS	
Current assets				
Cash	200,000		200,000	
Accounts receivable	300,000		300,000	
Inventory	500,000		500,000	
Total current assets		1,000,000		1,000,000
Gross plant, property, and equipment	10,000,000		10,000,000	
Accumulated depreciation	2,000,000		1,000,000	
Net plant, property, and equipment		8,000,000		9,000,000
Total assets		9,000,000		10,000,000

Liabilities

	TAX BOOKS		STOCKHOLDERS' BOOKS	
Current liabilities				
Accounts payable	500,000		500,000	
Deferred taxes payable			500,000	
Total current liabilities				1,000,000
Stockholders' equity				
Common stock	300,000		1,000,000	
Additional paid-in capital	500,000	1,000,000	7,000,000	1,000,000
Retained earnings		500,000		7,000,000
				1,000,000
Total liabilities		9,000,000		10,000,000

DEPRECIATION AND REPORTED INCOME

The use of accelerated depreciation methods such as DDB and SOY postpones the tax liability to the later years in the project's life. Over the life of the project, the total tax liability is not materially changed; the largest portion of the liability is simply shifted backwards (deferred). In the project's later years its tax liability is larger under the accelerated depreciation methods than under the comparable straightline methods.

This postponement of taxes has led to the common practice of keeping at least two sets of corporate accounting books, one for tax purposes (reporting to the IRS) and one for stockholders (those used in the annual report to the stockholders). The books for taxes use the accelerated methods of depreciation in order to reduce reported income and lower the tax liability. The books for stockholders use a straightline method on the same assets, which has the effect of raising reported net income (an attraction to stockholders). The difference between the two reported tax figures is represented to the stockholders as a deferred tax liability, payable in the future when the asset reaches later life and the taxes associated with accelerated depreciation are higher than those associated with straightline depreciation.[5] For example, examine Table 5A-4, assuming the firm represented is new, having completed only one year of operation with an initial $10 million in plant, property, and equipment (capital projects) with a 10-year expected life and no salvage value. Notice that on the stockholders' books the use of straightline depreciation lowers the depreciation charge and increases the reported net income. The difference between the two sets of books is accounted for on the balance sheet by the deferred tax liability.

Appendix 5B Some Problems with the Decision Criteria

Sometimes the decision rules we have discussed develop interpretational problems because of peculiarities of the situation to which they are applied. These problems do not detract from the application of the decision rules to capital budgeting

---

[5] It is possible to defer this tax liability indefinitely if the annual addition of new equipment generates a sufficiently large tax deferral under the accelerated method to more than offset the amount by which depreciation is less than that given by the straightline method in the older assets.

Frequently, an asset does not last its IRS-expected lifetime and is sold or scrapped. In order to recapture some of the taxes deferred under the accelerated methods, which the IRS had expected to collect if the asset had lasted its expected lifetime, the IRS taxes the difference between the depreciated value and what the value of the asset would have been under the straightline method at ordinary income tax rates rather than at the lower long-term capital gain tax rates usually associated with the sale of an asset above its depreciated value. The difference between the sale price and the value under the straightline method is taxed at the lower long-term capital gains rates.

procedure, but we must recognize potential variations which might be misleading if we remained unaware of them. It is usually a simple matter to make appropriate adjustments.

THE REINVESTMENT ASSUMPTION

With any of the techniques which discount future cash inflows back to the present, there is an implied reinvestment assumption. It is assumed that when the cash inflows are received, they are immediately reinvested in another project or asset which has the same return as the present project's internal rate of return (IRR) or, if the DCF or NPV method is being used, has the same return as the cost of capital (k).

This implied reinvestment assumption allows us to consider the projects under the NPV, DCF, or IRR procedures independently of any consideration for where the cash inflows are going once they are received. The assumption works well, provided we accept available projects which *do* return the cost of capital or the internal rate of return.

But what if the reinvestment rate at which the cash inflows may be invested is different from k or the internal rate of return? This would have a direct bearing on the attractiveness of the project. A higher reinvestment rate would make more attractive a project with a more rapid recovery of the invested capital (a concentration of the expected cash inflows in the earlier years of the project's expected life), because the returned funds could be reinvested more profitably than in the present project. Conversely, a lower reinvestment rate than that earned on the present product would make a rapid recovery less attractive, because the returned funds would have to be put into projects less rewarding than the present one. Examine the proposed projects in Table 5B-1. Instead of assuming there would be other projects available in which to reinvest the cash inflows when received at the IRR, let us assume the available reinvestment rate over the 5-year period is 20 percent. Then project A's terminal sum would be $21,672 compared to project B's terminal sum of $19,000. Project A, when taken in conjunction with the higher reinvestment consideration, is more attractive than project B, despite A's lower rate of return.[1]

One way to clear up any confusion that may arise because of the reinvestment assumption is to use the Terminal Value (TV) approach discussed earlier in this chapter.[2] Under TV, the reinvestment rate is explicitly incorporated into the cash inflows at rates which may vary from one period to the next. TV is the most flexible

Table 5B-1

Year	Project A	Project B
0	($10,000)	($10,000)
1	5,660	2,000
2	2,000	2,000
3	2,000	2,000
4	2,000	2,000
5	2,000	6,917
IRR	10%	12%

[1] G. David Quirin, *The Capital Budgeting Decision*, Irwin, Homewood, Ill., 1967, pp. 82–83.
[2] Jack Hirshleifer, *Investment, Interest, and Capital*, Prentice-Hall, Englewood Cliffs, N. J., 1970, p. 57.

approach to the problem, allowing the reinvestment rate to be adjusted at any time during the life of the project. At the other extreme are the assumed fixed reinvestment rates implied in the DCF, NPV, and IRR methods. Between the two extremes it is possible to make any number of different reinvestment assumptions. Typically the reinvestment problem is not a major one. It can be ignored unless there are clear indications that a significant change in the available reinvestment rate is going to occur during the life of the proposed project.

IRR COMPARED TO DCF

Occasionally the IRR and the DCF give conflicting results. Assume we have the projects shown in Table 5B-2. Using the DCF or IRR decision criterion, both projects are acceptable. However, Project C is *preferred* under the IRR criterion, while project D is preferred under the DCF criterion. Which should we choose, if we can only select one?

The solution lies with the reinvestment assumption. We would choose that project which provided the highest terminal sum, given a reinvestment rate. By compounding out the first year's cash inflow of $1,200 for project C until the fourth year so that the two projects have identical time horizons, we can decide between the two. If, for example, the reinvestment rate was assumed to be 20 percent, the terminal sum for project C in year four would be $2,073.60. Since this exceeds the $1,873.00 for project D, we would select project C.

If we could select both, we probably would; both seem highly profitable. The problem arises because we have assumed k in the DCF method to be different from the computed r in the IRR method and then proceeded to assume each as the reinvestment rate in its own method. If k and r had been identical the problem would not have arisen.

This illustrates the problem of time horizons. If we are using the same decision criterion to accept or reject proposed projects, assuming a constant reinvestment rate at k in the DCF method and at r in the IRR method allows us to ignore differences in the life expectancies of different projects. However, once we drop that assumption and allow the reinvestment rate to vary in different periods or in different methods, we must explicitly consider the time horizon.

MULTIPLE ROOTS

When using the IRR approach, it is possible to get more than one solution for r in finding the rate which equates the future stream of cash inflows to the original outlay. This occurs when there is a cash outflow among the cash inflows (a reversal

Table 5B-2 IRR versus DCF

Year	Project C	Project D
0	($1,000)	($1,000)
1	1,200	
2		
3		
4		1,873
IRR	20%	17%
DCF ($k = 10\%$)	$1,091	$1,279

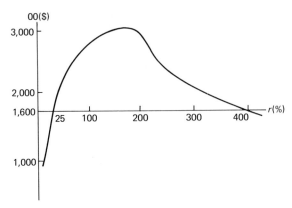

Figure 5B-1 The Multiple-Root Solution

of sign) as in a nonconventional capital project.[3] For example,[4] assume we are evaluating the installation of a high-power, $1,600 oil pump that will allow the firm to recover $10,000 worth of oil at the end of one year instead of at the end of two years. The project's cash flow pattern would bè:

Year	
0	($1,600)
1	+10,000
2	−10,000

Solving for the IRR, we would find that there were two rates of return which equated the future cash flows to the original outlay. The IRR equation:

$$\$1,600 = \frac{\$10,000}{(1+r)^1} - \frac{\$10,000}{(1+r)^2}$$

could be solved by both $r = 25$ percent and $r = 400$ percent. This is illustrated in Figure 5B-1, which shows at what r the future stream equates to the original outlay. This result leads to some very confusing and contradictory implications. If the new high-power pump costs nothing, $r = 0$ percent; if it costs $827, $r = 10$ percent, and if it costs $1,600, $r = 25$ percent. In fact, as the pump increases in cost, the return also increases for the same future stream—a very illogical conclusion.[5]

The solution to this problem is to isolate what exactly has been gained by installing the new pump. The answer is that a year has been gained: instead of waiting 2 years, all the oil is now pumped up in 1 year. We must determine how much that year's time is worth to the firm in terms of the project. The firm has actually, in a sense, borrowed $10,000 for the period of 1 year, between the end of year 1 and the end of year 2, for an investment of $1,600. The use of that $10,000 is worth whatever

[3] Since the IRR equation is a polynomial of degree n, there are n solutions, only one of which is real (not imaginary or negative) when the project is conventional. However, when the project is not conventional there is more than one real root, and we must resolve the confusion.

[4] For a more detailed discussion of this example, see James H. Lorie and Leonard J. Savage, "Three Problems in Capital Rationing", *Journal of Business*, October 1955, pp. 236–237. This article is reprinted in Ezra Solomon, *The Management of Corporate Capital*, University of Chicago Press, Chicago, 1959, pp. 56–66.

[5] *Ibid.*, pp. 74–79.

the firm's available reinvestment rate allows it to earn on $10,000. If, for example, the available reinvestment rate were 20 percent, that extra year is worth $2,000 (.20 × $10,000) to the firm. So the project is really a $1,600 original outlay to get back $2,000 at the end of 2 years. That is:

$$\$1,600 = \frac{\$2,000}{(1+r)^2}$$

$$r = 11.8\%$$

If the r to the year's investment of $10,000 is greater than k, the firm would accept the new pump; otherwise it would reject it.

It has also been suggested[6] that an appropriate way to avoid this confusion is to use the NPV approach, which does not give more than one solution to any proposed project.

INFORMATION

None of the capital budgeting decision criteria we have explored will be very accurate or reliable unless the information used as inputs for the equations is also accurate and reliable. Most firms use a formal procedure for gathering the information on the proposed project. A form similar to Table 5B-3 might be circulated among the interested parties. The purpose is to insure that all the expertise within the company is brought to bear on the evaluation. In your position as financial officer, you will route this type of information-gathering device to all the appropriate personnel.

Once the forms have been filled in and double-checked, it is your job to incorporate the information into one or more of the decision criteria and to present it in report form (Table 5B-4) to those who make the final capital budget decisions.[7]

INFLATION

Capital budgeting decisions very rarely consider inflation, but inflation can and does confuse the picture and distort the evaluation. Inflation is an increase in the price level of the commodities and other inputs which go into the purchase price and the operation of the project. If costs of operation were to rise without an offsetting rise in the selling price of the product produced by the project, the expected stream of cash inflows would be less than had been anticipated. An acceptable project might no longer be acceptable. The original outlay could also rise substantially if its procurement were spread over several years, such as when the firm builds a new factory or plant. These increased costs should actually be incorporated into the decision criteria at the initial evaluation, if they are expected to alter the project's attractiveness.

The financing aspect of the project is also affected by inflation. Dollars are essentially measured in their purchasing power, or what they can buy. When inflation occurs, the dollar is worth less. What a firm owes diminishes in purchasing power

---

[6] J. Hirshleifer, "On the Theory of Optimal Investment Decisions," *Journal of Political Economy*, August 1958, pp. 329–352.

[7] Harold J. Bierman, Jr. and Seymour Smidt, *The Capital Budgeting Decision*, 4th ed., Macmillan, New York, 1971, ch. 13.

Table 5B-3 Typical Project Information Sheet

Proposal   Project No.

	Year 1 19___ low med. high	Year 2 19___ low med. high	Year 3 19___ low med. high	Year 4 19___ low med. high	Year 5 19___ low med. high	Year 6 19___ low med. high
Estimated life:						
A. Sales						
B. Production expenses						
1. Labor						
2. Material						
3. Overhead						
4. Sales promotion						
5. Administrative						
C. Working capital						
1. Accounts receivable						
2. Inventory						
3. Cash balances						
D. Other cash savings and costs						
1. Salvage						
E. Taxes paid						
F. After-tax cash flows						

Routing: Marketing, Production, Finance

Table 5B-4   A Typical Project Reporting Sheet: The Capital Project Information Form

Plant or division:		Date:	
Proposal:		Project no.	

A. Description and justification summary
B. Cash flow estimates (annual)
    Estimated life _____

Year	low	medium	high
1			
2			
3			
4			
5			
6–10			

      Remarks:

C. Risks
D. Summary of decision criteria

	low	medium	high
1. DCF at ____%	_____	_____	_____
2. NPV at ____%	_____	_____	_____
3. IRR	_____	_____	_____
4. Payback	_____	_____	_____
5. Other			

E. Sponsor _____   Prepared by _____
F. Remarks   Date   Initials
    Engineering
    Production
    Marketing
    Comptroller

during inflation. This affects the firm's cost of capital by allowing it to pay off the principal and interest in cheaper dollars. These savings may be recorded by reducing the cost of capital used in the decision criteria.

The decision criteria may be adjusted to account for inflation by stating every component in real terms as if there had been no inflation. For example, we could adjust the estimated production costs upward by some index of inflation to determine how the cashflow might be affected. Despite the numerous examples, particularly in such long-term projects as jet fighter planes, management very rarely considers inflation until it is too late.

6

CAPITAL BUDGETING UNDER
CERTAINTY–MULTIPLE PROJECTS

NO FIRM IS A SINGLE-PROJECT OPERATION with but one investment opportunity for the financial officer to evaluate. Instead the financial officers must choose among many more projects than they could possibly fund. Of course they can immediately weed out those that do not meet their firm's decision criteria, but even then they will almost certainly have more acceptable projects than they can hope to fund. And they may find that they cannot consider each of the acceptable projects in isolation, but that interactions among the projects must be taken into consideration.

As financial officer, you have narrowed the field to a number of investment projects, each of which is acceptable using one or more of the decision criteria in Chapter 5. How do you further analyze them to select the best from among the acceptable? The technique that you will apply to answer that question depends on the firm's financial circumstances at the time and the characteristics of the projects themselves. If the firm has sufficient capital resources, the financial officer will budget as many of the acceptable projects as possible, for each additional project undertaken is another desirable employment of funds by the firm. Yet, even with unlimited capital, the financial officer must have techniques for ranking projects according to their relative attractiveness in an organized fashion which is easily communicated to others in the firm. If the firm has limited funds available, as most firms do, the financial officer must select that collection of acceptable projects which most helps maximize the corporate objective.

The characteristics of the projects themselves may dictate the financial officer's selection. Projects are often mutually exclusive: only one or the other may be selected. In those instances, financial officers have techniques which help them select the most advantageous. Other common special characteristics which may affect the financial officer's capital budgeting are the questions of replacement equipment, pollution abatement equipment, and contingency projects. These capital budgeting categories do not fit as neatly into the selection process as the typical project. How does the financial officer choose among those acceptable projects with special considerations so that the capital budget still maximizes the corporate objective?

RANKING PROCEDURES

How do I select the best from among the acceptable projects, if the firm has an unlimited recourse to the capital market?

It is unusual to find firms with an unlimited ability to raise funds; but even in this case, the financial officer must communicate to others in the firm which projects should be undertaken and in what order. For this, ranking procedures can be used. Further, even though the firm may have unlimited access to the capital markets, previously acceptable projects may become unacceptable because the cost of funds rises despite the fact that there is no limitation on the amount that the firm can raise. We will explore the case of unlimited funds under the unrealistic assumption of a constant cost of funds and under the more realistic assumptions of a rising and of a shifting cost of funds to see how each affects the financial officer's ranking procedures.

Unlimited Funds at a Constant Cost

This very unrealistic situation implies that the firm can raise as much as it wants without increasing the cost it has to pay for those funds. All firms, no matter how good their credit rating, eventually encounter a ceiling beyond which their creditors will not lend them any more or will do so only at a higher rate of interest.

Ranking with NPV Even in a firm which has more funds than it needs for all its acceptable projects, the financial officer will rank them in descending order in terms of the chosen decision criterion. In Table 6-1 the projects are ranked in descending order of their net present value (NPV). All the projects in Table 6-1 except number 8 are acceptable and would be undertaken by a firm with unlimited funds at a constant cost, in order to maximize the net present value of the entire firm. Project 8 is not undertaken because it is unacceptable under the NPV decision criterion. Similar ranking procedures would be used for other decision criteria that use the present-value discounting technique, such as discounted cash flow (DCF).

Ranking with IRR The financial officer can also rank the projects in descending order of their internal rates of return (IRR), as in Table 6-2. The financial officer would undertake the project with the highest IRR first and then proceed to the remaining projects in descending order of IRR until the cutoff point at the cost of funds. If the cost of funds is assumed to be 10 percent, you would undertake all the projects in Table 6-2 except number 8, which is rejected because its IRR is less than the assumed cost of funds.

We can graph the IRR curve as in Figure 6-1. The descending order of the IRR for the projects is reflected in the downward-sloping IRR curve. As the amount of

Table 6-1   Projects Ranked in Descending Order of NPV

Project number	Cost	NPV
1	$ 10,000	$33,000
5	100,000	27,500
3	50,000	26,388
4	67,500	24,732
2	32,000	24,000
6	5,000	18,000
7	43,000	10,000
9	26,000	7,500
10	45,000	3,221
8	125,000	−2,500

Table 6-2

Project number	Cost	IRR
1	$ 10,000	22%
5	100,000	19
4	67,500	18
3	50,000	16
2	32,500	15
6	5,000	14
9	26,000	13
7	43,000	12
10	45,000	11
8	125,000	8

funds invested increases, the firm undertakes an increasing number of projects and is forced to use the lower-yield projects as the ones with the higher IRR are used up. However, as long as the IRR remains above the constant cost of funds line (k), each project undertaken is profitable, and the total net cash inflows to the firm increase. Once the project's IRR drops below the constant cost of funds, the firm experiences a net outflow, and the project is unacceptable.

There are many reasons why the IRR declines. In most instances, the firm simply exhausts the relatively few, very high-yield projects it has immediately available and must start undertaking lower-yield, but nevertheless, profitable projects in order to maximize the firm's worth. Frequently the market for the firm's product may become increasingly saturated or there is a diminishing economy of scale as the operations become larger. Each of these circumstances will cause the next additional project to be less profitable than the prior one.

Ranking with BC The financial officer ranks the projects in descending order of the benefit cost (BC) ratio as illustrated in Table 6-3. Confronted with the ranking in Table 6-3, the finance committee or the board of directors would vote to undertake all the projects except number 8, which would be rejected immediately because its BC ratio is less than one.

Ranking with other decision criteria The financial officer would rank all the projects in a similar fashion regardless of the decision criterion used. If you were using the ter-

Figure 6-1 The IRR Curve at a Constant Cost of Capital

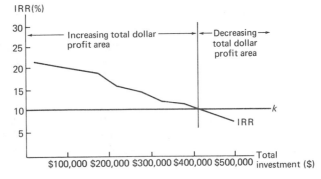

Table 6-3   Ranking with the Benefit/Cost Ratio

Project number	Cost	BC
1	$ 10,000	3.2
5	100,000	2.9
3	50,000	1.9
4	67,500	1.8
2	32,000	1.7
6	5,000	1.6
7	43,000	1.5
9	26,000	1.4
10	45,000	1.1
8	125,000	.9

minal value (TV) technique, you would rank the projects in descending order of their terminal value. Using the payback (PB) technique, you would rank the projects in descending order of the payback period, from the fastest to the slowest, and accept all projects with an acceptable payback period.

Unlimited Funds at a Rising Cost

Let us replace the highly unrealistic assumption of a constant cost of funds with that of a cost of funds which rises as the firm increases the amount of funds it raises. The cost of funds usually increases as the firm continues to go to the capital markets with additional securities to sell, because investors become less receptive to the firm's securities. The upward slope of the cost-of-capital curve is reflected in Figure 6-2. Investors naturally want to hold only a limited amount of any one firm's securities since to diversify is to avoid the risk of putting all their eggs in one basket and seeing that one firm falter because of unforeseen events. The only way additional securities can be sold is for the firm to give investors a greater return and increase the cost of funds. In the extreme, the firm can want so much funds that it influences the entire capital market with a big new issue of securities. (Merely announcing the intention to sell such a large issue causes the cost of funds to increase for every firm, including the issuer itself.)

The combination of the upward-sloping cost-of-funds curve (k) and the downward sloping IRR curve in Figure 6-2 leads to a different cut-off point in the ranking

Figure 6-2 Unlimited Funds at a Rising Cost of Capital

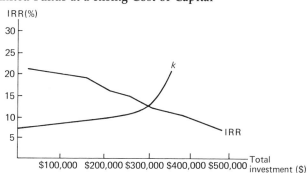

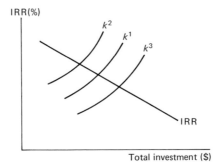

Figure 6-3 Unlimited Funds at a Shifting Cost of Capital

from that of Table 6-2, where we assumed a constant cost of funds. Figure 6-2 argues for acceptance of all projects except numbers 7, 8, and 10, for now those projects have a lower return than the cost of the funds it takes to finance them.

The BC and NPV rankings also reflect the rising cost of funds in their present-value discounting procedures, and fewer projects are acceptable under their rankings.

Unlimited Funds at a Shifting Cost

The real trick for you, as the financial officer, is not to be caught unaware of the shift-in-cost-of-funds curve (k) as illustrated in Figure 6-3. Not only does the cost of funds rise in relation to the volume of funds raised by the firm, but the cost also increases and decreases, or shifts, for any given volume of funds because of factors beyond the control of the financial officer and the firm. For example, interest rates for all securities in the entire capital market can shift upward because of such factors as increased economic activity, which encourages all firms to increase their fund-raising at the same time, putting increased demand on the limited supply of capital, and forcing up the cost of funds.

The effect on your ranking procedures is to increase the number of your acceptable projects, if the IRR curve remains stable and you can raise the funds during a period in which the cost of funds curve has shifted downward to the right (k^3), making funds less costly. If the cost of funds curve shifts up to the left (k^2), reflecting an increased cost, the number of acceptable projects decreases.

This illustrates that the successful financial officer must master the timing of security offerings (more commonly called *flotations*) so as to catch the periods of minimum capital cost—and certainly to avoid the periods of high capital cost. A good financial officer who does catch the period of low capital costs, say at k^3 in Figure 6-3, moves the firm much closer to maximizing its corporate objective, because less expensive capital allows the firm to undertake more acceptable projects and beat the competition.

CAPITAL RATIONING

As financial officer, what analytical techniques do I use to select the best group of projects when the firm has limited funds?

Most firms have a fixed amount of funds they can devote in any one year to investment in capital projects, and typically this amount will support fewer than the

Table 6-4   Projects Ranked by Descending NPV

Project number	Cost	NPV
4	$500	300
5	300	200
2	400	175
3	500	100
1	100	50

number of acceptable projects the firm has available for immediate investment. This situation necessitates what is known to financial officers as *capital rationing*. To carry out capital rationing, you will have to restructure your decision criteria to a certain extent. We will examine the following capital rationing methods and decision criteria: (1) the aggregation method under NPV and DCF; (2) the incremental method under IRR; (3) the BC criterion; (4) postponement analysis; and (5) conflicts in the criteria which result under capital rationing.

Aggregation

The aggregation method for selecting the best projects for the firm's limited funds using the NPV or DCF criterion simply adds together the NPV of all the projects which fit into the available funds and determines which combination of projects maximizes the total NPV, as long as the cost of capital is stable. In Table 6-4 the projects available to one firm with a $1,000 capital limitation are ranked in descending order of NPV.

Since there will be a substantial number of combinations for any relatively large list of projects, it has been suggested[1] that the maximum number in the combination can be narrowed down by ranking the projects in ascending order of their cost and accepting them until the available capital is exhausted. The minimum number in the combination can be narrowed down by ranking the projects in descending order

Table 6-5   Feasible Combinations of Projects within a $1,000 Capital Limitation

Feasible combinations	Aggregate NPV
4,5	$500
4,5,1	550
4,2	475
4,2,1	525
4,3	400
4,1	350
5,2	375
5,2,1	425
5,3	300
5,3,1	350
5,1	250
2,3	275
2,3,1	325
2,1	225
3,1	150

[1] William H. Jean, *Finance*, Dryden Press, Hinsdale, Ill. 1973, pp. 101–105.

of their NPV and accepting in this order until the budget is exhausted. In this way, given our $1,000 capital limitation, Table 6-4 would have immediately showed us that the minimum combination is two and the maximum combination three. We then list all possible project combinations to see which maximizes the aggregate NPV, as in Table 6-5. The combination of projects 4, 5, and 1 maximizes the aggregate NPV, so these should be selected, while the other projects must be either postponed or rejected. This process is tedious unless programmed on a computer, and it does not help us if we are using the IRR decision criterion.

Incremental Analysis and Indivisibilities

Incremental analysis has been suggested[2] as one method of incorporating capital rationing into the IRR decision criterion. As before, you rank the projects in descending order of their IRR. Then you proceed to undertake all projects from the highest IRR down, until the funds are exhausted or the cost of funds (k) is encountered. This is illustrated in Table 6-6. If you had $200,000 to spend, you would undertake projects 1, 5, and 4 for a total outlay of $177,500. You cannot undertake project 3 because you have exhausted your funds. Of course you can see by glancing down the list that project 6 is still acceptable and within your available funds, so you would also undertake that project too.

The problem of selecting the best combination arises because of the *indivisibility* of the projects, which causes leftover available funds. Notice that in Table 6-6 there is a substantial amount of funds left over after implementing project 4 which cannot be used to invest in project 3 because you cannot buy slightly less than half (22,500/50,000) of a project. You cannot buy half a truck or half a milling machine; you must buy all or none of it. Unless you can find an acceptable use for $22,500 excess dollars, you will not have maximized the total return from your available funds, for the excess will sit idle or earn less than your cost of capital in low-yield assets.

You could take the excess $22,500 and put it into a lower-yield project down the list such as project number 6, which is within the available funds. But, even if we undertake project 6, we are left with $17,500 of excess available funds and no acceptable projects. The funds would probably have to be placed in temporary security

Table 6-6   IRR Ranking under Capital Rationing

Project number	Cost	IRR	Funds available
1	$ 10,000	22%	$200,000
5	100,000	19	190,000
4	67,500	18	90,000
3	50,000	16	22,500
2	32,500	15	22,500
6	5,000	14	22,500
9	26,000	13	17,500
7	43,000	12	17,500
10	45,000	11	17,500
8	125,000	8	17,500

[2] James H. Lorie and Leonard J. Savage, "Three Problems in Capital Rationing," *Journal of Business*, October 1955, and reprinted in Ezra Solomon, *The Management of Corporate Capital*, The Free Press, New York, 1959, pp. 56–66.

investments yielding less than the firm's cost of funds and detracting from the maximization objective. Alternatively, the financial officer could stretch the firm's borrowings a little and come up with the additional $27,500 required to undertake project 3 and exactly exhaust the available funds. This is frequently more difficult than it would appear, however, because funds are raised in blocks at one time, and short-term borrowings available to stretch the budget may be inappropriate for investment in long-term projects.

Incremental analysis tells you whether giving up a relatively small but high-yield project frees enough funds for you to undertake a larger but lower-yield project *which will increase the total return.* In Table 6-6, you could forfeit project number 1 to free $10,000, which when added to the $22,500 excess would allow you to undertake project number 2. But is it worth giving up project 1 to invest the excess funds in project 2? The answer depends on the return to the additional $22,500 which you can now invest. You have given up project 1, the investment of the excess cash in a low-yield security, and project number 6, and the cashflow from each of those investments is lost. But the cashflow from investing $32,500 in project 2 at 15 percent is gained. You must determine if the additional inflow from the difference of the two streams is worth the incremental cost of the more expensive project. We can express the decision rule as follows:

$$\Delta C = \sum_{t=1}^{n} \frac{F_{tL} - [F_{tH} + F_{tE}]}{r} \tag{6-1}$$

where

ΔC = the incremental cost
F_{tL} = the net cashflows to the lower-yield project over its life
F_{tH} = the net cashflows to the higher-yield project(s)
F_{tE} = the net cashflow to the excess funds
r = the IRR of the incremental stream
$\sum_{t=1}^{n}$ = the sum of these cashflows over the life of the longest lived project

In our example from Table 6-6, assuming a 1-year life for each project and a 6 percent yield on the excess funds:

$\Delta C = \$17,500$
$F_{tL} = \$4875$
F_{tH} (project 1) = 2200
F_{tH} (project 6) = 700
$F_{tE} = \$1050$

$$\$17,500 = \frac{\$4875 - (\$2200 + \$700 + \$1050)}{r}$$

$r = 5.2\%$

Since the IRR for the incremental investment is a relatively low 5.2 percent, we would undertake projects 1 and 6 and reject project 2. Notice, however, that the plan did increase the total net cashflows to the firm to $4875 from the $3950 for projects 1 and 6 and excess cash combined. We must compare the IRR on the incremental investment to the cost of capital in order to judge the desirability of investing in the large project because, if for no other reason, the excess funds could be used to repurchase the shares of the company on the open market, which yields at least the going cost of capital. Or the excess funds could be temporarily invested if it were obvious that high-yield projects would be available the next year and the financial officer did not want to tie up funds for several years in a relatively large low-yield project.

NPV and Indivisibilities

When ranking by the NPV or the DCF, you will also encounter indivisibilities which may leave you with excess cash. And you have the same choices: (1) undertake a project with a lower NPV in order to absorb the excess funds; (2) stretch the budget a little and look for some additional funds; or (3) perform an incremental analysis to see if it might be desirable to sacrifice a few small projects with high NPV's, freeing enough funds for the firm to undertake a larger but lower-NPV project which would absorb all the excess funds.

Benefit/Cost Ratio and Capital Rationing

When ranking the projects in descending order of their BC ratios under capital rationing, the financial officer must be aware that some peculiarities may cause the ranking to deviate from under the NPV criterion and lead to contradictory results.

We can see in Table 6-7 that the BC criterion ranks the projects in a different order than the NPV criterion does. For example, project 5 is now more highly ranked (despite its lower NPV) than projects 3, 2, and 4. This is because the BC ratio reflects the benefits (present discounted value) per dollar of cost, while the NPV reflects the absolute amount of benefits in excess of cost. This may lead to a confusing dilemma. Which project, for example, should you recommend for adoption first: project 5 because it has the higher BC or project 3 because it has the higher NPV?

Confusion arises because of the scaling problem associated with the BC ratio and the indivisibilities at the cutoff point. The BC ratio compensates for the difference in cost of the projects by comparing every project in terms of a ratio which hides the differences in size. The financial officer may spend most of the available funds on many small projects, thereby cutting off some highly acceptable, larger project which might have produced an even higher aggregate NPV because of its size and its absorption of any excess funds which could not be put to use in the small projects with the higher BC ratios.

The confusion is resolved in the same way we handled the NPV and indivisibilities. We have already seen that, because of the indivisibilities, it may be preferable to invest all available funds at a higher total NPV than to invest part of the funds in relatively small projects with higher BC ratios and the remaining funds in low-BC projects. Of course, in Table 6-7, if there were sufficient funds available,

Table 6-7   Ranking by BC Ratio

Project number	PDV	Cost	NPV	BC
1	$ 7,500	$ 5,000	$2,500	1.5
5	1,500	1,000	500	1.5
3	7,000	5,000	2,000	1.4
2	12,000	10,000	2,000	1.2
4	21,000	20,000	1,000	1.05
6	5,000	5,000	0	1.0
7	5,500	6,000	−500	.88

you would have accepted all the projects with *either* a positive NPV or a BC ratio greater than one, and the contradictory rankings would have no affect on your capital budget.

Postponement Analysis

The firm may be able to postpone until another period some of the projects it cannot undertake in this period because of capital rationing. *Postponement analysis*[3] is a technique for determining which projects are the most postponable in the sense that their delay occasions the least cost to the firm. If we were using the BC ratio, the most postponable projects would be those which suffered the least decline in that ratio by waiting one period. It would not be advisable, for example, to postpone a project which depended for its sales on a temporary fad like the hula-hoop or some other fleeting fashion. Such a project will obviously be more adversely affected by postponement than a project which has a longer and more stable pattern of sales. If possible, of course, you would accept all projects which have a BC ratio greater than one and reject all projects with a BC ratio less than one, and postponement analysis would not be necessary. This technique is only needed when capital rationing makes it necessary to forego or postpone certain acceptable projects.

How do I determine the postponability of each project? First, you rank the acceptable projects in descending order of their BC ratio (as in Table 6-8) and then compute the net present value of each project (*i*) as of the present time (*t* = 0) to derive NPV_{i0} in Table 6-8. Next you must recompute each project's NPV as if the project had been started 1 year later, being sure to consider any increase in the cost of the project or changes in its expected cashflow pattern because of the 1-year post-

Table 6-8   Postponement Analysis

Project number	Cost	BC ($k = 10\%$)	NPV_{i0}	NPV_{i1}
1	$ 1,000	2.1	$1,100	$ 800
2	2,000	1.9	1,800	1,000
3	500	1.8	400	500
4	1,000	1.7	700	700
5	1,000	1.5	500	250
6	10,000	1.3	3,000	1,000
7	5,000	1.1	500	400

$$\text{Postponement Index} = \frac{NPV_{i0} - NPV_{i1}}{\text{Cost}}$$

Project number	Postponement index
1	.30
2	.40
3	−.20
4	0
5	.25
6	.20
7	.02

[3] G. David Quirin, *The Capital Expenditure Decision.* Irwin, Homewood, Ill., 1967, pp. 181–185.

ponement, and discount that back to the present time ($t = 0$) to derive the NPV_{i1} in Table 6-8. NPV_{i0} reflects the present value of the project if undertaken in this period, and NPV_{i1} reflects the present value of the project as of this period if undertaking it has been postponed until next period.

The difference between the two NPVs is the cost of postponement. We can rank each project according to its relative postponement cost, which is measured as the difference between the two NPVs in relation to the project's cost and is shown in the lower portion of Table 6-8. As the postponement index decreases, the loss to postponement also decreases. In fact, project 3 with its negative postponement index actually increases in value because of the 1-year delay and is clearly the most readily postponable, while project 4 experiences no expected loss because of the delay. As financial officer, you would recommend that the projects with the lowest postponement index be the first to be delayed. Of course you would not automatically undertake the postponed projects in the following year but would compare them to the projects available in the succeeding year, selecting the delayed ones only if they were among the best.

Ranking Under Capital Rationing—
A Review of the Problems

Let us pause here to review the various problems which have arisen in preparing the capital budget, particularly in a situation of capital rationing.

The scale problem Under capital rationing the size of the project may cause a different ranking order depending on whether you are using NPV or BC as the decision criterion, although the accept-reject decision will be the same for any project in either case.

The timing of the cashflows Whereas the IRR method assumes that the reinvestment rate is equal to the internal rate of return on the project itself, the NPV method assumes that the reinvestment rate is equal to the external cost of funds (k) for the firm (see Appendix 5B). Because of this assumption, we can sometimes get conflicting results in the decision criteria. In the following example, the DCF of project D is higher than the DCF of project C, but the IRR of project C is higher than the IRR of project D.

Year	Project C	Project D
0	($1,000)	($1,000)
1	1,200	
2		
3		
4		1,873
IRR	20%	17%
DCF ($k = 10\%$)	1,091	1,279

This contradiction in the decision criteria arises because of differences in the timing of the cash inflows and the assumed rate at which they can be reinvested. Projects with large and rapid cash inflows may appear attractive if the reinvestment rate is high, while the same projects may appear relatively less attractive than some other project if the reinvestment rate is low.

Indivisibilities Indivisibility may cause some acceptable project to be squeezed out of the budget because it can only be partly financed. Resulting excess funds may have to be invested at a relatively low rate of return, causing the aggregate return or NPV to the firm to be lower than it could be.

Postponement In a capital rationing situation, the firm may be forced to postpone acceptable projects because of a lack of funds. Under these circumstances the firm selects the projects which are the most postponable in the sense that they suffer the least reduction in their NPV because of the delay.

A Partial Resolution of the Problems

We can partially resolve some of the problems if we can stretch the firm's borrowing of funds past the capital rationing point CR to CR' in Figure 6-4, the point where the cost of capital on a continuously rising curve (k) intersects the downward-sloping IRR curve. At that point the internal reinvestment rate on the last acceptable whole project is equal to the external cost of capital for the firm. If we use that opportunity cutoff point as the discount factor in our NPV decision criterion, we have max-imized our position under both the NPV and the IRR methods. For example, of-fered the projects shown in Table 6-9, if we had $48,000 in available funds we would stretch our borrowings to $50,000 so that we could include the next whole project, number 5. This would raise our cost of capital to 16 percent on both an internal and external basis. If, in addition, we used the terminal-value approach to help us cope with changing reinvestment levels throughout the lives of the projects, we would have resolved still another ambiguity in the capital budget decision criteria.

By stretching our fund raising to the point where the external cost of capital equals the internal rate of return on the last acceptable project which exhausts our available funds, and then by using that rate in the terminal-value decision criterion to account for any fluctuations in the reinvestment rate over time, we partially resolve all four problems. The timing of the cashflow problem has been simplified because the reinvestment rate is equalized under both methods and adjusted for fluctuations over time. The postponement problem is resolved because we are forc-ing a cutoff point in this period by stretching our borrowing to the point where the increased cost of funds has made unacceptable all projects but those which fit into this period's budget. The indivisibilities have been taken care of by stretching the

Figure 6-4 The Effect of Stretching Our Borrowing

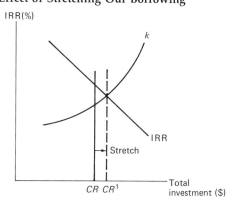

Table 6-9

	Project number	Cost	IRR	Available funds
	1	$10,000	25%	$48,000
	2	10,000	20	38,000
Original capital	3	10,000	19	38,000
rationing →	4	10,000	17	18,000
Stretched funds →	5	10,000	16	8,000
	6	10,000	15	0
	7	10,000	14	0
	8	10,000	13	0

budget to include the next whole project in the ranking. The scale problem has been eliminated because we undertake all acceptable projects in descending order of their relative attractiveness regardless of the size, for we have stretched the budget to include all the top-ranked projects. This also eliminated the ambiguities in ranking between the BC ratio and the NPV.

Not all the ambiguities have been resolved, because by stretching the funds and raising the cost of capital in this period, we still have not considered the projects which may be available in future periods to make it attractive for us to temporarily store some funds. We will discuss this problem later.

Other methods for resolving some of the problems and ambiguities of the capital budgeting decision criteria which develop under capital rationing are found in Appendix 6A. The more mathematically inclined student is referred there for a discussion of linear and mathematical programming applications to capital budgeting.

OTHER CONSIDERATIONS

As financial officer, how do I handle such other considerations in the capital budgeting process as mutually exclusive projects, contingency projects, replacement projects, pollution equipment, and multiperiod considerations?

Mutually Exclusive Projects

Sometimes two acceptable projects cannot both be undertaken because they have conflicting resource uses, such as the conflict which arises over whether to build a distributing center or a manufacturing plant on a piece of company-owned property, or whether to manufacture the product or buy it from another manufacturer. It is possible that both alternatives are acceptable projects under the decision criterion being used, but only one may be undertaken. How do we make sure that we undertake the best, and how does this mutually exclusive characteristic affect the ranking procedures we have been discussing?

The answer is relatively simple if the projects are ranked on a comparable basis such as the terminal-value approach, where the reinvestment rate is explicit. The project with the higher terminal value of the two alternatives is undertaken. For example, if projects 2 and 3 in Table 6-10 were mutually exclusive, the higher of the two in rank (project 2) is undertaken and the lower (project 3) is foregone entirely. If we had a $50,000 capital constraint, which would have been enough to finance the first 5 projects in Table 6-10, our inability to undertake project 3 has now freed $10,000, and we can now undertake the next highest ranking project (number 6).

Table 6-10   Ranking with Mutually Exclusive Projects

Project number	Cost	NPV of terminal value (terminal value − cost)
1	$10,000	$20,000
2	10,000	19,000
3	10,000	18,000
4	10,000	17,000
5	10,000	16,000
6	10,000	15,000
7	10,000	12,000
8	10,000	11,000

The incremental approach also helps select the best projects from among a group of mutually exclusive acceptable projects.[4] As financial officer, you can determine if the additional inflows warrant the additional investment in undertaking a large project in favor of dropping a less costly one, if the two are mutually exclusive. This can be done by first finding the project with the smallest outlay. Then determine the incremental IRR on the difference in the cash inflows between it and the project with the next to smallest cost. If the incremental IRR is greater than the cost of capital (k), we would undertake the larger project instead of the smaller one, since the extra investment is an acceptable project. If there were more than two mutually exclusive projects in this group, we would repeat the process to determine if the incremental IRR of the next least costly project is greater or less than that of the project just accepted. If its incremental IRR is greater than the cost of capital, we would accept it and forego the previously accepted project. For example, assume that the cost of capital is 6 percent and that all the projects in Table 6-11 are mutually exclusive so that we can choose only one. Incremental analysis first compares the smallest project (number 4) with the next smallest (number 3). The additional investment to move from project 4 to project 3 is $1,000, and the incremental cashflow

Table 6-11   Mutually Exclusive Acceptable Projects

Project number	Cost	IRR	Cashflows/year
1	$9,000	7%	$3,429.46 for 3 years
2	8,000	14	3,445.31 for 3 years
3	6,000	8	1,811.60 for 4 years
4	5,000	12	2,081.60 for 3 years

Incremental IRR

Project	Additional investment	Incremental cashflows	Incremental IRR
4 versus 3	$1,000	−$ 270.00 (years 1–3) + 1,811.60 (year 4)	less than 1%
4 versus 2	3,000	+ 1,363.71 (years 1–3)	16% approx.
2 versus 1	1,000	− 15.85 (years 1–3)	negative

[4] Lorie and Savage, *op. cit.* "Three Problems." pp. 227–239.

is −$270 in each of the first three years and $1,811.60 in the fourth year. However, this incremental cashflow has less than a 1 percent IRR and must be rejected. Still using project 4 as the standard, after rejecting project 3, we compare it to project 2 and see that the incremental cashflows provide a 16 percent return to the additional investment, so we accept project 2 in favor of project 4. Finally, we must compare project 2 with project 1. Here the decision is obvious: the incremental cashflow stream is negative, so there is no benefit at all of committing an additional $1,000 to undertake project 1. Of the four mutually exclusive projects, we would undertake number 2 since it has an incremental IRR in excess of the cost of capital.

Contingency Projects

Sometimes the firm can undertake a particular project if and only if it undertakes yet another project; the first project is contingent upon the undertaking of the second. But, the firm may wish to rank the projects separately, as if they were independent. For example, a large oil company was thinking of constructing an oil unloading and storage facility which would serve as a distribution center and which would be very profitable. However, they could only build the loading and storage facility if the water approach was deepened and if a very expensive sea wall was constructed. The facility and the sea wall were evaluated separately because the firm wanted to have the corps of engineers build the sea wall. The firm hoped to convince the corps of engineers of the sea wall's desirability since the corps had a much lower cost of capital which might make the project acceptable to them despite the fact that it was, by itself, unacceptable to the firm at its higher cost of capital.

Table 6-12 reflects this situation. Project 1 is the loading and storage facility and project 5 is the sea wall. Normally the firm would reject project 5 because its BC ratio is less than one, but since project 1 is contingent upon the undertaking of project 5, you would have to take the weighted average of projects 1 and 5 combined to determine their desirability, unless you could convince the corps of engineers to undertake project 5. For example,

$$
\begin{array}{rl}
10,000 \times 1.9 = & 19.0 \\
3,000 \times .9 = & \underline{2.7} \\
& 21.7
\end{array}
$$

The weighted average of 1 and $5 = \dfrac{21.7}{13,000} = 1.669$. The combined project is still acceptable, but now it would rank third on Table 6-12.

Replacement Projects

Sometimes, instead of analyzing a project as expansionary, the financial officer is required to evaluate the project as a replacement for an existing project. This could occur if the firm were replacing obsolescent equipment or plant. For example, an oil

Table 6-12   Ranking Contingency Projects

Project number	Cost	BC
1	$10,000	1.90
2	5,000	1.80
3	20,000	1.75
4	7,000	1.6
5	3,000	.9

Table 6-13   Replacement Project Analysis

Period	Net after-tax[5] cashflow, new pumps	Net after-tax cashflow, old pumps	Replacement cashflow
1	$70	$50	+20
2	50	40	+10
3	30	20	+10
4	20	10	+10
5	15	0	+15

New pump cost = $100
Old pump salvage value = 0
Present value of replacement stream ($k = 10\%$) = $50.10
Decision: Reject purchase of new pump

company may wish to replace a pump which, although still functioning, was considerably slower than the newer, more rapid pumps. By replacing the old pump, the firm can get the oil up faster, more efficiently, and more completely. This means the firm can get a larger cashflow stream sooner, but in the process, of course, it destroys the old cashflow stream of the original pump. The question is whether or not the additional cashflow generation of the new pump is worth the additional investment in the new pump. Table 6-13 shows that the purchase of the new pump at a cost of $100 will increase the cash inflows to the firm in each of the 5 years of the life of the new pump. In fact, since the new pump is able to get deeper into the well, the entire cashflow in year 5 is additional income. The difference between the newly created stream of inflows and the destroyed stream of old inflows is the stream of benefits to the replacement project itself. It is this stream which must be discounted to its present value, not the newly created stream. Since the replacement project's present value at 10 percent is less than the cost of the new pump, we reject the project and continue with the old pump.

Minimum average annual cumulative cost replacement analysis This method of replacement analysis concentrates on minimizing the operating cost in order to pinpoint the period in which to replace the equipment, rather than analyzing the increment stream of cash inflows associated with the replacement, as we did above. This operating efficiency analysis is typically applied to the equipment used in the daily operations of the firm, such as delivery trucks, as opposed to the larger capital replacement projects. Under this analysis we would determine the optimal trade-in point by locating the year in which the average operating costs were minimized. For example, in Table 6-14 it is clear that the minimum average annual cumulative cost for this equipment, costing $10,000 and depreciated over a 5-year life by the double declining balance method (see Appendix 5A), is minimized at the end of year 3. After year 3 the average annual cumulative cost begins to rise because of the greater operating cost; prior to year 3 the cost is higher because of the higher depreciation expense.

This method of replacement analysis has several drawbacks. It assumes that the replacement is equal to the original and that there is no improvement in operating efficiency gained by replacement. Furthermore, there is no consideration for the time value of money, since there is no discounting involved in determining the op-

---

[5] If there were a salvage value to be considered, it would have to be adjusted to include the effect of any taxes arising from the transaction.

Table 6-14   Minimum Average Annual Cumulative Replacement Analysis

1	2	3	4 = (2) + (3)	5	6 = (5)/(1)
Year	Depreciation	Operating costs	Annual total cost	Cumulative total cost	Average annual cumulative total cost
1	$4,000	$ 500	$4,500	$ 4,500	$4,500
2	2,400	1,000	3,400	7,900	3,950
3	1,440	1,500	2,940	10,840	3,613
4	864	3,500	4,364	15,204	3,801
5	518	5,000	5,518	20,712	4,142

Cost = $10,000
Depreciated by the double declining balance method over a 5-year expected life

timal replacement period. Drawbacks notwithstanding, this analysis is considerably better than no analysis or just waiting for the original equipment to wear out before replacing it.

Minimum average annual cumulative cost with increased operating efficiency replacement analysis More often, replacement analysis must consider the improved operating efficiencies to be gained by replacing the old equipment with the newer models. In that case, the financial officer would have to adjust the above analysis to include the operating improvements. If we assume that the model to be replaced has the cost figures shown in Table 6-14 and that the new model, which is twice as efficient, has the cost figures shown in Table 6-15, then the optimal replacement year for the new model is also year 3. But *should* the firm replace the old model of Table 6-14 with the new model of Table 6-15? The average annual cumulative cost for the old model in year 3 is $3,613; it is $3,650 for the new model. Since the new model does twice the work of the old model, we have to double the old model's cost figures before making the comparison:

$$\text{Old model} \quad (2 \times \$10,840)/3 = \$7,226.76$$
$$\text{New model} \quad (1 \times \$10,950)/3 = \$3,650.00$$

The new model is clearly the preferred choice.

MAPI replacement analysis The MAPI (Machinery and Allied Products Institute) method is associated with the name of George Terborgh.[6] It improves upon the minimum average annual cumulative cost analysis by considering the present

Table 6-15   Cost Figures for More Efficient Model

Year	Depreciation	Operating costs	Annual total	Cumulative total	Average annual cumulative total
1	$4,800	$ 300	$5,100	$ 5,100	$5,100
2	2,900	550	3,450	8,550	4,275
3	1,500	900	2,400	10,950	3,650
4	1,000	3,000	4,000	14,950	3,738
5	600	4,000	4,600	19,550	7,820

[6] George Terborgh, *Dynamic Equipment Policy*, McGraw-Hill, New York, 1949.

value of the deteriorating efficiency of the machinery and the present value of the capital costs to determine the optimal replacement point for similar equipment. Assuming a cost of $100,000 and no salvage value, the MAPI analysis would look like Table 6-16, where optimal replacement is at the end of year 5, the year of minimum time-adjusted average annual cost. This is typically called the *adverse minimum* and is associated with the optimal replacement point under the MAPI analysis. Notice that the operating deterioration not only reflects the increased cost of operating the equipment but is also discounted back to the present for the time value of money.

If this were a replacement analysis with increased efficiency of operation instead of the straight replacement, we would have to include a time-adjusted factor for the efficiency of the replacement. If the time-adjusted annual average total cost for the old equipment for the next year and each subsequent year to the end of its life is greater than that of the new equipment, we would replace the old.[7]

Table 6-16   MAPI Replacement Analysis

Year	(1) Deterioration in operating efficency	(2) Present value $(k = 10\%)$ of (1)	(3) Cumulative present value of (1)
1	0	0	0
2	$10,000	$ 8,260	$ 8,260
3	20,000	15,020	23,260
4	30,000	20,490	43,750
5	40,000	24,840	68,590
6	50,000	28,250	96,840

(4) Capital recovery factors[1]	(5) = (3) × (4) Annual coverage operating deterioration	(6) = $100,000 × (4) Capital costs	(7) = (5) + (6) Total cumulative costs
1.000	0	$100,000	$100,000
.5762	$ 4,759.00	57,620	62,379
.4021	9,353.00	40,210	49,563
.3155	13,803.00	31,550	45,353
.2638	18,094.00	26,380	44,474
.2296	22,234.00	22,960	45,194

[1] The capital recovery factor is:

$$\frac{i(1 + i)^n}{(1 + i)^{n-1}}$$

which can be read off tables of engineering economy available from MAPI, but which we should recognize as the compounding factor divided by the regular compound annuity factor, given n and i. The concept behind the capital recovery factor is to incorporate the compounding factor on the capital recovered and reinvested, while at the same time discounting for the time value of money lost while waiting for the capital recovery.

[7] Gerald A. Fleischer, *Capital Allocation Theory: The Study of Investment Decisions*, Appleton, 1969, Ch. 8, pp. 125–142. See also Eugene L. Grant, Lawrence F. Bell, and W. Grant Ireson, *Principles of Engineering Economy 4th ed.*, Ronald Press, New York, 1964.

Pollution Equipment

There are basically two ways of looking at pollution abatement projects: (1) they are compulsory under the law; or (2) the alternatives are to close, move, relocate internationally, take court action to stop the requirement, or pay the fines.

Compulsory under law If the installation of pollution abatement equipment is viewed as a legal requirement for the continuation of the firm, it must receive top priority in the capital budget despite the fact that it will not increase cash inflows to the firm. When society, through its governmental authorities, shifts the burden of reducing dirty water and air to the firm, the firm must bear the cost.

Pollution projects involving costly equipment must be undertaken to meet government regulations. The only way these projects can be budgeted is to determine the requirement under the law for the year and to set aside a corresponding amount of available funds off the top of the budget. Any remaining funds can then be allocated using the decision criteria and methods of analysis presented so far.

Alternatives The firm does not have to look upon pollution abatement projects as inevitable. It can relocate to an area with less stringent pollution regulations, either within the United States or in some other country. In the extreme it can close down a particular plant or the entire firm. The evaluation of the alternatives is similar to the evaluation of projects for their acceptability. Is the stream of cash inflows remaining in the life of the plant worth the incremental cost of the required pollution abatement equipment and the alternative use of the salvage value of the plant? The decision criterion is as follows:

$$S + C = \sum_{t=1}^{n} \frac{CF_t}{(1+r)^t}$$

where

  S = the salvage value of the old plant
  C = the cost of the pollution equipment
  r = the internal rate of return
  CF_t = the yearly cashflow in the remaining life of the project

If the internal rate of return (r) is less than the cost of capital, then the firm should close the plant and reinvest the salvage value elsewhere. If r is greater than the cost of capital, the firm should install the pollution equipment, for the investment is warranted.

Multiperiod Horizons

The financial officer may evaluate projects and plan his or her capital budget on a one-year basis. This, of course, has its limitations. A one-year time horizon and plan prevents you from knowing what acceptable projects may appear in the next period which might have to be foregone because of your decisions in this period. A very attractive project might have to be excluded from next year's capital budget because you did not set aside available funds this year.

Interrelationships among the periods are also not considered in a one-year time horizon. As a financial officer, you might attempt to handle this problem with postponement analysis, but that still does not give you more than one further period of analysis. It is also tempting, under one-period analysis, to bring in a few less attractive projects with quick cash throwoffs in their earlier years and relatively unattractive prospects thereafter to relieve the strain of capital rationing. This ties up your funds in later periods and may force you to forego high-yield projects which you might have seen coming if you had used *multiperiod analysis.* Although you should consider several consecutive periods in your capital budget preparation, it is a time-consuming and highly uncertain task. Appendix 6A explains how mathematical programming can help handle some of the problems of multiperiod analysis.

SUMMARY

After having read Chapter 6, you should be able to answer these questions:

1. Once I have selected a number of investment projects, each of which is acceptable using one or more of the criteria in Chapter 5, how do I distinguish among them to insure that I undertake the best, assuming that the firm has unlimited recourse to the capital markets?

Ranking procedures allow us to select the best from among the many acceptable projects. We list the projects in descending order of their relative attractiveness under the chosen decision criterion and undertake all projects as long as the funds are available and the project acceptable under the decision criterion. Even under the unrealistic assumption of unlimited recourse to the capital markets, the financial officer must anticipate shifts in the cost of funds in order to time investments for the least expensive capital cost and thereby make the firm more competitive and profitable.

2. If the firm's access to the capital markets is limited, how do I select the best set of acceptable projects within the capital constraints?

When operating under capital rationing, it is necessary to consider the effects of indivisibilities and scale on the ranking procedures. If excess funds remain available because the next lowest ranked project cannot be completely undertaken, it becomes necessary to determine if some aggregation of the acceptable projects will lead to a higher total NPV or yield because it allows employment of these excess funds (and despite the sacrifice of some smaller, high-yield projects). We also saw how the use of incremental analysis and postponement analysis helped in preparing a capital budget under rationing, and we examined the effect of stretching the budget in order to resolve the contradictory results of the different reinvestment assumptions.

3. How do I handle such other capital budgeting problems as mutually exclusive, contingency, replacement, and pollution abatement projects?

Incremental analysis, again, allows us to determine the best of a group of mutually exclusive projects. The replacement projects require that the incremental cashflow between that which was sacrificed in the replacement and the newly created cashflow had to have a greater present discounted value than the cost of the replacement equipment. We saw that replacement decisions are frequently based on operating efficiency criteria rather than capital budgeting criteria. Finally, we explored the alternatives to the required installation of pollution abatement equipment and decided that if the rate of return to the old plant with the abatement equipment was sufficiently high to justify its cost, we should install the equipment and continue in operation at the present location; otherwise we should close or relocate the plant.

QUESTIONS

6-1 Ranking projects with the net present value (NPV) and internal rate of return (IRR) methods sometimes yields conflicting preferences. What factors may account for these different rankings?

6-2 What is capital rationing?

6-3 Suppose the ranking of projects according to the IRR method leaves you with considerable funds that cannot be invested due to indivisibilities. As financial officer, what alternatives might you suggest?

6-4 Discuss, within the framework of the IRR method of ranking projects, how the following external factors may affect the capital budgeting decisions of the firm. Use a graph similar to Figure 6-2 to illustrate your analysis.
  (a) The Federal Reserve System engages in an effort to reduce the rate of growth in the money supply.
  (b) Congress passes a law allowing an investment tax credit of 10 percent.
  (c) Congress passes a law speeding up the rate of accelerated depreciation on capital projects.

6-5 The following graph depicts the cost of capital k and the IRR for a firm with only $100,000 in funds available for investment.

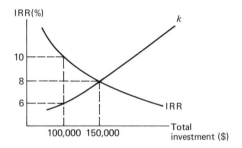

Discuss the following statement: "The reinvestment rate of the IRR and NPV methods are only equal at the margin where no indivisibilities or capital rationing occurs."

6-6 Under what conditions might a firm choose to pay a pollution tax rather than install pollution control equipment?

6-7 Many firms continue to use obsolete machinery long after new, more efficient equipment is available. Under what circumstances would this represent poor financial planning?

PROBLEMS

6-1 The Multiplex Company is considering expanding its investment budget to include projects A, B, and C. The expected costs and cashflows are as follows:

Year	Project A cashflow	Project B cashflow	Project C cashflow
1	$12,000	5,000	4,000
2	12,000	5,000	4,000
3	12,000	5,000	4,000
Cost	28,000	10,000	9,000

(a) Assuming the firm's cost of capital is 6 percent, rank the projects according to the following criteria:
  (1) Net present value (NPV)
  (2) Internal rate of return (IRR)
  (3) Benefit/cost ratio (BC)
(b) Note and discuss differences in the ranking order of the projects using the three methods in (a).
(c) Using the IRR method of ranking projects, which projects will be accepted if the firm's cost of capital is 6 percent and unlimited capital is available. Illustrate graphically.
(d) Using the IRR method of ranking projects, which projects will be invested in if the firm's cost of capital increases to 14 percent. Illustrate graphically.

6-2 The Multiplex company has estimated the cashflows for the following two mutually exclusive projects:

Year	Project A	Project B
0	-$100,000	-$200,000
1	40,000	0
2	40,000	0
3	40,000	0
4	40,000	0
5	40,000	400,000

(a) Calculate the internal rate of return for each project. Which project is preferred?
(b) Calculate the net present value of each project. Which project is preferred? Assume the firm's cost of capital is 6 percent.
(c) What assumptions embodied in the internal rate of return and net present value methods of project evaluation influenced your decisions in (a) and (b)? Can you reconcile the dilemma?

6-3 Using the incremental internal rate of return method, determine which of the following three mutually exclusive projects is preferable.

Project	Cost	IRR (approximate)	Cashflows per year
A	$20,000	13%	$5,000 for 6 years
B	15,000	10	4,000 for 5 years
C	10,000	8	3,000 for 4 years

Assume the firm's cost of capital is 7 percent.

6-4 Datamax Company is contemplating replacing its present computer printer with a new, more efficient model. The present printer has a remaining life of 3 years, with expected net cashflows of $10,000 per year, and no salvage value. The new printer will contribute an annual net cashflow of $15,000 for 5 years and has a salvage value of $10,000. The new printer costs $45,000.
(a) Using the internal rate of return method, should the firm replace its present computer printer with the newer model? The firm's cost of capital is 8 percent.
(b) Using the net present value method, should the firm replace its present printer with the newer model?

6-5 A county in which Goodtire Company manufactures automobile tires recently passed stringent air pollution standards that will apply to the firm. Engineers have estimated the cost of the required pollution abatement equipment to be $250,000. The Goodtire plant will be obsolete in 3 years, and its current salvage value is $400,000. If production is continued for the next 3 years, an annual cashflow of $300,000 is expected. Management is faced with the alternative of either installing the pollution control equipment or closing the plant now. Which alternative do you suggest Goodtire follow? Assume Goodtire has a cost of capital of 12 percent.

BIBLIOGRAPHY

Baumol, William J., and Richard E. Quandt. "Investment and Discount Rates Under Capital Rationing—A Programming Approach." *The Economic Journal,* LXXV (June 1965), 317–329.

Bernhard, Richard H. "Mathematical Programming Models for Capital Budgeting—A Survey, Generalization, and Critique." *Journal of Financial and Quantitative Analysis,* IV (June 1969), 111–158.

Lorie, James H., and Leonard J. Savage. "Three Problems in Rationing Capital." *Journal of Business,* XXVIII (October 1955), pp. 227–239.

Robichek, Alexander A., and James C. Van Horne. "Abandonment Value and Capital Budgeting." *Journal of Finance,* XXII (December 1967), 577–590.

Weingartner, H. Martin. "Capital Budgeting of Interrelated Projects: Survey and Synthesis." *Management Science,* 12 (March 1966), 485–516.

———. *Mathematical Programming and the Analysis of Capital Budgeting Problems.* Prentice-Hall, Englewood Cliffs, N.J., 1962.

Appendix 6A **Mathematical Programming in Capital Budgeting**

LINEAR PROGRAMMING

Linear programming is a common type of mathematical programming designed to maximize or minimize some objective function subject to the constraints of the situation. There is always some objective towards which the firm, through its management and its financial officer, strives. But we never completely get there because the resources we have are limited. Linear programming expresses both the objective and the resource constraints in a mathematical form and tells us how far we *can* progress toward maximizing our objective within our limitations.

The Objective Function

The objective function is a mathematical expression of our objective. It relates the use of the resources which are important in achieving that objective to the objective itself. For example, if we had a total profit maximization objective (P) and only two products (X_1 and X_2), each of which contributed $3 and $4 per unit, respectively, to total profits, we could state our profit-maximization objective function as:

$$P = 3X_1 + 4X_2 \qquad (6A\text{-}1)$$

The optimum point, where P is maximized, depends on our ability to produce X_1 and X_2. As the number of units produced and sold increases, total profit would also increase. However, since the situation is constrained, we cannot probably produce or sell as much of each product as we would like, but must allocate our limited resources between the two products so that total profit is maximized within the constraints.

Linear programming can also be applied to capital budgeting decisions. For example, our objective function might be to maximize the net present value of the projects undertaken. If we had four acceptable projects (X_1, X_2, X_3, X_4) which contributed a NPV of $10, $15, $20, and $25, respectively, our new profit-maximization objective function would be:

$$\text{NPV} = 10X_1 + 15X_2 + 20X_3 + 25X_4 \qquad (6A\text{-}2)$$

The optimum point, where NPV is maximized, depends on our ability to implement X_1, X_2, X_3, and X_4. Linear programming tells us what combination of the acceptable projects will maximize NPV within such constraints as capital rationing.

Constraints

Our ability to implement projects X_1 through X_4 in Equation 6A-2 or to produce and sell products X_1 and X_2 in Equation 6A-1 is constrained by our limited resources, particularly capital. We must operate within these constraints while still maximizing our objective function. For example, in our profit-maximizing objective function, the situation might be such that production is constrained by the availability of labor, machine time, and cash. Each of these necessary inputs in the production process is typically limited. Assume, for example, the following limits:

Labor = 300 hours
Machine time = 500 hours
Cash = $1,200

Further assume that each unit of X_1 and X_2 takes the following resources to produce:

	X_1	X_2
Labor	2 hours	3 hours
Machine time	5 hours	4 hours
Cash	$16	$6

The mathematical representation of the constraints for X_1 is the number of units of X_1 produced times the hours of labor, the hours of machine time, and the amount of cash required to produce each unit. The mathematical representation of the constraints for X_2 is the number of units of X_2 produced times the hours of labor, the hours of machine time, and the amount of cash required to produce each unit. In total, the required amount of each factor for both products must be equal to or less than the available total for each factor, such that:

$$2X_1 + 3X_2 \leqslant 300 \text{ hours}$$ Labor constraint   (6A-3)

$$5X_1 + 4X_2 \leqslant 500 \text{ hours}$$ Machine time constraint   (6A-4)

$$16X_1 + 6X_2 \leqslant \$1,200$$ Cash constraint   (6A-5)

In addition, we need the non-negativity constraints:

$$X_1 \geqslant 0$$
$$X_2 \geqslant 0$$

which state that the firm cannot produce a negative quantity of either product.

The Total Model

Now that we have the objective function and the constraints specified in mathematical form, the complete model is:

maximize $P = 3X_1 + 4X_2$ (6A-1)

subject to

$$2X_1 + 3X_2 \leqslant 300$$ (6A-3)
$$5X_1 + 4X_2 \leqslant 500$$ (6A-4)
$$16X_1 + 6X_2 \leqslant 1,200$$ (6A-5)
$$X_i \geqslant 0 \ (i = 1, 2)$$

Graphic Solution

When we have only two variables in the objective function, we can plot both the objective function and the constraints on a two-dimensional figure such as Figure 6A-1. The graphic solution first defines the feasible area within which production may take place without violating the constraints by overlapping one constraint func-

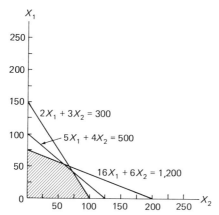

Figure 6A-1 Graphic Representation of the Feasible Area

tion (the lines in Figure 6A-1 above and to the right of which production cannot take place) with another. The feasible solutions are in the cross-hatched area in Figure 6A-1. Notice that the entire area lies to the left and below the most constraining of the constraint functions. From this feasible area, linear programming will pick the one solution with the highest value for the objective function.

Plotting the constraint functions In order to plot the constraint functions in Figure 6A-1, we must first convert the inequalities of the constraints to equalities such that:

$$2X_1 + 3X_2 = 300$$
$$5X_1 + 4X_2 = 500$$
$$16X_1 + 6X_2 = 1200$$

Now each constraint is a linear equation that can be solved for any given level of X_1 and X_2.

If all 300 available labor hours go into the production of X_1 and none goes into the production of X_2, the firm can produce 150 units of X_1, since each unit of X_1 requires 2 hours of labor. We can graph this point on Figure 6A-1 where X_1 on the vertical axis equals 150 units and X_2 on the horizontal axis equals 0. Conversely, if we were to devote our entire labor resource to the production of X_2 and none to X_1, we could produce 100 units of X_2 and none of X_1 and still be within the labor constraint. We can graph this point on Figure 6A-1 at 100 on the horizontal (X_2) axis and 0 on the vertical (X_1) axis. Since the function is linear and two points define a straight line, we can connect the two points and derive our labor constraint function.

We follow the same procedure for the machine time and cash constraints. If we were to devote our entire machine time to the production of X_1, we could produce 100 units of X_1 and none of X_2 within the machine time constraint. Conversely, if we were to devote all the machine time to the production of X_2 and none to X_1, we could produce 125 units of X_2 and none of X_1 within the machine time constraint. Again, we would plot these points on Figure 6A-1 and connect them with a straight line to derive the outer boundary of the feasible area within the machine time constraint.

If we were to devote all our cash resources to the production of X_1 and none to X_2, we could produce 75 units of X_1 and none of X_2. Conversely, if all the financial resources went into the production of X_2, we could produce 200 units of X_2 and none of X_1. Plotting these two points on Figure 6A-1 and connecting them with a straight line gives us the boundary for the cash constraint. Obviously, since we cannot exceed *any* individual constraint, the feasible area lies below *all* three boundaries and is represented by the cross-hatching. The non-negativity constraints prevent the feasible area from going below either axis, keeping it in the upper right-hand quadrant and precluding negative solutions.

Optimal point by trial-and-error   There remains the question of where within the feasible area the optimal solution lies. We recognize that one of the corners must be the optimal solution where total profits (P) are maximized, because it is only at the corners that the highest combination of X_1 and X_2 can occur. Any combination below a corner does not squeeze out the last unit of production and leaves additional resources which could produce still more of either one or both of the products. This can be proved on Figure 6A-1 by picking any spot within the feasible area and verifying by inspection that the total profit is lower here than at the nearest corner to that spot.

We have five (5) corners in Figure 6A-1:

Corner	X_1	X_2
0	0	0
A	75	0
D	0	100
B	51	61
C	46	67

The profits at each corner are:

Corner	$3X_1 + 4X_2$	= Profit
0	$3(0) + 4(0)$	$= 0$
A	$3(75) + 4(0)$	$= 225$
D	$3(0) + 4(100)$	$= 400$
B	$3(51) + 4(61)$	$= 397$
C	$3(46) + 4(67)$	$= 406$

Comparing the profits at all the corners, we discover that point C, representing production of 46 units of X_1 and 67 units of X_2, maximizes the total profit within the

Figure 6A-2   The Iso-Profit Line

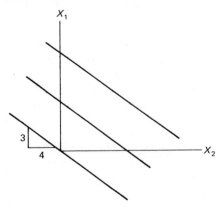

constraints. Notice that none of the constraints is violated at point C, for the combination of 46 units of X_1 and 67 units of X_2 requires 293 hours of labor, 498 hours of machine time, and $1,138 of cash. In the sense that it calls for collection of data and mechanical comparison, this is a trial-and-error method.

Optimal point by fitting the objective function We can also find the optimal solution by graphing the objective function over the feasible area. We start by plotting the *iso-profit line,* along which, regardless of the combination of the two products, the total profit remains the same. As the production of one is increased and that of the other decreased, there is an exact offset and total profits remain constant. The slope of the iso-profit line represents the trade-off between the two profit contributions. In our profit function of:

$$P = 3X_1 + 4X_2 \qquad (6A\text{-}6)$$

the trade-off is 3:4 as illustrated in Figure 6A-2. We can start overlaying the iso-profit line at the point $X_1 = X_2 = 0$ and extend it in either direction from that point at a slope of 3:4. Moving the line up and to the right (parallel, of course, to the original line) gives us the profit at any combination of the two products as we increase their output. This can be done by moving a straightedge up and to the right, keeping it parallel to the original line.

Superimposing Figure 6A-2 on top of Figure 6A-1 gives us Figure 6A-3. Examining Figure 6A-3, we can see that the highest point at which an iso-profit line is tangent to the feasible area occurs at point C. Any other point of tangency at the 0, A, B, or D corners does not provide so high a total profit.

Mathematical Solution

Several mathematical algorithms are commonly available to solve the linear programming model. The most frequently encountered is the *simplex model.* Essentially, it proceeds in an organized fashion to test each corner to see if it is the max-

Figure 6A-3 Figure 6A-2 Superimposed on Figure 6A-1

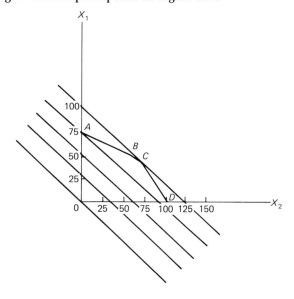

imizing solution. Whenever you encounter a model with more than three variables, it is usually appropriate and time-saving to use a computer-programmed algorithm to derive the solution.

The process describes the model in the same fashion as we have previously done. Our problem was:

maximize $P = 3X_1 + 4X_2$

subject to

$$2X_1 + 3X_2 \leqslant 300$$
$$5X_1 + 4X_2 \leqslant 500$$
$$16X_1 + 6X_2 \leqslant 1{,}200$$
$$X_i \geqslant 0 \ (i = 1, 2)$$

In order to turn the inequalities of the constraints into the necessary equalities, we use the slack variables, which represent the amount of each input factor left unused in the feasible area. We have to rewrite the constraint functions as:

$$2X_1 + 3X_2 + 1X_3 \qquad\qquad\quad = \quad 300$$
$$5X_1 + 4X_2 \qquad + 1X_4 \qquad = \quad 500$$
$$16X_1 + 6X_2 \qquad\qquad + 1X_5 = 1{,}200$$

We now have equalities with which the simplex method can determine the optimum solution to the objective function, where variables X_3, X_4, and X_5 are the slack variables.

Typically, this is represented in tableau format like the initial simplex tableau that follows:

	X_1	X_2	X_3	X_4	X_5	
X_3	2	3	1	0	0	300
X_4	5	4	0	1	0	500
X_5	16	6	0	0	1	1,200

We will not solve this for the solution is tedious, and the mathematics of the method are readily available in elementary business operations research textbooks.[1]

The Dual

Up to this point we have been concerned only with what is called the *primal*, or the solution which maximized or minimized the objective function. Every linear programming model also has a shadow solution, which is the minimum solution for a maximizing objective function and the maximum solution for a minimizing objective function. This shadow solution is called a *dual*.

In our example, the dual is computed by transposing the coefficient of the columns in the primal to become the coefficient of the rows in the dual such that:

$$2u_1 + 5u_2 + 16u_3 \geqslant 3$$
$$3u_1 + 4u_2 + 6u_3 \geqslant 4$$
$$u_i \geqslant 0 \ (i = 1, 3)$$

subject to

$$300u_1 + 500u_2 + 1{,}200u_3 = \text{minimized}$$

[1] C. D. Throsby, *Elementary Linear Programming*, Random House, New York, 1970, has a good discussion of the simplex method.

The objective function of the dual is now to minimize the use of the resources, and its coefficients are the former constraints of the primal model. The direction of the inequalities also changes.

If we solve the above model for the dual, we get the shadow effect on the primal. In other words, we can see how a change in u_1, u_2, or u_3 will affect the primal, for now the marginal effect of a one-unit change in any u_i has an effect on the maximization of total profits (P). This lets us know how much additional production we can engage in if we stretch one or several of the resource constraints.

Linear Programming Applied to Capital Budgeting under Capital Rationing

A typical capital budgeting model under capital rationing[2] might look like this:

$$\text{maximize} \quad \text{NPV} = \sum_{j=1}^{n} b_j X_j \tag{6A-7}$$

subject to

$$\sum_{j=1}^{n} C_{t_j} X_j \leq C_t \quad t = 1, 2 \tag{6A-8}$$

$$0 \leq X_j \leq 1$$

where

b_j = net present value of project j
X_j = the proportion of project j undertaken
C_{t_j} = net outlay for project j in time t
C_t = total funds available in period t

This particular capital budgeting model lets us maximize the NPV for the entire capital budget within the constraints of capital rationing in period 1 and period 2. Given the parameters just defined, this linear programming model tells us which projects and how much of each project we can undertake in this period under the capital constraint of this period and how much of each project we should postpone until next period. For example, if we had ten projects, we might accept them in the following fashion:

Project number (j)	Period 1 % undertaken	Period 2 % undertaken
1	0	50
2	100	0
3	0	0
4	50	50
5	75	25
6	0	100
7	100	0
8	25	0
9	0	0
10	35	50

This solution implies that we would undertake all of projects 2 and 7; none of projects 1, 3, 6, and 9; and fractional parts of projects 4, 5, 8, and 10 in the first period. In

[2] H. Martin Weingartner, *Mathematical Programming and the Analysis of Capital Budgeting Problems*, Prentice-Hall, Englewood Cliffs, N.J., 1962.

the second period we would undertake project 6, fractional parts of 1, 4, 5, and 10, and none of the remaining projects. This would, within the linear programming model, maximize the NPV of the capital budget.

The Dual Interpretation

In this particular capital budgeting model, the dual tells us how an additional dollar increase in the funds available in each period will affect the maximization of the NPV during that period. It reveals the effect, in other words, of relaxing the capital rationing by an additional dollar. If the dual solution were:

$$.95 = u_1$$
$$1.37 = u_2$$

this would imply that an additional dollar raised and invested in period one would yield only an additional $.95 in NPV; whereas an additional dollar raised in period two would yield an additional $1.37 in NPV in period two. As a financial officer then, you would not stretch your fund-raising in the first period because it would not be worth it in terms of maximizing your NPV objective. You would wait for the second period to stretch your fund-raising because at that time you could invest the additional money and move closer to maximizing your NPV objective.

Other Considerations in Applying Linear Programming Models to Capital Budgeting

When linear programming is applied to the capital budgeting procedure, there are other possible constraints which could be incorporated in addition to the available funds constraint we have discussed.[3] A more complete model would consider the production function and the impact of scarce materials used in the production process upon the firm's ability to undertake the capital projects under consideration. Further, the firm must maintain a sufficiently large cash balance not to suffer an embarrassing shortage because it has devoted too much of its funds to capital projects. Hence a financial liquidity constraint must be included in the model. It is also necessary to constrain the model so that the firm's terminal wealth is not only defined but is also constrained to some positive value at the chosen horizon date. It would be inappropriate to find that the model had given us a solution which maximized the NPV for the next few years but left the firm bankrupt at the end of some longer period of time. If you are not careful, this situation can occur under the simple capital budgeting model.

Several other constraints could be added. There might be an upper limit on the firm's borrowing. The simple capital budgeting model should have constraints against multiple adoptions of the same project so that the solution is not to undertake several of the same projects, since the firm only wants one of each acceptable project. Conversely, the model should have non-negativity constraints: the firm cannot disinvest in a project it is only considering. Finally, if the firm uses a payback objective function, the model should be constrained so that at any given date the net outlays to the group of undertaken projects is less than or equal to zero, so as to insure that at any given horizon date the firm is meeting its decision criterion.

As a financial officer, you want to specify your linear programming model in a fashion appropriate to your situation. The above constraints are among those you

[3] Richard H. Berhard, "Mathematical Programming Models for Capital Budgeting—A Survey, Generalization, and Critique," *Journal of Financial and Quantitative Analysis*, June 1969, 111–158.

might want to consider, but they are certainly not the only ones that might be applicable. Remember that you will have to determine the applicability of the constraints to your circumstances and construct the model with them in mind.

Mutually Exclusive and Contingency Projects

To handle mutually exclusive projects within the linear programming framework requires that we adjust the model.[4] We must add another restriction such that:

$$\sum_{j \epsilon J} \leq 1 \tag{6A-9}$$

where

ϵJ = the set of mutually exclusive projects from which one is to be chosen.

By restricting this set to one or fewer projects, we force the process to select only the most attractive project. Of course the problem is that the solution might give us a fractional adoption decision which we might not be able to undertake.[5] The remedy for fractional solutions is explained later in this appendix.

Contingency projects[6] within the linear programming framework are handled by constructing compound projects that treat the contingencies as one project. The solution would undertake or reject the compound project, never considering the two projects on an individual basis.

Alternatively, the linear program framework might be constrained such that, if project m is desirable only if project k is adopted, then:

$$X_m \leq X_k \tag{6A-10}$$

which implies that if $X_k = 0$, both projects are rejected by the solution, for under this constraint if X_k is zero and X_m must be less, then X_m must also be zero. However, this constraint does not simultaneously rule out the possibility that project k may still be undertaken while project m may still be rejected, because the solution to the model may be $X_k = 1$ and $X_m = 0$ and still satisfy the constraint.

Choice of the Objective Function

What should be the appropriate objective function for a capital budgeting model is far from agreed.

The NPV model[7] We have already seen that the selection of the NPV objective function is:

$$\max \text{NPV} = \sum_{j=1}^{n} b_j X_j \tag{6A-7}$$

The NPV model has been criticized[8] because it does not separate the project's cash inflows and its outflows, but rather considers the two as a net figure. This, critics

[4] G. David Quirin, *The Capital Expenditure Decision,* Irwin, Homewood, Ill., 1967, p. 191, and Weingartner, *Mathematical Programming,* pp. 32–34 and 39–44.

[5] *Ibid.,* p. 32.

[6] *Ibid.,* pp. 33–34.

[7] *Ibid.,* Ch. 3.

[8] Willard T. Carelton, "Linear Programming and Capital Budgeting Models: A New Interpretation," *Journal of Finance,* December 1969, 825–833, and William J. Baumol and Richard E. Quandt, "Investment and Discount Rates under Capital Rationing—A Programming Approach," *The Economic Journal,* June 1965, 317–329.

claim, prevents the model from considering the reinvestment in period 2 of the cash inflows from the projects undertaken in period 1. Since the cash inflows of period 1 could finance the projects undertaken in period 2, the available funds constraint may not be as harsh or as restrictive as the model and its solution imply.

The critics of the NPV model also question the cost of capital as it is used in the model. The problem, which we explore in more detail below, is that you must use the externally derived cost of capital to get the NPV (b_j) of each project before applying linear programming to determine which projects maximize NPV. But, the cost of capital is internal to the solution of the model and is not known until the actual time of solution. In the solution it appears in the dual as the implied marginal return to the additional funds raised. It is much like the chicken and the egg problem, for one must come before the other can be determined, and whichever is taken for granted may not be correct.

The cost of capital might actually be the discount rate applied to the value of not consuming this period, the time value, that is, of money for investors for one period. If this is the case, the stockholder dividends generated by the firm's investments in these projects—and not the flows to the projects themselves—are what should be discounted. This requires identity between the firm and its owners as to the timing of the future consumption of the cash inflows. If the objective is shareholder wealth maximization, the objective function should be stated in terms of investors' utility of dividends, and maximizing dividends is what capital budgeting should be considering, rather than the NPV of the projects in isolation.[9]

Baumol and Quandt model In response to these criticisms, Baumol and Quandt[10] have reformulated the NPV based on the maximization of shareholders wealth as measured by their utility for dividends:

$$\text{maximize} \quad \sum_{t=0}^{T} U_t W_t \tag{6A-11}$$

subject to

$$-\sum_{j=1}^{j} a_{jt} X_j + W_t \leqslant M_t \tag{6A-12}$$

$$X_j \geqslant 0 \tag{6A-13}$$

$$W_t \geqslant 0 \tag{6A-14}$$

where
$W_t =$ dollar withdrawal by owners (dividends) in period t
$U_t =$ owners' utility in period t
$a_{jt} =$ the jth project's dollar generation in period t
$M_t =$ the funds available from external sources
$X_j =$ the amount of the jth project accepted

The discount rate (k) is implied in the objective function as the time value of money which exactly equates the utility of the stockholders in the next period to the utility of the stockholders in this period, so that they are indifferent to whether they receive dividends now or one period later. This is implied in the model as follows:

$$\frac{U_t}{U_{t-1}} = (1 + k_t)^{-1} \tag{6A-15}$$

---

[9] Carelton, "Linear Programming," p. 829.
[10] Baumol and Quandt, Investment and Discount Rates."

Equation 6A-15 says that the stockholders' proportional loss of utility from waiting one period to receive the dividends is equal to the time value of money.

According to its originators, solving this model will remedy the problems of the NPV model. The fund generation from each project in each period is now explicitly considered. The cost of capital is still internally determined but is now the same as that implied externally as the time value of money for investors. And the capital budgeting and dividend policy are integrated into one model so that the model maximizes shareholder wealth.

The critics of the Baumol and Quandt model maintain that since the discount factor remains internally determined in the linear programming solution, it cannot be used *a priori* to derive the utility of the owners in both periods. Again, this is the conflict between the external and the internal discount factor which we explore in more detail below.

The critics[11] of this model also claim that a share-maximization objective function based on dividends requires a terminal-value proxy of the share price at the end of the decision period. Investors' utility depends not only on the dividends received but also on the share price at the end of the period under consideration, for any capital gain is also part of the investors' return and increases their expected utility. The Baumol and Quandt model does not include this.

Finally, the Baumol and Quandt model is criticized as being a little unrealistic.[12] In order to apply the model, "we must know the cash configuration of every project the firm can undertake during the planning horizon" in order to derive the dividend policy.

Horizon model The horizon model[13] has an objective function which maximizes the firm's value at some future terminal point instead of the NPV or present worth model. This differs from the other models in that it more clearly recognizes the intertemporal effects between periods, taking into consideration such things as the reinvestment of the inflows of prior periods. It also incorporates the financial transactions of lending and borrowing funds over the multiperiods. We could formulate this model as follows:[14]

maximize $\quad \sum_j \hat{a}_j X_j + V_T - W_T$ $\qquad\qquad$ (6A-16)

subject to

$$\sum_j a_1 X_j + V_1 - W_1 \leq D_1 \qquad\qquad (6A\text{-}17)$$

$$\sum_j a_{tj} X_j - (1+r)V_{t-1} + V_t + (1+r)W_{t-1} - W_t \leq D_t \qquad\qquad (6A\text{-}18)$$

$$t = 2, \ldots T$$

$$0 \leq X_j \leq 1 \qquad\qquad (6A\text{-}19)$$

$$V_t, W_t \geq 0 \qquad\qquad (6A\text{-}20)$$

---

[11] Carelton, "Linear Programming."
[12] Carelton, "Linear Programming," p. 829.
[13] Weingartner, *Mathematical Programming*, Ch. 8.
[14] *Ibid.*, p. 142.

where

$\hat{a}_j =$ the value of all subsequent future flows to the horizon
$a_{tj} =$ the inflow from project j undertaken in period t
$D_t =$ expected funds generated from operations in year t
$W_t =$ the borrowing in year t
$V_t =$ the lending over one period
$r =$ the borrowing and lending rate of interest

Notice how the horizon model incorporates the borrowing and lending as well as the reinvestment and gives the financial officer a model which specifies more of the long-range plans than the others. Nevertheless, this model is also criticized[15] because it does not contain a utility function, implying that utility is independent of time, despite the fact that we know the investor's utility is not independent of time. Further, in the horizon model the goal is to maximize only the dollar return on available projects at the horizon, and the opportunity cost of funds for the investor may not be known prior to the investment decision. Under these circumstances, the horizon model may not resolve the conflict between the external and internal determination of the cost of funds.

Models that incorporate the production function Some model builders[16] maintain that the model must be constrained by material input schedules, production functions, and demand schedules such that our simultaneous optimal solution in the linear programming application to capital budgeting includes the financial transactions of withdrawals and borrowings, as well as the production requirements of product mix, facilities, and labor. The complete linear programming model would simultaneously maximize investor utility while also determining the required internal level of inputs such as labor, plant, equipment, and the production schedule to meet demand. Such a model would be inclusive of all the considerations and allow coordination among the various elements of the firm. In concept, we would want a model such as that suggested by Lerner and Moag[17] which would maximize the sum of the utility of the withdrawals over the multiyear planning period subject to the following constraints:

1. In the initial period: total revenues − capital outlays − labor expenses − withdrawals + borrowings + the initial capital ≥ 0.
2. In the middle years: total revenues − repayments of borrowings − interest payments − labor costs − withdrawals ≥ 0.
3. In the final year: total revenues − repayment of borrowings − interest payments − labor costs − withdrawals ≥ 0.

Notice that a model constructed with the above format in mind incorporates all the production and financing decisions in a simultaneous solution. There is no need to first calculate the cashflow or net present value of any specific project. Further, the model overcomes some of the problems of interdependencies among the variables, such as the price of elasticity of demand.[18]

---

[15] L. J. Merville and L. A. Tavis, "A Generalized Model for Capital Investment," *Journal of Finance*, March 1973, 109–118.
[16] Joseph S. Moag and Eugene M. Lerner, "Capital Budgeting Decisions under Imperfect Market Conditions—A Systems Framework," *Journal of Finance*, September 1969, 613–621.
[17] *Ibid.*
[18] *Ibid.*, pp. 620–621.

Multiperiod Considerations

We can alter the basic NPV model to account for shifting funds between periods, assuming the funds carried over until needed are invested at the cost of capital,[19] by adding the following constraint:

$$\sum_j \sum_t X_j c_{jt} \le \sum_{t=1}^n C_t \tag{6A-21}$$

where

$X_j =$ the proportion of project j undertaken in period t

$c_{jt} =$ the outlay for project j in period t

$C_t =$ the capital constraint in period t

This constraint turns the single capital constraint in the simple NPV model into a multiperiod constraint such that the solution will take into account the movement of funds between periods.

This multiperiod planning horizon consideration has lead to still another criticism of the Baumol and Quandt model and most other models.[20] Unless the planning period horizon coincides with the terminal date of the last project to be completed, there is no guarantee that the models will maximize the cash accumulation during the period over which the investors' utility is being considered. Rather, it is possible that most of the benefits may accrue after the end of this period and leave the investor at a lower utility for the period, unless, as pointed out, the corporate planning period and the investors' utility period coincide.

The multiperiod consideration also resurrects the conflict between the internally and externally determined cost of funds. The multiperiod NPV model requires that "we have a complete specification of available projects for consideration in future periods."[21] In short, we must know the cost of capital and the net present value of each project in advance of the linear programming application.[22] This creates a direct conflict, because the cost of capital is calculated simultaneously when the NPV model is solved, but in order to solve it we must first know the cost of capital as input data to the model.[23] In finance this is called the Hirshleifer paradox.

The Hirshleifer Paradox[24]

This paradox says that the implied cost of capital for the company's stockholders comes externally from their time-preference utility of receiving the withdrawal, their desire, that is, to have the dividends now instead of in a later period. This means that the cost of capital must be known in advance of the investment decision and must be identical to the firm's cost of capital. But the linear programming application gives *another* cost of capital, which is computed simultaneously with the investment decision.

---

[19] Quirin, *The Capital Expenditure Decision*, p. 193.

[20] A. G. Lockett and C. Tomkins, "The Discount Rate Problem in Capital Rationing Situations: Comment," *Journal of Quantitative and Financial Analysis*, June 1970, 245–260.

[21] Quirin, *The Capital Expenditure Decision*, p. 196.

[22] James C. T. Mao, *Quantitative Analysis of Financial Decisions*, Macmillan, New York, 1969, p. 162.

[23] Merville and Tavis, "A Generalized Model," p. 110.

[24] J. Hirshleifer, "On the Theory of Optimal Investment Decisions," *The Journal of Political Economy*, August 1958, pp. 329–352.

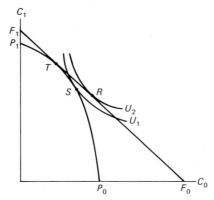

Figure 6A-4 Investor Utility Time Preference

The concept of the externally determined cost of capital as a utility preference over time is illustrated in Figure 6A-4, where:

C_0 = consumption in period 0
C_1 = consumption in period 1
P_0P_1 curve = the production possibility curve
U_1U_2 curve = the utility curves of investors
F_0F_1 curve = the financial market possibility curve (a borrowing-lending curve)

A firm can move along the F_0F_1 curve by either borrowing or lending at an interest rate r which is the slope of the F_0F_1 curve and represents the trade-off between consumption in the two periods. Without borrowing or lending, the firm's highest utility is on U_1 at point S but it can get to U_2, the higher utility curve, by investment on P_0P_1 to point T borrowing in period 1 to get to point R, and repaying the loan in period 2. This use of the production possibility curve in conjunction with the financial market possibility curve allows investors to reach a higher utility.

The interest rate representing the trade-off of consumption between the two periods is determined by the stockholders' desires and does not necessarily agree with the cost of capital derived by linear programming unless by chance the two utility functions are identical. This conflict leads us to ask which cost of capital is the correct one to use.

The Cost of Capital

Since there is a conflict between the internally and externally derived cost of capital, which should you, as the financial officer, choose? Despite the fact that almost all models use the internally determined cost of capital, it is by no means clear that they should. In fact, Elton[25] maintains that we should use the external cost of capital. Under capital rationing, a common situation, the financial market (lending-borrowing) curve does not exist because the firm cannot reach it. The highest utility attainable is on U_1 where P_0P_1 is tangent to U_1 at point S, and where the slope of the

[25] Edwin J. Elton, "Capital Rationing and External Discount Rates," *Journal of Finance*, June 1970, 573–584.

tangency is equal to the cost of capital. Since the slope of the investors' utility function (U) is now the cost of capital and that slope depends on the market time-discount for firms of the same risk, the external cost of capital is the firm's cost of capital and should be used to evaluate its capital projects. However, Elton demonstrates that this externally determined cost of capital can still be used in the utility-of-withdrawal models, such as Baumol and Quandt's, because in them the dual is the external rate, as described by Elton, and the internal cost of capital can even differ, if there are no withdrawals. The appropriate cost of capital for the linear programming investor utility models is the external rate, which shows up as the dual of the stockholders' utility constraints when the firm pays dividends as an alternative to the capital rationing of not borrowing and external evaluation and investor consumption preferences are considered.

Merville and Tavis[26] also attempt to adjust the utility model to resolve the conflict over the internal versus the external cost of capital by incorporating a specific desire for dividends over the period by stockholders. In addition, they try to resolve the cash accumulation problem of the horizon model by specifically including in the same model borrowing and lending at interest rates expected to prevail over the planning period. In the two-period case their model is:

maximize $\quad U(K) = \sum_{j=1}^{2} U_j K_j + U_2 \left(\sum_{i=1}^{I} \hat{d}_{2i} X_i \right)$ (6A-22)

subject to

$$-\sum_{i=1}^{I} d_{1i} X_i + V_1 - b_1 + K_1 \leq H_1 \tag{6A-23}$$

$$-\sum_{i=1}^{I} d_{2i} X_i - (1 + \bar{r}_L) V_1 + (1 + \bar{r}_B) b_1 + K_2 \leq H_2 \tag{6A-24}$$

$$0 \leq X_i \leq 1 \qquad i = 1, \ldots I \tag{6A-25}$$

$$V_1 \geq 0 \tag{6A-26}$$

$$b_i \geq 0 \tag{6A-27}$$

$$K_j \geq 0 \qquad j = 1, 2 \tag{6A-28}$$

where

U_j = the constant utility per dollar for all returns in period j
K_j = consumed dividends in period j
X_i = proportion of project i undertaken
d_{ji} = cashflow of project u in period j
V_1 = amount loaned in period 1
$\bar{r}_L$ = the lending rate
$\bar{r}_B$ = the borrowing rate
b_1 = amount borrowed in period 1
H_j = the cash throwoff from the current operations in period j
$\hat{d}_{2i}$ = the present value of all cashflows of project i past time period 2 discounted back to period 2 at the cost of capital

Notice the incorporation of the financial transactions of borrowing and lending and the utility trade-off of dividend versus consumption into the single period model.

---

[26] Merville and Tavis, "A Generalized Model," p. 113.

The Variability in Earnings per Share Model

Lerner and Rappaport[27] have suggested that a linear programming application may produce erratic reported earnings per share because of the variation in cash inflows under the maximizing solution. For example, the solution may undertake a highly profitable project which has a substantial amount of start-up cost, such as a deep-shaft mining operation. This may temporarily depress earnings per share. Lerner and Rappaport maintain that this variability should be eliminated in order to max-imize share price, since firms with a consistent growth pattern seem to command a higher price in relation to their earnings. This is accomplished by constraining the model so that reported earnings per share must rise at a stipulated annual rate, such that:

$$\text{maximize} \quad \sum_{j=1}^{n} \sum_{t=1}^{n+1} \frac{a_{jt}}{(1+k)^t} X_j \tag{6A-29}$$

subject to

$$\sum_{j=1}^{n} E_{jt}X_j - (1+g) \sum_{j=1}^{n} E_{j,t=1} X_j \geq 0 \tag{6A-30}$$

$$X_j + q_j = 1 \qquad (j = 1, 2 \ldots n)$$

$$X_j, q_j \geq 0$$

where

a_{jt} = cashflow to the jth project in period t
X_j = proportion of project j undertaken
q_j = proportion of project j not undertaken
E_{jt} = earnings of project j in period t
g = stipulated growth rate

Integer Programming

One of the problems in the application of linear programming to capital budgeting is the fractional acceptance of projects in the optimal solution. How do you under-take half a warehouse or half an oil tanker? The answer is that you do not, but rounding to the nearest integer may be misleading because it may fail to produce an optimal solution or put the budget over the available capital.

Various techniques have been developed for handling this problem. The most common is the use of integer programming.[28] Basically, integer programming ad-justs the model by restricting it such that X_j must be an integer and then solving with this additional constraint, so that the feasible region is cut down to only those optimal points which are integer solutions.

Goal Programming versus Linear Programming

Goal programming is a variation on linear programming which allows the specifica-tion of more than one objective (goal) function within the "true environmental"

[27] Eugene M. Lerner and Alfred Rappaport, "Limited DCF in Capital Budgeting," *Harvard Business Review*, September/October, 1968, 133–139.

[28] For example, see W. J. Baumol and R. E. Gomory, "Integer Programming and Pricing," *Econometrica*, July 1960, 521–550, and E. M. L. Beale and R. E. Small, "Mixed Integer Program-ming by a Branch and Bound Technique," *Proceedings of the 1965 IFIP Congress*.

constraints.[29] It is not necessary that each goal be attainable, but it must represent something that the builder of the model deems desirable. The goal programming technique then picks the most satisfying (if not optimal) solution.

The linear programming model is adjusted[30] by defining new surplus (Z^+) and slack (Z^-) variables such that:

$$Z^+, Z^- \geq 0$$
$$Z^+ \times Z^- = 0$$

The objective function incorporates the surplus and the slack variables to reach the new goal such that:

$$\sum_{j=1}^{n} b_j X_j - \text{NPV goal} = Z^+ - Z^-$$

and the objective function is:

$$\sum_{j=1}^{n} b_j X_j - Z^+ + Z^- = \text{NPV goal} \tag{6A-31}$$

This goal programming model can be solved with the simplex technique. Notice that the slack and surplus variables have to equally cancel each other out, so that the optimal solution is no more productive overall than the unadjusted model, although it tends to be more satisfying to more goals. This is implied in the symmetry of the slack and surplus variables. If the goal level is not attainable, the optimal solution will have $Z^+ = 0$ and $Z^- \geq 0$, and vice versa.

The satisfying aspect of goal programming makes it more applicable to government and nonprofit organizational planning where more than a profit maximization motive exists. It also makes goal programming better equipped to coordinate the diverse activities of a multidivisional firm as well as the operating departments of any one division. For example, the coordination of the other departments to a sales forecast goal is easier with this technique than in regular linear programming. As in linear programming, you can rank the multiple goals in order of their attractiveness.[31]

---

[29] Mao, *Quantitative Analysis,* Chs. 4 and 5.

[30] A. W. Charnes, W. W. Cooper, and Y. Ijiri, "Breakeven Budgeting and Programming to Goals," *Journal of Accounting Research,* Spring 1963, 16–43.

[31] George C. Philippatos, *Financial Management Theory and Techniques,* Holden-Day, San Francisco, 1973, p. 576.

7

CAPITAL BUDGETING UNDER RISK

No one can foretell the future; we can only make educated guesses about it. Capital budgeting requires the financial officer to make specific assumptions about the future and to derive specific estimates of a proposed project's future cash inflows and outflows. The financial officer who makes the most accurate estimates is the least surprised, the most prepared—and usually the best paid.

As a financial officer, you must be capable of coping with the uncertainty of the future. After all, you are the person most responsible for evaluating the firm's long-term investments. If your projections are incorrect, your analysis, no matter how sophisticated, will suffer, and the firm's progress toward its goal will be retarded. There is nothing so destructive to a highly sophisticated quantitative capital budgeting analysis as inaccurate estimates at the outset. If you start with bad information, calculation and computation will not rectify the original inaccuracy; they will perpetuate it through the entire evaluation procedure.

BASIC CONCEPTS

The necessity of incorporating an uncertain future into capital budgeting raises several questions which we will address in this chapter. What exactly is this uncertainty? We must understand the specific problem we are facing when we incorporate uncertainty considerations into the capital budget projections and calculations.

Certainty and Uncertainty

To get a working definition of the problem, let us first examine the condition of certainty. We all have an intuitive feel for certainty. We know it when we come across it, but what is it? For the financial officer looking from the present forward, *certainty* is a future which contains one possible outcome, and it is known in the present. In the jargon of the comedian, only death and taxes are certain; everything else is possible but not inevitable.

By contrast, *uncertainty* is the condition faced by the financial officer when the future contains an unknown number of possible outcomes, none of which is known.

Under uncertainty almost anything can occur. Of course, you can estimate what the outcome might be, but you are still in the dark about the chances of that outcome occurring.

Risk and Probability

The more realistic condition under which most financial officers operate is risk. In *risk,* there are a number of possible known outcomes, each with a known probability of occurrence, and any of which may occur. This is more realistic, since we typically make educated guesses to cover the range of possible occurrences from one extreme to the other. All the formal analysis of risk does is to shape our subjective feelings on the outcomes and their associated probabilities into a concrete, standardized format which can be readily communicated to those who must make decisions based on our risk analysis. For example, when you cross the street you automatically compute and explore in your mind the two possible outcomes: (1) death or injury by accident and (2) a safe crossing to the other side. You also quickly and subjectively calculate the odds of each outcome occurring: Outcome (1) has 1 chance out of 1,000 of occurring, and Outcome (2) has 999 chances out of 1,000 of occurring. Now you cross the street with a 99.9 percent probability that you will make it safely to the other side.

This example leads to our definition of probability. When you express the odds of the outcome as a percentage, such as 99.9 percent, you are saying that you believe there is a 99.9 percent probability (chance of occurrence) that you will arrive safely on the other side. There is only a .1 percent probability that you will *not* safely cross the street. *Probability,* therefore, is the chance of occurrence associated with any possible outcome. It is usually expressed as a percentage of the total probability of all occurrences. In our street-crossing example, the two outcomes represent all the possible outcomes of your journey across the street. Together, they add up to 100 percent of the outcomes—one or the other has to occur. In general, the probability of the outcomes has to include all the possible occurrences and must add up to 100 percent.[1] When the possible outcomes are arrayed over the associated probabilities, we derive the probability distribution.

When the financial officer formulates estimates of a project's cashflows, he or she is also considering the probabilities of each possible cashflow (outcome) which might occur. The capital budgeting situation has more outcomes, more complications, and more probabilities. The necessary thought process is also more complex than the automatic or ingrained process we use when crossing the street, and the conclusions must be put into a form which is easily communicated to others.

Statistical Techniques

As a financial officer you will have to derive estimates of future cashflows, but how do you make an educated guess as to the possible outcomes and their associated probabilities once you know you are dealing with risk? This involves isolating and understanding the significant factors which influence the outcome, making assumptions about the level of each influencing factor, and relating those assumptions to the specific estimates and their associated probabilities. When dealing with subjec-

[1] $\sum_{i=1}^{n} P_i = 100\%$, where $P_i =$ the probability of X_i, $i = 1, \ldots n$.

tive estimates such as these, you must understand what is important in determining the cashflows, for the starting point of your estimating procedure will be an appreciation of the environment which you expect to prevail during the period of your estimate. Only if you know that the level of general economic activity is a very important factor in the project's sales, for example, will you think to consider the expected level of that factor in subjectively estimating the project's cashflows.

Once you have these subjective estimates and their attached probabilities, how do you measure, quantify, and interpret the risk? It is necessary to quantify risk in some standard measure so that it can be communicated to others in the firm and used as input into the quantitative, statistically sophisticated risk-handling techniques of capital budgeting. We discover in this chapter that as a financial officer you will need to know such concepts of risk measurement as the probability distribution, the expected value (mean), the standard deviation, and other measures of the probability distribution. All these measures allow us to quantify and interpret our estimates. Further, once we have a uniform measure of risk, we can compare the degree of risk among proposed projects as well as judge the risk of an individual project.

Once you have arrived at quantified, educated estimates about the possible outcomes and their associated probabilities, how do you adjust your capital budgeting techniques to include risk? The capital budgeting techniques which incorporate risk are various, but they all help you handle the project's risk in a systematic fashion so that you are aware and can make others aware of the risks even if you cannot eliminate them from the project. Once you have made the firm's ultimate decision-makers aware of the project's risk, it is up to them to decide if undertaking it is worth the risk. If you do *not* inform them of the risk beforehand and the project is not successful, it is your fault and your reputation as a financial manager is damaged.

Once you have analyzed the risk of each project, how do you select the combination of interrelated, variously risky projects which best maximizes the firm's objective? Since under risk the outcome is not certain, the remote possibilities sometimes occur and lead to unexpected failure or outstanding success. Sometimes one central influencing factor, such as a general recession in economic activity, simultaneously affects all the firm's projects adversely. You will have to plan a strategy of project selection which will let you smooth over the fluke failure or the general disaster as much as possible. Such a strategy operates through the appropriate choice of interrelated risky projects. We will explore how this capital budgeting portfolio strategy can be quantified and communicated to others.

FORECASTING

How do we make an educated estimate about the possible outcomes and their associated probabilities once we know that we are dealing with risk?

Risk Implications of Mechanical Forecasting Techniques

In Chapter 3 we saw certain mechanical forecasting techniques used in the preparation of the budgets, but we intentionally ignored their risk implications. Let us look at these methods and their risk implications now.

Extrapolation This procedure merely extends forward the past performance to derive the next period's estimate. It ignores risk entirely. Therefore we cannot use extrapolation if we are looking for a mechanical technique which considers risk.

Trendline and scatter diagram These, too, ignore the risk component in their extrapolation of past performance into the future. They are of little use in capital budgeting under risk.

Field surveys Generally field surveys conducted, say, on the firm's sales force tend not to solicit information on the respondent's subjective feel for the risk of the situation, although these surveys could and should incorporate such questions.

Regression analysis This technique, which relates variables of influence in past estimates, provides the standard error of the estimate (discussed later in this chapter). This risk measurement tells us how reliable past estimates have been in relation to actual past occurrences. As estimates derived from the regression analysis move farther from actual outcomes, the standard error increases. A large standard error implies a large amount of risk that the estimated outcome will not be the one to occur, while a small standard error implies a small amount of risk that the estimated outcome will not be the one to occur, based on historical standards.

However, the standard error does not give us the distribution of all possible outcomes and their associated probabilities, since it only supplies one estimate for each future period. Despite this limiting factor, regression analysis is still a very useful forecasting tool for the financial manager, and the combination of the estimate and the standard error is used extensively in capital budgeting under risk, particularly in deriving an initial estimate.

The other major limiting factor is the failure of regression analysis to embody the financial officer's subjective thoughts in deriving a distribution of the possible outcomes and their associated probabilities. A reliance on the mechanical nature of the regression analysis does not reveal the underlying feel which the experienced financial forecaster might bring to the situation. Since we are dealing with the educated estimate anyway, it would be helpful to see exactly what the estimator considers important and what in the model no longer seems applicable. Of course, if the financial officer could adjust the parameters of the regression model based on that intuitive feel, we could get the best of both forecasts. Or if we made some comparison of the model's estimate to the financial officer's own, this limiting factor could be overcome. For example, the imposition of wage and price controls and ceilings on interest rates greatly changed the evaluation of capital projects. Unless the financial officer adjusted the regression model to compensate for these changes in the financial and operating environment, the model would not have forecasted correctly during the period.

Ingredients of an Estimate

An estimate is not pulled from the air. It comes from a working knowledge of the area and the experience required to anticipate and evaluate the environment. For our purposes, the estimating process falls into three parts: (1) identifying the influential factors; (2) making reasonable assumptions about the level of each factor; and (3) relating the first two parts to the specific influence.

Knowing and isolating the factors that significantly influence the possible outcomes usually comes through experience and training. The financial officer of a steel manufacturer would be aware that important influences upon the cashflows to a proposed new rolling mill include labor wage settlements, the level of economic activity and the ensuant demand for steel, the price competitiveness of foreign steel, the technology and production costs of the rolling mill and of competing metals and plastics, and other factors.

Once you are aware of the important factors, you must make reasonable assumptions as to the level of each which you expect to prevail during the periods of your estimates. Let us look again at our street-crossing example. We identify the important factors as visibility of traffic, the level of the traffic flow, the color of the traffic light, and the place of the crossing. If the traffic is highly visible, there is little traffic, the light is red, and we are crossing at the corner, our subjective probabilities might be:

Death or injury	.1%
A safe crossing	99.9%
Total probability	100.0%

We can make different assumptions about the influencing factors such that the traffic is hidden from view, there is a heavy traffic flow, the light is green, and we are crossing in the middle of the street. Our subjective probabilities might then be:

Death or injury	10%
A safe crossing	90%
Total probability	100%

We may or may not want to take the chance, but at least we are aware of the risk, and if appropriate we can communicate this to others.

The very same type of assumptions would be made by the financial officer of the steel company concerning the cashflow estimates for the proposed rolling mill. For example, it is probable that one of the two following sets of circumstances (scenarios), out of the many possible, is going to occur. The financial officer might also subjectively feel that there is a 75 percent probability of scenario 1 occurring, and only a 25 percent chance of scenario 2 occurring.

Important factor	Assumption	
	Scenario 1	Scenario 2
Labor wage settlement	No strike or decreased productivity per hour of labor	Strike and decreased productivity per hour of labor
Economic activity and steel demand	Sustained high level	Relatively large periodic recessions
Foreign competition	Eased by dollar devaluation	As strong as in the past
Technology and production costs	$1 reduction per ton	No reduction in costs
Competing materials	No increased competition	A decrease in the price of plastics

Table 7-1

Estimated average annual cashflow	Associated probability
$80,000,000	10%
65,000,000	20
55,000,000	40
45,000,000	20
30,000,000	10

With these two sets of assumptions, the financial officer would derive specific estimates of the annual cashflow the project will be able to generate. He or she would consider the influence on the estimates of each of the major factors and might forecast the following:

Factor	Scenario 1	Scenario 2
Labor wage settlement	$10,000,000	$-5,000,000
Economic activity	40,000,000	37,000,000
Foreign competition	10,000,000	0
Technology and production costs	20,000,000	0
Competing materials	0	-2,000,000
Average annual cashflow	$80,000,000	$30,000,000

The financial officer's subjective estimates of the average annual cashflows to the rolling mill are:

Estimated average annual cashflow	Associated probability
$30,000,000	25%
80,000,000	75

There are probably other estimates to be derived by postulating different assumptions and combinations of assumptions about the important factors. The typical financial officer will explore as many scenarios as are necessary to construct a full picture of the possible outcomes conceivable at this juncture. They might look like Table 7-1, which implies that there are five possible scenarios, each leading to one of the possible outcomes and its associated probability. If the array of outcomes is computed in the financial officer's head, there is a limit on the number of scenarios. If the scenarios are simulated on a computer under the direction of the financial officer, who picks the important factors and makes assumptions on the level of each, many scenarios can be quickly calculated and reviewed. This saves the time and effort of doing the mathematical computations, although the financial officer still has the hard job of deciding what should go into the computer model.

INTERPRETING RISK

How do we measure, quantify, and interpret risk now that we know that it is the distribution of possible outcomes and their associated probabilities?

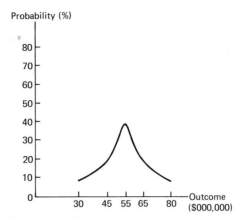

Figure 7-1 Probability Distribution

The Probability Distribution

The array of the possible outcomes and their associated probabilities is known as the *probability distribution.* We can graph it as in Figure 7-1, which is the plot of the probability distribution of Table 7-1, by marking the intersection of each possible outcome along the horizontal axis with the associated probability along the vertical axis and connecting these points with a continuous line.

Notice that Figure 7-1 gives us the same information on the risk of the project as Table 7-1. We can see from the probability distribution graph that there are five possible outcomes ranging from a low of $30,000,000 with a probability of occurrence of 10 percent to a high of $80,000,000 also with a probability of occurrence of 10 percent.

Distributions that resemble Figure 7-1 are known as *normal distributions.*[2] They resemble a bell-shaped curve in that they gradually fan out symmetrically from a top

Figure 7-2 A Graph of Certainty

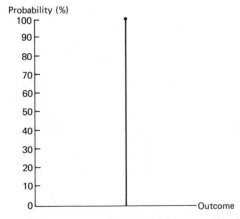

[2] There are other common shapes for the probability distribution, such as the rectangular, the bimodal, and the log normal. We will deal only with the normal distribution for the purposes of illustration since the measures of risk are identical for all distributions.

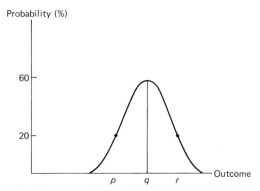

Figure 7-3 A Graphic Representation of Risk

point to either side, reaching smaller and smaller probabilities as the possible out-comes disperse on either side of the midpoint. The probability distribution gives us a picture of the risk in the project. We could even quantify and graph the condi-tion of certainty, as in Figure 7-2. Under absolute certainty there is only one pos-sible outcome, and it will certainly occur. This is represented in Figure 7-2 by the intersection of the single possible outcome at q with the associated probability of 100 percent.

As we move into a situation of risk, the dispersion from q will increase as other cashflows become possible. From Figure 7-3, it is obvious that under this particular situation of risk there is a chance that outcome p or outcome r, instead of outcome q, might occur. Of course, as the dispersion continues to increase around q, the proba-bility of q occurring decreases, for now outcomes p and r also make up some of the total chance of occurrence, which must remain at 100 percent. In Figure 7-3, the probability of q occurring has dropped to 60 percent, and p and r both have a proba-bility of 20 percent.

Now ask yourself: If q were my specific estimate, would I feel more secure that q would occur from distribution A or distribution B in Figure 7-4? The answer is that q is more likely to occur in B than in A because there is less dispersion around the specific estimate q—and of course the probability of q is higher. Provided you are confident that all possible outcomes are included in the distribution, you will prefer

Figure 7-4 Probability Distributions of Outcomes

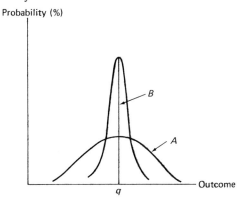

the project associated with distribution B over the project associated with distribution A, because for the same outcome, B has less risk. Of course, if the distribution has been poorly constructed in the first place and outcomes outside the distribution actually *could* occur, no amount of quantification or risk interpretation is going to improve your handling of the risk.

The Expected Value

We can be more precise in our measurement than merely looking at the graph in Figure 7-4 and visualizing the top point and the dispersion around q as represented by the distributions of A and B. Let us think of q as the weighted average of all the outcomes, where each outcome is weighted by its associated probability. This weighted average is known as the *mean* of the distribution.[3] The mean of the steel executive's forecast would be calculated as follows:

Possible outcome		Probability		
$80,000,000	×	.10	=	$ 8,000,000
65,000,000	×	.20	=	13,000,000
55,000,000	×	.40	=	22,000,000
45,000,000	×	.20	=	9,000,000
30,000,000	×	.10	=	3,000,000
			Mean =	$55,000,000

The $55,000,000 mean captures the financial officer's feeling as to what the probability distribution implies is most likely to occur among all the possible outcomes. In capital budgeting applications, the mean will frequently be used as the specific estimate of the occurrence, the dispersion around which represents the risk.

Measures of Dispersion

In addition to quantifying the expected value, we can also quantify the risk through various measures of dispersion, the most common of which are the variance and the standard deviation.

The variance The variance measures the dispersion around the mean by calculating the weighted average of the square difference between each outcome and the mean, such that:

$$\text{var} = \sum_{i=1}^{n} (X_i - \overline{X})^2 P_i \qquad (7\text{-}1)$$

where
    var = the variance
    X_i = outcome
    $\overline{X}$ = the mean
    P_i = the associated probability of outcome i

[3] Other common measures of central tendency are the median, which is the center outcome halfway between the extremes, and the mode, which is the most frequently observed outcome in the distribution.

In the distribution of possible outcomes of the steel company's financial officer, the variance would be:

$(X_i - \overline{X})^2$		P_i		
($80 million − $55 million)^2	×	.10	=	$ 62.5 million
$(65 - 55)^2$	×	.20	=	20.0
$(55 - 55)^2$	×	.40	=	0.0
$(45 - 55)^2$	×	.20	=	20.0
$(30 - 55)^2$	×	.10	=	62.5
		Variance =		$165.0 million

The variance increases as the dispersion of the possible outcomes from the mean increases. Notice that the outcomes below and above the mean are separately included and do not offset each other because of the squared differences. The steel company's financial officer is forecasting a mean of $55,000,000 as the average annual cashflow and a variance of $165,000,000.

The standard deviation The more useful measure of dispersion is the standard deviation, which is the square root of the variance. This still prevents the outcomes above the mean from offsetting those below the mean, but it compensates for the enlarging effect of squaring.

The standard deviation is then:

$$\sigma = \sqrt{\sum_{i=1}^{n} (X_i - \overline{X})^2 P_i} \qquad (7\text{-}2)$$

where

$$\sqrt{\sum_{i=1}^{n} (X_i - \overline{X})^2 P_i} = \text{the square root of the variance}$$

$$\sigma = \text{the standard deviation}$$

In our example, the standard deviation is $12.8 million.

Interpretation of the standard deviation The standard deviation in the normal distribution is unique in that one standard deviation to either side of the mean incorporates 68.3 percent of all the possible outcomes. We can infer a 68.3 percent certainty that, if the distribution is correctly specified in the first place, the occurrence will be within one standard deviation above or below the mean. This is illustrated in Figure 7-5. In fact, as can be seen from Figure 7-5,

$$\overline{X} \pm 1\,\sigma = 68.3\% \text{ of all possible outcomes}$$
$$\overline{X} \pm 2\,\sigma = 95.0\% \text{ of all possible outcomes}$$
$$\overline{X} \pm 3\,\sigma = 99.7\% \text{ of all possible outcomes}$$

Two standard deviations to either side of the mean implies that we can be 95 percent certain that one of the possible outcomes within that area will occur. We can extend this to 99.7 percent certainty by taking the area under three standard deviations to either side of the mean of a normal distribution.

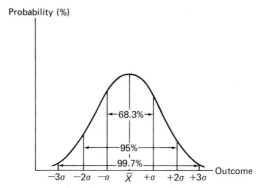

Figure 7-5 The Area Under the Normal Distribution

Other Measures of Dispersion

The variance and the standard deviation are not the only measures of dispersion that may be useful in interpreting risk, although they are the most commonly used. Among the other measures are the standard error of the estimate and skewness.

The standard error of the estimate We have already discussed the fact that the standard error of the estimate is the measure of risk associated with regression analysis. As illustrated in Figure 7-6, the regression analysis estimate (Y_x) is the mean of the distribution, whose measure of dispersion is the standard error. We can use this measure as the risk associated with the regression-derived estimate.

Skewness In addition to the mean and the standard deviation, all probability distributions are characterized by skewness, which reflects the degree of symmetry of the dispersion around the mean. In the normal distribution there is perfect symmetry, such that the dispersions to both sides of the mean are equal. However, in other distributions the symmetry is not perfect. Sometimes there may be a greater number of possible outcomes to the right or to the left. If the distribution is lopsided to the left, it is positively skewed. If it is lopsided to the right, it is negatively skewed. As extreme possible outcomes in either direction are introduced, the mean is shifted beyond the median (the middle possible outcome) and the mode (the most

Figure 7-6 Standard Error of the Estimate

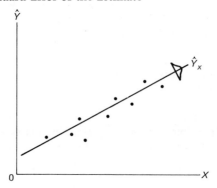

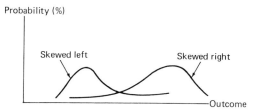

Figure 7-7 Skewness

commonly observed possible outcome), and the distribution takes on the shape of one of those in Figure 7-7.

We can measure the skewness of any distribution as follows:

$$\alpha_3 = \sum_{i=1}^{n} \frac{(X_i - \overline{X})^3 P_i}{s^3}$$

(7-3)

where

α_3 = skewness
s = the standard deviation
X_i = possible outcome i
$\overline{X}$ = the mean
P_i = the probability associated with outcome i

The interpretation of the measure is straightforward. A positive skewness implies an increased number of possible outcomes above the mean—and a pleasant surprise in that the expected value is frequently exceeded. A negative skewness implies an increased incidence of possible unpleasant outcomes, which fall below our expected value. If you have to miss the expected value, it is always more expedient to underestimate than to overestimate. This is not to say you should underestimate intentionally; an accurate estimate is the best on which to base your plans. But confronted with the choice of two projects, each of which had the same mean but one of which had a positively skewed distribution while the other was negatively skewed, you might prefer the positively skewed distribution, because if the unexpected did occur, the outcome would be more likely to exceed your expectations.[4]

---

[4] Another measure of the distribution is the kurtosis or the peakedness of the distribution, which is measured as:

$$\alpha_4 = \sum_{i=1}^{n} \frac{(x_i - \overline{X})^4}{s^4}$$

where

α_4 = kurtosis
s = the standard deviation

Even with skewness equal to zero, the distributions can have different peaknesses, as illustrated in the following figure:

See Wm. C. Merrill and Karl A. Fox, *Introduction to Economic Statistics*, Wiley, New York, 1970, p. 32.

Coefficient of Variation

The coefficient of variation[5] is a measure of relative dispersion, which allows us to compare the risks among projects of different size.

The coefficient of variation is measured as the standard deviation of the project's distribution divided by its own mean, such that:

$$V = \frac{\sigma}{\overline{X}}$$

where

   $V =$ coefficient of variation
   $\sigma =$ standard deviation
   $\overline{X} =$ mean

For example, the coefficient of variation of the rolling mill project would be:

$$V = \frac{\$12.8 \text{ million}}{55.0 \text{ million}}$$

$$= .2327$$

The usefulness of the coefficient of variation is best illustrated when dealing with a scale size problem. If project A and project B had the following means and standard deviations, it would be difficult to say which had the greater attractiveness.

Project	A	B
Mean	$14,000	$10,000
Standard deviation	$ 2,000	$ 2,000

Project A has a higher risk, but it also has a higher mean than project B. If we computed the coefficient of variation, we would see that:

$$V_A = .143$$
$$V_B = .100$$

which implies that project B has less risk per dollar of expected return than project A. This comparison is only possible when we use the coefficient of variation.

INCORPORATING RISK INTO THE CAPITAL BUDGET

How does the financial officer adjust capital budgeting techniques to include risk considerations and the risk measurements we have just discussed?

There are many approaches to the incorporation of risk. Their applicability varies among the decision criteria and the situation.

Mean-Standard Deviation Approach

This approach is perhaps the most straightforward incorporation of risk into the decision criteria that use present value as a decision variable. For illustration let us use the DCF (discounted cashflow) criterion, which from Chapter 5, is:

$$\text{DCF} = \sum_{t=1}^{n} \frac{\overline{\text{CF}_t}}{(1 + k)^t} \tag{7-4}$$

[5] Other common measures of dispersion include the mean absolute deviation and the relative variance.

where

DCF = the present value of the discounted cashflow
$\overline{CF}_t$ = the expected value of the cashflow in period t
k = the cost of capital[6]

Notice the distinction between the cashflow estimate of this DCF approach and the one developed in Chapter 5. In the DCF criterion under certainty, we used the point estimates of just one figure for each period's cashflow. In contrast, the incorporation of risk leads us to use the mean of a distribution of possible outcomes in each year. The difference is that by using the mean, we are forced into considering the dispersion.

In the DCF risk criterion, the financial officer starts out by collecting the distributions of possible outcomes and their associated probabilities for each project in each year for which a cashflow estimate is needed, such as illustrated in Table 7-2.

Once the financial officer has derived the mean and the standard deviation as in Table 7-2, he or she can compute the DCF risk criterion, if the cost of capital (k) equals 10 percent, as:

$$\overline{DCF} = \frac{\$2,000}{(1+.10)^1} + \frac{\$2,625}{(1+.10)^2} + \frac{\$2,275}{(1+.10)^3}$$

$$= \$1,818.18 + \$2,169.43 + \$1,709.23$$

$$= \$5,696.84$$

$$\sigma = \sqrt{\frac{\$547.72^2}{(1+.10)^2} + \frac{\$450.69^2}{(1+.10)^4} + \frac{\$346.32^2}{(1+.10)^6}} \qquad (7\text{-}5)$$

$$= \$674.07$$

Table 7-2   Projected Probability Distribution of Cashflows

Year	Project A cashflow outcomes	Probability	$\overline{X}$	σ
1	$1,000	.10		
	1,500	.20		
	2,000	.40	$2,000	$547.72
	2,500	.20		
	3,000	.10		
2	2,000	.20		
	2,500	.30		
	2,750	.20	$2,625	$450.69
	3,250	.30		
3	1,500	.10		
	2,250	.70	$2,275	$346.32
	2,500	.10		
	3,000	.10		

[6] This assumes independence among the cashflows. Some (James C. Van Horne, *Financial Management and Policy*, 2nd ed., p. 132) maintain that in the analysis we should use the risk-free rate (i) to discount the cashflows, but this is not the case. As we shall see, the cost of capital (k) is externally determined by the suppliers of the capital based on the expected value of their own cashflow stream of dividends, which must be higher than the risk-free rate if there is any distribution around that expected cashflow. As the dispersion increases, the firm's cost of capital rises.

The first important difference between the certain and the risk-inclusive criteria is that in the latter you do get a standard deviation which is an explicit reflection of the risk. Notice that the standard deviation for the project is computed by squaring each term to comply with the standard deviation formula.

Also notice that the use of the mean cashflow in each year may give considerably different results from the use of one point estimate. The mean includes an explicit consideration for the entire range of possible outcomes, not just the one that subjectively feels the best to the financial officer. Under this method, you are forced to consider the other possible outcomes and their potential effect on the occurrence.

The interpretation of the result under the risk-inclusive DCF criterion is that the expected DCF is $5,696.84 and the associated risk, as measured by the standard deviation, is $674.07. We now have indications of the project's risk as well as its reward. Those who have to make an accept-reject decision are now equipped to consider whether the expected return is worth the risk. It is no longer a matter of simply accepting if the DCF exceeds the project's cost. It is very possible that this explicit consideration of risk will cause a reappraisal of many projects which were previously accepted without question.

Probability of Acceptance Error Approach

This method works best with the net present value decision criterion, although it is by no means entirely limited to it. When applied to the NPV decision criterion, its general objective is to determine the probability that the actual NPV occurrence is going to be less than zero and that the project has, therefore, been accepted in error. This is illustrated in Figure 7-8. All the possible outcomes of the distribution which lie to the left of NPV = 0 imply that the project should not be accepted. Of course, as we can see from Figure 7-8, the mean NPV of the project is greater than zero, and based on that we might accept the project. If the outcome that did occur lay to the left of zero, then in accepting the project based on the positive mean NPV value, we have made an error. In this approach we quantify the probability of committing that error and treat it as our risk measure.

We know that in a normal distribution, 50 percent of the possible outcomes lie to the right of the mean and 50 percent to the left. The shaded area in Figure 7-8 represents that portion of the left side of the distribution which has an NPV greater than zero. The question is: What portion of the distribution (commonly referred to as the

Figure 7-8 The Probability of Acceptance Error

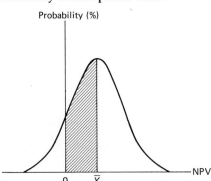

area under the curve) lies still farther to the left, where NPV is less than zero? Expressed as a percentage of the total area, that proportion indicates the chance of the occurrence being less than NPV = 0.

We can determine the area under the curve to the left of NPV = 0 by standardizing the division of the area under the curve to conform to a table which divides the area under a normal curve through the use of Equation 7-6.

$$Z = \frac{0 - \overline{X}}{\sigma}$$
(7-6)

where

Z = the standardized value
$\overline{X}$ = the mean NPV
σ = the standard deviation

In Equation 7-6, we are standardizing the variation under the normal curve from the point NPV = 0.

In our example of the last approach, the mean present value of the project was $5,696.84 and its standard deviation was $674.07. If the project cost $5,000, then its expected net present value would be $696.84. Its Z value would be:

$$Z = \frac{\$696.84}{\$674.07} = -1.03$$

Reading that Z value from the table of area under the normal curve, we find that 15 percent of the area would lie to the left of NPV = 0. This implies that if we accept this project, there is a 15 percent chance that we have erred and that the actual occurrence will be NPV less than zero. Again, risk is incorporated into the analysis by providing the decision-makers with an easily communicated measure which allows them to judge whether the expected net present value is worth the risk. If they feel it is, the project is undertaken. If they feel the project is too risky for their liking, they reject it.

Risk-Adjusted Discount Rate Approach

This is another method for incorporating risk into the capital budgeting decision criteria that use the present-value approach. In this method the discount factor is adjusted to compensate for the risk. As the risk increases, the discount rate increases and the present value of any given stream of cashflows is reduced. The effect is to make the project less attractive as the risk increases because of the lower present value. In contrast to the mean-standard deviation and the probability of acceptance error approaches, which give a return and a risk measure, this method has only one measure on which to base an accept-reject decision. If the risk-adjusted present value of the project is less than the cost, we reject it.

To understand the concept of the risk adjusted discount rate (cost of capital), it is necessary to realize that there exists a risk-free rate (alternatively called the default-free rate) associated with projects and investments that have certainty in their cashflow stream: one known possible set of cashflow estimates. However, the United States government debt obligation is the only investment afforded this characteristic of certainty in its cashflow. There is no chance that lenders of funds to the United States government will not get the dollar amount of their loans back and the dollar amount of interest due when promised, because all the government has to do is print up some more money. We can observe this risk-free rate as the yield on government securities (see Chapters 8–11), and we signify it as i.

When the financial officer considers other possible investments besides the risk-free government securities, it is necessary to adjust the cost of capital (discount rate) in the present-value capital budgeting procedures to reflect that additional risk such that:

$$k_A = i + \alpha_A$$

where
$\quad k_A$ = the risk-adjusted cost of capital for project A
$\quad\quad i$ = the risk-free rate
$\quad \alpha_A$ = the risk-adjustment premium

The risk-adjustment premium added to the risk-free rate (i) reflects the greater risk attached to this project than attached to a government debt obligation. As the risk increases, the risk-adjustment premium also increases and the risk-adjusted cost of capital to the project rises.

In order to get some feel for the size of the risk adjustment, the financial officer will again turn to the dispersion in the distribution of cashflows. As the dispersion increases, α_A and k_A also increase. In fact, we can express α_A as a function of the proportional relationship between the standard deviation of the project's cashflows and the standard deviation of the total firm's cashflows, such that:

$$\alpha_A = \left(\frac{V_A}{V_{Firm}}\right)\alpha_{Firm}$$

where
$\quad \alpha_A$ = the risk premium to project A
$\quad V_A$ = the coefficient of variation of project A
$\quad V_{Firm}$ = the coefficient of variation of the firm
$\quad \alpha_{Firm}$ = the risk premium associated with the entire firm

In a somewhat arbitrary fashion, the financial officer will determine the risk premium for the entire firm (α_{Firm}) in comparison to the risk-free rate. The next step is to divide the coefficient of variation of the project (V_A) by the coefficient of variation of the firm's cashflows (V_{Firm}) and decide if the project has a greater or lesser risk than the entire firm. This relationship between V_A and V_{Firm} will proportionally increase k_A above or below the risk free rate (i) such that if:

$$\frac{V_A}{V_{Firm}} > 1 \quad \text{then} \quad k_A > k_{Firm}$$

and if:

$$\frac{V_A}{V_{Firm}} < 1 \quad \text{then} \quad k_A < k_{Firm}$$

If the coefficient of variation of the project is less than that of the firm's, then the risk-adjusted discount rate for the project is less than that of the firm, and vice versa.

Using the expected value of the cashflow distributions for each year in the project's life and the risk-adjusted discount rate, the financial officer will find the risk-adjusted net present value for the project. For example, if:

$$NPV = -C + \sum_{t=1}^{n} \frac{\overline{CF}_t}{(1 + k_A)^t}$$ (7-7)

and the following figures are available on the firm and the project:

Year	$\overline{CF}_t$	i	V_{Firm}	V_A	α_{Firm}	$k_A = i + \dfrac{V_A}{V_{Firm}}(\alpha_{Firm})$
1	$3,000	7%	.16	.08	.06	.10
2	3,000	7	.16	.08	.06	.10
3	3,000	7	.16	.08	.06	.10

and if, in this example, the project costs $5,000, then its risk-adjusted NPV would be:

$$NPV = -\$5,000 + \frac{3,000}{(1 + .10)^1} + \frac{3,000}{(1 + .10)^2} + \frac{3,000}{(1 + .10)^3}$$

$$= \$2,461.00$$

We would undertake this project because its risk-adjusted NPV is greater than zero. If the risk-adjusted NPV were less than zero, we would reject the project.

Notice the advantages of the risk-adjusted discount approach. Each project is adjusted separately so that an appropriate level of risk for the project itself can be used in its evaluation. Lower-risk projects might become more attractive despite their lower cashflow stream, while high-risk/high-cashflow projects might become unattractive. This could be very helpful in guiding the firm to lower-risk projects that might offset the higher risk of the firm in general. Another advantage is that the cost of capital of the entire firm as it is determined in the financial markets can be used as a guide in calculating the discount rate for the individual project, which can and should fluctuate with the cost of capital. Also, this analysis still utilizes the probability distribution of the cashflows to get the mean cashflow in each year, which is used in deriving the risk-adjusted NPV of Equation 7-7. We forfeit none of the subjective analysis which goes into deriving the mean cashflow estimates. Finally, the risk-adjusted NPV is a single figure on which to base an accept-reject decision, unlike some of the other methods which provide both a risk and a return measure and are open to interpretation.

Hurdle Rate Approach

When the general technique of the risk-adjusted discount rate is applied to the internal rate of return decision criterion (IRR), it becomes the hurdle rate. The hurdle rate is the adjusted cost of capital and is calculated in the same manner as:

$$k_A = i + \alpha_A$$

Now, k_A becomes the hurdle rate which has to be exceeded by the IRR for the firm to undertake the project. If:

$$IRR_A > k_A \qquad \text{undertake the project}$$
$$IRR_A < k_A \qquad \text{reject the project}$$

For example, if the IRR for the project were 23.5 percent and the hurdle rate (k_A) were 16 percent, we would undertake the project.

The hurdle rate approach has the same advantages as the risk-adjusted discount rate, although it is not uncommon to find that financial officers who use the hurdle rate throw in a "fudge factor" of a few additional percentage points in an effort to provide a cushion against errors of judgment. Of course, inasmuch as it eliminates some projects which should have been undertaken, this cushion also hinders the firm from maximizing its position. Also, it frequently happens that a particular hurdle rate becomes fixed as the decision criterion and is inflexible, regardless of changes in the financial markets or the firm's cost of capital. This, too, leads to a less-than-optimal position and your actual cost of capital may exceed the hurdle rate during periods of high interest rates and expensive capital. This would be sheer folly.

Simulation Approach

Applying the concept of Monte Carlo simulation to capital budgeting is relatively straightforward[7] and, with the aid of a computer, relatively easy. Envision each possible outcome assigned a random number corresponding to those on a roulette wheel. As the wheel turns and the little silver ball drops into a numbered slot, the possible outcome with the corresponding number is selected as the outcome for this round of simulation. For example, assume we had the following possible outcomes, their associated probabilities, and the assigned numbers:

Possible outcomes	Associated probabilities	Assigned random numbers
$1,000	.10	1
1,500	.20	5 and 10
2,000	.40	2, 3, 4, and 9
2,500	.20	7 and 6
3,000	.10	8

Each outcome is assigned one or more of the random numbers *depending on its probability*. If, as in this example, there is a 1 in 10 chance of the occurrence being $1,000, that possible outcome is assigned 1 out of the 10 possible random numbers. Similarly, since the $2,000 possible outcome has a 40 percent chance of occurring, it is assigned 4 out of the 10 possible numbers on our roulette wheel.

When the wheel is spun, one of the ten numbers appears, and the possible outcome with the corresponding assigned number is selected as the occurrence. Of course, those outcomes with more assigned numbers have a larger chance of being selected, because the silver ball can drop into one of their assigned numbers more frequently. In Monte Carlo simulation, we repeat the process of spinning the ball and selecting an occurrence until we have a sufficient number such that the average of all the selected occurrences truly reflects what might actually occur if the situation were composed of random occurrences.

When Monte Carlo simulation is applied to capital budgeting the procedure remains the same. We select the variables that we feel represent the important ele-

[7] David B. Hertz, "Risk Analysis in Capital Investment," *Harvard Business Review*, January-February 1964, 95–106.

ments of the capital budgeting evaluation process. These variables would most likely reflect the thinking and estimates of the various persons responsible for each of the necessary inputs into the decision criterion being used. For example, we would need estimates on the market size (m) and the selling price per unit (s) of the product from the marketing vice-president. We would need estimates on the life of the machine (n) and the cost of the machine (c) from the engineering vice-president. We would need an estimate of the cost of capital (k) from the financial officer and an estimate of the unit cost of production (u) from the vice-president in charge of production.

We would require the complete feelings of each on the estimates given. This means that we want a subjectively derived probability distribution of the possible outcomes for each variable, not just a single-point estimate. In this fashion we get the benefit of the estimator's experience as it relates not only to the outcome but also to the risk of that outcome occurring, as measured by the dispersion in the probability distribution. Graphically, we would expect that the six variables we are using here (there could be as many as you felt were necessary), would have probability distributions like those in Figure 7-9.

These are the necessary inputs to the NPV decision criterion, assuming straight-line depreciation and no salvage value. We can see this from the NPV formula:

$$NPV = -C + \sum_{t=1}^{n} \frac{CF_t}{(1 + k)^t}$$

where the cashflow in any period is:

$$CF_t = (m \times s) - (u \times s) + \left(\frac{c}{n}\right)$$

Figure 7-9 Probability Distributions of Input Variables

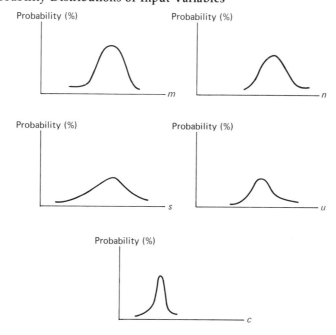

where

> m = market size
> s = the selling price per unit
> u = the unit cost of the product
> c = the cost of the machine
> n = the life of the machine in years

Each one of these variables has been given a probability distribution by the person responsible for the area. In an effort to coordinate all this information into the capital budgeting evaluation, the financial officer would apply the simulation technique by assigning random numbers to each of the possible outcomes in each distribution and selecting one possible outcome from each. For example, the random selection process might result in:

> m = 100,000 units
> s = \$1.00
> u = \$.75
> c = \$10,000
> n = 3
> k = 10%

The combination of this particular selection would produce a net present value of:

$$NPV = -\$10,000 + \frac{\$28,334}{(1+.10)^1} + \frac{\$28,334}{(1+.10)^2} + \frac{\$28,334}{(1+.10)^3}$$

$$= \$60,461$$

We repeat the process of random selection with a different set of necessary input variables and recompute the NPV for the second combination. We continue to repeat the selection and recomputation of the NPV until we are convinced that we have a sufficient number of combinations, usually over 100, which represent a reasonable sampling of what the NPV might look like under a condition of random occurrence in each of the input variables.

When we have compiled this list of 100 or more simulated NPV values, we will find that there is a tendency for many of them to group around some value, despite the fact that no two sets of variables have to be identical. This is because the set may have randomly included a high value for one variable and a low value for another variable in this combination, while randomly including a low value for the first variable and a high value for the second variable in a later combination, so that the reversal of values offset one another. Of course, among the 100 or more combinations there will be extremely low combinations and extremely high combinations, but there will also be a tendency for the combinations to cluster at a particular NPV.

We depict this list of combinations in Figure 7-10 as a normal distribution (despite the fact that none of the distributions on the individual variables *has* to be normal), because of the statistical law of large numbers which states that the mean of a large sampling of means tends to be normally distributed.

As in any normal distribution, we can now compute a mean ($\overline{NPV}$) and a standard deviation (σ_{NPV}), which we could not do before based on the individual factors. In fact, since the individual variables were not normally distributed, it would have been very difficult to apply some of the approaches to capital budgeting under risk, such as the probability of acceptance error.

The major advantage of the simulation technique is that we now have a normal distribution from which we can get a mean and a standard deviation for use in other

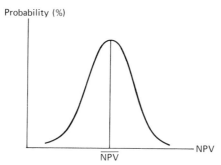

Figure 7-10 The Distribution of the Combinations

analysis or for use in our decision to accept or reject the project. The appealing characteristic of the distribution is that it incorporates all the areas that impact the NPV decision criterion with the subjective opinions of the experts in the area, yet it lets us coordinate those diverse opinions into easily communicated and uniform measurements upon which a decision can be made.

The major disadvantage of the simulation technique is that it works best if there is no dependence among the variables. Since we are drawing random values for the variables from each distribution, one at a time, we are implying that the value of the first variable drawn has no relationship to the value of any subsequent variables. Of course, the simulation technique can be applied to any of the other decision criteria, such as the internal rate of return, by identifying the important variables in that decision criterion and simulating with them.

Sensitivity Analysis

Sensitivity analysis is not really a risk-reducing or risk-measuring technique. It is a technique for evaluating the impact that the various changes the financial officer can make in each important variable would have on the possible outcomes. For example, if the financial officer were estimating the cashflow in period t and using the following model to do so:

$$CF_t = (m \times s) - (m \times u) + \left(\frac{c}{n}\right)$$

the following values would give a cashflow estimate of $28,334 in period t:

$$m = 100,000 \text{ units}$$
$$s = \$1$$
$$u = \$.75$$
$$n = 3$$
$$c = \$10,000$$

Now the financial officer might wonder what would be the effect on the cashflow during the period of raising the selling price per unit (s) to $1.25. Sensitivity analysis will pretest this on the model, to give an indication of what the effect might be. If, in the opinion of the marketing expert, the increase in the selling price will also cause a decline in demand to 80,000 units, the cashflow for the period will be:

$$CF_t = (80,000 \times \$1.25) - (80,000 \times \$.75) + (\$10,000/3)$$
$$= \$43,334$$

In this particular case, the increase in the selling price will apparently have a favorable impact on the cashflow during the period. Therefore, judging from the sensitivity analysis, the financial officer should suggest that the selling price be raised. Of course, the analysis may also reveal that the impact is unfavorable or that the change in the variable's value has no significant impact and that it would be a waste of time for the firm to devote any of its resources to analyzing or considering it. Finally, an analysis of this type often reveals the riskiness of the project by highlighting the fact that a small miscalculation in a highly sensitive area about which you feel very unsure can have a dramatic effect on the occurrence. If this is the case, your risk might be higher than if you were sure of the very sensitive areas and uncertain of the very insensitive areas.

Contingency Budgeting Approach

Although we have already discussed the concept of contingency budgeting in Chapter 3, it deserves brief mention here as an effective method of risk analysis. It is based on the dispersion of a low, medium, and high forecast and is readily communicated to others for their accept-reject decision. Examining the budget under all three possible situations gives insight into the potential risk. Further, it prepares the firm for a more rapid mobilization of its forces should the expected not occur.

Decision Tree Approach

Alternative strategies for the implementation of a project or the evaluation of that project frequently require a sequential decision-making process, whereas the accept-reject decision is made in stages. For example, the financial officer might have to decide between immediately launching a full-scale project and undertaking a small pilot project now with a second-stage decision about going full-scale to be made later. The small-scale pilot project, if successful, could lead to a larger investment; immediate full-scale production, if successful, could capture the market ahead of the competition. The question is to decide which alternative under the conditions of risk is more acceptable, if either.

In such a situation, it is often more realistic to examine the future cashflows under different assumed conditions such as different levels of demand. That is, we can assume different conditions under which different possible outcomes might occur during the next period. We can make another set of different assumptions concerning the period after that, and so on. Then we can examine the possible outcomes in each period to evaluate the project.

Analysis of a small pilot project versus immediate full-scale production is represented graphically in Figure 7-11. Assume the cost of the project is $20,000, which can be invested immediately in full-scale production or $5,000 in stage 1 and $15,000 in stage 2, 2 years later. At the end of the second year, we have to make a decision to either remain small or go into full-scale production. The assumed life-expectancy of either alternative is 5 years. Figure 7-11 shows that at stage 1, the initial decision, the firm can expect a high, medium, or low demand response for either alternative. Whether the firm chooses the pilot project or full-scale production, it has a .5 chance of encountering a high demand, a .1 chance of encountering a low demand, and a .4 chance of encountering a medium demand. These are the possible demand outcomes and their associated probabilities, based on estimates made at the initial decision point.

As you can see from Figure 7-11, the possible demand outcomes and probabilities of the full-scale production alternative hold for the entire 5-year period. The pos-

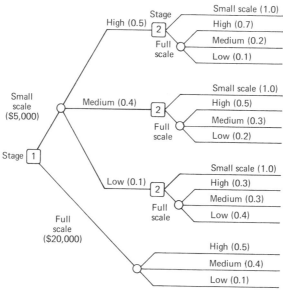

Figure 7-11 A Decision Tree Set of Assumptions with Associated Probabilities

sible demand outcomes and probabilities for the pilot project cover only the first 2 years of stage 1. We must also estimate, at the initial decision point, the possible demand outcomes and their associated probabilities that could occur during stage 2 if we move into full scale production. Figure 7-11 shows that *if demand were high for the pilot project through stage 1,* the probability that demand will remain high during stage 2 is assigned a relatively high value of .7—against relatively small probabilities of .2 for medium demand and .1 for low demand.

If, on the other hand, the pilot project encounters only medium demand during stage 1, then the probability of encountering high demand during stage 2 is estimated to be only .5. The probability of medium demand is estimated at .3, and the probability of low demand is estimated at .2. If the pilot project encounters low demand during stage 1, the probabilities for stage 2 would be: .3 for high demand, .3 for medium demand, and .4 for low demand. Of course, at the end of stage 1 we also have the choice of remaining at the pilot project (small-scale) level during stage 2, which would assure us of continuing at the same level as in stage 1, whether that level was small, medium, or high demand. This is represented by a certain probability of 1.0 in Figure 7-11.

Table 7-3 shows the 5-year cashflow stream for each alternative and the NPV of those streams at a cost of capital of 10 percent.

The question is: Which alternative is preferred under the projected cashflows and their associated probabilities? We can answer that question by determining which alternative has the higher NPV by working from right to left in Figure 7-12, on which we find the calculated NPV's of Table 7-3. Starting at the righthand side, we can compute the NPV of each alternative by working left. From Figure 7-12, we see that the expected NPV of full-scale production in stage 2 after encountering high demand for a pilot project in stage one is:

$$\overline{\text{NPV}} \text{ (high demand/full-scale)} = .7(\$35{,}854) + .2(\$5{,}029) + .1(-\$15{,}521)$$
$$= \$24{,}552$$

Table 7-3   Cashflow and NPV of Alternative Projects

Demand	Year						
Stage 1/stage 2	0	1	2	3	4	5	NPV
Pilot/pilot							
High demand	−$5,000	$ 7,000	$ 7,000	$ 7,000	$ 7,000	$ 7,000	$21,536
Medium demand	−5,000	5,000	5,000	5,000	5,000	5,000	13,954
Low demand	−5,000	1,000	1,000	1,000	1,000	1,000	−1,210
Pilot/full-scale							
High/high	−5,000	7,000	−8,000	20,000	20,000	20,000	35,854
High/medium	−5,000	7,000	−8,000	5,000	5,000	5,000	5,029
High/low	−5,000	7,000	−8,000	−5,000	−5,000	−5,000	−15,521
Medium/high	−5,000	5,000	−10,000	20,000	20,000	20,000	32,385
Medium/medium	−5,000	5,000	−10,000	5,000	5,000	5,000	1,560
Medium/low	−5,000	5,000	−10,000	−5,000	−5,000	−5,000	−18,990
Low/high	−5,000	1,000	−14,000	20,000	20,000	20,000	26,359
Low/medium	−5,000	1,000	−14,000	5,000	5,000	5,000	−9,348
Low/low	−5,000	1,000	−14,000	−5,000	−5,000	−5,000	−33,202
Full-scale/full-scale							
High demand	−20,000	20,000	20,000	20,000	20,000	20,000	55,816
Medium demand	−20,000	5,000	5,000	5,000	5,000	5,000	−1,046
Low demand	−20,000	−5,000	−5,000	−5,000	−5,000	−5,000	−38,954

Figure 7-12   Decision Tree Showing NPVs

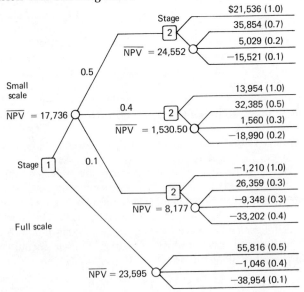

We can do this for each possible pilot project demand outcome in stage 1 followed by full-scale production in stage 2 such that:

Stage 1 demand $\overline{\text{NPV}}$

High $24,552

Medium   .5($37,267) + .3($1,560) + .2(−$18,990)

= $1,530.50

Low   .3($26,359) + .3(−$9,348) + .4(−$33,202)

= −$8,177

On the other hand, the $\overline{\text{NPV}}$s for initiating a pilot project in stage 1 and remaining with it through stage 2 are:

Stage 1 demand $\overline{\text{NPV}}$

High $21,536

Medium $13,954

Low   −$1,210

Notice that only if a high demand occurs during the stage-1 pilot project is it worth going into full-scale production during stage 2, for the expected NPV under full-scale production in stage 2 after encountering either medium or low demand during the stage-1 pilot is less than if we remained at the pilot project level *throughout* stage 2. We have two alternatives. We either go into immediate full-scale production, or we start with a pilot project which will shift to full-scale production only if the stage-1 demand is high; otherwise it will stay as a pilot project during stage 2.

The selection of the better alternative depends on the expected NPVs of the alternatives, which are:

$$\overline{\text{NPV}} = .5(\$55,810) + .4(-\$1,046) + .1(-\$38,954)$$
$$= \$23,595 \text{ for the immediate full scale project}$$
$$\overline{\text{NPV}} = .5(\$24,552) + .4(\$13,954) + .1(-\$1,210)$$
$$= \$17,736 \text{ for running the pilot project first}$$

Obviously, in this particular example we would go immediately into full-scale production, because the expected NPV of that alternative is higher than the expected NPV of any pilot project/full-scale alternative.

Notice, however, how the decision tree technique has given us a sequential outlook, and we can deal with the consequences of future decisions as they impact our need for a decision in the present period. The technique also forces us to deal more explicitly with the risk associated with future periods, and we could incorporate the standard deviation of the expected NPV, as we did in the mean-standard deviation approach.

Utility in a Capital Budgeting Technique

Utility analysis Utility may be loosely thought of as the satisfaction that the individual or the firm receives from the funds employed. Each firm and each individual has a different set of preferences; two people or firms can, therefore, assign different degrees of relative attractiveness to the identical project. Thus, we frequently observe that some of us prefer more leisure to more money, while others prefer more money to more leisure. Each of us has a combination of the two which will maximize our own preferences or, in other words, our *utility*.

In an analogous fashion, it is not the actual amount of money to be received from the project but the utility of the amount to be received at the degree of risk associated with the project that we might want to maximize. Some firms have a distinct preference for the absolute amount of money and are willing to undertake substantial risks to get it. Other firms prefer less risk and are willing to undertake projects with less expected return and lower risk exposure. Each firm has a combination of return and risk which maximizes its utility.

Measuring utility[8] Financial theorists have classified the firm's utility for money into the three general categories as: diminishing marginal utility (A), constant marginal utility (B), and increasing marginal utility (C), illustrated in Figure 7-13. Though each firm and individual may differ in the degree of fit into a particular category, as reflected by the steepness of the line (slope) in Figure 7-13, we all fit into at least one category and all rational firms fit into category A (diminishing marginal utility for money).

In the *diminishing marginal utility* of money category, curve A in Figure 7-13, as our holding of dollars increases, our utility (pleasure) from each additional dollar decreases but never becomes negative. In other words our utility increases but at a decreasing rate. The last dollar received does not give us as much utility as the one before it, but it increases our total utility by some additional positive amount. We can see this in the slope of curve A, which continually rises but at an ever-smaller rate as we move out the money ($) axis. For example, the first dollar you receive may mean a lot since it may be the difference between starvation and survival, but the 10 millionth dollar you receive will most certainly not give you as much pleasure.

The diminishing marginal utility curve represents the typical utility posture of most people and firms and implies that they are risk averters. The risk averter may be thought of as a person or firm that, in choosing between two equal outcomes, derives greater utility out of the one with the higher degree of certainty. This agrees with our intuitive feeling at the beginning of the chapter that we should select the project with the less dispersion if we had to choose between two projects with the same expected net present value.

We can demonstrate that we get a greater utility from a project with less dispersion than from another project with the same expected value but greater dispersion. Our use of dispersion as a measure for risk implies that people with a diminishing marginal utility for money are risk averters, as shown in Figure 7-14. In Figure 7-14, we measure the amount of satisfaction a firm or individual receives on a vertical axis calibrated in "utils," a traditional standard of utility measurement. We measure the

---

[8] The measurement of utility depends upon an entire series of axioms. They are beyond the scope of this text and will only be listed here. The interested reader is referred to John Von Neumann and Osker Morgenstern, *Theory of Games and Economic Behavior*, 2nd ed., Princeton University Press, Princeton, N.J., 1947.
The axioms are:
1. Transitivity—the ranking of outcomes in order of preference such that outcome 1 is preferred to outcome 2.
2. Certainty-equivalence—the expression of the uncertain outcome in certainty form.
3. Substitutability—the interchange of one certainty-equivalence for another without a loss or gain in utility.
4. The higher probability of occurrence for equal outcomes is preferred.
5. The pleasure of gambling as an end in itself is ruled out.

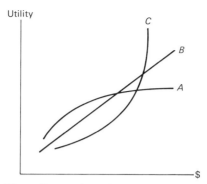

Figure 7-13 The Three Categories of Utility

expected value of the possible outcomes on the horizontal axis. We can see from Figure 7-14 that there are 3.5 utils associated with a certain occurrence of $90. However, there are only 3.2 utils associated with the expected value of $90 from a probability distribution which has a 50 percent chance of a $60 occurrence and a 50 percent chance of a $120 occurrence. This is represented in Figure 7-14 by the midpoint of the line connecting the $60 and $120 points on curve A. Despite the fact that the expected value of this 50-50 chance of $60 or $120 is identical to the $90 from the certain occurrence, our utility has declined because of the risk associated with the wider dispersion of the chance alternative. If we were to increase the dispersion as represented by the line connecting points $0 and $180 on curve A, corresponding to a probability distribution of possible outcome $0 with an associated probability of 50 percent and possible outcome $180 with an associated probability of 50 percent, the derived utility would be 1.8 utils, despite the fact that the expected value of the occurrence is still $90.

As the dispersion around any expected value increases, the utility derived from that expected value of the occurrence decreases. This has to be the case under a diminishing marginal utility of money curve because the higher outcomes to the right of the certain occurrence have a proportionally smaller utility per dollar than do the ones to the left of the certain occurrence. Even if you received the $180, for example, your utility associated with that high occurrence is proportionally less per

Figure 7-14 Risk-Aversion with a Diminishing Marginal Utility of Money

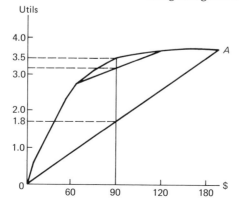

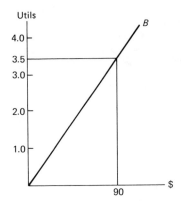

Figure 7-15 Constant Marginal Utility of Money

dollar than the utility received farther to the left, because the curve flattens out at $180. When we combine the utils, we find that the weighted average is less than the utils associated with the certain occurrence.

A second general category of utility curve is the *constant marginal utility* for money, as illustrated in Figure 7-15. The constant, upward slope of the constant marginal utility curve (B) implies that the firm receives the same amount of utility from every additional dollar of return. Consequently, these firms are risk-neutral in the sense that their utility remains constant at 3.5 utils for any project with an expected value of the occurrence of $90. A certain $90 occurrence or the midpoint between a $0 possible outcome with a 50 percent chance of occurrence and a $180 possible outcome with a 50 percent chance of occurrence both lie on the B curve opposite 3.5 utils.

The third general category of utility curve is the *increasing marginal utility* for money curve, as illustrated in Figure 7-16. Firms and individuals with this type of utility curve are thought of as risk-seekers and, in most instances, as irrational

Figure 7-16 Risk-Seeking with Increasing Marginal Utility for Money

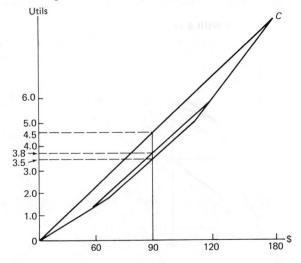

decision-makers. They get increasingly more utility from each additional dollar received, as represented by the upward slope of curve C. This makes them go after the long-shot, big reward, despite the risks. Notice in Figure 7-15 that there are still 3.5 utils associated with the $90 certain occurrence, but there are now 3.8 utils associated with the 50-50 chance of either $60 or $120 and 4.5 utils associated with the 50-50 chance of $0 and $180. The chance of a large, long-shot ($180 in this case) outweighs the additional risk of the increased dispersion because of the proportionally higher utility of the additional dollar received for outcomes to the right of the certain occurrence.

A firm in this category, although rare, would undertake the most risky ventures in hopes of large rewards. There are, for example, mineral prospectors who search the desert for the big strike, but who, except for the sensational rare find, generally fail. The financial officer of a firm should never be a risk-seeker in all cases. The occasional risky project with a relatively small investment and potentially large payoff might be included on occasion as a balance to the more conservative projects, but the repeatedly risk-seeking financial officer will guide a firm to ruin.

The utility capital budgeting model Once the financial officer has specified the firm's utility function, he or she can judge its degree of risk-aversion[9] and evaluate each proposed project accordingly. However, you should note that measuring the utility is not an easy task, and, even once you have some idea of management's risk aversion, you still may not know (or have it agree with) the stockholders' utility. These reasons tend to discourage the use of utility analysis in capital budgeting, although it would be a mistake not to consider at least the general risk attitudes of the people to whom you, as financial officer, are presenting your evaluation. No financial officer causes more displeasure among supervisors than the one who keeps suggesting very high-risk projects to a very risk-averse board of directors, and vice versa. As a financial officer, you just would not go into a capital budget presentation suggesting that a very conservative bank undertake an expedition to the Amazon to look for diamonds.

If we could precisely measure the utility curve, we could relate it to any particular project through that project's probability distribution of possible cashflow outcomes to get the expected utility occurrence. For example, we can derive an expected utility of 2.01 for project A in the following fashion.

Possible NPV outcomes	Utility of each NPV outcome	Associated probability of outcome	Weighted utility of each outcome
−$100,000	−3.5	.1	−.35
0	0	.2	.00
200,000	+3.0	.6	1.80
400,000	+5.6	.1	.56
			Expected utility 2.01

We take the possible NPV outcomes, which we can derive by computing the NPV of the project at each possible set of cashflows in the subjectively postulated probability distribution of cashflows, and then measure the utils associated with each pos-

---

[9] We assume risk-aversion because it is by far the typical utility function of financial management, although the degree of risk-aversion varies among firms.

sible outcome. In this case, there are a negative 3.5 utils associated with the possible loss. This rises to a positive 5.6 utils at an outcome of $400,000. Finding the weighted average gives us the expected utility of 2.01. We now have a measure of the relative attractiveness of the project when it is compared to the expected utility of other projects under consideration. The project with the higher expected utility is the preferable one.

Notice that the utility capital budgeting model allows the financial officer to incorporate the utility function of the decision-makers directly into the evaluation of the project. This replaces the necessity of weighing the expected return against the expected risk, as must be done in the capital budgeting techniques that provide both figures, such as the mean-standard deviation approaches. Unfortunately, because of the difficulty of measuring the utility curve, this method is rarely used. However, the concept of differing risk-aversion levels among firms and individuals must be understood by you if you want to avoid the pitfalls of presenting an inappropriate project proposal to your superiors. Do we want to undertake that much risk? It is a question that is always weighed into the decision-making process somehow. You must be aware that risk-aversion differs among firms and individuals.

CAPITAL BUDGETING AND THE FIRM'S OBJECTIVE

Once you have analyzed the risk of the individual projects, how do you select the portfolio of interrelated projects under risk which maximizes the firm's objective?

Combining Projects

Combining projects affects the absolute magnitude of the variation in the cashflow streams over time as compared to the variation in the cashflow of each product. If, for example, as illustrated in Figure 7-17a, the expected cashflow streams over time for projects A and B exactly offset each other, the effect of the combination is to reduce the dispersion around the expected occurrence to zero, represented by the

Figure 7-17 Variation in Cashflow Streams of Combined Projects

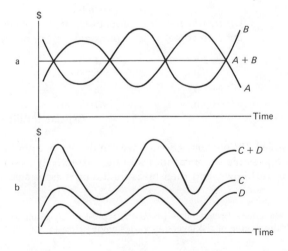

horizontal straight line. In other words, the combination of the two has leveled out the two cycles.

If the variations in the expected cashflows of the two projects over time complement each other, like projects C and D in Figure 7-17b, the magnitude of the variation caused by combining them increases. For this portfolio of projects, the dispersion as measured by the standard deviation would increase. The firm might then experience strains on its cash reserves during the cyclical downturns and would certainly be exposing itself to increased risk.

The degree to which the cashflows of different projects move together is expressed as the correlation between the projects. Since projects A and B in Figure 7-17a exactly offset one another, they have perfect negative correlation, as signified by a correlation coefficient of -1. Such a combination, although rare, might arise from undertaking a project which fluctuated with the level of general economic activity along with another project which fluctuated inversely with the level of general economic activity. Projects C and D, on the other hand, have perfect positive correlation, signified by the correlation coefficient of $+1$, since their cashflows move in an exactly complementary fashion with each other. Obviously, the closer we get to a portfolio of projects that are perfectly negatively correlated one with the other, the more risk we can remove from the firm's capital budget.[10]

If we have more than two projects under evaluation, a number of combinations of projects exist. Each has its own expected return (which could be measured as the expected IRR, NPV, or the expected value of any other decision criterion) and its expected risk (the standard deviation around that expected value). For example, the financial officer could be faced with the possible combinations shown in Table 7-4. We could graph these expected return-risk profiles as in Figure 7-18.

Table 7-4   Expected Return-Risk Profiles of Various Project Portfolios

Portfolio number	$\overline{\text{IRR}}_p$	σ_p
1	12%	4%
2	14	6
3	8	2
4	20	12
5	19	11
6	11	7
7	12	6
8	16	8
9	17	9
10	8	4

[10] As long as the cashflows are less than perfectly positively correlated, there is a reduction in the standard deviation of the portfolio of projects because:

$$\sigma_p = \sqrt{\sum_{j=1}^{m} \sum_{t=1}^{m} r_{jt}\, \sigma_j\, \sigma_t}$$

where

σ_p = the standard deviation of the portfolio
r_{jt} = correlation coefficient between project j and project t
σ_j and σ_t = the standard deviation for each project

See Harry M. Markowitz, *Portfolio Selection: Efficient Diversification of Investments,* Wiley, New York, 1959.

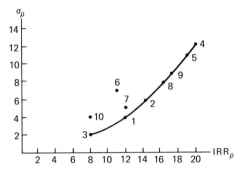

Figure 7-18 Graph of Expected Return-Risk Profiles

Notice that as the expected return increases (moves to the right on the horizontal axis), the expected risk of that portfolio also increases. Conversely, as the expected risk increases, the expected return increases. This is the typical relationship found between return and risk, implying the usual banality that you get nothing for nothing. If your expected return is high, it is almost certain that your risk is high also.

Notice from Table 7-4 and from Figure 7-18 that we can immediately eliminate some portfolios of projects because they are dominated by other portfolios; that is, there are other portfolios with both a higher expected return and a lower expected risk. In our illustration, we can immediately eliminate portfolio 10 because it is dominated by portfolio 3, which has the same return but a lower risk. Portfolio 1 also dominates portfolio 10 because the former has a higher return for the same risk. Portfolio 1 dominates portfolio 7 because it has the same return for a lower risk. Portfolio 2 dominates portfolio 6.

A portfolio of projects is preferred if it offers the highest expected return for a given level of risk *or* the lowest expected risk for any given level of expected return. Under those conditions, the only portfolios of projects we are interested in are those on the outer edge connected by the curve in Figure 7-18. Those to the left of that curve are dominated by some other portfolio. In finance parlance, that curve is known as the *efficiency frontier.*

We cannot yet make any selection among the portfolios on the efficiency frontier, although we can see that the riskier portfolios are to the upper right of the frontier and the less risky ones to the lower left. Each individual firm will prefer the portfolio that most satisfies its utility preference for risk. In this case we measure risk through the indifference curve.

The Indifference Curve

The *indifference curve* measures the various expected return-risk profiles from which we derive equal utility such that we are indifferent as to which portfolio of projects on the indifference curve we would prefer. For example, we might be indifferent between the portfolio with an expected IRR of 8 percent and a standard deviation of 2 percent and another portfolio with an expected return-risk profile of 10 percent and 2.5 percent. The increased return expectations exactly offset the increase in the expected risk, so we feel the higher return for the riskier project is worth the extra risk. Therefore the projects offer equal utility.

The indifference curve (Figure 7-19) is constructed from the utility curve, using a

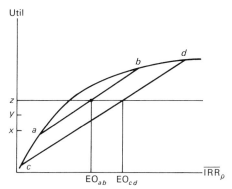

Figure 7-19 Derivation of the Indifference Curve

diminishing marginal utility function. We are looking for the combination of possible outcomes on the utility curve which, regardless of the associated expected occurrence (E.O.) gives us the same amount of utils, Z in this case. In Figure 7-19 we can see that the combination of possible outcomes a and b with its corresponding expected occurrence (E.O._{ab}) has the same utility as the combination of possible outcomes c and d, despite the fact that the latter's expected occurrence (E.O._{cd}) is larger. The reason for the same level of utility despite the higher expected occurrence is the higher risk represented by the greater dispersion between points c and d.

There is an entire series of different combinations which lie on the utility level Z. Some of these combinations will have a lower return and lower risk, while others will have a higher return and higher risk. If we plotted the expected return-risk profiles of all combinations which had their midpoint (E.O.) on utility level Z, we would get the indifference curve of Figure 7-20. Here we are indifferent among the combinations which lie on the curve, for each gives us the same utility. This is so because all have Z utils.

For every level of utility there is another indifference curve representing the plot of combinations whose midpoints (E.O.) lie on that level. This entire series of indifference curves may be plotted on the indifference curve mapping shown in Figure 7-21. Each curve reflects a given utility level, such that we are indifferent among the portfolios of projects anywhere along the curve. But we would prefer to be on the

Figure 7-20 The Indifference Curve

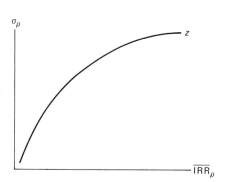

Figure 7-21 Indifference Curve Map

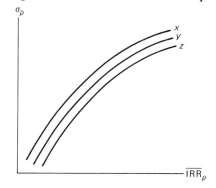

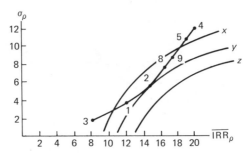

Figure 7-22 Available Portfolios Compared to Indifference Curve Map

curve representing the highest utility level. In this case, the Z indifference curve is the highest level. This can be seen because the Z indifference curve gives the highest return at any particular risk. As we move down to the right, we encounter still more indifference curves at higher utility levels.

If we superimpose the indifference map of Figure 7-21 on the expected return-risk profiles of the project portfolios of Figure 7-18, we can relate the available portfolios to our preferred risk position, as shown in Figure 7-22. The portfolio of projects which allows us to get to the highest indifference curve obviously maximizes our utility and is the one we will undertake. In Figure 7-22, it is clear that portfolio 2 maximizes our utility, because it allows us to reach indifference curve Y, the highest indifference curve we *can* reach. We cannot reach indifference curve Z, for we have no portfolio which comes into contact with it. We would not undertake any of the portfolios on indifference curve X because we can reach a higher indifference curve by undertaking portfolio 2. In general, the highest indifference curve we can reach is the one tangent to the efficiency frontier. In Figure 7-22, tangency occurs at portfolio 2.

Notice that it is possible that the portfolio of projects which are finally undertaken may actually include some of the individual projects which were originally far down the list of available, acceptable projects. This is because their negative correlation with the other projects in the portfolio is of value. Their inclusion reduces the risk of the entire portfolio which, in turn, dampens the amplitude of the variation in the firm's overall capital budget.[11] It is the expected return-risk profile of the possible whole packages, or portfolios, of projects which must be considered within the risk preferences of the decision-makers.

SUMMARY

After having read Chapter 7, you should be able to answer these questions:

1. What is uncertainty?

We distinguished between uncertainty and risk. Operating under uncertainty, we face an unknown number of possible outcomes, none of which is known. Operating under risk, we face a known number of possible outcomes, each of which has a value and an associated probability of occurrence.

[11] Wilbur G. Lewellen and Michael S. Long, "Simulation versus Single Value Estimates in Capital Expenditure Analysis," *Decision Sciences*, Vol. 3, 1972, pp. 19–33.

2. How do I estimate the possible outcomes and their associated probabilities of occurrence?

The derivation of the estimates may involve many forecasting techniques such as extrapolation, trendline and scatter diagram analysis, field surveys and regression analysis. But much of the distribution of the outcomes is derived from the subjective thought process of the financial officer, who has to know and isolate the factors of significant influence on the occurrence, make reasonable assumptions about each of the influences, and derive specific estimates of the cashflows.

3. How do I measure, quantify, and interpret risk once I have the distribution of the possible outcomes and their associated probabilities?

Once we have probability distribution, we can derive measures of central tendency and dispersion which reflect our expectations on the occurrence and risk associated with achieving that occurrence. These measures include the commonly used mean and standard deviation, although we saw that there are other measures, such as the standard error of the estimate and the skewness of the distribution.

4. How do I adjust the capital budgeting techniques to include risk?

We explored many approaches, including the incorporation of the mean and the standard deviation of the cashflows to replace the point estimates. We looked at risk-adjusted methods which increased the discount factor (the cost of capital) to compensate for the risk.

We examined simulation and sensitivity analysis to see how they could aid the financial officer in improving the accuracy of our models. Decision tree approaches allowed us to look at the independent and the correlated sequential outcomes over the life of the project. We also saw how we could incorporate the utility of the decision-makers directly into the capital budgeting evaluation process so as to reflect their risk-aversion and coordinate their selection of the project which best suited their own individual attitudes toward risk.

5. Once I have analyzed the risk of each separate project, how do I select the portfolio of interrelated projects under risk which best maximizes the firm's objective?

The combination of projects could have a lower risk than the projects taken separately because the variations in the cashflows over time could be dampened if there were less than perfectly positive correlation among the projects. Thus, we would select the portfolio of projects that gives us the highest return for that level of risk which best reflects the decision-makers' attitude toward risk.

QUESTIONS

7-1 Distinguish between risk and uncertainty.
7-2 Define the following terms and phrases:
  (a) Probability
  (b) Probability distribution
  (c) Normal distribution
  (d) Mean outcome of a probability distribution
  (e) Standard deviation
  (f) Coefficient of variation
7-3 The net present values (NPV) of projects A, B, and C have been estimated for various possible circumstances that might affect the firm. Similarly, probabili-

ties of each occurrence have been estimated, and the mean NPVs and their respective standard deviations are given below:

Project	A	B	C
Mean NPV	$100,000	$200,000	$300,000
Standard deviation	$ 5,000	$ 8,000	$ 25,000

   (a) Calculate and rank the projects according to their risk, as measured by the coefficient of variation.
   (b) Explain why you ranked the projects as you did.
7-4 Suppose your boss is interested in knowing the likelihood (probability) of the actual net present value (NPV) being negative for a particular project. How would you provide a reasonable estimate?
7-5 Discuss some of the differences and similarities in the risk-adjusted discount rate and certainty-equivalent approaches for incorporating risk into capital budgeting. (The certainty-equivalent approach is discussed in Appendix 7A.)
7-6 Under what circumstances might the decision tree technique in capital budgeting analysis be useful?
7-7 (a) Define and graphically illustrate an efficiency frontier.
   (b) Define and graphically illustrate an indifference curve map for a risk averter.
   (c) How are the efficiency frontier and the indifference map useful in selecting a portfolio of projects? Illustrate graphically.
7-8 What decision rule can be used to determine if an investment project should be continued or abandoned? (Abandonment is discussed in Appendix 7A.)

PROBLEMS

7-1 A proposed project is estimated to have the following initial cost, cashflows, and abandonment value:

Year	Cashflow	Abandonment value
0	−$50,000	
1	40,000	$30,000
2	30,000	25,000
3	20,000	20,000
4	10,000	0

Assuming the firm's cost of capital is 8 percent:
   (a) What is the optimum life of the project? That is, should the project be abandoned prior to the end of the fourth year after completion? (Abandonment is discussed in Appendix 7A.)
   (b) If after one year in operation the cashflows are revised downward for the remaining years of the projects as follows, is the abandonment decision affected?

Year	Revised cashflows	Abandonment value
2	$20,000	$25,000
3	15,000	20,000
4	5,000	0

7-2 Union Company has estimated the cashflows for its proposed Suburban Skill Project for the two-year life of the project. The principal variable affecting the expected cashflows is House Bill 201, which will provide financial assistance to suburban residents who participate in the project. Without the government aid, the cashflows will be severely reduced. Union management has estimated there is an 80 percent probability that HB 201 will be passed and a 20 percent probability that it will fail. If HB 201 passes, the estimated cashflow in year 1 is $20,000. Similarly, if HB 201 fails the estimated cashflow is $5,000. During the second year of the project, management is concerned about possible competing programs and has estimated that there is a 50 percent chance that competing programs will develop if HB 201 passes. If HB 201 passes and competing programs do develop, the cashflow in year 2 is estimated to be $25,000; if competing programs do not develop, the estimated cashflow in year 2 is $35,000. On the other hand, if HB 201 fails there is a 90 percent chance that no competing programs will develop and only a 10 percent chance that such programs will be initiated. If HB 201 fails and competing programs develop, the estimated cashflow for year 2 is $10,000. If HB 201 fails and no competing programs develop, the estimated cashflow for year 2 is $15,000.

Assume that Union has a cost of capital of 8 percent and that the Suburban Skill Project costs $20,000 and has a salvage value of $16,000 and $0 at the end of years 1 and 2, respectively.

(a) Draw a decision tree diagram of the proposed project.
(b) Ignoring salvage values, compute the expected NPV and standard deviation for the project.
(c) Utilizing the salvage values, is the expected NPV and risk of the project different from (b)?

7-3 Cashflows for project A have been estimated for the three-year life of the project under various assumptions regarding future events and the probabilities of such events occurring.

Year 1		Year 2		Year 3	
Cashflow	Probability	Cashflow	Probability	Cashflow	Probability
$1,000	.10	$3,000	.05	$2,000	.10
2,000	.40	4,000	.45	3,000	.30
3,000	.40	5,000	.45	4,000	.40
4,000	.10	6,000	.05	5,000	.20

Assume the firm has a cost of capital of 10 percent, the project has no salvage value, and the project costs $5,000.

(a) Calculate the expected net present value (NPV) and standard deviation of the project.
(b) What is the project's coefficient of variation?
(c) What is the probability that the actual NPV of the project will be negative?

7-4 Texflex is contemplating investing in one of two mutually exclusive projects and is currently using the risk-adjusted discount rate approach in its capital budgeting decisions. Excluding the present investment proposals, the firm's coefficient of expected cashflows is .40, and it anticipates a required rate of return by marginal investors of 16 percent. Presently, long-term United States Treasury bonds are yielding 6 percent. The expected cashflows and standard deviations for each project are as follows:

	Project A			Project B	
Year (t)	$\overline{CF}_t$	σ_t	Year (t)	$\overline{CF}_t$	σ_t
1	$2,500	$1,000	1	$4,000	$2,000
2	2,500	1,000	2	4,000	2,000
3	2,500	1,000	3	4,000	2,000
			4	4,000	2,000
			5	4,000	2,000

(a) What is the coefficient of variation for project A?
(b) What is the coefficient of variation for project B?
(c) What is the risk-adjusted discount rate for project A? For project B?
(d) If project A costs $5,000 and B costs $15,000, which project is preferred? (Compare the projects' risk adjusted NPVs.)

7-5 The Rowe Company uses a certainty-equivalent approach in the evaluation of its risky capital budgeting proposals. (The certainty-equivalent approach is discussed in Appendix 7A.) Currently, two mutually exclusive projects are under consideration. The expected net cashflows and standard deviations for each project during each year of its life are as follows:

	Project A		Project B	
Year (t)	$\overline{CF}_t$	σ_t	$\overline{CF}_t$	σ_t
0	-$18,000	0	-$30,000	0
1	15,000	1,000	15,000	1,000
2	10,000	1,000	15,000	1,000
3	10,000	2,000	10,000	1,000
4	0	0	10,000	2,000
5	0	0	10,000	3,000

Assume the risk-free discount rate is currently 6 percent.
(a) What is the certainty-equivalent NPV for each project? Which project is preferred?
(b) Suppose management chooses to ignore the standard deviations of each period's expected net cashflows (σ_t), but utilizes instead the following certainty-equivalent coefficients (B_t):

	Project A	Project B
Year (t)	B_t	B_t
0	1.0	1.0
1	0.80	0.80
2	0.70	0.80
3	0.65	0.75
4		0.60
5		0.50

What is the certainty-equivalent NPV for each project? Which project is preferred?

7-6 The XYZ Company is contemplating introducing a new product, Zape, either on a limited scale in Texas or on a broader scale throughout the Southwest. The initial costs of the pilot projects are $50,000 in Texas and $300,000 for the entire Southwest. The equipment for each project has the same 3-year life and no salvage value beyond the initial year. Presently, the risk-free discount rate is 6 percent. Management has estimated the following expected net cashflows for each project under certain levels of demand (High, Normal, and Low) and assigned the following probabilities of each demand level occurring (probabilities are the same for each year):

Texas Project	Probability	Year			
		0	1	2	3
High demand	.20	$−50,000	$70,000	$70,000	$70,000
Normal demand	.60	−50,000	60,000	60,000	60,000
Low demand	.20	−50,000	40,000	40,000	40,000
Southwest Project					
High demand	.30	−300,000	200,000	200,000	200,000
Normal demand	.40	−300,000	150,000	150,000	150,000
Low demand	.30	−300,000	100,000	100,000	100 000

Should Zape be introduced in Texas or the entire Southwest?

BIBLIOGRAPHY

Adler, Michael. "On Risk-Adjusted Capitalization Rates and Valuation by Individuals." *Journal of Finance*, XXV (September 1970), 819–836.

Bierman, Harold, Jr. "Discounted Cash Flows, Price Level Adjustments and Expectations." *Accounting Review*, XLVI (October 1971), 693–699.

Blume, Marshall E. "On the Assessment of Risk." *Journal of Finance*, XXVI (March 1971), 1–10.

Byrne, R., A. Charnes, A. Cooper, and K. Kortanek. "Some New Approaches to Risk." *Accounting Review*, LXIII (January 1968), 18–37.

Cohen, Kalman J., and Edwin J. Elton. "Inter-Temporal Portfolio Analysis Based Upon Simulation of Joint Returns." *Management Science*, 14 (September 1967), 5–18.

Grayson, C. Jackson, Jr. *Decisions Under Uncertainty: Drilling Decisions by Oil and Gas Operators*. Division of Research, Harvard Business School, Boston, 1960.

Greer, Willis, R., Jr. "Capital Budgeting Analysis with the Timing of Events Uncertain." *Accounting Review*, XLV (January 1970), 103–114.

Hertz, David B. "Investment Policies that Pay Off." *Harvard Business Review*, 46 (January-February 1968), 96–108.

———. "Risk Analysis in Capital Investment." *Harvard Business Review*, 42 (January-February 1964), 95–106.

Hillier, Frederick S. "The Derivation of Probabilistic Information for the Evaluation of Risky Investments." *Management Science*, 9 (April 1963), pp 443–457.

Klausner, Robert F. "The Evaluation of Risk in Marine Capital Investments." *Engineering Economist*, 14 (Summer 1969), 183–214.

Kryzanowski, Lawrence, Peter Lasztiz and Bernhard Schwab. "Monte Carlo Simulation and Capital Expenditure Decisions: A Case Study." *The Engineering Economist*, 18 (Fall 1972), 31–48.

Lerner, Eugene M., and Alfred Rappaport. "Limit DCF in Capital Budgeting." *Harvard Business Review*, 46 (July-August 1968), 133–139.

Magee, J. F., "How to Use Decision Trees in Capital Investment." *Harvard Business Review*, 42 (September-October 1964), 79–96.

Mao, James C. T., "Survey of Capital Budgeting: Theory and Practice." *Journal of Finance*, XXV (May 1970), 349–360.

Merville, L. J., and L. A. Travis, "Optimal Working Capital Policies: A Chance-Constrained Programming Approach." *Journal of Financial and Quantitative Analysis,* VIII (January 1973), 47–60.

Moag, Joseph S., and Eugene M. Lerner, "Capital Budgeting Decisions Under Imperfect Market Conditions—A System Framework." *Journal of Finance,* XXIV (September 1969), 613–621.

Myers, Stewart C., "A Note on Linear Programming and Capital Budgeting." *Journal of Finance,* XXVII (March 1972), 89–92.

———. "Procedures for Capital Budgeting Under Uncertainty." *Industrial Management Review,* 9 (Spring 1968), 1–15.

Naslund, Berthel, and Andrew Whinston, "A Model of Multi-period Investment Under Uncertainty." *Management Science,* 9 (January 1962), 184–200.

Paine, Neil R., "Uncertainty and Capital Budgeting." *Accounting Review,* XXXIX (April 1964), 330–332.

Quirin, G. David, *The Capital Expenditure Decision.* Irwin, Homewood, Ill., 1967.

Robichek, Alexander A., and Stewart C. Myers, *Optimal Financing Decisions.* Prentice-Hall, Englewood Cliffs, N. J., 1965, Ch. 5.

Salazar, Rudolfo C., and Subrata K. Sen, "A Simulation Model of Capital Budgeting Under Uncertainty." *Management Science,* 15 (December 1968), 161–179.

Schwab, Bernard, and Peter Lusztig, "A Note on Investment Evaluations In Light of Uncertain Future Opportunities." *Journal of Finance,* XXVII (December 1972), 1093–1100.

Stapleton, Richard C., "Portfolio Analysis, Stock Valuation and Capital Budgeting Decision Rules For Risky Projects." *Journal of Finance,* XXVI (March 1971), 95–118.

Tuttle, Donald L., and Robert H. Litzenberger, "Leverage, Diversification and Capital Market Effects on a Risk Adjusted Capital Budgeting Framework." *Journal of Finance,* XXIII (June 1968), 427–443.

Van Horne, James C., "Capital-Budgeting Decisions Involving Combinations of Risky Investments." *Management Science,* 13 (October 1966), 84–92.

Westerfield, Randolph, and Robert Keeley," A Problem in Probability Distribution Techniques For Capital Budgeting." *Journal of Finance,* XXVII (June 1972), 703–710.

Whitmore, G. A., and S. Darkazanli, "A Linear Risk Constraint in Capital Budgeting." *Management Science,* 18 (December 1971), B-155–B-157.

Appendix 7A **Other Techniques in Capital Budgeting**

CERTAINTY-EQUIVALENT APPROACH

Instead of adjusting the demoninator (the discount factor or the cost of capital) in the present-value approaches to capital budgeting, we can adjust the cashflow estimates for risk. We saw in Chapter 5 that when dealing with certainty the cost of funds was the pure interest rate or risk-free interest rate. By reducing the uncertain expected cashflows to certainty in this method, we return, in effect, to the evaluation of the project under certainty as in Chapter 5 and must use the risk-free rate. When not using certainty or the certainty equivalent cashflow, we must use the risk-adjusted cost of capital (k) discussed in Part Three. If we were to reduce the cashflow estimate in each year over the life of the project to a point of certainty such that we felt 100 percent certain that the estimate would occur, we would have effectively eliminated all risk. This certain cashflow is equivalent to the cashflow on a United States government security.

The appropriate discount rate to use when the cashflow estimate is equivalent to certainty is the risk-free rate, since there is no longer any risk left in the cashflow estimate. The discount rate will still vary, of course, as the financial markets change, but the rate for the project is the same as the rate for a United States government security.

The decision rule associated with the certainty equivalent approach is to undertake the project if its certainty-equivalent NPV is greater than zero. For any of the other present-value decision criteria, the rule is similarly altered to reflect the present value of the certainty-equivalent cashflows in relation to the project's cost.

We can calculate the certainty equivalent of the cashflows (CF_t) in several ways. First, we can reduce the cashflow estimate by a sufficient number of standard deviations to insure that, under the normal distribution, the occurrence will be certain to occur. This can be done by taking the mean of the cashflow estimates for each period and reducing it by three standard deviations as follows:

$$C.E._t = \overline{CF_t} - 3\sigma$$

where

$C.E._t$ = the certainty equivalent for period t
$\overline{CF_t}$ = the mean cashflow estimate for period t
σ = the standard deviation

As we have seen, this reduction of the mean by three standard deviations makes us 99.7 percent certain that the occurrence will be at least equal to the certainty equivalent. Of course, we could use any multiple of the standard deviation that we felt produced certainty. For example, if:

$$\overline{CF_t} = \$3,000$$
$$\sigma = 500$$

then:

$$C.E._t = \$3,000 - 3(\$500)$$
$$= \$1,500$$

If the project had a 3-year life, no salvage value, cost $5,000, and the risk-free discount rate were 7 percent, the project's certainty-equivalent NPV would be:

$$NPV = \frac{\$1,500}{(1+.07)^1} + \frac{\$1,500}{(1+.07)^2} + \frac{\$1,500}{(1+.07)^3} - \$5,000$$

$$= -\$1,063.55$$

Since the certainty-equivalent NPV is negative, we would reject the project. Notice that the discount factor used was the risk-free rate of 7 percent, but that the reduced cashflow estimates more than offset the lower rate of discount.

A second method of calculating the certainty equivalent is to reduce the estimate by a factor (B_t) that reflects your particular willingness to trade the risky estimate for the certainty equivalent:

$$B_t = \frac{\text{Certain cashflow}_t}{\text{Estimated cashflow}_t}$$

B_t increases as the certainty equivalent increases relative to any estimate for the period. If you subjectively feel that there is great certainty of the estimate occurring, B_t will be close to (if not exactly) 1.0, implying that the certain cashflow and the estimated cashflow are equal. As you become less certain that the estimated cashflow and the certain cashflow are equal, B_t decreases; in the extreme, it sinks to zero.

This B_t factor is then applied to the numerator of the NPV formula, reducing the estimated cashflows to certainty and forcing the discount factor in the denominator to be the risk-free rate. In our example, if the risk-free discount rate were 7 percent and B_t was:

$$B_t = \frac{\$2,000}{\$3,000}$$

$$= .67$$

then the NPV would be:

$$NPV = -\$5,000 + \frac{.67(\$3,000)}{(1+.07)^1} + \frac{.67(\$3,000)}{(1+.07)^2} + \frac{.67(\$3,000)}{(1+.07)^3}$$

$$= \$248.60$$

A third method of calculating the certainty equivalent is the time-adjusted method. If you felt less certain of your estimated cashflow as the length of time over which you have to estimate increases, you might want to increase B_t to account for any increased uncertainty associated with the futurity of the estimate. For example, instead of having B_t remain constant at .67, you might want to have B_t decline as time progresses such that:

$$B_1 = .67$$
$$B_2 = .50$$
$$B_3 = .40$$

The NPV would be:

$$NPV = -\$5,000 + \frac{.67(\$3,000)}{(1+.07)^1} + \frac{.50(\$3,000)}{(1+.07)^2} + \frac{.40(\$3,000)}{(1+.07)^3}$$

$$= -\$841.12$$

We would now reject this project, since it has a negative certainty-equivalent net present value.

Notice how the B_t factor effectively decreases the certainty equivalent of the estimated cashflow over time. Of course the financial officer has great flexibility in determining the exact value of the B_t factor, since this is basically done by subjective feel.

HILLIER MODEL APPROACH

Like the decision tree technique, this approach allows us to consider the relationship of the cashflows between periods within the mean-standard deviation framework. Whereas the previous mean-standard deviation approach assumed that the cashflow in one period was independent of the cashflow in succeeding periods, this mean-standard deviation approach explicitly incorporates the correlation of the cashflows between periods. In other words, this approach allows us to consider the possibility that a bad occurrence below our expectations *now* is indicative of a still worse period, also below our expectations, in the future. This is true if the two periods are correlated. We could say that, if the periods are correlated, once you start to deviate from the expected, you would continue to deviate again in the next period, making the total deviation over the entire life of the project rather large, since the deviations would cumulate. Once you start downhill, you gather momentum and continue into the pit at the bottom.

The decision-makers should at least be aware of this possibility. The financial officer can make them aware of it by specifying the correlation coefficient (ρ) among the cashflows of the different periods as:

$$\rho = \frac{\text{cov } (\text{CF}_t, \text{CF}_{t+1})}{\sigma_{\text{CF}_t} \sigma_{\text{CF}_{t+1}}}$$

where

$\rho =$ the correlation coefficient which can go from 0 to +1 in this case

cov $(\text{CF}_t, \text{CF}_{t+1}) =$ the covariance or the degree to which the cashflow of one period moves in union with the cashflow of the next period

$\sigma_{\text{CF}_t} =$ the standard deviation of the cashflow in the period t

When the correlation coefficient equals zero, the cashflows are independent between periods, and we can use the simple mean-standard deviation approach. When the correlation coefficient reaches one, the cashflows in the different periods are perfectly positively correlated so that as this period's cashflow deviates from its expected value, next period's cashflow will also deviate from its expected value by a proportional amount. If the cashflows are perfectly positively correlated, the effect of the deviations from the expected value cumulates, causing a relatively large deviation from the expected value for the entire project. We must account for this in our calculations of the expected NPV and standard deviation.

The expected NPV for the project does not change even with perfectly positively correlated cashflows between periods, so we can continue to calculate the expected NPV as:

$$\overline{\text{NPV}} = \sum_{t=1}^{n} \frac{\overline{\text{CF}_t}}{(1+k)^t} - \text{C}$$

The presence of a perfectly positive cashflow stream does, however, change the computations for the variance and its square root, the standard deviation, such that for the two-period case, the variance is:

$$\sigma^2_{\text{NPV}} = \sigma^2_{\text{CF}_0} + \frac{\sigma^2_{\text{CF}_1}}{(1+k)^2} + \frac{\sigma^2_{\text{CF}_2}}{(1+k)^4} + \frac{2}{(1+k)} \text{ cov } (\text{CF}_0, \text{CF}_1)$$

$$+ \frac{2}{(1+k)^2} \text{ cov } (\text{CF}_0, \text{CF}_2) + \frac{2}{(1+k)^3} \text{ cov } (\text{CF}_1, \text{CF}_2) \qquad \text{(7A-1)}$$

which since cov $(\text{CF}_t, \text{CF}_{t+1}) = \sigma_{\text{CF}_1} \sigma_{\text{CF}_2}$ when $\rho = 1$ reduces to:

$$\sigma^2_{\text{NPV}} = \sigma^2_{\text{CF}_0} + \frac{\sigma^2_{\text{CF}_1}}{(1+k)^2} + \frac{\sigma^2_{\text{CF}_2}}{(1+k)^4} + \frac{2\sigma_{\text{CF}_0}\sigma_{\text{CF}_1}}{(1+k)} + \frac{2\sigma_{\text{CF}_0}\sigma_{\text{CF}_2}}{(1+k)^2} + \frac{2\sigma_{\text{CF}_1}\sigma_{\text{CF}_2}}{(1+k)^3}$$

$$= \left[\sigma_{\text{CF}_0} + \frac{\sigma_{\text{CF}_1}}{(1+k)} + \frac{\sigma_{\text{CF}_2}}{(1+k)^2} \right]^2 \qquad \text{(7A-2)}$$

All we have done in the above equation is to include the covariance in our calculation of the standard deviation as we first computed it in the simple mean–standard deviation approach earlier in the chapter. The addition of the covariance terms in Equations 7A-1 and 7A-2 to reflect the correlation among the cashflows of different periods is the only difference between this and Equation 7-5. If we take the square root of Equation 7A-2, we get the standard deviation. We now have the expected NPV and the standard deviation of that NPV if the cashflows are correlated.

Notice, also, that the incorporation of the covariance[1] has forced us to consider the correlation among the cashflows of different periods so that we are not taken by surprise if we are below estimates and keep getting worse. Even if, as financial officer, you do not explicitly incorporate this correlation between periods, it is advisable to at least recognize the possibility that an initial deviation from expectation may only worsen in the next periods instead of correcting itself. Your contingency budgets should reflect this possibility.

ABANDONMENT IN CAPITAL BUDGETING

The financial officer is often faced with deciding whether to abandon a capital project which has failed or has become outmoded before its time. How do you conduct a periodic evaluation during the project's life to decide if it should be abandoned? Also, how is the initial decision to undertake or reject the project affected by the explicit incorporation of abandonment into the capital budgeting process?

Periodic Abandonment Evaluation

Once the project is in place, the abandonment alternative is always available.[2] At each juncture, usually at the end of each year or accounting period, the financial of-

---

[1] George C. Philappatos, *Financial Management Theory and Techniques*, Holden-Day, San Francisco, 1973, p. 220.

If some of the cashflows are independent while others are correlated, then:

$$\overline{\text{NPV}} = \sum_{t=0}^{n} \frac{\overline{\text{CF}_t}}{(1+k)^t} = \sum_{t=0}^{n} E(Y_t) + \sum_{r=1}^{m} E(X_t^{(r)})$$

$$\sigma^2_{\text{NPV}} = \sum_{t=0}^{n} \left[\frac{\sigma^2(Y_t)}{(1+k)^{2t}} \right] = \sum_{r=1}^{m} \left\{ \sum_{t=0}^{n} \left[\frac{\sqrt{\sigma^2(X_t^{(r)})}}{(1+k)^t} \right] \right\}^2$$

where
    Y_t = the independent cashflows
    $X_t^{(r)}$ = the tth cashflows correlated with the rth future cashflows

[2] Alexander A. Robichek and James C. Van Horne, "Abandonment Value and Capital Budgeting," *Journal of Finance*, December 1967, 577–589.

Table 7A-1

Year	Cashflow	Scrap value
1	$5,000	$7,000
2	4,000	5,000
3	3,000	3,000
4	2,000	1,000
5	1,000	0

ficer compares the abandonment value with the net present value of the project for the years remaining in its life. If the abandonment value exceeds the NPV at that time, the decision-makers may want to abandon it.

For example, let us take a 5-year project with a cost of $10,000, the cashflows and scrap values at the end of each year as shown in Table 7A-1, and a given cost of capital (k) of 10 percent. The NPV of the project at the initial decision period (year 0) is:

$$NPV_0 = -\$10,000 + 4,545 + 3,304 + 2,253 + 1,336 + 621$$
$$= \$2,059$$

Since the NPV_0 is greater than zero, we undertake the project. If we view the scrap value as the cost of acquiring the subsequent cashflows, the NPV at the review at the end of year 1 would be:

$$NPV_1 = -\$7,000 + 3,636 + 2,478 + 1,502 + 613$$
$$= \$1,229$$

Since the NPV_1 is greater than zero, we would continue with the project at the end of year 1 and not abandon it. In other words, the salvage value is worth less than the value of continuing the project. Reviewing the project at the end of year 2 shows that:

$$NPV_2 = -\$5,000 + 2,727 + 1,652 + 751$$
$$= \$130$$

Since NPV_2 remains positive, we continue with the project. Reviewing the project at the end of year 3 shows that:

$$NPV_3 = -\$3,000 + 1,818 + 826$$
$$= -\$356$$

Since the NPV_3 is less than zero, we would abandon the project in order to realize the salvage value, which is now in excess of what we expect to realize from continuing the project.[3] Obviously, any time the salvage value exceeds the present value of the subsequent years' cashflows, the project should be abandoned. This periodic review procedure is a very important function of the financial officer. It makes it possible to weed out projects which have failed to perform as expected and whose subsequent cashflow expectations have been reduced because of a disappointing first year or two of operations. It can trigger contingency capital budget programs and prevent the firm from riding a losing project for an unnecessarily extended period of time.

[3] William H. Jean, *Finance*, Dryden Press, 1973, pp. 158–161.

Optimum Life and Abandonment

In addition to the periodic review, the explicit recognition of the abandonment alternative allows us to evaluate the optimum life of the project at the initial accept-reject decision. This is very useful for the financial officer's planning as it suggests when to abandon the project and when to expect receipt of the salvage value for future reinvestment.

The question facing you, as the financial officer, is to find the optimum life which gives the highest NPV_0 at year 0, considering both the expected cashflows and the salvage value. Taking our example in Table 7A-1, we can work backwards from a full, 5-year life to determine what year is the optimum year in which to abandon the project:

$$\begin{aligned}
NPV_0 \text{ for 5 years} &= -\$10{,}000 + \$5{,}000(.909) + \$4{,}000(.826) + \$3{,}000(.751) \\
&\quad + \$2{,}000(.683) + \$1{,}000(.621) + 0 \\
&= \$2{,}059 \\
NPV_0 \text{ for 4 years} &= -\$10{,}000 + \$5{,}000(.909) + \$4{,}000(.826) + \$3{,}000(.751) \\
&\quad + \$2{,}000(.683) + \$1{,}000(.683) \\
&= \$1{,}997 \\
NPV_0 \text{ for 3 years} &= -\$10{,}000 + \$5{,}000(.909) + \$4{,}000(.826) + \$3{,}000(.751) \\
&\quad + \$3{,}000(.751) \\
&= \$2{,}355 \\
NPV_0 \text{ for 2 years} &= -\$10{,}000 + \$5{,}000(.909) + \$4{,}000(.826) \\
&= \$1{,}979 \\
NPV_0 \text{ for 1 year} &= -\$10{,}000 + \$5{,}000(.909) + \$7{,}000(.909) \\
&= \$908
\end{aligned}$$

Notice that in each computed NPV_0 the salvage value is the last cashflow to be discounted. As the number of years of operation declines, the salvage value becomes larger and more important in determining the NPV_0, but the expected operating cashflows become less significant. The trade-off between these two determines the optimum life of the project.

In our example, the optimum life is 3 years, because the NPV_0 for the 3-year operation is highest. As the financial officer, you would recommend that the project be abandoned after 3 years and the salvage value reinvested in other projects.

Abandonment and the Expected Return-Risk Profile

As we have just seen, if we consider abandonment as an alternative to continuing the project, we would accept the salvage value whenever it was greater than the expected present value of the subsequent cashflows. This explicit consideration for abandonment alters not only the expected return of the project but also its risk, because in our evaluation we substitute the abandonment value whenever it is higher than the present value for the subsequent cashflows. This raises our expected return and lowers our expected risk for the project.

For example, Table 7A-2 represents the financial officer's expectations for a 2-year project costing $10,000 at a cost of capital of 10 percent. It is clear from Table 7A-2 that the financial officer is forecasting a 90 percent probability that the first year's cashflow will be $7,000 and a 10 percent probability that the first year's cashflow will be only $2,000. The forecast for the second year is obviously influenced by whatever happens in the first year, such that a small cashflow in the first year leads to a forecast of a small cashflow in the second year. If the first year's larger forecast is

Table 7A-2

	Year 1		Year 2	
Cashflow	Associated probability	Cashflow		Associated probability
$7,000	.9	$10,000		.7
		9,000		.3
$2,000	.1	2,000		.5
		1,000		.5

the one to occur, the financial officer is projecting a 70 percent probability of a $10,000 second-year cashflow or a 30 percent probability of a $9,000 second-year cashflow. If the first year's smaller forecast is the one to occur, the financial officer is forecasting a 50 percent probability of either a $2,000 or a $1,000 cashflow in the second year.

The possible outcomes and associated probabilities for the entire two years of the project are:

Combined cashflows	Associated probability
$7,000 + 10,000	(.9) (.7) = .63
7,000 + 9,000	(.9) (.3) = .27
2,000 + 2,000	(.1) (.5) = .05
2,000 + 1,000	(.1) (.5) = .05
	1.00

The NPVs for each possible combined cashflow discounted at a cost of capital of 10 percent are:

$$NPV = -\$10,000 + \$7,000(.909) + \$10,000(.826) = \$4,623$$
$$NPV = -\ 10,000 + \ 7,000(.909) + \ 9,000(.826) = \ 3,797$$
$$NPV = -\ 10,000 + \ 2,000(.909) + \ 2,000(.826) = -6,530$$
$$NPV = -\ 10,000 + \ 2,000(.909) + \ 1,000(.826) = -7,356$$

The expected NPV_0 and the standard deviation (σ_{NPV}) are calculated as they were for the mean-standard deviation approach, such that:

$$\overline{NPV_0} = 4,623(.63) + 3,797(.27) - 6,530(.05) - 7,356(.05)$$
$$= \$3,424$$

$$\sigma_{NPV} = \sqrt{\begin{array}{l}[4,623 - 3,242]^2(.63) + [3,797 - 3,242]^2(.27) \\ + [-6,530 - 3,242]^2(.05) + [-7,356 - 3,242]^2(.05)\end{array}}$$
$$= \$3,416.9$$

If the project has an expected salvage value of $3,000 at the end of period 1, then the expected cashflows would be:

Combined cashflows		Probability
Year 1	Year 2	
-$10,000 + 7,000 + 10,000		.63
- 10,000 + 7,000 + 9,000		.27
- 10,000 + 5,000 + 0		.05
- 10,000 + 5,000 + 0		.05

In the last two combinations the second-year cashflows have been forfeited in favor of abandoning the project and receiving the $3,000 salvage value, because the salvage value at the end of year 1 exceeded the present value of the subsequent year's expected cashflow in the last two combinations.

Under the circumstances, the NPVs at a 10 percent cost of capital are:

$$NPV = -\$10,000 + 7,000(.909) + 10,000(.826) = \$4,623$$
$$NPV = -\ 10,000 + 7,000(.909) + 9,000(.826) = \ 3,797$$
$$NPV = -\ 10,000 + 5,000(.909) + \quad 0 \quad = -5,455$$
$$NPV = -\ 10,000 + 5,000(.909) + \quad 0 \quad = -5,455$$

Then the expected NPV and associated standard deviation are:

$$\overline{NPV} = \$4,623(.63) + 3,797(.27) - 5,455(.05) - 5,455(.05)$$
$$= \$3,391$$

$$\sigma_{NPV} = \sqrt{\begin{array}{l}[\$4,623 - 3,391]^2(.63) + [3,797 - 3,391]^2(.27) \\ + [-5,455 - 3,391]^2(.05) + [-5,455 - 3,391]^2(.05)\end{array}}$$
$$= \$2,970.9$$

Notice that the explicit incorporation of the abandonment alternative has increased the expected NPV and simultaneously decreased the associated risk. Specifically, we have substituted the abandonment value for the second-year operating cashflow in the last two combinations. Explicit consideration of the abandonment alternative is obviously a useful device for financial planning.

Appendix 7B Capital Budgeting Techniques Without Probabilities

Various strategies have been developed by which the financial officer can evaluate projects even if there are no probabilities associated with the possible outcomes— almost a condition of uncertainty. These techniques generally still allow the financial officer to select the most satisfactory project(s) in terms of the decision makers' attitude toward risk.

The financial officer, without specifying the probabilities or having any idea of the risk, could think of the possible outcomes under the various conditions (states of nature) which might prevail, such as presented in Table 7B-1 (also known as a *payoff matrix*).

Table 7B-1 summarizes the financial officer's opinion about the net present value of project 1 and project 2 under the three possible levels of economic activity. If we experience a recession, the NPV_1 would be $0, while the NPV_2 would be $-\$1,000$. The payoff in terms of NPV during a normal period would be:

$$NPV_1 = \$1,000 \qquad NPV_2 = \$1,500$$

Table 7B-1   Payoff Matrix

	Recession	Normal	Boom	State of Nature
NPV$_1$	0	$1,000	$2,000	
NPV$_2$	−$1,000	$1,500	$6,000	

while during a boom period the payoff would be:

$$NPV_1 = \$2,000 \qquad NPV_2 = \$6,000$$

Which project do you undertake?

MAXIMIN STRATEGY

The maximin strategy deals with this question by maximizing the minimum of the possible outcomes. Even if the worst state of nature (general level of economic activity) occurs, the firm has maximized its position. This is a very conservative approach because the firm has, in this example, given up the opportunity for larger outcomes in a normal or boom period for assurance that it would achieve the best possible position under the worst circumstances. In our example, the maximin strategy would lead us to undertake project 1, because under the worst state of nature, the lowest we can get is a zero net present value.

MAXIMAX CRITERION

The maximax criterion maximizes the maximum possible outcome. If the best state of nature occurs (a boom), the firm achieves the highest NPV position. Obviously this is a very optimistic strategy. In our example, the maximax criterion leads us to undertake project 2 because it has the highest possible outcome of $6,000. In contrast, we could never get that high a NPV with project 1, regardless of the state of nature. As in the maximin strategy, we reached this decision without specifying the probabilities.

ASSIGNED PROBABILITY CRITERION

As a partial return to the probability analysis, the assigned probability criterion specifies a subjective probability (α) to the maximum payoff depending on how optimistic you are, and the complement of that probability ($1 - \alpha$) to the minimum payoff. For example, if you felt 70 percent sure that the boom would occur, α would equal .70 and its complement ($1 - \alpha$) would equal .3. Assigning each of those to the maximum and the minimum payoff for each project would give you the expected NPV:

$$E(NPV_1) = .7(\$2,000) + .3(0) = \$1,400$$
$$E(NPV_2) = .7(\$6,000) + .3(-\$1,000) = \$3,900$$

In this example, you would undertake project 2 because the expected net present value based on the assigned probabilities is larger.

MINIMIZING THE REGRET STRATEGY[1]

This strategy is a very pessimistic one. It attempts to minimize the regret you might feel at missing the maximum payoff, should it occur. We can construct the regret matrix (Table 7B-2) to tell us the difference between each payoff and the maximum payoff that could occur for that project. Each regret payoff in each box of Table 7B-2 reflects how much NPV you miss if the boom does occur. Under either project, you miss nothing and have no regret if the boom occurs. However, if the recession occurs, you have only $2,000 worth of regret for project 1 but $7,000 of regret with project 2. In order to minimize the regret, you apply the minimax strategy to the regret matrix and, in this example, find that project 1 minimizes your regret because the most regret that you can have is $2,000, while the largest regret in project 2 is $7,000.

MIXED STRATEGIES

Under some circumstances you can interchange the projects so that a strategy comprised of parts of both projects maximizes your position. The timing of stocks and bonds in your investment portfolio, where the two are interchangeable and where the direction of the financial markets is the state of nature, lends itself to a mixed strategy.

We want to be put in a position where we are equally as well off with either strategy over a series of repeated trials. If n equals the percentage of the time we are invested in stocks, $1 - n$ equals the percentage of the time we are invested in bonds, and the stock strategy must equal the bond strategy, the payoff matrix might be as shown in Table 7B-3. If the bond and the stock strategies have to return the same, and n is the percentage of time we are invested in stocks:

$$n(-.10) + (1 - n).30 = n(.07) + (1 - n)(.08)$$
$$n = 56.4\%$$

The optimum mixed strategy is to be invested in stocks 56.4 percent of the time, and the remainder of the time in bonds. At those percentages we would be equally well

Table 7B-2   Regret Matrix

	Recession	Normal	Boom	State of Nature
NPV$_1$ regret	$2,000	$1,000	0	
NPV$_2$ regret	$7,000	$4,500	0	

Table 7B-3

	Market down	Market up
Return on stocks	−10%	+30%
Return on bonds	+ 7%	+ 8%

[1] L. J. Savage, "The Theory of Statistical Decisions," *Journal of the American Statistical Association*, 1951, 55–57.

off in bonds or in stocks and would maximize our position. A word of caution is appropriate in this example: the mixed strategies method assumes the state of nature occurs randomly, that bond and stock returns are random occurrences.

DECISION THEORY[2]

In contrast to the strategies which involve uncertainty, the decision theory technique allows us to incorporate additional information into a situation of risk where we already have subjectively derived probabilities. It affords an even more refined probability associated with any given outcome.

Assume we have the two projects shown in Table 7B-1 and have decided to sample a group of economists on their opinion about the likelihood of a recession, normal conditions, or a boom level of general economic activity. Since this is a situation of risk, we already feel that the probabilities, as shown in column 2 of Table 7B-4, are: recession 20 percent, normal 50 percent, and boom 30 percent. Experience has shown that when our surveyed group of economists thought there was going to be a normal period, they were correct 60 percent of the time. But 20 percent of the time when they predicted a normal period, there was actually a recession. In addition, 10 percent of the time when there had actually been a boom, the economists had predicted a normal level of general economic activity. This is summarized in column 2 of Table 7B-4.

Armed with that information, we can answer the question: What is the probability of a normal period if the economists predict a normal period? The probabilities are shown in Table 7B-4. The joint probabilities (column 4 in Table 7B-4) represent the refined estimates of a recessionary, normal, or boom period occurring when we combine our own subjective feel with that of the economists. With all this additional information, we can say that the associated probabilities after refinement are:

$$
\begin{array}{llll}
\text{Recession} & = .04/.37 = & .108 \\
\text{Normal} & = .30/.37 = & .811 \\
\text{Boom} & = .03/.37 = & \underline{.081} \\
& & 1.000
\end{array}
$$

These new probabilities tell us that there is an .811 percent chance of normal economic activity, while the other two possibilities are now lower than our previous estimates.

Table 7B-4

Economic activity	(1) Probability of economic activity	(2) Probability of normal given forecast	(3) = (1) × (2) Joint probability (refined by prediction)
Recession	.2	.2	.04
Normal	.5	.6	.30
Boom	.3	.1	.03
			.37

[2] Morris Hamburg, *Statistical Analysis for Decision Making*, Harcourt, New York, 1970, Chap. 14.

Using these refined probabilities, we can compute the expected NPV of the two projects in Table 7B-1 as:

$$E(NPV_1) = .108(0) + .811(\$1{,}000) + .081(\$6{,}000)$$
$$= \$1297$$
$$E(NPV_2) = .108(-\$1{,}000) + .811(\$1{,}500) + .081(\$6{,}000)$$
$$= \$1{,}594.50$$

We would choose project 2 because its expected NPV is larger. The risk is also lowered because the weights assigned to the extreme outcomes in calculating the standard derivation are reduced as the probability of a normal period is increased.

Appendix 7C Capital Budgeting for Small Businesses

The small business must employ its capital under the same criteria of profitability as the large corporation. Capital investment projects for the small business must also yield a return in excess of the cost of capital, must also have a present value of expected cashflows in excess of their cost, and must generally be acceptable under the decision criteria employed by the larger corporations.

The major difference between the proprietor of a small business and the financial officer of a larger corporation is that the larger firm has or employs specialists, such as architects and engineers, to check on the practicality of projects. Their assurances allow the financial officer to analyze the situation almost entirely on a financial basis. In contrast, the small business proprietor may have to check on the functionality of the project as well as perform the financial analysis.[1] In a small business there are a smaller selection of projects from which to choose, and the owner must personally consider all the implementing factors of the project. Sometimes the projects are the natural outgrowth of one item or product or marketing channel in which the firm is already operating.

The expansion of plant to increase capacity (because sales are good and promise to remain so) is a natural outgrowth of the business. Other considerations include a survey of the building itself to insure adequate space for machinery and personnel, efficient loading facilities, easy accessibility, sound and pleasing exterior and interior appearances—such as lighting and floor support. One must check to see that the facilities meet the fire, zoning, and other laws of the area. If the facility caters to the public, the small business must offer convenient entrances for customers, shoplifting-prevention equipment, customer comforts such as air conditioning and toilets, and a location convenient to parking. The layout of the store or office must encourage efficiency of operation and establish a pleasant atmosphere for the customer and the employee.

[1] H. N. Broom and Justin G. Longenecker, *Small Business Management*, 3d ed., South-Western Publishing Co., 1971.

three

the cost of capital

LET US LOOK AT SOME OF THE MAJOR QUESTIONS which you, as the financial officer, must be able to answer in advising your firm on how to raise capital. As you read Part Three, look for the answers to the following questions:

1. What do I have to know in order to get the least expensive package of securities for my firm's financing?

2. What is a financial market, who participates, and what are the securities in those markets?

3. How do particular segments of the financial markets behave over time?

4. What are the theoretical underpinnings of the financial markets?

5. What is the cost of capital (k) for a particular security?

6. Can the financial officer determine the package of securities with the least cost to the firm?

7. What is the appropriate dividend policy for the firm?

8

the concept of the cost of capital

As a financial officer you should be aware that capital, the source of funds for the firm, is not costless. Why does capital cost and how is it priced? Capital costs because it is a scarce resource, and the firm must compensate the providers of that capital for giving up their funds to the firm, even if only temporarily. For their part, the providers demand compensation from the firm for giving up their capital to it. A negotiated point between the two parties represents the price the firm pays to the suppliers of capital. Usually, this price is expressed as an interest rate in the same fashion as when you supply funds to your local savings and loan association at 5¼ percent. As financial officer for the firm, you might have negotiated a 7 percent loan from an insurance company, thus committing the firm to pay the insurance company an annual interest of $70 for each $1,000 borrowed. It is traditional to express the cost of these funds in terms of the interest rate per year, so that even a 6-month loan has a yearly interest cost of, for example, 8 percent per annum. The return required by the lender or investor in the firm is considered part compensation for the use of the money and part compensation for the risks involved in lending to or investing in the firm. Traditionally, the former is known as the default-free rate (i), and the latter is known as the risk adjustment. Together, they form the cost of capital (k).

As the financial officer of a firm concerned with raising funds, you obviously need an intimate knowledge of the financial markets wherein you raise funds. But what is a financial market? If we do not know what financial markets are available to us as a source of funds, we cannot choose among them to find the appropriate buyers for our security offerings. Good financial officers know where to raise funds. We shall discover that a financial market is essentially a place where suppliers and demanders of capital come together.

Good financial officers also know that they are competing against other firms who are also trying to sell their securities to potential investors. Who are the participants in the market? We shall see that individuals and financial institutions in which people save their money are the major potential purchasers of our securities.

Good financial officers know what securities they have available to sell. After all, by merely offering a different type of security more suited to the potential investor's need, you might reduce your cost for any particular amount of funds you raise. Later sections of the text describe in detail the alternative securities you, as a financial officer, have available.

Good financial officers have acquired familiarity with the financial markets either through experience or through a careful study of their historical performance. What can we learn from such a study? First, we hopefully learn not to repeat the mistakes of the past. Security offerings which were incorrectly timed so that they were sold at the peak in capital costs are a reminder to offer securities at cyclical lows in the cost of capital instead. In order to do this, good financial officers must learn to recognize those characteristics, signs, and other indications and variables which are representative of the financial environment. We shall see that financial markets do have cyclical movements that can be anticipated by careful analysis of the important economic and financial factors which influence the supply of and the demand for funds.

There are patterns in the various financial markets over time that the financial officer might concentrate on in order to time securities offerings to cyclical lows in the cost of capital. Are there any insights into the cost of capital or any significance in these patterns, and how can they help us time our securities offerings? We shall see that there is a distinct pattern in interest rates over the term to maturity (the length of time remaining until the loan is repaid). The structure of interest rates over the various terms to maturity offers insight into the financial market's collective opinion about the direction future interest rates will take. And it provides indications of the cost of capital for various alternative maturities the financial officer may consider offering. (*Maturities,* or repayment dates, may range from one day to many years.)

Good financial officers acquaint themselves with the theory of the financial markets and study their historical performance, because financial market theory suggests how to time and tailor security offerings in order to lower the cost of capital. We shall see that financial theory helps us understand the reasons why investors demand the required return on the securities we offer. It also helps us tailor our offerings so that they are more attractive to the investor, who then requires a lower rate of return.

INVESTMENT CAPITAL AS A SCARCE COMMODITY

Why does capital cost, and how is the price of capital usually expressed?

Investment Capital

Investment capital is the funds raised by the firm to finance what the financial officer and the firm have selected to invest in. The projects are not necessarily selected and then financed; rather the two processes work in conjunction. During the course of project evaluation, the financial officer is continually providing feedback on the state of the financial markets and the appropriate cost of capital to use in the decision criteria.

Supply Factors

The supply of investment capital is obviously limited, for unlimited money and credit are not floating around in the economy. The desire and abilities of the lenders and investors to supply funds to the firm restricts the amount of fundraising a particular firm or firms in general can do. For example, banks cannot continue indefinitely to lend without running afoul of the credit restrictions placed on them by the government. Too, banks and other potential lenders and investors may not *want* to purchase the securities offered because the return is unattractive or the security does not complement their investment objectives or does not fit into their portfolios.

In some areas of the world and for some types of securities, the financial markets are insufficiently developed and cannot accommodate frequent or large offerings. The market may be unaccustomed or unwilling to purchase securities of all different maturities, which to the financial officer constitutes a lack of breadth. The market may also be unable to provide capital for large offerings (a lack of depth) or to absorb large issues without being unduly depressed and causing the cost of capital for all firms to rise (a lack of resiliency). Whenever there is an insufficient number of participants, the ease with which financial markets bring the firm and potential purchasers of its securities together may be impaired and the supply of capital limited.

If, on the other hand, people in general increase savings and put more of their income either directly into the financial markets or into the financial institutions who invest funds in the securities of firms, the supply of investment capital is increased. Any savings channel which discourages people from hoarding their income and encourages them to save their income by investing or banking it increases the supply of funds. During periods in which the flow of funds into the financial markets and into the financial intermediaries is increased, the offering of securities by the financial officer is easier and probably less costly.

The government also influences the supply of capital through the use of monetary policy by which it directly restricts or expands the supply of funds in the economy. Obviously if the federal government, through the Federal Reserve System, withdraws funds from the financial markets, the financial officer will find it more difficult and probably more costly to sell securities.

All these factors which affect supply tend to follow a cyclical pattern, as we shall see later in this chapter. At certain times, many of the factors react in unison to the economic environment and curtail the supply. For example, it is common to find the government intentionally withdrawing funds at the same time investors are also saving less in financial intermediaries, putting pressure on the financial markets and tending to raise the cost of capital.

Demand Factors

The other side of the market which the financial officer must consider is competition from other firms for the limited supply. This competition is the demand for funds. Most firms need funds at about the same time, as their profit prospects pick up with the increase in economic activity, and they decide to enlarge the number of projects undertaken. Firms become more optimistic, and previously marginal projects become acceptable with more optimistic cashflow projects (see Chapter 5). Like supply, demand describes a cycle which the financial officer should be aware of and which the good financial officer tries to anticipate, in order not to offer securities at the peak in the demand cycle.

The Price of Capital

The price of the funds for which the financial officer must negotiate is expressed as the annual interest rate for loans and as a price per share for stock. Typically, as is the case with all supply and demand situations, the price is the mechanism that equates the supply and demand. As demand increases in relation to the supply, interest rates rise, and vice versa. In this fashion some of the increased demand is choked off and the supply of funds is increased. As the financial officer, you are participating in the financial markets as a demander or as a supplier of funds, depending on the circumstances of your individual firm. You would ideally like to be a demander during periods when the supply is high relative to demand and interest rates are low and to be a supplier when interest rates are high. When interest rates were low, you might even raise funds not needed for any specific project, in anticipation of the need arising at some future date when interest rates and the cost of capital were high.[1]

When financial officers talk about the cost of capital for the loan or the debt security they have offered, they are referring to the actual interest rate they have contracted to pay the lender. Of course, for other securities, particularly stocks, the cost of capital differs from the interest rate paid on the firm's debt securities. However, the cost of capital for all securities is, in part, compensation to the supplier for the firm's use of the funds—without compensation for risk attached in owning the securities. This part is typically known as the *default-free interest rate* or the pure interest rate and can be observed on loans and the debt securities of borrowers with no risk. For example, the Treasury bonds of the United States government are default-free because the government can always print the dollar bills with which to meet the interest payments and the return of principal when due. Typically, the default-free rate is symbolized as i by the financial officer.

The other part of the cost of capital, over and above the default-free rate, is compensation to the supplier for the risk that the borrower may not be able to meet the interest payment or to return the original principal when promised. As investors and suppliers of capital believe the firm has increased chances of not meeting these obligations, they demand greater compensation for the risk involved in supplying the capital to the firm and, in the extreme, refuse to supply capital at any price. It is more typical for the cost of capital to increase moderately, perhaps a few percentage points, as the risk increases to a certain point—and then to jump sharply upward beyond that point.

We can imagine how this additional compensation for risk might work in practice. Envision yourself as a potential supplier of capital faced with the decision of which demander of funds you are going to lend to and at what price. Would you, for example, be willing to pay the same price for the 7 percent United States government Treasury bonds of 1990, which promised to pay you $70 a year interest for each year from now until 1990 and to return $1,000 to you in 1990, and a 7 percent bond of the bankrupt PennCentral Railroad, which, although promising to pay you $70 a year for each year from now until 1990 and to return $1,000 in 1990, has not paid any interest in recent years and may not be able to return that $1,000 in 1990? Of course you are not willing to pay the same price for the two bonds. In fact if you bought the PennCentral bond at all, you would have to be expecting a very large return, perhaps based on the possibility that the federal government might take over the PennCentral and pay off its bonds.

Why would you not be willing to pay the same price for the two bonds? The Penn-Central bonds are far more risky than the United States government bonds. For

---

[1] In a speech before the Detroit Security Analysts, the Masco Corporation identified its policy of raising funds during periods of low interest rate in anticipation of future investment projects.

the same promised interest payments and return of principal it is obvious that you will want to pay a lower price for the riskier PennCentral bonds. The chances of that firm's fulfilling its promise are minimal, whereas the chances of the United States government's fulfilling *its* financial promises are 100 percent.

There are, of course, varying degrees of risk between the two extremes of the United States government and a bankrupt northeastern railroad. While the United States government Treasury bonds may be the least risky security, we, as providers of capital, are continually faced with the necessity of deciding how much riskier investments may be and, consequently, how much higher the firm's cost of capital should be for securities of increasingly more risk exposure. For example, the bonds of the American Telephone and Telegraph Company (ATT) are considered to be of limited risk, yet they are certainly slightly riskier than the bonds of the United States government. Investors are willing to supply funds to ATT only at a higher interest rate, even if only slightly higher, than that paid by the United States government. This increases the cost of capital to ATT above that which the United States government pays.

The process of assigning risk and requiring higher interest rates, thus raising a firm's cost of capital even further above the default-free interest rate, continues throughout the entire spectrum of risk exposures. The potential supplier of capital has to decide upon what interest rate to demand from firms slightly more risky than ATT, such as Ford Motor Company. The process continues as investors continue to increase their required return and raise the firm's cost of capital as they work their way down through increasingly risky demanders.

The cost of capital, which financial officers traditionally symbolize as k, is an annualized interest rate that equates the supply of funds available for a particular type of security with the demand for those funds, including an adequate consideration for risk. We might symbolize the cost of capital in general as:

$$k = i + \phi$$

where
i = the default-free interest rate
ϕ = the compensation for risk

As the risk premium increases, the firm's cost of capital also increases. But let us not forget that the cost of capital can fluctuate in response to the supply-demand conditions in the financial markets at any time and particularly when investors perceive changes in the particular degree of risk associated with the firm. As a financial officer, if you want to catch the bottom of the cost-of-capital fluctuations, you not only have to time your securities offerings to the periods where the supply of capital is relatively high in relation to the demand, but you must also project an image to potential suppliers of capital which keeps them thinking your firm has a low degree of risk.

CAPITAL MARKETS—AN HISTORICAL EXAMINATION

What is a capital market? Who participates? What insights about raising funds and keeping the cost of capital to a minimum does an historical examination of the capital markets give the financial officer?

The Capital Market

A *capital market* is generally associated with the raising of longer-term funds, as opposed to the money market in which shorter-term funds are raised. In the capital market we find financial officers offering such securities as stocks (equity claims) and long-term bonds which promise return of the original principal more than one year in the future. In the money market we find financial officers raising funds through securities which typically must be repaid in one year. Hence, the maturity of one year is the traditional dividing line between the capital markets and the money markets.

It is in the capital markets that the demanders of funds and the suppliers of funds get together to arrange the transfer of the funds. They usually do this through intermediaries who handle the savers' funds and who have professional expertise and experience in the capital markets, such as life insurance companies and investment bankers. These intermediaries make a business of taking the savers' funds and investing them in the securities offered by the corporations or taking the securities of the corporation and selling them to the intermediaries or individual investors.

Capital Market Participants

The participants in the capital markets are varied, although most suppliers could be classified as either financial institutions who represent the saver or the individual saver and most demanders could be classified as corporations, governments, or individuals.

Demanders of capital As we can see in Table 8-1, funds are generally demanded for:
1. Real estate mortgages on both residential and commercial properties, which are used to finance the purchase of property
2. Corporate securities such as stocks and bonds
3. State and local government securities used to finance such projects as school and sewer construction
4. Foreign securities sold in this country by foreign governments and corporations in order to raise funds for their investment projects
5. Business loans that are the borrowings of corporations, mainly at commercial banks
6. Consumer and other bank loans primarily used by individuals to finance such items as automobiles and other consumer durables
7. Open market paper, which are short-term loans sold by corporations to short-term lenders in order to raise funds
8. United States government treasury and its agencies established to raise funds and reloan those funds to certain designated sectors of the economy. When the government borrows, it channels away funds from corporate securities to other sectors of the economy. This is particularly true during periods of large government deficits that must be financed through the sale of government debt securities. At a time when the government is coming to the financial markets with a large offering, interest rates tend to rise for your firm's offering because of the competition for the limited supply of credit.

As a financial officer of a corporation, you should realize that you are competing for funds against a host of others who want to raise funds for their own investment projects. These include state and local governmental units as well as other corpora-

Table 8-1 Summary of Supply and Demand for Credit ($ Billions)

	Annual net increases in amounts outstanding							Amounts outstanding 12/31/72E
	1967	1968	1969	1970	1971	1972E	1973E	
Net demand								
Privately held mortgages	19.8	24.0	22.7	20.2	41.8	58.6	49.2	519.1
Corporate bonds	16.0	14.0	13.8	22.8	23.7	19.4	19.7	236.3
State and local securities	9.0	10.3	7.1	14.7	21.3	12.5	7.7	178.3
Domestically held foreign bonds	1.2	1.1	1.0	0.9	0.9	0.9	1.0	16.8
Subtotal long-term nonfederal	46.0	49.4	44.6	58.6	87.7	91.4	77.6	950.5
Business loans	5.1	15.4	18.4	3.8	8.0	21.6	28.8	171.8
Consumer loans	4.5	10.0	9.4	6.0	11.2	19.1	23.0	157.5
All other bank loans	3.7	4.1	2.6	2.2	6.9	11.2	9.7	63.8
Open market paper	3.9	4.1	12.1	1.7	−1.0	0.8	8.4	39.9
Subtotal short-term private	17.2	33.6	42.5	13.7	25.1	52.7	69.9	433.0
Privately held treasury debt	3.4	6.2	−6.3	6.1	19.4	14.0	6.1	259.7
Privately held federal agency debt	3.7	5.3	8.1	9.0	2.8	9.7	16.2	60.7
Subtotal federal	7.1	11.5	1.8	15.1	22.2	23.7	22.3	320.4
Total net demand for credit	70.3	94.5	88.9	87.4	135.0	167.8	169.8	1703.9
Net supply[1]								
Mutual savings banks	5.1	4.2	2.5	3.4	8.9	10.1	7.2	93.1
Savings and loan associations	9.1	10.3	9.7	12.6	29.6	35.8	30.7	229.9
Life insurance companies	6.4	6.0	4.4	5.0	7.2	8.9	9.1	174.6
Fire and casualty companies	1.4	1.9	2.4	3.8	3.7	3.6	3.3	38.1
Private noninsured pension funds	0.8	1.2	1.0	2.6	−1.8	−0.6	−0.1	35.3
State and local retirement funds	3.0	4.5	3.7	3.8	3.7	4.4	5.0	56.0
Open-end mutual funds	−0.5	0.9	0.9	0.5	−0.5	0.2	0.5	7.2
Total nonbank investing institutions	25.3	29.0	24.6	31.7	50.8	62.4	55.7	634.2
Commercial banks[2]	36.8	39.6	15.6	33.7	51.0	70.0	62.2	570.7
Finance companies	0.6	5.3	7.7	1.5	4.0	7.9	7.5	68.3
Credit unions	0.8	1.5	1.8	1.6	3.0	3.4	2.9	21.5
Business corporations	0.9	5.6	7.6	−1.8	5.4	5.2	7.0	69.5
State and local governments	0.7	3.1	3.4	−0.5	−1.5	4.1	7.0	23.2
Foreigners	1.2	1.0	−0.7	10.7	26.8	8.7	3.8	65.9
Subtotal	66.3	85.1	60.0	76.9	139.5	161.7	146.1	1453.3
Residual: individuals and miscellaneous	4.0	9.4	28.9	10.5	−4.5	6.1	23.7	250.6
Total net supply of credit	70.3	94.5	88.9	87.4	135.0	167.8	169.8	1703.9

[1] Excludes funds for equities, cash and miscellaneous demands not tabulated above.   [2] Includes non-operating holding and other bank related companies.

SOURCE: *Supply and Demand for Credit in 1973,* Salomon Brothers, New York, p. 2.

tions within and without your own industry. You are going to have to keep constant track of what the other demanders appear to be going to do and to make judgments on the degree of competition you face in order to minimize your firm's cost of capital for any security offering.

Suppliers of capital On the other side of the capital market are the suppliers who have collected the funds in order to invest in securities offerings. It is up to you to convince them they should invest in your firm's securities at a relatively low cost, and that is no easy task. Among the suppliers are:

1. Savings and loan associations, mutual savings banks, and credit unions, who all collect savers' funds and invest them, as long as those funds remain on deposit, in the securities offerings of corporations and other demanders of funds, particularly real estate purchasers

2. Life insurance companies, who collect funds in the form of premiums from their policy holders and invest them in the interim before they are needed to pay death benefits

3. Fire and casualty insurance companies, who collect premiums and invest those funds in the securities offerings of corporations and others until they are needed to pay to policy holders as indemnification for a fire or casualty loss

4. Private noninsured pension funds, who collect funds from their members and invest those funds in the securities offerings of corporations and others between the time the funds are collected and the time they are paid out in retirement benefits

5. State and local government retirement funds, which do the identical task for employees of governments

6. Mutual funds, which channel funds from the saver to the user of funds

7. Commercial banks, which take in deposits of savers and of people who want to keep a checking account and channel those funds into the securities of users, such as your corporation

8. Finance companies, which supply credit to smaller borrowers and individuals

9. Business corporations and state and local governments, which occasionally find themselves with excess funds to invest in the securities of other corporations, rather than allowing them to sit idle.

10. Foreign investors, who supply funds to the financial markets when they purchase the security offerings of domestic users of capital

11. Individuals, the final category of suppliers, to whom the financial officer turns if financial institutions do not purchase the securities offered.

As a good financial officer, you must be alert to the developing patterns of supply in the capital market and gear your securities offerings to those financial intermediaries or individuals who have the most abundant supply of capital available at the time. This requires you to cultivate contacts with the representatives of various financial intermediaries so that you can reach them when you want to offer your securities. You also need to know which types of financial intermediaries—and which particular companies within each type—are most amenable to purchasing your securities.[2]

Capital market equilibrium   You should be aware that the total supply must equal the total demand and that this occurs because of the price-equilibrating mechanism of the interest rate. If the amount that users (demanders) of funds had originally hoped to raise exceeds the funds that suppliers had originally intended to make available, the interest rate could be expected to increase, and vice versa. If the various signs and indications appear to foreshadow an upsurge in demand or a curtailment of supply, it is your responsibility to so inform your firm's decision-makers so they can formulate their plans accordingly.

1965–1974   If we undertake an historical examination of a past period in the financial markets, looking at certain variables that may be key indicators and relating them to the performance of the financial markets of that time, we should be in a better position to avoid repeating past mistakes. As hard as it is, even in retrospect, to correlate the key variables to the actual performance of interest rates, a study of

---

[2] This is usually covered in a course on financial institutions and involves a considerably more detailed study of the capital markets than is appropriate to this text. The interested student is referred to a course in financial institutions.

Table 8-2   Summary of Figure 8-1 for Yield of AAA Corporate Bonds

Market at local trough[1]	Rising market	Relatively stable market	Market at local peak[2]	Falling market
Mid 1965	1966		End 1966	Early 1967
Early 1967	Latter 1967	1968		
	1969		Late 1969	Early 1970
Early 1970	Mid 1970		Mid 1970	Late 1970–early 1971
Early 1971	Mid 1971		Mid 1971	Latter 1971
Early 1972		First half 1972	1972	Latter 1972
End 1972	1973–1974			

[1] Local trough is the low point in that immediate time period.   [2] Local peak is the high point in that immediate time period.

the past may show how a good financial officer might try to determine the prevailing and expected future market environment. In any event, we should be able to identify some economic and financial variables which you can use in making your own analysis of future markets.

Let us examine the 1965–1974 period, which was characterized by many varied market environments both favorable and hostile to the offering of securities. Figure 8-1 reveals a cyclical pattern within what appears to be an upward trend in the corporate AAA bond yield (the interest rate on the highest quality long-term corporate bonds). We can pinpoint the troughs (bottoms) and peaks along with the periods of rising, stable, and falling yields during the period as shown in Table 8-2.

Figure 8-1, as summarized in Table 8-2, reveals that within a relatively brief 7-year period, interest rates and the cost of capital have been highly cyclical, reaching 5 local peaks and 6 local troughs and covering a range of approximately 4½ to 8½ percent. Obviously, not only is the cost of capital fairly volatile, but a mistiming of the security offering can be very expensive, nearly doubling the cost if the firm had waited until 1970 to raise long-term funds that it could have and, in retrospect, should have raised in 1965. Of course, looking out from the end of 1972, the finan-

Figure 8-1   Bond Yields

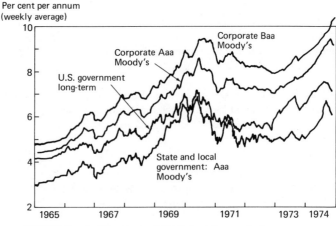

SOURCE: Board of Governors of the Federal Reserve System

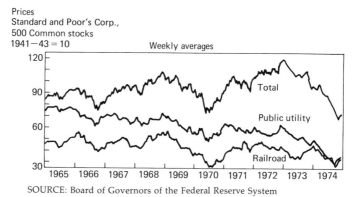

Figure 8-2 Stock Prices

Figure 8-2 Stock Prices

cial officer would have to decide if interest rates were going to fall still further from their 1970 peaks or return to those levels or higher. It is also obvious from Figure 8-1 that there are relatively few periods of stable interest rates and cost of capital in which the financial officer can work. The financial officer must cope not only with cyclical volatility but also with the frequency and speed which characterize changes in the market.

   The pattern of rapid, cyclical volatility is also found in the performance of stock prices, which reflect the cost of equity capital, Figure 8-2. As we shall see, high stock prices imply a lower cost of equity capital. Shifts in the supply and demand factors cause this cyclical pattern. Let us see if we can pinpoint some of the more important supply-demand factors which a financial officer might watch in an effort to understand the reasons for cyclicality and to judge the timing of securities offerings to the troughs in the cost of capital.

Demand Factors

Among the most important economic and financial factors that influence the demand for capital are: (1) the profitability of capital projects; (2) the general level of economic activity; (3) government fiscal policy; and (4) inflation prospects.

Project profitability If firms begin to believe that they have an increased number of acceptable projects, they will try to raise increased amounts of capital to undertake those projects, enlarging the demand for capital in the financial markets. This frequently occurs during periods when the entire schedule of projects along the internal rate of return curve (IRR, see Chapter 6) shifts upward and to the right (IRR^1), as shown in Figure 8-3. The attractiveness of each project along the entire schedule is increased, implying that additional investment as measured along the horizontal axis is also increased, and the cost of capital (k) rises to k^*. This upward shift in the IRR curve usually happens because the decision-makers in all firms simultaneously become more optimistic about the expected cashflows to all projects. This reflects improvement in the economic outlook and reduced uncertainty in the atmosphere in which the forecasts are made.

Economic activity As prospects for the general level of economic activity improve, firms see the need for expansion and additional investment in projects to supply the increased consumer demand which usually accompanies increased economic activ-

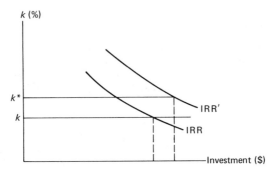

Figure 8-3 A Shift in the IRR

ity. This puts further demands on the capital markets as firms try to sell their securities to finance their expansion. Typically, the general level of economic activity and the improved profit prospects for investment projects complement one another, enlarging the demand for capital and putting upward pressure on the cost of capital.

Government fiscal policy If the government is running a deficit which it must finance by selling its securities in competition to the firm's, further demand pressures are exerted on the capital markets. The good financial officer tries to anticipate periods in which the government is going to be a large competitor for funds. The government tries to raise capital when the other sectors of the economy are not trying to raise their own capital, in a countercyclical fashion, but often the government's timing of its need for funds has not been accurate, and it comes to the market at exactly the same time you do.

Inflation expectations Expectations of rising costs and prices have the effect of accelerating the firm's demand for capital and of causing the suppliers of capital to raise the return they require before they will lend to the firm. Both these factors put upward pressure on the cost of capital. Expectation of a higher-than-previous rate of inflation promises to increase the cost of the project and makes the financial officer rush to undertake it before the price goes up. By borrowing the capital now, the officer can make the amount go further before prices rise and can pay back the amount borrowed to the lenders in "cheaper" dollars which do not have as much purchasing power and may be easier for the firm to earn.

On the other hand, suppliers of capital are not foolish and will raise their required return in inflationary periods, to compensate for the expected loss of purchasing power. The combination of the borrowers' increased willingness to borrow and the lenders' reduced desire to lend unless interest rates are increased puts upward pressure on the firm's cost of capital as the expectations of inflation grow stronger, and vice versa. This contributes to the cyclicality of the cost of capital.

Supply Factors

The two major supply factors in the capital markets are: (1) the savings which are available either directly or indirectly through financial intermediaries to purchase the securities offered and (2) the government's monetary action in providing or withdrawing funds from the markets.

Savings Savings of individuals tend to increase as their income increases. During periods of high economic activity, savers tend to make more money available to the financial intermediaries, unless the interest rate that the financial intermediaries is paying is considerably less than the rate savers can get by investing their funds directly in securities offered. As the flow of savings into the financial intermediaries increases, the amount of funds they supply to the capital markets increases. Alert financial officers will look for signs that the financial intermediaries to whom they typically sell their firms' securities are experiencing a stepped-up inflow, implying a receptive mood to securities, or a decreased inflow or possibly outflow of funds, implying a mood less receptive to securities offerings.

Monetary policy Working through the Federal Reserve System (the United States monetary authority) the government attempts to control the flow of funds into and out of the financial markets. This is accomplished mostly through the commercial banks, which, because they are the largest suppliers of capital to nonfinancial corporations, have great influence on the financial officer's ability to raise funds. If the Federal Reserve System withdraws funds from the financial markets by curtailing the ability of the commercial banks to lend to corporations, the financial officer is going to have to turn to less receptive, perhaps more expensive, sources and will face stiffer competition for the remaining pool of funds from other firms who have been cut off by the banks.

The alert financial officer continually monitors the Federal Reserve System to try to tell whether it is intending to restrict or expand the availability of capital. You can predict this to a certain degree by examining the Federal Reserve System's objectives and relating their activity in the financial markets to those objectives. Primarily the Federal Reserve is interested in conducting a countercyclical policy that restricts credit (funds availability) during periods of accelerating economic activity. The goal is to prevent the economy from experiencing an uncontrollable, runaway boom with the undesirable side-effects of excessive inflation and subsequent depression. During periods of slow economic activity, the Federal Reserve expands credit to prevent recessions and stimulate recovery.

Each Federal Reserve objective elicits a Federal Reserve policy action in the financial markets which the financial officer should be aware of in order not to be frustrated by Federal Reserve actions in attempts to raise inexpensive capital. We can summarize the association between the objective and the policy as:

Objective	Policy	Effect on bond yields
Control inflation	Tighten the supply of credit	Higher
Stimulate the economy	Expand the supply of credit	Lower
Achieve full employment	Expand the supply of credit	Lower
Achieve balance in United States international payments	Tighten the supply of credit	Higher

As a financial officer, if you saw that inflation was at a higher rate than you believe the government will allow to continue, you could reasonably expect that the Federal Reserve would initiate action to alleviate the upward pressures on prices by curtailing consumer and business expenditures. Since the Federal Reserve tries to accomplish this through the financial markets, it restricts credit and raises interest rates and the cost of capital in the process.

1965–1974 examined Let us look at the data in Figure 8-4 and relate it to the pattern of interest rates found in Figure 8-1. In this manner we may be able to discover what the supply and demand factors discussed above look like during periods of low-cost and high-cost capital. As financial officers we can use this knowledge to guide us in the timing of our security offerings. If these factors start developing in a manner which resembles previous periods of high cost of capital, we should be alerted to the possibility of an impending increase in our financing costs.

We would expect that high costs of capital would be associated with the high demand for capital caused by increased profit expectations of corporations, and vice versa. For the most part, we find this to be true in comparing panel (a) of Figure 8-4 to Figure 8-1. Rising corporate profits were accompanied by rising interest rates in 1965–1966, while falling interest rates accompanied the fall in profits for 1967. In 1968, rising profits were accompanied by stable to rising interest rates. However, the falling corporate profits of 1969–1970 were accompanied by rising interest rates, and the rising profits of 1971 were accompanied by raising and then falling interest rates. These unexpected relationships between profits and interest rates during 1969–1970 and 1971 illustrate the difficulty of interpreting the developing pattern. They highlight the fact that as a financial officer you should not rely on one factor but should examine the entire profile of all of them to get a feel for both prevailing and impending financial market conditions. In the first half of 1972, the expected relationship returned, with profits and interest rates falling. During the rising profits of later 1972 and 1973, interest rates rose.

Figure 8-4 Factors Influencing the Capital Markets

PROFITS AFTER TAXES OF LARGE CORPORATIONS

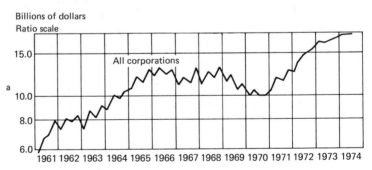

ECONOMIC ACTIVITY IN INDUSTRIAL PRODUCTION

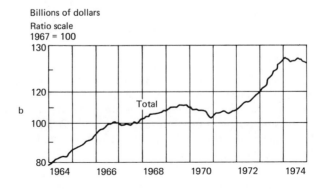

RECEIPTS AND EXPENDITURES OF THE UNITED STATES GOVERNMENT

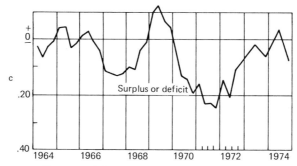

c

SOURCE: Treasury and Commerce Departments and Bureau of the Budget

WHOLESALE PRICES

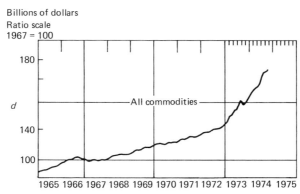

d

SOURCE: Bureau of Labor Statistics

SAVING RATIO: PERCENTAGE OF DISPOSABLE INCOME

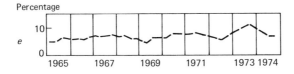

e

TOTAL MONEY STOCK

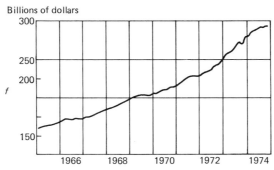

f

SOURCE: Board of Governors of the Federal Reserve System

We would expect our examination of economic activity as measured by industrial production in panel (b) of Figure 8-4 to also show interest rates rising along with rising general economic activity. For the most part, this is true. As in the case of corporate profits, the 1965–1966 rise in general economic activity was associated with rising interest rates. The 1968–1969 recovery period was, as expected, accompanied by stable to rising interest rates as the expansion gathered steam. The 1970–1971 dip in economic activity saw interest rates also dip but only after a lag of a few months. The 1972 recovery, on the other hand, saw interest rates fall at first with rising industrial production, contrary to normal expectations. However, climbing interest rates accompanied the recovery in economic activity during latter 1972 and 1973. In 1974 interest rates rose despite a slowing in production, primarily because of increased inflation expectations.

The federal government budget, Figure 8-4(c), is only sometimes a reliable indicator of the developing pattern of interest rates. But it is an important element in the financial officer's construction of a financial market profile. In mid 1965 the budget had a peak surplus (high) and, as we would expect, interest rates were at or near their trough (bottom). In late 1965, the budget had a local trough, and interest rates were rising. In mid 1966, there was another peak surplus, but interest rates showed no sign of declining and continued to rise. In late 1967, the expected relationship returned, with the budget running a large deficit and interest rates hitting new peaks. In mid 1969 the budget ran a surplus, but interest rates rose. In mid 1971 the budget hit a new all-time deficit, and, as expected, interest rates hit a local peak. Throughout 1973 and 1974, the smaller deficits and accompanying rising interest rates were caused by other factors such as inflation.

The relationship between inflation and the interest rate appears more consistently reliable than that of the other demand factors discussed so far, although the other relationships have been useful in constructing the entire profile of the market. Between mid 1965 and late 1966 rising inflation rates, as revealed in the steepening slope of the wholesale price index in panel (d) of Figure 8-4, were accompanied by rising interest rates. Conversely, the stable inflation rates of early 1967 saw interest rates fall, only to return to a rising pattern with the acceleration of inflation in late 1967 through mid 1970. When inflation rates subsided in the latter part of 1970, interest rates again tapered off. Notice that the hump in interest rates in mid 1970, which seemed to be contradictory to our expected relationship with corporate profits and general economic activity, fits into place when we add the effect of the rapid acceleration in inflation, which started in 1969 and culminated in the middle of 1970. If we give a little leeway for a lag while suppliers of capital recognized the full extent of the degree and the duration of inflation, the mid 1970 hump in interest rates is understandable. The rekindling of rapid inflation in early to mid 1971 and its subsequent dampening in late 1971 can be directly traced in interest rates, which also rose sharply and then fell sharply. In the first part of 1972, interest rates remained stable despite the rise in the rate of inflation, but they declined, as did the rate of inflation, in the latter part of 1972. In 1973 and 1974, historically high inflation caused the rapid rise in interest rates.

On the supply side of the market, we can see that the savings factor (revealed in panel (e) of Figure 8-4 by the savings ratio), which is the percentage of disposable or spending income that is saved instead of spent, typically peaks when interest rates bottom out or fall and troughs when interest rates peak or rise. When the savings ratio peaked in 1965, interest rates troughed. In mid 1966, when the savings ratio troughed, interest rates were rising. In mid 1968, when the savings ratio again peaked, interest rates again troughed. In early 1969, the savings ratio hit a local trough while interest rates were rising, and in mid 1971, when the savings ratio peaked, interest rates started falling. Through the 1973–1974 rapid rise in interest rates, savings first increased as higher interest rates attracted savers, and then fell as people's ability to save eroded with inflation.

Federal Reserve policy is revealed in the growth of the money stock in panel (f) of Figure 8-4. It may be the most influential of all factors during the 1965–1974 period. Without fail, when the money stock (supply) growth rate accelerated, as represented by a steepening in the slope of the money stock line in panel (f), interest rates stabilized or fell. When the rate of growth in the money stock flattened, interest rates rose. In 1965, a year of accelerating growth in the total money stock, financial officers saw a trough in interest rates, while in 1966, a year of flat growth in the total money stock, financial officers saw rising interest rates. Although the rate of growth in the money stock picked up toward the end of the first quarter of 1967 and continued to accelerate throughout 1968, it was not until 1968 that interest rates stabilized. However, in 1969 when the rate of growth in the money stock again flattened, interest rates resumed their rise, only to fall again in 1970 when the money stock expanded rapidly. In mid 1971, a flattened growth rate in the money stock was accompanied by rising interest rates. In 1972, the rising growth of the money stock was accompanied by falling interest rates, but the 1973 growth in the money supply did not dampen the rise in interest rates. The slow growth of the money supply in 1974 only served to increase the strain on the capital markets and to cause still higher interest rates.

The relationship between the supply-demand factors and interest rates and the reliability of the expected relationship during the 1965–1974 period is summarized below:

Factor	Expected relationship	Reliability, 1965–1974
Project profitability	As factor increases, interest rate increases	Accurate 70% of the time
Economic activity	As factor increases, interest rate increases	Accurate 75% of the time
Government fiscal policy	As surplus increases, interest rate decreases; as deficit increases, interest rate increases	Accurate 50% of the time
Inflation expectations	As factor increases, interest rate increases, usually with a lag	Accurate 75% of the time
Savings	As savings increase, interest rate decreases	Accurate 60% of the time
Monetary policy	As credit loosens, interest rate decreases; as credit tightens, interest rate increases	Accurate 100% of the time

The lesson for the financial officer in this brief examination of one period in the history of the financial markets is that there appears to be a relationship among the supply and demand factors which accompany, if not foreshadow, the cyclical pattern of the cost of capital. A good financial officer keeps abreast of the trends in these supply-demand factors. In general, when the profile of factors indicates a slowing in the demand for funds because the pace of economic activity is slackening and the rate of inflation is slowing, it also indicates an acceleration in the supply of funds, because of the actions of the Federal Reserve System. At the same time savers, interest rates and the cost of capital show signs of declining. When the demand for funds steps up, the other factors react in the opposite manner, but by and large the *relationships* hold.

THE STRUCTURE OF INTEREST RATES

We have seen that there is a cyclical pattern in interest rates over time. Is there also a pattern of interest rates among the various maturities of debt that I can offer at any particular point in that cycle? Will such a pattern in the term (maturity) structure of interest rates help me answer the question: Is the interest rate less if I raise short-term or long-term capital for the firm?

As a financial officer, you will want to use any differences in the cost of capital among maturities, when appropriate, to lessen your firm's cost of capital. For example, you can raise money for the firm from the sale of bonds which mature from one year to perhaps thirty or fifty years from now. Whether the long-term or the short-term bond is the least costly depends on present and expected economic conditions and the supply-demand factors for each maturity segment and the total capital market.

If we do find that there is a term structure pattern as well as a cycle pattern, we should study it to determine what interest rate the financial markets may expect to prevail during some relatively near future time when we may want to sell securities.

Table 8-3   The Term Structure of Treasury Bonds as of August 3, 1973

Decimals in bid-and-asked and bid changes represent 32nds (101.1 means 101 1-32). a-Plus 1-64. b-Yield to call date. d-Minus 1-64.

TREASURY BONDS

Rate	Mat. date		Bid	Asked	Bid Chg.	Yld.
$4^{1}/_{8}$s,	1973	Nov	97.18	97.22	−1.3	8.77
$4^{1}/_{8}$s,	1974	Feb	97.20	97.24	.....	8.62
$4^{1}/_{4}$s,	1974	May	96.18	96.22	− .2	8.78
$3^{7}/_{8}$s,	1974	Nov	94.12	94.20	− .3	8.42
4s,	1980	Feb	81.12	82.28	− .4	7.57
$3^{1}/_{2}$s,	1980	Nov	77.6	77.22	− .2	7.54
7s,	1981	Aug	98.10	98.26	− .2	7.20
$6^{3}/_{8}$s,	1982	Feb	92.22	92.30	− .2	7.51
$3^{1}/_{4}$s,	1978–83	Jun	69.14	70.14	− .2	7.55
$6^{3}/_{8}$s,	1984	Aug	91.16	91.24	− .4	7.48
$4^{1}/_{4}$s,	1975–85	May	74.28	75.28	− .2	7.35
$6^{1}/_{8}$s,	1986	Nov	89.28	90.12	− .2	7.27
$3^{1}/_{2}$s,	1990	Feb	68.22	69.22	− .4	6.53
$4^{1}/_{4}$s,	1987–92	Aug	70.8	71.8	.....	7.01
4s,	1988–93	Feb	69.30	70.30	+ .4	6.69
$4^{1}/_{8}$s,	1989–94	May	68.24	69.24	− .8	6.88
7s,	1993–98	May	91.0	91.8	− .4	7.80

SOURCE: *Wall Street Journal*

The Yield Curve

The pattern of interest rates (yields) over the various maturities (future years in which the bonds will be redeemed) on bonds of equal risk, such as, for example, the bonds of the United States Treasury as illustrated in Table 8-3 is the term structure. Obviously, all Treasury bonds are of equal risk since they are all issued by the same borrower under the same terms and are all default free. But the yield on each of the bonds is different, depending on the maturity date ("mat. date" in Table 8-3). Interest rates as of August 3, 1973 ("yld." in Table 8-3) were considerably higher among the bonds which matured within the next several years than among most of the bonds which did not mature for many years to come.

The term structure revealed in Table 8-3 can be graphed as shown in Figure 8-5, producing what is known as the *yield curve*. From the yield curve the financial officer can quickly see if it is cheaper to finance the investment projects with long-term or short-term sources of funds. In this particular period, it is clear that short-term funds are more expensive than longer-term funds. Yield curves showing lower interest rates in the longer term are shown as downward-sloping yield curves.

Downward-sloping yield curve   The economic rationale for the downward-sloping yield curve tells the financial officer what the financial markets are expecting the future state of the economy and interest rates to be. Typically, the downward-sloping yield curve occurs during a very high, unsustainable level of economic activity which is likely to be followed by a recessionary phase within a relatively short time. Since present demand for funds is very high but should taper off during the ensuing recession, the term structure of interest rates reflects this with very high yields in the immediate maturities tapering off to lower yields in the more distant maturities.

We can see how this condition of expected declines in interest rates forces the yield curve to slope downward.[3] Since lower yields are expected to prevail among the more distant periods, the presently outstanding bonds which mature in the more distant periods include expectations of those lower yields as well as the higher

Figure 8-5 The Yield Curve for Treasury Bonds as of August 3, 1973

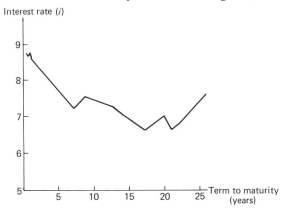

[3] This is known as the *expectations theory* of the term structure of interest rates. Under that theory the yield on any one long-term bond has to equal the yield expected to be attained on a series of bonds of shorter maturities within that identical time period when those shorter-term bonds are issued. See Burton G. Malkiel, *The Term Structure of Interest Rates: Expectations and Behavior Patterns*, Princeton University Press, Princeton, N.J., 1966.

yields they would have if they were short-term bonds during the prevailing high level of interest rates. Long-term bonds are in many ways a combination of a short maturity and a longer maturity, and their yield over the entire time is some combination of the higher short-term yield and the lower long-term yield expected to prevail in the more distant period when we get there. The averaging of the high and the expected low yields produces a lower yield for the longer-term bonds and gives the yield curve a downward slope.

Reinforcing the downward slope caused by expectations of lower interest rates and the prevailing inflationary boom is the tight supply relative to the large demand in the short-term segment of the market. Even as the Federal Reserve tightens and consumers save less, optimism on the part of firms sends the demand soaring for funds to finance such things as inventory. Simultaneously, in the longer-term segment of the market, the demand for real estate mortgages dries up at the higher interest rates, and the United States Treasury reduces its demand for long-term funds as the government budget runs a surplus because of the higher tax revenues generated by the booming economy. The combination of the expectation of lower yields and the supply-demand factors in the separate sections of the market push up short-term interest rates and push down long-term interest rates to enhance the yield curves downward slope.

The downward-sloping yield curve tells the financial officer that the market place is expecting a recession during which interest rates may be expected to fall. If the firm can wait, it might be advisable to postpone financing until interest rates move down. It might also be advisable for the financial officer to take a closer look at the prospects for general economic activity and re-evaluate parts of the firm's capital budget.

Upward-sloping yield curve If the short-term interest rate is less than the long-term interest rate, the yield curve slopes upward, as illustrated in Figure 8-6.

The message of the upward-sloping yield curve is the reverse of what the downward-sloping yield curve revealed. The low interest rates in the short-term segment reflect a prevailing recession with its relatively low demand for and large supply of funds. The longer-term segment reflects the expectations of the financial markets that interest rates will rise in the future, and the prevailing relatively high demand for long-term funds by the United States Treasury is a result of lower tax revenues. Financial officers should anticipate that future security offerings may cost more if they wait a while and that because of the foreshadowed recovery in economic activity, they might consider re-evaluating the firm's capital budget.

Figure 8-6 Upward-Sloping Yield Curve

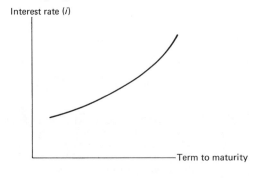

Interest rate (*i*)

Term to maturity

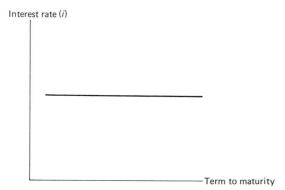

Figure 8-7 Flat Yield Curve

Flat yield curve The flat yield curve, as illustrated in Figure 8-7, reflects a period during which the financial markets expect little change in the prevailing economic conditions or interest rates. Typically, this yield curve is transitory, existing for only a little while as the yield curve moves from a downward-sloping configuration to an upward-sloping one, or vice versa. Unfortunately, economic and financial conditions are never stable for any length of time, and, as a consequence, the flat yield curve that implies stability is rarely observed.

Humped yield curve The humped yield curve, as illustrated in Figure 8-8, is characterized by both the shorter- and the longer-term segments of the term structure having lower yields than the intermediate maturities. This type of curve is not uncommon. It is typical of periods during which the financial markets expect the boom to reach its unsustainable peak within a relatively short period of time. The peakness of the hump is also aggravated by the preference of suppliers of long-term capital, such as life insurance companies which do not need short-term investments, to put their funds exclusively in long-term investments and to reject totally the short- and intermediate-term maturities. Simultaneously, the short-term lenders, such as commercial banks, provide funds exclusively to the shorter maturities and totally reject the longer- and intermediate-term maturities. This leaves the inter-

Figure 8-8 Humped Yield Curve

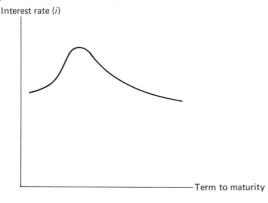

mediate-term maturities with few buyers and a lower price and higher yield for any given amount of bonds with intermediate terms.

As a financial officer, you should be aware that the sale of intermediate-term securities during a period in which the yield curve is humped will probably result in a higher cost of capital than the sale of either short- or long-term maturities. It is typical of the yield curve to become humped shortly before the peak in economic activity, and we can use this as one additional piece of information in our capital budgeting deliberations.

Two Very Important Caveats

In examining the yield curve to gather information on the prospects for the economy and interest rates, it is extremely important not to lose sight of the fact that: (1) interest rates throughout the entire term structure tend to move up and down in unison, although shorter-term yields are more erratic than longer-term yields; and (2) it is typically more prudent on the part of the good financial officer to try to finance the acquisition and investment in long-term assets with long-term funds.

The shift from the downward-sloping to the upward-sloping curve generally sees all interest rates fall. For example, if the short-term interest rate were 8 percent and the long-term interest rate were 7.5 percent, we would have a downward-sloping yield curve. To get to the upward-sloping yield curve all interest rates fall, but the shorter-term interest rates fall more, such that the short-term interest rate might drop to 4 percent and the long-term rate only to 6 percent. The yield curve would now slope upward, but all interest rates would be below their former levels when the yield curve sloped down.

It is not prudent to finance highly illiquid and long-term assets with a disproportionate amount of short-term funds. A good financial officer would never finance a fleet of railroad locomotive engines or jumbo jets exclusively with short-term borrowing, even if the short-term interest rate were considerably less than the longer-term interest rate. You should avoid the necessity of returning frequently to the markets to refinance the short-term loans that have come due. The firm may be severely hurt if such refinancing coincides with a credit crunch during which funds are either not available at all or extremely expensive, probably offsetting all that was saved by using the shorter and less expensive funds in the first place. On the other hand, the long-term financing could have allowed the financial officer to set the annual repayments at a pace with which the firm could comfortably ride out any credit crunch or severe restriction of funds.

Some general guidelines for the financial officer are: (1) time the sale of the firm's securities to troughs in the interest-rate cycle; (2) tailor your securities to the segment of the market with the lowest interest rates; (3) do not, however, finance long-term assets with a disproportionate amount of short-term funds; and (4) if you have to sell your securities during a period of high interest rates, be sure you get the right to redeem the bond at your option in the near future so that, if interest rates do drop, you can refinance (issue new bonds to replace the old ones) at a lower cost of capital.

Yield Spreads

In contrast to the yield curve, which shows the term structure of yields for bonds of the same degree of risk, the *yield spread* shows the differences in yields between bonds of the same maturity but different degrees of risk. This is important to the financial officer in judging the cost of capital because it makes it possible to compare the firm's security offerings to the already outstanding securities of other companies. For example, if our bonds are rated Baa (medium grade), as in Figure 8-1, we would expect that they would bear a higher interest rate than the bonds of an Aaa (highest quality) firm. Although the yields on the two qualities of bonds tend to move in unison and the typical spread might be about 1 percent, there are short periods of time when the spread widens, such as the latter part of 1970. During those periods, the financial officer of the Baa firm might be advised to wait until the spread narrows again, since the market might then be more receptive to riskier securities. In addition, it is typical for this spread to narrow at peaks in the general level of economic activity, such as the peak in interest rates in 1969 on Figure 8-1. The alert financial officer would realize that the rapid narrowing of the yield spread foreshadowed a slowing economy and a decline in interest rates. He would make every effort to convince the financial markets that the firm's Baa rating should be better, for as the rating improves, the cost of capital to the firm declines.

THE FINANCIAL MARKET ENVIRONMENT

What does the theory of financial markets tell us about the timing and tailoring of security offerings so that as financial officers we can attempt to reduce the firm's cost of capital? In other words, how does the financial market view risk so that financial officers know what to do in order to make the securities more attractive and less risky to potential investors and thereby lower the cost of capital?

The Risk-Return Trade-off

The fundamental relationship at the heart of all financial markets is that as the risk associated with any security increases, the return expected by the purchaser of that security must also increase.[4] The suppliers of capital must expect to be compensated for undertaking that additional risk or they will not supply the capital.

We have already seen that we would not buy the bonds of the American Motors Corporation at an expected 7 percent yield if the bonds of the United States Treasury were selling at a 7 percent yield, because the difference in risk makes the American Motors bonds considerably less attractive at the same yield. However, there are investors who might be willing to commit their funds to the American Motors bonds if the yield from the investment could be 13 percent, 15 percent or 20 percent. The exact expected return where you would buy the American Motors bonds depends on your individual desire and ability to undertake the risk, but most people have some large expected return where they might buy some of the riskier bonds for their portfolio. Since there is a whole spectrum of risk among the bonds offered, it is the financial market's function, financial theory tells us, to assign the appropriate return to the level of risk associated with each security. Thus, for example, we might find the bonds of the General Motors Corporation selling at a yield above the yield on the Treasury bond but below the yield on the American Motors bond. Similarly, as financial officers, if we lower our firm's risk, we can lower its cost of capital.

Figure 8-9 reflects a proportional trade-off between the expected return necessary to induce potential investors to purchase our security and the associated risk. As

---

[4] The interested student is referred to Appendix 8A to see how the trade-off between expected return and risk is derived.

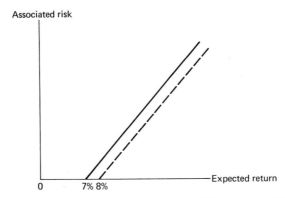

Figure 8-9 Proportional Trade-Off Between Expected Return and Risk

the associated risk increases, investors require a higher expected return on their investment in order to compensate them for undertaking the risk. Of course, the realized return may *not* be there, and the investors may actually take a loss. But in order for the firm to sell the securities in the first place, it is necessary for the financial officer to convince potential investors that they can expect a particular return. If there is increased uncertainty among potential investors because of, say, confusion over the profit prospects of the firm, these investors require a higher compensation for the increased risk. Where investors see your firm on the trade-off line in Figure 8-9 (commonly called the capital market line) determines your cost of capital. If, like the United States government, you have no risk exposure, you would pay only 7 percent for your capital, which lies on the horizontal axis at zero risk. A higher risk exposure puts your cost of capital up and to the right on the capital market line.

It is also clear from Figure 8-9 that if the trade-off line moves to the right, the cost of capital for all firms increases, whether or not their risk exposure has changed. Thus, if the cost of capital to the United States government bonds moves from 7 to 8 percent (the dashed line in Figure 8-9), the cost of capital for a firm half-way up the trade-off line in its risk exposure also increases one percentage point. This is because all securities compete for investors' funds; if one increases its promised return, the others must also. The trade-off line can also shift to the right, pivoting on the 7 percent risk-free rate, and raising the cost of capital for all firms, if investors in general see the risk exposure of all firms rising simultaneously, such as in times of governmental crisis.

The Diversification Effect

In addition to the trade-off of expected return and associated risk, the theory of finance also tells us that there is a diversification effect which the financial officer can exploit to lower the cost of capital. Imagine for a moment that you are responsible for making the investment decisions for a large portfolio of securities. You decide what securities to buy from among those offered. If you are right you get rewarded; if you are wrong, you lose your high-paying job. Obviously you are not willing to take excessive chances, so you hedge your decisions by diversifying over several different types of securities and situations in the hope that if you have made a wrong decision on one, the others will still preserve your reputation as a fine portfolio manager and investor.

Now envision a financial officer coming to you and trying to sell you his or her latest security offering. If you already have what you consider a sufficiently large amount of your funds invested in securities of this type or in this firm or industry, you would be very unwilling to increase your risk exposure by purchasing the securities. Only if the financial officer increased your expected return might you consider purchasing the securities. On the other hand, if you did not have sufficient diversification because you lacked the type of security being offered by this financial officer, you would be very willing to purchase the security, even at a slightly lower expected return because it fills a need in your diversification program.

If you simply expand this need for diversification to investors in general, you can see how a surfeit of one type of security causes the cost of capital associated with that particular type of security to rise, and a shortage of that particular type of security comes to lower its cost of capital. As an alert financial officer, you would try not to offer securities already in oversupply. You would try to offer securities in short supply to take advantage of the cheaper cost of capital afforded securities which fill the prevailing diversification needs of investors. In fact, you might even sit down with your large potential suppliers of capital and design a security for them with the specific terms and characteristics they desire in exchange for a lower cost of capital.

Implications for the Financial Officer

The implications of this proportional trade-off between expected return and risk as revealed in the straightline (the capital market line)[5] of Figure 8-9 and the diversification effect are: (1) there is a trade-off which the financial officer can exploit to lower the cost of capital, and (2) the type and terms of the security that the firm offers can either mesh or not mesh with investors' diversification needs and *this affects the cost of the capital.*

Your firm's securities will fluctuate to a great extent with the fluctuations of security prices in general, and, as a consequence, your firm's cost of capital will fluctuate with the cost of capital of all securities in general. According to Figure 8-9 this has to be so, because the yield on competing securities rises, forcing your cost of capital as measured by the yield on your securities to rise also. (Alternatively, the risk of every security in the market can rise because of a general factor which makes investors demand a higher compensation from all securities, including yours.) The first lesson for financial officers is that they must expect the cost of capital to vary with the markets in a fashion that is beyond their control. Of course they can still try to lower the firm's cost of capital by *timing* security offerings to the troughs in the cost of capital.

The second lesson for alert financial officers is that they can lower the cost of capital by a proportionate amount if they can lower their firm's risk image to investors. Decreasing the firm's risk image moves the firm down the trade-off line and causes a decrease in the expected return investors require from the company. That is why financial officers are always giving addresses before security analysts societies. They are trying to convince the analysts who purchase their securities that they have everything under control and that the firm actually has a lower risk exposure than that which is presently being assigned to it by investors. Therefore, it should have a lower cost of capital.

---

[5] See J. Fred Weston, "Investment Decisions Using the Capital Asset Pricing Model," *Financial Management*, Spring, 1973; Wm. F. Sharpe, *Portfolio Theory and Capital Markets*, McGraw-Hill, New York, 1970; or Michael C. Jensen, "Capital Markets in Theory and Evidence," *Bell Journal of Economics and Management Science*, Autumn 1972.

The third lesson for financial officers is that it is within their control to offer investors securities which, because of their particular characteristics, fill the need in investors' diversification plans and make them more willing to buy the securities offered at a lower cost of capital.

In a market where investors are not able to diversify particularly well, good financial officers can tailor their security offerings to the diversification needs of their potential investors, thereby making the securities more attractive to them and giving their firms a lower cost of capital. For example, if you were negotiating with a life insurance company to provide expansion capital to your firm, they might not be interested in acquiring your firm's debt, because they might already have sufficient debt of equal risk. They could only be induced to purchase your debt if the return were raised. Instead, you might offer the insurance company a debt which also allows them to convert into the common stock of your company. This may be attractive to them because they have no other equity securities in their portfolio and this semiequity balances the risks of their all-bond portfolio. You should then be able to negotiate a lower cost of capital for the convertible bond than for the straight bond. Interestingly, you could probably get a lower cost of capital from the insurance company on this semiequity bond than if you tried to sell your stock (equity) to other potential investors who already had your stock or other large equity holdings, because adding additional shares of your firm's stock would not have met their diversification plans. Tailoring the security offerings to the diversification needs of the particular investor should lower your cost of capital.

The External versus the Internal View

As a financial officer, you must look beyond the immediate surroundings of your firm and step outside its confines to view it as the potential suppliers of capital view it. In other words, you must adopt the external viewpoint of those outside your firm and understand their position, because your cost of capital is essentially their required rate of return. Thus, your cost of capital is determined in the financial markets and is partly beyond your control, since the capital markets obviously fluctuate in response to factors other than what is going on in your firm. But you still control that aspect of the cost of capital which allows *tailoring the security offered* to make it more attractive to the portfolio needs of the investor and *altering the risk image* associated with your type of business and your financial transactions. And you can still have a highly significant impact on the firm's cost of capital by *timing security offerings* to troughs in interest rates or to periods of high equity prices, even though you have no control over the factors that cause these fluctuations.

SUMMARY

After having read Chapter 8, you should be able to answer these questions:

1. Why does capital cost?

Capital costs because it is a scarce commodity which must be allocated among the demanders (users). Since it is in limited supply, firms compete for capital by compensating investors for the use of the funds they supply. Each security offered must provide an interest rate to compensate the investor for both giving up the use of the funds for a period of time and the risk undertaken in so doing. The total compensation is the firm's cost of capital.

2. What is a financial market and who participates?

A financial market is simply the meeting place of suppliers of capital (lenders) and demanders of capital (borrowers). The typical demanders are corporations, real estate purchasers, state and local governments, foreign corporations and governments, and frequently the federal government. The suppliers are generally savers (via such financial intermediaries as savings and loan associations and insurance companies), the Federal Reserve System through its control of the money supply, and commercial banks.

3. Is there any pattern in interest rates which can help financial officers lower the cost of capital for their firms?

Interest rates and security prices are distinctly cyclical over time. The cost of capital reflects this and tends to be lowest during periods when the rate of growth in the money supply and in savings is highest, when the federal government is operating at a surplus, the profit outlook is depressed, and the economy in general is at a low ebb. Of course the cost of capital tends to be highest when the opposite conditions prevail. Security offerings timed to the cyclically low periods have a reduced cost of capital.

4. What is the pattern of interest rates over the maturity schedule, and how does this help the financial officer lower the cost of capital?

The pattern of interest rates over the maturity schedule is known as the term structure, and its graphic representation is the yield curve. Depending on its configuration, the financial officer can get an indication of the financial markets' expectations for interest rates over the near future. A downward-sloping yield curve indicates expectations of a decline in interest rates, while an upward-sloping yield curve indicates expectations of higher interest rates to come.

The financial officer might be able to lower the cost of capital by offering securities in the least-cost segment of the market, although this can be dangerous if carried to the extreme that the firm's debt burden becomes excessively short-term and its repayment commitments become too high to be refinanced in periods of tight credit.

Although the interest rates on all maturities tend to move up and down in unison, relative changes among the maturity segments may allow the alert financial officer to decrease the firm's cost of capital.

5. What does the theory of financial markets tell the financial officer about lowering the firm's cost of capital?

Financial theory postulates proportional relationships between the return a security has to give an investor in order to make the investor purchase it and the risk attached to that purchase. As the risk increases, the return expected by the investor has to increase also. This proportional relationship means that a well-functioning market will see all securities fluctuate in unison in response to changes in interest rates in general and to changes in increased general uncertainty. The fluctuations related to these general market factors are beyond the control of the financial officer.

On the other hand, the theory of financial markets demonstrates that the financial officer who can lower the risk image of the firm among investors will proportionately lower the cost of capital to the firm. Also, the financial officer who specifically tailors securities to fill a void in the diversification plans of the specific investor will make the investor willing to pay more for the security and thus lower the firm's cost of capital. A general application of this concept is to offer the types of securities that are relatively rare on the market and to avoid selling those that are in abundant supply.

QUESTIONS

8-1 Define in general terms what the concept of the cost of capital means to the financial officer. Do you think IBM and Control Data Corporation would have comparable costs of capital?

8-2 How might the Federal Reserve System cause the cost of capital to increase for all firms?

8-3 Distinguish between the terms *capital markets* and *money markets*.

8-4 Identify some of the major buyer and seller groups in the capital markets.

8-5 Indicate whether interest rates should generally increase or decrease if the following events occur:

	Interest Rate	
	Increase	Decrease

(a) Corporate profits decrease
(b) Industrial production increases
(c) Federal budget deficit
(d) Consumer price index decreases
(e) Money stock increases
(f) Consumers savings increase

8-6 Define the expression *term structure of interest rates*. Give an example of your definition. What is a yield curve?

8-7 Suppose the following yields on treasury bonds were observed in the *Wall Street Journal* on December 31, 1974.

Date of Maturity	Yield (%)
12/31/75	6.45
12/31/76	6.50
12/31/77	6.75
12/31/78	7.25
12/31/79	6.40
12/31/80	6.35
12/31/85	6.00
12/31/90	5.85

(a) Graph the yield curve.
(b) Explain what factors may be contributing to the shape of the yield curve.
(c) If your firm were faced with financing an intermediate term project of four years, how might the yield curve influence the maturity-of-bond financing decision of your firm? Assume bond financing is to be used exclusively.
(d) If your firm were faced with financing some long-term investments with a life of 15 years, would you choose short-term or long-term bonds? Why? Assume bond financing is to be used exclusively.

8-8 Why is the "yield spread" on bonds important to the financial officer?

Appendix 8A **The Derivation of the Capital Market Line**

How is the capital market line (the trade-off line between expected return and associated risk) derived? Under the assumptions of the idealized market,[1] it is derived through the action of investors in their efforts to achieve an optimum position in their portfolios.

The financial markets can be viewed as a series of possible securities where investors can put their funds. Each security has an expected return and an associated expected risk which in many ways represent the average of what every potential investor expects to gain by investing in the security and the average of what every investor thinks is the associated risk of receiving that expected return. Typically, the expected return of each security is thought of as the mean of the entire distribution of investors' expectations of return ($\overline{R}$), and the associated expected risk is thought of as the standard deviation ($\overline{\sigma}$) of that distribution of expected returns.

Individual securities are always combined into a portfolio of investments by investors, because it is not prudent to put all your eggs in one basket. Otherwise an unforeseen unfavorable event could wipe out your entire investment. When investors combine the individual securities into the portfolio of their choice, the portfolio itself takes on an expected return, which is nothing more than the weighted average of the expected returns to each of the securities in the portfolio, and an associated risk, which is the weighted standard deviation of the individual securities in the portfolio adjusted for the correlation among the expected returns (see Chapter 7).

In choosing their preferred portfolios, investors would first rank all portfolios in descending order of their expected return ($\overline{R}$) with its associated expected risk—the standard deviation of the expected return, ($\overline{\sigma}$), as shown in Table 8A-1. Obviously, some of these portfolios are more attractive than others in Table 8A-1 because they offer a higher expected return with a lower or equal associated risk. For example, portfolio number 2 dominates portfolio number 3 because it has a higher expected return (18 percent versus 17 percent) and a lower associated risk (10 percent versus 11 percent)! Likewise portfolio number 6 dominates portfolio number 5. Among the portfolios which are not dominated, individual investors would choose that portfolio with which they felt most comfortable; in other words, the portfolio with the level of risk exposure they could live with. Those who can live with more risk will select the higher-risk, higher-return portfolios. Those unwilling to tolerate risk exposure will select the lower-risk, lower-return portfolios. We can illustrate the investors' choice as shown in Figure 8A-1, which illustrates what finance people call

---

[1] The assumptions upon which the idealized market are built are: (1) investors are risk avoiders, (2) investors try to maximize one-period wealth, period by period, (3) all investors have the same information and expectations, (4) there are no transactions costs, and (5) investors can borrow and lend at the same rate. See John Lintner, "Security Prices, Risk and Maximal Gains from Diversification," *Journal of Finance,* December, 1965, pp. 587–615; Jan Mossin, *Theory of Financial Markets,* Prentice-Hall, Englewood Cliffs, N.J., 1973; and William F. Sharpe, "Capital Asset Prices: A Theory of Market Equilibrium under Conditions of Risk," *Journal of Finance,* September 1964, pp. 425–442.

Table 8A-1

Portfolio number	$\overline{R}$	$\overline{\alpha}$
1	20 %	12 %
2	18	10
3	17	11
4	16.5	9
5	15	8
6	15	7
7	12	6
8	10	5.5
9	8	5
10	7	4.5

the efficient frontier. Lower-risk, lower-return portfolios appear on the lower left of the efficient frontier; higher-risk, higher-return portfolios appear on the upper right.

The efficient frontier in Figure 8A-1 cannot, however, remain in that configuration because: (1) the dominated portfolios, number 3 and number 5, are not desired by any investors (in fact, the securities in these portfolios are sold off as investors try to move into the more desirable portfolios along the efficient frontier); and (2) the opportunity to borrow and/or lend at the default free-rate (*i*) must be considered.

In the process of selling off the securities in the dominated portfolios and rein-vesting those funds into portfolios along the efficient frontier, investors force down the prices of the securities in portfolios numbers 3 and 5, increasing their expected return, and force up the prices of securities in portfolios along the frontier, de-creasing their expected return, until *all* the portfolios fall on the efficient frontier. Simultaneously, investors have an opportunity to buy not only the risk securities of the firms but also the default-free, riskless securities of the United States govern-ment.[2] This default-free rate would fall on the horizontal axis at zero associated risk

Figure 8A-1 The Efficient Frontier of Securities Portfolios

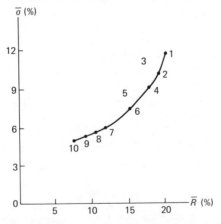

[2] This is accomplished under what is known as the separation theorem, which allows in-vestors of all degrees of risk-aversion to hold a representative portfolio of all stocks and achieve their optimal position through borrowing or lending. See J. Francis and S. Archer, *Portfolio Analysis*, Prentice-Hall, Englewood Cliffs, N.J., 1971, p. 117.

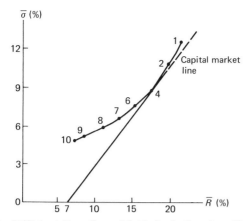

Figure 8A-2 The Efficient Frontier with Default-Free Lending/Borrowing

and the prevailing interest rate on government bonds, such as the 7 percent illustrated in Figure 8A-2.

It is clear from Figure 8A-2 that portfolio number 10 is dominated by the portfolio of all government bonds yielding 7 percent because the return is higher and the risk is lower for the latter. Investors start selling off the dominated portfolio, forcing its security prices down and its expected return up, until it becomes more in line with the expected return-risk relationships of the other portfolios.

It is also clear from Figure 8A-2 that investors can make up a portfolio consisting of various combinations of risky securities and the default-free securities. Depending on the exact proportion of investors' funds placed into portfolio number 4 and the default-free securities, for example, their expected return-risk relationship could lie on the straight line between portfolio number 4 and 7 percent on the horizontal axis. The investor with 50 percent of his or her funds in the default-free securities and 50 percent in the securities of portfolio number 4, would have an expected return of 11.75 percent and the expected risk would be 4.5 percent, which is a higher return and a lower risk than portfolio number 8 with its expected return of 10 percent and risk of 5.5 percent.[3] This means that investors have a more attractive alternative than portfolio number 8, and they sell off the securities in that portfolio, forcing it more in line with the expected return and risk relationships of other combinations of portfolio number 4 and the default-free securities that lie on the straight line connecting the two.

If investors do the reverse and borrow at 7 percent to finance the purchase of additional securities from portfolio number 4, they can derive portfolios with various expected return-risk relationships by varying the proportions of the amount they borrow and the amount of portfolio number 4 they buy. These derived portfolios are more attractive than the portfolios with higher expected return-risk relationships which were above portfolio number 4 on the efficient frontier before we introduced the ability to borrow and to lend at 7 percent. This gives us the extension of the ef-

[3] The expected return is calculated as:

$$.5(.165) + .5(.07)$$

The risk is calculated as:

$$.5(.09) + .5(0)$$

ficient frontier illustrated by the dashed line in Figure 8A-2 (the entire straightline is known as the capital market line).

The investor can get *any* expected return-risk relationship by simply altering the proportions of the securities in the entire market place and the default-free securities. All the securities have taken on a relationship with the market which reflects their ability to add diversification to investors' portfolios and thereby reduce their risk. With the introduction of the default-free securities, the other securities with risk become more attractive for inclusion in investors' portfolios as they aid in diversification plans and help reduce risk. If securities do not help very much in this regard, the investor must receive a higher return, which is a higher cost of capital to the firm. This trade-off determines the capital market line and gives us the diversification effect of Chapter 8.

9

The Cost of Capital for Individual Securities

After studying chapter 8, we are aware that the cost of capital is the equivalent of the risk-adjusted rate of return on a firm's security offerings required by the investors (suppliers of capital) at any point in time. Now we must try to estimate the cost of capital for each particular type of security offering that you, as the financial officer, may want to consider.

How does the financial officer know which type of security is the cheapest (lowest cost of capital) and helps advance the firm most towards its objective? To answer this question, you will first have to understand what factors determine the cost of capital for the individual securities the firm can offer for sale. These factors are contained in the financial markets as well as in the firm and in the security itself. They are what investors examine in their evaluation of your security to set their required rate of return. Among the many factors which affect investors' determination of this risk-adjusted required rate of return are interest rates on competing securities, purchasing-power risk, the firm's business and financial risk, and the marketability risk of the security itself.

When investors determine their risk-adjusted required rate of return, which is your firm's cost of capital, it shows up in the financial market place as the collective evaluation of all investors at that time. Of course, the evaluation and required rate of return can vary among individual investors and from time to time, but what the financial officer observes in the securities markets as the cost of capital is what it takes at that moment to sell out the firm's security offerings: the required rate of return for the last investor to buy the last bond or share of stock offered. In this chapter we will examine those factors which impact the risk-adjusted rate of return required by the financial markets of your firm's various types of securities.

The second question the financial officer must be able to answer in order to identify the least costly security to use in raising funds is: What types of securities are there and what specific factors affect each type's cost of capital? We shall discuss debt, common equity (stock), retained earnings, and preferred stock.

The cost of capital for the firm's debt (k_d) is the risk-adjusted required rate of return needed to sell such securities as the firm's bonds, loan agreements, long-term promissory notes, and other securities under which the firm borrows the funds at an interest rate and promises to repay the original amount borrowed at some future time.

The cost of capital for common equity (k_e) is the risk-adjusted rate of return required to sell the common stock of the firm, which entitles the stockholder to all the dividends that the firm declares in the future.

The cost of capital for the firm's retained earnings (k_{re}) is the risk-adjusted required rate of return that makes stockholders willing to let you reinvest that portion of the firm's earnings not declared as dividends to the stockholders.

The cost of capital for the firm's preferred stock (k_p) is the risk-adjusted required rate of return necessary to sell the preferred stock of the company, representing *a priori* equity ownership in the firm, which entitles the owner to a claim on a specific amount of dividends and liquidation value prior to the common stockholders.

THE PERTINENT FACTORS

What factors determine the cost of capital for the firm's securities?

As we have seen, there are basically two major categories of factors which affect the cost of capital for the firm's securities. These are (1) the supply-demand consideration in the financial markets which affects the cost of capital for all securities by changing the default-free interest rate (i) and forcing the cost of capital of competing securities to change in the same direction, and (2) the risk associated with the individual firm and the individual security, which increases the cost of capital above the default-free interest rate in an amount proportional to the associated risk. The cost of capital (k) is then:

$$k = i + \phi$$

where
$i =$ the default-free interest rate which reflects the real interest rate and the purchasing-power risk premium
$\phi =$ the risk adjustment associated with the business and financial risk exposure of the firm and the marketability risk of the security itself

The interest rate is the price mechanism which equates the supply of funds with the demand for funds. In other words, if the supply is larger than the demand, interest rates drop; and if the demand is larger than the supply, interest rates rise. We now observe that the default-free interest rate (i) part of the compensation is really the sum of two components: the real interest rate and the purchasing-power risk premium.

The Real Interest Rate

We can observe the interest rate (yield) on any bond by merely opening our newspapers to the financial page and looking. The yield on the United States government bonds represents compensation to the lender (purchaser of those bonds) not only for surrendering the use of that money but also for forfeiting the purchase of something else. The *real interest rate* compensates the purchaser for surrendering the money, while the *purchasing-power risk premium* compensates the purchaser for any increase in the price of the item *not* purchased with the money instead. What we observe in the financial markets as the interest rate is more correctly labeled the market or nominal interest rate. The market interest rate is then:

$$i = r.i. + p$$

where

$i =$ the nominal interest rate (risk-free rate)

$r.i. =$ the real interest rate

$p =$ the purchasing-power risk premium

The Purchasing-Power Risk Premium

If inflation—an increase in the cost of goods and services—is expected to occur during the period for which potential investors surrender control of their funds by purchasing the firm's securities, the value of the dollar returned to the investors when they sell these securities is reduced in terms of what it will buy. If you were lending the firm your money by buying its bonds, you would certainly want to get back every dollar you lent the firm and enough interest on top of that to have made it worth your while. In other words, because you lent your money you want to feel richer when your loan is repaid, and the only way to feel richer is to have command over more goods and services than you had before you purchased the bond. For example, suppose you had your eye on a new motorcycle which costs $1,000, but instead of buying it you loaned out your $1,000 for one year at 5 percent. At the end of that year, you would receive $1,050 in return of the original principal and the interest. But, if the price of that motorcycle has risen to $1,100 by the end of the same year, you have actually *lost* in terms of real purchasing power because you can no longer afford the motorcycle and have forfeited one year's riding pleasure.

If, however, you had anticipated that 10 percent rise in the price of the motorcycle, then you would have only loaned out your $1,000 at an interest rate sufficient to at least keep pace with inflation and provide some compensation over and above that for surrendering control of your funds. If you had demanded 13 percent interest for one year, for example, you would have received $1,130 at the end of the year, bought your motorcycle for $1,100 and still been $30 richer than you were one year ago. If you had not been able to get an interest rate high enough to compensate you for the anticipated 10 percent loss of purchasing power, then you would have bought the motorcycle instead of loaning your funds.

Potential investors refrain from buying the firm's securities until they are compensated for anticipated inflation, so financial officers are forced to raise the interest rate they are willing to pay until they can attract the funds. This forces up the cost of capital to the firm during periods of anticipated acceleration in the rate of inflation among all types of securities, including stocks, bonds, and even default-free United States Treasury bonds. Even with their iron-clad promise to pay you your principal and interest, United States government securities still do not promise that the dollars used to repay you will be worth as much in terms of their purchasing power as they were when you first loaned them to the government. As the expectation of inflation accelerates, the purchasing-power risk premium also increases, and interest rates and the firm's cost of capital rise. Of course, if decelerating inflation is expected, then interest rates and the cost of capital tend to decline. For example, if $r.i. = 3$ percent, and $p = 6$ percent, then $i = 9$ percent. But, if p rose to 7 percent, then i would be 10 percent. Of course, $r.i.$ can also change in relation to fundamental shifts in the supply-demand conditions in the capital markets. If, for example, $r.i.$ rose to 4 percent, while $p = 6$ percent, then i would be 10 percent.

Business Risk

In addition to the real interest rate and the purchasing-power risk premium, potential investors must feel they are being compensated for any risk associated with the individual firm's promise to pay the interest on its bonds and the dividends expected by the shareholders. Notice that this part of the compensation, which is also included in the firm's cost of capital, differs from the interest rate and purchasing-power risk premium parts of the compensation. It is strictly related to the firm and not to the general market and economic factors of supply-demand conditions in the financial markets or the rate of anticipated inflation.

As a firm's risk of not meeting its obligations increases, its cost of capital (k) also increases, because investors demand a greater return to undertake the greater risk. This does not mean that the firm is shaky, but it is just relatively more risky than the default-free bonds of the United States government. For example, American Telephone and Telegraph Company or General Motors Corporation bonds are secure bonds, but they do have more risk than the United States government bonds, so investors require a higher interest rate. For example, the yields on these bonds might be:

Firm and bond	Yield
United States Government 7s 1993	7.24%
American Telephone and Telegraph 8s 2000	7.50
General Motors 6⁷/₈s 1995	7.70
Martin-Marietta Corporation 9s 1985	8.30
United Merchants and Manufacturers 9¹/₂s 1995	8.90
Edo Corporation 5¹/₄s 1987	9.50

The *business risk* (b) associated with the firm's securities arises from the very nature of the firm's operating environment, which imparts a degree of uncertainty into even the most secure firm with the most honorable intention of meeting its debt obligations and investors' expectations of dividends. Those operating environments which are relatively less stable lead investors to infer a greater risk of default, demand a higher interest rate, and increase the firm's cost of capital. Of course, the degree of greater risk can vary from very small to very large, depending on the circumstances of the firm.

Several conditions in the general operating environment can affect investor interpretation of the degree of risk. First, if the firm's prospects are clouded at the moment, investors typically require a higher rate of return. Second, if the firm's history has been shaky, erratic and hard to predict, or relatively less stable, perhaps dotted with extremely bad years in which the repayment of principal and interest was less than certain, investors will require a higher rate of return. Third, if the firm's prospects change such that the relative certainty connected with the firm's payment of its obligations deteriorates, investors will demand a higher rate of return. Fourth, if the firm's operations are inherently unstable, subject for instance to the business cycle or the vagaries of politically unstable countries, investors require a higher rate of return, forcing up the firm's cost of capital. The cost of capital for the firm will be lowered, of course, if the firm can lessen the impact of any factor in the eyes of the investors.

Notice that all these general influences have the central theme of variability in operating earnings, which impairs the firm's ability to meet its promised or expected payments. We can, therefore, represent the cost of capital to the firm as:

$$k = r.i. + p + b$$

where

k = the cost of capital
$r.i.$ = the real interest rate
p = the purchasing power risk premium
b = the business risk

We can see how a deterioration in the business environment (increase in business risk) affected the yield on Ling Temco Vought debenture bonds between 1968 and 1970. The firm's earnings went from $3.43 a share in 1968 to a deficit of $10.59 a share in 1969 and a deficit of $17.18 a share in 1970, as the demand for its products dampened and as exceptionally large interest charges (financial risk) were incurred. As the situation worsened and business risk increased, Ling Temco Vought's 5 percent debentures of 1988 fell dramatically in price and rose dramatically in yield, as we can see:

Date	Price	Current yield
January, 1969	$60\frac{1}{2}$	8.26%
January, 1970	40	12.5%
January, 1971	$22\frac{7}{8}$	21.85%

Financial Risk

We shall see in Chapter 10 that the particular method by which a firm finances its investments can increase the variability of earnings available to meet debt obligations and expected dividends *over and above* the variability imparted by the firm's operating environment (business risk). This is known as *financial risk* (f). As it increases, investors infer a greater degree of risk to purchasing the firm's securities and require a higher rate of return, increasing the firm's cost of capital.

Basically, financial risk can come about either through the use of too much debt (fixed obligations) in the financial structure of the firm or through inept matching of the debt-repayment obligations to the firm's cash inflows. For example, it is typically not prudent to finance the acquisition of railroad locomotives with commercial paper (debt which matures every three months). A good financial officer does not use highly liquid debt securities to finance highly illiquid assets, for in periods of restricted credit availability, the firm may not be able to refinance the maturing short-term securities. If investors do see an unduly large amount of debt maturing in the near future, they will demand a very high return for providing you with additional capital. Notice that financial risk, like business risk, is particular to an individual firm and not related to more general influences such as capital market supply-demand conditions or inflation expectations.

The financial officer now faces a cost of capital k of:

$$k = r.i. + p + b + f$$

Taking together the effect of business and financial risk on the variability of earnings, Firm A would, from its historical record of earnings, probably have a higher cost of capital than Firm B, despite the fact that both firms have identical average annual earnings during the period.

Year	Firm A earnings	Firm B earnings
1	$3,600	$1,500
2	3,400	1,600
3	(300)	1,700
4	4,000	1,800
5	3,000	1,900
6	(2,000)	2,000
7	3,000	2,200
8	1,000	2,400
9	800	2,600
10	4,000	2,800
Average annual earnings	2,050	2,050

Marketability

Investors also require that they can realize the going market value of the securities in cash if and when they decide to sell. The relative degree to which investors can liquidate their holdings of the firm's securities at or near the going market price is known as *marketability,* and it influences their willingness to purchase your security offerings.

Marketability is a time-dimensioned variable, dependent upon the relative supply and demand conditions, which affects the volatility of price changes between sales, given all the other risk factors constant. The market value of any security will be adversely affected in a transaction only if the sale has to be made in a very short time and/or the offering constitutes a relatively large supply of securities in relation to the number of bids that can be solicited over the available time. If the number of potential bidders is usually small when the owner of the security goes to sell it, or if the amount of the security offered for immediate sale is large in relation to the typical amount that could be expected to be bought at one time by potential bidders, the owner of the security runs the risk of having to take a lower-than-prevailing market price to induce buyers to absorb the entire offering. Under those circumstances, the financial officer should realize that potential investors will require a higher rate of return to compensate for this marketability risk.

To insure that investors do not require a higher rate of return from your security offerings because of a relatively low degree of marketability, a good financial officer tries to make securities plainly visible in large markets where numerous buyers and sellers exist. This makes potential investors feel the firm's securities have a high degree of marketability and can be sold with relatively little deviation from the going price. This is one reason why a firm and its financial officer may choose to list the firm on an organized stock exchange such as the New York Stock Exchange. The good financial officer also realizes that one must usually sell a relatively large amount of any particular security at less than the prevailing price.[1]

As the degree of marketability risk (m) increases, the cost of capital also increases, such that:

$$k = r.i. + p + b + f + m$$

---

[1] The financial officer can regularly judge the degree of marketability by such factors as the number of shares outstanding, the number of stockholders, the number of shares in the floating supply (those shares not closely held but actively traded), and the number of shares traded during the average day.

Implications for the Financial Officer

The alert financial officer realizes that the firm's cost of capital can be affected by the general factors of real interest rates, inflation, business risk, financial risk, and marketability. There is very little control over the real interest rate or the expected rate of inflation, but through proper timing of security offerings, the financial officer *can* effectively lower the firm's cost of capital. By projecting an image which leads investors to expect less volatility and uncertainty in the firm's earnings because of an improved operating environment or a more conservative capital structure, the financial officer can further lower the cost of capital. In addition, the marketability of the firm's securities can be promoted by trying to increase the number of persons who own the securities, widely publicizing activities and financial operating results, acquainting security analysts with the firm, and making the firm's securities more easily traded.

THE COST OF CAPITAL FOR DEBT

Given the firm's promise to pay its lenders a specific dollar amount each year on a particular debt security, what return does the aggregate of all investors (that is, the market place) require at any given time and can we, as financial officers, observe this?

The cost of capital for debt (k_d) is the return potential investors require of the firm's debt securities, such as its bonds. In relation to the general factors of risk, we can see that:

$$k_d = r.i. + p + b + f_d + m$$

where

k_d = the cost of debt
$r.i.$ = the real interest rate
p = the purchasing-power risk premium
b = the business risk
f_d = the firm's financial risk associated with its debt[2]
m = the marketability risk associated with the particular security

If any of the general risk factors rise, the cost of debt for the firm rises. If any of the general risk factors fall, the cost of debt falls.

Let us examine a typical bond and see if we can observe the cost of debt as it would appear in the market place. If we, as financial officers, are selling a 15-year bond which promises to pay $70 in interest payments at the end of each year for the next 15 years and return the original $1,000 investment at the end of 15 years, the potential investor in that bond would have to examine the worth of the interest and return-of-principal flows in Table 9-1.

Having read Chapter 4, we recognize that potential investors consider the time value of money when they evaluate this stream of flows to derive a price for the bond that will provide them with their required rate of return. Clearly the more

---

[2] The financial risk for the debt differs slightly from the financial risk for the equity, since the former takes priority over the latter in the distribution of the firm's revenues. The financial risk for the debt depends to a great extent on the variability in the firm's interest coverage and fixed charges earned, while the financial risk to the equity depends to a great extent on the variability in the firm's earnings per share.

Table 9-1   Interest and Return-of-Principal Flows on a 15-Year Bond

Year	Interest payment	Return of principal
1	$70	$0
2	70	0
3	70	0
4	70	0
5	70	0
6	70	0
7	70	0
8	70	0
9	70	0
10	70	0
11	70	0
12	70	0
13	70	0
14	70	0
15	70	1,000

distant interest payments and the return of principal are not worth as much now as the nearer interest payments. The investor must be compensated at a rate of return (the discount rate in Equation 9-1 below) that considers all the general factors: compensation for the real interest rate, expected inflation, and business, financial, and marketability risks. That required rate of return, which is the firm's cost of capital for debt, is used as the discount factor in Equation 9-1, such that:

$$P_0 = \sum_{t=1}^{15} \frac{\$70}{(1+k_d)^t} + \frac{\$1,000}{(1+k_d)^{15}} \tag{9-1}$$

where

P_0 = the price of the bond at this point in time

k_d = the cost of debt

What actually happens is that potential investors look at the expected cashflows, decide what is the required rate of return, and then use that return to discount the cashflows to the present. For example, if the required return were 7 percent, the price of the bond would be:

$$\$1,000 = \sum_{t=1}^{15} \frac{\$70}{(1+.07)^t} + \frac{\$1,000}{(1+.07)^{15}}$$

As financial officers, we could not read the minds of investors to determine k_d, but we can look in the financial pages of our newspapers and find the price at which investors are now buying the bonds described in Table 9-1. From there we can calculate the k_d of Equation 9-1, since we know the cashflows and the price (P_0), in the following manner:

$$\$1,000 = \sum_{t=1}^{15} \frac{\$70}{(1+k_d)^t} + \frac{\$1,000}{(1+k_d)^{15}} \tag{9-2}$$

This procedure is identical to determining the internal rate of return (IRR), as we did in Chapters 4 and 5. If we solve Equation 9-2 for k_d, we will find the cost of debt to be 7 percent.

Now the cost of debt does not have to remain constant from one time to another.

Should it rise, we would find investors less attracted to our bond and demanding a higher rate of return, raising our cost of debt. This increase could happen if any of the general risk factors increased. If we opened our financial pages and found the price of the bond had sunk to say $769.40, we could be sure that our cost of debt had increased. We could figure out the new cost of debt as:

$$\$769.40 = \sum_{t=1}^{15} \frac{\$70}{(1 + k_d)^t} + \frac{\$1,000}{(1 + k_d)^{15}} \tag{9-3}$$

$$k_d = 10\%$$

Since the interest payments and the return of principal remain constant regardless of the change in investors' required rate of return, only the bond price and the cost of debt can change. It is obvious, therefore, that *as the observed bond price changes, the firm's cost of debt has changed in the opposite direction.* A financial officer can pinpoint the exact cost of debt after the price change by calculating k_d in generalized Equation 9-4.

$$P_0 = \sum_{t=1}^{n} \frac{IP_t}{(1 + k_d)^t} + \frac{P_n}{(1 + k_d)^n} \tag{9-4}$$

where
  P_0 = the observed market price of the bond
  IP_t = the interest payments
  P_n = the return of principal
  k_d = the cost of debt
  n = the number of years until the bond matures

In our bond of Table 9-1, IP_t equals $70, $P_n = \$1,000$, and $n = 15$ years. Just to be complete, we can also see that as the price of the bond rises, the cost of debt must fall. For example, assume the price of the bond in Table 9-1 rose to $1,090.80. Using Equation 9-4, the financial officer could determine that the cost of debt had declined to 6 percent.

Yield to Maturity

The calculations of the k_d which we performed above also give us the *yield to maturity,* which is synonymous with the cost of debt. We can continue to calculate the k_d as above, using such aids as the present-value tables of Appendix B or precalculated bond tables, or we can resort to the approximation method of Equation 9-5.

$$Y_{TM} = \frac{IP_t + \dfrac{P_n - P_0}{n}}{\dfrac{P_0 + P_n}{2}} \tag{9-5}$$

where
  Y_{TM} = the yield to maturity
  IP_t = the annual interest payments
  P_n = the return of the principal
  P_0 = the observed price of the bond
  $P_n - P_0$ = the difference between the observed price and the return of principal, which is a capital gain if P_n is larger than P_0 and a capital loss if P_0 is greater than P_n

Equation 9-5 says that the yield to maturity (k_d) increases as the bond price declines because investors have less invested in the bond to get the annual interest payments and the return of principal; and because by paying less than $1,000 for the bond and getting back $1,000 at maturity, they have a capital gain which accrues to them proportionally each year if they hold the bond to maturity. Notice that the adjustment in the yield to maturity occurs through the price change, as investors demand a higher return from your securities, they are willing to pay a lesser price for any given interest and return-of-principal cashflow stream. Approximation is very rarely used among financial officers and their advisors. Almost all use the precalculated bond yield tables illustrated in Table 9-2 instead.

After-Tax Cost of Debt

Since interest is a tax-deductible expense, as financial officers we have to consider the after-tax cost of debt, especially if we want to judge its impact on the firm's after-tax profitability or compare it to the cost of other types of securities we could offer whose cashflow streams are not tax-deductible, such as preferred and common stock. We can calculate the after-tax cost of debt by adjusting the pre-tax cost for the tax rate such that:

$$k_{dt} = k_d(1 - t) \tag{9-6}$$

where
　　t = the tax rate
　　k_{dt} = the after-tax cost of debt
　　k_d = the pre-tax cost of debt

For example, if:

$$k_d = 10\%$$
$$t = 50\%$$

then:

$$k_{dt} = .10(1 - .50)$$
$$= 5\%$$

Implications for the Financial Officer

As financial officers, we can measure the cost of debt capital as the yield to maturity investors require, as reflected in the price they are willing to pay for the interest payments and return-of-principal cashflow schedule of any particular bond. Notice that we can estimate the cost of debt capital very quickly by looking at the prevailing bond price and computing the k_d.

If you are going to offer a bond to potential investors, you can judge the cost of capital for that bond by examining similar bonds of similar companies. For example, if you are thinking of offering 10-year bonds and the 10-year bonds of your nearest competitor have a yield to maturity of 8 percent, you can predict that your cost of debt will be close to 8 percent, as well.

Since the required rate of return on bonds is an investor-determined function of the real interest rate, expected inflation, and business, financial, and marketability risks, an alert financial officer can affect the cost of debt by offering the securities at a low point in the real interest rate cycle and by changing investors' attitudes towards the firm's risk image.

Table 9-2 A Bond Yield Table

7%				YEARS				7%
Yield	*15*	*16*	*17*	*18*	*19*	*20*	*21*	*22*
6	109.80	110.19	110.57	110.92	111.25	111.56	111.85	112.13
1/8	108.51	108.84	109.16	109.46	109.75	110.01	110.26	110.50
1/4	107.23	107.52	107.78	108.04	108.27	108.50	108.70	108.90
3/8	105.98	106.21	106.43	106.64	106.83	107.01	107.18	107.34
6 1/2	104.75	104.93	105.10	105.26	105.41	105.55	105.68	105.81
5/8	103.53	103.67	103.79	103.91	104.02	104.12	104.22	104.31
3/4	102.34	102.42	102.51	102.58	102.65	102.72	102.78	102.84
7/8	101.16	101.20	101.24	101.28	101.31	101.35	101.38	101.41
7	100.00	100.00	100.00	100.00	100.00	100.00	100.00	100.00
1/8	98.86	98.82	98.78	98.74	98.71	98.68	98.65	98.62
1/4	97.74	97.66	97.58	97.51	97.44	97.38	97.32	97.27
3/8	96.63	96.51	96.40	96.30	96.20	96.11	96.03	95.95
7 1/2	95.54	95.39	95.24	95.10	94.86	94.86	94.75	94.65
5/8	94.47	94.28	94.10	93.93	93.78	93.64	93.51	93.38
3/4	93.42	93.19	92.98	92.79	92.60	92.44	92.28	92.14
7/8	92.38	92.12	91.88	91.66	91.45	91.26	91.08	90.92
8	91.35	91.06	90.79	90.55	90.32	90.10	89.91	89.73
1/8	90.35	90.03	89.73	89.46	89.20	88.97	88.75	88.55
1/4	89.35	89.00	88.68	88.38	88.11	87.86	87.62	87.41
3/8	88.38	88.00	87.65	87.33	87.04	86.76	86.51	86.28
8 1/2	87.42	87.01	86.64	86.30	85.98	85.69	85.43	85.18
5/8	86.47	86.04	85.64	85.28	84.95	84.64	84.36	84.10
3/4	85.54	85.08	84.66	84.28	83.93	83.61	83.31	83.04
7/8	84.62	84.14	83.70	83.30	82.93	82.59	82.28	82.00
9	83.71	83.21	82.75	82.33	81.95	81.60	81.28	80.98
1/8	82.82	82.30	81.82	81.39	80.99	80.62	80.29	79.98
1/4	81.94	81.40	80.90	80.45	80.04	79.66	79.32	79.00
3/8	81.08	80.52	80.00	79.54	79.11	78.72	78.37	78.04
9 1/2	80.22	79.64	79.12	78.63	78.20	77.80	77.43	77.10
5/8	79.39	78.79	78.24	77.75	77.30	76.89	76.52	76.18
3/4	78.56	77.94	77.39	76.88	76.42	76.00	75.62	75.27
7/8	77.74	77.11	76.54	76.02	75.55	75.12	74.73	74.38
10	76.94	76.30	75.71	75.18	74.70	74.26	73.87	73.51
1/4	75.37	74.70	74.09	73.54	73.04	72.59	72.18	71.81
1/2	73.85	73.15	72.52	71.95	71.44	70.97	70.55	70.18
3/4	72.37	71.65	71.00	70.41	69.89	69.41	68.99	68.60
11	70.93	70.19	69.53	68.93	68.39	67.91	67.47	67.08
1/4	69.54	68.78	68.10	67.49	66.94	66.45	66.02	65.62
1/2	68.18	67.41	66.72	66.10	65.55	65.05	64.61	64.21
3/4	66.87	66.08	65.38	64.75	64.19	63.69	63.25	62.85
12	65.59	64.79	64.08	63.45	62.88	62.38	61.94	61.54
1/4	64.35	63.54	62.82	62.18	61.62	61.12	60.67	60.28
1/2	63.14	62.32	61.60	60.96	60.39	59.89	59.45	59.05
3/4	61.96	61.14	60.42	59.78	59.21	58.71	58.27	57.88
13	60.82	60.00	59.27	58.63	58.06	57.56	57.12	56.74
1/4	59.72	58.89	58.16	57.52	56.95	56.46	56.02	55.63
1/2	58.64	57.81	57.08	56.44	55.88	55.38	54.95	54.57
3/4	57.59	56.76	56.03	55.39	54.83	54.34	53.92	53.54
14	56.57	55.74	55.01	54.38	53.82	53.34	52.92	52.55
1/4	55.58	54.75	54.02	53.39	52.84	52.37	51.95	51.59
1/2	54.61	53.78	53.06	52.44	51.89	51.42	51.01	50.65
3/4	53.67	52.85	52.13	51.51	50.97	50.51	50.10	49.75
15	52.76	51.94	51.23	50.61	50.08	49.62	49.22	48.88

1.00 = $10.

SOURCE: *High Yield Bond Basis Book*, Financial Publishing Co., 1969, p. 128.

THE COST OF EQUITY CAPITAL

What rate of return do the potential investors for the firm's common stock (equity) require, and can we observe this in the stock market?

Just as in the case of debt capital, investors will purchase the equity capital of the firm, in the form of its common stock, only if they expect to receive a return which will compensate them for surrendering control of their funds during the period they own the stock—adjusted for the appropriate risk in ownership. Again, they may not *realize* the expected return, but they require that in order to purchase the stock they must be able to *expect* that return. This required rate of return is, like its counterpart for debt capital, a function of the general risk factors of real interest rates, expected inflation, and business, financial, and marketability risks as evaluated by all market participants, such that:

$$k_e = r.i. + p + b + f_e + m \qquad (9\text{-}7)$$

where

k_e = the cost of equity capital
$r.i.$ = the real interest rate
p = the purchasing-power risk premium
b = the business risk
f_e = the financial risk associated with the common stock
m = the marketability risk associated with the particular security

Any of the risks may increase or decrease at any time, causing the firm's cost of equity (k_e) to change accordingly.

The price investors are willing to pay for the common stock is the present discounted value of the expected cashflow stream which accrues to the stock, since the stream is to be received in the future and must be discounted for the time value of money. But unlike the bonds, for which the dollar cashflows are expressly known in the interest payments and the return of principal, the dollar reward to the common stock is what the stock certificate entitles the owner to receive, namely the dividends that the company declares as long as the firm is a going concern. Ownership of the stock does not include the right to anything else.

Potential investors in common stock must estimate the expected stream of dividends and discount that stream to the present at the required rate of return (k_e) to determine the price that gives them their required rate of return at any given time. The relationships are summarized as follows:

$$P_0 = \sum_{t=1}^{\infty} \frac{\hat{D}_t}{(1 + k_e)^t} \qquad (9\text{-}8)$$

where

$\hat{D}_t$ = the investors' estimated stream of future dividends
k_e = the cost of equity, reflecting the time value of money adjusted for risk
P_0 = the prevailing market price

$\sum_{t=1}^{\infty}$ = the summation of the dividend stream over the life of the firm which is assumed to be infinite (∞) for the going concern

Since we, as financial officers, can immediately observe the stock price (P_0) by looking up the trading price of stock in the financial pages of the newspaper, we can get some idea of our prevailing equity cost by making an assumption about what investors expect the dividend stream to be and then solving Equation 9-8 for k_e. There are four typical assumptions which we can make, each of which allows us to derive our prevailing cost of equity capital as implied in the prevailing stock price. These are (1) a constant dividend with no growth, (2) a dividend growing at a constant rate, (3) a dividend growing at intermittent rates of growth at different times, and (4) a growing company which pays no dividends.

Constant Dividend with No Growth

If the present dividend is assumed to remain constant at its present level for the assumed perpetual life of the going concern, Equation 9-8 becomes:

$$k_e = \frac{D_1}{P_0} \tag{9-9}$$

which is the solution for a perpetuity of a constant dividend from now until infinity.[3] It simply says that the cost of equity capital for the constant perpetual dividend is the dividend (D_1) divided by the prevailing stock price (P_0). For example, if we assume that investors are expecting a constant annual dividend of $1 per share from our firm because of its relatively stable and nongrowth characteristics, and if we observe that our stock is selling for $10 per share in the stock market, the firm's cost of equity is:

$$k_e = \frac{\$1.00}{\$10.00}$$

$$= 10\%$$

The Dividend Growing at a Constant Rate

If we can reasonably make the assumption that investors expect our present dividend to grow throughout the perpetual life of the firm at a constant rate (g), then Equation 9-8 can be altered to include this consideration, such that:

$$P_0 = \sum_{t=1}^{\infty} \frac{D_0(1+g)^t}{(1+k_e)^t} \tag{9-10}$$

[3]

$$P_0 = \frac{D_1}{(1+k_e)} + \frac{D_2}{(1+k_e)^2} + \frac{D_3}{(1+k_e)^3} \cdots \cdots + \frac{D_n}{(1+k_e)^n} \tag{1}$$

Multiplying Equation (1) by $(1 + k_e)$ gives:

$$(1+k_e)P_0 = D + \frac{D_2}{(1+k_e)^1} + \frac{D_3}{(1+k_e)^2} \cdots \cdots + \frac{D_n}{(1+k_e)^{n-1}} \tag{2}$$

Subtracting Equation (1) from Equation (2) gives:

$$(1+k_e)P_0 - P_0 = D_1 - \frac{D_n}{(1+k_e)^n} \tag{3}$$

As $n \to \infty$

$$(1+k_e)P_0 - P_0 = D_1$$

$$P_0 = \frac{D_1}{k_e}$$

where

P_0 = the prevailing stock price
D_0 = the prevailing dividend
g = the assumed rate of growth in the dividend
k_e = the cost of equity
$k_e > g$

Notice that in Equation 9-10, the dividend will get larger and larger as time passes because of the constant growth factor (g). For example, an initial $1 dividend this year growing at a constant 10 percent will be $1.10 next year, $1.21 the year after that, and so on. This is clearly different from both the bond, which has a constant interest payment for a specific number of years, and the no-growth dividend, which is expected to remain the same in perpetuity.

We can solve the growth perpetuity[4] to derive Equations 9-11 and 9-12 in a similar manner to our solution for Equation 9-9.

$$P_0 = \frac{D_1}{k_e - g} \tag{9-11}$$

$$k_e = \frac{D_1}{P_0} + g \tag{9-12}$$

If, as financial officers, we assumed investors were expecting our present $1 dividend to grow at 8 percent a year over the remaining life of the firm, which is assumed to be infinite, and we observed the price of our stock to be $20, then:

$$k_e = \frac{\$1.00}{\$20.00} + .08$$
$$= 13\%$$

[4]
$$P_0 = \frac{D_0(1+g)}{(1+k_e)} + \frac{D_0(1+g)^2}{(1+k_e)^2} + \frac{D_0(1+g)^3}{(1+k_e)^3} \cdots + \frac{D_0(1+g)^n}{(1+k_e)^n} \tag{1}$$

Multiplying Equation (1) by $\frac{(1+k_e)}{(1+g)}$ gives:

$$\frac{(1+k_e)}{(1+g)} P_0 = D_0 + \frac{D_0(1+g)}{(1+k_e)} + \frac{D_0(1+g)^2}{(1+k_e)^2} \cdots + \frac{D_0(1+g)^{n-1}}{(1+k_e)^{n-1}} \tag{2}$$

Subtracting Equation (1) from Equation (2) gives:

$$\frac{(1+k_e)}{(1+g)} P_0 - P_0 = D_0 - \frac{D_0(1+g)^n}{(1+k_e)^n} \tag{3}$$

As $n \to \infty$, the second term on the right side of Equation (3) disappears:

$$\frac{(1+k_e)}{(1+g)} P_0 - P_0 = D_0 \tag{4}$$

$$P_0 \left[\frac{(1+k_e)}{(1+g)} - 1 \right] = D_0 \tag{5}$$

$$P_0 \left[\frac{(1+k_e) - (1+g)}{(1+g)} \right] = D_0 \tag{6}$$

$$P_0 [(1+k_e) - (1+g)] = D_0(1+g) \tag{7}$$

$$P_0(k_e - g) = D_1 \tag{8}$$

$$P_0 = \frac{D_1}{k_e - g} \tag{9}$$

Our cost of equity capital under the assumption of a constant growth in our dividend is the present dividend yield plus the growth rate, which, in this example, is 13 percent.

Intermittent Dividend Growth

If we assume in our attempt to infer the cost of equity capital that investors expect intermittent growth in our dividend, then we would substitute as follows:

$$P_0 = \sum_{t=1}^{5} \frac{D_1(1+g_1)^t}{(1+k_e)^t} + \sum_{t=6}^{10} \frac{\hat{D}_5(1+g_2)^{t-5}}{(1+k_e)^t} + \cdots + \sum_{t=11}^{\infty} \frac{\hat{D}_{10}(1+g_3)^{t-10}}{(1+k_e)^t} \qquad (9\text{-}13)$$

where

$\quad P_0 =$ the prevailing market price of the firm's stock
$\quad D_1 =$ the prevailing dividend per share
$\quad \hat{D}_5 =$ the dividend expected to prevail at the end of 5 years from now
$\quad \hat{D}_{10} =$ the dividend expected to prevail at the end of 10 years from now
$\quad k_e =$ the cost of equity capital
$\quad g_1 =$ the assumed growth rate in dividend for the next 5 years
$\quad g_2 =$ the assumed growth rate in dividend for years 6 through 10
$\quad g_3 =$ the assumed growth rate in dividend for years subsequent to year 10

For example, if $g_1 = 10$ percent, $g_2 = 5$ percent, and $g_3 = 0$, k_e is the rate which equates the investors' anticipated dividend stream at the various growth rates to the prevailing price (P_0).[5]

No Dividend

If the firm has decided to reinvest its entire earnings, which is typical of many growth companies which can reinvest now in the anticipation of higher earnings later, and pays no dividend, how can the cost of equity be determined?

The first thing to remember is that investors do not change their required rate of return (the firm's k_e) just because there is no dividend and all earnings are reinvested. Investors just look to get their dollar reward and the return from an increase in share price made possible by the reinvestment. The idea is that the firm has so many high-yield investment projects available that by keeping the earnings, investors' expectations of larger, future dividends are increased, and this leads to an increase in the stock price. The required rate of return then accrues to the stockholders in the form of a capital gain which they receive when they sell their shares at a later date and at a higher price (P_n) than they paid (P_0), such that:

$$P_0 = \frac{P_n}{(1+k_e)^n} \qquad (9\text{-}14)$$

[5] The financial officer can make many assumptions about the shape of the growth stream. For example, following the industry life cycle in which the firm grows rapidly at first, then grows at a decreasing rate, and finally declines, the financial officer can assume a quadratic pattern in the dividend stream such that:

$$P_0 = \sum_{t=1}^{\infty} \frac{D_0 \prod_{t=1}^{\infty} (1 + at^2 - bt + c)}{(1+k_e)^t}$$

where

P_0 = the original price paid

P_n = the price for which the potential investor expects to sell the shares at the end of n periods

k_e = the cost of equity

n = the expected number of periods over which the shares are held in investors' portfolios

Investors can reasonably expect P_n to be greater than P_0 because, if the firm has been successful in reinvesting its earnings, the dividends stockholders will receive once the firm starts paying dividends should be larger than would have been the case if the firm had started paying dividends earlier. Also, by the time n periods have gone by, the initiation of the dividend stream is closer and more valuable because of the time-value of money. For example, if investors had expected to receive $1 in dividends 10 years from now, that $1 would have a present worth of only $.385 if the required rate of return is 10 percent. But, 5 years from now that same $1 of expected dividends will then have a present value of $.62 if the required rate of return has remained constant at 10 percent.

If we assume a particular P_n greater than P_0, the cost of equity for the no-dividend firm is:

$$k_e = \frac{P_n}{P_0} - 1 \qquad (9\text{-}15)$$

The particular P_n that we assume reflects the present value of the future stream of dividends for the years after year n, provided k_e and investors' expectations about the stream do not change. In other words, as financial officers we must try to estimate what the selling price of the stock will be in year n (P_n), which is the present value of the stream of dividends that investors in year n expect to receive in every year subsequent to year n, discounted at the required rate of return prevailing at year n.[6]

Obviously it is very difficult, if not impossible, for financial officers to estimate the price of the firm's stock several years ahead. Accordingly, many financial officers have developed price/earnings ratio (P/E) approximations, which use the prevailing stock price and the latest earnings per share to approximate investors' required rate of return and the firm's cost of equity.

As financial officers, we will typically encounter three different P/E approximation methods: (1) the earnings yield, (2) the earnings yield plus growth, and (3) the

---

[6] It is not very appealing and certainly not to be taken seriously by the astute investor, but there may be occasions when the financial officer feels that the stock price at the end of period n is whatever a bigger fool will pay. This may happen when the stock market is in a highly speculative period, such as before the 1929 crash. During those periods the financial officer is well advised to undertake immediately a large common stock offering.

In those situations where investors expect to receive a dividend and a capital gain, the no-dividend derivation of the cost of equity capital in Equation 9-15 can be adjusted to consider the capital gain, as follows:

$$k_e = \frac{\sum_{t=1}^{n} D_t + P_n}{P_0} - 1$$

simulated dividend plus growth. The earnings yield method simply (and incorrectly) says that:

$$k_e = \frac{E_0}{P_0} \qquad (9\text{-}16)$$

where

k_e = the cost of equity
E_0 = the latest earnings per share
P_0 = the prevailing stock price

For example, if $E_0 = \$1$ and $P_0 = \$10$, k_e would be 10 percent. It must be emphasized that the *earnings yield* method is misleading and incorrect. While the latest earnings reflect only this past period, the prevailing price reflects the entire stream of future earnings that investors expect to receive. It is like comparing apples and oranges, because the two are not concerned with the same factors. We could derive a misleadingly low earnings yield for a growth stock like IBM because its price reflects much larger earnings anticipated in the near and further future, while its latest earnings per share are already history and much too low in comparison to what investors are anticipating. Such situations can produce obviously misleading results. For example, if $E_0 = \$.25$, $P_0 = \$100$, then $k_e = \frac{1}{4}$ percent, which is clearly incorrect but can often be observed among the more glamorous growth stocks.

In instances where there is no dividend and the firm is growing at a fairly constant rate, financial officers would be better off using the *earnings yield plus growth* approximation:

$$k_e = \frac{E_0}{P_0} + g \qquad (9\text{-}17)$$

For example, if $E_0 = \$1$, $P_0 = \$100$, and $g = 10$ percent, then:

$$k_e = \frac{\$1.00}{\$100} + 10\%$$
$$= 11\%$$

It is also possible to refine the approximation a little more by assuming a retention rate which would prevail as if the firm had been paying dividends, such that:

$$k_e = \frac{E_0(1-\lambda)}{P_0} + g \qquad (9\text{-}17)$$

where

λ = the assumed retention rate
$E_0(1-\lambda)$ = the implied dividend if the firm had been paying dividends

Under this method, the financial officer has attempted to convert the earnings to a dividend in order to bring the cost of equity approximation more into line with the dividend stream that investors are anticipating. For example, if $E_0 = \$1$, $P_0 = \$100$, $\lambda = 50$ percent and $g = 10$ percent, then:

$$k_e = \frac{\$1.00(1-.50)}{\$100} + 10\%$$
$$= 10.5\%$$

While the *simulated dividend plus growth* method is perhaps the most refined, it is only an approximation like the others. The earnings yield method is inferior and should be avoided. The other two methods may be used, providing they are understood as approximations of the true cost of equity, which is very difficult to measure.

After-Tax Cost of Equity

Unlike the cost of debt, which must be adjusted for the tax rate to be expressed on an after-tax basis, the cost of equity is already expressed on an after-tax basis because dividends and earnings per share are after-tax items on the firm's income statement. In other words, because of the tax-deductible nature of interest, the government is essentially picking up half the cost (at tax rates equal to 50 percent), whereas the government picks up none of the cost of equity.

Implications for Security Analysis

Since the cost of equity for the firm is the required rate of return for investors, it is reasonable to assume that the evaluation of the stock by investors has an impact on the firm's cost of capital. If, as financial officers, we can understand a little of how security analysis works, we may be in a better position to understand the impact of security price changes on our cost of equity.

First, it is clear from Equation 9-8 that the cost of equity (k_e) can be solved:

$$P_0 = \sum_{t=1}^{\infty} \frac{\hat{D}_t}{(1 + k_e)^t} \tag{9-8}$$

From Equation 9-4, it is clear that the cost of debt can be solved:

$$P_0 = \sum_{t=1}^{n} \frac{IP_t}{(1 + k_d)^t} + \frac{P_n}{(1 + k_d)^n} \tag{9-4}$$

And we know that the general factors in the required rate of return, or the firm's cost of either debt (k_d) or equity (k_e), are:

$$k_e = r.i. + p + f_e + b + m$$
$$k_d = r.i. + p + f_d + b + m$$

where
  $r.i.$ = the real interest rate
  p = the purchasing-power risk premium
  f = financial risk for either debt (f_d) or equity (f_e) securities
  b = business risk
  m = marketability risk

We can see that if there are changes in any of the general factors in the required rate of return or in the expected dividend stream, our stock price changes. The exact effect on the stock price depends on the relative magnitudes of the changes in the denominator or the numerator of Equation 9-8. Similarly, if there are changes in the required rate of return, the price of the bond will also change in an opposite direction, but the entire price change depends on what happens to the denominator of Equation 9-4, since the numerator (reward) is fixed.

Table 9-3   Probable Effects on Stock Prices

$$P_0 = \sum_{t=1}^{\infty} \frac{\hat{D}_t}{(1 + k_e)^t}$$

A. No Change in the Required Rate of Return (k_e)
   1. If dividend expectations increase, then P_0 rises.
   2. If dividend expectations decrease, then P_0 falls.

B. No Change in Dividend Expectations $(\hat{D}_t)$
   1. If the required rate of return rises, then P_0 falls.
   2. If the required rate of return falls, then P_0 rises.

C. Both $\hat{D}_t$ and k_e Change
   1. If $\hat{D}_t$ rises and k_e rises, $\Big\{$ P_0 rises or falls, depending

       or   then $\Big\{$ on the proportional relationship

       If $\hat{D}_t$ falls and k_e falls, $\Big\{$ in the changes.
   2. If $\hat{D}_t$ falls and k_e rises, then P_0 falls.
   3. If $\hat{D}_t$ rises and k_e falls, then P_0 rises.

Table 9-3 illustrates the changes we could expect in our stock price in relation to changes in the expected dividend stream or the required rate of return.

Financial officers who want to maximize their firm's share price must attempt to get to those combinations of k_e and $\hat{D}_t$ which raise P_0 and avoid those combinations which lower P_0. Since several of the factors that influence investors' return requirements are beyond control, such as the real interest rate, financial officers must anticipate changes in k_e or $\hat{D}_t$ to take advantage of favorable changes in the firm's stock price when offering securities to raise capital.

THE COST OF RETAINED EARNINGS

The cost of retained earnings (k_{re}) is the cost of equity we have just developed, because we have been talking about the cost of raising new funds through the reinvestment of earnings. Since the financial officer can raise equity capital by either selling new shares or retaining earnings, we have been answering the question: At what rate of return are investors indifferent to whether the firm pays out its earnings in dividends or reinvests the earnings for future growth, excluding individual tax considerations? This point is reflected in the share price financial officers use to determine the firm's cost of equity. If investors are not getting the return they had expected from the firm's reinvestment of its earnings, they will sell the stock, forcing down the price until they get the required rate of return. By lowering the stock price in response to a lower expected dollar reward in the form of dividends or capital gains, potential investors maintain the required rate of return they need in order to purchase the stock. However, the previous owners from whom they may buy the stock suffer a loss because the dividend expectations have declined since they purchased the stock. Of course, we have seen in Table 9-3 that the required rate of return (k_e) can also increase and cause the stock price to fall. What the financial officer sees reflected in the stock price as the implied cost of capital is the cost of equity retained in the firm.

THE COST OF NEWLY ISSUED EQUITY

What is the cost of equity capital raised as newly issued common stock, and can we observe this?

The cost of newly issued common equity, or the sale of stock to the public or financial institutions, differs only slightly from the cost of retained equity. The basic differences arise because when it issues new equity the firm has to bear additional expenses which it did not have to bear when retaining earnings. These additional expenses are known as flotation costs and include commissions to the investment banker for selling the stock, printing expenses, registration with the government for permission to sell the stock, advertising, and any discount from the prevailing stock price which may have to be given to potential investors to induce a sufficient number of them to purchase all the shares offered. Frequently the number of new shares issued at once to raise the equity capital is rather large in relation to the typical number of shares which may be traded on any one day. Therefore, to lure purchasers during the new stock offering, the firm has to lower the stock price temporarily, raising the firm's cost of capital. The cost of newly issued common equity is calculated as follows:

$$k_{en} = \frac{D_1}{P_f} + g \tag{9-18}$$

where

k_{en} = the cost of newly issued common equity
D_1 = the prevailing dividend
P_f = the prevailing share price less flotation costs; $(P_0 - f) = P_f$
g = assumed growth rate

If:

$D_1 = \$1.00$
$P_0 = \$12.00$
$f = \$2.00$
$P_f = \$10.00$
$g = 8\%$

then:

$$k_{en} = \frac{\$1.00}{\$10.00} + 8\% \qquad k_{en} = 18\%$$

The 18 percent is a higher cost of capital than the cost of retained earnings, which would be 16.5 percent, because of the flotation costs.

THE COST OF PREFERRED EQUITY CAPITAL

The financial officer may also raise equity capital through the sale of preferred stock which, like debt, entitles investors to a fixed cashflow known as the preferred dividend. Unlike debt, preferred stock is usually redeemable at the option of the company at any time in the future. If the financial officer assumes that the redemption date is unknown, then the cost of preferred equity capital is:

$$k_p = \frac{D_p}{P_p} \tag{9-19}$$

where

k_p = the cost of preferred equity
P_p = the prevailing price of the preferred stock
D_p = the preferred dividend, which is usually fixed

For example, if:

$$D_p = \$8.00$$
$$P_p = \$100$$

then:

$$k_p = \frac{\$8.00}{\$100}$$
$$k_p = 8\%$$

If the price of the preferred stock drops because investors require a higher rate of return, the cost of preferred equity capital rises, and vice versa.

As in the case of the cost of common equity, the k_p is already figured on an after-tax basis since its dividend is not a tax-deductible expense.

SUMMARY

After having read Chapter 9, you should be able to answer these questions:

1. What general factors determine the cost of capital for individual securities?

The cost of capital for individual securities is the rate of return investors require in order to purchase the security. The major factors influencing what investors require are the real rate of interest, inflation expectations, business risk, financial risk, and marketability risk. The first two are essentially beyond the control of the financial officer. The second two are characteristic of the particular firm and its operating environment and capital structure, while marketability risk is peculiar to the particular security.

We also saw that the sum of these general factors is the return investors require for the time value of money adjusted for the risk involved in the investment. Thus, the cost of capital equates the expected reward stream to the going price of the security. The financial officer has to infer the cost of capital from the observed market price and the assumed reward stream.

2. What is the cost of debt capital?

The cost of debt capital is the yield to maturity which equates the prevailing price of the bond to the expected cashflow stream, such that:

$$P_0 = \sum_{t=1}^{n} \frac{IP_t}{(1+k_d)^t} + \frac{P_n}{(1+k_d)^n}$$

Which on an after-tax basis is:

$$k_{dt} = k_d(1-t)$$

3. What is the cost of common equity?

The cost of common equity (k_e) is the rate of return investors require to purchase your already outstanding stock, such that:

$$P_0 = \sum_{t=1}^{\infty} \frac{\hat{D}_t}{(1+k_e)^t}$$

where k_e equates the future stream of expected dividends, which is the reward to the stockholder, to the present value or selling price of the share, at an appropriate discount rate for the time-value of money adjusted for the risk.

We saw, however, that if the financial officer could assume a constant growth rate in the firm's dividend in perpetuity, then the cost of equity capital could be approximated as:

$$k_e = \frac{D_1}{P_0} + g$$

If the firm paid no dividends, the financial officer could approximate k_e as the simulated dividend plus growth:

$$k_e = \frac{E_0(1 + \lambda)}{P_0} + g$$

4. What is the cost of newly issued common equity capital?

Because of the expenses incurred by the firm in issuing new common stock, the cost of newly issued equity capital has to be adjusted upward such that wherever P_0 was found in the cost of equity determinations, P_f, which is the prevailing price adjusted downward for the flotation costs, has to be substituted.

5. What is the cost of preferred equity capital?

The cost of preferred equity capital is simply the preferred dividend divided by the prevailing price of the preferred stock.

QUESTIONS

9-1 Distinguish between the real interest rate and the nominal interest rate.

9-2 Do you think long-term bonds issued by ATT or a relatively small, defense-contract-oriented firm would have a higher cost of debt? Why?

9-3 Distinguish between business risk and purchasing-power risk and the effect each has on the cost of capital of any security.

9-4 List the general factors that may affect the cost of capital for any security.

9-5 (a) Why is the cost of debt adjusted to reflect the after-tax cost to the firm?
(b) If a firm's pre-tax cost of debt is 12 percent and its corporate tax rate is 48 percent, what is its after-tax cost of debt?

9-6 In what ways is the cost of debt similar to the cost of preferred capital? Are there any differences?

9-7 Do you think a firm's cost of newly issued equity should differ from the cost of outstanding equity?

9-8 The price/earnings ratios (P/E) of Gromax Corporation and Steadynow Company were recently observed to be 100, and 10, respectively. Can we infer anything about these firms' respective costs of equity capital?

PROBLEMS

9-1 (a) Compute the cost of debt of an outstanding long-term corporate bond selling at $100,000 and promising to pay $8,000 per year for 30 years and $150,000 at the end of 30 years. Assume the firm has a marginal tax rate of 50 percent.

(b) If the nominal interest rate increases, what do you think will happen to the price of the bond?

9-2 In December Bolcon was priced at $75 per common share based upon an expected annual growth rate in dividends of 10 percent. In April the nominal interest rate rose due to Federal Reserve credit restrictions and investors revised Bolcon's expected growth rate downward to 8 percent. Assuming Bolcon's current dividend is $2, what is its cost of equity capital? What happened to its price per share in April?

9-3 The common stocks of Firms A and B are currently selling at the same price—$50 per share. However, investors anticipate that Firm A will pay a constant dividend of $4 per share in the foreseeable future, whereas Firm B is expected to pay a $4 dividend this year and thereafter pay a 5 percent greater dividend each year than in the prior year. What are the costs of equity capital for Firms A and B?

9-4 Growmod is a young company that is expected to grow quite rapidly for the next 5 years and then experience a slower rate of growth. The firm's financial officers expect a 20 percent annual growth rate in earnings for the next 5 years and then an annual growth rate of 8 percent in the foreseeable future. The firm's current market price per share of common equity is $38.39, and its dividend this year will be $.50. What is the minimum rate of return that the marginal investors are requiring on Growmod's common stock?

9-5 The market price per share of preferred stock of Firm C is $25 and it promises to pay an annual dividend of $2 with an indefinite redemption date. What is the firm's cost of preferred equity capital?

9-6 MBA Enterprises is a relatively small company which is considering raising additional capital by issuing 20,000 new shares of common stock. Presently the firm's common stock has a market price of $50 per share, a current dividend of $4, and an annual growth rate in dividends of 5 percent for the foreseeable future. The costs of issuing the new securities are given below:

Commissions to investment bank	$20,000
Printing of stocks	2,000
Government registration	1,000
Advertising	5,000
Total flotation costs	$28,000

(a) Compute the cost of the newly issued common capital to the firm.
(b) How does this compare to the cost of capital on existing common stock?

9-7 Firms D and E are young, growth-oriented companies whose common stock have price/earning multiples of 80 and 60, even though neither firm has paid any dividends in the past nor expects to pay any for the next several years. Likewise, firms D and E have had annual rates of growth in earnings of 18 percent and 12 percent, respectively, and these rates are anticipated for the foreseeable future. Compare the costs of equity capital for the two firms.

BIBLIOGRAPHY

Bauman, W. Scott. "Investment Returns and Present Values." *Financial Analysts' Journal*, 25 (November–December 1969), 107–118.

Baxter, Nevins D. "Leverage, Risk of Ruin, and the Cost of Capital." *Journal of Finance*, XXII (September 1967), 395–404.

Ben-Shahar, Haim, and Abraham Ascher. "Capital Budgeting and Stock Valuation: Comment." *American Economic Review*, LVII (March 1967), 209–214.

Bodenhorn, Diran. "A Cash Flow Concept of Profit." *Journal of Finance*, XIX (March 1964), 16–31.

Brewer, D. E., and J. Michaelson. "The Cost of Capital, Corporation Finance, and the Theory of Investment: Comment." *American Economic Review*, LV (June 1965), 516–524.

Brigham, Eugene F., and Keith V. Smith. "The Cost of Capital to the Small Firm." *Engineering Economist*, 13 (Fall 1967), 1–26.

Crockett, Jean, and Irwin Friend. "Capital Budgeting and Stock Valuation: Comment." *American Economic Review*, LVII (March 1967), 214–220.

Elton, Edwin J., and Martin J. Gruber. "The Cost of Retained Earnings—Implications of Share Repurchase." *Industrial Management Review*, 9 (Spring 1968), 87–104.

Fama, Eugene F. "Multiperiod Consumption—Investment Decisions." *American Economic Review*, LX (March 1970), 163–174.

Gordon, Myron J. *The Investment, Financing and Valuation of the Corporation*. Irwin, Homewood, Ill, 1962.

Haley, Charles, W. "A Note on the Cost of Debt." *Journal of Financial and Quantitative Analysis*, I (December 1966), 72–93.

Hirshleifer, Jack. "Investment Decisions Under Uncertainty: Applications of the State-Preference Approach." *Quarterly Journal of Economics* (May 1966), 252–277.

Lerner, Eugene M., and Willard T. Carleton. "The Integration of Capital Budgeting and Stock Valuation." *American Economic Review*, LIV (September 1964), 683–702. "Reply." *American Economic Review*, LVII (March 1967), 220–222.

Lewellan, Wilbur G. *The Cost of Capital*. Wadsworth, Belmont, Calif., 1969, 3–4.

McDonald, John G. "Market Measures of Capital Cost." *Journal of Business Finance* (Autumn 1970), 27–36.

Porterfield, James T. S. *Investment Decisions and Capital Costs*. Prentice-Hall, Englewood Cliffs, N. J., 1965.

Robichek, Alexander A., and John G. McDonald. "The Cost of Capital Concept: Potential Use and Misuse," *Financial Executive*, XXXIII (June 1965), 2–8.

———, J. G. McDonald, and R. C. Higgins. "Some Estimates of the Cost of Capital to Electric Utilities, 1954–1957: Comment." *American Economic Review*, LVII (December 1967), 1278–1288.

Van Horne, James C. *The Function and Analysis of Capital Market Rates*. Prentice-Hall, Englewood Cliffs, N. J., 1970.

Appendix 9A Beta Analysis and the Cost of Equity Capital

It may be possible to use the risk-return trade-off to derive the cost of equity capital (k_e).[1] If we can relate the risk associated with a particular stock to the single factor of stock price volatility instead of the several general risk factors that we used in Chapter 9, the proportional relationship between the particular stock's price volatility and the price volatility of all stocks can give the financial officer the firm's cost of equity capital.

If your stock's price movements are more volatile than the price movements of all stocks in general, investors might demand a higher required rate of return (k_e) because of the additional risk associated with owning your particular stock. Conversely, if your stock's price movements are less volatile than the market in general, investors might require a lower return because there is less risk with your stock. Obviously, if your stock has the identical price movements of the market average, investors require a return equal to that of the average market return.

We can illustrate this relationship graphically as in Figure 9A-1.

As the relative risk increases, as measured by the price volatility of your stock divided by the price volatility of the market averages, there is a shift to the right along the horizontal axis in Figure 9A-1, indicating that investors now see your stock as riskier. They interpret this along the k_e function (line) in Figure 9A-1 to a cost of equity capital on the vertical axis; the upward slope of the k_e function indicates that your k_e increases as your risk increases. For example, if your stock's volatility were at point X on the horizontal axis, your k_e would be at point Y on the vertical axis. This is the same trade-off of risk for return that we explored in Chapter 9.

We can quantify the k_e function of Figure 9A-1 as:

$$k_e = R_f + B_j[\overline{R}_m - R_f] \tag{9A-1}$$

Figure 9A-1 The Relationship Between Relative Stock Price Volatility and the Cost of Equity Capital

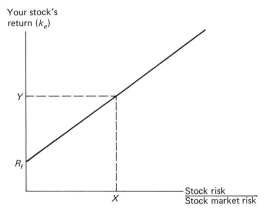

[1] See, for example, J. Fred Weston, "Investment Decisions Using the Capital Asset Pricing Model," *FMA Journal*, Spring 1973, 25–33.

where

k_e = the required rate of return (R_j)

R_f = the risk-free rate of return to a default-free security such as a United States government treasury bill

$\overline{R}_m$ = the average return to the market in general

$\overline{R}_m - R_f$ = the difference between the average return to the market in general and the default-free return, also commonly called the excess return

B_j = the Beta coefficient

Notice from Figure 9A-1 and Equation 9A-1 that since all stocks must possess some risk, all stocks must be expected to return in excess of the default-free rate (R_f), so the k_e function starts at the positive return on the vertical axis which corresponds to the prevailing default-free rate.

Any particular stock has a history of being more or less risky (volatile) than the market average, although the perception of this relationship is sometimes biased, and it may be over- or under-estimated.[2] The amount by which the required rate of return will exceed the default-free rate, therefore, depends on how volatile the stock is historically in relation to the market average. The degree of this relationship is revealed in the Beta coefficient (B_j). A B_j greater than 1 reflects a greater-than-average risk for the stock, judged on its historical volatility. In Equation 9A-1, a B_j greater than 1 obviously increases k_e by a proportionate amount of the excess return. For example, if R_f = 7 percent, B_j = 1.5, and R_m = 10 percent, then:

$$k_e = .07 + 1.5[.10 - .07]$$
$$= 11.5\%$$

On the other hand, if B_j is less than 1 because your stock's price volatility has been historically low in relation to that of the market in general, the required rate of return would be closer to the default-free rate. If, for example, R_f = 7 percent, B_j = .75, and $\overline{R}_m$ = 10 percent, then:

$$k_e = .07 + .75[.10 - .07]$$
$$= 9.25\%$$

If B_j equals 1.0, then:

$$k_e = .07 + 1.0[.10 - .07]$$
$$= 10\%$$

Since k_e, the required rate of return, is the firm's cost of equity capital, it is clear that as the firm's stock price volatility increases relative to the market, the firm's cost of capital may also increase. The financial officer can get a reasonably good idea of the firm's stock price volatility as measured by the Beta coefficient by regressing the realized k_e in the form of dividends and capital gains over particular periods with the realized excess returns ($\overline{R}_m - R_f$) over the same periods, although there is no guarantee that the relationship will hold in the future.

The implications of Beta analysis on altering the cost of equity capital for the financial officer are somewhat vague at this point. Since the analysis allows the financial officer to focus only on the single factor of stock price volatility (and since actually attempting to regulate the market price is illegal), there is little the financial officer can do besides passively measuring the relative volatility.

---

[2] See, for example, Franco Modigliani and Gerald A. Progue, "An Introduction to Risk and Return," *Financial Analysts' Journal*, May–June 1974, 69–86.

10

CAPITAL STRUCTURE AND THE COST OF CAPITAL

ONCE FINANCIAL OFFICERS KNOW the cost of capital for each type of security, how do they combine different securities to get the least overall cost of capital (k_o)? As we shall see, this depends to a great extent on the firm's *capital structure,* which is the combination of long-term securities used to finance the firm. The judicious use of long-term debt and common equity (financial leverage) can, if properly handled, lead to a lower cost of capital and higher profits and share prices for the firm.

Unfortunately, it is not as simple as determining which type of security has the lowest individual cost of capital and financing the entire firm with it because there are side effects on the cost of other types of securities when the financial officer combines them. It is imperative that we understand that financing with long-term debt, for example, not only affects the cost of debt capital but also affects the cost of common equity capital. The financial officer must be aware of the interaction among the different types of securities.

Once we understand the interaction among the securities and how the combined package of debt and equity affects both the cost of debt (k_d) and the cost of equity (k_e), how do we measure the overall cost of capital (k_o)? We shall see that there are two methods which we can use: the weighted average cost of capital and the marginal cost of capital. We will concentrate primarily on the weighted average cost of capital since it is the most commonly used by financial officers. We shall also see that there are ancillary questions in measuring the overall cost of capital, such as whether we use the book value or the prevailing market value of the securities as the weights in the weighted average cost of capital.

Once they have measured the overall cost of capital, how do financial officers actually go about raising capital so that, through the judicious use of debt and equity, they can minimize the firm's overall cost of capital? Many financial officers believe that by appropriate adjustment in the capital structure—changing the proportion of debt to equity—they can lower the firm's cost of capital to a minimum.

FINANCIAL LEVERAGE

How does the injection of debt in the capital structure affect the firm's profits? How does it affect the cost of debt capital? How does it affect the cost of equity?

When the proportion of debt in relation to equity is increased for any given capital structure, the potential variability introduced into the earnings stream increases, causing investors to demand higher required rates of return for *both* debt and equity securities. They are responding to the increased risk of not receiving the promised payment of interest and principal or the previously anticipated dividend stream. And financial leverage is a two-edged sword. In addition to affecting the firm's cost of debt and cost of equity, it can affect the earnings in a negative or a positive fashion. With positive financial leverage, the firm's earnings per share will increase; with negative financial leverage, earnings per share will decrease.

Financial leverage is advantageous to the firm when the proportional increase in the per-share earnings is greater than the proportional increase in the cost of equity capital, for then the share price will rise. Financial leverage is also advantageous if the combination of debt and equity leads to an overall minimum cost of capital. On the other hand, if the proportional increase in the firm's earnings per share is less than the proportional increase in the firm's cost of equity, financial leverage is disadvantageous to the firm, for its stock price will fall. Financial leverage is also disadvantageous to the firm if its use increases the overall cost of capital above the minimum which can be attained.

Positive Financial Leverage

Positive financial leverage occurs when the profits of the firm are increased because of the injection of debt into the capital structure. Table 10-1 illustrates that introducing $20 million of 5 percent debt into Firm B, which is identical to Firm A in all other respects, boosted earnings per share from $4.00 for Firm A to $7.00 for Firm B without a single change in any other aspect of either firm's operations. Firm A has not employed financial leverage at all, since it has not used any debt. The positive financial leverage employed by Firm B has enabled it to earn $7.00 a share compared to Firm A's $4.00, despite the identical rate of return, revenues, and expenses for both companies.

How did Firm B manage to increase its earnings per share by merely financing

Table 10-1   Positive Financial Leverage

	Firm A	Firm B
Assets	$ 40,000,000	$ 40,000,000
Debt	0	20,000,000 (5% bonds)
Equity	40,000,000	20,000,000
	(1 million shares)	(500,000 shares)
Return on total assets before taxes and interest	20%	20%
Sales	$100,000,000	$100,000,000
Cost of goods sold	60,000,000	60,000,000
Gross profit	40,000,000	40,000,000
Selling and general administrative expense	32,000,000	32,000,000
Operating profit	8,000,000	8,000,000
Interest expense	0	1,000,000
Net income before taxes	8,000,000	7,000,000
Taxes (50%)	4,000,000	3,500,000
Net income after taxes	4,000,000	3,500,000
Earnings per share	$4.00	$7.00

with half debt instead of all equity as Firm A did? The answer is twofold. First, Firm B paid 5 percent for its debt funds to acquire assets upon which it earned 20 percent. The 15 percent difference accrued to the shareholders as the owners of the firm who are entitled to the residual earnings after all prior claims on earnings, such as interest payments, have been made. The dollar difference in this example is $3 million before taxes and $1.5 million after taxes, which is figured as:

Earnings on assets acquired by debt at 20%	$4,000,000
Interest payments on debt at 5%	1,000,000
Positive leverage	3,000,000
Taxes (50%)	1,500,000
After tax leverage effect	1,500,000

Second, Firm B sold only half the number of shares that Firm A had to sell in order to raise the necessary funds, because Firm B raised half of *its* funds through the sale of debt capital. Therefore, the additional after-tax leverage effect of $1,500,000 was divided among the 500,000 shares such that each share received an additional $3.00 in earnings.

Negative Financial Leverage

Before we become engrossed with the power of financial leverage and rush out as financial officers to inject huge amounts of debt financing into our firm's capital structure, let us quickly illustrate that financial leverage can also lower your earnings per share in situations where the rate of return on your assets is less than the cost of debt capital. This negative financial leverage is illustrated in Table 10-2, where the cost of debt is 8 percent, while the return on assets is only 5 percent before taxes. Of course, no alert financial officer is intentionally going to finance at 8 percent a project returning 5 percent, but in numerous situations a project's anticipated return is higher than its realized return, and the financial officer only discovers after the proj-

Table 10-2   Negative Financial Leverage

	Firm C	Firm D
Assets	$ 40,000,000	$ 40,000,000
Debt	0	20,000,000 (8% bonds)
Equity	40,000,000	20,000,000
	(1 million shares)	(500,000 shares)
Return on total assets before taxes and interest	5%	5%
Sales	$100,000,000	$100,000,000
Cost of goods sold	74,000,000	74,000,000
Gross profit	26,000,000	26,000,000
Selling and general administrative expenses	24,000,000	24,000,000
Operating profit	2,000,000	2,000,000
Interest expense	0	1,600,000
Net income before taxes	2,000,000	400,000
Taxes (50%)	1,000,000	200,000
Net income after taxes	1,000,000	200,000
Earnings per share	$1.00	$.40

ect failed that it was costing more to finance than it was returning. The error in judgment is then compounded by the negative effect of the financial leverage. Furthermore the cost of debt can float upward as interest rates in general rise, under conditions when the cost of debt is tied to some other market interest rate. One such influence is the *prime rate*, the rate banks charge their most creditworthy customers. As the demand for funds relative to the supply increases, the prime rate rises, and the firm's cost of debt capital increases—perhaps to a point where it exceeds the return on the project.

Turning to Table 10-2, we can see that Firm C and Firm D are identical in every way except that Firm D has used debt to finance half its $40 million of assets. Consequently Firm D sold only 500,000 shares of stock to raise the other $20 million of capital, while Firm C sold 1,000,000 shares and used no debt.

Firm D experienced considerably lower earnings per share than its twin, Firm C, because of the negative leverage. First, Firm D paid 8 percent for capital used to acquire assets which returned only 5 percent. The stockholders had to make up the 3 percent deficiency out of their own earnings, since they are the owners. In dollar terms, this 3 percent deficit amounted to $600,000 before taxes on the $20 million in debt, or $300,000 after taxes. Second, the $300,000 cost each share $.60 since there are only 500,000 shares of Firm D outstanding and each share had to bear its proportional amount. This $.60 is the exact difference between the earnings per share of Firm C, which used no debt, and Firm D which used debt unsuccessfully.

The Effect of Financial Leverage on the Cost of Debt Capital

In addition to affecting earnings per share positively or negatively, injecting debt also affects the cost of both equity and debt. As illustrated in Table 10-3, any given change in the sales or expenses affects the earnings of a financially leveraged firm more than it affects the earnings of an unleveraged firm. The earnings per share for Firm F vary more in response to the $10,000,000 decline in sales than do the earnings per share for Firm E, despite the fact that they are identical in every way except that Firm F has a capital structure which is half debt while Firm E has no debt in its capital structure.

Notice in Table 10-3 that the 10 percent drop in the sales from $100,000,000 to $90,000,000 has caused earnings per share for Firm E to decline 62.5 percent, from $4.00 to $1.50. The same drop in sales has caused Firm F's earnings per share to decline 83.3 percent, from $6.00 to $1.00. Financial leverage has obviously magnified the percentage and the absolute decline in the earnings per share for Firm F.

Of course financial leverage also magnifies the increase in earnings per share for any given increase in sales or decrease in expenses. For example, a 10 percent increase over the original $100 million sales level for both Firm E and Firm F without any increase in expenses would see Firm E's earnings per share rise to $9.00, while Firm F's earnings per share would rise to $16.00. In percentage terms, Firm E's earnings per share would rise 125 percent, but Firm F's earnings per share would rise 166 percent.

As variability in earnings is magnified by the financial leverage, the dispersion around the mean earnings per share increases. Table 10-4 compares Firm E and Firm F's earnings per share under the three heretofore-mentioned situations: at the expected $100 million sales level, at the 10 percent decline in sales, and at the 10 percent increase in sales. Because of its use of debt, Firm F's earnings per share vary as much as $15.00 from the lowest to the highest figure, while Firm E's range is only $7.50.

Table 10-3   Variability in Earnings with Financial Leverage

	Firm E		Firm F	
Assets	$40,000,000		$40,000,000	
Debt	0		20,000,000 (10% bonds)	
Equity	40,000,000		20,000,000	
	(1 million shares)		(500,000 shares)	
Return on total assets before taxes and interest (pre-change)	20%		20%	

	Pre Change	After Change	Pre Change	After Change
Sales (in thousands)	$100,000	$90,000	$100,000	$90,000
Cost of goods sold	60,000	57,000	60,000	57,000
Gross profit	40,000	33,000	40,000	33,000
Selling and general administrative expenses	32,000	30,000	32,000	30,000
Operating profit	8,000	3,000	8,000	3,000
Interest expense	0	0	2,000	2,000
Net income before taxes	8,000	3,000	6,000	1,000
Taxes (50%)	4,000	1,500	3,000	500
Net income after taxes	4,000	1,500	3,000	500
Earnings per share	$4.00	$1.50	$6.00	$1.00

Potential investors in the bonds of these firms would naturally demand a higher rate of return from Firm F than from Firm E because of this greater dispersion. As the dispersion increases, the chance increases that the firm will encounter a difficult period and not be able to meet its interest payments or principal repayments. On the other hand, a firm with no debt would not have to worry about meeting its debt obligations and could more readily ride out a bad year. For example, Firm E in Table 10-3 could withstand a further decline of $3,000,000 in its net income before taxes and still not be in trouble with any of its creditors, while a further drop of that size in net income before taxes would leave Firm F short $2 million on the interest it owed bondholders. If Firm F could not raise the funds to meet the interest payment, the bondholders could put the firm into bankruptcy. The use of financial leverage exposes Firm F's bondholders to greater risk, so they require a higher rate of ex-

Table 10-4

Sales	Firm E earnings per share	Firm F earnings per share
+10%	$9.00	$16.00
Expected	4.00	6.00
−10%	1.50	1.00
Range	7.50	15.00

pected return to purchase its bonds. Hence the cost of debt capital (k_d) has to increase because the financial risk (f_d) part of the required rate of return increases as the proportion of debt to equity in the firm's capital structure rises. In terms of our formula:

$$k_d = r.i. + p + b + f_d + m$$

where

k_d = the cost of debt capital
$r.i.$ = the real interest rate
p = the purchasing-power risk premium
b = the business risk
f_d = the financial risk to the bondholders, which varies directly with the proportion of debt in the capital structure
m = the marketability risk of the particular security

The Effect of Financial Leverage on the Cost of Equity Capital

In a similar fashion, the cost of equity capital (k_e) will also increase as the variability in the firm's earnings per share increases because of the presence of financial leverage.

Investors require a higher rate of return as the dispersion around the expected dividend stream increases, since the risk of not receiving the anticipated benefits also increases. Using our illustration of Firms E and F, it is apparent that potential purchasers of Firm F's common stock require a higher rate of return (a higher k_e for the firm) than they do for the stock of Firm E because of the larger risk associated with Firm F's stock. In terms of the cost of equity capital we can see that:

$$k_e = r.i. + p + b + f_e + m$$

where

k_e = the cost of equity capital
$r.i.$ = the real interest rate
p = the purchasing-power risk premium
b = the business risk
f_e = the financial risk to the stockholders, which varies directly with the proportion of debt in the capital structure
m = the marketability risk of the particular security

The Effect of Financial Leverage on the Firm's Securities Prices

The effect of financial leverage on the price at which the firm's bonds sell is quite direct. As the amount of debt relative to the equity in the capital structure increases, the financial risk to the bondholders increases; for any given interest payment, the price of the bond has to fall. We can see this in the following familiar equation:

$$P_0 = \sum_{t=1}^{n} \frac{IP_t}{(1 + k_d)^t} + \frac{P_n}{(1 + k_d)^n} \qquad (10\text{-}1)$$

where
P_0 = the bond price
IP_t = the annual interest payment
P_n = the return of the principal at maturity in year n
k_d = the cost of debt

In Equation 10-1 we can see that as k_d rises because of the increased financial risk associated with any greater use of debt, the bond price has to fall since IP_t and P_n are fixed.

The effect on the stock price, however, is not so clear. The stock price can rise or fall depending on the relationship between the effect the greater use of debt has on earnings and on the cost of equity (k_e). Since the increased use of debt in the capital structure can affect both the earnings per share and the cost of capital in the familiar share price evaluation model of Equation 10-2, the two effects may offset one another.

$$P_0 = \sum_{t=1}^{\infty} \frac{\hat{D}_t}{(1 + k_e)^t} \qquad (10\text{-}2)$$

where
P_0 = stock price
$\hat{D}_t$ = anticipated dividends derived from anticipated earnings
k_e = the cost of equity

Positive financial leverage leads to an increase in expected earnings and dividends per share, which in Equation 10-2 raises the price of the stock if nothing else changes. But the cost of equity (k_e) does change when financial leverage is employed. The increase in k_e puts downward pressure on the stock price, as can also be seen in Equation 10-2. We are faced with a situation in which the use of financial leverage has exerted counteracting influences on the stock price. Positive leverage has increased earnings and dividends per share and put upward pressure on the stock price, while the increase in financial risk to the stockholders has raised k_e and put downward pressure on the stock price.

Table 10-5 summarizes the potential positive and negative effects of financial leverage on the stock price. Notice that as the proportionate use of debt increases the cost of equity always increases, regardless of the effect on expected dividends. Thus, if the financial leverage is negative, the firm's stock price falls because both factors are putting downward pressure on the stock price. In the case of positive financial leverage, the exact effect on the stock price depends on the relationship between the two factors. For example, if because of financial leverage expected dividends rose 10 percent from a perpetual $1.00 a share to a perpetual $1.10 a share, but the cost of equity rose from 10 percent to 12 percent, the price of the stock would fall

Table 10-5   Financial Leverage and Stock Prices

As the use of debt relative to equity increases:

	Stock price:
Positive financial leverage	
1. $\hat{D}_t$ increases greater than k_e increases:	rises
2. $\hat{D}_t$ increases less than k_e increases:	falls
Negative financial leverage	
1. $\hat{D}_t$ decreases and k_e increases:	falls

from \$10.00 a share to \$9.25. This decline occurs, despite the increase in dividend expectations brought on by the positive leverage, because of the greater increase in the cost of capital.

The implications for the financial officer are obvious. Before you undertake additional financial leverage, make sure that it will be positive financial leverage and that the increase in the cost of capital for the firm's securities does not offset the favorable benefits to the firm's stock price. Check to see how much additional variability would be imparted to the firm's earnings stream by the presence of the additional debt and be certain that, even in an unusually bad year, your firm could meet its debt obligations.

Measures of Financial Leverage

As financial officers how do we measure the degree of financial leverage in the capital structure?

There are basically three standard measures employed by financial officers and their creditors, the bondholders and bankers. These are the debt/equity ratio (see Chapter 3), the interest coverage ratio (EBIT), and the elasticity of earnings per share to earnings coverage. The debt/equity ratio simply measures the proportion of the debt to the equity in the capital structure. As more financial leverage is undertaken, the debt/equity ratio increases. As with most ratios, there is usually an accepted industry standard to which the firm's debt/equity ratio is compared. If the firm's ratio is reasonable in comparison, potential lenders and stockholders penalize the firm only slightly. If the firm's debt/equity ratio is out of line with the industry standard, potential investors in the firm's securities substantially raise their required rate of return and, hence, the firm's cost of capital.

The problem with the debt/equity ratio is that it does not tell us the impact of financial leverage on the earnings per share or indicate the risk of not meeting the increased debt obligations. The interest coverage ratio relates the earnings before interest and taxes (EBIT) to interest (I), such that:

$$EBIT = \frac{EBIT}{I}$$

It conveys the degree of coverage of the interest payments required at any given level of financial leverage. Again, by comparing the firm's EBIT ratio to an acceptable industry standard, potential investors in the firm's securities can get some idea of the degree of financial risk involved in purchasing that security.

The elasticity of earnings per share (EPS) to earnings coverage relates the proportionate change in earnings per share to the proportionate change in the EBIT ratio, such that:

$$F.L. = \frac{\dfrac{\Delta EPS}{EPS}}{\dfrac{\Delta EBIT}{EBIT}} \tag{10-3}$$

where

$F.L.$ = the degree of financial leverage
EPS = earnings per share
$EBIT$ = the earnings coverage ratio
ΔEPS = the change in EPS
$\Delta EBIT$ = the change in EBIT ratio

For example, if EBIT = $1,000,000, EPS = $100, and an increase in the relative use of debt is expected to make ΔEBIT = $200,000, and ΔEPS = $.25, then:

$$\text{F.L.} = \frac{\dfrac{\$.25}{1.00}}{\dfrac{200,000}{1,000,000}}$$

$$= 1.25$$

This 1.25 implies that as EBIT ratio increases (decreases) by 1 percent, earnings per share will increase (decrease) by 1.25 percent, a relatively high degree of financial leverage. But this measure of financial leverage does not tell the financial officer the effect on the cost of debt or equity. For that, you must return to the increased variability in earnings per share or the change in the debt/equity or EBIT ratios caused by the financial leverage and relate it to the financial risk factor in the cost of debt or equity.

THE WEIGHTED AVERAGE COST OF CAPITAL

Once we understand how the cost of debt (k_d) and the cost of equity (k_e) interact when the two types of securities are combined, how do we measure the cost of capital for the overall package of securities?

The financial officer typically uses the weighted average cost of capital to measure the firm's overall cost of capital (k_o) when debt and equity are combined in the capital structure. Accordingly:

$$k_o = \frac{D}{D + E}\,(k_d) + \frac{E}{D + E}\,(k_e) \qquad (10\text{-}4)$$

where

k_o = the overall cost of capital
D = the amount of debt in the capital structure
E = the amount of equity in the capital structure
k_d = the cost of debt capital
k_e = the cost of equity capital

Equation 10-4 is merely a weighted average in which the percentage of debt in the capital structure weights the cost of debt capital and the percentage of equity in the capital structure weights the cost of equity capital. Before giving an example for Equation 10-4, let us first look at the two common situations in which the weighted average cost of capital might be calculated: (1) the financial officer and the firm have successfully convinced potential investors that they have a target debt/equity ratio which shall be constant, although from time to time, after the issue of new debt, the ratio may temporarily rise; or (2) the financial officer and the firm have not convinced potential investors that the debt/equity ratio is constant, despite only minor deviations from some known target.

In the first situation, the financial officer and the firm have made efforts, such as presentations before security analysts' societies, to communicate to potential investors that the firm intends to keep the debt/equity ratio constant at its present proportions, although any particular financing may temporarily raise or lower the ratio because new issues of stocks and bonds are intermittently sold in large chunks. (Of course, the firm also has to compile an historical record of keeping its

Table 10-6

Type of financing	k	After-tax k (tax = 50%)	Proportions	k_0
Debt	8%	4%	30%	1.2%
Equity	12%	12%	70%	8.4%
				9.6%

debt/equity ratio at approximately the announced target, or the financial markets will quickly stop believing these claims, creating situation number two.)

Assuming you have convinced the financial markets that the debt/equity ratio is going to be constant, potential investors will keep the financial risk components of their required rates of return for stock (f_e) and for bonds (f_d)[1] constant, simplifying the calculations in Equation 10-4. For example, from information in Table 10-6, we can see that the firm's overall cost of capital (k_0) is 9.6 percent. This can also be calculated directly from Equation 10-4, such that:

$$k_0 = \frac{D}{D + E} (k_d) + \frac{E}{D + E} (k_e) \tag{10-4}$$

$$k_0 = \frac{30}{30 + 70} (.07) + \frac{70}{30 + 70} (.12) \tag{10-5}$$

$$= 9.6\%$$

The 9.6 percent is the cost to the total capital structure, which tells the financial officer what the after-tax cost of capital for the firm is at this particular time and at this particular debt/equity combination. As financial officers, however, we should never lose sight of the fact that both the weighting factors and the cost of each type of capital in Equation 10-4 can change if we change the proportion of debt to equity in the capital structure, unless we have convinced potential investors to ignore temporary deviations from the target debt/equity combination. The weights will change because the amount in each type of security has changed, and the cost of each type of capital will change because the financial risk has changed. The cost of capital for each security can also change if the other general risk factors such as real interest rates, purchasing-power premiums and business or marketability risks change, even if investors are willing to ignore temporary deviations from what we have communicated as our constant debt/equity combination. However, if the financial markets are convinced that our debt/equity ratio is constant, they tend to ignore the temporary changes in the weighting factors and in the cost of capital caused by the financial risk factor, allowing the financial officer to spend more time trying to lower the firm's cost of capital by concentrating on the other risk factors.

If we have *not* successfuly convinced the financial markets that our debt/equity proportion is constant, investors will react each time we change the proportions.

---

[1] As financial officers, we might get some idea of the financial risk imparted to the debt (f_d) by examining the EBIT ratio or the fixed-charges-earned ratio, which is:

$$\frac{EBIT}{IP + P[1/(1 - t)]}$$

where
    IP = interest payment due
    P = principal repayments due
    t = the tax rate

This reaction will be particularly sharp if we have maintained that our debt/equity proportions are constant while, the markets have come to believe through our security offerings that they are not constant. Under the situation of a fluctuating debt/equity ratio, investors change the weightings and the cost of each type of capital because of the change in the financial risk every time we offer securities. If we offered additional debt securities which increased the debt/equity ratio, the cost of capital for both the debt and the equity would rise, provided the other factors which determine investors' required rate of return remained constant. Both k_d and k_e and the weightings in Equation 10-4 change with each offering. If we issued more debt, raising the percentage of debt in the capital structure from the 30 percent of Table 10-6 to 40 percent and k_d to 5 percent after tax, the percentage of equity in the capital structure has to sink to 60 percent from the previous 70 percent and its cost might rise to 13 percent. Then the overall cost of capital for the firm would be:

$$k_o = \frac{D}{D + E} (k_d) + \frac{E}{D + E} (k_e) \qquad (10\text{-}4)$$

$$= \frac{40}{40 + 60} (.05) + \frac{60}{40 + 60} (.13) \qquad (10\text{-}5A)$$

$$= 9.8\%$$

Notice that k_o has increased as the percentage of debt in the capital structure increased, because the weighting factors *and* the cost of each type of capital have changed. If the financial officer had effectively communicated that the change in the proportions was only temporary, the overall cost of capital might have remained closer to the original 9.6 percent, because the financial markets might have continued to use the long-run proportions of Equation 10-5, instead of adjusting immediately to the short-run changes of Equation (10-5A).

The degree to which the financial officer can communicate the constancy of the debt/equity proportions affects the degree to which investors overlook short-run changes in the capital structure and calculate the required rate of return on the assumed long-run proportions. If we want to avoid some of the fluctuations in our cost of capital caused by large chunks of either debt or equity capital being raised at once, we have to convince the financial markets that the accompanying deviations from the target debt/equity combinations are temporary and should be ignored.

THE MARGINAL COST OF CAPITAL

Instead of using the weighted average overall cost of capital, some financial officers use the marginal cost of capital. Under this procedure, the financial officer ranks the various securities in ascending order of their cost of capital so as to start with the least costly source and proceeds down the list, tapping each successively least costly source as the demand for funds arises. For example, we can see from Table 10-7 that the least costly source of funds for this firm at this time is debt. The first additional amount of debt is $2 million, available at an after-tax cost of 6 percent. However, while the next least costly source is also debt, it is more expensive than before because the firm's debt/equity ratio has increased, causing the financial markets to increase the cost. After using the $4 million in debt from the first two least costly sources of funds, the financial officer will use preferred stock at 9 percent to finance the next most attractive projects, although there appears to be a relatively small amount of capital to buy the preferred stock and only $1 million can be sold. This is

Table 10-7   Marginal Cost of Funds

Source	Quantity available at this cost	After-tax k	D/E after offering
Debt	$2,000,000	6%	40%
Debt	2,000,000	7	57
Preferred stock	1,000,000	9	50
Retained earnings	2,000,000	12	44
Common stock issue	3,000,000	15	33
Debt	1,000,000	5	38

probably due to the smaller number of potential preferred stock investors. After using preferred stock, the financial officer might find that retained earnings and a new stock issue are the least costly, although still expensive. Notice how investors keep increasing the cost of each type of security along the lines of evaluation we discussed in Chapter 9. Finally, after issuing the relatively costly common stock and using retained earnings, the firm has brought its debt/equity ratio back to a point where the next least costly source is debt, and the cycle of debt followed by additional equity starts anew.

Figure 10-1 illustrates the marginal cost of funds. The marginal cost of funds (MCF) rises from the least expensive sources up and to the right in Figure 10-1 as the firm undertakes further investments, the profitability of which is measured graphically by the internal rate of return (IRR) line. The IRR diminishes, as shown, as the amount of investment increases.

The financial officer will tap sources of capital until the MCF line crosses the IRR line, for beyond that point additional investment is no longer profitable. Above and to the right of that intersection, the cost of capital to finance the project exceeds the expected return from the project. Notice that even though the use of debt after the issuance of the expensive equity is again lower than the IRR on some available investments (to the right of point q,) the firm cannot undertake them for it must sell the equity first before it can sell the lower-costing debt. The firm's investment, therefore, stops at the intersection of MCF and IRR, unless there is a shift in either of the lines.

Under this method of determining the cost of capital, the financial officer would match the particular project and its IRR to the particular financing source and the

Figure 10-1   The Marginal Cost of Funds

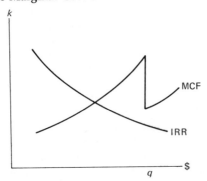

cost that was necessary to finance the project. For example, the next project might be financed with the preferred stock of Table 10-7, meaning we would compare its IRR to a 9 percent cost of capital in our capital budgeting decision. Critics of the marginal cost say this is incorrect because it is the firm as a whole that raises the funds and not the project itself, and we cannot pinpoint sources with particular projects unless we assign the proportionate sources, as the weighted average cost does, to each project. Under the weighted average cost of capital, the financial officer uses the overall cost of capital to evaluate each project, regardless of the particular source of funds raised to finance the project. In the weighted average overall cost of capital, it is as if the projects were being financed out of a pool of funds raised by the firm, while in the marginal cost of capital each project is evaluated along with its own source.

The desired package of securities under the marginal cost of capital is where the MCF intersects the IRR. The financial officer will use all sources up to that point because it is profitable to do so. The package of securities will emerge in a ranking like Table 10-7, from the least costly down through and including the last source necessary to finance all the projects up until the intersection of MCF and IRR. For example, if our MCF intersected our IRR at 12 percent, our debt/equity ratio in Table 10-7 would be 44 percent and our capital structure would include debt, preferred stock, and retained earnings in addition to our original stock issue. On the other hand, the package of securities under the weighted average overall cost of capital will be that combination of debt and equity which gives us the least overall cost of capital (k_o).

OTHER CONSIDERATIONS IN MEASURING THE OVERALL COST OF CAPITAL

As financial officers, we must also consider the appropriate weights to use in calculating the overall cost of capital (k_o). We should use the market value of debt and the market value of equity, instead of their book values, as the weighting factors in Equation 10-4, because these more realistically reflect the cost of capital under the prevailing financial environment and at the present capital structure. We can compute the market values by simply looking at the prevailing price of the firm's bonds and stock and multiplying each by the number of bonds and shares outstanding. For example, if the prevailing market price of the firm's stock was $10 a share and it had 1 million shares outstanding, the market value of the equity would be $10,000,000. If the firm had two bond issues outstanding, one of which was selling in the financial markets for $900 for each of the 1000 bonds in that issue and the other of which was selling for $1,000 a bond for each of the 1000 bonds in that issue, the firm's market value of its debt would be $1,900,000. The firm's overall cost of capital, if its k_d were 6 percent and its k_e 15 percent, would be:

$$k_o = \frac{\$1,900,000}{1,900,000 + 10,000,000}(.06) + \frac{\$10,000,000}{1,900,000 + 10,000,000}(.15)$$
$$= 13.56\%$$

Using the historic book values of the debt and the equity can be misleading, since they reflect the cost of capital which prevailed at the time of their original issue and not the prevailing cost of capital, which reflects any changes in the financial market environment or the firm itself since the original issue. If the book value of the equity is lower than the market value of the equity, which is typical, the use of book values as the weighting factor usually leads to a lower overall cost of capital. If the book value of equity is greater than the prevailing market value, the cost of capital is usually higher than it should be. If the book value of the debt is greater than its market value, which is typical in periods of high interest rates, the use of the book value of the bonds will understate the firm's cost of capital, and vice versa.

While market values should be used as the weighting factors in computing the overall cost of capital, we should be aware that certain financial institutions, particularly banks, give great emphasis to the book values. When we are negotiating a loan with them we should understand their position and can even use it as a bargaining point. These institutions use book values because they feel it gives them more insight into the protection they will get in case of liquidation. If things do not work out for the firm as expected, the financial markets will adjust quickly, slashing the prevailing price of the firm's stock and bonds before the lenders, such as banks, have a chance to get their money back. At that point the banks must look to the firm's assets to recover their loans, and assets are best judged by the book value. Guarding against the worst, bankers always pay attention to the book value of the equity as the cushion they can use to assure repayment of the loan in case of liquidation. These institutions may also look to the book value rather than the prevailing market values in trying to derive your cost of capital because fluctuations in the prevailing market price of your securities may occur too often for them to feel it is a reliable indicator. This is not valid, of course, for the markets are merely reflecting what may be a very rapidly changing financial environment, but a few financial officers and lenders may want a more permanent weighting factor, while a few others maintain that the changing market environment is reflected in the changing cost of capital for each type of security and not the weighting factors. Be alert for opportunities to use such views as negotiating points, surrendering to the other view where it is not important to you but gives the lender a feeling of safety in return for a lower interest rate.

In computing the overall cost of capital, the financial officer must never lose sight of any important considerations. One of these is avoidance of a credit crunch. It is important to space your debt maturities so that you are not forced to refinance a large portion of your debt during a period of exceptionally high interest rates. You might consider a slightly higher than minimum overall cost of capital in your effort to achieve the proper spacing of your maturities. A record of poor timing, showing that you were always forced to refinance at the peak in interest rates, will give you and your firm a bad name and force investors to reconsider their appraisal of the firm before buying any more of its securities. This also means that as a financial officer you must give careful attention to matching your repayment schedules with the expected inflow of funds. Sometimes this will involve lengthening the firm's maturity schedule, even though doing so may not minimize the overall cost of capital.

MINIMIZING THE OVERALL COST OF CAPITAL

How does the financial officer minimize the overall cost of capital in designing the firm's capital structure?

Traditionally, it is assumed that by adroitly manipulating the proportions of debt and equity in the capital structure, the financial officer can minimize the overall cost of capital.

The first logical step any financial officer would take in order to lower the firm's overall cost of capital would be to increase the proportion of the least costly source of capital in the capital structure. For example, if the after-tax cost of debt is 5 percent, the cost of equity is 15 percent, and the capital structure is presently 30 percent debt, the firm's cost of capital (k_o) is:

$$k_o = \frac{30}{100}(.05) + \frac{70}{100}(.15)$$

$$= 12\%$$

Now if the financial officer increased the percentage of debt in the capital structure to 50 percent without raising the cost of capital for either equity or debt, the firm's overall cost of capital would be:

$$k_o = \frac{50}{100}(.05) + \frac{50}{100}(.15)$$

$$= 10\%$$

But as we have already seen, the cost of equity (k_e) and the cost of debt (k_d) do not remain the same as the percentage of debt in the capital structure increases, unless the financial market is convinced the increase is only minor and temporary. As the debt/equity ratio rises, k_e and k_d also rise, partially or completely offsetting the drop in k_o. If, for example, as we increased the percentage of debt in the capital structure to 50 percent, k_e rose to 20 percent and k_d rose to 10 percent because of the increased financial risk, the firm's k_o would be:

$$k_o = \frac{50}{100}(.10) + \frac{50}{100}(.20)$$

$$= 15\%$$

The overall cost of capital would have actually *risen* when the financial officer tried to use more of what appeared, at the previous debt/equity ratio, to be the least costly debt capital. Failure to consider the consequences of raising the percentage of debt to 50 percent on the cost of both the equity and the debt would have raised the overall cost of capital.

It is the financial officer's job to judge the two offsetting effects of increasing the proportion of debt in the capital structure: the rise in the cost of debt and equity and the decrease or increase in the overall cost of capital generated by using a greater proportion of debt.

We can graph the relationship between these factors as in Figure 10-2. As the proportion of debt in the capital structure increases (moves right on the horizontal axis), both the cost of equity and the cost of debt begin to rise as a reflection of the increased financial risk. The two do not necessarily rise in the same proportion. Simultaneously with the increasing use of debt, the overall cost of capital begins to fall because the after-tax cost of debt is typically cheaper than the cost of equity. And as the weighting factor shifts more to the debt factor because of the enlarged use of debt, the weighted average sinks. The drop in k_o continues until the minimum point (q) is reached, because of increased use of the cheaper debt. After point q, the accelerating rise in k_e and k_d, associated with what the financial markets are now beginning to think may be signs of approaching excessive use of debt and too much financial risk, completely offsets the advantage of using the lower-cost debt.

By minimizing the overall cost of capital, the financial officer can maximize the

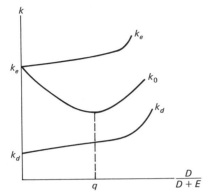

Figure 10-2 The Overall Cost of Capital

value of the firm, which is a likely objective. At point q in Figure 10-2, the cost of capital is minimized, which means that potential investors are willing to pay a higher price for any given stream of expected benefits. At any other point besides q, the cost of capital is not minimized, and the firm's total market value is not maximized. For example, assume the following firm offers $300,000 in 5 percent bonds selling at par ($1,000 a bond) and, for purposes of illustration, pays no taxes:

Net operating earnings	$100,000
Interest	15,000
Net earnings (N)	85,000
k_e	.15
Total market value of equity (S)	= 566,667

$$S = \frac{N}{k_e}$$

Total market value of debt (B)	= 300,000
Total market value of the firm (B + S)	= 866,667

$$B = \sum_{t=1}^{n} \frac{IP_t}{(1 + k_d)^t} + \frac{P_n}{(1 + k_d)^n}$$

$$k_o = \frac{300,000}{866,667} \,(.05) + \frac{566,667}{866,667} \,(.15)$$

$$= 11.5\%$$

However, if the financial officer raised the proportion of debt to 50 percent without affecting k_e or k_d, the total value of the firm would increase and k_o would decrease:

Net operating earnings	$100,000
Interest	25,000
Net earnings	75,000
k_e	.15
Total market value of equity (S)	= 500,000
Total market value of debt (B)	= 500,000
Total market value of the firm (B + S)	= 1,000,000

$$k_o = \frac{500,000}{1,000,000} (.05) + \frac{500,000}{1,000,000} (.15)$$

$$= 10\%$$

Notice that the total market value of the firm increases as k_o decreases for any given net operating earnings.

If, however, as we increased the proportion of debt to $500,000, k_e rose to 20 percent and k_d rose to 10 percent, the total value of the firm would have decreased, and k_o would have risen:

Net operating earnings	$100,000
Interest	50,000
Net earnings	50,000
k_e	.20
Total market value of the equity (S)	= 250,000
Total market value of the debt (B)	= 500,000
Total market value of the firm (B + S)	750,000

$$k_o = \frac{500,000}{750,000} (.10) + \frac{250,000}{750,000} (.20)$$

$$= 13.3\%$$

It is clear from these examples that as we minimize k_o, we maximize the value of the firm.

Realistically, of course, it is probably not possible to compute the minimum overall cost of capital to a specific point on Figure 10-2 or to the third decimal place. The actual situation may look more like Figure 10-3, which depicts a range over which the overall cost of capital is minimized. Within the "saucer bottom" of k_o, the financial officer can gauge financial offerings to be sure that the firm does not go to the left or to the right of the saucer part of the curve. To the left, sell debt. To the right, sell equity. This range concept is also more in keeping with the financial officer's attempts to communicate to the financial market that the firm intends to keep its capital proportions reasonably constant and that any movement within the range should not be interpreted by investors as a change in the target debt/equity ratio.

Figure 10-3 The Overall Cost of Capital within a Range

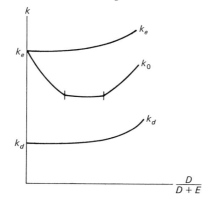

MATCHING MATURITIES

How do financial officers avoid the credit crunch? What happens if the availability of capital from any source dries up to the point where we cannot raise funds almost regardless of the interest rate we are willing to pay?

This is not as unlikely as it sounds. In 1969, credit was so tight that bankruptcy was feared imminent for several large companies, as well as many smaller companies, who needed capital to continue. In fact, lack of credit was said to be the final straw that forced the PennCentral Company, the nation's largest railroad, into bankruptcy. As financial officers, we must always be prepared to cope with unexpected credit crunches.

There are two basic approaches to avoiding a crunch: (1) lengthen the debt schedule, and (2) match the maturities with the expected cashflows. Lengthening the maturities at every opportunity before the scheduled repayment of the original principal, and particularly during periods of low long-term interest rates, means that the firm will never encounter a large principal repayment during a credit crunch. For example, if we had a large principal repayment coming up in three years, we should not wait for the time to run out before making arrangements to refinance that debt. Rather, we should take the first opportunity of low, long-term interest rates. By not waiting until the last minute when we no longer have a choice, we have some flexibility and some negotiating power. As long as we continue to take advantage of low points in the cycle of interest rates to refinance the debt and keep extending the maturity dates, we will preserve that flexibility and avoid having to arrange large refinancings at disadvantageous times.

Secondly, we can try to arrange the interest payments and the repayment of principal to coincide with the expected cashflows from the projects financed by that particular issue of debt. Therefore, as the interest and the repayment of the principal come due, we can expect to have the funds available. For example, we might try to get our debt obligations in line with our cash inflows as in Table 10-8, which shows that the scheduled repayment of each bond issue is more than covered by the expected cash inflows to the projects which that issue financed. The excess coverage comes from profits and that portion of the projects financed by equity. This excess provides a cushion for error in case the expected cash inflows are not as large as anticipated. Such matching nearly guarantees that we will never find ourselves in the real bind of the firm that financed its purchase of long-term assets with 90-day notes and found that, at the end of one of the 90-day periods within the life of the long-term assets, refinancing was simply not available at any price. That firm went bankrupt.

Table 10-8   Matching Payment Outflows with Expected Inflows

Amount of issue	Description of issue	Annual repayment schedule	Expected cash inflow
$100 million	4¾s 1995	$ 5 million	$ 6 million
75 million	7s 1984	7.5 million	10 million
2 million	3s 1976	1 million	1.2 million
50 million	7⅛s 2001	1.9 million	2.0 million
Total		15.4 million	19.2 million

SUMMARY

After having read Chapter 10, you should be able to answer these questions:

1. What are the effects on the cost of equity capital and the cost of debt capital when the financial officer combines debt and equity in the firm's capital structure?

As the proportion of debt to equity in the capital structure increases, the firm's earnings per share can increase if there is positive financial leverage or can decrease if there is negative financial leverage, simply because of the very *use* of financial leverage. At the same time, the use of financial leverage, whether positive or negative, increases the cost of equity capital and the cost of debt capital because of the associated increased financial risk caused by the increased variability of earnings when financial leverage is used.

2. What are the effects on the firm's bond and share prices if financial leverage is increased?

The effect on the firm's bond prices is clear: as the financial risk increases because of the use of financial leverage, the bond price has to sink. The effect on the firm's stock price is not so evident. If, because of the positive financial leverage, the firm's expected earnings and dividends are increased proportionately more than the firm's cost of equity is increased, the stock price rises, and vice versa.

3. How does the financial officer measure the overall cost of capital for the combination of debt and equity in the capital structure?

The overall cost of capital for the firm can be measured as the weighted average of the firm's cost of equity and cost of debt, where the weights used are the market values of the stock and the equity in relation to the total market value of the entire firm. We saw, though, that some financial institutions which lend to the firm may use book values instead.

4. How does the financial officer minimize the firm's overall cost of capital?

The financial officer can minimize the firm's overall cost of capital by adding additional amounts of the least costly security to force the overall cost of capital to decline. Since the after-tax cost of debt capital is usually the least, the financial officer continues to add debt to the capital structure until the offsetting effect of the attendant rising cost of equity and debt exceeds the advantage of using more debt, and the overall cost of capital starts to turn upward.

We may observe this more clearly in actual practice as a *range* of relatively low overall cost of capital rather than a specific point. This is particularly true if the financial officer and the firm have successfully communicated to the financial markets that any deviation from the target debt/equity proportions of the capital structure is only temporary.

QUESTIONS

10-1 What is the difference between positive and negative financial leverage?

10-2 Firms A and B are the same asset size and sell their products in the same market. However, Firm A has only 10 percent debt in its capital structure, whereas Firm B has 60 percent debt in its capital structure. If the industry demand is erratic (and hence both firms' sales are volatile), which firm will have the higher cost of debt?

10-3 Indicate the effect of each of the following occurrences on the cost of debt (k_d), the cost of equity (k_e), and the weighted average cost of capital (k_o) for Firm B in question 10-2.

Occurrence	k_d	k_e	k_o
(a) Increase in inflation			
(b) Downturn in economic activity			
(c) More stable industry demand			
(d) Firm B increases its leverage			

10-4 Indicate the effect of each of the following occurrences on the price of bonds issued by Firm B and on the price of common stock of Firm B.

Occurrence	Price of Bonds	Price of stock
(a) Increase in inflation		
(b) Downturn in economic activity		
(c) More stable industry demand		
(d) Firm B increases its leverage		

10-5 Distinguish between the debt/equity ratio, the interest coverage ratio (EBIT), and the elasticity of earnings per share to earnings coverage as measures of financial leverage.

10-6 What is the principal criticism of the use of the marginal cost of capital as opposed to the weighted average cost of capital in capital budgeting decisions?

10-7 Under what conditions should the market values of equity and debt be used in calculating the weighted average cost of capital as opposed to the book values?

10-8 On what basis does the traditional view contend that minimum cost capital structure exists for each firm?

10-9 The financial managers of the PennCentral railroad are often accused of contributing to the railroad's bankrupt status due to the large amount of debt used to finance investments (railroad and nonrailroad related). What is the basis of this criticism, and do you agree?

PROBLEMS

10-1 Suppose Firms X and Y are identical in every way except for the composition of their capital structure. Each firm's present structure and selected income statement items are shown below.

	Capital Structure	
	Firm X	Firm Y
Debt (8% bonds)	$ 20,000,000	0
Equity (shares)	80,000,000	10,000,000
	(800,000 shares)	(1,000,000 shares)
Total assets	$100,000,000	$100,000,000

Selected Income Statement Items

	Firm X	Firm Y
Operating income		
Interest expense		
Net income before taxes		
Taxes (50%)		
Net income after taxes		
Earnings per share		

(a) Assuming each firm's operating income return is 10 percent on total assets, fill in the above items for each firm. How can the difference in earnings per share be explained? Is this an example of positive or negative financial leverage?

(b) Assuming each firm's operating income return on total assets is 6 percent, fill in the following selected items:

Selected Income Statement Items

	Firm X	Firm Y
Operating income		
Interest expense		
Net income before taxes		
Taxes (50%)		
Net income after taxes		
Earnings per share		

How can the difference in earnings per share be explained? Is this an example of positive or negative financial leverage?

(c) What must the operating income return on total assets be for financial leverage to exercise a neutral effect on earnings per share?

(d) For (a), what are the debt/equity and EBIT ratios for each firm?

(e) Suppose management is interested in knowing the effect of financial leverage on each firm's earnings per share if operating income in (a) should vary by ±$1,000,000 in the next year. Specifically, two questions have been posed: (1) If operating income varies by +10 percent, what will be the percentage change in earnings per share for each firm? (2) What is the degree of financial leverage for each firm?

10-2 The capital structure of the XYZ Company consists of the following:

Debt (8% bonds)	$ 500,000
Equity ($10 per 200,000 shares)	2,000,000
Total	$2,500,000

The firm's tax rate is 50% and its common stock presently sells for $20. The book value and market value of debt are the same. The cost of equity capital is 10%.

(a) Using book values, what is the overall weighted average cost of capital?

(b) Using market values, what is the overall weighted average cost of capital?

10-3 Suppose the McCoin Peanut Company is trying to determine the capital structure that minimizes its overall weighted average cost of capital (k_o). For total capital assets of $1,000,000 it has estimated the after-tax cost of debt (k_{dt}) and equity (k_e) for the following capital structures:

Structure	Debt financed	Equity financed	k_{dt}	k_e
A	$800,000	$200,000	9%	10%
B	500,000	500,000	6	11
C	200,000	800,000	5	14

What is the optimal capital structure?

10-4 The Moyer Company has the following capital structure as of December 31, 1975:

Debt (7%)		$20,000,000
Preferred stock (8%)		5,000,000
Common stock	$20,000,000	
Retained earnings	5,000,000	
Common equity		25,000,000
Total capital assets		$50,000,000

The above capital structure is considered optimal. The firm is considering an expansion program that will increase the firm's total capital assets to $75,000,000 by the end of 1976. During 1976 an additional $10,000,000 will be added to retained earnings. New bonds issued up to $20,000,000 will have a coupon rate of 8 percent and will be sold at par. Preferred stock can be sold with a 9 percent rate of return up to $10,000,000. The dividend paid on common stock for 1975 was $5 per share and dividends are expected to grow at a 7 percent annual rate in the foreseeable future. Presently the price per share of existing common stock is $60, but newly issued common stock will have a $5 per share flotation cost. The firm's marginal tax is 50 percent.

(a) To finance the $25,000,000 expansion and maintain its current optimal capital structure, how much must the firm finance with debt? What is the after-tax cost of new debt capital?

(b) To finance the $25,000,000 expansion and maintain its current optimal capital structure, how much must the firm finance with preferred stock? What is the after-tax cost of the newly issued preferred stock?

(c) To finance the $25,000,000 and maintain its current optimal capital structure, how much must the firm finance with common equity? Externally? Internally? What are the after-tax costs of retained earnings and newly issued common stock?

(d) What is the weighted average cost of funds raised during 1976?

(e) If a capital expansion program of $15,000,000 had been planned would the weighted average cost of capital on the new funds be different? (A numerical answer is not necessary.)

(f) If a capital expansion program of $50,000,000 had been planned, would the weighted average cost of capital on the new funds be different from (d)? (A numerical answer is not necessary.)

BIBLIOGRAPHY

Barges, Alexander. *The Effects of Capital Structure on the Cost of Capital.* Prentice-Hall, Engle-wood Cliffs, N.J., 1963.

Baumol, William and Barton G. Malkiel. "The Firm's Optimal Debt-Equity Combination and the Cost of Capital." *Quarterly Journal of Economics,* LXXXI (November 1967), 547–578.

Ben-Shahar, Haim. "The Capital Structure and the Cost of Capital: A Suggested Exposition." *Journal of Finance,* XXIII (September 1968), 639–653.

Bierman, Harold, Jr., and Richard West. "The Acquisition of Common Stock by the Corporate Issuer." *Journal of Finance,* XXI (December 1966), 687–696.

_____. "Risk and the Addition of Debt to the Capital Structure." *Journal of Financial and Quantitative Analysis,* III (December 1968), 415–423.

Brigham, Eugene F., and Myron J. Gordon. "Leverage, Dividend Policy, and the Cost of Capital." *Journal of Finance,* XXIII (March 1968), 85–104.

Donaldson, Gordon. *Corporate Debt Capacity.* Division of Research, Harvard Business School, Boston, 1961.

Elton, Edwin J. "The Cost of Retained Earnings—Implications of Share Repurchase," *Industrial Management Review,* 9 (Spring 1968), 87–104.

Haugen, Robert A., and James L. Pappas. "Equilibrium in the Pricing of Capital Assets, Risk-Bearing Debt Instruments, and the Question of Optimal Capital Structure." *Journal of Financial and Quantitative Analysis,* VI (June 1971), 943–954.

Heins, A. James, and Case M. Sprenkle. "A Comment on the Modigliani-Miller Cost of Capital Thesis." *American Economic Review,* LIX (September 1969), 590–592.

Krouse, Clement G. "Optimal Financing and Capital Structure Programs in the Firm." *Journal of Finance,* XXVII (December 1972), 1057–1072.

Lintner, John. "The Cost of Capital and Optimal Financing of Corporate Growth." *Journal of Finance,* XVIII (May 1963), 292–310.

_____. "Dividends, Earnings, Leverage, Stock Prices and the Supply of Capital to Corpora-tions," *Review of Economics and Statistics,* 44 (August 1962), 243–269.

Melnyk, Lew Z. "Cost of Capital as a Function of Financial Leverage." *Decision Sciences* (July-October 1970), 327–356.

Modigliani, Franco, and M. H. Miller. "The Cost of Capital, Corporation Finance and the Theory of Investment." *American Economic Review,* XLVIII (June 1958), reprinted in *Foundations for Financial Management,* ed. James Van Horne. Irwin, Homewood, Ill., 1966, pp. 367–405.

_____, and M. H. Miller. "The Cost of Capital, Corporation Finance and the Theory of In-vestment: Reply." *American Economic Review,* IL (September 1958), 555–569; "Taxes and the Cost of Capital: A Correction." *Ibid.,* LIII (June 1963), 433–443; "Reply." *Ibid.,* LV (June 1965), 524–527; "Reply to Heins and Sprenkle." *Ibid.,* LIX (September 1969), 592–595.

Mossin, Jan. "Security Pricing and Investment Criteria in Competitive Markets." *American Economic Review,* LIX (December 1969), 749–756.

Pfahl, John K., David T. Crary, and R. Hayden Howard. "The Limits of Leverage." *Financial Executive* (May 1970), 48–55.

_____, and David T. Crary. "Leverage and the Rate of Return Required by Equity." *The Investment Process.* The International Textbook Company, Scranton, Pa., 1970, 175–191.

Reilly, Raymond R., and William E. Wecker. "On the Weighted Average Cost of Capital." *Journal of Financial and Quantitative Analysis,* VIII (January 1973), 123–126.

Robichek, Alexander A., and Stewart C. Myers. *Optimal Financing Decisions.* Prentice-Hall, Englewood Cliffs, N.J., 1965.

_____. "Problems in the Theory of Optimal Capital Structure." *Journal of Financial and Quantitative Analysis,* I (June 1966), 1–35.

Schall, Lawrence D. "Firm Financial Structure and Investment." *Journal of Financial and Quantitative Analysis,* VI (June 1971), 925–942.

Schwartz, Eli. "Theory of the Capital Structure of the Firm." *Journal of Finance,* XIV (March 1959), reprinted in *Foundations for Financial Management,* ed. James Van Horne. Irwin, Homewood, Ill., 1966, pp. 413–433.

_____, and J. Richard Aronson. "Some Surrogate Evidence in Support of the Concept of Op-timal Capital Structure." *Journal of Finance,* XXII (March 1967), 10–18.

Solomon, Ezra, "Leverage and the Cost of Capital." *Journal of Finance,* XVIII (May 1963), reprinted in *Foundations of Financial Management,* ed. James Van Horne. Irwin, Homewood, Ill., 1966, pp. 406–412.

––––––. "Measuring a Company's Cost of Capital." *Journal of Business,* XXVIII (October 1955), 240–252.

Stiglitz, Joseph E. "A Re-Examination of the Modigliani-Miller Theorem." *American Economic Review,* LIX (December 1969), 784–793.

Wippern, Ronald F. "Financial Structure and the Value of the Firm." *Journal of Finance,* XXI (December 1966), 615–634.

Appendix 10A **The Modigliani and Miller Cost of Capital Approach**

Modigliani and Miller (MM)[1] have led a dissenting school of thought in opposition to the traditional approach, which, as we saw in Chapter 10, maintains that through judicious use of the proportion of debt to equity in the firm's capital structure the financial officer can minimize the firm's overall cost of capital. MM, in contrast, maintain that the financial officer cannot change the firm's overall cost of capital, regardless of the proportion of debt to equity in the capital structure. In other words, the firm's overall cost of capital is constant. Let us briefly examine their argument.

MM'S ASSUMPTIONS

First, MM make certain assumptions which we must accept for now in order to facilitate their argument, but which, upon closer examination, reveal weaknesses in their stand. These assumptions are: (1) Capital markets are perfect. There are no transactions cost of buying or selling stocks or bonds, and every investor has the same information and can borrow or lend at the same interest rate. (2) Every investor is perfectly rational so that each has the same expectation of earnings with which to evaluate the shares of any firm. (3) Business risk is equal among firms with similar operating environments. (4) There are no taxes.

HOMEMADE LEVERAGE

Under their assumptions, MM argue that investors will adjust their own holdings of a firm's securities so that the firm's overall cost of capital will not change, regardless of the proportion of debt in the firm's capital structure. In essence, their homemade leverage argument rests on the assumption that individual investors will borrow to finance their purchase of the stock if the firm does not use its own financial leverage. If the firm uses financial leverage, individual investors will not borrow to finance their own purchases of the stock because the firm already has enough financial leverage for both of them. If this is done as MM envision it, there will be an exact offset so that the combination of firm and individual financial leverage will be identical for all firms in a given business risk class. We can illustrate their argument through the following example: Assuming we have two firms, A and B, which are identical in every fashion except that Firm A has no debt while Firm B has $300,000 in 5 percent debt. Firm B's cost of capital is therefore slightly higher at 15 percent than Firm A's cost of capital at 12 percent because of the associated financial risk.

---

[1] Franco Modigliani and Merton H. Miller, "The Cost of Capital, Corporation Finance and the Theory of Investment," *American Economic Review*, XLVIII (June 1958), pp. 261–297; and "Taxes and the Cost of Capital: A Correction," *American Economic Review*, LIII (June 1963), 433–443.

Table 10A-1   Total Market Values of Firms A and B

	Firm A	Firm B
Net operating income	$100,000	$100,000
Interest	–	15,000
Net earnings	100,000	85,000
k_e	.12	.15
Total value of the equity (S)	833,333	566,667
Total value of the debt (B)	–	300,000
Total value of the firm ($B + S$)	833,333	866,667

The total market value for Firm A would, however, be less than the total market value of Firm B as shown in Table 10A-1.

According to MM, the situation shown in Table 10A-1 cannot exist for any length of time, for Firm B cannot have a higher total market value than Firm A simply because it used financial leverage and Firm A did not. According to MM, since Firm A and Firm B are identical in every other aspect, their total market value should also be identical and investors, through their actions of selling off shares in Firm B (which MM consider overvalued) and buying shares in Firm A (which MM consider undervalued), will insure that the total market values become identical. This is done through homemade leverage, which operates as follows.

If the stockholders of Firm B sell off 1 percent of the shares in Firm B, they will receive $566.67, which they will invest in Firm A because it is undervalued. However, before investing in Firm A, they will notice that Firm A does not have the debt nor the associated financial risk that Firm B has. They will, therefore, borrow enough on their own to come back to the same level of risk that they had as stockholders of Firm B and invest the proceeds from the sale of Firm B stock *and* the loan in the stock of Firm A. The investors, then:

1. Sell 1 percent of Firm B, receiving $566.67
2. Borrow an amount equal to 1 percent of Firm B's debt, $300 (the same amount a 1 percent stock holding would bear in Firm B at 5 percent interest, since all can borrow and lend at the same rate)
3. Buy 1 percent of Firm A's stock for $833.33 and have $34.34 left over in cash, which can also be invested in the stock of Firm A

These steps have let stockholders exchange their 1 percent interest in Firm B for a 1 percent interest in Firm A, but the process creates excess cash, which should not happen if the two firms are identical.

This uneven trade leaves the investors who sold Firm B stock and bought Firm A stock in a better position, as illustrated in Table 10A-2.

Obviously, according to MM, this situation in which the stockholders of Firm A are getting a larger return ($89) than the stockholders of Firm B ($85) for the same risk as measured by the debt/equity ratio, cannot exist for very long before investors wake up to the opportunity of getting more for the same investment and risk. They continue to sell Firm B's stock and buy Firm A's stock, driving down the price of B and raising the price of A until the return to both firm's stock are the same.

In the process of bringing the returns of the firms to equality, stockholders also raise B's overall cost of capital by lowering its stock price and lower A's overall cost of capital by raising its stock price until the two firms have an equal overall cost of capital. So it does not matter what the capital structure of Firm B is, its cost of capital after investors exercise their homemade leverage is constant, because investors exactly offset the firm's financial leverage with their own.

Table 10A-2   Comparison of Stockholders Position in Firm A and Firm B

	Firm A	Firm B
Gross return on stock investment	$104 (12% on $866.67)	$85 (15% on $566.67)
Interest on personal borrowing (5%)	15	0
Net return	89	85
Risk exposure (f_d) as measured by debt/equity	$\dfrac{300}{566.67} = 52.9\%$	$\dfrac{300}{566.67} = 52.9\%$
k_0	12%	$52.9(.05) + 42.1(.15) = 9.72\%$

PROBLEMS WITH MM

There are several problems with the MM argument, particularly with its assumptions. First, contrary to the MM assumption, it is commonly observed that borrowing costs and the availability of funds do vary among borrowers. The most creditworthy borrowers tend to get the lowest rates and the most ready access to funds, while the less creditworthy tend to pay higher rates and have less ready access to funds. Since corporations are traditionally better known and considered more creditworthy than individuals, it is difficult to imagine individuals substituting their own homemade leverage at the same interest cost as the corporation. Under the more realistic situation in which the individual would pay a higher interest rate, the advantage of homemade leverage would probably disappear and render the MM example invalid.

Second, there are many institutional restrictions that would also make it difficult for the homemade leverage to exist. These would include less-than-perfect markets and transactions costs which may make it unprofitable for the investor to switch from Firm A to Firm B in our example. Further, there are additional expenses connected with purchasing the odd lot (less than commonly traded number of shares) necessary to create homemade leverage, and there are margin requirements set by

Table 10A-3   After-tax Value of Firms A and B

	A	B
Net operating earnings	$100,000	$100,000
Interest	0	15,000
Net earnings before taxes	100,000	85,000
Taxes (50%)	50,000	42,500
Net income	50,000	42,500
k_e	10%	15.45%
k_d	—	5%
k_0	10%	10%

If the MM argument holds and k_0 is identical for both firms at 10 percent, then the total market value should be equal, but is not:

Total market value of the equity (S)	$500,000	$275,000
Total market value of the debt (B)	—	300,000
Total market value ($B + S$)	500,000	575,000

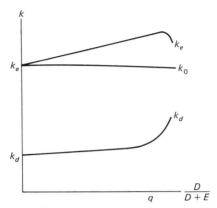

Figure 10A-1 Extreme Financial Leverage in the MM Argument

the federal government which prohibit the individual from borrowing a sufficient amount of funds to create the homemade leverage.

Third, there are taxes to be paid which disrupt the MM argument. Since the interest cost is a tax-deductible expense, Firm B saves, at a 50 percent tax rate, half of its interest cost, while Firm A does not get the same advantage. This, as shown in Table 10A-3, increases the total market value of Firm B, regardless of the effect of homemade leverage.

Firm B has a higher total market value because of the tax savings on its interest, $7,500 a year, which at the overall cost of capital of 10 percent is the difference in the total market value between the two firms. No matter what the individual investor does, the two firms will never have the identical value MM postulate.

Fourth, the argument of a constant overall cost of capital reduces to the absurd when the extreme cases of financial leverage are considered. If MM's arguments are taken literally, it means that the increase in the cost of equity capital is exactly offset by the injection of further lower-cost debt capital. But in the extreme, where lenders insist upon higher interest rates for further lending, the cost of debt capital has to eventually turn up as at point q in Figure 10A-1. After point q, there is no longer an exact offset to the rising cost of equity because of the injection of additional debt, for the debt itself has become more costly. In order for MM's claim of a constant overall cost of capital to hold here, the cost of equity capital has to start falling, which is absurd since no rational investor is all of a sudden going to require less return for a higher level of risk exposure. It would take irrational investors to decide that the equity position at these extremely levered positions was less risky than at less extremely levered positions.

Appendix 10B **Some Empirical Evidence on the Modigliani and Miller Hypothesis**

Various studies have been undertaken to see whether the MM approach of a constant overall cost of capital or the traditional approach of a minimum overall cost of capital is observable in practice. Let us briefly review a few of the better known studies to see what was observed.

THE BARGES STUDY

Barges[1] supported the traditional conception of a saucer-shaped overall cost of capital curve which could be minimized. Using book values instead of market values for the weighting factors and ignoring any growth, he found that the average overall cost of capital in his regression (Equation 10B-1) first rose and then declined as the ratio of long-term debt to the total permanent capital increased for Class I railroads, such that:

$$Y = 12.39 - 0.244X + 0.00258X^2 \qquad (10B-1)$$

where
Y = the average cost of capital
X = the ratio of long-term debt to total permanent capital

THE WIPPERN STUDY

Wippern[2] tried to improve upon the Barges study by incorporating into his regression more variables which, since they were left out of the Barge regression, might have biased the results in favor of the traditional approach. He also concentrated on the cost of equity function instead of the overall cost of capital function. By doing this, Wippern could show that the cost of equity function was sufficiently linear and increased at an appropriate rate to exactly offset the injection of debt into the capital structure and keep the overall cost of capital constant. However, while Wippern did find some indication that the cost of equity capital was more linear and the overall cost of capital a little less saucer-shaped than Barges had estimated, the cost of equity did not increase fast enough to keep the overall cost of capital constant.

Wippern's specific regression model used the earnings yield (see Chapter 9) as the imputed cost of equity capital, such that:

$$E/P = a + b_1(\text{F.L.}) + b_2(g) + b_3(\text{DIVID}) + b_4(S) + b_5 \ldots + b_{10}(D_t) \qquad (10B-2)$$

[1] Alexander Barges, *The Effects of Capital Structure on the Cost of Capital,* Prentice-Hall, Englewood Cliffs, N.J., 1963.
[2] Ronald F. Wippern, "Financial Structure and the Value of the Firm," *Journal of Finance,* XXI (December 1966), 615–634.

where

E/P = the earnings price ratio (earnings yield)

$F.L.$ = financial leverage as measured by $\dfrac{i}{C - 2s}$, where i was the most recent year's reported fixed charges, C was the 10-year trendline average of cash inflow, and $2s$ was twice the standard deviation around that trendline

g = the growth

DIVID = the payout ratio (see Chapter 3) for the firm

S = the logarithm of the firm's size as measured by its assets

D_t = dummy variables assigned to each industry to insure that no bias because of business risk and operating environment distorts the relationship between financial leverage and the cost of equity

Notice that Wippern has taken great pains to insure that his financial leverage measure is not distorted by the book value or the market value weightings and to include almost all the other variables to be sure that the results are not biased by the omission of an important factor.

MM EMPIRICAL STUDY

Modigliani and Miller[3] themselves have supported their claim with empirical evidence. Using 43 electrical companies for the 1947–1948 period, they used total earnings after taxes divided by the market value of all the firm's securities as a measure of the overall cost of capital and regressed that on the financial structure of the firm, which they measured as the market value of the firm's senior securities (debt and preferred stock) divided by the total market value of all the firm's securities. They found that:

$$X = 5.3 + .006d$$
$$(\pm.008) \tag{10B-3}$$

where

X = the overall cost of capital

d = their measure of financial leverage

Equation 10B-3 says that the overall cost of capital for electrical utilities during the 1947–1948 period was 5.3 percent, and that the increase of .006 percent for each unit of additional financial leverage was so small as to be statistically insignificant, as indicated by the fact that its standard deviation (in parentheses) was larger than the coefficient itself. MM interpreted this as meaning that the overall cost of capital was constant, because the slope of the line, as measured by the second term of Equation 10B-3, is insignificant. They found similar results for 42 oil companies during 1953, such that:

$$X = 8.5 + .00057d$$
$$(\pm.024) \tag{10B-4}$$

where, again, the slope of the k_o line was insignificant.

---

[3] F. Modigliani and M. H. Miller, "The Cost of Capital, Corporation Finance, and the Theory of Investment," *American Economic Review*, XLVIII (June 1958), pp. 261–297.

On the other hand, MM found that the slope of the line for the cost of equity capital *was* significant, in contrast to Wippern, and sufficient to exactly offset the injection of lower-cost debt and keep the overall cost of capital constant. They found for the 43 electrical utilities that the cost of equity capital (Z), as measured by the net income to stockholders after taxes divided by the total market value of the common stock when regressed on the financial leverage variables (which again was the total market value of the senior securities divided by the total market value of the firm h), was:

$$Z = 6.6 + .017h$$
$$(\pm.004)$$
\hfill (10B-5)

and for the 42 oil companies was:

$$Z = 8.9 + .051h$$
$$(\pm.012)$$
\hfill (10B-6)

Since the second term of each equation was significant, MM concluded that the cost of equity (Z) rose at a sufficient rate as financial leverage increased to exactly offset the injection of lower-cost debt capital and to keep the overall cost of capital constant.

BRIGHAM AND GORDON

Brigham and Gordon[4] (BG) used a slightly different model to test the behavior of the cost of equity capital over the range of financial leverage. Their model was:

$$\frac{D_0}{P_0} = a_0 + a_1 g + a_2 h + a_3 u$$
\hfill (10B-7)

where

$\dfrac{D_0}{P_0}$ = the current dividend yield

g = the growth rate of the firm
h = the degree of the financial leverage
u = an index of stability in the firm's earnings

Using 69 utility stock from 1958–1962, BG found that the cost of equity as measured by the current dividend yield rose as the degree of financial leverage rose, but that the implied slope was insufficient to maintain a constant overall cost of capital and that the traditional saucer-shaped k_0 function was supported.

THE WESTON STUDY

Weston[5] made one of the earlier attempts to refine the MM empirical work by including the firm's size and growth in the determination of the overall cost of capi-

---

[4] Eugene F. Brigham and Myron J. Gordon, "Leverage, Dividend Policy, and the Cost of Capital," *Journal of Finance*, XXIII (March 1968), 85–104.

[5] J. Fred Weston, "A Test of Cost of Capital Propositions," *Southern Economic Journal*, XXX (October 1963), 105–112.

tal, such that:

$$k_o = a + b_1 \left(\frac{D}{E}\right) + b_2(A) + b_3(g) \qquad (10B-8)$$

where

k_o = the overall cost of capital after tax

$\dfrac{D}{E}$ = the firm's debt/equity ratio

A = the firm's asset value

g = the firm's growth rate

Regressing Equation 10B-8 on 59 utilities for 1959, Weston found that the financial leverage variable $\left(\dfrac{D}{E}\right)$ had a significant negative sign which to him supported the traditional concept of a saucer-shaped overall cost of capital function. He also found similar results when he used the pre-tax k_o and when he excluded the preferred stock from the debt/equity ratio.

IMPLICATIONS FOR THE FINANCIAL OFFICER

While there are still other empirical tests we could explore, it is clear from these few that the question of the shape of the overall cost of capital function is far from definitively settled. The preponderance of evidence seems to indicate, however, that the function is saucer-shaped, particularly when taxes are considered. As financial officers, we should base our financing strategy on the fact that we can minimize our overall cost of capital through the judicious use of financial leverage.

11

DIVIDENDS

WE HAVE SEEN IN THE CHAPTERS to this point that dividends are an important consideration used by potential stockholders in evaluating the firm's stock price. Prevailing and anticipated dividends are, therefore, important in determining the firm's cost of equity capital. The firm's management must have a dividend policy which complements its objective and helps lower its cost of equity capital and maximize its share price. But what is dividend policy, and how does a good financial officer go about selecting the best dividend policy for his or her firm? We shall examine what dividend policy is, how dividend policy functions, and what the financial officer must know in order to select the best dividend policy.

Once we know what dividend policy is, we must know how it is implemented. In other words, how are dividends actually paid to shareholders? Financial officers must understand the mechanics of dividend payments, for they customarily execute the dividend policy decided upon by the firm's management.

Even before implementing the chosen dividend policy, however, the financial officer plays a large role in its selection. When called upon by the board of directors, you must be able to answer the question: What are the possible dividend policy objectives? As we shall see there are several different objectives, such as maintaining stability in the amount of the dividend or the payout ratio (the proportion of the earnings per share paid to the stockholders as dividends).

What must the financial officer consider in selecting an appropriate objective? If we, as financial officers, are to make sure that the chosen dividend policy objective is compatible with the firm's overall objective and operations, we must consider such factors as the legal implications of paying the dividend and the general need for capital within the firm, as well as the desires of our stockholders. A good financial officer has considered all the variables affected by the firm's choice of dividend policy and which, in turn, affect that choice, before advising the firm's decision-makers as to which dividend policy objective they should implement.

One of the most important considerations in selecting a dividend policy is its impact on the firm's cost of capital, its growth, and its share price. How does the dividend policy influence these factors? As an alert financial officer, you must be prepared to analyze the effects of a particular dividend policy on the firm's share price, especially if the firm's objective is maximizing share price.

Finally, what alternatives can you suggest to the payment of a cash dividend and how do these alternatives affect the firm? We shall see that among the options available to the financial officer is the stock dividend, which may be more appropriate in certain instances than the payment of the more typical cash dividend.

DIVIDEND POLICY

What is dividend policy?

Dividends, as we have seen, are that portion of the firm's retained earnings paid out to the stockholders. Companies usually decide what percentage of the past period's earnings to retain and what percentage to pay out as dividends. Since dividends are not a contractual obligation of the firm to its stockholders as are interest payments on the firm's bonds, the amount of the dividend, if any, is vested in management's best judgment as one of its options on how to use the firm's income. The board of directors, who are ultimately responsible for setting dividend policy, can choose not to pay out any dividends, using the firm's earnings to acquire additional assets instead.

Dividend policy is the guiding principle in determining what portion of earnings should be paid out in dividends during the coming period. The policy may be expressed in any one of several different objectives, which we shall explore shortly, such as the target payout ratio, which represents the percentage of earnings per share that the firm would like to pay in dividends, or the absolute dollar amount of the dividend itself, or some criterion which combines the payout ratio and the absolute dollar amount of the dividend per share.

THE MECHANICS OF DIVIDEND PAYMENTS

Once the firm has adopted a dividend policy, how does the financial officer, who usually must implement the policy, actually pay the dividends to the stockholders?

First, the board of directors meets to consider a dividend payment to the stockholders. If they decide to declare a dividend, they will issue a statement specifying its dollar amount, the date it was declared, the date it will be paid, and who is entitled to receive it. Figure 11-1 illustrates a newspaper account of such an announcement. On December 3, 1973, The Stanley Works will compile a list of all its stockholders through the company's registrar. Any new ownership must be recorded on the registrar's official list of stockholders through the transfer process on or before December 3, 1973. A new owner of the stock will not receive the dividend from the company if the transfer process has not been completed by that time, and the old shareholder of record as of December 3, 1973 receives the dividend.

Since paperwork causes a delay in the transfer process between the time of the sale and the recording of the new owner's title on the registrar's books, convention has decreed that five business days prior to the close of the transfer books, the stock trades *ex-dividend,* meaning that it is no longer entitled to the most recently declared dividend as of that date and that any new purchaser of the stock does not receive such a dividend. In our example, November 28, 1973 would be the ex-dividend date (assuming there were no intervening weekends or holidays).

On December 18, 1973 the company's disbursing agent, at the financial officer's direction, mails out a $.24 per share dividend payment check to the stockholders of record as of December 3, 1973.

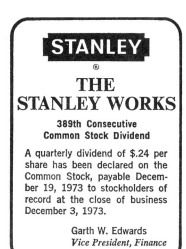

Figure 11-1 A Dividend Announcement Appearing November 23, 1973

DIVIDEND POLICY OBJECTIVES

In advising your board of directors, what are the possible dividend policy objectives you might consider?

After all, when the board selects the particular dividend policy for the firm upon your advice, they want to be sure you have considered all the alternative policies, and you must be prepared to answer their questions about the alternatives in justifying your own selection.

Stability of the Dollar Amount of the Dividend

It is generally felt that investors favor stable dividends which never recede from the prior period's level, but which still have good prospects for steady upward growth. If the firm develops such a dividend pattern, it may make investors more willing to pay a higher price for stock and lower the firm's cost of equity capital because the risk attached to estimating the expected dividend stream is lessened when the dividend does not fluctuate or recede. Further, there is a group of stockholders who are dependent on a regular dividend income, such as retired persons, who would certainly favor a stock whose dollar dividend they could depend on and use in their budgeting. They may be willing to pay a higher stock price for the avoidance of a cut in expected dividend which could disrupt their budgeting.

Many regulated financial institutions which purchase stocks in the course of their business, such as trust departments of banks, are sometimes and in certain states limited to the stock of those companies on what is known as the "legal list," a list of stocks compiled by the regulatory authority. Since, in many instances, a stock makes the list only if it has a record of continuous and stable dividends, any firm wishing to expand the ownership of its stock to these institutions must consider a stable dividend policy. Such expansion might also increase the general demand for the stock and raise its price, perhaps because of a decreased marketability risk, and thus lower the firm's cost of equity capital.

Still another reason for pursuing a stable dividend policy objective is that investors are thought to use dividends and changes in dividends as a source of information about the firm's profitability. An increasing dividend is said to convey the message that the firm is experiencing a favorable upswing of a somewhat permanent nature. Investors may assume that the board of directors has confidence in maintaining the higher dividend or it would not have declared it. A stable dividend is thought to give the firm itself an aura of stability, whereas a reduced dividend is said to signal a permanently unfavorable change in the firm's profit outlook.[1]

One consequence of a very stable dividend policy in the face of fluctuating earnings per share is that the payout ratio, which is the percentage of any particular year's earnings per share paid to stockholders as a dividend per share, also fluctuates. In those years with higher earnings per share, a constant dividend leads to a lower payout ratio; in those years with a lower earnings per share than that which prevailed in the year the dividend was originally declared, the payout ratio is higher.

Most firms, in addition to desiring a stable dollar amount of dividend, also have a target payout ratio which they aim for, such as paying out 50 percent of the earnings per share as dividends. The desire to maintain the present dividend level conflicts with strict adherence to any particular target payout ratio especially when earnings per share drop off, even temporarily.

To avoid the necessity of reducing the dividend because of an off year, but to still progress toward the target payout ratio, firms raise their dividends per share gradually, as the earnings per share rises. They increase dividends enough to advance toward the target payout ratio, but they leave a cushion in case the following year's earnings per share dip. Even in an off year, the firm's stable image will remain intact.[2] For example, if the target payout ratio were 50 percent and the present dividend were $1 a share, the firm would not go immediately to a dividend of $1.50 if the earnings per share rose to $3.00, since that would expose the firm to the necessity of reducing the dividend in the following year if earnings per share then fell below $3.00. Rather, the firm might elect to gradually ease toward the 50 percent target payout by declaring a $1.25 dividend. With the $1.25 dividend, the firm's earnings per share could drop to $2.50 in the following year and still be at the 50 percent target payout ratio, avoiding the necessity of reducing the dividend.

We can formulate this dividend policy as the financial officer might use it in determining the dollar amount of the dividend to declare:

$$D_{t+1} = D_t + a \left(P^* - \frac{D_t}{E_t} \right) E_t \tag{11-1}$$

where
$\quad D_{t+1}$ = the dividend amount under consideration
$\quad D_t$ = the prevailing dividend
$\quad \dfrac{D_t}{E_t}$ = the prevailing payout ratio
$\quad P^*$ = the target payout ratio
$\quad E_t$ = the latest earnings per share
$\quad a$ = the adjustment cushion

[1] M. Miller and F. Modigliani, "Dividend Policy, Growth, and the Valuation of Shares," *Journal of Business,* XXXIV (October 1961), 411–433.
[2] J. Lintner, "Distribution of Income of Corporations Among Dividends, Retained Earnings, and Taxes," *American Economic Review,* XLVI (May 1956), 97–113.

The board of directors could come to you, as the financial officer, asking for your advice as to what dividend to declare. If you ascertained that they wanted to leave a cushion of about 50 percent and that they had a target payout ratio of 50 percent, and if you knew that the current dividend was $1 and the current earnings per share $3.00, you could determine that the dividend should be $1.25 by using Equation 11-1:

$$D_{t+1} = \$1.00 + .50 \left(.50 - \frac{\$1.00}{\$3.00} \right) \$3.00$$

$$= \$1.25$$

Stability of the Payout Ratio

Alternatively, as the financial officer, you might consider stability of the payout ratio instead of stability of the dividend itself as your dividend policy objective. However, this always leads to fluctuations in the dividends per share, which may cause investors to decrease their evaluation of your firm's worth. This objective seems to be clearly inferior to others.

A Policy of Extra Dividends

An extra dividend is usually declared at the end of the period, after the results are already known, in recognition of a better earnings performance for a particular period and, as the name implies, in addition to the regular dividend. The year-end extra does not seem as permanent as the regular dividend to investors, so if it is not declared the following year-end, investors are not as likely to consider it a reduction in the dividend. A firm like General Motors, for example, will declare an extra dividend instead of raising the dividend when it has a good model year, so that it can avoid reducing the regular dividend if the next year is less profitable. In 1973, General Motors declared an extra dividend of $1.85, in recognition of the record-breaking 1973 model year, above the regular dividend of $3.40. This approach allowed them to reduce the total payment in the following year without cutting back on the regular dividend, by simply reducing the size of the extra.

A Residual Dividend Policy

On occasion you will encounter a firm which uses a residual dividend policy. They pay out whatever is left over after the firm's capital needs are satisfied. Obviously this leads to an erratic dividend pattern and investor dissatisfaction with the stock. It should be avoided.

All this discussion does not mean that you should always pay a dividend. There are firms, as we shall see shortly, who might retain all their earnings to help finance their investment projects.

OTHER CONSIDERATIONS IN DIVIDEND POLICY

Beyond dividend stability and the target payout ratio, there are other less quantifiable considerations which have to be taken into account by the financial officer.

Ability to Borrow

If the firm has relatively easy access to inexpensive and plentiful capital, it may be willing to adopt a more liberal dividend policy, represented by a higher payout ratio. Since the firm is not pressed for funds and can raise all the capital it needs to finance its investment projects, it may be foolish to keep idle funds around or to insist upon using relatively expensive retained earnings when less costly debt capital is available.

Liquidity

If there is already excess liquidity, as typified by a relatively large amount of cash and other near-cash securities, the firm might consider a more liberal dividend policy since there appears to be no pressing need for funds. On the other hand, a firm strapped for funds by the pressing need to finance what appear to be attractive projects would probably have a lower payout ratio.

Control

Sometimes, if a firm's management has only a slight control over the firm, the board of directors will retain a substantial portion of the earnings rather than pay dividends so as to avoid the necessity of selling any more voting stock to the public, which might further dilute their control. As a financial officer, you should be aware of how important this consideration is to the board of directors, although in few instances is control an important factor.

Taxes

Federal and state taxes on the income of the firm and of its stockholders can influence your dividend policy recommendations to the board of directors. You have to avoid two aspects of the tax. First, you do not want the federal taxing authorities to impose additional taxes upon your firm because they feel it has excessively accumulated retained earnings so as to avoid taxes. Certain firms, particularly smaller and more closely held firms, can run afoul of the tax ruling that they cannot retain funds so that their shareholders can avoid paying personal income taxes on the dividends. If the taxing authority finds the firm in violation of this, it can impose additional taxes (see Appendix 2A).

Second, you must consider the tax position of your shareholders. While it may be difficult for a firm with many shareholders to identify a typical stockholder tax position, certain types of firms frequently attract certain types of stockholders. For example, a new venture firm attracts risk capital more interested in growth of the original investment than does an established firm in a stable industry, which attracts stockholders because of its generous dividends.

If, as financial officer, you can isolate a genuinely typical tax position, consider it in your dividend policy recommendation. Stockholders in a high tax bracket tend to favor retention of earnings for reinvestment, expecting that this will lead to a higher stock price, which, in turn, leads to a capital gain for the stockholders when they sell the shares. Since the capital gain is taxed at a lower rate than the dividends, it is worth more after taxes to the individual in a high tax bracket. On the other hand, stockholders in a lower tax bracket would probably favor a generous current dividend because of their need for current income and the greater certainty associated with receiving the dividend now instead of the less certain prospect of a capital gain later.

Availability of Acceptable Investment Projects

If the firm has a large number of acceptable investment projects in which it can place all the funds it can raise, the firm will favor a low payout ratio. Numerous attractive investment opportunities create a pressing need for funds, and the retention of earnings is convenient and less costly than selling a new issue of equity. Retained earnings also provide a base upon which the firm can borrow additional funds, because the retention keeps the debt/equity proportions of the capital structure in line. On the other hand, if the firm has few attractive investment opportunities available, it will probably have a very generous dividend policy, for it will not have a pressing need for funds.

Loan Restrictions

Probably the most common influence on the dividend policy of most firms, outside of the need for internal financing, is the loan restriction on the payment of dividends. Typically, the lenders insist that the stockholders provide insurance that the interest and loan repayment obligations will be met. Towards this end they limit, in the loan agreement, the firm's ability to pay dividends to the stockholders, forcing the firm's retained earnings to be reinvested in the firm. Reinvestment leads to a lower debt/equity ratio and a larger cushion for the lenders. This dividend restriction may apply either to the declaration of new dividends on stocks which never paid a dividend before or to increased dividends on stocks which already pay a dividend. It may be stated such that the firm has to attain a certain dollar amount of retained earnings before it can declare a dividend, which must be from retained earnings in excess of the required amount. If, as a financial officer, you are negotiating a loan for a firm which wants to reinvest all its earnings, you can bargain for a lower interest rate by "conceding" the lenders a restriction on your dividends, since you never intended to pay dividends anyway.

Legal Considerations

Some states regulate the corporation's ability to pay dividends if that payment will impair the capital, where the capital can be defined as the common stock and additional paid-in capital. For example, if your corporation had the following capital accounts:

Common stock (1 million shares, $10 par value)	$10,000,000
Additional paid-in capital	15,000,000
Retained earnings	5,000,000
	$30,000,000

it could not declare a dividend of more than $5,000,000, because to do so would impair the capital. The corporation is usually limited to dividend payments out of its retained earnings by the regulations of the state in which the corporation is chartered.

State regulations may also restrict the corporation from borrowing funds to pay common stockholder dividends. And if the firm is insolvent, it cannot pay dividends at all until all creditors' claims against the firm have been satisfied.

Debt Repayment

As a financial officer, you may well have to make the choice between early repayment of the firm's debt or payment of a dividend. If, in your opinion, the early repayment of the debt is more pressing than the need to declare a dividend, you would retain the earnings in order to pay off the debt. You could judge this by examining the effect on the firm's share price. Repaying the debt reduces the firm's financial risk, but omitting an expected dividend reduces the stockholders' anticipation of dividends. Since the former tends to increase share prices and the latter tends to decrease share prices, your judgment as to the final effect on the share price will guide your advice to the board of directors.

Inflation

Some firms view depreciation as a source of funds for replacing worn machinery and other capital assets, but inflation usually leaves the depreciation generated short of allowing the firm sufficient funds to replace the old equipment. These firms tend to look upon retained earnings as a source of funds to make up the shortfall in the depreciation. Under those circumstances, their dividend payout tends to be less generous during periods of more rapid inflation.

Frequency of Payment

Established firms commonly pay their dividends on a quarterly basis. Other firms pay at other intervals, such as semiannually and annually, and a few firms have adopted monthly payments, such as William Wrigley and Company, the chewing gum manufacturer. Some investors who may rely on dividends for income may be attracted to firms with more frequent payments, and this could influence the firm's stock price. Depending on the type of stockholders and their needs, the financial officer may consider recommending more or less frequent payments.

DIVIDEND POLICY AND SHARE PRICE

Much of your advice as financial officer will spring from your analysis of how dividend policy impacts the firm's share price. We have already seen that stability in the dividend policy seems to increase the share price. Dividend policy also affects investors' expectations of our growth and the risk they associate with any given stream of anticipated dividends.

Stable Dividend Policy

Just for the sake of completeness, we can restate here what we have already seen: a stable dividend policy which avoids occasional reduction of dividends reflects favorably on the firm in the minds of stockholders. This helps increase the share price by reducing the uncertainty that investors associate with the anticipated stream of dividends. A stable dividend projects an image of a stable operating environment, and an increase in the dividend communicates the feeling of a firm entering a new period of prosperity.

Dividend Policy and Growth

The dividend policy we select also influences the growth investors expect in our earnings (see the Walter model in Appendix 11A). If the firm can reinvest retained earnings in projects with a higher rate of return than what stockholders could expect to receive if they themselves reinvested the earnings in the form of dividends, then investors should encourage the firm to reinvest the earnings for them in anticipation of increased future earnings and higher stock prices. Reinvestment of retained earnings expands the firm's earnings asset base and should lead to a growing earnings per share and a higher stock price. We can see this in our share evaluation models from Chapter 9:

$$P_0 = \frac{D_0}{k_e - g}$$

(11-2)

or:

$$P_0 = \sum_{t=1}^{\infty} \frac{\hat{D}_t}{(1 + k_e)^t}$$

(11-3)

In Equation 11-2, a retention of earnings which leads to an increased growth rate (g) will lower the denominator (which in essence is a decrease in the cost of equity capital and the rate of return required by stockholders) and increase our stock price (P_0). In Equation 11-3, it is obvious that an increase in expected dividends (D_t) in future years, years $t = 1$ and beyond, increases the numerator—and our firm's share price.

Dividend Policy and Risk

Offsetting the positive effects on the stock price as dividend and dividend growth estimates are upwardly revised because of the retention and reinvestment of earnings is the risk associated with the postponement of the dividends and the increased uncertainty associated with receiving the capital gain expected because of the reinvestment of the retained earnings. (See the Gordon model in Appendix 11A.) As the firm postpones the declaration of dividends so that it can reinvest earnings in the hopes of increasing future earnings and stock prices, there is a greater risk that the stockholder may never realize the expected dividends because the firm may not succeed in the projects it chooses to reinvest in. This uncertainty, coupled with the longer wait to receive the dividends even if they are increased, may actually lower the stock price if the effect is greater than that of the increased growth of dividends expected from the reinvestment of the retained earnings. As the financial officer, you must weigh the counterbalancing factors and decide which is the more influential, the increased growth in expected earnings and dividends or the increased risk associated with any particular payout rate.

This still leaves us with a question: Do investors consider dividends or earnings the more important factor in the evaluation and determination of our stock price? Is the dividend now worth more than the expectation of increased dividends later? Unfortunately, there is no definite agreement on this point, but the suggestions of Graham and Dodd[3] and of Friend and Puckett[4] seem to indicate that dividends per share are more important. To Graham and Dodd, investors considered the dividend

---

[3] B. Graham, D. Dodd, and S. Cottle, *Security Analysis*, McGraw-Hill, New York, 1962.
[4] I. Friend and M. Puckett, "Dividends and Stock Prices," *American Economic Review*, LIV (September 1964), 656–682.

three times more valuable than the reinvestment of earnings. This is reflected in their famous evaluation model of the 1930s and 1940s which states that:

$$P_0 = M \left(\frac{E}{3} + D \right)$$
(11-4)

where
P_0 = the prevailing price
E = the earnings per share
D = the dividend per share
M = a market-determined multiple

Friend and Puckett generally found dividends to be more important in determining share price than retained earnings, particularly among companies with lower growth prospects. In their study relating normalized earnings, dividends, and retained earnings to the price/earnings ratio[5] they found that the P/E ratio tended to be more influenced by the dividends than by the earnings. This confirmed to them their first indications that low-growth companies should have higher payout ratios than high-growth companies, although in either situation dividends were still the dominant influence on the P/E ratio.

STOCK DIVIDENDS

Stock dividends are in the form of additional stock instead of cash. For example, a 2 percent stock dividend means that the owner of record of 100 shares of stock receives an additional 2 shares on the payment date. The effect of a stock dividend on the accounting books, on the price of the stock, and in the considerations of the financial officer differs from that of a regular cash dividend.

Accounting for Stock Dividends

Accounting for a stock dividend payment is similar to accounting for a cash dividend in that both must be paid out of retained earnings. But the stock dividend is charged to retained earnings at the prevailing market price of the stock, as illustrated in Table 11-1.

---

[5] The normalized earnings were used so that random variations in the earnings which did not influence the declaration of dividends were eliminated. The tested model was:

$$P_t = a + b\, D_t + cR^n{}_t$$

where
P_t = the prevailing price
D_t = the prevailing dividend
$R^n{}_t$ = the normalized retained earnings

The results for the chemical industry in 1958 were:

$$P_t = -5.87 + 25.78\, D_t + 18.82\, R^n{}_t$$

and for the 1958 food industry were:

$$P_t = 3.00 + 15.11\, D_t + 3.83\, R^n{}_t$$

which to Friend and Puckett implied that for the growth chemical industry dividends were only slightly more important than retained earnings, while in the nongrowth food industry dividends were almost five times as important, as reflected in the value of the coefficients.

Table 11-1   Accounting for a Stock Dividend

Prior to Payment of the Stock Dividend:

Common stock (1 million shares, $10 par value)	$10,000,000
Additional paid-in capital	20,000,000
Retained earnings	50,000,000
Total stockholders' equity	$80,000,000

After a 10 percent stock dividend paid at a $20 per share market price:

Common stock (1,100,000 shares, $10 par value)	$11,000,000
Additional paid-in capital	21,000,000
Retained earnings	48,000,000
Total stockholders' equity	$80,000,000

It is clear that the sole accounting effect of the stock dividend has been to transfer the market value of the stock dividend to the common stock and the additional paid-in capital accounts. In this case a 10 percent stock dividend is 100,000 shares, which at a prevailing market price of $20 a share means that $2,000,000 has to be transferred from the retained earnings to the other two accounts. The amount transferred to the common stock account is the number of shares times the stock's par value, which in this case is 100,000 times $10 a share, or $1,000,000. The remainder of the market value of the transfer which is $1 million, the difference between the par value and the market value of the stock dividend, is transferred to the additional paid-in capital account. The net effect on the total stockholders' equity has been absolutely zero.

Stock Dividends, Earnings Per Share, and Stock Price

When a firm pays a stock dividend, the previously reported earnings per share (based upon the smaller number of shares outstanding before the stock dividend) have to be adjusted to provide a uniform basis of comparison. Therefore, if the firm in Table 11-1 had reported a $1 per share earnings before the 10 percent stock dividend, it would have to adjust its earnings per share downward to $.91, which is calculated as:

$$\frac{E_0}{1 + D_s}$$

where

E_0 = the original earnings per share
D_s = the stock dividend rate

$$\frac{\$1.00}{1 + .10} = \$.91$$

Future earnings per share do not have to be adjusted, because they will automatically be computed on the enlarged number of shares outstanding after the payment of the stock dividend.

The effect on the stock price of a stock dividend is similar. On the ex-dividend date, if the stock price were $20 a share as in our example, then the ex-dividend price would be:

$$\frac{\$20.00}{1 + .10} = \$18.18$$

This adjustment means that the total value of the stockholders' shares will not increase simply because the number of shares each stockholder owns increases. In our example, the total value of the stockholders' shares would remain $20 if each owned one share, because 1.10 shares times $18.18 per share = $20. Theoretically there is no advantage to a stock dividend, for it merely keeps each shareholder at the same proportional ownership interest by giving each a greater number of shares in the same size pie, so to speak. In addition, we would expect that a stock dividend would have no effect on the investors' attitude toward the firm's risk and would not change the firm's cost of equity or the rate of return required by investors.

But in practice stock dividends sometimes do have advantages to the stockholders. First, they are not taxed at the time stockholders receive them, as are regular cash dividends. Instead, they are taxed when the stockholder chooses to sell the shares and then only at the capital gains rates rather than the regular income tax rates, which are higher. The stockholder can delay paying the taxes by not selling the stock received as the dividend. A stock dividend can lead to a wider ownership of the firm's shares, if the stock dividend is sold by some of the present shareholders, as it frequently is. This can increase the marketability of the firm's stock if the market for the shares is thin. Frequently, a small 2% to 3% stock dividend is not totally adjusted for in the stock price and may give the present stockholders a slight increase in the total value of their present holdings, even though this effect should theoretically not exist. For a firm which is already paying a dividend, a stock dividend also increases the total cash payout to stockholders and is like a hike in the cash dividend. For example, if a firm which is paying a dividend of $1 a share declares a 10 percent stock dividend as well, the total dividends received by a 100-share stockholder increase from $100 to $110.

Other Considerations

In addition to finding that the firm's stockholders may like stock dividends because of their advantages, the financial officer must also consider their use in light of the firm's situation. When the firm may want to preserve cash for other investments but still wants to give the stockholders something, the stock dividend frequently communicates to stockholders that they are being kept in mind by the board of directors and that the omission of the cash dividend is for internal growth needs. This tends to support the stock price and keep the stockholders content, although it has been abused frequently by firms which wish to mislead stockholders and cover up a deteriorating profit situation. These firms offer the explanation that the stock dividend is needed to conserve internally-generated capital to finance projects—when it is actually declared because the earnings from which to pay dividends are no longer there.

SUMMARY

After having read Chapter 11, you should be able to answer these questions:

1. What is dividend policy?

The heart of the dividend policy is the percentage of the earnings to be paid out as dividends, also known as the payout ratio. The particular percentage that is paid out has impact on the firm's stock price and growth prospects.

2. How are dividends paid?

The board of directors declares a specific dollar amount of dividends payable on a specific future date to stockholders of record as of an earlier date. Because of book-keeping delay, stocks go ex-dividend five business days before the record date and the purchaser of the stock after the ex-dividend date is not entitled to receive the declared dividend.

3. What are possible dividend policy objectives?

The major dividend policy objectives are to avoid reducing the dividend and to progress toward a previously determined target payout ratio. Within that frame-work, firms tend to set their dividends as a percentage of the earnings slightly lower than the target payout ratio in order to avoid reducing the dividend if the suc-ceeding period's earnings should drop below those of the previous period.

Alternatively, a firm can adopt a dividend policy objective such as a year-end extra dividend in recognition of a good year without implying a permanency to the dividend increase. The firm should not adopt any dividend policy which promotes fluctuations in the dividend.

4. As a financial officer, what factors should you consider in selecting a dividend policy?

In addition to the objective itself, you should consider such factors as the firm's ability to borrow, the firm's liquidity, control of the firm, the average tax bracket of your stockholders, loan restrictions, legal considerations, debt repayment needs, and the availability of attractive investment projects.

5. How does the dividend policy influence the firm's stock price and growth pros-pects?

The stock price could be influenced by the informational content of the dividend. If an increased dividend communicated to the stockholders that the firm had en-tered a new era of better earnings prospects, the stock price might react favorably. Of course, a reduction in the dividend might have just the opposite effect.

If retention of the firm's earnings leads investors to anticipate an increased stream of future dividends, the stock price might rise, provided the additional uncertainty associated with the postponement of the dividend payment did not offset the antici-pation of higher future dividends caused by the reinvestment.

There is little evidence to support the contention, but most financial theorists feel that dividends are more valuable to stockholders than are retained earnings and their associated hope of higher future dividends. However, almost all the theorists and the empirical studies suggest that the dividend payout ratio should be lower among those firms with good growth prospects than among less growth-oriented firms.

QUESTIONS

11-1 (a) Distinguish between a cash dividend and a stock dividend.
     (b) From a stockholder's viewpoint would one be preferred to the other?
11-2 On July 15, the board of directors of Eatherly Company declared an annual div-idend of $1 per share to the common stockholders of record as of July 25, pay-able on July 30. Mr. Smith bought several shares of Eatherly common on July 23, and Mr. Jones purchased several shares on July 16. Will both Mr. Smith and Mr. Jones receive the announced dividends? Why?
11-3 (a) What is the dividend payout ratio?
     (b) Under normal circumstance is it possible for a firm to maintain both stable dividends and stable payout ratios?

11-4 What are some of the factors, besides stability of dividends and/or payout ratio, that the financial officer must consider before making dividend recommendations?

11-5 Does the payment of a stock dividend affect a firm's total stockholder's equity?

11-6 A major criticism of the bankrupt PennCentral Railroad was that it maintained a constant dividend payout ratio for many years. Under what circumstances would this criticism be valid?

11-7 Do you agree with the following statement: "Firms like United States Steel and Texaco will probably have higher dividend payout ratios than Xerox or Polaroid because of the differences in their industry growth potentials."

11-8 Indicate how each of the following events would probably affect the average aggregate dividend payout ratio for all United States industrial firms:

Event	Dividend payout ratio		
	Increase	Decrease	Indeterminant
Reduction in capital gains tax			
An increase in investment opportunities			
Substantial wage increases			
Reduction in worker productivity			
A decrease in interest rates			

PROBLEMS

11-1 Suppose Firm A is principally concerned with showing a steady rise in its dividends per share and avoiding, if possible, a decline in its dividends per share. Likewise, the firm has a dividend payout ratio target of 50 percent and its most recent dividend was $2.00 a share. The present earnings per share of the firm is $5.00. (a) If the firm wishes to maintain its target payout ratio, what will be its dividend? (b) If management decides it would like a cushion of 30 percent in case next year's earnings fall off, what will be the dividend this year? What is the payout ratio?

11-2 Smith Company has the following capital accounts:

Common stock (300,000 shares, $10 par value)	$ 3,000,000
Additional paid-in capital	10,000,000
Retained earnings	2,000,000
Total stockholders' equity	$15,000,000

(a) In most states what would be the maximum total cash dividend the firm could legally pay?

(b) If the firm pays a dividend of $5.00 per share, what is the effect on total stockholders' equity?

(c) If a 20% stock dividend is paid at a market price of $30 per common share, what happens to the above capital accounts? What is the adjusted earnings per share if present earnings were $300,000?

11-3 The management of Rowe Company has been comparing P/E ratios for the past five years with one of its closest competitors, Dow Company. Selected data follow:

Rowe Company

Year	Earnings/share	Dividends/share	Payout ratio	P/E
1975	$3.80	$1.90	.50	13.6
1974	3.00	1.50	.50	11.7
1973	3.50	1.75	.50	12.5
1972	2.90	1.95	.50	11.6
1971	3.00	1.50	.50	12.9

Dow Company

Year	Earnings/share	Dividends/share	Payout ratio	P/E
1975	$3.90	$1.75	.45	17.8
1974	3.10	1.55	.50	17.2
1973	3.50	1.40	.40	16.8
1972	2.80	1.32	.55	17.3
1971	3.10	1.24	.40	16.9

If both firms are in the same market and have similar capital structures, what factors might be contributing to Dow's relatively higher P/E ratios?

BIBLIOGRAPHY

Bodenhorn, Diran. "A Cash Flow Concept of Profit." *Journal of Finance,* XIX (March 1964), 16–31.

Brennan, Michael. "A Note on Dividend Irrelevance and the Gordon Valuation Model." *Journal of Finance,* XXVI (December 1971), 1115–1122.

Brittain, John A. *Corporate Dividend Policy.* The Brookings Institution, Washington, D.C., 1966.

Dailing, Paul G. "The Influence of Expectations and Liquidity on Dividend Policy." *Journal of Political Economy,* LXV (June 1957), 209–224.

Davenport, Michael. "Leverage, Dividend Policy and the Cost of Capital: A Comment." *Journal of Finance,* XXV (September 1970), 893–897.

Dhrymes, Phoebus J., and Mordecai Kurz. "On the Dividend Policy of Electric Utilities." *Review of Economics and Statistics,* 46 (February 1964), 76–81.

Fama, Eugene F., and Harvey Babeak. "Dividend Policy: An Empirical Analysis," *Journal of the American Statistical Association,* 63 (December 1968), 1132–1161.

Friend, Irwin, and Marshall Puckett. "Dividends and Stock Prices." *American Economic Review,* LIV (September 1964), 656–682.

Gordon, Myron J. "Dividends, Earnings and Stock Prices." *Review of Economics and Statistics,* 41 (May 1959), 99–105.

Hausman, W. H., R. R. West, and J. A. Largay. "Stock Splits, Price Changes, and Trading Profits: A Synthesis." *Journal of Business,* XLIV (January 1971), 69–77.

Higgins, Robert C., "Dividend Policy and the Valuation of Corporate Shares Under Uncertainty." Ph.D. dissertation, Stanford University, 1968.

Holland, Daniel M. *Dividends Under the Income Tax.* National Bureau of Economic Research, New York, 1962.

Krainer, Robert E. "A Pedagogic Note on Dividend Policy." *Journal of Financial and Quantitative Analysis,* VI (September 1971), 1147–1154.

Lintner, John. "Distribution of Income of Corporations Among Dividends, Retained Earnings, and Taxes." *American Economic Review,* XLVI (May 1956), 97–113.

Miller, M. H., and Franco Modigliani. "Dividend Policy, Growth, and the Valuation of Shares." *Journal of Business*, XXXIV (October 1961), 411–433.

———, and Franco Modigliani, "Some Estimates of the Cost of Capital to the Electric Utility Industry." *American Economic Review*, LVI (June 1966), 333–391.

Porterfield, James T. S., "Dividends, Dilution, and Delusion." *Harvard Business Review*, 37 (November-December 1959), 156–161.

Sussman, M. R. *The Stock Dividend.* Bureau of Business Research, University of Michigan, Ann Arbor, Mich., 1962.

Van Horne, James C., and John G. McDonald. "Dividend Policy and New Equity Financing." *Journal of Finance*, XXVI (May 1971), 507–520.

Walter, James E. "Dividend Policies and Common Stock Prices." *Journal of Finance*, XI (March 1956), 29–41.

———. "Dividend Policy: Its Influence on the Value of the Enterprise." *Journal of Finance*, XVIII (May 1963), 280–291.

Watts, Ross, "The Information Content of Dividends." *Journal of Business*, 46 (April 1973), 191–211.

Woods, Donald H., and Eugene F. Brigham. "Stockholder Distribution Decisions: Share Repurchase or Dividends." *Journal of Financial and Quantitative Analysis*, I (March 1966), 15–28.

Appendix 11A **Some Dividend Policy Models**

Various models have been proposed to evaluate the dividend policy decision in relation to the objective of maximizing share price. While agreement is not found among the models as to the precise relationship, it pays to examine some of the more famous models to gain insight into the effect dividend policy might have on share-price evaluation. As financial officers, we would want to incorporate the appropriate insights into our own thinking and dividend policy considerations.

WALTER MODEL

The Walter model[1] is:

$$P = \frac{D + \dfrac{r}{k_e}(E - D)}{k_e} \tag{11A-1}$$

where

P = the prevailing share price
D = the dividend per share
r = the return on investment
k_e = the cost of equity capital
E = the earnings per share

This model says that if the return on investment is greater than the cost of capital, retained earnings, as measured by the difference between E and D, more than proportionately increase P. In that case, stockholders desire the firm to retain earnings if r is greater than k_e. If, for example:

$r = .20$
$k_e = .10$
$E = \$2.00$
$D = \$.50$

then:

$$P = \frac{.50 + \dfrac{.20}{.10}(\$2.00 - .50)}{.10}$$

$$= \$35.00$$

In this example, if the firm increased its retained earnings, Walter claims the share price would rise. Conversely, if r had been less than k_e, then a decrease in the retained earnings would have increased the share price. As a result, Walter concludes that if the firm has a large number of profitable projects such that r is greater than k_e, the firm should pay little or no dividends.

---

[1] J. E. Walter, "Dividend Policies and Common Stock Prices," *Journal of Finance*, XI (March 1956), 29–41.

MM MODEL

Modigliani and Miller[2] maintain that dividend policy has no effect on the firm's share price and therefore does not matter. This is, of course, an extreme view opposed by the majority of financial thinkers. They attempt to prove their argument in the following manner, postulating that the prevailing price of the stock (P_0) is:

$$P_0 = \frac{1}{(1 + k_e)} (D_1 + P_1) \qquad (11A\text{-}2)$$

where
  P_0 = the prevailing stock price
  k_e = the cost of equity capital
  D_1 = the dividend to be received during period one
  P_1 = the prevailing stock price one period hence

We recognize P_0 in Equation 11A-2 as the capitalized value of the one-period dividend and expected capital gain. The total capitalized value of the firm is simply the number of shares (n) times the price of each share, P_0, from Equation 11A-2 such that:

$$nP_0 = \frac{1}{(1 + k_e)} [nD_1 + (n + \Delta n)P_1 - \Delta nP_1] \qquad (11A\text{-}3)$$

where
  D_1 = the dividend per share during one period
  n = the number of shares outstanding at the beginning of the period
  Δn = the change in the number of shares outstanding during the period

Equation 11A-3 simply states that the total value of the firm is the capitalized value of the dividends to be received during the period plus the value of the number of shares to be outstanding at the end of the period, considering any newly issued shares, less the value of the newly issued shares. If we worked through Equation 11A-3, we would see that it reduces to Equation 11A-2 times a factor of n, such that:

$$nP_0 = \frac{1}{(1 + k_e)} [nD_1 + nP_1] \qquad (11A\text{-}4)$$

If, as financial officers, we were to finance all our investment projects by either the sale of new stock or retained earnings, the dollar value of new stock that we would have to sell is:

$$\Delta nP_1 = I - (E - nD_1) \qquad (11A\text{-}5)$$

where
  ΔnP_1 = the dollar value of new stock sold to finance our projects
  I = the total dollar volume of new financing needed
  E = earnings during the period
  nD_1 = total dividends paid

Equation 11A-5 simply states that whatever of our capital needs (I) are *not* financed by retained earnings ($E - nD_1$) must be financed through the sale of stock.

[2] M. Miller and F. Modigliani, "Dividend Policy, Growth, and the Valuation of Shares," *Journal of Business*, XXXIV (October 1961), 411–433.

If we substitute Equation 11A-5 into Equation 11A-3, we derive:

$$nP_0 = \frac{1}{(1 + k_e)} \left[(n + \Delta n)P_1 - I + E \right] \tag{11A-6}$$

Since dividends (D) are not found in Equation 11A-6, MM conclude that dividends do not count, and that dividend policy has no effect on the stock price.

The problems with the MM argument are that: (1) It is only effectively logical under the assumption of no taxes, which eliminates the differential tax between the firm and its shareholders. (2) There are assumed to be no flotation or transaction costs which, since they do exist, make it very hard to have the exact offset between retained earnings and the sale of newly issued stock envisioned in the model. (3) The MM model ignores the uncertainty associated with the postponement of dividends to finance growth. In their model the interchange between present dividends and future dividends financed by retained earnings is exactly even. They also fail to consider that dividends convey information to investors which may make them more confident of the firm's prospects—and which means that the interchange is not as exactly even, as MM suggest.

GORDON MODEL

Based on the investor's aversion for risk, Gordon[3] suggests that since retained earnings are evaluated as a risky promise of higher future dividends, investors would require a higher rate of return as the retention rate increased, and this could adversely affect the stock price, such that:

$$P = \frac{D_0}{(1 + k_e)} + \frac{D_0}{(1 + k_e)^2} \tag{11A-7}$$

where D_0 is constant because the firm pays out 100 percent of its earnings in dividends and does not grow. But if that firm started to retain earnings for reinvestment, two things would happen. First, expected future dividends would start to grow as some function of the retained earnings (r.e.); and second, investors would start demanding a higher rate of return (k_e) because of the increased risk associated with the futurity of receiving the more distant dividends. Gordon expressed this in Equation 11A-8:

$$P = \frac{D_0}{(1 + k_e)^1} + \frac{D_0 + b(\text{r.e.})}{(1 + [k_e + k_e'])^2} \tag{11A-8}$$

where
   $b(\text{r.e.})$ = the increased expectations in dividends caused by retaining earnings
   k_e' = the increase in the cost of equity capital (k_e) caused by retaining earnings (postponing dividend payments)

Gordon concludes that if the policy of retaining earnings increases the numerator of Equation 11A-8 proportionately more than it increases the denominator, the share price will rise. If the cost of equity rises proportionately more than the increased dividend expectations, then the share price will fall. A significant factor is obviously investors' expectations as to the profitability of the projects in which the retained earnings are reinvested.

[3] M. J. Gordon, "Optimal Investment and Financing Policy," *Journal of Finance*, XVIII (May 1963), 264–272.

THE GORDON-BRIGHAM MODEL

To test if dividends or earnings were the more important to stockholders in their evaluation of the firm's shares, Gordon and Brigham[4] used Equation 11A-9:

$$\frac{D_0}{P_0} = a_0 + a_1 g + a_2 h + a_3 u + a_4 e + a_5 s \tag{11A-9}$$

where

g = the firm's growth rate

h = the firm's debt/equity ratio

u = an index of the firm's stability in earnings

s = the firm's size

e = the proportion of the firm's business in electricity, to reflect that the sample used was composed of electrical utilities

GB reasoned that if investors were indifferent between dividends now or dividends later as reflected in the current growth rate (g), the coefficient of a_1 would be -1, since that would be an exact trade-off between the dividends in the dependent variable (D_0/P_0). As it turned out, a_1 was equal to $-.4$, considerably less than the trade-off value of -1 and implying that investors really did prefer dividends to retained earnings about $2\frac{1}{2}$ to 1.

GENERAL IMPLICATIONS

While the empirical evidence is rather inconclusive, the indications are that dividends are preferred to retained earnings. This is probably true because they are more certain and investors have a tendency to assign a higher value to a more certain stream.

The implications for the financial officer are probably not as clear cut as that, for you certainly do not see many firms paying out 100 percent of their annual earnings in an effort to maximize their share price. Rather, the optimum point probably lies somewhere in the middle. Too much payout in the face of profitable reinvestment opportunities causes investors to penalize the stock price. Too little payout in relation to the reinvestment opportunities of the firm also causes investors to penalize the firm's stock price.

Financial officers should never forget, however, that they can attract different types of stockholders by altering their dividend policy. A low payout and an associated high growth rate attract the more risk-oriented investors, while a high payout associated with a lower growth rate attracts the more conservative investors.

[4] M. J. Gordon and E. F. Brigham, "Leverage, Dividend Policy, and the Cost of Capital," *Journal of Finance*, XXIII (March 1968), 85–104.

FOUR
WORKING CAPITAL MANAGEMENT

LET US LOOK AT SOME OF THE IMPORTANT QUESTIONS about working capital management. As you read Part Four look for the answers to the following questions:

1. What are cash and marketable securities?
2. What is the objective of cash and marketable securities management?
3. What factors must you, as the financial officer, consider in determining the firm's minimum cash and marketable securities needs?
4. How do you coordinate these considerations into a careful analysis to determine the minimum needs?
5. What techniques are available to lessen your need for cash reserves?
6. What marketable securities are available for the temporary investment of idle cash?
7. What is inventory and what is the appropriate objective for inventory management?
8. What factors would you consider in determining the firm's inventory needs?
9. What is the firm's objective in its accounts receivable policy?
10. What factors must the financial officer consider in attempting to determine the optimal accounts receivable policy for the firm?
11. How does the financial officer implement and monitor the accounts receivable policy the firm selects?

12
CASh AND MARKETABLE SECURITIES

CASH AND MARKETABLE SECURITIES are the two components of cash management for which you, as the financial officer, are responsible. It is up to you to see that adequate cash balances are maintained. It is also up to you to see that the entire cash management is efficiently operated at as low a cost as possible. In addition, you are probably required to look upon the firm's cash management as a profit center, whereby investment of temporarily idle cash balances in marketable securities can lead to additional profits.

First, however, we must be sure we can answer the question: What are cash and marketable securities? *Cash* is the currency that we have on hand or in the checking account (demand deposit) balances that we maintain at the bank. By far the larger portion of cash is in the form of checking accounts, which are distinguished by their lack of earning power and their immediacy of use. In other words, those accounts pay no interest, but we can simply write a check against the account as payment of the firm's bills.

If cash balances do not earn any money, why does the firm hold them? The three motives commonly used to explain the maintenance of cash balances are the transaction motive, the precautionary motive, and the speculative motive. *Transaction balances* are kept in order to meet routine cash needs such as the purchase of raw materials and payrolls. *Precautionary balances* are kept to meet unanticipated cash needs occasioned by such things as sharp increases in raw material costs, strikes, and unexpected slowdowns in the collections of accounts receivable. *Speculative balances* are kept in order to allow the firm to take advantage of opportunities which present themselves at unexpected moments and which are typically outside of the normal course of business, such as a drop in securities prices or a merger proposal. It is the financial officer's job to determine the amount of cash that should be kept in each category.

We now know what cash is and why firms hold cash balances, but what are marketable securities and why do firms hold them? *Marketable securities* are usually securities which can be converted rather quickly into cash, although there is no guarantee that the securities' prices will not fluctuate, giving the firm a profit or a loss on that conversion into cash. Typically, these securities are short-term, ranging from overnight loans to maturities of less than a year, although there is no restriction against using securities with longer terms. We shall see that among the more common types are United States Treasury bills, Federal Funds, commercial paper, and repurchase agreements.

Why might you want to own marketable securities? First, they serve as an alternative to idle, nonearning cash balances. Second, the adroit use of marketable securities can have a relatively large impact on the firm's earnings per share. For example, $2 million in idle cash invested at 7 percent for one year can add $140,000 in pre-tax earnings, or $.14 a share on 1 million shares. Obviously, a financial officer does not want idle cash in excess of the firm's minimum needs lying fallow if it can be invested. Third, marketable securities are an attractive place to keep some cash reserves to meet precautionary or speculative needs. If the conversion back to cash can be accomplished quickly, it is only sensible to use marketable securities instead of idle cash balances for your precautionary and speculative balances, because the former earns money until they are needed.

What is your objective in cash and marketable securities management? It is really twofold. You want to minimize idle cash balances because they do not earn anything for the firm. Yet you must have sufficient cash balances to meet the anticipated as well as the unanticipated cash needs of the firm. As financial officer, you must insure that the firm has enough cash so that the orderly processes of production and marketing are not interfered with. You must consider the firm's known needs for cash, a cushion for unanticipated cash needs, a policy on speculative balances, and a procedure for selecting the right investments for temporarily warehousing those speculative, precautionary, or otherwise generally excessive cash balances. Among other things, for example, a good cash management policy will enable the firm to take trade discounts for early payment of its accounts payable.

What factors must the financial officer specifically consider in order to determine the firm's needed cash balance? The general factors are the synchronization of the cash inflows and the cash outflows, the costs associated with a shortfall in the firm's cash needs, the costs associated with maintaining excess idle cash, the costs associated with managing the firm's cash balances and marketable securities, and the associated uncertainties.

In order to synchronize the cashflows, you will have to examine such cash inflow characteristics as the seasonal and cyclical pattern of the firm's sales, its collection of accounts receivable, and its borrowings. You will also have to examine such cash outflow characteristics as the firm's payroll, raw material costs, interest payments, accounts payable pattern, debt amortization, and taxes. To determine the costs associated with a shortfall in the firm's cash needs, you will have to examine the firm's transaction costs of raising cash, its borrowing costs, the forfeiture of trade discounts and other valuable opportunities, the deterioration in the firm's credit rating, and the increased banking charges. To determine the cost associated with maintaining excess idle cash, you will have to examine the missed opportunities from which the firm could have profited if it had invested those funds, particularly the interest passed up on marketable securities. To determine the operating costs associated with the cash management, you will have to examine the cost of maintaining a staff and of buying and storing the securities.

In addition to the synchronization and the costs aspects of cash management, financial officers also have to cope with the associated uncertainty. If there were perfect certainty, you would keep your cash balances at zero, since they do not earn anything, converting just enough marketable securities to cash the minute before they are needed. But unfortunately there are irregularities in the cashflows caused by delays in collections and disbursements. Your ability to cope with these uncertainties and thus minimize the amount of necessary cash balances depends on the degree to which you can borrow, your forecasting ability, management's desire to avoid shortfalls and keep precautionary balances, and management's desire to speculate with the firm's cash and marketable securities. We shall also examine the impact of uncertainty on your cash management operations and strategy.

Once you have examined and estimated all the pertinent factors and costs, how do you derive an optimal cash balance? We shall see that the cash budget (introduced in Chapter 3) is the main tool that the financial officer uses to synchronize the firm's cashflows and determine cash needs. But in order to optimize, you must turn to the cash management techniques models. We shall see how one model, under certainty, allows the financial officer to establish optimal cash balances using the pertinent factors. We shall also see that the financial officer can, with the addition of a safety stock balance, cope with the uncertainty of the cashflows, depending on how willing the firm is to risk a shortfall.

Once the financial officer has established the optimal cash and marketable securities balances, what specific techniques are available to lessen the need for cash? There are techniques which speed up the cash inflows, such as lock boxes and techniques which slow down the disbursals, such as float management. We shall examine some of these methods in this chapter.

Finally, once we have determined the optimal cash balance, what marketable securities are available to the financial officer to temporarily invest idle cash in excess of that optimal level? There are United States Treasury bills, tax anticipation notes, Federal agencies' notes, repurchase agreements, bankers' acceptances, and many other types which may be used for the temporary investment of idle cash balances.

THE OBJECTIVE OF CASH MANAGEMENT

Once the financial officer knows what cash and marketable securities are, what is the appropriate cash management objective?

Basically, it is a twofold objective: (1) meet the cash disbursement needs (the payments schedule), and (2) minimize the funds committed to transactions and precautionary cash balances. Some firms also keep speculative cash balances, but that generally depends on management. Since most firms do not speculate as such, but only use marketable securities as a haven for temporary, excess cash, we will not analyze speculative balances.

Meeting the Payments Schedule

In the normal course of business, all firms experience a flow of cash through the corporate treasury. Cash flows in from the collection of accounts receivable generated when the firm's goods and services are sold, and cash flows out to the firm's suppliers of raw material and to its employees. We might look upon cash as oil to lubricate the ever-turning wheels of business: without it the process grinds to a stop. Since almost all firms consider themselves continuing operations, it is up to the financial officer to see that the firm has enough cash on hand to meet its payments schedule. You could keep a lot of idle cash lying around to insure that you never miss a due date on your payments schedule. But this would be poor financial management to say the least and at best a very costly practice, because idle cash does not earn any return.

There are, however, advantages to making payments on time which tend to push financial officers in the direction of excess cash balances. Certainly, excessive cash prevents insolvency, for if you always have cash on hand to meet all payments, no creditor can force you into an embarrassing situation—or perhaps bankruptcy. Your banker will be very pleased to see you maintaining large inactive cash balances in your checking account, for he or she can turn around and lend that money at a profit. So, if you do keep sufficient cash in your checking account, your relationship with your banker will not be strained, but this can be accomplished with less than excessive idle balances in the account. Large cash balances also help maintain a good relationship with your trade creditors and material suppliers, for you may never miss a payment and probably pay early, helping them plan their own cash management. In addition, large cash balances let you take advantage of trade discounts if you pay your bills earlier than their due date. And, of course, larger than necessary cash balances allow you to meet any unanticipated cash expenditures with limited strain on the firm.

Despite all these considerations, it is very costly to keep larger-than-necessary cash balances on hand. After all, you can maintain good relationships with your bankers and your trade creditors, prevent embarrassing cash shortages, and meet unanticipated needs with *sufficient* funds, instead of excessive reserves, through properly planned cash management. And you can use the excess cash for profitable investment elsewhere.

Minimizing Funds Committed to Cash Balances

The other half of the cash management objective is to minimize your firm's investment in idle cash balances. If there were perfect synchronization and certainty in your cash receipts and payments schedule, you would obviously avoid cash balances entirely. Unfortunately, this situation does not exist, and some cash balances must be maintained. As you minimize the cash balances, you increase the chance of a shortfall and a failure to meet the payments schedule. Conversely, as you increase the cash balances, you decrease the chance of a shortfall and a failure to meet the payments schedule, but you forego possible profits.

A shortfall does not immediately force the firm into bankruptcy, but it is costly. As the financial officer, you must weigh that cost against what it costs your firm to keep idle cash on hand. Of course, if you do have a shortfall enough times and in sufficient amounts over a sustained period of time, you will be bankrupt.

You must also realize that in minimizing the firm's cash balances you should consider a cushion of precautionary cash balances to meet the unexpected. These are costly since they do not earn a profit for the firm. They should be minimized. This raises the same conflict in the objective, for by keeping precautionary cash balances you avoid the costs of the unexpected shortfall, but you incur the cost of idle balances. The level to which precautionary balances should be minimized depends on the degree of shortfall exposure and costs that management is willing to tolerate.

CONSIDERATIONS IN DETERMINING THE CASH NEED

Once the financial officer understands the twofold, conflicting aspects of the cash management objective, what specific factors must be considered to determine the firm's required cash balance?

Synchronization of the Cashflows

Synchronizing the cashflows requires the financial officer to first select a planning horizon over which to estimate the cash inflows and the cash outflows as they are expected to occur in each of the subperiods within the horizon. The typical planning horizon for each management is one year, with each of the twelve months being a subperiod. Thus the financial officer forecasts the firm's cash inflows and outflows for each month within the coming year.

Forecasting the inflows, as we have seen in Chapter 3 when we constructed the cash budget, centers on forecasts for the collections of accounts receivable. You must consider when the account is collected, not the time when the sale is made. This means that you must be alert to seasonal and cyclical patterns of payment as well as to delays, defaults, returns, and discounts in the collections. You must also estimate cash sales, interest and dividend income, borrowing proceeds, and the sale of the firm's securities or fixed assets.

The forecasting of the cash outflows as they are expected to be incurred in each month of the planning horizon requires the financial officer to consider all the accounts payable on the payments schedule. Among the more typical accounts payable are those for the purchase of raw materials, payroll, selling and general administrative expenses—less, of course, any trade discounts expected to apply during the month. You also have to consider such financial cash outflows as the repayment of loans, the repurchase of the firm's securities in the open market, the purchase of fixed assets such as plant and equipment, interest and dividends payable, and taxes.

An accurate forecast by the financial officer means that the uncertainty is reduced and the firm has to maintain fewer precautionary balances. It also pinpoints those months in which the firm will have excess cash to invest temporarily in marketable securities and those months in which the firm will have a cash shortfall. Knowing in advance, you can make the most convenient arrangements to borrow temporarily.

Short Costs

Even with a carefully constructed cash budget, the firm could still have a shortfall in its cash needs. The shortfall could be expected and arrangements made to cover the shortage. In fact, the cash budget is designed to pinpoint those times when you can expect a shortfall. The shortfall could also be unexpected. But whether expected or not, every shortfall will incur certain costs, depending on the severity, duration, and frequency of the shortfall and how you cover the shortage. Expenses incurred as a result of a shortfall are called *short costs.*

One of the most common short costs is transactions costs associated with raising cash. For example, if you convert some of the firm's liquid reserve assets (such as its investment in United States Treasury bills), you might pay a commission to the broker who sells them for you and transfer taxes on the sale.

There are borrowing costs if you borrow to cover the shortage. These include such items as the interest on the loan, any placement fees, and the other costs associated with arranging the loan.

If the shortage causes you to lose trade discounts which you might otherwise have taken, there is a relatively substantial cost involved. For example, if you can get a 2 percent discount off the purchase price by paying in 10 days instead of 30 days, you can save what amounts to about 36 percent a year. In order to get the 2 percent discount, all you give up is 20 days' use of the money (the difference between paying at the end of 10 days and paying at the end of 30 days). That is 2 percent for a period of one-eighteenth of a year ($^{20}/_{360}$)—or 36 percent on an annual basis. That is substantial savings to forego because of a temporary shortage of cash.

There is also the cost associated with a deterioration of the firm's credit rating. As shortfalls increase in severity and frequency, banks will start charging more for borrowings and the cost of capital will rise. And there are the less quantifiable aspects of a deteriorated credit standing. Your suppliers might stop extending you credit, some may demand cash payment upon delivery, and others may refuse to sell to you. The firm's image among its customers may decline, adversely affecting sales and profits.

If you draw down your checking account balances below the level you have agreed to maintain, typically called compensating balances, in order to cover the shortfall, your bank will charge you a penalty rate. These compensating balances are usually required by the bank, particularly in connection with a loan, to compensate them for the banking services they provide. The bank earns money on these balances by lending them out to other borrowers and can therefore afford to provide such services as credit referrals, check clearing, and business consultation. Typically, the penalty rate for failing to maintain your compensating balance is steep enough to discourage shortfalls.

Excess Cash Balance Costs

On the other side of the picture, you incur costs if you have excessively large cash balances. Too much idle cash means that the firm has missed opportunities to invest those funds, if only temporarily, at a positive rate of interest. As the forfeited interest rate rises, it becomes increasingly more expensive to maintain idle funds. For example, keeping $1 million in a checking account above the required minimum for only 3 months means a forfeiture of $10,000 if the 3-month Treasury bill rate were 4 percent. If the bill rate were 8 percent, the firm would have lost $20,000 in those 3 months. General Motors had cash items of $2,946,900,000 in 1972. If we assume that the prevailing interest rate during the period was 7 percent, it would have cost General Motors $206,283,000 in 1972 not to invest those cash items. Even smaller firms than General Motors frequently find that they have large amounts of cash on hand which can be invested. The question for the financial officer is to determine how much of that cash can be invested.

Of course, the appropriate amount may vary at different times for any particular firm. Some firms have pronounced seasonal patterns in their cash balances. Other firms have pronounced cyclical patterns in their operations such that during economic recessions they have excess cash. Sometimes, after the sale of a debt issue but before the money can be totally invested in the projects to be undertaken, the financial officer should temporarily invest those funds. For example, an electrical utility might sell a large bond issue to finance construction over the next several years. Until the funds are actually spent upon completion of the construction, the alert financial officer would invest them. Ideally, you want to have no idle funds; you want every possible dollar invested and working for you at all times.

Procurement and Management Costs

In addition to the shortfall and the excess balance costs, there are the costs associated with establishing and operating a cash management staff and activities. These costs are generally fixed and are mainly accounted for by salaries, bookkeeping expenses, and the storage and handling of the securities. The firm has to pay you or one of your assistants to supervise the operations and to make the appropriate decisions such as the amount and type of marketable securities to purchase. This in turn requires bookkeeping to keep track of the transactions and storage facilities, such as safe deposit boxes.

Uncertainty and Cash Management

Since cash inflows and cash outflows can never be exactly synchronized and never predicted with complete accuracy, the financial officer has to recognize the impact of uncertainty on cash management strategy. First, a precautionary cushion against shortfalls is needed to cope with the uncertainty caused by irregularities in the cashflows, unexpected delays in collection and disbursement, defaults, and unanticipated cash needs.

The impact of uncertainty on cash management can be mitigated through improved forecasting, use of cashflows over which the financial officer has control, and an increased ability to borrow. Certain cashflows such as tax payments, payrolls, planned capital expenditures, and dividends, for example, can be anticipated. Tax payments become due regularly at specific dates during the year. It is relatively easy for the financial officer to prepare for these predictable cash outflows by accumulating cash over the immediately preceding months or by making arrangements to borrow enough funds well in advance to cover the taxes. The funds set aside each month for this purpose can be temporarily invested in interest-earning securities, which might be selected to mature on the same date the payment is due. We shall see that the federal government sells tax-anticipation securities designed for just this purpose.

The alert financial officer can mitigate the potential impact of uncertainty on cash management through borrowing agreements with a bank. Under these agreements the bank automatically covers any shortages in your checking account (overdrafts) up to a prearranged limit. As the financial officer, you will probably be in a better position if you approach your banker before any shortages occur. Explain that you do not envision any unexpected shortages, but just in case, you would like to have an understanding with the bank that any that *do* arise will be temporary and that the bank will help you cover the shortages. This way, you maintain good relations with your banker even if there is an unexpected shortfall. In a slightly more formal approach you can arrange a line of credit, which, as the name implies, is a loan you can draw upon when you desire. For this drawing privilege and the bank's guarantee that the funds will be there when you want them, you pay a small interest rate on the unused portion of the loan and a larger rate on the portion that you draw upon.

The financial officer can, of course, mitigate the impact of uncertainty on cash management by improved forecasting of the cashflows. As the accuracy of the forecast increases, there is less need for precautionary balances. Much depends on the degree to which management desires to avoid unexpected shortfalls in the first place. As the desire of avoiding them increases, the precautionary cash balances which must be maintained also increase.

DETERMINING THE CASH NEED

Once financial officers have examined all the pertinent considerations and costs, how do they derive an optimal cash balance?

The three basic approaches are the cash budget, the minimizing-cost model, and the minimizing-cost model with precautionary balances.

The Cash Budget

We have already seen in Chapter 3 that the cash budget is the financial officer's basic tool for coordinating and forecasting the firm's cashflows. Table 12-1 is an example of a cash budget. As financial officers, we must forecast the monthly cash inflows, such as cash sales and accounts receivable collections, as well as the monthly cash outflows, including such items as accounts payable. Notice that there are no accruals in the cash budget; each item is an actual receipt or disbursement of cash. Once we have estimated the total monthly receipts and expenditures, we can readily see if we are going to have an unexpected shortfall or not. In Table 12-1, shortfalls are expected in months 1 and 2. The good financial officer will make advance arrangements for coverage of those anticipated shortfalls. He or she will also plan to temporarily invest at some positive rate of interest the excess cash balances expected in months 5 and 6, after repaying the short-term borrowings in months 3, 4, and 5. Notice that the minimum balance in this example is $1 million. It appears that the financial officer has decided that $1 million is the optimal cash balance for the firm. But where did that figure come from? The cash budget does not tell us.

The Optimal Cash Balance

Let us turn our attention to determining the optimal cash balance[1] that the firm should try to maintain. Essentially we want to minimize the firm's cost of maintaining cash balances. Recognizing the three basic cost categories of short costs, excessive cash costs, and procurement costs, the financial officer has to examine each and minimize the total of all three.

Short costs Short costs rise as the firm holds less and less cash. This is evident when we consider that the firm will more frequently fail to meet its payments schedule and maintain its required compensating balance at the bank if it has lower cash balances. We can see from Figure 12-1(a) that bank-associated short costs are zero if the firm maintains the required compensating bank balance. However, as the firm's cash balance at the bank falls below the required minimum (to the left of point A), the short costs increase, rising quite steeply and at an accelerated rate as the bank cash balances approach zero.

We can see a similar pattern of short costs in Figure 12-1(b), which relates short costs to the cash balances needed to meet the firm's payments schedule. As in the case of the bank short costs, the payments short costs are also zero if we have enough cash to meet all the payments, as at point B. To the left of point B, the payments-associated short costs, such as lost trade discounts, deteriorating credit rating, and an increased cost of financing, rise quite steeply.

We can combine the bank-associated short costs and the payments-associated short costs into one as in Figure 12-1(c), where point C is the total required cash balance (the sum of A plus B). Total short costs rise as we maintain a lower cash balance.

Long costs The costs incurred because the firm has forfeited opportunities for profit by holding rather than investing idle cost are called *long costs.* The opportunity cost increases as the size of the idle cash balance increases. For example, if the firm had excess cash of $100, the forfeited profit at 7 percent would have been only $7 in the

---

[1] W. J. Baumol, "The Transactions Demand for Cash: An Inventory Theoretic Approach," *Quarterly Journal of Economics,* LXV (November 1952), 545–556.

Table 12-1 Cash Budget

Month	First Six Months 19xx					
	1	2	3	4	5	6
Cash receipts						
Cash sales	$200,000	$250,000	$300,000	$300,000	$300,000	$200,000
Accounts receivable collection	—	882,000	1,984,500	2,425,000	2,646,000	2,646,000
Interest received	50,000	—	—	—	—	50,000
Dividends received	—	—	100,000	—	—	100,000
Sale of stock	—	—	—	—	—	8,000,000
Total receipts	250,000	1,132,000	2,384,500	2,725,000	2,946,000	10,996,000
Cash disbursements						
Purchases	50,000	75,000	100,000	100,000	100,000	50,000
Direct labor	300,000	350,000	400,000	400,000	400,000	300,000
Manufacturing overhead	650,000	675,000	700,000	700,000	700,000	650,000
Administrative, distribution and advertising	100,000	100,000	100,000	100,000	100,000	100,000
Raw materials	100,000	150,000	200,000	200,000	200,000	100,000
	—	700,000	750,000	800,000	800,000	800,000
Interest paid	20,000	—	—	—	—	—
Dividends paid	100,000	—	—	100,000	—	—
Installment payments on machinery	—	—	—	—	—	1,000,000
Long-term debt repayment	—	—	—	—	—	4,000,000
Total disbursements	1,320,000	2,050,000	2,250,000	2,400,000	2,300,000	7,000,000

Net receipts (disbursements)	(1,070,000)	(918,000)	134,500	325,000	646,000	3,996,000
Cash on hand beginning of month	2,000,000	1,000,000	1,000,000	1,000,000	1,000,000	1,117,500
Cash on hand end of month	930,000	82,000	1,134,500	1,325,000	1,646,000	5,113,500
Minimum required balance	1,000,000	1,000,000	1,000,000	1,000,000	1,000,000	1,000,000
Short-term financing needs	70,000	918,000	—	—	—	—
Repayment of short-term financing	—	—	134,500	325,000	528,500	—
Short-term borrowing outstanding end of month	70,000	988,000	853,500	528,500	0	0

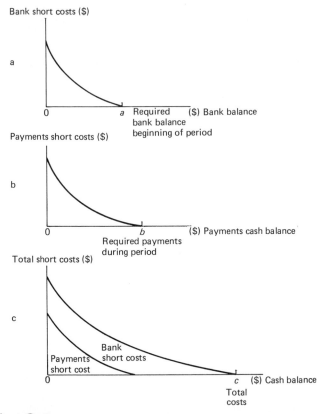

Figure 12-1   Short Costs

year, but would have been $140,000 on $2 million of excess cash. The long costs also increase as the yield on the securities into which the firm could have put its excess cash increases. If the opportunity interest rate were 9 percent, it would be more costly to hold idle cash than if the opportunity interest rate were only 3 percent. We can schematically illustrate the relationship between long costs and the size of the idle balances as shown in Figure 12-2(a). If we have no cash balances (zero on the horizontal axis), there are obviously no long costs because we have invested all our idle funds. As we increase our cash balances (move to the right on the horizontal axis) total long cost increases (on the vertical axis). The long cost associated with our presently maintained cash balances K will be z. In other words at K, our present cash holdings, we have incurred as large a long cost as we could without acquiring more cash and increasing our idle balances. We could decrease the long costs by decreasing our present cash balances (moving to the left of K on the horizontal axis). Since the firm typically sells its least liquid, highest-yield securities first, the total long cost rises more rapidly at first than later when the firm sells its more liquid, lower-yield securities as it moves toward K.

Now, if we wish to increase our cash on hand beyond point K, we have to either (1) sell some temporary investments, converting the securities to cash and incurring extra costs such as the transaction expenses of brokerage fees or even a loss on the sale or (2) borrow additional funds, incurring the extra costs of interest expense, which is typically higher than the firm can obtain on its investments. These extra

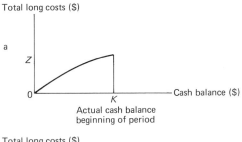

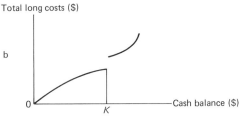

Figure 12-2   Long Costs

costs are reflected in Figure 12-2(b) by the discontinuous rise after point K, where the firm's present cash holding end and increased cash balances must be raised. As the firm continues to raise additional cash beyond its present holdings, it increases the total long costs at an accelerating rate, reflecting the increased cost of borrowing.

Procurement costs   In addition to the short and long costs, we have to consider the procurement costs associated with operating the cash management program. Some one has to supervise the operation. There are clerks and bookkeepers who run the daily routine. There is the overhead of an office. All these costs must also be considered. But they are fixed, which means that at almost any level of cash balances their cost remains constant. There is no way the financial officer can minimize the procurement costs by adjusting the firm's cash balances.

Minimizing total cash management costs   First, let us represent total cash management costs as follows:

$$TC = P + TSC + TLC \tag{12-1}$$

where
TC = total cash management costs
P = procurement costs
TSC = total short costs
TLC = total long costs

We can see this relationship in Figure 12-3, which is Figure 12-1(c) superimposed on Figure 12-2(b). Total cash management cost (TC) is the sum of the LC, and SC, and the P costs. Notice, however, that the short costs decrease as the cash balance increases, while the long costs increase as the cash balance increases. The offsetting effect of the two costs as the cash balances are increased depends on the slope of the two lines (the rate of increase or decrease in each cost). Typically, the reduction in short costs is greater at first than the increase in the long costs as the cash holdings are enlarged, forcing the total cost down. However, after a certain point (in this fig-

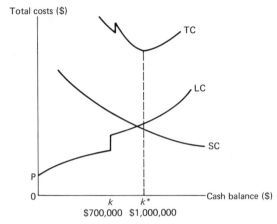

Figure 12-3   Total Cash Management Costs

ure K^*), the long costs start to increase faster than the short costs are reduced—and total costs rise. That low point in the total costs indicates that the firm's optimal cash balance is at K^*, or $1 million. In this figure, K represents the firm's actual cash balance. To attain the ideal level of cash balances, the financial officer would have to sell $K^* - K$ dollars of securities, which in this figure is $300,000. If the optimal cash balance were to the left of K, the financial officer would have to purchase additional securities, reducing the idle cash holdings.

Notice that K^* is at the low point on the total cost curve in Figure 12-3, but that is not necessarily at the intersection of the LC and SC curves. Further, notice that since the procurement costs are fixed, the total cost curve is raised by an amount P along the entire length of the horizontal axis, implying that there is no change in the procurement costs regardless of the level of cash balances.

An example   Table 12-2 reveals how the total cost first declines to a minimum and then rises as the cash balances are increased. The optimal cash balance, where the total cost is minimized, is at $1 million. At cash balances more or less than $1 million, the total is increased.

In this example, the financial officer calculated the long costs as 7 percent on the first $500,000, which reflected the prevailing yield on United States Treasury bills, and at 10 percent on all idle cash balances in excess of $500,000, reflecting the higher long costs associated with raising additional cash balances above that amount. He or she calculated the short costs as the sum of the bank charges, lost trade discounts, and other borrowing costs. Notice that the short costs fall to a relatively small amount as the cash balances become excessive. The procurement costs do not

Table 12-2   Cash Management Costs

Cash Balance	TC	=	P	+	SC	+	LC
$ 500,000	$14,000	=	$3,000	+	$7,500	+	$ 3,500
700,000	13,000	=	3,000	+	4,500	+	5,500
1,000,000	12,500	=	3,000	+	1,000	+	8,500
1,300,000	15,000	=	3,000	+	500	+	11,500
1,500,000	16,600	=	3,000	+	100	+	13,500

change regardless of the size of the cash balance, and total cost is minimized by the offsetting interactions of the short and the long costs. The optimal cash balance used in constructing the cash budget is that which minimizes the total cost of cash management.

Precautionary Cash Balances

We have, up to this point, determined the optimal cash balance where the cost of maintaining those balances is minimized. We have not allowed for any cash cushion to meet unanticipated cash needs. We must now determine the appropriate amount of such precautionary balances. We can look upon them as a safety well of cash to tap when the need arises. The question is how much more cash in addition to the optimal cash balance (K^*) should the financial officer maintain.

In order to answer that question, the financial officer has to (1) estimate, from the firm's experience, what it has previously encountered as unanticipated cash needs above the optimal balance, (2) determine the cost to the firm of not having those precautionary balances to meet the unexpected cash needs when they arise, and (3) determine management's aversion to not meeting unanticipated cash needs.

Estimating the probability of need   The financial officer can estimate the probability that the firm will encounter cash needs above the optimal balance by examining the firm's records for representative periods in the past. For example, in examining the last 10 years for the firm (Table 12-3), you would find that there were typically three separate months in the year during which the cash demands on the firm exceeded the optimal cash balance. Six months of each year saw the cash needs of the firm exactly equal to the optimal balance, while three months of the typical year saw the firm's cash needs well below the optimal balance.

Table 12-3 tells the financial officer that 75 percent of the time there is no need for precautionary balances since the optimal balance has been sufficient. In fact, in one typical month the cash need was $10,000 less than the optimal balance and in two typical months the cash need was $5,000 less than the optimal balance. On the other hand, there is typically one month in the year (8 percent of the time) when the cash needs are $10,000 greater than the optimal balance and two months of the year (16 percent of the time) when the cash needs are $5,000 greater than the optimal cash balance. From this information, we can construct the probability distribution shown in Figure 12-4.

Precautionary balance benefits and costs   The benefits of having precautionary balances are the profit opportunities that suddenly pop up and the costs that the firm avoids in quickly raising funds to meet sudden cash needs. For example, with precautionary cash balances on hand, the firm could take advantage of a quantity

Table 12-3

Number of periods per year	Amount of unanticipated cash needs in excess of K^*
1	$10,000
2	5,000
6	0
2	−5,000
1	−10,000

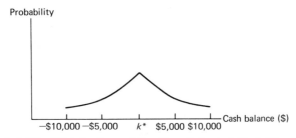

Figure 12-4   Probability Distribution of the Unanticipated Cash Needs

discount offered by its suppliers or meet the additional costs of increased fringe benefits from a recently negotiated labor contract without incurring the costs of borrowing.

The cost of having precautionary balances is the forfeited interest that could otherwise have been earned if those cash balances were invested. The task before the financial officer is to find the optimal level of precautionary cash balances to take advantage of a sufficient number of unanticipated profit opportunities but not to tie up too much cash.

In order to determine what that level is, the financial officer has to weigh the benefits against the costs to find where to maximize the total net profits (benefits minus costs) from holding precautionary balances. We can measure the benefits as follows:

$$B = R \times N \times PCB \qquad (12\text{-}2)$$

where

$B =$ benefits in dollars
$R =$ the average return on the unexpected profit opportunity
$PCB =$ precautionary cash balance level
$N =$ the fraction of a year over which the opportunity occurred

For example, if the average return on the unexpected profit opportunity (R) were 12 percent, the benefits from keeping $5,000 in precautionary balances in our example from Table 12-3 would be:

$$B = .12 \times \text{\textonesuperior/6} \times \$5,000$$
$$= \$100$$

We can measure the cost of the precautionary balances for the year as follows:

$$C = Y \times PCB \qquad (12\text{-}3)$$

where

$C =$ the cost in dollars
$Y =$ the forfeited yield on securities for the period held
$PCB =$ the precautionary balance level

For example, if the forfeited yield were 7 percent, the cost of $5,000 in precautionary balances would be:

$$C = .07 \times \$5,000$$
$$= \$350$$

The period held is assumed to be one year in this case, as this firm does not know the months in which the precautionary balances are needed.

Obviously, in this particular example, the financial officer should not keep $5,000 of precautionary balances, because the net cost to the firm would be $250, the difference between the $100 benefits and the $350 costs. Of course, the financial officer is counting on history repeating itself and producing two profit opportunities at the $5,000 level as revealed in Table 12-3.

The financial officer would perform this analysis at each separate level of precautionary balances and also examine the costs and the benefits of keeping $10,000 in those balances. At that level the profit opportunity which historically has occurred one month in the year would be accessible. The benefit of catching that one opportunity per year would be:

$$B = .12 \times \frac{1}{12} \times \$10,000$$
$$= \$100$$

the cost would be:

$$C = .07 \times \$10,000$$
$$= \$700$$

The net cost on the $10,000 opportunity would have been $600.

The total cost of keeping precautionary balances of $10,000 is, therefore, the $600 on the $10,000 opportunity plus the $250 net cost on the two $5,000 opportunities, for if we keep $10,000 it certainly is enough to take care of the $5,000 opportunities as well. The total cost of the $10,000 level is, in this example, $850. Since both levels of precautionary balances have a higher cost than benefits, the financial officer should not keep any precautionary cash balances on hand.

If the financial officer had decided to increase idle, precautionary balances to the $15,000 level, he or she would have found that there were still no benefits to keeping the larger amount. There were no profit opportunities of that size, while the cost of holding $15,000 in idle precautionary cash balances would have been $1,050 (7 percent of $15,000). The $1,050 net loss would include the total costs of the $5,000 and $10,000 balances.

The financial officer's determination of the benefits and the costs of the various precautionary cash balances are really only the first step. Let us not forget that there are many highly liquid and temporary investments into which the financial officer can put funds. After determining the desirability of a particular level of precautionary balances, as illustrated here, the astute financial officer will invest them in appropriate interest-bearing obligations.

Management's aversion to missed opportunities   In addition to the total net profit at each level of precautionary balances, the financial officer must assess management's aversion to missing profit opportunities. Some managements would actually prefer to have excessively large precautionary balances, above the most profitable level, because they want to meet every emergency cash need. In our example, the very averse management might insist upon holding $15,000 in precautionary balances, despite the cost, because they want to be prepared to meet all future needs, even those greater than ever experienced before. This is an extreme position which you are not likely to encounter, but there are frequent cases of less extreme aversions which have led firms to hold more in precautionary balances than necessary.[2]

---

[2] Montgomery Ward, under the leadership of Sewell Avery, kept tens of millions of dollars in precautionary balances, cutting off the firm's expansion and allowing the leadership in the retail field to pass to Sears, Roebuck and Co. Eventually these excessively large cash balances attracted the attention of corporate raiders who ousted Avery and distributed the cash to the stockholders.

TECHNIQUES FOR LESSENING CASH NEEDS

What specific techniques are available for lessening the firm's need for idle cash balances?

Part of your cash management job is to manage the cash so that the firm can maintain the same level of activity and profitability without using as much cash as before you started managing the cash. As financial officer, you can accomplish this mainly by accelerating collections, slowing disbursements, or other actions which lessen the need for transactions and precautionary idle cash balances.

Accelerating Collections

Any method which accelerates collection lessens the firm's need for cash. As the collection process speeds up, there is more cash coming into the firm's treasury at any time than there previously was. This lessens the need for cash.

Prompt billing One of the simplest methods of accelerating collections is to bill promptly and accurately. A surprisingly large number of firms do not do so. One large department store in New York, for example, actually forgot to bill a substantial number of its customers because of an error in the computerized billing operations, for which, as financial officer, you are responsible. Another department store actually went out of business because its computerized billing system was so inaccurate that no one was billed correctly and no one could figure out who owed what.

Trade discounts Offering a trade discount for early payment frequently speeds collection, as your customers take advantage of the offer. We have already seen that the savings to customers can be substantial on a relatively small discount of, say 2 percent, and they may very well pay early to get that discount. From your point of view the early payments mean that you have less cash tied up in financing the accounts receivable and, therefore, less need for cash balances.

Mechanical procedures The simple enclosure of self-addressed return envelopes with the bill speeds up collection by making it easier for the customer to mail payments and reducing the chance of their going astray because of an incorrect address.

Lock box In order to speed up the collection of accounts receivable and avoid the delays associated with long-distance mailing, the financial officer can arrange to have the payment sent to a *lock box*. A lock box is nothing more than a regional bank payment center located in the area of the customer. The financial officer instructs the customer to mail payment to a nearby post office box from which a regional bank picks it up and deposits it to the firm's account. This saves the mailing time and the check-clearing time, since the post office and the bank are geographically closer than you are to the customer.

Once the bank has picked up the customer's payment and deposited it to the firm's account, it issues you a deposit slip notifying the firm and showing how much is now in the account at that regional bank. If the balance in the account is larger than the firm wishes to maintain or is required to maintain as a compensating balance by the regional bank, it transfers the funds to its own working balances account for use in the firm's operations. Usually, the lock box is only economical if there is a relatively large number of checks to be received in the area because of the expenses attached to maintaining a lock box and establishing regional banking relations.

Regional collection office   Along the same lines as a lock box, the firm might find it more economical to establish a regional office where the firm's customers can send their payments. This also cuts down on the mailing and check-clearing time.

Slowing Disbursements

Any action on the part of the financial officer which slows the disbursement of funds lessens the need for cash balances. Slower payments mean there is less cash going out of the firm's treasury on the average and therefore less need for cash.

Delaying payment   If you are not going to take advantage of any offered trade discounts for early payment, you might as well delay the maximum time since there is no advantage to paying any earlier, provided this practice does not sacrifice the good trade relations the firm has with its suppliers. If your supplier has extended 30-days credit, you should take the entire 30 days at the very minimum, temporarily investing the funds at some positive rate of interest.

Float   It could be several days between the time you write a check and the time it is actually received by your supplier, deposited in the bank, and presented by that bank to your bank for payment against your checking account. That difference between the bank balance and the book balance of your checking account over the period is known as *float*. You still have the use of the funds in your checking account during that period, even though you have written a check against those funds, because your bank has no way of knowing that you have written that check until it is presented to it for payment. For example, if you paid your supplier in San Francisco with a check drawn on a New York City bank, it might take days for the mail to reach San Francisco and several more days before it was deposited and returned to New York for payment against your checking account. In the intervening time you could have temporarily used those funds for other purposes, provided you returned them to the checking account in time to meet the payment.

One technique of using float is the *delay draft*. This check (draft) on your account is not payable until your office has physically examined it and accepted it for payment against your account. So, you could write the check and wait to deposit sufficient funds until it showed up in your office, using that cash elsewhere in the firm's operations in the meantime.

The use of float, however, is becoming increasingly more difficult since the introduction of high-speed electronic communications and data processing systems and the concerted efforts of federal monetary authorities to speed up the process of check-clearing among banks.

Less frequent payrolls   If you meet your payrolls once a month instead of every other week, you slow the disbursements and lessen the cash need. You must be careful, however, not to violate state laws which may require meeting the payroll at least twice in the month.

Reducing the Need for Precautionary Balances

In addition to lessening the need for transactions balances, there are techniques available to you, as the financial officer, for lessening the need for precautionary balances.

Overdraft system   In the overdraft system the bank automatically extends credit to the firm by clearing checks in excess of the amount of cash in the firm's checking account. For this service the bank charges you interest on the money advanced to cover the shortage. Of course, there are limits on the amount that the bank will advance to the firm, but such details are prearranged with the bank.

Lines of credit   The line of credit is a prearranged loan you can draw upon instantly. Instead of keeping idle precautionary balances, you might rely on a line of credit. However, you must weigh the cost of the line of credit against the cost of precautionary balances to determine which is more economical. Typically, banks charge an initial fee for extending the line of credit even if you do not draw upon it—in addition to interest on the amount that you actually do use.

Temporary investments   Instead of holding idle precautionary cash balances, many financial officers maintain reserves in highly liquid securities which they can convert into needed cash at a moment's notice with little chance of loss or expense. In fact, several financial officers claim that alert cash management may allow the financial officer to do away with precautionary cash balances entirely. The presence of highly liquid securities which can be converted to cash on demand has replaced the need for precautionary cash balances in their view. Certainly there is an increasing trend toward using these marketable securities instead of precautionary cash balances, particularly as interest rates on them have risen to historically high levels in excess of 10 percent. As good financial officers, we must be familiar with the more common types of these marketable securities.

MARKETABLE SECURITIES

What marketable securities can the financial officer choose from as a place to temporarily invest any cash balances in excess of the optimal amount for the firm?

There are many such financial instruments (securities), but their basic common characteristic is their temporary nature. The financial officer wants to be able to convert the securities back to cash quickly and with little, if any, loss. In financial terms these features are typically referred to as *liquidity*. Let us explore this and other important characteristics the financial officer might look for in a marketable security before enumerating specific financial instruments.

General Considerations

In addition to liquidity, the financial officer might also examine a security's risk and price volatility to judge the merits of using that security as a temporary haven for excess cash.

Liquidity   The characteristic of liquidity varies among securities. As the degree of liquidity increases, there is an increase in the speed at which the security can be converted into cash without sustaining an appreciable loss from the prevailing market price. We generally find that highly liquid financial instruments have active markets involving many participants (buyers and sellers) who are capable of handling a transaction of your size without a significant drop in the prevailing price. We would also usually find readily available price quotations as to what those participants are presently willing to pay for the security, and we would expect relatively small transactions costs and easy entry by all who wish to participate.

Risk   Since the financial officer wants the funds to be there when needed, he or she is typically unwilling to invest in securities which may default on their promised interest payment or redemption. It is poor cash management, for example, to buy a financial instrument in the expectation that it will mature in time to use the redemption proceeds for your tax payments only to have it default. The financial instrument with the least default risk, essentially zero, is the United States Treasury security. As we move away from that default-free security, the default risk increases along with the prevailing interest rate on the security. The temptation is always before the financial officer to sacrifice safety for a higher return. Some do. But it is typically more prudent in cash management to invest in the less risky securities and sacrifice the additional yield for the sake of safety.

Price volatility   A financial instrument with a high price volatility exposes the firm to a potential loss if the price has dropped since its purchase and the firm must convert. Because the firm's cash management is generally concerned with being able to convert to a particular amount of cash when needed, financial officers tend to shy away from the more volatile securities and use the more stable ones in their cash management. Of course, if financial officers wish to take the chance, they may buy the more price-volatile securities in hopes that the price will have increased by the time the firm needs the cash and has to convert.

Typically, the more price-volatile securities are those with longer maturities. The least volatile securities may have a maturity of one night or just a few days. As the maturity increases to months and to years, the price volatility increases until we get to common stocks, which are the most volatile of all since they have an infinite maturity.

Liquid Marketable Securities

As a financial officer, you must know the common types of securities that you can use in cash management and be familiar with their liquidity, default risk, and price volatility.

Treasury bills   Commonly referred to as T bills, these are the shortest-term securities of the United States Treasury. The typical maturities at issue are 90 and 182 days although there are less frequent issues of 6 months and 1 year. Of course, as the T bills approach maturity, they can be purchased from prior owners in the secondary market with maturities as short as a few days.

T bills are highly liquid instruments with a large, well organized secondary market, small transactions costs, and easy entry for orders exceeding $100,000.

There is no default risk because they are the direct obligation of the United States government. T bills have little price volatility because of their short maturities, compared to the longer-term treasury securities such as notes, certificates, and bonds (up to 30-year terms).

T bills are traded on a discounted basis, which means that the interest is computed as the difference between the price you have paid and the $1,000 per bill you get at redemption. If you paid $990 for a 3-month bill, your effective interest rate would be $10 on a $990 investment. At an annual rate based on the traditional 360-day year used when computing the implied yield, that return is 4.04 percent. We can observe this in the daily government securities price quotations in our newspapers as the bid yield and asked yield, where the *bid yield* is based on the prevailing price that buyers are willing to pay and the *asked yield* is based on the prevailing price sellers are willing to accept. Since the market buyers are always willing to pay less than the market sellers are willing to accept, the bid price (yield) is always lower (higher) than the asked price (yield) until they agree on a transaction price.

Tax anticipation bills (TAB) TABs are very similar to T bills except that they are accepted by the United States Treasury as payment for taxes, and consequently the difference between the price paid and the $1,000 each TAB is worth for tax payments is free of federal taxes. For example, if you buy the TAB for $990 and use it to pay $1,000 of your tax bill, it is as if you were getting a $10 reduction on your tax liability. Since they are used mainly for tax purposes, they usually mature within one week after the quarterly tax date and are usually issued by the United States Treasury, although public agencies backed by the federal or state government are sometimes empowered to issue them.

The TAB liquidity, default risk, price volatility, and trading basis are identical to those of the T bill.

Federal agency obligations These are generally short-term obligations of such federal agencies as the Veteran's Administration, Housing and Urban Development, Federal Home Loan Bank Board, and the Bank for Cooperatives, among others. All these agencies are empowered by the government to sell their securities in the open market in order to raise funds to channel to particular groups within the society. For example, the Federal Home Loan Bank Board raises funds to lend to savings and loan associations in order to encourage mortgage lending.

These agencies' obligations have a relatively high degree of liquidity with a large secondary market and readily available price quotations, which we can observe, in many cases, in the daily newspapers. The default risk is relatively small since payment of interest and principal are guaranteed by the United States Treasury, yet most market participants consider them slightly more risky than the T bill or other direct obligations of the government. The price volatility among the shorter-term instruments of these agencies is very similar to the T bill, although the longer-term maturities these agencies issue tend to fluctuate substantially more.

They are traded on a yield-to-maturity basis, rather than on the discounted basis characteristic of T bills and TABs.

Bankers' acceptances Bankers' acceptances are simply checks (drafts) payable at some future date and guaranteed (accepted) as to payment at that future date by a bank. They usually originate in the course of international trade when a check on the account of an importer is drawn to the order of an exporter. When the bank accepts the check against the account of the importer (usually secured by a line of credit for the importer at the accepting bank), it becomes a negotiable instrument. It is then sold by the exporter to whose order it is drawn at a discount from the face value to financial officers who use them in their cash management and who present them to the guaranteeing bank for payment upon the due date.

The liquidity of these bankers' acceptances is very high and a large, well organized secondary market exists where they can be purchased or sold. The market is easily entered by those financial officers who want to deal in them, although acceptances generally range from $25,000 to $1 million each.

The default risk is relatively small since the bank stands behind the payment and is obligated to make good if the issuer of the check defaults. Of course, you should be familiar with the guarantor bank. There are a very few banks who may be unable to honor their own guarantee, and occasional fraudulent guarantees have been encountered.

Commercial paper   Commercial paper consists of the unsecured promissory notes of larger corporations, such as the General Motors Acceptance Corporation, the financing subsidiary of General Motors. In addition to the financing companies, which are large users of commercial paper, many industrial concerns also issue "paper." The larger firms tend to sell their paper directly to such buyers as financial officers by announcing a forthcoming sale and the effective yield on that issue. If, as a financial officer, you are interested in purchasing part of the issue, you must contact the issuer. The smaller issuers tend to sell (place) their paper through dealers who buy it from them and resell it to financial officers and others.

The secondary market is rather limited, and the paper is rather illiquid. If you use commercial paper in your cash management, you should be prepared to hold it until it matures, which ranges from 30 days to as much as 1 year. (Issues over 270 days are unusual because they must be registered with the Securities and Exchange Commission.)

The default risk had been thought to be very low since the paper was issued only by the most creditworthy corporations and was usually rated as to quality by an independent rating agency. However, the collapse of the Penn Central saw many large and sophisticated purchasers of its commercial paper take total losses in their holdings despite the high quality rating which had been accorded the Penn Central paper. The lesson to be learned by a good financial officer is not to rely solely on the credit rating and to remember that commercial paper does have its risks. Reflecting those risks, the yield on paper is usually 1.5–2 percent higher than the yield on T bills.

The price volatility is larger than on other short-term instruments because of the poor secondary market, which frequently forces a financial officer who must convert the paper to cash before its maturity date to take a loss. The paper is sold on a discounted basis as are T bills.

Repurchase agreements   Repurchase agreements, or "repos" as they are called in the trade, are negotiated arrangements whereby the financial officer agrees to buy some of a security dealer's inventory of a particular security for a specified number of days. The security dealer, *at the same time,* agrees to buy them back from the financial officer at the end of the specified period for a slightly higher price. In effect the difference between the prices represents the interest to the firm. Such agreements are usually arranged between the firm and a government bond dealer and involve Treasury securities, although the principles can be applied to any type of dealer and any type of security.

The liquidity is very high since the arrangement is self-liquidating. The firm has a guaranteed resale at a known price. And, importantly to the financial officer, the repro can be tailored to the firm's specific needs at the time. Repros have been arranged for as short a term as overnight.

The default risk is slight since, if the dealer cannot buy back the securities as agreed, the firm can sell the securities which were given to it as collateral. Since the prices are fixed at the time of negotiation there is no price volatility.

Negotiable certificates of deposit   Certificates of deposits (CDs) are time deposits at banks, the ownership of which is evidenced by a certificate instead of a passbook. Typically the CD has a maturity of under one year although, since they can be individually negotiated, the exact term can be any length the bank agrees to. CDs with maturities over 90 days and in excess of $100,000 are, under present banking regulations, totally negotiable as to the interest rate the bank will pay. During periods of tight money when the banks need funds, the rate can be relatively high and has been as much as 3½–4 percent higher than the yield on T bills.

The liquidity of CDs is thinner than that of T bills, even though most of them are negotiable and can be resold, because the secondary market is not as fully developed. If, as a financial officer, you purchase CDs you should plan to hold them until maturity.

The default risk is generally slight since this is a direct obligation of the bank probably insured by the Federal Deposit Insurance Corporation (FDIC) for up to $40,000. However, the bank's guarantee is only as good as the bank itself. If the bank defaults, as a very few have, you may never get all of your money back, and you may even wait awhile until the FDIC pays you the amount that they had insured.

The price of a negotiable CD tends to move up and down with other market instruments of the same maturity. However, because of the lack of a good secondary market, a forced conversion to cash may drop the price below what might be expected to prevail in relation to the yield on other similar securities with a better secondary market.

Eurodollars Eurodollars are time deposits in foreign banks or foreign branches of United States banks. They are denominated in dollars instead of the local currency. Thus, if the London branch of a New York bank were paying a higher rate for time deposits than its parent in New York, you, as financial officer, could wire a time deposit to that branch, creating a Eurodollar deposit. As in the case of United States domestic bank CDs, the maturities and the interest rate are negotiable between you and the London bank. While the typical term is less than a year, it has been known to approach ten years.

The liquidity of Eurodollar deposits is somewhat limited since an organized secondary market is still developing, but some participants in the market make a practice of buying Eurodollar deposits before they reach maturity. The price of Eurodollars tends to move in tandem with other international money-market rates and particularly with interest rates at New York banks. Occasionally, if United States domestic banks are strapped for funds, the Eurodollar rate will move up substantially higher than the domestic market rate for similar maturities, as the United States banks turn to overseas sources to borrow dollars at higher rates than they may be allowed to pay under United States banking regulations.

The default risk varies among the banks, to whom you must turn for payment. If the bank defaults, you will probably suffer a substantial loss. It is always best to know your bank.

Federal funds Federal Funds are simply overnight loans to banks that use them to meet the reserve requirements established for the banks by banking authorities. Entry into the market is restricted to amounts of $500,000 or more. You can either place the funds directly with a bank, who might contact you if you have spread the word that you do lend, or arrange the loan through a dealer.

The liquidity of Federal Funds is high since it is a self-liquidating, overnight loan repaid the next day into your checking account. The default risk is slight since the term is so short, and it is highly unlikely you will be a creditor of that bank on the night it defaults. There is no price volatility since at the time of the loan you are given a deposit, good the next day at the bank. The deposit is slightly higher than the loan, and the difference is your effective interest.

Foreign treasury bills   These are very similar to United States Treasury bills except that they are issued by foreign governments and denominated in foreign currency. United Kingdom treasury bills are examples of foreign T bills. Sometimes they are attractive because of a higher yield than on domestic T bills, but you always have to be careful of fluctuations in the conversion price of the foreign currency back into United States dollars, since the foreign bills are denominated in foreign currency.

The liquidity of foreign T bills is quite high in larger money market centers such as London, where there are many active dealers in the security. The T bills of foreign countries with smaller international financial centers are, of course, less liquid.

The risk of default is quite slim if the government is solid. Of course, the Treasury bills of an unstable government are no more default-free than those of a nearly bankrupt corporation. And there is always foreign exchange risk associated with foreign T bills. For example, if between the time you purchased the United Kingdom bill and the time you want to convert back into cash and United States dollars, the British pound had been devalued 5 percent against the dollar, your effective interest rate would have been reduced by 5 percent. If the United Kingdom bill yielded 13 percent, your actual yield would be only 8 percent after the devaluation loss. We will see in Chapter 24 how you might protect yourself from a potential devaluation.

Local agency short-term tax-exempt notes   Frequently, such local agencies as regional urban redevelopment and housing authorities issue short-term notes. The interest on these notes is not taxed by the federal government since it cannot tax another governmental authority.

The secondary market for these local agency notes is rather well developed and relatively easy to enter. The denominations of the notes range from $1,000 to $1 million. Their liquidity is high. Their default record has been good, with relatively few defaults. Their prices tend to move in line with those of other short-term, highly liquid instruments, such as T bills.

Less Liquid Marketable Securities

Despite their lack of liquidity, there are marketable securities with longer maturities which the financial officer may, on infrequent occasions, want to use in cash management. As long as you are willing to expose your firm to the risk that the price of the security when you convert it back to cash may be less than what you originally paid for it, you can use any security regardless of its term. However, these less liquid financial instruments are typically not used in cash management because of that risk.

Corporate bonds   Corporate bonds are the longer-term debt obligations of firms. The average maturity at issue is approximately 20–30 years. As time passes and the maturity date approaches, the bond takes on the characteristics of shorter-term corporate obligations.

Since there is such a large number of issuers and bonds to choose from, their liquidity and default risk tend to be quite varied. Larger issues of the more well known firms traded on an organized bond exchange such as the New York Bond

Exchange unit of the New York Stock Exchange tend to be the most liquid, although certainly nowhere near as liquid as T bills. Smaller issues traded on something other than an organized bond exchange may have no functioning secondary market whatsoever.

The default risk also varies among the companies who issue these bonds and ranges all the way from highest quality to total default. The independent bond rating agencies have tried to capture the varying degrees of quality in synopsis form. For example, Standard and Poor's *Bond Guide*[3] rates the bonds according to the following categories:

AAA	highest grade
AA	almost as good as AAA
A	upper medium grade
BBB	medium grade
BB	lower medium grade
B	speculative
CCC-CC	outright speculation
C	income bonds on which no interest is being paid
DDD-D	bonds in default with various degrees of recovery prospects

As a financial officer, you would probably never have occasion to use any bond rated lower than A, particularly in cash management.

Since the maturity of these bonds tends to be lengthy, they have the highest degree of price volatility among debt securities. If forced to convert at a time when interest rates were high, you would probably suffer a loss, which could be considerable. Some price fluctuations in recent years have been as much as 25 percent of the bond's value, for example. Of course, the opportunity to profit is also there, but in cash management, the emphasis is more on safety of principal than on speculative profit.

Preferred stocks Preferred stocks, as we shall see in Chapter 21, are fixed claims on the earnings of the firm and on a particular amount of assets in liquidation prior to the common stock's claim on those after-tax earnings. As with corporate bonds, the liquidity of the issue varies with its size and with trading on an organized exchange. But, even a large issue traded on the New York Stock Exchange is typically highly illiquid.

The default risk varies with the quality of the issuer in much the same manner as the risk of long-term corporate bonds, and the price volatility is large, fluctuating with the general level of interest rates.

Common stock Common stock represents the residual, and by far the least certain, claim on the firm's earnings. The liquidity of any particular issue of common stock depends on the size of the issue, the number of active participants in the market for the stock, and where the stock is traded. A large issue actively traded on the New York Stock Exchange may be relatively liquid up to a certain number of shares. But if the number of shares you want to sell is large in relation to the typical number traded, the market is illiquid and you will have to suffer a significant drop from the prevailing price in order to entice enough potential purchasers of the security to buy it.

---

[3] Standard and Poor's *Bond Guide*, p. 6.

Default risk varies among the corporations issuing the stock, ranging from highest quality issues, such as American Telephone and Telegraph common, to speculative issues. Since common stocks have an infinite life, they have the greatest price volatility of any security. Of course, along with all the risk, there is a possibility of large capital gains. However, it must be emphasized again that it is usually more prudent in cash management to preserve the principal than to speculate for large capital gains.

Equipment trust certificates   These are financial instruments traditionally issued by railroads to finance their acquisitions of rolling stock (freight cars). The certificate represents a lien (claim) on or ownership of the rolling stock. They are not very liquid, as there is no well developed secondary market, but they have had an exceptionally good record of not defaulting. Though typically issued with longer-term maturities, they are sometimes given shorter maturities that might be convenient for your cash management program.

Municipal securities   Municipal securities are the debt obligations of local and state governments, and they are usually tax-exempt so that, in effect, their after-tax yield is double that of the coupon payment to a corporation in the 50 percent tax bracket. For example, a 5 percent tax-free interest rate is equivalent to a 10 percent taxable interest rate. Most municipal securities are highly illiquid, particularly in large quantity. The default risk varies among the issuers, and the price tends to fluctuate with the general movement in interest rates.

SUMMARY

After having read Chapter 12, you should be able to answer these questions:
1. What are cash and marketable securities?
Cash is comprised of currency and demand deposits in the form of checking accounts at your bank. The vast majority of cash is in the form of demand deposits. Marketable securities are financial instruments that can be resold by a prior owner. In cash management, the financial officer emphasizes the more liquid marketable securities, which are characterized by their quick convertibility into cash at a price relatively close to the prevailing market price.
2. What is the financial officer's objective in cash and marketable securities management?
The objective is really twofold. As the financial officer responsible for cash management, it is your job to see that the firm has sufficient cash on hand to meet its payments schedule. It is also your job to see that the firm's investment in cash is minimized, because idle cash balances do not earn anything for the firm.
3. What specific factors must the financial officer examine to determine the firm's needed cash balance?
First, the financial officer must synchronize the firm's cash inflows and outflows as effectively as possible. This is done through the use of a cash budget which reflects the financial officer's forecasting accuracy for each of the subperiods (typically one month) within the planning horizon (typically one year).
Second, the financial officer has to estimate the short costs, the long costs, and the procurement costs associated with the cash management as well as the firm's aversion to the uncertainty of the cashflows. We saw that short costs arose whenever

the firm failed to maintain an adequate level of cash to meet its payments schedule and had to draw down its checking account balances below the required compensating balance level, convert some marketable securities to cash, or borrow. We saw that long costs arise whenever the firm has cash balances which are not invested. As the size of the firm's idle cash balances rise, its short costs decline because it has fewer shortfalls, but its long costs rise, because it has more idle cash. Procurement costs remain constant at all levels of idle cash balances because they are essentially fixed.

4. How does the financial officer determine the optimal cash balance?

If the financial officer minimizes the total costs, both long and short, the optimal cash balance appears at that point. If the actual cash balance is larger than the optimal, the idle balances should be reduced by investing the excess amount, and vice versa.

5. How does the financial officer determine the optimal level of precautionary balances for the firm?

The optimal level of precautionary balances depends on the firm's historical experience of unexpected cash needs, management's willingness to experience shortfalls because of these unexpected cash needs, and the net benefits to holding idle precautionary balances. The optimal level of precautionary balances is where the net benefits of holding those balances are maximized.

6. What specific techniques do financial officers have for lessening the firm's cash needs?

Basically, they can either accelerate collections or slow disbursements. Acceleration techniques included the use of lock boxes, regional payment offices, prompt and accurate billing, and trade discounts for early payment. Slowing techniques included the use of float and delay drafts. To lessen the need for idle precautionary cash balances, the financial officer can arrange lines of credit or an overdraft agreement with the firm's bank and can use marketable securities.

7. What marketable securities are available to the financial officer in his or her cash management strategy?

There are many common financial instruments which are relatively liquid and can be used in the firm's cash management. Among these are T bills, tax anticipation notes, commercial paper, bankers' acceptances, repurchase agreements, Federal Funds, foreign T bills, and Eurodollars.

QUESTIONS

12-1 Explain why the firm's demand deposits, or bank checking accounts, are considered a cash asset rather than a marketable security.

12-2 What are the two conflicting objectives of cash management?

12-3 What are some of the explicit and implicit costs to the firm resulting from nonsynchronization of cash inflows and outflows?

12-4 Distinguish between short costs, long costs, and procurement costs, giving examples of each.

12-5 Explain why the total cost schedule (see Figure 12-3) is generally thought to be U-shaped. What is the effect of an increase in procurement costs on the optimal level of cash balances?

12-6 Briefly define the following terms:
   (a) Lock box   (c) Float
   (b) Trade discount   (d) Line of credit

12-7 The "asked yield" and "bid yield" on United States Treasury bills is given daily in the financial section of most newspapers. What do these expressions mean and how do they differ?

12-8 Suppose your firm has excess cash reserves of $100,000 for a three-day period. What marketable securities might you consider as a source of temporary profits?

12-9 What factors might contribute to the yield differential between foreign treasury bills and United States Treasury bills?

PROBLEMS

12-1 The Bolcon Company has analyzed its short costs (SC), long costs (LC) and procurement costs (PC) for various levels of cash balances (K) and found that the following equations accurately describe the various costs at given levels of cash balances:

$$SC = \$10,000 - 2K - .0007K^2$$
$$LC = .5K + .0008K^2$$
$$PC = \$20,000$$

(a) What is the approximate optimal level of cash balances (K^*) the firm should maintain? What is the total cost (TC) at K^*? Graphically illustrate the above relationships. (Hint: Let K be 6,500; 7,000; 7,500; 8,000; and 8,500. Then find the TC at each level of K.)

(b) If the SC function is redefined as:

$$SC = \$15,000 - 2K - .0007K^2$$

what is the effect on the optimal level of K^*? On TC at K^*?

(c) If PC increased to $30,000 what would be the effect on K^*? On TC at K^*?

12-2 Bolcon is concerned with the level of precautionary cash balances it should maintain in addition to the optimal cash balances (K^*) from question 12-1. A review of the past twelve months illustrates the relation of K^* to the actual cash balances needed (K):

Number of Months	$K - K^*$
1	3,000
3	1,500
4	0
3	-1,500
1	-3,000

The average return on the unexpected profit opportunities is 10 percent while the opportunity cost of the cash balances is 8 percent.

(a) Graph the probability distribution of the unanticipated cash balances needed by Bolcon.

(b) What is the optimal level of precautionary cash balances above K^*?

(c) If the opportunity cost of cash balances was 12 percent, and the average profit return 10 percent, what is the optimal level of precautionary cash balances above K^*?

12-3 At the present time the Zapco Company has a centralized billing system. That is, both billings and customer payments originate and return to one locality. On the average, it takes four days for the customer's payment to reach the central office and another full day until the payment is deposited and recorded at Zapco's bank. The daily average payments received are $250,000.

Zapco is considering initiating a lock box system that will speed up mail delivery of customers' payments and bank deposits to one and a half days.

(a) What would the reduction in cash balances be if the lock box system was initiated?

(b) If Zapco has a 7 percent profit opportunity on its short-term investment instruments, what is the opportunity cost of maintaining the central billing and payments system?

(c) If the net annual cost of the lock box system is $40,000, should the system be implemented?

BIBLIOGRAPHY

Anderson, Clay J. "Managing the Corporate 'Money' Position." *Business Review.* Federal Reserve Bank of Philadelphia, Philadelphia, March 1961, 3–10.

Archer, Stephen H. "A Model for the Determination of Firm Cash Balances." *Journal of Financial and Quantitative Analysis,* I (March 1966), 1–11.

Baumol, William J. "The Transactions Demand for Cash: An Inventory Theoretic Approach." *Quarterly Journal of Economics,* LXV (November 1952), 545–556.

Bierman, Harold, Jr. and Alan K. McAdams. *Management Decisions for Cash and Marketable Securities.* Graduate School of Business, Cornell University, Ithaca, N. Y., 1962.

Calman, Robert F. *Linear Programming and Cash Management/CASHALPHA.* The M.I.T. Press, Cambridge, Mass., 1968.

DeSalvo, Alfred. "Cash Management Converts Dollars Into Working Assets." *Harvard Business Review,* 50 (May–June 1972), 92–100.

Eppen, Gary D., and Eugene F. Fama. "Solutions for Cash-Balance and Simple Dynamic Portfolio Problems." *Journal of Business,* XLI, 1 (January 1968), 94–112.

Jeffers, James R., and Jere Kevon. "A Portfolio Approach to Corporate Demands for Government Securities." *Journal of Finance,* XXIV (December 1969), 905–920.

King, Alfred M. *Increasing the Productivity of Company Cash.* Prentice-Hall, Englewood Cliffs, N. J., 1969, Chs. 4 and 5.

"Lock Box Banking—Key to Faster Collections." *Credit and Financial Management,* LXIX (June 1967), 16–21.

Miller, M. H., and Daniel Orr. "The Demand for Money by Firms: Extension of Analytic Results." *Journal of Finance,* XXIII (December 1968), 735–759.

Miller, M. H., and Daniel Orr. "A Model of the Demand for Money by Firms." *Quarterly Journal of Economics,* LXXX (August 1966), 413–435.

Neave, Edwin H. "The Stochastic Cash-Balance Problem with Fixed Costs for Increases and Decreases." *Management Science,* 16 (March 1970), 472–490.

Orgler, Yair E. *Cash Management: Methods and Models.* Wadsworth Publishing Co., Belmont, Calif., 1970.

Orgler, Yair E. "An Unequal-Period Model for Cash-Management Decisions." *Management Science,* 16 (October 1969), 77–92.

Reed, Ward L. "Profits From Better Cash Management." *Financial Executive,* XL (May 1972), 40–57.

Soldofsky, Robert M., and Dennis R. Schwartz. "How Companies Manage Cash." *Financial Executive,* XL (October 1972), 40–46.

Sprenkle, Case M. "The Uselessness of Transactions Demand Models." *The Journal of Finance,* XXIV (December 1969), 835–848.

White, D. J., and J. M. Norman. "Control of Cash Reserves." *Operational Research Quarterly,* XVI, 3 (September 1965).

Appendix 12A **Cash Management Models**

What attempts have financial people made to provide a more precise analytical model for cash management? As financial officers we do not necessarily have to follow the models exactly, but let us see what they tell us about how cash management should be conducted.

BAUMOL MODEL

In his model, William J. Baumol tries to determine the minimum cost amount of cash (C) that the financial officer can obtain by converting securities to cash, considering the cost of conversion and the counterbalancing cost of keeping idle cash balances which otherwise could have been invested in marketable securities.[1]

The Costs

What are the costs which Baumol feels are associated with cash management and which have to be minimized?

1. The cost of converting from marketable securities to cash, which he assumes to be fixed at an amount b, must be minimized. These conversions costs are incurred each time a conversion from marketable securities to cash takes place and are assumed to be independent of the size of the transaction. However, the total conversion costs increase with the number of times conversion takes place, which, if the total transactions cash needs for the period were T, would be $\frac{T}{C}$ times. That is, the total transactions needs divided by the dollar value of the marketable securities sold at each conversion gives us the number of conversions per period. The total conversions costs per period are then the number of conversions, $\frac{T}{C}$, multiplied by the cost per conversion, b, or:

$$\frac{Tb}{C}$$

2. The lost opportunity cost which is derived from the forfeited interest rate (i) that could have been earned on the investment of the cash balances is the second cost. The total lost opportunity cost is the interest rate times the average cash balances kept by the firm.

The total cost to be minimized, according to Baumol, is the sum of these two costs, but before we can determine the conversion amount which leads to that minimization, we must determine the amount of cash the firm, on average, keeps in idle cash balances for transaction purposes so that we can compute the total lost opportunity cost.

---

[1] William J. Baumol, "The Transactions Demand for Cash: An Inventory Theoretic Approach," *Quarterly Journal of Economics,* LXV (November 1952), 545–556.

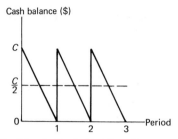

Figure 12A-1   The Firm's Cash Outflow Pattern

The Average Cash Balance

Baumol assumed a constant and certain pattern for the firm's cash outflows, as illustrated in Figure 12A-1. We can see from that figure that the firm has regular and certain cash needs over the period. At the beginning of each period, the firm starts with a cash balance of C, which it gradually spends until at the end of the period it has a zero cash balance and must replenish its cash supply back to the level of C.

Over any single period, then, the firm has an average cash balance which is the sum of the beginning cash balance (C) plus the ending cash balance (zero) divided by 2. Using the notation of Figure 12A-1, we can represent the average cash balance as:

$$\frac{C + 0}{2} \text{ or } \frac{C}{2}$$

The average lost-opportunity cost is, therefore,

$$i\left(\frac{C}{2}\right)$$

Determining the Optimal Conversion Amount

Now, Baumol asks: Why keep all that beginning cash balance during the entire period when you do not need it all at the beginning of the period? For example, if the period were one thirty-day month, you would need only one-thirtieth of the beginning cash balance each day. This means if you withdrew only one-thirtieth of the entire amount, you could leave the rest in interest-earning securities. On the one-thirtieth of the cash not needed to the last day of the month, you could earn twenty-nine days' interest. On the one-thirtieth of the cash not needed until the next to the last day of the month, you could earn twenty-eight days' interest, and so on.

The total costs to be minimized are, therefore, the sum of the total conversion costs plus the lost-opportunity cost of not investing the cash until needed in interest-bearing instruments. We can express this as:

$$TC = i\left(\frac{C}{2}\right) + \frac{bT}{C} \tag{12A-1}$$

The cash withdrawal which costs the least—the optimal conversion amount (C^*)—is calculated through the calculus[2] as:

$$C^* = \sqrt{\frac{2bT}{i}} \qquad (12A\text{-}2)$$

Implications for the Financial Officer

Baumol's solution in Equation 12A-2 shows that the optimal withdrawal (C^*) is a direct function of the square root of the conversion costs (bT) and an inverse function of the opportunity interest rate (i). This implies that as the total cash needs for transactions (T) rises because of additional projects and expanded sales, the optimal withdrawal increases less than proportionally. This is so because of the economies of scale which can be achieved in cash management. Each project does not need its own additional cash balances. It only needs enough added to the general cash balances of the corporation to facilitate the expanded operations.

On the other hand, as the opportunity interest rate (i) increases, the optimal cash withdrawal decreases as the square root function implies in Equation 12A-2. This is so because as i increases it is more costly to forfeit the investment opportunity, and financial officers want to keep as much cash invested in securities for as long as possible. They can afford to do this at the higher interest rates because at those higher rates any shortfall costs caused by a lower withdrawal are offset.

Before leaving the model, let us note that it is a very simplistic one which might mislead us. The model's assumptions of certainty and regularity of withdrawal do not really reflect the situation as we would most probably find it in the actual operations of the firm. The model is concerned only with transaction balances and not with precautionary balances. The assumed fixed cost nature of the withdrawals is also not particularly realistic. Nevertheless the model does clearly and concisely demonstrate the economies of scale and the counteracting nature of the conversion and lost-opportunity costs, major considerations in any financial officer's cash management strategy.

MILLER-ORR MODEL

In order to make the Baumol model more realistic, Miller and Orr (MO)[3] suggested that the cash balances of the firm resemble those in Figure 12A-2 more than they resemble the uniform and certain levels of Baumol's model (Figure 12A-1). We can

[2]
$$\frac{\delta TC}{C} = \frac{i}{2} - \frac{bT}{C^2}$$

$$0 = \frac{i}{2} - \frac{bT}{C^2}$$

$$\frac{bT}{C^2} = \frac{i}{2}$$

$$C^2 = \frac{2bT}{i}$$

$$C^* = \sqrt{\frac{2bT}{i}}$$

[3] M. H. Miller and D. Orr, "A Model of the Demand for Money in Firms," *Quarterly Journal of Economics*, LXXX (August 1966), 413–435.

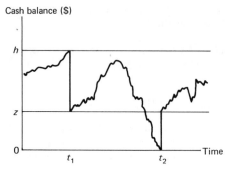

Figure 12A-2   Random Cash Balances

see from Figure 12A-2 that MO have assumed that the cash balances randomly fluctuate between an upper bound (h) and a lower bound (0). When the cash balances hit the upper bound, the firm has too much cash and should buy enough securities to bring the cash balances back to the optimal bound (z). Specifically, the financial officer has to buy $h - z$ dollars of securities, returning the firm's cash balances to the z boundary, as represented by the straight vertical drop in the cash balances line from h to z at time t_1. When the cash balances hit 0 at time t_2, the financial officer must return them to the optimal bound (z) by selling (converting to cash) $z - 0$ dollars of securities, as represented by the straight vertical rise in the cash balances line from 0 to z at time t_2.

The objective of cash management, according to MO, is to determine the optimal cash balance level (z), which minimizes the cost of cash management. MO express the costs as follows:

$$C = \frac{bE(N)}{t} + iE(M) \qquad (12A\text{-}3)$$

where

b = the fixed costs per conversion
$E(M)$ = the expected average daily cash balance
$E(N)$ = the expected number of conversions
t = the number of days in the period
i = the lost-opportunity costs
C = total cash management costs

As in the Baumol model, the optimal cash balance level (z^*) can be determined through the calculus as:

$$z^* = \sqrt[3]{\frac{3b\sigma^2}{4i}} \qquad (12A\text{-}4)$$

where

σ^2 = the variance of the daily changes in the firm's cash balances

Equation 12A-4 tells the financial officer that the optimal cash balance is a direct function of the cube root of the conversion cost and the variance in the daily balances and the inverse function of the cube root of the lost-opportunity interest rate. As in the Baumol model, there are economies of scale in cash management, and the two basic costs of conversion and lost interest that have to be minimized.

MO go on to further specify the optimal upper boundary (h^*) as three times the optimal cash balance level, such that:

$$h^* = 3z^* \tag{12A-5}$$

In a later suggestion,[4] they also maintain that the financial officer could consider the use of less liquid, potentially more profitable securities as investments for the firm's cash balances in excess of h^*.

ORGLER'S MODEL

Orgler suggests that an optimal cash management strategy can be determined through the use of a multiple linear programming model. The model, according to Orgler,[5] would have to be constructed in three sections: (1) selection of the appropriate planning horizon, (2) selection of the appropriate decision variables, and (3) formulation of the cash management strategy itself. The advantage of the linear programming model is that it lets the financial officer coordinate the optimal cash management strategy with the other operations of the firm, such as production, and with loan restrictions on working capital balances.

Horizon Selection

Orgler basically resorts to a one-year planning horizon with twelve monthly periods because of its simplicity, although he probably would have preferred to have a less subjectively chosen horizon. However, as long as the equations and constraints used in the linear programming model "incorporate the decision variables from several periods" such that the cashflow equations from each period reflect the prior periods' cashflows, the selected horizon is appropriate. In other words, Orgler wants to be sure that the operations of the firm in earlier periods are accurately reflected in the periods in which the associated cashflow will occur. For example, we have already seen that there is a lag of up to several months between the time of the sale and the cash inflow when the accounts receivable are collected.

Decision Variables

Orgler has four basic sets of decision variables which impact the firm's cash management and which must be incorporated into the linear programming model. These are: (1) the firm's payments schedule, (2) the firm's short-term financing, (3) the firm's purchase and sale of marketable securities, and (4) the cash balance itself. We shall see that the optimal payments schedule is derived along with the other decision variables when the model is solved. The cash balance is the minimal cash balance required and serves to constrain the model, meaning that the solution will not allow us to fall below that minimum cash balance, which according to Orgler can be either the average daily minimum cash balance over the entire planning horizon of one year or the absolute minimum at each monthly period. Of course, the model also assumes that cash balances in excess of the required minimum do not earn any profit.

---

[4] *Ibid.,* "The Demand for Money by Firms: Extension of Analytical Results," *Journal of Finance,* December 1968, 735–759.

[5] Yair E. Orgler, *Cash Management: Methods and Models,* Wadsworth Publishing Co., Belmont, Calif., 1970.

The Formulation of the Model

The formulation of the model requires that the financial officer first specify an objective function and then specify a set of constraints. We shall also explore the interpretation of the dual and an example of the model.

The objective function   Orgler's objective function is to "minimize the horizon value of the net revenues from the cash budget over the entire planning period." Using the assumptions that all revenue generated is immediately reinvested and that any cost is immediately financed, the objective function represents the value of the net income from the cash budget at the horizon "by adding the net returns over the planning period." Thus, the objective function recognizes each operation of the firm that generates cash inflow or cash outflow as adding or subtracting profit opportunities for the firm from its cash management operations. In the objective function, decision variables which cause inflows, such as payments on accounts receivable, have positive coefficients, while decision variables which generate cash outflows, such as the interest on short-term borrowings, have negative coefficients. The purchase of marketable securities would, for example, produce revenue and thus have a positive coefficient, while the sale of those securities would incur conversion costs and have a negative coefficient.

The constraints   Orgler's suggested constraints could be either institutional or policy constraints. The institutional constraints are those imposed upon the firm by external forces such as a bank-required compensating balance. Policy constraints are imposed upon the firm's cash management by the firm itself. For example, an internally imposed constraint might prohibit the financial officer from selling securities until they mature. Either constraint can occur in the model during one monthly period or over several or all the months in the one-year planning horizon.

An example of the constraints which we shall use in the model is the payments constraint that says we can control our accounts payable policy to conform to such things as the taking of early-payment trade discounts. The financing constraint might exclude the conversion of marketable securities as a source of funds, since that is a separate decision variable. The cash balance constraint could prohibit the firm from holding less cash than the required minimum. The cashflows themselves would be constrained such that the cash balances at the beginning of the period plus all cash inflows minus all cash outflows during the period would equal the cash balance at the end of the period.

The duals   Although we will not specifically explore the dual here in this cash management model (see Appendix 6A), we should at least point out that a linear programming model for cash budgeting such as Orgler's does have a dual which provides valuable information to the financial officer. Since each dual reflects the marginal impact of the financial officer's action in relaxing or tightening a particular constraint on the objective function, we can judge—or prejudge—the effect of our cash management strategy and possibly take action to improve the profit potential of our cash management. For example, the dual of the minimum required cash balance constraint gives the financial officer the opportunity cost of this restriction. If, for example, the minimum cash balance required is equal to the compensating balance required at the firm's bank, we would then be in a position to know what it would save the firm if the agreement with the bank were modified, according to Orgler.

An example   The objective function is:

$$\text{Maximize profit} = a_1 X_1 + a_2 X_2 \tag{12A-6}$$

where
    X_i = units of products 1, 2
    a_i = profit per unit of product 1, 2

subject to the following production constraints:

$$b_1 X_1 \le \left\{ \begin{array}{l} \text{production constraints such as} \\ \text{assembly time, labor time, raw} \end{array} \right. \tag{12A-7}$$
$$b_1 X_2 \le \left. \text{material inventory} \right. \tag{12A-8}$$

and the following cash constraints:

$$C_1 X_1 + C_2 X_2 \le \text{cash available} \tag{12A-9}$$

where
    cash available = beginning cash balance + accounts receivable collection − loan
                  repayments − rent − minimum cash balance

and the following capital constraints:[6]

$$CR = \frac{C + A/R + INV}{CL} = 2.0 \tag{12A-10}$$

where
    CR = the firm's current ratio
    C = the firm's cash, which is comprised of minimum cash balance (MB) + available cash (AC) − labor costs, such that:

$$\text{Cash} = MB + AC - (d_1 X_1 + d_2 X_2) \tag{12A-11}$$

where
    AC = the cash available constraint of Equation 12A-9
    d_1 = the labor cost per unit of X_1
    d_2 = the labor cost per unit of X_2

A/R = accounts receivable at the beginning of the period (BAR) − collections (COL) during the period + sales on accounts receivable, such that:

$$BAR - COL + (e_1 X_1 + e_2 X_2) \tag{12A-12}$$

INV (inventory) = beginning inventory (BAI) + new stock (NS) − inventory sold, such that:

$$BAI + NS - (f_1 X_1 + f_2 X_2) \tag{12A-13}$$

Current Assets (CA) = $C + A/R + INV$, which we can derive by adding Equation 12A-11, Equation 12A-12, and Equation 12A-13 to get:

$$MB + AC - (d_1 X_1 + d_2 X_2) + BAR - COL + (e_1 X_1 + e_2 X_2)$$
$$+ BAI + NS - (f_1 X_1 + f_2 X_2) \tag{12A-14}$$

Current Liabilities (CL) = beginning current liabilities
$$\qquad\qquad\qquad - \text{loan repayment} + \text{new accounts payable} \tag{12A-15}$$

---

[6] See also William Beranek, *Working Capital Management,* Wadsworth Publishing Co., Belmont, Calif., 1966.

Then, the current ratio (CR) constraint is:

$$CR = \frac{CA}{CL} > 2.0 \qquad (12A\text{-}16)$$

where 2.0 was selected as a standard, acceptable current ratio level.

We can now solve for CR in terms of X_1 and X_2, since all other input data in Equations 12A-11 through 12A-16 are given in terms of X_1 and X_2 to derive Equation 12A-17 as:

$$g_1 X_1 + g_2 X_2 > \text{amount of } CA \text{ to keep } CR > 2.0 \qquad (12A\text{-}17)$$

For example, substituting the following hypothetical data:

$$
\begin{array}{ll}
MB = \$200 & e_1 = 10 \\
AC = \$300 & e_2 = 15 \\
d_1 = 1 & BAI = \$300 \\
d_2 = 2 & NS = \$500 \\
BAR = \$500 & f_1 = 3 \\
COL = \$200 & f_2 = 9
\end{array}
$$

into Equations 12A-14 through 12A-16 gives us:

$$
\begin{aligned}
CA &= 200 + 300 - (1X_1 + 2X_2) + 500 + 200 + (10X_1 + 15X_2) \\
&\quad + 300 + 500 - (3X_1 + 9X_2) = 2000 + 6X_1 + 4X_2 \qquad (12A\text{-}14A)
\end{aligned}
$$

$$CL = \$1,200 \qquad (12A\text{-}15A)$$

$CR > 2.0$ requires:

$$\frac{2000 + 6X_1 + 4X_2}{1,200} > 2.0 \qquad (12A\text{-}16A)$$

which is:

$$2000 + 6X_1 + 4X_2 \geqslant 2,400 \qquad (12A\text{-}16B)$$
$$6X_1 + 4X_2 \geqslant 400 \qquad (12A\text{-}16C)$$

The linear programming model is, therefore:

$$\text{Maximize profits} = a_1 X_1 + a_2 X_2 \qquad (12A\text{-}6)$$

subject to

$$b_1 X_1 \leqslant \left\{ \begin{array}{l} \text{production} \end{array} \right. \qquad (12A\text{-}7)$$
$$b_2 X_2 \leqslant \left. \begin{array}{l} \text{constraints} \end{array} \right\} \qquad (12A\text{-}8)$$
$$c_1 X_1 + c_2 X_2 \leqslant \text{cash available constraint} \qquad (12A\text{-}9)$$
$$g_1 X_1 + g_2 X_2 > \text{current asset requirement constraint} \qquad (12A\text{-}17)$$
$$X_i \geqslant 0 \; i = 1,n \text{ non-negativity constraint} \qquad (12A\text{-}18)$$

Notice how the model allows the financial officer to integrate cash management with production and other aspects of the firm. All cashflows in the cash budget are considered, including such items as accounts receivable collection (Equation 12A-12) and loan repayments (Equation 12A-11). The minimum balance of the cash budget is minimized when the model is solved (Equation 12A-9), while the working capital asset requirements are met (Equation 12A-17).

A CONTROL THEORY MODEL APPROACH

Sethi and Thompson (ST)[7] have used control theory to build a cash management model which is self-stabilizing within the control limits. As in most models, the objective is to determine the optimal level of cash balances at a point where the "minimum total discounted cost" is least by establishing a program of exchanging securities for cash, and vice versa, within the appropriate constraints, patterns of behavior for cash, and cost variables.

Using ST's notation:

$x(K) =$ the initial dollar cash balance for the kth period
$y(K) =$ the initial securities balance for the kth period
$d(K) =$ the firm's demand for cash in the kth period
$u(K) =$ the dollar amount of the conversion of securities into cash during the kth period such that if $u(K)$ is less than zero, securities have been purchased

The control variable constraints would be:

$$-M_2 \leq u(K) \leq M_1 \tag{12A-19}$$

Equation 12A-19 means that $u(K)$, the buying and selling of securities, is the control variable used by the financial officer to reach the minimum total discounted cost of maintaining cash balances. M_1 and M_2 are the constraints; they must be positive, since the financial officer cannot buy a negative amount of securities. The lower limit is M_2 and the upper limit on securities purchases is M_1. Above M_1 the firm cannot transact a security purchase or sale.

Like any cash model we have explored, ST's model considers the following costs, which have to be minimized:

$r_2(K) =$ the interest rate earned on the security balance $y(K)$ during period k
$\alpha =$ the dollar amount of the broker's commission for buying or selling one dollar's worth of securities
$r_1(K) =$ the interest rate earned on the cash balance $x(K)$ during the kth period (frequently not mentioned in the other cash models)

The change in the cash balances during period k is:

$$\Delta x(K) = r_1(K)x(K) - d(K) + u(K) - \alpha|u(K)|$$

$$\text{given } x(0) = x_0 \tag{12A-20}$$

which says that the change in the cash balance during period k equals the interest earned on the cash balances of the period minus the cash outflow during the period plus the sale of securities minus the commissions on that sale, given the initial cash balance of x_0.

A change in the securities position during k period, $y(K)$, is:

$$\Delta y(K) = r_2(K)y(K) - u(K)$$

$$\text{given } y(0) = Y_0 \tag{12A-21}$$

which says that the change in the securities balance equals the interest rate earned on the security balance in the kth period times the amount of the securities balance minus the sale of the securities in period k.

[7] S. P. Sethi and G. L. Thompson, "An Application of Mathematical Control Theory to Finance: Modeling Simple Dynamic Cash Balance Problems," *Journal of Financial and Quantitative Analysis*, December 1970, 381–394.

The objective function is, therefore, to maximize the terminal values of the cash, $x(N)$, and of the securities, $y(N)$, subject to the constraints of Equation 12A-19 and using the process described in Equations 12A-20 and 12A-21 (the transition equations) as time passes from $k = 0$ to $k = N$, the terminal year.

ST choose to state their terminal objective function as minimizing the negatives of $x(N)$ and $y(N)$ such that:

$$\text{Minimize } u(K) - x(N) - y(N) \tag{12A-22}$$

which says using the sale or purchase of securities as the control variable, minimize the negative of the cash and of the securities balances as of the terminal period.

But before solving Equation 12A-22 subject to the constraint and transition equations, we must first identify variables which define the path or movement through time from $k = 1$ to $k = 2$ . . . $k = N$ of the cash, $x(K)$, and the security, $y(K)$, balances. These are known as *adjoint variables,* and ST symbolize them as $\lambda_1(K)$ and $\lambda_2(K)$ for cash balances and for securities balances, respectively.

We can see the effect of the adjoint variables in Equation 12A-23:

$$H(K) = \lambda_1(K + 1) \; \Delta x(K) + \lambda_2(K + 1) \; \Delta y(K) \tag{12A-23}$$

which by substitution into Equations 12A-20 and 12A-21 gives us:

$$H(K) = \lambda_1(K + 1) [r_1(K)x(K) - d(K)] + \lambda_2(K + 1)r_2(K)y(K)$$
$$+ \{\lambda_1(K + 1)[u(K) - \alpha|u(K)|] - \lambda_2(K + 1)u(K)\} \tag{12A-24}$$

where the control variable $u(K)$ lies entirely within the "curly brackets."

To maximize the objective function, all we have to do is maximize Equation 12A-24 with respect to $x(K)$ and $y(K)$, such that:

$$\frac{\partial H(K)}{\partial x(K)} = -\lambda_1(K + 1)r_1(K); \; \lambda_1(N) = 1 \tag{12A-25}$$

$$\frac{\partial H(K)}{\partial y(K)} = -\lambda_2(K + 1)r_2(K); \; \lambda_2(N) = 1 \tag{12A-26}$$

Solving for $\lambda_1(K)$ and $\lambda_2(K)$ gives us:

$$\lambda_1(K) = \prod_{j=K}^{N} [1 + r_1(j)] \tag{12A-27}$$

$$\lambda_2(K) = \prod_{j=K}^{N} [1 + r_2(j)] \tag{12A-28}$$

which simply identifies the cost variables which must be minimized by our use of securities balances $u(K)$. In this case:

$\lambda_1(K) = $ the compound sum of the dollar amount of the cash balances held from present k period until the terminal period, N, in the future

$\lambda_2(K) = $ the compound sum of one dollar worth of securities held from the present k period until the terminal period, N, in the future.

Now we must derive the optimal cash management policy which, given $\lambda_1(K)$ and $\lambda_2(K)$, establishes the trade-off between cash and securities (our $u(K)$ control variable) to minimize the objective function. ST do this by writing the control variable as the definition of two non-negative variables such that:

$$u(K) = u_1(K) - u_2(K) \tag{12A-29}$$

given $u_1(K) \geqslant 0$, $u_2(K) > 0$

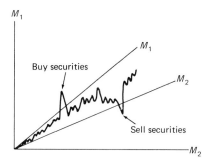

Figure 12A-3   A Bounded Cash Management Control Path

Arranging terms in Equation 12A-29, we get:

$$|u(K)| = u_1(K) + u_2(K) \tag{12A-30}$$

and substituting into the "curly brackets" expression of Equation 12A-24 gives us:

$$w(K) = \\ u_1(K)[(1 - \alpha)\lambda_1(K + 1) - \lambda_2(K + 1)] - u_2(K)[(1 + \alpha)\lambda_1(K + 1) - \lambda_2(K + 1)] \tag{12A-31}$$

which when solved for $u_1(K)$ gives an optimal cash balance policy of:

$$\frac{\partial w(K)}{\partial u_1(K)} = u_1(K) = \begin{cases} M_1 \text{ if } (1 - \alpha)\lambda_1(K + 1) > \lambda_2(K + 1) \\ \text{undetermined if } (1 - \alpha)\lambda_1(K + 1) = \lambda_2(K + 1) \\ 0 \text{ if } (1 - \alpha)\lambda_1(K + 1) < \lambda_2(K + 1) \end{cases} \tag{12A-32}$$

and:

$$\frac{\partial w(K)}{\partial u_2(K)} = u_2(K) = \begin{cases} 0 \text{ if } (1 + \alpha)\lambda_1(K + 1) > \lambda_2(K + 1) \\ \text{undetermined if } (1 + \alpha)\lambda_1(K + 1) = \lambda_2(K + 1) \\ M_2 \text{ if } (1 + \alpha)\lambda_1(K + 1) < \lambda_2(K + 1) \end{cases} \tag{12A-33}$$

where M_1 is the constrained upper bound and M_2 the constrained lower bound in Figure 12A-3.

If the time path of the cash balances and the securities balances as guided by the variables $\lambda_1(K)$ and $\lambda_2(K)$ exceeds M_1, the firm buys securities; but if the time path as guided by $\lambda_1(K)$ and $\lambda_2(K)$ falls below M_2, the firm sells securities.

Equation 12A-32 says "the optimal policy is to sell securities at the maximum rate if the future value of one dollar (cash) less the brokers' commission is greater than one dollar's worth of securities." If the future of one dollar of securities less commission is greater than the future worth of one dollar in cash, the firm should buy securities.

This application of control theory, although using sophisticated mathematics, simply specifies the upper bounds on the cash/securities portfolio mix (M_1) by portraying the expected path of the cash and the securities balances over time. First, the pertinent cost variables are defined, which in this case are $\lambda_1(K)$ and $\lambda_2(K)$ as related to the interest earned on cash and securities balances during any period. Second, the path through time, $K = 1 \ldots N$, is guided by those cost variables and our cash/securities balances. Third, the appropriate upper and lower bounds for our portfolio mix are determined, given these factors. Finally, the optimal policy is determined by comparing the time path with the bounds, which serve as a correctional guide as the path moves through time occasionally running into the bounds.

13

İNVENTORY MANAGEMENT

As FINANCIAL OFFICERS, WE ARE RESPONSIBLE for financing the firm's inventory. We would like to devote as little of our capital to the inventory as possible, since the firm does not want to tie up funds in excessive or slow-moving inventory. We must also see to it that a sufficient amount of inventory is maintained to insure the smooth operation of the firm's production and marketing functions. But what exactly is inventory? Generally, inventory is the stockpile of the product the firm is offering for sale and the components that make up the product. For example, the firm's finished-product inventory might be the number of automobiles, refrigerators, or groceries on hand waiting to be sold. The inventory of the intermediary components which go into the final product would consist of the raw materials, the work-in-process, and the supporting supplies. For example, the raw materials inventory of a steel manufacturer would include the iron ore on hand for use in the manufacturing process, while the raw materials inventory for an electric utility would be the coal or fuel oil on hand to be burned in generating electricity. The work-in-process for the automobile manufacturer would be the partially assembled cars on hand. The inventory of supplies would be such supporting materials as stationery, paper clips, heating oil for keeping the plant warm, and other similar items not directly used in the production process.

If inventory is expensive to maintain, why keep any inventory at all? First, inventory allows the manufacturer to bridge time. Since there is no instantaneous production or delivery, there must be a stockpile of the product which can be quickly tapped so that the actual sale does not wait upon a lengthy production process. Second, inventory is used to meet the competition. If the firm does not meet the customer's demand rapidly or completely, the firm may lose that customer to a competitor who can. This leads firms to stock not only enough inventory to satisfy the expected demand but also an additional amount (safety stock) to satisfy unexpected demand. Third, inventory allows the firm to lessen the costs of discontinuities in the production process. Since it is often very costly to stop the production of one model and set up for the production of another model, it is frequently less expensive to produce one model in excess of the current demand than it is to start and stop the production process. The excess is then placed in inventory to meet future demands. This is known as *production leveling* and is only possible because of inventory. Fourth, inventories serve as hedges against price increases and shortages in raw materials. If, as the financial officer, you envision extensive price increases in the basic raw materials, you should consider stockpiling a sufficiently large supply at the lower, presently prevailing prices. Similarly, if you anticipate a shortage in a necessary raw material or supply, a stockpile which would allow you to continue normal operations might be an advisable inventory strategy.

Once we know what inventory is and why it is used, what is the financial officer's objective in inventory management? The objective in inventory management, like that of cash management, consists of two counterbalancing parts. One, you want to minimize your investment in inventory since funds not committed to financing inventory can be invested in other acceptable projects which could not otherwise be funded. Two, you are responsible at the same time for insuring that the firm has enough inventory to meet demand when it arises and to keep the firm's production and marketing operations functioning smoothly. We can see that the two parts of the objective conflict with one another. By holding less inventory, we minimize our investment but run the risk of not meeting demand and disrupting the firm's operations. Conversely, by holding large amounts of inventory, we diminish the chance of not meeting demand and of disrupting the firm's production and marketing operations, but we increase our investment in inventory. How do we find the optimal level of inventory to maintain?

Before we can determine the optimal level, what factors must we, as financial officers, examine? Since the optimal level is associated with the minimum cost of inventory, we must look at the costs, which fall into two basic categories. One category is the costs associated with ordering the inventory. These consist of such expenses as those involved with placing the order to replenish the stockpile. The total ordering costs, as we shall see, rise as the number of orders rises.

The second category consists of costs associated with maintaining the inventory, traditionally called *carrying costs*. Such warehousing expenses as lights, maintenance, taxes, depreciation, janitorial services, insurance, and the cost of capital used to finance the inventory purchases would be in this category. As we shall see, the total of these carrying costs varies with the quantity ordered and placed into inventory. As the quantity of each order increases, the total carrying costs also increase.

Once we have examined the pertinent costs, how do we determine the optimal inventory quantity to order? The optimal order quantity, traditionally referred to as the economic order quantity (EOQ) is determined where the total of the carrying costs and the ordering costs is minimized. If we know demand, we can balance the two categories of costs to find a minimum, since the carrying costs rise as the quantity ordered increases, while the ordering costs decline as the quantity of each order increases. We shall also see that the EOQ allows the financial officer to incorporate the *economies of scale* associated with inventory management. The required number of additional units of inventory connected with each expansionary project undertaken is typically not as many as the last project because the inventory can be pooled to service all the projects producing this particular item.

Once financial officers know the optimal order quantity, how do they consider the uncertainty that the demand upon which they have based their calculations may be incorrect? In other words, how does the financial officer analyze the problem of unanticipated spurts or declines in demand so as to cover satisfactorily those unexpected events at a minimum additional cost above the EOQ? We shall see that the judicious use of *safety stocks* allows the financial officer to cover this uncertainty.

Once the financial officer has determined the firm's EOQ and appropriate safety stock, how does he or she keep track of this inventory and when is the time to reorder? An alert financial officer depends on current status reports on inventory in order to make the necessary readjustments to an ever-changing business environment. You must know your inventory situation at any moment, for outdated information can lead to misjudgments costly for the firm and for the financial officer's reputation. For example, if you do not know until three months after the drop in demand occurred that product X is not selling and that the firm is accumulating unsalable inventory of this item, you are at a considerable disadvantage. A competitor who has that information within one week after the change in demand is in a better position to deal with the situation. Your firm will be stuck with unwanted inventory and incur an extraordinary expense. Both could have been avoided if you had been apprised of the situation sooner.

We shall also see that modern communication techniques such as computers aid the financial officer's effort to keep abreast of the firm's inventory situation and help derive the appropriate reorder point for restocking that inventory.

THE OBJECTIVE OF INVENTORY MANAGEMENT

Once you know what inventory is and what functions it serves, such as bridging time, what is the objective of inventory management which, as the financial officer, you must keep in mind in order to focus your analysis and recommendations?

The two parts of the objective are: (1) to minimize the firm's investment in inventory and (2) to meet the demand for the product by facilitating the firm's marketing and production.

Minimizing the Investment in Inventory

The absolute minimum inventory is zero. The firm would keep no inventory and would produce on an individual, custom order basis. However, this is not practical for the vast majority of firms since they must meet customers' demand now or lose the order to competitors who can, and they must also store inventory to insure smooth production schedules.

Any good financial officer wants to minimize inventory because maintaining inventory is costly. For example, keeping $1 million invested in inventory means that the firm has had to raise $1 million in capital at its prevailing cost of capital to pay the wages of the employees who fabricated the product and the suppliers who provided the raw materials. If, for example, that cost was 10 percent, the cost of inventory financing would be $100,000 a year. In addition, the firm would also have to bear the costs associated with storing the inventory.

Meeting Demand

On the other hand, if the objective of inventory management were solely to maximize sales by instantaneously meeting all demand, the firm would keep excessively large amounts of the product stockpiled in inventory. The firm would never experience the costs associated with shortfalls in meeting that demand. It would never suffer the costs of losing a customer to a competitor, of losing the customer's goodwill, of losing the sale and profits, or of incurring production disruptions and delays.

It is extremely costly, however, to have inventory sitting around tying up capital that could be profitably employed elsewhere just so you can avoid shortfalls. As the financial officer, you have to determine the appropriate level of inventory in terms of the trade-off between the expected benefits of not experiencing shortfalls in meeting demand and the cost of maintaining the necessary inventory. In other words, is it worth it to keep so many units of additional inventory or is it too costly?

CONSIDERATIONS IN DETERMINING THE OPTIMAL INVENTORY ORDER

We can express the objective of minimizing the firm's investment in inventory in terms of the associated costs. What are these associated costs that you, as the financial officer, have to consider?

Basically they are: (1) the costs associated with ordering and (2) the costs associated with carrying the inventory.

Ordering Costs

Ordering costs are essentially those expenses incurred each time an order is placed. Upon placing an order with either an outside supplier or with the firm's own production department, there is the cost of preparing the invoice (order requisition form) which includes secretarial, stationery, and bookkeeping expenses. The secretary has to type the form, the bookkeeper has to record it, and the computer operator has to keypunch the form and process it, if the firm's inventory management is computerized.

After the order form has been filled out, the firm incurs the costs of setting up the production changes if the product is manufactured by the firm itself. This may entail retooling the machinery to conform to the specifications of the new product, and the scrap and test items of the first run occasion another expense. If the order is placed with an outside supplier, there are the expenses of receiving and inspecting the goods to insure that the quantity and the quality ordered is actually received.

Carrying Costs

The carrying costs are essentially associated with the warehousing and financing of the inventory. Because the inventory has to be stored, the firm incurs warehousing expenses such as property taxes, depreciation of the buildings, maintenance, utilities, and janitorial services. The firm also has to pay for insurance to protect the inventory against fire and theft and, in some states, has to pay an inventory tax. The firm must also bear the cost of deterioration in the inventory because of pilferage or obsolescence. If the inventory spoils because of age or becomes outmoded or outdated because of technological advances or changes in tastes, it may not command as high a price as before, if it is still salable at all. The firm has to absorb that loss. Finally, the firm must also raise the capital to finance the acquisition of the inventory, and since capital is costly, as we have seen in Chapters 8–11, the firm bears this expense.

DETERMINING THE OPTIMAL ORDER QUANTITY

Once the financial officer knows what pertinent costs must be minimized, how can they be formulated into a concise analysis to determine the optimal, or economic, order quantity (EOQ)?

Graphic Determination of the EOQ

We can see from Figure 13-1 that the total ordering costs rise with the number of times an order is placed during the operating period. If, as in Figure 13-1, each order cost $50 to place, the total ordering costs for one order would be $50. The total ordering costs for two orders would be $100, and so on. Table 13-1 illustrates this increment.

We can express Figure 13-1 and its complementary Table 13-1 as a formula:

$$TOC = N \times P \tag{13-1}$$

where
TOC = total ordering costs
N = the number of orders placed during the period
P = the ordering cost per order

For example, if N equals 30 and P equals $50, the total ordering costs (TOC) for the period would be $1,500. Alternatively, we can express N as the total demand for the period divided by the quantity of inventory received each time an order is placed. In symbols this would be:

$$N = \frac{D}{Q}$$

where
D = the expected demand for the product during the period
Q = the quantity of inventory received each time an order is placed

For example, if the period's demand (D) is expected to be 3,000 units and the quantity ordered each time (Q) is 100 units, the firm would place an order 30 times during the year. We can calculate the total ordering costs as:

$$TOC = \frac{D}{Q} P \tag{13-2}$$

where we have substituted $\frac{D}{Q}$ for N in Equation 13-1.

Figure 13-1 Total Ordering Cost in Relation to the Number of Orders Placed

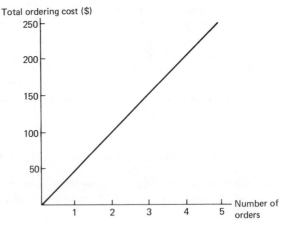

Table 13-1

Number of orders	Ordering costs per order	Total ordering costs
1	$50	$50
2	50	100
3	50	150
4	50	200
5	50	250

Equation 13-2 reveals that the total ordering costs (TOC) decline as Q increases, because the number of orders placed in the period $\left(\dfrac{D}{Q}\right)$ also declines. For example, if we ordered 500 units, instead of the 100 units ordered in the previous example, for a demand of 3,000 units, the number of times the firm would order drops to 6 (3,000 divided by 500) from the previous 30. The total ordering costs if we ordered 500 units at a time would be:

$$TOC = \frac{D}{Q} P$$
$$= \frac{3,000}{500} (\$50)$$
$$= \$300$$

instead of the $1,500 (30 × $50) incurred when the firm ordered 100 units at a time.

Figure 13-2 illustrates that total ordering costs decline as the quantity received with each order increases. In that figure, the total ordering costs are $1,500 when each order is for 100 units and only $300 when each order is for 500 units.

On the other hand, total carrying costs (TCC) increase as the quantity received with each order is increased, for with the arrival of each order the firm has more inventory on hand to store, insure, and finance. In our example, the 500-unit order would have a larger total carrying cost than the 100-unit order, as illustrated in Figure 13-3. If the carrying costs for the period are $2 per unit, then 100 units would have total carrying costs of $200, while 500 units would have total carrying costs of $1,000. Figure 13-3 is expressed in Table 13-2.

Just as we expressed total ordering costs in a formula (Equation 13-2) we can

Figure 13-2   Total Ordering Costs in Relation to the Quantity Received with Each Order

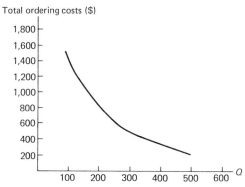

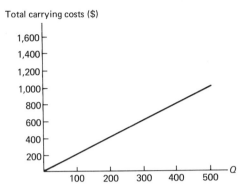

Figure 13-3 Total Carrying Costs in Relation to the Quantity Received with Each Order

express the total carrying costs, as portrayed in Figure 13-3 and Table 13-2, as follows:

$$TCC = INV \times C \qquad (13\text{-}3)$$

where
    TCC = total carrying costs
    INV = the average units in inventory at any time
    C = the carrying costs per unit

For example, if the average inventory (INV) were 100 units and the carrying costs per unit (C) were $2, total carrying costs (TCC) would be $200.

We can see from Figure 13-2 that total ordering costs (TOC) decline as the quantity received with each order (Q) rises, while we can see from Figure 13-3 that the total carrying costs (TCC) rise as the quantity received with each order (Q) rises. By superimposing Figure 13-2 on Figure 13-3, we can derive Figure 13-4 to illustrate the total of all costs in relation to the quantity received with each order.

In Figure 13-4 the total-cost (TC) curve declines to a minimum at Q^* and then rises. Obviously, as financial officers, we want to order the quantity Q^* each time, since it minimizes our inventory costs. Keeping with the traditional terminology, we shall call the quantity Q^* the economic order quantity (EOQ). How do we derive a specific figure for the EOQ? We have to turn from the graphs to more precise mathematical determination.

Table 13-2

Number of units received per order	Carrying costs per unit	Total carrying costs
100	$2	$200
200	2	400
300	2	600
400	2	800
500	2	1,000

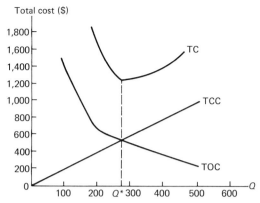

Figure 13-4   Total Inventory Costs in Relation to the Quantity Received with Each Order

Mathematical Determination of the EOQ

We can find the total cost (TC) by adding the total ordering costs (TOC) to the total carrying costs (TCC):

$$TC = TOC + TCC \tag{13-4}$$

where
  TC = total costs
  TOC = total ordering costs
  TCC = total carrying costs

Now we have already seen in Equation 13-2 that:

$$TOC = \frac{D}{Q} P \tag{13-2}$$

and in Equation 13-3 that:

$$TCC = INV \times C \tag{13-3}$$

Now we have to define the average inventory (INV) more carefully and in terms of the quantity ordered (Q). We can define the average inventory as $\frac{Q}{2}$ because if we had ordered and received, say, 500 units at the beginning of the period, knowing with certainty that we would sell exactly 500 units during the period, we would have zero units on hand at the end of the period. Averaging the beginning and the ending inventory, we would find that the average inventory for the entire period was 250 units. In symbols the calculation is:

$$INV = \frac{Q + 0}{2} = \frac{Q}{2}$$

where
  INV = average inventory
  Q = the original order size, or the beginning inventory

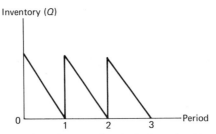

Figure 13-5 Inventory Levels over the Period under Certainty

We can see this in Figure 13-5, where at the beginning of each period we have Q amount of inventory which just arrived on our order and we steadily sell off that inventory until at the exact end of the period we are left with no inventory. Under the certainty of timing assumed here, the next shipment of Q amount of inventory arrives just as the last unit of the prior period's inventory is being shipped out. Notice that Figure 13-5 is constructed assuming that demand is known with certainty and is evenly spread throughout the period, otherwise we could not draw the uniform, downward-sloping straight lines which represent the inventory level.

Now, instead of expressing carrying costs per unit (C) as a dollar amount, we can express C as an annual percentage rate (I) of the dollar value of the inventory. For example, it might cost the firm 25 percent of the inventory value as carrying costs. This might be derived by the financial officer as follows:

Storage	10%
Insurance and taxes	2
Deterioration	3
Capital costs	10
Carrying costs	25%

It is more common to express the carrying cost as a percentage of the dollar value of the inventory than as a dollar cost per unit, because most of the individual costs are themselves expressed as an annual percentage of the inventory value. For example, the cost of capital is always expressed as an annual interest rate. Deterioration is typically expressed as the expected percentage of the units on hand, and taxes are always assessed as a percentage of the value.

Since we are now expressing our carrying costs per unit (C) as an annual percentage of the dollar value of the average inventory, we must find an expression for that dollar amount. If the average number of units in inventory at any time is $\frac{Q}{2}$, then the dollar value of the average inventory, if each unit cost S dollars to acquire, is $\frac{Q}{2} S$ and the total carrying costs are:

$$TCC = \frac{Q}{2} SI \qquad (13\text{-}5)$$

where
TCC = total carrying costs
$\frac{Q}{2}$ = average inventory in units

S = the value of one unit of inventory

I = the carrying costs expressed as an annual percentage of the total dollar value of the inventory

For example, if:

$$Q = 500$$
$$I = 25\%$$
$$S = \$100$$
$$TCC = \frac{500}{2}(.25)(100)$$
$$= \$6,250$$

The total cost (TC) can be expressed as:

$$TC = \frac{D}{Q}P + \frac{Q}{2}SI \tag{13-6}$$

which can be minimized[1] to:

$$Q^* = \sqrt{\frac{2DP}{IS}} \tag{13-7}$$

where

Q^* is the EOQ

If:

$$D = 3,000 \text{ units}$$
$$P = \$50$$
$$I = 25\%$$
$$S = \$100$$

Then:

$$Q^* = \sqrt{\frac{2(3,000)(50)}{(.25)(100)}}$$
$$\cong 109 \text{ units per order}$$

This means that the firm can minimize its total costs of ordering inventory by ordering 109 units at a time. If the annual demand is 3,000 units, the total cost is minimized by ordering 27 times a year, or approximately every 13 days.

----

[1]
$$\frac{\delta TC}{\delta Q} = -\frac{DP}{Q^2} + \frac{IS}{2}$$

Setting the above equal to zero to minimize it:

$$0 = -\frac{DP}{Q^2} + \frac{IS}{2}$$

$$\frac{DP}{Q^2} = -\frac{IS}{2}$$

$$Q^2 = \frac{2DP}{IS}$$

$$Q^* = \sqrt{\frac{2DP}{IS}}$$

At 109 units per order every 13 days, the total cost is:

$$TC = 27(50) + 55(100)(.25)$$
$$= \$2,725$$

If the order had been for 100 units instead, the total cost would have been \$2,750, while if the order quantity had been 120 units, the total cost would also have been \$2,750. Order quantities slightly larger and slightly smaller than 109 units lead to a higher total cost.

Implications for the Financial Officer

The economic order quantity (EOQ) tells the financial officer that the relationship between it and the demand (D), the ordering costs (P), the inventory value (A), and the carrying costs (I) is not proportional. Rather, Q^* is related to the other variables by a square root function, and such a relationship implies that there are economies of scale which allow the financial officer to lower the firm's investment in inventory as the firm expands. Each additional increase in demand requires a less-than-proportional increase in the inventory. For example, the first project to manufacture widgets might require an inventory of 1,000 widgets on hand at the beginning of the period, but the second project to double widget production might require only another 500 units, half of the inventory required for the first widget project. This means that in our capital budgeting analysis the investment in inventory that is part of the original outlay for the second project is only half of what it was for the first project.

The EOQ also tells the financial officer that the order quantity (Q^*) should be increased as the ordering costs (P) increase. On the other hand, if the carrying costs (I) or the value of the inventory increases, the order quantity (Q^*) should be decreased.

The EOQ is a starting point for the financial officer's inventory management strategy. It supplies the minimum cost order quantity, given a certain demand and a certain lead time between the placing of the order and the receipt of the goods. Let us explore how the EOQ can be expanded to handle variability in demand and delivery lead times.

SAFETY STOCKS

Once the financial officer knows the EOQ, how does he or she incorporate the uncertainty of demand?

Most firms must maintain a cushion (safety stock) against larger-than-expected demand. As the financial officer, you are responsible for determining how large that safety stock, if any, should be.

The Problem

Instead of running out of inventory exactly at the end of the period, just as the new shipment arrives, we may be short of the actual demand, which for some reason is greater than we had anticipated, or because our resupply is late in arriving. To avoid running out and disappointing the firm's customers, losing the sales and the accompanying profits, or disrupting the production schedule because of a lack of raw material inventory, we must keep some safety stock, consisting of additional

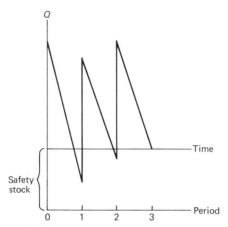

Figure 13-6 Safety Stock

units of inventory in excess of the expected demand and above the EOQ level of inventory at the beginning of the period. We can schematically illustrate the safety stock principle as shown in Figure 13-6. Without the safety stock, the firm would have run out of inventory before the end of period 1 and period 2. With the safety stock available, the firm merely dipped into the extra units on hand and satisfied the demand.

Carrying additional units of inventory, however, is expensive, just as if they were part of the regular inventory which the firm keeps to meet its regular demand. Conversely, there is a cost to being short of inventory when the unexpected demand arises. The most clearly identifiable stockout cost is the lost profit from the sales that could not be made because the firm was out of stock. More difficult to measure, although perhaps equally important, is the damage to customer relations when the firm cannot satisfy the customer's needs. The customer may be lost to the competition forever if the shortages are crucial and interfere with operations. Finally, the firm's production schedule may be disrupted because of a shortage of raw material inventory. This is costly because of the idle downtime and the unnecessary start-up costs incurred. Obviously, if you keep excessively large safety stocks, the firm experiences no short costs, but it bears the unduly large carrying costs of maintaining these excessive inventories. It is your job, as the financial officer, to weigh the counterbalancing costs and find the appropriate safety stock where the total cost is minimized. In other words, how large should the safety stock be so that the firm can meet unexpected demand without carrying an unduly large and overly expensive safety stock?

Determining the Optimal Safety Stock

How can the financial officer combine the carrying and the stockout costs into a systematic analysis in order to determine the optimal (least-cost) safety stock inventory? The first thing to notice is that again we have a situation where the carrying costs rise as the size of the safety stock increases, while the stockout costs decline as the size of the safety stock increases.

The second thing to notice is that since we are dealing with an uncertain demand, we must estimate the probability of being out of stock at each safety stock level so that we can derive the expected total cost (carrying costs plus stockout costs) at that level. For example, after examining the firm's records for the last 100 quarters, we might find that the firm had been short (out of stock) by the following amounts in the following number of quarters:

Number of units short	Number of quarters
100	1
80	2
50	3
20	4
10	10
0	80
	100

This compilation says that the firm had been short 100 units only once in the last 100 quarters, or 1 percent of the time, but it had been 10 units short 10 percent of the time.

It is clear, judging by history, that if the firm kept 100 units in the safety stock, it would never be short. It is also clear that by carrying those 100 units in safety stock, the firm would experience a carrying cost of $2,500, using the 25 percent carrying

Table 13-3   Expected Stockout Costs

Safety stock level	Stockout (units)	Stockout costs ($50/unit)	Probability of stockout	Expected stockout cost at this level	Total expected stockout costs
100	0	0	0	0	0
80	20	$1,000	.01	$10	$10
50	50	2,500	.01	25	
	30	1,500	.02	30	65
20	80	4,000	.01	40	
	60	3,000	.02	60	
	30	1,500	.03	45	210
10	90	4,500	.01	45	
	70	3,500	.02	70	
	40	2,000	.03	60	
	10	500	.04	20	405
	100	5,000	.01	50	
	80	4,000	.02	80	
0	50	2,500	.03	75	
	20	1,000	.04	40	
	10	500	.10	50	700

Table 13-4   Total Safety Stock Costs

Safety stock level	Expected stockout costs (from Table 13-3)	Carrying costs ($25/unit)	Total cost
0	$700	$ 0	$ 700
10	405	250	655
20	210	500	710
50	65	1,250	1,315
80	10	2,000	2,010
100	0	2,500	2,500

cost per unit and a unit value of $100 from our previous example. The total cost of a 100-unit safety stock is therefore:

Safety stock	Carrying cost ($25 per unit)	Stockout costs	Total cost
100	$2,500	$0	$2,500

If our safety stock level were 80 units, there is a 1 percent probability that the firm could be short 20 units—the 1 percent chance that an unexpected demand of 100 units will materialize. If stockout costs were $50 per unit, this would cost the firm $1,000. However, since this particular shortage is expected to arise only 1 percent of the time, the expected stockout costs are only $10, i.e., (.01 × $1,000). We can determine the expected stockout costs for each level of safety stock as in Table 13-3.

Notice in Table 13-3 that as the safety stock level decreases, providing a smaller cushion against any demand in excess of what had been anticipated, the expected stockout costs rise, because there is more opportunity for the firm to be out of stock. For example, if the firm kept a safety stock level of 20 units, it would be 80 units short of demand if demand were 100 units greater than expected, 60 units short of demand if demand were 80 units greater than anticipated, and 30 units short of demand if demand were 50 units more than anticipated. Therefore, we must consider the probability of being out of stock at each safety stock level for each possible demand greater than that level.

In order to derive the total costs, the financial officer must add the carrying costs to the expected stockout costs at each safety stock level,[2] as shown in Table 13-4.

We can see from Table 13-4 that the optimal (least-cost) safety stock inventory is 10 units. If we maintain less than 10 units or more than 10 units, the total cost increases. The minimum is reached when the carrying costs, which increase as the safety stock level rises, counterbalance the stockout costs, which decrease as the safety stock level increases. The firm in our example will give up its attempt to satisfy any unexpected demand in excess of 10 units because it is too costly.

CONTROLLING INVENTORY

Once the financial officer has determined the economic order quantity and the optimal safety stock, how does he or she know when to reorder?

---

[2] See, for example, M. C. Findlay and E. E. Williams, *An Integrated Analysis for Managerial Finance*, Prentice-Hall, Englewood Cliffs, N. J., 1970, p. 87.

The answer lies in the financial officer's physical control over the inventory—keeping constant track of it and establishing the appropriate reorder point.

A Method of Inventory Control

As financial officer, you must keep very close account of how much inventory is left so that you know when to reorder. Failure to keep an accurate and updated status report can mislead you into thinking that you have a sufficient supply on hand when you are actually dangerously low already and will run out before you have a chance to reorder. It could also mislead you into believing that your inventory is selling as expected when in truth the demand for the item has not materialized, and the firm is stuck with unsalable merchandise.

The more modern systems of inventory control utilize the speed and the capacity of the computer. You might even observe such a system the next time you are in a department store. Those electronic cash registers are actually terminals for a computer. When the cashier records the inventory number of the item, the computer immediately picks it up and subtracts one unit from the inventory it maintains in its memory. Then, at very short intervals, it issues an inventory report to the financial officer revealing how much was sold, at what price, and how much is left. The computer can also print up a reorder form for an economic order quantity when it shows that the current number of units left in inventory has reached a predetermined level. That computer-printed reorder form is then sent out to the firm's supplier, who ships the firm its new supply.

Determining the Reorder Point

Because it takes time for the firm to actually receive the inventory it has ordered, the financial officer must reorder before the present inventory is depleted. The alert financial officer considers the number of days required for the supplier to receive and process the order as well as the number of days during which the goods will be in transit from the supplier. For example, if it takes seven days for the quantity ordered to reach the firm from the supplier, we must have seven days' inventory on hand when we reorder.

We can illustrate this in Figure 13-7, where we have assumed a 28-day inventory cycle, from the time the order is received until the end of the period when we expect the entire order to have been sold and shipped to our customers. If we have a 7-day

Figure 13-7 The Reorder Point

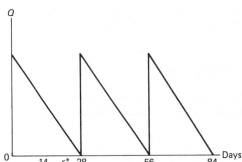

lead time, we must reorder at point r^*, which in this case would be the end of the twenty-first day, so that we have 7 days' inventory left to cover the expected delays in processing and transit. In terms of the number of units, we would have to reorder when our inventory on hand was one quarter of the original level at the beginning of the period, which is calculated as 7 days' lead time divided by the 28-day cycle. For example, if the beginning inventory were 109 units, our reorder point would be approximately 27 units. When the inventory on hand reached 27 units, we would initiate an order for another 109 units, the EOQ. Notice the necessity of knowing when we reached that 27-unit reorder point. If we had a reporting delay of 7 days and were consequently 7 days behind in reordering, the firm would have been entirely without inventory for a week, unless it had a safety stock.

If, at the reorder point, we observe that we have used some or all of our safety stock, we must increase the order quantity to replenish it. If in the previous case we had used all our regular inventory plus 8 units of the safety stock, we would have had to reorder 117 units (109 for regular inventory and 8 units for the safety stock) to restore the optimal safety stock level.

SMALL BUSINESS ALTERNATIVES

Sometimes the rather sophisticated versions of the EOQ are too expensive to develop or too elaborate for small business applications. Instead, the small business may resort to simpler applications of ratios for inventory management. For example, small business owners may keep a running inventory of items sold by describing the item on a duplicate sales slip or marking a shelf inventory slip attached to the item's storage area when one unit is used. When the number of units left reaches a predetermined point, reflecting a specified number of days' inventory, the item is reordered. When adjusted for seasonal variations, a simple "bin count," a running tabulation of the number of units remaining in the storage area, is sufficient to indicate a reorder point.

Alternatively, when the inventory-to-sales ratio falls below a certain predetermined point, the small businessperson might automatically reorder. This is another relatively simple but effective inventory management system.

SUMMARY

After having read Chapter 13, you should be able to answer these questions:
1. What is inventory?
Inventory is the stockpile of finished goods, work-in-process, and supplies which the firm stores in anticipation of need.
2. Why have inventory?
Inventory serves to bridge the lapse in time between production and sale of the item. It also helps the firm coordinate its production scheduling so as to avoid disruptions and the accompanying expenses. It serves as a competitive marketing tool enabling the firm's marketing department to meet demand when it arises and thus keep, as well as gain, customers. Finally, we saw that inventory also serves as a hedge against expected price increases and shortages in the firm's raw material and supplies needs.
3. What is the objective of inventory management?

Inventory management should minimize the firm's investment in inventory and costs of managing that inventory, while at the same time insuring a sufficient inventory to meet customer demand. Thus, the twofold objective of inventory has conflicting elements. A large inventory assures the firm of meeting demand, but does not minimize the firm's investment or costs of inventory. A minimal inventory keeps the firm's investment and costs low, but exposes it to the possibility that it may not be able to meet its customers' needs.

4. What are the costs of inventory management that the financial officer tries to minimize?

The two basic costs are the ordering costs, which consist of those expenses associated with placing the order (such as bookkeeping and salaries), and carrying costs, which consist of those expenses associated with the warehousing and financing of the inventory (such as insurance, rent, and the cost of capital).

5. How does the financial officer determine the optimal ordering quantity?

Once we had isolated the pertinent costs, we observed that the carrying costs increase as the quantity ordered increases, while the ordering costs decrease as the quantity ordered increases. Using the counterbalancing effect of the two costs, we found that there was an order quantity which minimized the firm's cost. We called that order quantity the economic order quantity (EOQ).

6. How does the financial officer incorporate uncertainty into inventory management?

The financial officer uses safety stocks of inventory above what is anticipated to be the normal demand, in order to cover any abnormally high, unexpected demand that may materialize. The optimal level of safety stocks was determined where the sum of the carrying costs of that safety stock plus the stockout costs of being unable to meet demand was minimized.

7. How does the financial officer control the firm's inventory?

It is very important that, in addition to setting the EOQ and the optimal safety stock, the financial officer also keep accurate, current records of inventory so as to detect slow-selling items and to know when to reorder, considering the lead time between the placement of that order and the receipt of the goods. You reorder in time to cover the days during which the order is being processed and the goods are in transit.

QUESTIONS

13-1 Define *inventory* and give a few examples.

13-2 How are the objectives of inventory management and cash balance management similar?

13-3 A famous economist recently remarked, "One way to distinguish profit maximizing firms from sales maximizing firms is to observe their inventory levels." What was meant by this statement?

13-4 Distinguish between inventory ordering costs and inventory carrying costs, and give examples of each.

13-5 The total ordering costs (*TOC*) from Equation 13-2 are defined as $N \cdot P$ where N is number of orders and P the ordering cost per order.

(a) What assumptions regarding P and expected demand (D) must hold if *TOC* and N are linearly related as shown in Figure 13-1?

(b) Under what conditions might the *TOC* curve be nonlinearly related to N?

13-6 Explain why total ordering costs decline at a decreasing rate as the quantity received with each order increases, as shown in Figure 13-2. Under what conditions might the curve appear differently?

13-7 Explain briefly what the formula to find the optimal order quantity (Q^*) should suggest to the financial analyst:

$$Q^* = \sqrt{\frac{2DP}{IS}}$$

13-8 What purpose does safety stock serve? What are some of the benefits and costs associated with safety stock?

13-9 Describe the likely effects on inventory levels of the following events:
(a) A major supplier announces a 5 percent price increase.
(b) Several major suppliers improve their delivery time of materials to your firm.
(c) Demand for the firm's product increases.
(d) The firm increases its number of styles of products.

PROBLEMS

13-1 The Aby-Crocker Company manufactures wooden crocks used for storing and aging liquids of various kinds. The firm has incurred difficulties in the past due to inappropriate inventory levels, and management has decided to try to establish a more suitable inventory policy. The demand for crocks at their present price has been about 12,500 crocks per year. The cost of placing an order for materials used in producing crocks is $100 and is invariant. Each unit of inventory is valued at $50. Additional carrying costs are estimated as follows as a percent of total inventory value:

Storage costs	7%
Insurance and taxes	2%
Deterioration	3%
Capital costs	8%

(a) What is the optimal order quantity (Q^*)?
(b) What is the optimal number of times inventory should be ordered each year?
(c) Illustrate in tabular display that Q^* is indeed the optimal order quantity by calculating the total cost of inventory if EOQ = Q^*, $Q^* - 50$; $Q^* - 100$, $Q^* + 50$, and $Q^* + 100$.
(d) If the estimate for demand were revised upward to 15,000 per year what is the effect on the optimal order quantity (Q^*) and the number of orders per year?
(e) If ordering costs increase to $120 per order, what is the effect on Q^*? (Assume demand is 12,500 crocks per year.)
(f) If the value of each unit of inventory increases to $60, what is the effect on Q^*? (Assume demand is 12,500 and the ordering cost per order is $100.)
(g) If the firm's cost of capital increases to 10 percent, what is the effect on Q^*? (Assume original values for all other variables.)

13-2 The previous problem assumed certainty with respect to the level of demand for crocks produced by Aby-Crocker. But the following figures illustrate the number of months that demand exceeded available crocks for the past 50 months:

Number of crocks short	Number of months
200	2
150	3
100	5
50	10
0	30
	50

Crocks are currently selling at $100 per crock. The carrying costs are the same as in Problem 13-1 (20 percent carrying cost per inventory unit and inventory valued at $50 per unit).

(a) If the firm wished to never miss a sale, what would be its safety stock? What is the total cost associated with this level of safety stock?

(b) What are the total expected costs associated with a safety stock of 150? Of 100? Of 50? Of 0?

(c) What is the optimal safety stock inventory level? Is it 200, 150, 100, 50, or 0?

(d) What is the total cost associated with the optimal safety stock?

13-3 Figure 13-4 suggests that total cost is minimized at the same level of Q where the total carrying cost function (TCC) intersects the total operating cost function (TOC). Does the level of Q at this intersection equal the same Q^* found in Equation 13-7? Why or why not?

BIBLIOGRAPHY

Arrow, K. J., S. Karlin, and H. Searf. *Studies in the Mathematical Theory of Inventory and Production.* Stanford University Press, Stanford, Calif., 1958.

Beranek, William, "Financial Implications of Lot-Size Inventory Models." *Management Science,* 13 (April 1967), 401–408.

Buffa, Elwood S. *Production-Inventory Systems: Planning & Control.* Irwin, Homewood, Ill., 1968.

Hadley, G., and T. M. Whitin. *Analysis of Inventory Systems.* Prentice-Hall, Englewood Cliffs, N. J., 1963.

Magee, John F. "Guide to Inventory Policy, I, II, and III." *Harvard Business Review,* January–February 1956, 49–60; March–April 1956, 103–116; and May–June, 57–70.

Snyder, Arthur, "Principles of Inventory Management," *Financial Executive,* 32 (April 1964), reprinted in *Foundations for Financial Management,* ed. James Van Horne. Irwin, Homewood, Ill., 1966, pp. 70–80.

Starr, Martin K., and David W. Miller. *Inventory Control—Theory and Practice.* Prentice-Hall, Englewood Cliffs, N. J., 1962.

14

ACCOUNTS RECEIVABLE

As FINANCIAL OFFICERS, IT IS OUR RESPONSIBILITY to fund the firm's accounts receivable. Accounts receivable are simply extensions of credit to the firm's customers, allowing them a reasonable period of time in which to pay for the goods after they have been received. Most firms treat accounts receivable as a marketing tool to promote sales and profits. The objective of the firm's accounts receivable policy is usually to encourage sales and gain additional customers by extending credit.

As financial officers, we are involved because we must finance the firm's investment in accounts receivable, implement the firm's chosen credit policy, including the screening of potential customers for their creditworthiness, and enforce collection. The financial officer must analyze how much the firm should invest in accounts receivable, for there is always the temptation to extend too much credit in an effort to boost sales beyond the point where the return on the investment in accounts receivable is no longer as attractive as the return on other investment opportunities. It is the financial officer's responsibility to guard against overinvestment in accounts receivable.

What factors must the financial officer consider in order to derive the most attractive accounts receivable policy? We shall see that the pertinent cost factors are interest on the capital used to finance the investment in receivables, the cost of operating a credit department, and possible delays and defaults in payment by the customers. On the other hand, the pertinent benefits are increased sales and profits.

What typical accounts receivable policy terms might you, as the financial officer, consider? The general policy specifies the length of time before the customer is expected to pay, any discount for early payment that is allowed the customer, and sometimes seasonal billing dates which allow the customer to pay after a particular selling season, such as after Christmas. When we translate the general policy into more specific credit terms, the most common are cash, which requires immediate payment on the part of the customer; net 30, which requires payment within 30 days; and 2/10, net 30, which requires payment within 30 days but allows a 2 percent discount if the customer pays within 10 days.

Once the terms of the accounts receivable policy have been chosen, how does the financial officer implement and monitor them? You will first determine the credit risk of the potential customer through a selection process which relies heavily on sources of information which you must gather. You then decide if the risk is worth the expected extra profit. If it is, you recommend that an appropriate amount of credit be extended to the customer. You are also required to monitor the credit once it has been extended to detect any deterioration in its quality and to act quickly to prevent the firm from suffering a loss if the quality deteriorates too far.

An alert financial officer will also be aware of other methods of financing the firm's accounts receivable to see if they are less costly than if the firm financed them itself. These alternative sources of financing for accounts receivable include factoring, credit insurance, and captive finance companies.

OBJECTIVE OF ACCOUNTS RECEIVABLE POLICY

What is the objective of accounts receivable policy?

While it is mostly a marketing tool to promote sales, the financial officer must see that its use still maximizes profit and return on investment and is not abused to a point beyond which the extension of credit is unprofitable or unattractive in terms of a return on investment.

The marketing department of the firm generally tends to look upon accounts receivable as a tool with which to sell the product and outdo the competition. We typically find most salespeople, for example, favoring a very liberal credit policy because it helps their sales. If the competition is offering credit, your firm might also have to offer credit to protect your marketing position. This can apply to a department store which finds that it must offer charge plates to its customers in order to compete, as well as to an international engineering firm which finds it must also extend or arrange long-term credit as part of the entire selling package in order to bid successfully on such projects as dams, refineries, and other large capital projects. It has frequently happened that the firm offering credit arrangements as part of the sales package has won the bid, despite the fact that other firms, who did not arrange credit, bid lower.

No matter how liberal your firm's salespeople want the credit policy, it is still your responsibility, as the financial officer, to see that the amount of credit extended is optimal and progresses the firm toward its corporate goal. This requires that the accounts receivable maximize profits and have an attractive return. You must weigh the costs and risks of the credit policy against the increased profits it is expected to generate. You must also try to avoid extending credit to potential customers who are likely not to pay or to tie up the firm's funds for a long time by delaying payment. You do not want to finance those customers who are too great a risk or who need such a large amount of total receivables that the investment in them becomes only marginally profitable, draining off funds which could be used to finance more attractive projects. As we shall see, if the return on investment in additional accounts receivable is less than the cost of funds raised to finance that additional credit, you must reject the additional investment in those receivables.

FACTORS IN DETERMINING ACCOUNTS RECEIVABLE POLICY

Once the financial officer and the marketing department have agreed that the objective of accounts receivable policy is to promote sales and profits *until* that point is reached where the return on investment in the further funding of receivables is less than the cost of capital, what specific cost and benefit factors must you consider in your analysis?

Costs

The major categories of costs associated with accounts receivable are (1) collection costs, (2) capital costs, (3) delinquency costs, and (4) default costs.

Collection costs If the firm's credit policy is strictly cash it has no collection costs, since all customer payments are immediate upon receipt of the goods. If the firm starts extending credit, however, in the anticipation of attracting more business, it incurs the collection costs of hiring a credit manager plus assistants and bookkeepers within the finance department; of acquiring credit information sources to aid in deciding which potential customer is creditworthy; and of generally maintaining and operating a credit department, providing such essentials as stationery, postage, and computer time.

Capital costs Once the firm extends credit, it must raise funds in order to finance it. The firm must pay its employees, its raw material suppliers, and all others who manufactured or distributed the product while waiting for the customer to pay for the product. This time gap means that the firm has to go out and raise funds (or use internally generated funds it could invest more profitably elsewhere) to meet its payments while waiting for payment from the customer. Capital is expensive, and the firm must bear the cost.

Delinquency costs The firm incurs delinquency costs when the customer is late in paying. This failure of the customer to pay on time adds collection costs above those associated with a normal collection. The firm has to bear the costs of written reminders, law suits, phone calls, and all other collection efforts. If the firm has to turn the account over to a collection agency, it usually loses a substantial portion of any amount recovered as payment to the collection agency. Delinquency also ties up funds which could be earning money elsewhere, creating an opportunity cost for any additional time the funds are tied up after the normal collection period.

Default costs The firm incurs default costs when the customer fails to pay at all. In addition to the collection costs, capital costs, and delinquent costs incurred up to this point, the firm loses the cost of goods sold but not paid for. It has to write off the entire sale once it decides the delinquent account has defaulted and is no longer collectable.

Benefits

The firm incurs benefits from the accounts receivable policy which must be weighed against the costs in order to determine the profitability of any particular accounts receivable policy. The benefits are the increased sales and profits anticipated because of a more liberal policy.

DETERMINING THE APPROPRIATE ACCOUNTS RECEIVABLE POLICY

Once financial officers know the costs and the benefits, how do they incorporate them into their analyses to achieve the objective of maximizing profits without undue risk or having the return from the extension of credit exceed the cost of capital?

Let us take the three most common accounts receivable policies, cash, net 30, and 2/10 net 30, and analyze them in order to demonstrate how the financial officer might proceed.[1]

In conjunction with the marketing department, the financial officer can alter the credit terms by extending the length of time over which the customer can pay and/or granting the customer a discount for paying earlier than the maximum time extended by the firm. In our example, a cash policy requires immediate payment. The net 30 policy allows the customer a maximum of 30 days within which to pay. The 2/10 net 30 policy allows the customer a maximum of 30 days in which to pay; but, if payment is made within 10 days, the customer can deduct 2 percent of the purchase cost. The 2 percent acts as an incentive to encourage the customer to pay within 10 days of the purchase.

Cash Policy

If the firm's accounts receivable policy is cash, the firm extends no trade credit. There are no collection costs and no capital costs since the firm has no money tied up in financing accounts receivable. There are obviously no delinquent or default costs, and the total cost of a cash accounts receivable policy is zero, as illustrated in Figure 14-1.

Since there are no costs to weigh, we have to examine the benefits (profits) that accrue to the cash policy. We can compute the total profits as follows:

$$TP = S(M) - C(M) - A \tag{14-1}$$

where
TP = total profits under this policy
S = the selling price per unit
C = the cost of goods sold per unit
M = the number of units sold under the cash policy
A = the accounts receivable costs

Figure 14-1 Accounts Receivable Costs in Relation to Policy

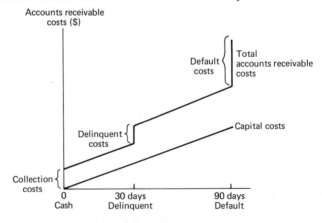

[1] R. Lindsay and A. Sametz, *Financial Management: An Analytical Approach*, Irwin, Homewood, Ill., 1967, Ch. 7.

If, for example, we assume that:

$$S = \$12$$
$$C = \$10$$
$$M = 100 \text{ units}$$
$$A = 0, \text{ since there is no trade credit extended}$$

then:

$$TP = \$12(100) - \$10(100) - 0$$
$$= \$200$$

In other words, the total profit to the firm under this cash policy is $200. The question is to determine if the other policies might not be more profitable.

Net 30 Policy

If the firm extends 30-day trade credit, it immediately incurs two types of accounts receivable costs: (1) the cost of the capital needed to finance the accounts receivable for 30 days and (2) such collection costs as billing, postage, bookkeeping, and credit management salaries. We can see in Figure 14-1 that the capital costs increase the longer the account is uncollected, for the firm must pay interest on the capital raised with each passing day. For example, if the cost of capital were 12 percent, it would cost the firm 1 percent of the amount of the trade credit extended for each month that the account remained uncollected. Each passing *day* would cost the firm .033 percent interest.

On top of the capital costs, the firm incurs the collection costs of billing, postage, and so on, which are constant regardless of the number of days the account remains uncollected, since they are typically incurred but once, on the first day. We see collection costs in Figure 14-1 as the constant cost added to the capital costs throughout the first 30 days during which the account is uncollected.

Offsetting the increased collection costs are the expected increases in sales and profits anticipated by our marketing department because of our adoption of the net 30 trade policy instead of the cash policy.

We can weigh the additional annual costs against the additional annual profits to determine if the adoption of net 30 is more profitable than remaining with the cash policy. For example, if the number of units sold increased from 100 units (M) under the cash policy to 300 units (N) under the net 30 policy, total revenue would have increased to $S(N) = \$12(300) = \$3,600$. Total cost of goods sold would have increased to $C(N) = \$10(300) = \$3,000$. Accounts receivable costs would now be:

$$AR = [C(N)]k + CC(N) \tag{14-2}$$

where

$k =$ the cost of capital for the funds used to finance the accounts receivable

$C(N) =$ the dollar value of the accounts receivable financed (cost of goods sold)

$CC =$ the collection costs per unit

$CC(N) =$ the total collection costs

$[C(N)]k =$ the total capital costs

Equation 14-2 simply says that the total accounts receivable costs to the net 30 policy are the capital costs plus the collection costs. The total capital costs are derived by multiplying the cost of capital (k) times the dollar value of the receivables which have to be financed, $C(N)$. The total collection costs are derived by multiplying the collection costs per unit (CC) times the number of units sold (N).

The total profit to the net 30 policy is the total revenue generated less the total cost of goods sold and the total accounts receivable costs, as follows:

$$TP = S(N) - C(N) - [C(N)]k - CC(N) \tag{14-3}$$

Assuming a selling price (S) of $12, a cost per unit ($C$) of $10, a cost of capital ($k$) of 10 percent, and collection costs of $.25 per unit, we could calculate total profits (TP) from the net 30 policy as:

$$TP = \$3,600 - \$3,000 - [3,000].10 - .25(300)$$
$$= \$225$$

Since the total profit from the net 30 policy is $225, compared to the $200 total profit under the cash policy, the firm would choose the net 30 policy.

2/10 Net 30 Policy

Under this policy the customer can either: (1) buy the goods and not take the discount or (2) buy the goods and take the discount for early payment. It is as if the firm has two different groups of customers. One group does not take the discount. These customers would be the same as those under the net 30 policy. There is no incentive for them to buy more from the firm than there was under the former accounts receivable policy. Total profits to this group would, as a consequence, remain unchanged at $225, assuming that none of the net 30 customers decides to pay early and take the 2 percent discount.

The adoption of the 2 percent early-payment discount would, however, attract additional customers and increase the anticipated sales. We must examine the additional benefits and costs associated with the early payment discount in order to determine the total profit to the 2/10 net 30 policy and compare it with the total profits of the other policies we might adopt. The additional revenue generated by offering the 2 percent discount is calculated as follows:

$$\text{Additional revenue} = (1 - d)S(N') \tag{14-4}$$

where

$S =$ selling price per unit
$d =$ the 2 percent discount
$N' =$ the additional number of units expected to be sold by the marketing department because of the 2 percent discount policy

The additional cost of goods sold because of the 2 percent discount would be:

$$\text{Additional cost of goods sold} = C(N') \tag{14-5}$$

where

$C =$ the cost of goods sold per unit as before
$N' =$ the additional number of units expected to be sold by the marketing department because of the 2 percent discount

The additional accounts receivable (AR) costs incurred by the firm because of the 2 percent discount would be:

$$\text{Additional AR costs} = \left[C(N') \frac{k}{3} \right] + CC(N') \tag{14-6}$$

where the cost of capital (k) is divided by 3 to reflect the fact that since the payment is received on the tenth day, the firm has to finance that account for only 1/3 of the time consumed if the account were collected on the thirtieth day without the discount.

If we assume that the additional number of units (N') sold because of the 2 percent discount is 500 and continue with the assumed figures from the prior example, the total profit (TP) to the 2/10 net 30 policy would be computed as shown in Equation 14-7, which combines Equations 14-4, 14-5, and 14-6:

$$TP_{2/10,n/30} = TP_{n/30} + (1 - d)S(N') - C(N') - [C(N')]\frac{k}{3} - CC(N') \qquad (14\text{-}7)$$

where

$TP_{n/30}$ = the total profit of the net 30 policy

In our example:

$$TP_{2/10,n/30} = \$225 + .98(12)(500) - 10(500) - [10(500)].33 - .25(500)$$
$$= \$815$$

Clearly, the 2/10 net 30 policy is preferred over either the cash or the net 30 policy since it maximizes the firm's profit.

Delinquency and Default

Up to this point we have considered the effect of the three most common accounts receivable policies on the firm's profits without considering the delinquency and default costs. Under either the net 30 or the 2/10 net 30 policy, there will be some customers who will delay and others who will default entirely, increasing the total accounts receivable costs as illustrated in Figure 14-1. After the allowable 30-day credit period in Figure 14-1, the uncollected account is considered delinquent, and the firm incurs such additional costs as further reminders and other measures to prod the customer into paying. The firm also continues to pay interest or incurs opportunity costs on the funds used to finance the account. After 90 days in Figure 14-1, the firm considers any uncollected account to have defaulted and writes off the total sale as an expense. Therefore, under both the net 30 and the 2/10, net 30 policies, the financial officer has to deduct the expected delinquency and default costs in order to determine the total profits.

Delinquency costs (DC) are those expenses associated with that portion of total sales which remain uncollected beyond 30 days in our example, and they force the company to spend an additional dollar amount per account (D) in an attempt to collect. We can express total delinquent costs of the 2/10 net 30 policy as follows:

$$DC = D(N + N')(p_d) \qquad (14\text{-}8)$$

where
$\quad DC$ = total delinquency costs
$\quad N'$ = the additional units sold to customers because of the 2 percent discount
$\quad N$ = the number of units sold to the net 30 customers
$\quad p_d$ = the percentage of total sales that are not paid for within 30 days
$\quad D$ = the average additional cost caused by delinquency

For example, if 3 percent of the total sales are not paid for within 30 days $(p_d = 3$ percent), the firm's total delinquency costs using the sales of our prior example and a \$5 average delinquency cost would be:

$$DC = \$5(300 + 500)(.03)$$
$$= \$120$$

In other words, total profits under the 2/10 net 30 policy must be reduced by $120 in our example. We would expect to encounter that much additional cost because of delayed payments. Under the net 30 policy, the firm's delinquency costs would be $45, since it sells only 300 units.

We also have to deduct the default cost (FC) which arises when the firm gives up trying to collect on the account and charges the entire cost of the goods sold as an expense. A certain portion (p_f) of the total sales $(N + N')$ under the 2/10 net 30 policy is expected to default. We can express the cost of goods that have to be written off as follows:

$$FC = C(N + N')(p_f) \hspace{3cm} (14\text{-}9)$$

where
$\qquad FC$ = total default costs
$\qquad C$ = the cost of goods sold per unit
$\qquad N$ = the number of units sold to the net 30 customers
$\qquad N'$ = the number of units sold under the 2/10 policy
$\qquad p_f$ = the percentage of sales that default

For example, if the percentage of defaulted sales (p_f) were .5 percent, then total default costs in our example would be:

$$FC = \$10(800)(.005)$$
$$= \$40$$

Under the net 30 policy, the default cost would be $15 since the firm sells only 300 units (N) under that policy. Therefore, $40 of default costs would have to be deducted from the 2/10 net 30 policy and $15 from the net 30 policy to derive the total profit to each.

Comparing the Three Policies

A comparison of the three common accounts receivable policies reveals that the 2/10 net 30 policy has an expected total profit, after deducting the delinquency and default costs, of $655. We derive this by subtracting the delinquency and default costs of $120 and $40, respectively, from the previously computed profit before those costs of $815.

The net 30 policy has a total profit, after deducting the delinquency and default costs, of $165. This is calculated by subtracting the delinquency cost of $45 and the default cost of $15 from the previously computed profit before those costs of $225.

The total profit to the cash policy does not change at all from the previously computed $200, since there are no delinquency or default costs associated with a cash policy. Obviously, the most attractive policy for this firm is the 2/10 net 30 policy, because it maximizes the profits when using accounts receivable policy as a competitive tool. As the financial officer, you should be willing to finance the marketing department if it selects this policy; you should encourage further study if the marketing department wants a different policy.

IMPLEMENTING AND MONITORING THE
ACCOUNTS RECEIVABLE POLICY

Once you have chosen the profit-maximizing accounts receivable policy, which in our example is 2/10 net 30, how do you implement and monitor it?

You cannot just extend credit to any potential customer who simply asks for it. You must carefully screen each and weed out the potential defaults and delinquents as much as possible before they inflict losses on the firm. This requires a careful selection process and determination of the rate of the return we can expect from extending credit. As financial officers we do not want to extend credit, even if it is profitable, if the return to that extension is less than the cost of capital used to finance it.

After the initial screening, the financial officer is required to continually monitor the existing accounts receivable to detect any deterioration or troublesome accounts early and rectify the situation before the firm incurs large losses. We do not want to keep extending credit to a customer who defaults just because we originally thought the customer would be a good credit risk. We shall explore various monitoring indications which we, as financial officers, might employ.

The Selection Process

How does the financial officer evaluate the risk of extending credit to any particular customer? What standards exist for extending credit?

Traditional standards The traditional standards are somewhat vaguely referred to as the five Cs of capital, character, conditions, capacity, and collateral.[2] *Capital* is typically measured by the size and financial strength of customers, as reflected in their financial statements. Our analysis, in the case of a corporation, might focus on the potential customer's capital accounts, stockholders' equity, and total assets. In the case of a personal account, we would focus on the analogous aspects of the individual's financial statements.

The potential customer's *character* is typically judged by reputation and determination for paying. Look at the customer's past record of business and payment practices. Satisfy yourself that the management has always operated with the fullest intent of meeting its obligations and has never been involved in other than desirable relationships with previous suppliers. Do not be swayed by the fast talk of a potential customer who insists that if you do not immediately grant credit he or she will go to your competitors. Reputable customers understand that you need a reasonable amount of time to investigate their creditworthiness and are willing to cooperate.

In screening potential customers, you must judge their past payment records against the general economic *conditions* which prevailed during the period of time you are investigating. Frequently marginal credit risks may appear more creditworthy than they should because of the crest in an economic boom which they may be riding. You should really examine customers' records to see that they have paid their bills even during recessionary economic climates. Extending credit to customers who have had trouble paying their bills in economic recessions may find your firm the next creditor to suffer after the economic boom has passed.

---

[2] J. F. Weston and E. Brigham, *Managerial Finance,* Holt, New York, 1972, pp. 536 ff.

The potential customer's *capacity* to pay has typically been judged by the extent of the more liquid assets, such as cash, marketable securities, inventories, and accounts receivable on the grounds that it is to these that the customer will turn to pay your bills. Of course you must judge the quality of those current assets. If, for example, the inventory appears to be obsolete or unsalable, you should not rely on current assets as a good indication of capacity to pay.

You might extend credit to a customer, despite reservations about credit-worthiness, if you can secure *collateral* which you could sell to satisfy your claim in the event of default. Sometimes the product you have delivered to the customer can be used as collateral. Under the system of consignment, for example, you retain title (ownership) of the product, until the customer sells it for a commission. Since you already own it, you can repossess it any time the customer appears too shaky.

Quantifying the risk The financial officer develops an intuitive feel for the credit-worthiness of potential customers after screening several thousand accounts receivable. But there are also techniques which make it possible to attach a more precise risk label on each customer. One of these techniques is discriminant analysis, discussed in Appendix 14A, which attempts to determine the potentially good and potentially bad risks through a statistical application. We can similarly distinguish the potentially good from the potentially bad without the use of the statistical application by identifying the various characteristics which have historically affected the customer's creditworthiness and by comparing the value of those characteristics against the historical standards for good and bad risks. For example, after looking at the firm's trade credit records for the last decade, we might select the 10 characteristics listed in Table 14-1 as the most indicative of credit risk. Then we could calculate the average value for each of these indicators for both historically good and historically bad (nonpaying) customers, using the financial statements of those customers for the worst year of general business conditions in the preceding decade.

Next compute the values of these indicators from the prospective customer's financial statements and compare them to the historical averages in Table 14-1. Every time the customer is at or below the historically bad value of any indicator, we can arbitrarily increase the risk of the customer not paying by 10 percent, representing one out of ten indicators which were typical of historically bad credit risks. Each time the value of the prospective customer's indicator lies between the historically bad level and the historically good level, we can increase the risk of not paying by 5 percent. For example, if the indicator levels for the prospective customer are as represented in Table 14-2, we can see that the acid-test ratio lies

Table 14-1   Historical Standards for Various Creditworthiness Indicators

Indicator	Good risk	Bad risk
1. Current ratio	2.0:1	1.5:1
2. Acid-test ratio	1.0:1	.7:1
3. Working capital	$ 1 million	$300,000
4. Debt/equity ratio	$2/1$	$4/1$
5. Total assets	$10 million	$ 2 million
6. Accounts receivable turnover	12 times	9.7 times
7. Inventory turnover	4.5 times	3.7 times
8. Total revenue	$50 million	$22 million
9. Credit payment record that year	On time	Delayed
10. Total accounts payable	$ 50,000	$700,000

Table 14-2 Prospective Customer's Indicator Values

Indicator	Value	Cumulative credit risk
1. Current ratio	2.0:1	0
2. Acid-test ratio	.9:1	5%
3. Working capital	$ 1.5 million	5
4. Debt/equity ratio	4/1	15
5. Total assets	$15 million	15
6. Accounts receivable turnover	14 times	15
7. Inventory turnover	4.5 times	15
8. Total revenue	$55 million	15
9. Credit record	On time	15
10. Total accounts payable	$600,000	20

between the historically good and historically bad level, and we increase the risk of not paying by 5 percent. Similarly, the customer's debt/equity ratio is at the historically bad risk level, so we would increase the customer's chance of not paying by another 10 percent to a cumulative total of 15 percent. The total accounts payable lie between the historically good and bad standards, so we would increase the risk another 5 percent to a total cumulative risk of 20 percent. In sum, we have assigned a 20 percent chance that this prospective customer will not pay the accounts receivable.

If we analyze the credit risk of each customer by comparing his indicators value to the standards developed as in Table 14-1, we can rank each customer in a category of credit risk. There would be those who fall into the 5 percent chance of not paying, the 10 percent chance, the 15 percent chance, and so on down to the higher risk categories. Naturally we would want to extend trade credit to the lowest risk category first and then, if profitable, to the next lowest risk category and so on. While somewhat crude, this method allows the financial officer to assign a quantitative ranking to each customer. And it can be refined by such subjective inputs as the financial officer's intuitive judgments on the customer's character and on any collateral that may be offered.

Sources of Information

Where do we, as financial officers, get the information we use in quantifying and evaluating the customer's credit risk?

Dun and Bradstreet Figure 14-2 is a sample Dun and Bradstreet Report (D and B) on the hypothetical Arnold Metal Products Company. We can see from the summary section of the report that this firm typically takes the early payment discount on its trade credit, makes sales of $177,250, has a net worth of $42,961, and employs 10 people. The summary also gives the name and address of the customer, the principals in the business, the number of years in operation, and the nature of the business.

The payments section tells us the customer's record of meeting trade credit obligations during the past period. The highest amount (HC) of trade credit granted this customer by other firms was $3,000 of which it still owes $1,500, although none of the amount is past due. Other firms have extended credit on an early payment discount basis for at least the last three years. This payments section provides the financial officer with insight into what other firms have experienced in their exten-

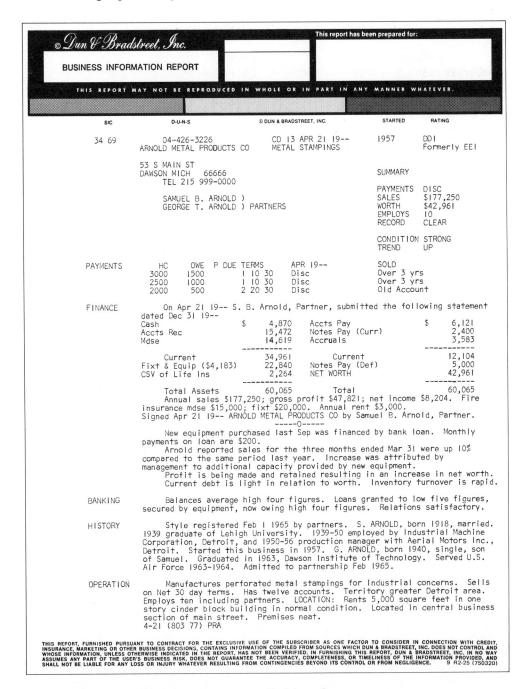

Figure 14-2 Dun and Bradstreet Report on a Ficticious Company

sion of trade credit to this customer. We can also judge the credit terms we might have to offer, if we plan to compete with this potential customer's present suppliers.

The finance section of the Dun and Bradstreet report gives us information on the customer's financial position. We are given a current balance sheet and highlights of the customer's income statement, including such items as annual rents and the amount of insurance coverage. We also get information on the age of the customer's plant and equipment and on the current state of profitability. Any of the information contained here could be used as an indicator in Table 14-1, if the financial officer's experience shows that it has been a reliable indicator in the past.

The banking section reveals the current status of the customer's relationship with the banker. Since the banker can typically keep close tabs on the customer because of the flow of funds through the bank, a good banking relationship may be highly indicative of a good trade credit risk. It also might indicate that the customer could resort to bank finance, if a seasonal cash bind developed, in order to pay the firm's trade credit.

The history section reveals the personal qualifications of the management. We can see in this sample report that the customer is a family business run by a father and son who appear to be technically competent.

The operations section of the report indicates the customer's relationship with his clients. We can see that the customer has only twelve accounts, mainly in the Detroit area. This could be troublesome if one of the larger accounts delayed payments, because it would disrupt a relatively large proportion of the Arnold Metal Product's cash inflow. This could, in turn, jeopardize the payment of the trade credit your firm has extended to Arnold Metal Products. We can also see from this section where the firm is located and the condition in which it keeps its operating facilities. Again, if the financial officer's experience shows that any of the operating information contained in the report is indicative of the customer's creditworthiness, he or she can incorporate it among the variables of Table 14-1.

From their investigation, Dun and Bradstreet give the potential customer an overall credit rating, which is stated in the upper right hand corner of this sample report. For the Arnold Metal Products Company this rating is DD1, which according to the rating explanations in Figure 14-3, tells us that Dun and Bradstreet estimates the financial strength of this customer to be between $35,000 to $50,000 and the creditworthiness of this customer to be high.

Financial statements The public financial statements of those firms that issue them are another source of information which the alert financial officer would use in evaluating a prospective customer's credit risk. If the firm does not issue public statements, the financial officer can use the Dun and Bradstreet report to get needed information. If the potential customer does not have a Dun and Bradstreet listing or refuses to cooperate in the report, the financial officer should be wary of extending credit.

Bank references As financial officers, we should check with the prospective customer's bank as a routine part of the screening process. The banker has the most current information on the customer's financial position and can give you, *with the customer's permission,* an idea of the prospect's current checking account balance, record of bad checks, and financial history. The banker might even give you some personal insights into the customer's character and operations.

Key to Ratings

ESTIMATED FINANCIAL STRENGTH			COMPOSITE CREDIT APPRAISAL			
			HIGH	GOOD	FAIR	LIMITED
5A	Over	$50,000,000	1	2	3	4
4A	$10,000,000 to	50,000,000	1	2	3	4
3A	1,000,000 to	10,000,000	1	2	3	4
2A	750,000 to	1,000,000	1	2	3	4
1A	500,000 to	750,000	1	2	3	4
BA	300,000 to	500,000	1	2	3	4
BB	200,000 to	300,000	1	2	3	4
CB	125,000 to	200,000	1	2	3	4
CC	75,000 to	125,000	1	2	3	4
DC	50,000 to	75,000	1	2	3	4
DD	35,000 to	50,000	1	2	3	4
EE	20,000 to	35,000	1	2	3	4
FF	10,000 to	20,000	1	2	3	4
GG	5,000 to	10,000	1	2	3	4
HH	to	5,000	1	2	3	4

**CLASSIFICATION FOR BOTH
ESTIMATED FINANCIAL STRENGTH AND CREDIT APPRAISAL**

FINANCIAL STRENGTH BRACKET

1 $125,000 and Over

2   20,000 to 125,000

EXPLANATION

When only the numeral (1 or 2) appears, it is an indication that the estimated financial strength, while not definitely classified, is presumed to be within the range of the ($) figures in the corresponding bracket and that a condition is believed to exist which warrants credit in keeping with that assumption.

ABSENCE OF RATING DESIGNATION FOLLOWING NAMES LISTED IN THE REFERENCE BOOK

The absence of a rating, expressed by two hyphens (--), is not to be construed as unfavorable but signifies circumstances difficult to classify within condensed rating symbols. It suggests the advisability of obtaining a report for additional information.

EMPLOYEE RANGE DESIGNATIONS IN REPORTS OR NAMES NOT LISTED IN THE REFERENCE BOOK

Certain businesses do not lend themselves to a Dun & Bradstreet rating and are not listed in the Reference Book. Information on these names, however, continues to be stored and updated in the D&B Business Data Bank. Reports are available on such businesses and instead of a rating they carry an Employee Range Designation (ER) which is indicative of size in terms of number of employees. No other significance should be attached.

**KEY TO EMPLOYEE
RANGE DESIGNATIONS**

ER 1	Over 1000 Employees
ER 2	500-1000 Employees
ER 3	100 - 499 Employees
ER 4	50 - 99 Employees
ER 5	20 - 49 Employees
ER 6	10 - 19 Employees
ER 7	5 - 9 Employees
ER 8	1 - 4 Employees
ER N	Not Available

© *Dun & Bradstreet, Inc.* 1975
99 Church Street, New York, N.Y. 10007   18B-7 (740308)

Figure 14-3   Dun and Bradstreet's Key to Ratings

Credit bureaus The financial officer should also check with such centralized credit bureaus as the National Association of Credit Men, which gathers credit information from many sources and geographical areas into one report. The experiences of other trade creditors with this prospective customer are centralized at the bureau and give the financial officer an extensive history of the prospect on such points as the maximum credit other firms have extended, the length of the credit terms, the amount of credit used by the customer, and the promptness of payments.

Evaluating the Credit Lines

Once we have decided on which accounts receivable policy maximizes the firm's profit and know how to classify potential customers according to credit risk, how much credit risk in total should the firm undertake? How much credit should it extend to members of a particular credit risk category?

Individual customer line How much credit does the firm extend to any one customer? We do not want to extend too much credit to any one customer to avoid a crushing blow to the firm's financial integrity if that customer did unexpectedly default. We must set a limit on the extension of credit to any one customer, even if we consider the change of default to be slight. The more creditworthy customers will be extended more credit than the less creditworthy. For example, once we have ranked the customers by credit risk category using the procedure illustrated in Table 14-2, we can determine the amount of credit the firm should extend to any one customer in a particular risk category.

Table 14-3 shows that we have decided to extend no more than $100,000 in credit to our best customers, those with but a 5 percent chance of default. If there is a 40 percent or higher chance of default in our opinion, after we have screened the prospective customer, the firm demands cash payment upon delivery of the goods. And between these extremes, as the chance of a bad account increases, the amount of credit we should be willing to extend diminishes. Of course, we can always make exceptions because of such circumstances as the offer of collateral.

Notice that the limits are set somewhat arbitrarily depending on the amount the financial officer feels comfortable with in each risk category and do not consider the benefits to be gained by extending credit. Limiting the amount of credit to any one customer does, however, set a clear policy which prevents your more zealous salespeople from extending too much credit in order to make a sale. It is your job as the financial officer to insure that the marketing department does not push the firm into overextending credit to any one individual, or total credit, just for the sake of increasing sales.

Total credit extended Not only should there be a limit on the amount of credit that the firm extends to any one customer, but there also should be a limit on how much risk the firm should undertake in its total extension of credit. At what level of overall risk should the firm cut off credit and insist on a cash-only payment basis?

The answer lies in the firm's expected return to financing the higher risk categories. In other words, does the return on the additional sales generated by extending credit to the next higher risk category qualify as an attractive investment?

Let us assume that the firm now extends credit to the 5 percent risk category (95 percent chance of paying) only. Does it pay the firm to extend credit to the 10 per-

Table 14-3 Assigning Credit Limits

Credit risk category (from Table 14-2)	Maximum credit line
5%	$100,000
10	50,000
20	30,000
30	5,000
40 or larger	cash

cent (90 percent chance of paying) risk category? That depends on the additional revenues and profits generated by the extension, the amount of funds needed to finance the additional accounts receivables, and the firm's cost of capital for those funds. For example, let us assume that the extension of credit to the 10 percent risk category would add $200,000 in annual sales. Assuming that the firm's cost of goods sold and selling and general administrative expenses are 60 percent of the selling price (a 40 percent operating profit margin), that the additional collection costs are $30,000, and that the cost of capital is 12%, we can express the amount of additional financing needed to support the additional accounts receivable as well as the return on the investment of those funds as follows:

Additional annual sales	$200,000	
Uncollected accounts receivable (10%)	20,000	
Net additional revenue		$180,000
Additional cost of goods sold and selling		
and general administrative expense (60%)	120,000	
Additional collection costs	30,000	
Total additional costs		150,000
Additional annual net income		30,000
Taxes (50%)		15,000
Additional annual net income after taxes		15,000

Notice that the expected default of 10 percent of the additional sales ($20,000) is subtracted directly from the annual increase in sales. The additional collection costs associated with the delay in payments and other collection costs of $30,000 are treated as a separate expense.

The total investment needed to support the additional annual sales is not $200,000. The firm need only finance that amount of accounts receivable which is outstanding on average during any one period during the year. For example, if the accounts receivable turned over four times a year, the average amount outstanding during any quarterly period would be $50,000; that is one-fourth of the annual amount. Of course, over all four quarterly periods within the year, the total amount would be $200,000, or four times $50,000, which is our annual additional sales. We can envision this as selling $50,000 of the product in the first quarter and having the accounts receivable generated by those sales paid off in the first quarter. The firm would finance only $50,000 of accounts receivable in that first quarter and at the end of that quarter would have no funds invested in accounts receivable. Then, if the firm sold another $50,000 of goods in the second quarter, it would generate $50,000 in accounts receivable, which would be paid off by the end of the second quarter. Total sales for both quarters would have been $100,000, but the total required investment in accounts receivable would have been only $50,000. Extending this to a full year of four quarters gives us annual sales of $200,000 and a needed investment of $50,000.

But even that $50,000 is an overstatement of the amount needed, for that includes the firm's profit, which we do not have to finance since we only fund the expenses incurred in creating the sales which lead to those profits. In this case, the expenses would be the additional cost of goods sold and the additional selling and administrative expense plus the additional collection costs, which in this case represent 75 percent of the selling price (derived as $150,000/$200,000). Our additional needed investment in this case would be only 75 percent of the $50,000, or $37,500, enough to cover expenses incurred in producing the additional revenue.

The return on that additional investment of $37,500 would be derived as the additional after-tax profit of $15,000 in relation to the additional investment, or:

$$\frac{\$15,000}{\$37,500} = 40\%$$

That 40 percent return is a good return and certainly in excess of our 12 percent cost of capital. It is clear that the firm should extend credit to the 10 percent risk category.

As financial officers, we should be encouraged by this large expected return and continue our analysis in a similar fashion to see if the expected returns generated by extending credit to the 20 percent risk category also exceed the firm's cost of capital. If so, the firm should extend credit to that group and so on. We keep extending credit to greater risk categories as long as the return on the additional investment exceeds the cost of capital, unless there are other projects with higher returns which should be funded first.

Monitoring Accounts Receivable

Just because the financial officer establishes a line of trade credit for an individual customer and a total credit line for the entire firm does not mean he or she can ignore accounts receivable management thereafter. It is important to continually monitor the receivables for indications of deterioration in an individual customer's ability to pay and of an overextension of credit to all customers. And you must trouble-scout for mechanical and procedural failures on the part of credit department equipment and personnel.

Monitoring individual customer credit[3]   The financial officer can check for deterioration in the creditworthiness of an individual customer by keeping a careful watch on certain telltale signs. The age of the oldest balance is one useful sign. You want to be sure that customers are not letting their records of promptness slip beyond the customary point. You want to also check the total amount each customer owes the firm to insure that each does not exceed the credit limit set for that particular risk category. You should check the amount of any past-due payment; an increasing amount should lead you to investigate further. You should know the date each account was opened and the record of promptness with which it has been paid. You should also periodically determine if there has been a payment in each account since the last due date. All these factors should be reviewed for each account at frequent and regular intervals so that you can quickly detect any deterioration and take remedial steps.

Monitoring the firm's entire credit line   It is also up to the financial officer to continually check certain indicators which can foreshadow need for a change in the accounts receivable policy. The accounts receivable turnover ratio (Chapter 3) or average collection period must be continually monitored to see that it remains within acceptable limits. For example, if the average collection period approaches 90 days when the firm only extends a maximum of 30 days' credit, there is clearly a deterioration and a problem with the accounts receivable policy or screening process which requires immediate attention. Similarly, a turnover ratio of four times a year

---

[3] J. B. Cohen and S. M. Robbins, *The Financial Manager,* Harper and Row, New York, 1966, p. 476.

when twelve times a year is the industry standard is a clear indication of a receivables problem. However, the financial officer must also be aware that there may be a seasonal pattern in the collection period caused by the Christmas selling season or seasonal billing dates. In those cases, the collection period must be compared to the acceptable limit under the circumstances.

Another check is required to see if the percentage of accounts receivable that do default is higher or lower than you would expect in the risk category. For example, if we had expected 20 percent of the sales to a particular risk category to default, but only 10 percent actually defaulted, we must review our credit standards to determine if they are too restrictive and discourage additional business which the firm could gain by lowering the standards and extending credit to other potential customers. On the other hand, if we had expected 20 percent of the sales to default and 30 percent actually defaulted, we would have to review our standards because they may have been too lax. Further, if the percentage of orders rejected for credit reasons seems too high (low), we will have to review the credit standards to see if they are too restrictive (lax).

Still another monitoring indicator is the age of the accounts receivable. We can categorize the accounts receivable by the number of days they have been outstanding, as shown in Table 14-4. If our accounts receivable policy was net 30, yet a disproportionate percentage of the accounts were over 30 days old, we would have to review our policy and credit standards. We could check against the historical record of the ages of accounts receivable and see if too many of the present receivables were over age.

Notice, however, that the aging of the total accounts receivable does not indicate the ability of the collection department to follow up on delinquent accounts. The aging schedule may be misleading in that regard because of seasonal sales patterns.[4] For example, if the firm extended $100 in 30-day credit in January and $900 in 30-day credit in February, the aging schedule at the end of February might show 91 percent ($900) of the accounts under 30 days old and 9 percent ($90) of the accounts between 31 and 60 days old. That may look like a highly acceptable aging schedule at first, but it hides the fact that the firm has collected only 10 percent of its January accounts, not a very good collection record.

In order to avoid this distortion and to get a better indication of the firm's ability to follow up and collect, we should determine the percentage of the amount still outstanding in relation to the amount of accounts receivable which originally gave rise to these accounts. For example, if $90 of the original $100 of January accounts remained uncollected at the end of February, we would say 90 percent of the January accounts were between 31 and 60 days old—not a very good record for a firm with a net 30 policy. Yet in terms of all the accounts for both January and February, only 9

Table 14-4   Aging Accounts Receivable

Age	Percent of total accounts receivable
Under 30 days	70%
31–60 days	20
61–90 days	7
Over 90 days	3
	100%

[4] W. G. Lewellen and R. J. Johnson, "Better Way to Monitor the Accounts Receivable," *Harvard Business Review*, May–June 1972, pp. 101–107.

percent of the accounts are between 31 and 60 days old. By relating the uncollected amount to the original sales month, we can get a better picture of the firm's collection results. In this case they are poor.

ALTERNATIVE METHODS OF FINANCING ACCOUNTS RECEIVABLE

Instead of financing the accounts receivable by raising funds to be invested in the receivables, the financial officer might use special methods of accounts-receivable financing which might be less costly or lower the firm's risk exposure to default. Among several relatively common methods are: (1) factoring, (2) credit insurance, (3) captive finance companies, and (4) various ways of reducing the firm's risk exposure.

Factoring

Factoring[5] is the sale of the firm's accounts receivable to a factor (a buyer of accounts receivable) under a previously negotiated, and usually flexible, agreement. Typically the firm's customers are instructed to pay their accounts directly to the factor, who acts as the firm's credit department. When the payment is received, the factor keeps part of it as factor's fee and credits the remainder to the firm's account.

Most factors will perform all the functions of the firm's credit department. They will screen and evaluate the potential customers for credit risk. They will collect the accounts receivable. They will sometimes assume all the risk of default under an arrangement whereby they purchase the accounts receivable from the firm without recourse. If the receivable has been purchased without recourse, the factor must bear the loss of any default. However, most accounts receivable are purchased with recourse to the firm, such that if the factor cannot collect, the firm has to reimburse the amount of the default by either making a cash payment or replacing the defaulted account with another, more viable account. Of course, the factor's fee is higher if the factor buys the receivables without recourse.

The factor may also lend the firm funds in advance of the anticipated payments on the receivables, to be repaid when the customer pays off the account. The factor charges interest on the loan, and the rates are typically higher than those which a bank might charge when it lends against the firm's pledge of the accounts receivable.

Benefits of factoring The major benefits of factoring lie in the costs the firm saves by not running its own credit operation. There are no collection costs, as the factor is responsible for collecting the account. There are no credit department costs such as bookkeeping or salaries. The firm can avoid the risk of default if it chooses to sell its accounts without recourse, although this is usually more expensive. The firm can get funds very quickly and almost without any of the delay or cost of applying for a loan or selling securities. The factor almost automatically advances the firm funds as soon as the account is opened.

---

[5] William J. Beranek, *Working Capital Management,* Wadsworth, Belmont, Calif., 1966, pp. 134 ff.

Costs of factoring The factor usually charges a service fee or discounts the face value of the account when it is purchased from the firm. For example, if the account were for $1,000, the factor might pay the firm only $950 for it. That would be a 5 percent discount on a 90-day account receivable, or an effective annual interest rate of 20 percent (4 times 5 percent). This is the factor's compensation for servicing your accounts. If the factor also lends the firm money in advance and you take the $950 before the account is collected by the factor, your firm is also charged interest.

Implications for the financial officer You will be called upon by the firm's decision makers to analyze the alternatives of financing the firm's accounts receivable internally or financing them through factoring. If the cost of factoring is less than the cost of internally financing them, you should recommend that the firm factor, and vice versa. For example, let us assume that the firm had $1,000 in 30-day accounts receivable which it could sell to the factor without recourse at a 5 percent discount (service fee) from the face value and would receive an advance loan for the $950 at 10 percent per annum. Alternatively, the firm could internally finance the receivables at an annual after-tax cost of capital of 10 percent and expect that 10 percent of the face value of the accounts would default and have to be expensed as bad debts. The costs of these alternatives are compared below:

Factored		Internally financed	
Service fee	$50	Cost of capital	$ 25
Interest on advance	23.75	Expected bad debt expense	100
Total costs	$73.75	Total costs	$125

Since the factoring alternative is the less expensive of the two, you should recommend that the firm factor its receivables.

Credit Insurance[6]

There are a few specialized insurance companies that will insure the firm against unusually large defaults of the firm's accounts receivable in any one period. For example, if the average expected default for the period is $20,000, but the firm actually suffers $40,000 in credit losses, the insurance company would reimburse the firm for 80 percent of the loss over the expected amount, which, in this case, is $16,000. That reimbursement figure is derived by determining that there was $20,000 more in losses during the period than had been anticipated and then taking 80 percent of that. The firm suffers the other $4,000 in unexpected losses. This 80 percent coverage is known as a coinsurance factor. The insurance company hopes having to bear part of the loss will prevent firms from carelessly or intentionally encountering unexpected losses.

Credit insurance may be particularly valuable if the firm has only a few large accounts receivable. Under these conditions, if any account defaulted it would be a devastating blow to the firm. It may also be useful to firms with many small, higher-than-average-risk accounts. Credit insurance is sometimes required by a bank before it will lend the firm funds on the pledge of accounts receivable as collateral; the bank wants to make sure the collateral is not going to be worthless if it has to seize it as payment for the loan.

[6] *Ibid.*, pp. 127–134.

There are also less attractive aspects to credit insurance. It tends to be relatively costly, varying with the credit risk of the accounts receivable and figured as a percentage of the firm's sales. The insurance company may refuse to insure those particular accounts which are in most need of insurance. And sometimes the interference of the insurer in the firm's handling of its credit department may be unacceptable to the firm's management.

Captive Finance Companies

Some firms have established wholly-owned subsidiaries to finance the firm's accounts receivable. For example, General Motors Acceptance Corporation, Ford Motor Credit, and Sears Roebuck Acceptance Corporation are captive finance companies. Sometimes the creation of a captive finance company makes it easier to raise funds because of its expertise in such financial instruments as commercial paper, and, of course, it gives the parent firm greater flexibility in extending credit to encourage sales. However, the borrowing capacity of the firm is probably not increased.[7] It is almost certainly more profitable than factoring or borrowing at a bank to finance the firm's receivables, because its cost of capital is typically cheaper than bank loans.

Other Accounts Receivable Strategies

As the financial officer, you can adapt your firm's accounts receivable policy to reduce its exposure to the default risk. One method is *consignment* of your product to the customer instead of outright sale. Under the consignment arrangement, the firm keeps the title to the goods and collects for the product as the customer sells it. If for some reason the customer no longer appears creditworthy, the firm can immediately repossess the goods since it already owns them. The speed and the legal ease with which consignment allows the firm to get back its goods (instead of the more difficult task of enforcing collection when trade credit is extended) can reduce your risk.

The firm can insist upon *collateral* to secure the line of trade credit it grants the customer. The collateral will hopefully be converted to the firm's ownership and sold to satisfy the amount of the credit extended if the customer should default. However, it is not always easy to convert the pledged collateral or to insure that it will be sufficiently valuable to satisfy the entire claim.

Of course, the firm can insist upon a cash-only policy for some or all of its customers, eliminating the credit risk. Finally, the firm may extend only small amounts of credit to a customer at first and gradually extend more as the trade relationship develops. In that fashion, the financial officer can more accurately observe the customer's character over time, preventing unduly large losses from unknown customers.

SUMMARY

After having read Chapter 14, you should be able to answer these questions:
1. What are accounts receivable?
Accounts receivable are extensions of trade credit to a firm's customer.

---

[7] W. G. Lewellen, "Finance Subsidiaries and Corporate Borrowing Capacity," *Financial Management,* Spring 1972, pp. 21–32.

2. What is the objective of accounts receivable policy?

The accounts receivable policy is basically a marketing tool to encourage sales. By extending credit, the firm expects to sell to more customers and meet the competition. However, it is the financial officer's responsibility to see that the policy adopted maximizes the firm's profits and moves it furthest towards its corporate goal. We must see to it that the firm does not overextend its trade credit beyond a point where the return on the investment required to support the receivable is unattractive in comparison to other available projects which the firm could undertake and that the firm's exposure to default risk is not more than it should be.

3. What accounts receivable policies are available to the financial officer?

The three most common accounts receivable policies are the cash policy, the net 30 days policy, and the 2/10 net 30 days policy. Under the cash policy the firm demands payment for the product when delivered and exposes itself to no credit risk. Under the net 30 policy, the firm allows its customers 30 days in which to pay. Under the 2/10 net 30 policy, the firm gives the customer a 2 percent discount for payment within 10 days and up to 30 days within which to pay without a discount. The idea is to encourage early and prompt payment by the customer. Of course the firm can vary any of the terms by changing the discount allowed for early payment, the number of days within which the customer can pay and still take the discount, or the number of total days the customer can take without the discount.

4. How does the financial officer implement and monitor the accounts receivable policy?

It is the financial officer's responsibility to evaluate each of the possible policies and determine which is the most profitable. You must weigh the additional sales that the firm can expect from extending more generous credit terms against the additional financing and collection costs associated with the more generous terms. The financing cost will rise as the length of time for payment increases, while the collection costs tend to be relatively fixed until the account goes beyond the due date. At that time the firm incurs additional costs associated with the delinquency, such as the expense of further collection efforts. If the account eventually defaults, the firm incurs a total write-off of the full amount of the account as a bad debt expense. The financial officer must consider the financing costs as well as the collection costs, the expected delinquency costs, and the expected default costs in determining which policy is the most profitable.

Once the firm has selected the appropriate policy, the financial officer must still monitor the accounts to insure that the firm's collection procedures are working well: that there is no deterioration in the creditworthiness of individual customers and that each potential customer is properly screened to determine the risk of extending credit. We saw that we can evaluate the credit risk by carefully examining the firm's historical experience with good and with bad risk and seeing how the prospective customer compares. If the customer resembles the characteristics of the historically bad risk more than the historically good risk, we should be very careful about extending credit. We also saw that the firm should continue to extend credit to less creditworthy customers provided the expected return to the investment in those additional accounts receivable warrants it.

5. What alternative financing methods are available to reduce the cost or risk of accounts receivable financing?

We saw that the firm can factor its receivables. It can also partially insure against an excessively large amount of default, and it can use a captive finance company for internally funding its receivables.

QUESTIONS

14-1 What is the general objective of accounts receivable management? In what ways is it similar and different from cash balance management and inventory management?

14-2 Explain what the following terms mean:
(a) net 30
(b) net 45
(c) 2/10 net 30
(d) 1/15 net 29

14-3 Identify some of the costs associated with accounts receivable and give examples of each type of cost.

14-4 What are the principal benefits of a liberal accounts receivable policy? Would you expect the firm's salespeople or stockholders to be more supportive of an easier credit policy?

14-5 Widget Company currently has an accounts receivable policy of cash only, but is considering initiating a net 30 accounts receivable policy. Generally speaking, how would you evaluate the proposed new policy?

14-6 What are the five traditional "Cs" the financial officer might consider in evaluating the creditworthiness of a potential customer?

14-7 What are some of the sources of information regarding a potential customer's credit risk that might be available to the financial officer?

14-8 Identify some of the advantages and disadvantages of the following methods of financing accounts receivable:
(a) Factoring
(b) Credit insurance
(c) Captive finance companies

14-9 What are some of the methods that can be used to monitor the firm's entire credit line?

PROBLEMS

14-1 The Public-Favor Company is contemplating a change in its accounts receivable policy from cash to either a net 30 policy or 1/15 net 30 policy. Expected demand is for 2,000 units of output (G-Posts) if the cash-only AR policy is maintained. If the net 30 AR policy is initiated, expected demand will increase to 2,500 G-Posts. The 1/15 net 30 AR policy will increase expected demand to 3,000 G-Posts, of which 500 units will be attributable to the 1/15 trade policy. The current price per G-Post is $5,000 and is expected to remain the same regardless of the AR policy used. The cost of goods used per G-Post is $3,000 and is invariant.

The cost of capital for the firm is 15 percent. Collection costs are estimated to be $200 per G-Post. Delinquency costs are expected to be $400 per G-Post for 5 percent of the total G-Posts sold. Defaults on payment are expected to be 8 percent of sales.
(a) Which AR policy would you recommend if the firm wishes to maximize profits?
(b) Which AR policy would you recommend if the firm wishes to maximize sales?

14-2 The Letme Company has compiled the following set of average indicators for their excellent, good, and poor credit customers for the past five years:

Indicator	Excellent risk	Good risk	Poor risk
Current ratio	2.5	2.0	1.5
Acid test ratio	1.0	0.8	0.6
Debt/equity	0.4	0.8	1.0
Total assets	$10 million	$5 million	$500,000
Accounts receivable turnover	16	12	8
Inventory turnover	7.0	5.5	3.5

In evaluating a potential customer's creditworthiness, the Letme Company assigns a probability of default for each indicator of 15 percent if it is below the poor risk benchmark, 10 percent if it is between the good risk and poor risk categories, 5 percent if it is between the excellent risk and good risk categories and 0 percent if it is greater than the excellent risk benchmark.

A customer recently applied for credit with Letme Company with the following values for its indicators:

Indicator	Customer's indicators	Probability of default	Cumulative probability of default
Current ratio	1.8		
Acid test ratio	0.9		
Debt/equity	0.3		
Total assets	$8 million		
Accounts receivable turnover	14		
Inventory turnover	4.5		

(a) Fill in the probability of default for each indicator and the customer's cumulative probability of default.
(b) Enumerate some of the sources of information the firm could use to obtain the above credit information.
(c) If the following maximum credit lines have been established for the associated cumulative probability of default categories, what is this customer's maximum credit line?

Cumulative probability of default	Maximum credit line
0–5%	$50,000
6–15%	30,000
16–25%	10,000
26–35%	5,000
36–45%	2,000
46–100%	Cash

14-3 The Wilmax Company is presently extending credit only to those customers in the 10 percent risk of default class or less. But a recent increase in credit applications in the 20 percent and 30 percent risk classes has caused the firm to reconsider its credit policy. Additional sales from the 20 percent risk category are estimated to be $500,000 and $300,000 for the 30 percent risk class. The cost of goods sold are 60 percent of sale value, and the firm's cost of capital is 10 percent. The additional collection and delinquency costs on sales to the 20 percent and 30 percent risk classes are $20,000 and $25,000, respectively. The firm's tax rate is 50 percent and the accounts receivable turnover ratio is 5.

(a) What is the incremental annual net income after taxes that would result from extending credit to the 20 percent risk class? The 30 percent risk class?

(b) What is the total investment required to finance the incremental sales in the 20 percent risk class? In the 30 percent risk class?

(c) What is the rate of return earned on the funds used to finance the sales to the 20 percent risk class? The 30 percent risk class?

(d) Should credit be extended to the 20 percent risk class? The 30 percent risk class?

14-4 Whoopla Company has $20,000 in 90-day accounts receivable which it can sell to Factorus Company without recourse for a 7 percent service fee and receive the advance loan at 12 percent per annum. If the accounts receivable are sold with recourse, the service fee is 4 percent and the advanced loan costs 10 percent per annum. Expected default costs are 15 percent of the original value of the accounts receivable. Whoopla's cost of capital is 12 percent.

Should Whoopla finance the accounts receivable internally, by factoring with recourse, or by factoring without recourse?

BIBLIOGRAPHY

Beneshay, Haskel. "Managerial Controls of Accounts Receivable—A Deterministic Approach." *Journal of Accounting Research*, 3 (Spring 1965), 114–133.

———. "A Stockastic Model of Credit Sales Debt." *Journal of the American Statistical Association*, LXI (December 1966), 1010–1028.

Beranek, William. *Analysis for Financial Decisions*. Irwin, Homewood, Ill., 1963, Ch. 10.

Greer, Cecil C. "The Optimal Credit Acceptance Policy." *Journal of Financial and Quantitative Analysis*, II (December 1967), 399–415.

Marrah, George L. "Managing Receivables." *Financial Executive*, XXXVIII (July 1970), 40–44.

Mehta, Dileep. "The Formulation of Credit Policy Models." *Management Science*, 15 (October 1968), 30–50.

———. "Optimal Credit Policy Selection: A Dynamic Approach." *Journal of Financial and Quantitative Analysis*, V (December 1970), 421–444.

Mitchner, Morton, and Raymond P. Peterson. "An Operations-Research Study of the Collection of Defaulted Loans." *Operations Research*, 5 (August 1957), 522–545.

Myers, James H., and Edward W. Forgy. "The Development of Numerical Credit Evaluation Systems." *Journal of the American Statistical Association*, LVIII (September 1963), 799–806.

Welshans, Merle T. "Using Credit for Profit Making." *Harvard Business Review*, 45 (January–February 1967), 141–156.

Wrightsman, Dwayne. "Optimal Credit Terms for Accounts Receivable." *Quarterly Review of Economics and Business*, 9 (Summer 1969), 59–66.

Appendix 14A **Discriminant Analysis as a Credit Screening Tool**

Discriminant analysis is a statistical technique using the characteristics of potential customers to classify them into either a bad credit risk group or a good credit risk group. For example, we can describe the customer by such financial characteristics as current ratio, total asset size, annual revenue, debt/equity ratio and others. We can find the value of each characteristic for historically bad and historically good credit risks and, using discriminant analysis, combine these characteristics into an index of credit risk.

For example, let us describe the good credit risks (G) and the bad credit risks (B) by the value of each customer's current ratio and each customer's asset size. Taking samples from the firm's records of both groups, we could plot the G customers and the B customers as in Figure 14A-1.

We can see from Figure 14A-1 that the B accounts cluster around one area where the current ratio (X_1) and the asset size (X_2) are both relatively low, while the G customers have historically grouped around relatively higher values for those variables, for the most part. Discriminant analysis allows the financial officer to fit a characteristic line which states the value of the G and of the B observations as a function of the variables X_1 and X_2 such that:

$$Z = a_1X_1 + a_2X_2 \qquad (14\text{A-1})$$

Figure 14A-1 G(ood) and B(ad) Customers Plotted by Asset Size and Current Ratio

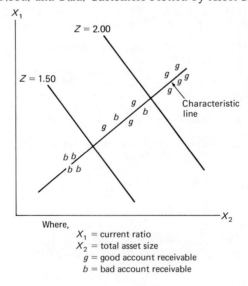

Where,
X_1 = current ratio
X_2 = total asset size
g = good account receivable
b = bad account receivable

Equation 14A-1 combines the values of X_1 and X_2 into an index (Z) weighted by the coefficients a_1 and a_2. A high value of X_1 and of X_2 for any firm puts the Z value in the upper right corner of Figure 14A-1 with the historically good accounts. A low value for each of those variables puts the firm on the characteristic line in the lower left corner with the historically bad risks. For example, let us assume we have two prospective customers, A and B, whose current ratios and asset sizes are:

Firm	Current ratio	Asset size
A	2.0:1	$20 million
B	1.0:1	10 million

If $Z = .4(X_1) + .0000001(X_2)$, the financial officer can determine that A has a Z value of 2.8 while B has a Z value of 1.4. Clearly B fits among the bad risks and should not be extended credit, while A fits into the G group as depicted in Figure 14A-1.

If the financial officer computes the historical Z value for all customers, with both good and bad records, a ranking like that in Table 14A-1 might emerge. In Table 14A-1 we can see that all firms with Z values above 2.0 are clearly good risks, while all firms with Z values below 1.5 are clearly bad risks. Between the 1.5 and the 2.0 value, is a grey area where some of the historically good credit risks actually have lower Z values than some of the historically bad credit risks, and vice versa. There are nine firms in the grey area, four of which were good and five of which were bad. If we extend credit to those firms with a Z value of between 1.9 and 1.99, there is a 33 percent chance that the customer will default, judging by the historical record which shows that 1 out of the 3 firms within that Z-value range was a bad credit risk. If we extend credit to those firms in the 1.8–1.99 Z-value range, the chance of a bad credit risk increases to 40 percent, judging by the historical record which shows 3 good firms and 2 bad firms within that range. Similarly, if we extend credit to the

Table 14A-1   Discriminant Analysis

(a) Arbitrary order			(b) Ranked by Z value		
Customer	Value	Historical record	Customer	Value	Historical record
A	2.8	G	A	2.8	G
B	1.4	B	D	2.1	G
C	2.0	G	J	2.1	G
D	2.1	G	C	2.0	G
E	1.5	B	H	1.9	B
F	1.0	B	M	1.9	G
G	1.7	B	N	1.9	G
H	1.90	B	O	1.85	B
I	1.65	B	K	1.80	G
J	2.1	G	G	1.7	B
K	1.8	G	I	1.65	B
L	1.60	G	L	1.6	G
M	1.90	G	P	1.6	B
N	1.90	G	E	1.5	B
O	1.85	B	B	1.4	B
P	1.60	B	F	1.0	B

1.7–1.99 range, we can expect a 50 percent chance of a bad credit risk. In the 1.6–1.99 range we can expect a 55.5 percent chance of a bad risk.

You can use discriminant analysis to determine into which risk category a particular potential customer fits simply by plugging in the appropriate values for the X variables. You can also rank the customers in descending order of their Z values and use that ranking to determine how far down the Z value the firm should extend credit.

five

short-term sources of funds

LET US LOOK AT SOME OF THE MAJOR QUESTIONS you may face as a financial officer in advising your firm on raising short-term capital. As you read through Part Five, look for the answers to the following questions:

1. What are the major sources of short-term financing?
2. How costly is each source?
3. When is it appropriate to use a particular type of short-term financing?
4. When should the firm lease instead of purchase assets?

15

CRADE CREDIC

WHAT IS TRADE CREDIT? Trade credit typically consists of the financial officer's use of the firm's accounts payable, accrued current liabilities such as taxes payable, and accounts receivable and inventory financing as sources of funds. Adroit use of these sources can contribute to more balanced and less costly fund-raising.

When and how does trade credit arise? As financial officers we must be thoroughly familiar with the answer to that question if we are to use trade credit to the firm's advantage. We shall see that trade credit traditionally arises in the normal course of daily operations. When the firm incurs expenses for later payment or builds up the amount it owes its suppliers, for example, it is temporarily borrowing from those vendors. Alternatively, the financial officer can actively seek additional loans by offering to pledge the firm's inventory or accounts receivable as collateral. We shall see that there are lenders who specialize in these types of loans, and we shall explore the loan characteristics peculiar to them.

Once we know when and how trade credit arises, when is it appropriate for the financial officer to use it as a source of funds? Typically, the general rule is to use trade credit to finance short-term funding because of its short-term repayment characteristic. Long-term maturities tend to be matched with longer-term assets. Although this rule is considered prudent by many, it is not always practiced by financial officers, nor is it necessarily binding in all cases, as we shall see.

TRADE CREDIT—ACCOUNTS PAYABLE

One form of trade credit is the accounts payable. These are the short term credits extended to the firm by its suppliers. Among the specific types of accounts payable which you may encounter are the open account, trade acceptances, promissory notes, and the consignment.

Open Account

An open account is the prearranged extension of credit to the firm by its suppliers, allowing the firm to take possession of the goods and some traditionally determined short-term period of time in which to pay. We have seen in Chapter 14 that typical terms of open accounts might be 30 days. The length of the credit period varies, however, among industries and even between companies within an industry.

The procedure is very simple in that the invoice which accompanies the shipment's delivery is the bill and the only formal acknowledgment of the debt. When the firm's receiving department signs the invoice upon taking delivery, the firm has recognized that it owes the amount on the bill. The receiving department notifies the financial officer's staff in charge of paying these accounts that the goods have been received and are in acceptable condition. Then it is up to you, as financial officer, to decide when to issue the payment check.

The cost of using this extended credit as a source of funds depends on the terms under which it is implemented. If the terms are net 30 days, for example, there is nothing to be gained by paying earlier than 30 days. In fact, earlier payment is costly to the extent that you have to take the funds from some other interest-earning or profitable investment in order to pay. In the process you lose that interest. So as long as the supplier is willing to wait 30 days, you might as well use the funds for the entire period before issuing the check. Of course if you take more than 30 days to pay, you can keep the funds working even longer. But you run the risk of jeopardizing the firm's credit standing, which can be costly and inconvenient, if this leads suppliers to stop extending credit.

If there is a discount for early payment, we can determine the cost of funds incurred by foregoing the discount and using the funds instead for the entire number of days before the account is overdue. For example, if the terms were 2/10, net 30 days, the firm could deduct 2 percent from its bill if it paid within 10 days, but must pay the entire amount if it chooses to use the funds for the entire 30 days. The cost of using those funds for the entire 30 days is 2 percent for an additional 20 days; that is the forfeited 2 percent discount for keeping the funds for the additional 20 days between the tenth day and the thirtieth day. A 20-day 2 percent loan works out to an annual interest rate of approximately 36 percent a year. This is a relatively high rate of interest, and financial officers are generally advised to take such discounts. Of course, smaller discounts or longer credit periods will lower the effective rate of interest and may make the early-payment discount unattractive. If you are not going to take the early-payment discount for some reason, then you should wait until the last day to issue the check, for once the discount is forfeited we might as well use the money, if only in an interest-bearing marketable security, for the few remaining days.

Trade Acceptances

Trade acceptances are essentially checks payable to the supplier at the future date noted on the check. For example, an importer of French wines might draw a check to the order of the French wine exporter, which the exporter could cash in 90 days. The exporter is able to draw the check payable to himself or herself against an account which the importer has set up at a bank. This *letter of credit* states that the importer has established credit with the bank, against which it has authorized the exporter to draw upon providing proof of shipment to the bank.

We, as the importer in our example, can either sign the draft formally acknowledging the debt or the bank can accept the responsibility for its payment in the event of the firm's default. Once accepted by the bank, the draft becomes a negotiable instrument which the exporter can sell at a discount from its face amount to raise funds. At the date on the draft, the owner at that time presents it for collection at the guarantor bank.

Promissory Notes

A promissory note is a formal acknowledgment of the trade credit extended, unlike the open account where there is no formal document which accompanies the extension of the credit. Its use is traditional in some industries, such as the fur industry, for example.

Consignment

Under the consignment process, no credit is extended and ownership of the merchandise never passes from the supplier to the firm. Rather, the merchandise is shipped to the firm under the agreement that it will sell the goods for the supplier's benefit, keeping only a small commission for itself as profit. The firm has no financing costs since it puts up no money, although it still incurs all the selling expenses.

Such suppliers are obligated to make it very plain to the firm that title has not passed by marking the merchandise as their property and insuring that the proceeds generated from the sale of the goods are segregated from the firm's other revenues and remitted to them. The phonograph record displays at most supermarkets are typically consignments. A separate company other than the supermarket sets up and maintains the display, while the consignee (the supermarket in this case) collects the proceeds of the sale and turns them over to the supplier, after deducting its commission.

TERMS OF CREDIT

Our suppliers could also designate the terms under which they expect to get paid when they extend credit to us. Typical terms of payment can range from the restrictive immediate cash payment to very liberal and lengthy credit periods, depending on the industry custom and how the supplier feels about our firm's credit-worthiness.

C. B. D.

Cash before delivery (C. B. D.) is used if the supplier is very wary of the customer's ability or desire to pay. The supplier will often wait for the check to clear the bank before shipping the merchandise to the firm.

C. O. D.

Cash on delivery (C. O. D.) terms are used by the supplier to insure prompt payment. The supplier instructs the transporter, who may be a trucking company or railroad, for example, not to turn over the merchandise to the firm unless the driver collects for them on the spot. If the goods are refused by the firm, the transporter returns the merchandise to the supplier, who bears the transportation costs of both trips.

S. D.–B. L.

The sight draft–bill of lading (S. D.–B. L.) terms assure the supplier payment before the firm takes possession of the merchandise. The bill of lading is the invoice of shipment signifying that the goods have been loaded on the transport and are on their way. The firm needs to present the bill of lading in order to take possession of the goods. The sight draft is the document requiring immediate payment from the firm (payment upon seeing it). The supplier ships the goods and forwards both the sight draft and the bill of lading to a designated bank. The firm must contact the bank and pay off the sight draft to the bank account of the supplier before the bank releases the bill of lading to the firm. Only after presenting the bill of lading to the transporter can the firm physically receive the merchandise.

Cash—No Discount

Under these terms the supplier has extended a reasonable length of time in which the firm is expected to pay after receiving the merchandise. There is no discount for early payment.

Discount Terms

As we have already seen in Chapter 14, the supplier may grant the firm a discount from the purchase price if the firm pays earlier than the full length of the extended credit period. For example, 2/10 net 30 means that if the firm pays within 10 days instead of taking the full 30 days, the supplier will allow it to deduct 2 percent from the payment.

Seasonal Dating

In businesses with a seasonal sales pattern such as Christmas toys, the supplier may be willing to ship early in the year and wait for payment until later in the year around the time the sale of toys picks up. In this fashion, the supplier is able to smooth out the production process and lessen warehousing costs. The firm, on the other hand, has possession of the merchandise earlier in the year and can start to sell some of the items before the major part of the selling season. It can also sell the items during the season before paying for them, if the payment date is after the end of the season. Of course the firm must bear the additional inventory expense it incurs when it takes the merchandise earlier in the year.

F. O. B.

Free on board (F. O. B.) means that the supplier covers all the delivery, inspection, and other costs to the point designated. After the merchandise reaches that point, the firm must cover the costs. For example, F. O. B. Dublin, Ireland means that the United States importer pays for and arranges the transportation, custom inspections, and other costs from the moment that the goods leave Dublin. F. O. B. New York means that the Irish exporter pays the costs to New York City.

C. I. F.

Cost, insurance, and freight (C. I. F.) means that the price quoted by the supplier includes the cost of the merchandise, the insurance charges, and the packing and freight charges to a specific destination.

ACCRUED CURRENT LIABILITIES

In addition to the accounts payable, the financial officer can generate short-term funds, which the firm can use at least temporarily, by postponing payments on current liabilities. If these current liabilities are paid immediately, cash is drained from the firm's treasury. Delaying payment of current liabilities is known as accruing current liabilities. The firm explicitly recognizes the fact that it owes these amounts but it postpones payment, temporarily using the cash elsewhere. Of course, when the firm can no longer postpone payment, it must have the cash available.

Typical accrued current liabilities include the quarterly payment of taxes, for example. Throughout the quarter the firm builds up a tax debt to the federal government as it earns a profit. At the end of the quarter, the firm must pay off the accrued debt. Until that time the financial officer recognizes the existence of the debt but does not pay it, using the cash elsewhere in the firm. Accrued expenses such as salaries, wages, and interest payable are treated in the same fashion.

The deferred income liability is slightly different in that it arises from advance payments to the firm by its customers. The firm has the early use of that money; however, it must fulfill the terms of the advance, usually by delivering the merchandise.

ACCOUNTS RECEIVABLE PLEDGING

We have already seen in Chapter 14 that the financial officer can use the firm's accounts receivable to raise money by factoring them. Alternatively, you can pledge the accounts receivable as collateral to a bank and borrow against the collateral.

The procedure is relatively simple. The financial officer gathers the available accounts-receivable information and presents it to the bank loan officer with a request to borrow funds. The officer will examine the authenticity and creditworthiness of the receivables and, if satisfied, will accept them as collateral with recourse for a loan. This means that if the accounts do not pay, the bank can call upon the firm to substitute another, more viable receivable as replacement for the defaulted account. The firm will be required to pledge formally the accounts receivable to the bank as collateral by signing a security agreement such as that illustrated in Figure 15-1. The agreement sets forth the terms and conditions under which the loan is made, particularly the rights of the bank to satisfy its claim should the firm default on the loan. It also specifies the duties of the firm in fulfilling the terms of the loan, such as the maintenance of accurate records.

In addition to the security agreement, the bank will file a financing statement under the Uniform Commercial Code with the appropriate state authorities. This second agreement has the effect of legally registering the loan under terms which define the rights and obligations of the lender and borrower. This is said to "perfect" the collateral to the benefit of the lender, who is now on public record as having a lien on the collateral. This public record serves to notify other potential lenders that the collateral is already pledged and will be checked by the bank before it makes the loan. A typical Uniform Commercial Code filing form is illustrated in Figure 15-2, and a typical Uniform Commercial Code form to change the original filing is illustrated in Figure 15-3.

In the usual accounts receivable financing, the bank will loan the firm a specified percentage of the total collateral value, so as to provide a cushion in case the receivables default. For example, the bank might loan us 70 percent of the total value of the receivables. Thirty percent of the accounts could default and the bank would still have enough viable collateral to secure the entire loan.

INVENTORY PLEDGING

As financial officers, we can use the firm's inventory as a source of funds in much the same way we use accounts receivable. By pledging the inventory as collateral for a loan, we can arrange to borrow funds under the specific forms of financing peculiar to inventory such as terminal warehousing, field warehousing, trust receipts, floating security and chattel mortgages.

The principle behind using inventory as collateral for a loan is similar to that of accounts receivable or the pledging of any other asset where the firm gives a lien to the lender which entitles the lender to possession of the asset if the firm defaults on the loan. In the specific case of inventory, the goods are usually required to be durable, identifiable, and readily resalable at a prevailing market price. The lender must also be able to get a valid lien on the goods, so that if taking possession becomes necessary, the claim is not disputed.

The inventory pledge must be formalized in a security agreement of some type which gives evidence of the existence of the collateral. The formal security agreement with a bank specifies not only the collateral but also the rights of the bank and the obligations of the borrower, among other items. As financial officer you would sign an agreement like this on behalf of your firm upon pledging collateral such as inventory.

You may come across other documents of collateral evidence besides the illustrated security agreement. These include the trust receipt and the warehouse receipt, which we shall cover shortly. But whatever the particular arrangement, inventory financing always involves a security agreement.

The cost to the borrower using inventory financing involves more than just the interest on the loan, although that is the major cost. In addition the firm is responsible for service charges incurred in maintaining the inventory. These might include such items as storage, inspection by the lender's representatives, and handling, which fall under the obligation of the firm to maintain the inventory so that its collateral value does not diminish. Typically, the borrower must also bear the cost of insuring the inventory against loss by fire or theft.

The typical inventory loan is negotiable on all points. When dealing with the loan officer, it is wise to remember that such items as who bears the inspection costs can be bargained. That does not mean the bank is going to change its demands, but it does mean you should not assume that in order to get the loan you have to agree to *everything* the bank demands. The interest rate charged, for example, will depend on the marketability of the collateral, the creditworthiness of the borrower, and other factors. If the collateral is readily marketable foodstuffs, for example, and the borrower has a prime credit rating, the interest rate should be relatively low.

Floating Collateral Liens

The floating collateral lien is a pledge of inventory without regard to specific inventory items. The borrower simply pledges a certain quantity of inventory or inventory value, reserving the right to substitute specific items of similar type or value for those already pledged.

This type of arrangement has the advantage of not restricting the borrower from

SECURITY AGREEMENT -- ACCOUNTS RECEIVABLE

The undersigned, _____, _____
                            (NAME)   (ADDRESS)

a _____ (hereinafter called "Debtor"), hereby grants to FIRST CITY NATIONAL BANK OF
  (CORPORATION, PARTNERSHIP)
HOUSTON, a national banking association with banking quarters in Houston, Harris County, Texas, whose address is 1001 Main Street, Houston, Texas, the secured party hereunder (hereinafter called "Bank"), a security interest in, and agrees and acknowledges that Bank has and shall continue to have a security interest in, all the Debtor's accounts, contract rights, notes, drafts, acceptances, instruments and chattel paper now owned by Debtor, as well as any and all thereof that may be hereafter acquired by the Debtor, and in and to all the proceeds and products thereof, and in and to all returned or repossessed goods arising from or relating to any contract rights, accounts or other proceeds of any sale or other disposition of inventory, to secure the payment of any and all indebtedness and liabilities whatsoever of the Debtor to Bank, whether direct or indirect, absolute or contingent, due or to become due, and whether now existing or hereafter arising and howsoever evidenced or acquired, and whether several, joint or joint and several.

1. Definitions:

(a) The terms "contract rights," "accounts," "notes," "drafts," "acceptances," "instruments" and "chattel paper" as used herein shall include not only such thereof as arise out of the sale or other disposition at any time and from time to time of inventory, but also such thereof as arise out of or for furnishing services, or the furnishing of, or the furnishing of the use of, or the lease of, any goods, except that the following shall be deemed to be excluded therefrom:

(b) As used herein the term "collateral" means all property from time to time subject to the security interest pursuant hereto.

(c) Subject to further express definitions set forth in subparagraphs (a) and (b) above, all terms used herein which are defined in the Uniform Commercial Code of the State of Texas ("Code") have the same meaning herein as in the Code.

2. General Representations and Warranties:

Debtor represents and warrants:

(a) Except for the security interest of Bank therein, the Debtor is, and as to collateral acquired after the date hereof the Debtor shall and will be, the owner of all collateral free from any liens, security interest, encumbrance or other right, title or interest of any other person, firm or corporation, and Debtor shall defend the collateral against all claims and demands of all persons at any time claiming the same or any interest therein adverse to Bank.

(b) There is no financing statement now on file in any public office covering any property of the Debtor of any kind, real or personal, tangible or intangible, or in which the Debtor is named as or signs as the Debtor, and so long as any amount remains unpaid on any indebtedness or liabilities of Debtor to Bank or any credit from Bank to Debtor is in use by or available to Debtor, the Debtor will not execute and there will not be on file in any public office any such financing statement or statements except the following:

    (i) The financing statement filed or to be filed in respect of and for the security interest in Bank hereby granted or provided for.

(c) In addition to the location at the address shown at the beginning of this agreement, Debtor has only the following places of business:

(d) The only office or offices where the Debtor keeps records concerning any accounts or contract rights are:

    (i) At the address shown at the beginning of this agreement, and _____

_____

    (ii) The Debtor will promptly notify Bank of any change in or additions to the locations specified in (c) and (d) above set forth.

3. Loan Formula:

Except to the extent that Bank may from time to time otherwise agree in writing, the amount of all the loans, and the interest rate thereon and the maturity or maturities thereof, shall be such as Bank shall in its discretion from time to time determine. Without limiting the foregoing it is understood that except to the extent Bank may from time to time otherwise agree in writing, Bank intends to limit its loans, advances or other extensions of credit so that the aggregate principal amount at any one time remaining unpaid on all indebtedness and liabilities of Debtor to Bank secured hereby shall not be in excess of _____% of the aggregate amount owing to the Debtor for shipments of products previously made and for services rendered for which invoices have been issued and in respect of which the Debtor has furnished Bank with the assignments and other information required under paragraph 4(d) hereof. The Debtor warrants that each and all of the accounts at any time included in the computation of the loan formula will be paid in full on or before _____ days from the respective dates of the billing thereof, and accounts which remain unpaid in whole or in part beyond such period are in respect of which set-offs, defenses or counterclaims are claimed by the account Debtor shall not be included in the loan formula. Notwithstanding the delivery of an assignment or identification pursuant to paragraph 4(d) or the making of any loan in connection therewith, Bank may within twenty (20) days after the date of each such assignment or identification, respectively, by notice in writing to the Debtor reject as unacceptable any one or more or all of the accounts included in such assignment or identification; and in the event of any such rejection the Debtor shall forthwith pay and apply on its indebtedness to Bank an amount equal to the loan formula value of such rejected account or accounts and such account or accounts shall not thereafter be included in the loan formula. Any such rejection may be for any reason deemed by Bank to be sufficient and notice of such rejection shall be deemed sufficiently given if mailed to Debtor by Bank within such twenty (20) day period.

4. Special Provisions re Accounts Receivable:

(a) The term "account," "accounts," or "accounts receivable" as used herein includes all contract rights, accounts, notes, drafts, acceptances and chattel paper in which at any time or from time to time Bank has or is intended to have a security interest under or pursuant hereto. As of the time any account becomes subject to such security interest, including without limitation as of each time any specific assignment or transfer or identification is made to Bank of any account, Debtor shall be deemed to have warranted as to each and all of such accounts that each account and all papers and documents relating thereto are genuine and in all respects what they purport to be; that each account is valid and subsisting and arises out of a bona fide sale of goods sold and delivered by the Debtor to, or in the process of being delivered to, or out of and for services theretofore actually rendered by the Debtor to, the account Debtor named in the account; that the amount of the account represented as owing is the correct amount actually and unconditionally owing except for normal cash discounts and is not subject to any set-offs, credits, deductions or counter-charges; that the Debtor is the owner thereof free and clear of all liens, encumbrances and security interest of any nature whatsoever; and that no surety bond was required or given in connection with said account or the contracts or purchase orders out of which the same arose.

(b) Bank shall have the privilege at any time upon request of inspecting during reasonable business hours any of the business locations or premises of the Debtor and the books and records of the Debtor relating to said accounts or the collection thereof as well as those relating to its general business and financial condition. The Debtor further agrees from time to time to furnish such other reports, data and financial statements including audits by independent public accountants, in respect of its business and financial condition as Bank may reasonably require. Bank shall have the right at any time, whether before or after default by the Debtor, to notify any and all account debtors to make payment thereof directly to Bank; but to the extent Bank does not so elect, Debtor shall continue to collect the accounts. Except as otherwise permitted by the proviso to this sentence, all proceeds of collection of accounts received by the Debtor shall be forthwith accounted for and transmitted to Bank in the form as received by Debtor and shall not be commingled with any funds of the Debtor; provided, however, that prior to default by the Debtor in the payment of any principal of or interest on any indebtedness to Bank, or until the privilege given to Debtor by this proviso shall be revoked by Bank in writing, the Debtor need transmit to Bank only the proceeds of accounts included in the identifications or assignments made pursuant to paragraph 4(d) hereof. In the event the account Debtor on any account included in any identification or assignment shall also be indebted to the Debtor in respect of other accounts not so included and such account Debtor shall make payment without designating the particular indebtedness against which it is to apply, such payment shall be conclusively presumed to be payment on the account of such account debtor included in the identification or assignment made pursuant hereto. The proceeds so transmitted to Bank shall be handled and administered by Bank in and through a Remittance or similar account; but the Debtor acknowledges that the maintenance of such an account by Bank is solely for its convenience in facilitating its own operations pursuant hereto and that Debtor has not and shall not have any right, title or interest in said account or in the amounts at any time to the credit thereof. Except to the extent Bank may from time to time in its discretion release proceeds to the Debtor for use in its business, all proceeds received by Bank shall be applied on the indebtedness secured hereby, whether or not such indebtedness shall have by its terms matured, such application to be made at such intervals, and first to principal and then to interest or exclusively to principal (the interest from time to time accruing to be charged to the general account of the Debtor or to be paid separately by the Debtor) as Bank may determine; but such application shall not be made less often than once each week, except that Bank need not apply or give credit for any item included in such proceeds until Bank has received final payment thereof at its office in cash or solvent credits accepted as such by Bank.

(c) Bank shall have the right in its own name or in the name of the Debtor to demand, collect, receive, receipt for, sue for, compound and give acquittance for, any and all amounts due or to become due on the accounts and to endorse the name of the Debtor on all commercial paper given in payment or part payment thereof, and in its discretion to file any claim or take any other action proceeding which Bank may deem necessary or appropriate to protect and preserve and realize upon the security interest of Bank in the accounts and the proceeds thereof.

(d) Debtor will from time to time execute such further instruments and do such further acts and things as Bank may reasonably require by way of further assurance to Bank of the matters and things herein provided for or intended so to be. Without limiting the foregoing, Debtor agrees to execute and deliver to Bank an assignment or other form of identification in the form required by Bank of all accounts at any time included in the computation of the loan formula, together with such other evidence of the existence and identity of such accounts as Bank may reasonably require; and Debtor will mark its books and records to reflect the assignment of such accounts. Debtor will accompany each transmission of proceeds to Bank pursuant to subparagraph (b) above with a report in such form as Bank may require in order to identify the accounts to which such proceeds apply.

(e) Returned or repossessed goods arising from or relating to any accounts shall, if requested by Bank, be held separate and apart from any other property. Debtor shall, as often as requested by Bank, but not less often than weekly even though no special request has been made, report to Bank the appropriate identifying information with respect to such returned or repossessed goods relating to accounts included in assignments, or identifications made pursuant to paragraph 4(d) hereof. At the same time, the Debtor shall report the appropriate identifying information with respect to all accounts included in such assignments or identifications which remain unpaid in whole or in part beyond the period specified in the third sentence of the first paragraph of paragraph 3 hereof or in respect of which set-offs, defenses or counter-claims are claimed by the account debtor. The Debtor shall forthwith pay and apply on its indebtedness to Bank an amount equal to the loan formula value of all accounts included in such reports.

5. Notes:

Each loan shall be evidenced by the promissory note of the Debtor bearing such interest rate and having such maturity as Bank may require, and all such notes shall bear a legend reading substantially as follows:

"This note evidences a loan pursuant to and is entitled to the benefit of the Security Agreement dated the _____ day of _____, 19____, executed by the undersigned in favor of First City National Bank of Houston."

6. General Covenants:

(a) The Debtor agrees to pay promptly when due all taxes, assessments and governmental charges upon or against the Debtor or the property or operations of the Debtor, in each case before the same become delinquent and before penalties accrue thereon, unless and to the extent that the same are being contested in good faith by appropriate proceedings.

(b) Debtor agrees to execute and deliver such financing statement or statements, or amendments thereof or supplements thereto, or other instruments as Bank may from time to time require in order to comply with the Code and to preserve and protect the security interest hereby granted. In the event for any reason, the law of any other jurisdiction other than Texas becomes or is applicable to the collateral or any part thereof, or to any loan by Bank, the Debtor agrees to execute and deliver all such instruments and to do all such other things as may be necessary or appropriate to preserve, protect and enforce the security interest and lien of Bank under the law of such other jurisdiction to at least the same extent as such security interest would be protected under the Code.

(c) In the event Debtor shall fail to maintain insurance, pay taxes, assessments, costs and expenses which Debtor is under any of the terms hereof required to pay, or fails to keep the collateral free from other security interest, liens or encumbrances, Bank may make expenditures for any or all such purposes and the amount so expended together with interest thereon at the rate of _____% per annum shall become immediately due and payable by Debtor to Bank and shall have the benefit of and be secured by the security interest herein granted and agreed to. All costs and expenses of Bank in retaking, holding, preparing for sale and selling or otherwise realizing upon any collateral in the event of any default by Debtor, including court costs and reasonable attorney's fees and legal expenses, shall likewise constitute additional indebtedness of Debtor which Debtor promises to pay on demand and which shall be entitled to the benefit of and be secured by said security interest.

7. Remedies and General:

(a) All indebtedness and liability of Debtor to Bank shall without demand or notice of any kind and notwithstanding the maturity date or dates expressed in any evidence of such indebtedness or liability, become immediately due and payable in the event of the dissolution, termination of existence, insolvency or business failure of the Debtor, or upon the application for the appointment of a receiver of any part of the property of the Debtor, or the commencement by or against the Debtor of any proceeding under any bankruptcy arrangement, reorganization, insolvency or similar law for the relief of debtors, or by or against any guarantor or surety for the Debtor, or upon the service of any warrant, attachment, levy or similar process in relation to a tax lien or assessment.

(b) Any one or more of the following shall also constitute events of default:

(i) failure of Debtor to pay when due any interest on or any principal or installment of principal of any indebtedness of Debtor to Bank,

(ii) the occurence and continuation of any event which under the terms of any evidence of indebtedness, indenture, loan agreement or similar instrument permits the acceleration of maturity of any indebtedness of Debtor to others than Bank,

(iii) any representation or warranty made by Debtor herein or made in any statement or certificate furnished to Bank by the Debtor pursuant hereto or in connection with any loan or loans proves untrue in any material respect as of the date of the making or issuance thereof, or

(iv) default shall occur in the observance of performance by Debtor of any provision of this agreement or of any note, assignment or transfer under or pursuant hereto.

When any event of default described in this subparagraph (b) has occurred and is continuing, Bank may, by notice in writing sent by registered mail to Debtor, declare the principal of and any accrued interest on all outstanding indebtedness and liabilities of Debtor to Bank immediately due and payable, and thereupon all such indebtedness and liabilities shall become and be immediately due and payable.

(c) When any indebtedness or liability of Debtor is due and payable and is unpaid in whole or in part, Bank shall, in addition to all other rights and remedies, have all the rights and remedies of a secured party under the Code (regardless of whether the Code is the law of the jurisdiction where the rights or remedies are asserted). Bank may require Debtor to assemble the collateral and make it available to Bank at a place designated by Bank which is reasonably convenient. Any requirement of the Code for reasonable notice to the Debtor shall be met if such notice is mailed, postage prepaid, to the Debtor at the address shown at the commencement of this agreement, at least 5 days before the time of the sale, disposition or other event or thing giving rise to the required notice.

(d) Any indebtedness owing from Bank to Debtor may be set off and applied by Bank on any indebtedness or liability of the Debtor to Bank at any time and from time to time either before or after maturity and without demand upon or notice to anyone.

(e) This agreement and all rights and liabilities hereunder and in and to any and all collateral shall inure to the benefit of Bank and its successors and assigns, and shall be binding upon the Debtor and its successors and assigns. Each and all of the terms hereof shall govern and apply to each and all of the loans heretofore made by Bank to Debtor and now outstanding, and to any and all collateral therefor, to the same extent as though such loans had been made and the collateral therefor assigned, transferred and delivered subsequent to the date of this agreement. This agreement and all rights and obligations hereunder, including matters of construction, validity and performance, shall be governed by the laws of the State of Texas.

8. Termination:

This agreement may be terminated by either the Debtor or Bank giving to the other 10 days notice in writing of such termination, but no such termination shall in any way affect the rights, duties, obligations or liabilities of either Bank or Debtor with respect to transactions occurring prior to such termination. Prior to such termination this shall be a continuing agreement in every respect.

9. Special Provisions Applicable to Loans to Debtor:

This agreement shall be deemed to be and shall become effective upon the execution hereof by Debtor and delivery of the same to Bank, and it shall not be necessary for Bank to execute any acceptance hereof or otherwise signify or express its acceptance hereof.

DATED_____

ATTEST:

_____   _____

                                         By_____

FORM N-27

Uniform Commercial Code—FINANCING STATEMENT—Form UCC-1 (Rev. 9-71)

FORM E1353—CLARKE & COURTS, INC.

IMPORTANT—Read instructions on back before filling out form

This Financing Statement is presented to a Filing Officer for filing pursuant to the Uniform Commercial Code | 3. Maturity Date (if any):

| 1. Debtor(s) (Last name first) and Mailing Address: | 2. Secured Party(ies) Name and Address: | 4. For Filing Officer (Date, Time, Number and Filing Office): |

FIRST CITY NATIONAL BANK
OF HOUSTON
1001 MAIN STREET
P. O. BOX 2557
HOUSTON, TEXAS 77001

5. This Financing Statement covers the following types (or items) of collateral. (WARNING: If collateral is crops or fixtures, read instructions on back.)

6. Name and Address of Assignee of Secured Party: (Use this space to describe collateral, if needed)

Check ☒ if covered: ☐ Proceeds of collateral are also covered. ☐ Products of collateral are also covered. Number of additional sheets presented _____

7. This Statement is filed without the Debtor's signature to perfect a security interest in collateral
   (Please check   ☐ already subject to a security interest in another jurisdiction when it was brought into this state, or
   appropriate box)   ☐ which is proceeds of the original collateral described above in which a security interest was perfected, or
                          ☐ already subject to a financing statement filed in another county, or
                          ☐ already subject to a pre-code perfected security interest.

FIRST CITY NATIONAL BANK OF HOUSTON

By_____   By_____
         Signature(s) of Debtor(s)   Signature(s) of Secured Party(ies)

(1) Filing Officer Copy—Numerical

STANDARD FORM—FORM UCC-1 (REV. 9-71)—APPROVED BY THE SECRETARY OF STATE OF TEXAS—FORM E-1353—CLARKE & COURTS, INC.

Figure 15-2   Uniform Commercial Code Filing Form

Figure 15-3   Uniform Commercial Code Form for Changing the Original Filing

---

Uniform Commercial Code—FINANCING STATEMENT CHANGE—Form UCC-3 (Rev. 9-69)

FORMCRAFT Inc.
"BUSINESS FORMS SPECIALISTS"
PHONE (713) 426-3060 • HOUSTON, TEXAS

IMPORTANT—Read Instructions on back before filling out form.

This Statement is presented to a Filing Officer for filing pursuant to the Uniform Commercial Code | 3. Maturity Date (if any):

| 1. Debtor(s) (Last name first) and mailing address: | 2. Secured Party(ies) Name and Address: | 4. For Filing Officer (Date, Time, Number and Filing Office): |

5. This statement refers to original Financing Statement No._____   Date Filed_____, 19____

| 6. A. Continuation ......☐ | B. Assignment ......☐ | C. Termination ......☐ | D. Partial Release ......☐ | E. Amendment ......☐ |
| The original Financing Statement is still effective. | The Secured Party of record has assigned his interest in the following collateral to: | The Secured Party of record no longer claims a security interest under the Financing Statement | The Secured Party of record releases the following collateral: | The Financing Statement is amended as set forth below: |

7.

By_____   By_____
         Signature(s) of Debtor(s)   Signature(s) of Secured Party(ies)

(1) Filing Officer Copy — Numerical

STANDARD FORM—FORM UCC-3 (REV. 9-69)—APPROVED BY SECRETARY OF STATE OF TEXAS selling the specific item of collateral and allows the firm to maintain control over the inventory. On the other hand, it is less attractive to the lender for those very same reasons. The lender's loss of control affords less security. Therefore, it is common to find this type of lien used only in conjunction with specific inventory liens as additional protection to the lender, over and above the protection of the floating lien.

Trust Receipts

Under this arrangement, title to the specific item passes to the lender when the loan is made. The lender returns the title to the borrower for use in the sale under the explicit agreement that the borrower only holds the goods and the proceeds from the sale in trust for the lender. At any time, the lender can take possession of the specific items, which usually have been identified by serial numbers. This type of agreement is also known as a flooring plan. Automobile dealers arrange for the manufacturer to send the bill directly to their bank, which advances a portion of the amount to the dealers on a short-term note. The cars, however, go to the dealers, who use the proceeds of their sale to repay the bank advance. In effect, the automobile dealer is holding the cars in trust for the bank.

Terminal Warehouse Receipts

When the firm puts the merchandise into a public warehouse for storage, warehouse personnel give the firm a receipt showing that the goods are in storage. The firm may request a formal receipt as illustrated in Figure 15-4, which is typically required if the firm wishes to pledge the inventory in storage as collateral for a loan. The receipt is usually issued in favor of the lending institution, and the name of the storer is shown on the face of the receipt along with other information needed to describe the merchandise.

As financial officers, we would most likely have made prior arrangements with the bank for the loan, and could start using the funds upon presentation of the warehouse receipt issued to the bank. In order to get to the stored inventory, the firm must get a release from the lender and present it to the warehouse. Only then can it remove the specific amount or items which the bank has authorized.

The typical warehouse receipt is non-negotiable and issued in favor of the bank. Some warehouse receipts, however, are negotiable and can be transferred by endorsement. This allows transfer of title from one party to another, provided the merchandise does not leave the warehouse.

Field Warehouse Receipts

The field warehouse receipt is similar to the terminal warehouse receipt except that it allows the merchandise to remain on the borrower's premises. This is particularly useful in those instances when it is impractical to move the goods. Under this arrangement, the borrower leases a portion of its own warehouse to a third party, the public warehouseperson, who limits and controls the access to this area by usually fencing it off and posting a guard. The public warehouseperson then issues a field warehouse receipt upon which the lender advances funds to the firm. Again the field warehouse receipt is issued in favor of the lender, and the borrower can obtain physical possession of the goods from behind the fence only when the lender issues a release.

This type of inventory financing does place a special burden on the lender to be

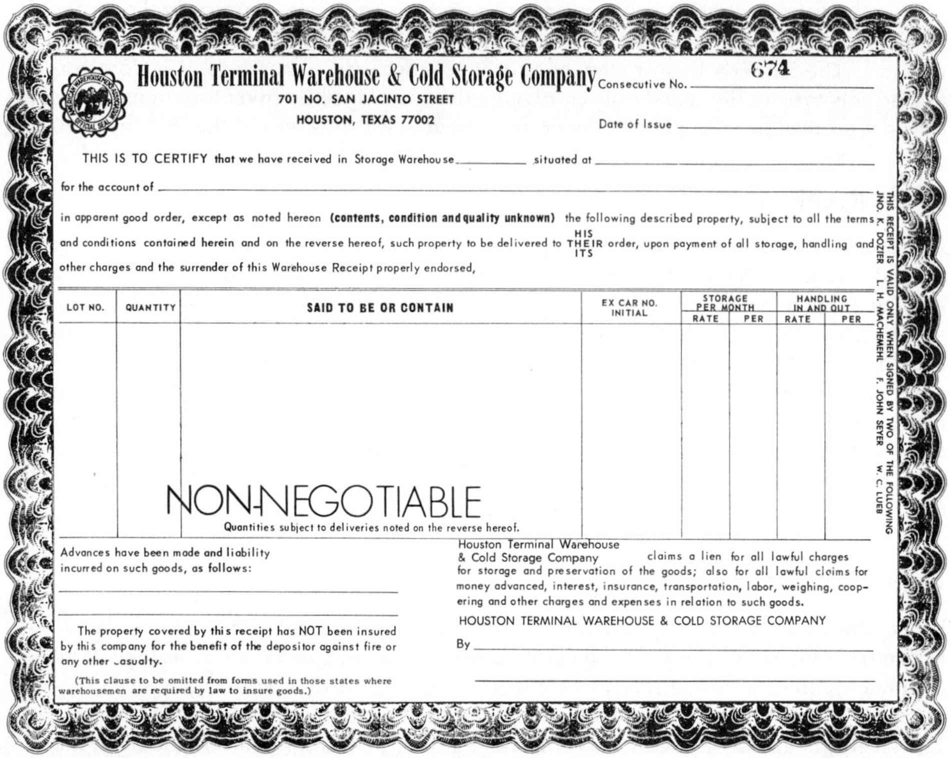

Houston Terminal Warehouse & Cold Storage Company
701 NO. SAN JACINTO STREET
HOUSTON, TEXAS 77002

Consecutive No. 674

Date of Issue ____________

THIS IS TO CERTIFY that we have received in Storage Warehouse ________ situated at ____________

for the account of ____________

in apparent good order, except as noted hereon **(contents, condition and quality unknown)** the following described property, subject to all the terms and conditions contained herein and on the reverse hereof, such property to be delivered to HIS / THEIR / ITS order, upon payment of all storage, handling and other charges and the surrender of this Warehouse Receipt properly endorsed,

LOT NO.	QUANTITY	SAID TO BE OR CONTAIN	EX CAR NO. INITIAL	STORAGE PER MONTH		HANDLING IN AND OUT	
				RATE	PER	RATE	PER
		NON-NEGOTIABLE Quantities subject to deliveries noted on the reverse hereof.					

THIS RECEIPT IS VALID ONLY WHEN SIGNED BY TWO OF THE FOLLOWING
JNO. K. DOZIER L. H. MACHEMEHL F. JOHN SEYER W. C. LUEB

Advances have been made and liability incurred on such goods, as follows:

The property covered by this receipt has NOT been insured by this company for the benefit of the depositor against fire or any other casualty.

(This clause to be omitted from forms used in those states where warehousemen are required by law to insure goods.)

Houston Terminal Warehouse & Cold Storage Company claims a lien for all lawful charges for storage and preservation of the goods; also for all lawful claims for money advanced, interest, insurance, transportation, labor, weighing, coopering and other charges and expenses in relation to such goods.

HOUSTON TERMINAL WAREHOUSE & COLD STORAGE COMPANY

By ____________

Figure 15-4 A Terminal Warehouse Receipt

extremely careful of fraud. Since the merchandise is so close to the borrower, there have been several instances in which the borrower has removed the collateral. In the famous Salad Oil Scandal, the borrower replaced the stolen collateral with water and then bribed or deceived the guards and inspectors into thinking the salad oil was still in the storage tanks.[1]

The field warehousing technique is rather costly to the firm not only because of the risk to the lender but because the firm must bear the costs of installing the field warehouse within its own facilities, and pay warehousing charges, the guards, the insurance and the other associated expenses in addition to the interest the lender charges on the advance.

Chattel Mortgages

This type of financing lets the borrower hold the title to the specific asset pledged, but requires that the lender give consent to the sale. Not having the title and the somewhat cumbersome necessity of seeking the lender's consent to the sale are disadvantages to the lender and the borrower, respectively. These drawbacks limit the use of this type of arrangement for inventory financing.

Frequently, the chattel mortgage gives the lender ownership equity in the merchandise much as a stockholder has in a firm, rather than specific title, and the

[1] Norman C. Miller, *The Great Salad Oil Swindle,* Penguin Books.

lender must go to court and have the merchandise sold under court order to satisfy its claim. This is also cumbersome and a big disadvantage to the lender, particularly in light of court rulings restricting the ability of such lenders to repossess items without due process of court action and proper notification to the borrower, two actions which are not required if the lender retains title.

On the other hand, the chattel mortgage has the advantage of facilitating bank financing where the bank needs a high degree of control but does not want the title. It also limits the lender's liability against legal judgments.

A TABULATION

Table 15-1 illustrates the considerable number of factors—besides the cost of the product and the interest cost—associated with your decision to use a particular type of trade credit. The convenience factor is frequently a consideration, as in the case of accounts payable and trade acceptances. The convenience and flexibility of the procedure may outweigh the costs incurred. The possible deterioration of relations with creditors makes many financial officers unwilling to stretch their accrued liabilities to the limit, even though they may be a less costly source of funds than a bank loan. When negotiating a loan, you may decide to pay a higher interest rate and retain control of your firm's inventory. Sometimes, you may find that the customs and traditions surrounding the typical uses for each type of trade credit dictate your choice.

SUMMARY

After having read Chapter 15, you should be able to answer these questions:

1. What is trade credit?

Trade credit consists of credit extended to the firm by its suppliers in the normal course of business. The more common types of trade credit are the open account, trade acceptances, promissory notes, and consignment. The largest of these is the open account, under which the extension of credit is usually prearranged and the invoice of shipment is usually the bill and the only formal acknowledgment of the debt.

2. What are the common terms of credit?

The common terms of credit specify such procedures as the time within which the supplier expects to be paid, any discounts the supplier will allow, and specification as to who pays the shipping and other costs. The payment time can range from before delivery to several months after shipment. The discount can be nothing or rather substantial, depending on the traditions of the industry and the competition. The transportation or other costs can be borne by either the supplier or the firm. If the shipment were F. O. B. point of shipment, the firm bears the cost. If the shipment is F. O. B. point of receipt, the supplier bears the cost.

3. How can the financial officer use the accrued current liabilities and the pledging of accounts receivable as sources of funds?

By postponing the payment of such expenses as federal income taxes until the due date, the financial officer has the use of money that otherwise would have been paid to the government. In effect, this is a no-interest loan from the government until the payment is made.

Table 15-1   Summary of Trade Credit Sources

Type	Typical Use	Typical Cost Considerations	Advantages and Disadvantages
1. Accounts payable	Short-term inventory	a. Early-payment discounts b. No interest c. Supplier relations d. Product price for cash	a. Flexible b. Convenient c. Payment delay
2. Trade acceptances	International inventory transactions	a. Letter of credit b. Delayed payment	a. Smoother, long-distance negotiations
3. Consignment	Specialized merchandise	a. Floor and storage space b. Forfeited profits	a. Lower profits b. No spoilage or unsold items c. Expanded sales line d. No investment e. Lower servicing costs
4. Seasonal dating	Seasonal merchandise	a. Storage space b. Spoilage c. Theft	a. Early sales and cash generation b. Lower supply price
5. Accrued current liabilities	Temporary funds	a. Relations with creditors b. Forfeit of early-payment discounts	a. No negotiations with lender b. Risk of insolvency
6. Bank accounts receivable pledge	Short-term revolving funds	a. Interest costs b. Recourse c. Loan restrictions d. Extra bookkeeping	a. Loss of control

7. Factoring	Short-term revolving funds	a. Factor's charges b. Interest c. Recourse d. Bookkeeping e. Account servicing	a. Loss of control
8. Floating collateral lien	Many items with rapid turnover	a. Interest cost b. Negotiation	a. Flexible
9. Trust receipts	Large, higher-priced items	a. Interest cost b. Negotiations	a. Bank pays supplier b. Bank retains title
10. Terminal warehouse receipt	Revolving inventory loan	a. Warehousing costs b. Interest cost c. Insurance	a. You retain title b. Inconvenience c. Loss of control
11. Field warehouse receipt	Revolving inventory loan for bulky items	a. Warehousing b. Interest c. Insurance	a. You retain title b. Less transportation c. Loss of control
12. Chattel mortgage	Larger, specific items	a. Interest costs b. Negotiations	a. You retain title b. Loss of control

The financial officer can pledge the firm's accounts receivable as collateral for a loan. The typical accounts receivable pledge entails signing a security agreement which, among other items, has the firm promise to replace defaulted accounts.

4. How can the financial officer use inventory pledging as a short-term source of funds?

There are several techniques. The general security agreement can be used to pledge inventory for a loan. The terminal warehouse receipt, evidencing the existence of the inventory in storage at a public warehouse, can be used as collateral for a loan. The field warehouse receipt, evidencing the existence of the inventory in a segregated area of the borrower's own storage facilities, can be used as collateral for a loan.

The floating collateral inventory lien arrangement allows the firm to freely substitute different, specific items, unlike most other liens which identify specific assets as collateral. Because of this ability to substitute and the increased difficulty this causes in supervising the collateral, the floating lien is used mainly for protection over and above a specific lien by the lender.

QUESTIONS

15-1 What purpose does the Uniform Commercial Code Filing Form serve?

15-2 Do you think a bank would loan a firm 100 percent of the value of that firm's accounts receivable even if all the accounts receivable were established as collateral?

15-3 What is a floating inventory collateral lien? How does it differ from an inventory trust receipt?

15-4 Does the risk to the lender differ in a terminal warehouse receipt as opposed to a field warehouse receipt?

15-5 What is a chattel mortgage?

15-6 How is the consignment method of trade credit different from the open account, trade acceptance, and promissory note?

15-7 Identify and briefly explain the terms of credit known as C. B. D., C. O. D., and S. D.–B. L.

15-8 Suppose a firm in New York orders some merchandise from a company in Chicago. Who bears the transport cost if the goods are shipped:

(a) F. O. B. New York

(b) F. O. B. Chicago

PROBLEMS

15-1 What is the effective annual interest rate being charged to the debtor if the trade discount is not taken on the following accounts receivable:

(a) 1/10 net 30

(b) 2/15 net 30

(c) 2/15 net 60

(d) net 30

15-2 The Bolcon Company has an accounts payable liability that is aged as follows:

0–30 days	$200,000
31–60 days	150,000
61–90 days	50,000

The firm wishes to borrow sufficient funds to pay off the 31–90-day-old accounts payable. The financial officer has included the most recent balance sheet in the loan request:

Bolcon Balance Sheet

Cash	$ 50,000	Accounts payable	$400,000
Accounts receivable	120,000	Bank loans	350,000
Inventory	800,000	Accruals	175,000
Current assets	970,000	Current debt	925,000
Fixed assets	600,000	Long-term debt	300,000
		Common stock	200,000
		Retained earnings	145,000
Total assets	$1,570,000	Total liabilities	$1,570,000

Sales in the previous year were $3 million, and earnings after taxes were 3 percent of total assets.

(a) How much bank financing is required to eliminate the 31–90-day accounts payable?

(b) If you were the bank loan officer, would you provide the loan? Explain.

BIBLIOGRAPHY

Addison, Edward T. "Factoring: A Case History." *Financial Executive,* XXI (November 1963), 32–33.

Beckman, T. N., and R. Bartel. *Credit and Collections: Management and Theory,* 7th ed. McGraw-Hill, New York, 1962.

Moore, Carroll G. "Factoring—A Unique Important Form of Financing and Service." *Business Lawyer,* XIV (April 1959), 703–727.

Polamnia, Francis J. "Commercial Financing: An Economic Tool." *Financial Executive,* 32 (January 1964), 52–54.

Reinhardt, Hedwig. "Economies of Mercantile Credit: A Study in Methodology." *Review of Economics and Statistics,* XXXIX (November 1957), 436–467.

Robichek, A. A., D. Teichroew, and J. M. Jones. "Optimal Short Term Financing Decision." *Management Science,* 12 (September 1965), 1–36.

Rogers, Robert W. "Warehouse Receipts and Their Use in Financing." *Bulletin of the Robert Morris Associates,* XLVI (April 1964).

16

Short-Term Borrowing

What types of short-term borrowings are available to the financial officer as a source of funds? We shall see that as financial officers we will be dealing mainly with bank loans as the firm's primary source of short-term money. However, we could use other financial instruments such as commercial paper, Eurodollar loans, conditional sales contracts, and business finance company loans.

Once you see that the bank is an obvious source of short-term borrowing, what do you look for in selecting a bank with which to start a continuing financial relationship? We shall see that you want to be sure the bank can serve your needs both as a depository for your funds and as a source of loans and other valuable services. As the financial officer, you should start to build a financial relationship only with those banks that are willing to aid you in your business. Some banks may be too large for your purposes and others too small or inadequately equipped to serve you. An alert financial officer starts with an appropriate bank and continues to build a permanent relationship with it.

After you have decided on a particular bank, how do you approach the officers for a loan? Obviously, an approach which impresses the banker with the fact that your firm is competent and capable of handling the loan will help in your banking relationship. This means you will have to be familiar with how the banker computes the interest on your loan, since banks compute loan interest in many ways. And you should know the general loan characteristics that you will be negotiating with the loan officer. Beyond these, a well-conceived cash budget showing the loan officer how you intend to repay the loan and demonstrating other signs of managerial competence also help in communicating with your banker.

What types of loans can you generally negotiate at a bank? This is important because you want to get the most appropriate type of loan for your firm and its prevailing needs. We shall see that among the more common types are the single loan, the revolving credit arrangement, and the line of credit.

Besides the bank, what other short-term sources are available to the financial officer? We can go outside the banking relationship directly to the short-term money markets. There we can offer the firm's short-term securities such as commercial paper in exchange for a short-term loan. Alternatively, we can negotiate with other types of lending institutions such as specialized business finance companies or even borrow internationally from overseas lending institutions.

490

BANKS AS A SOURCE OF SHORT-TERM FUNDS

Most financial officers find that they do a major portion of their short-term financing with banks where they have an established working relationship. These banks are almost entirely commercial banks which deal with business accounts, since this type of bank has the broadest lending power under the present banking laws and regulations and provides the most services to business.[1] Since the financial officer resorts so frequently to the commercial bank for short-term funding, selection of a particular bank requires careful consideration. The financial officer wants to feel confident that the bank will take care of the firm's short-term cash needs when they arise.

Selecting A Bank[2]

You must be sure that the bank offers the services your firm needs both now and for its immediate future growth. Among the important services to look for are the checking account procedures. Lower service charges are more attractive than higher service charges, though the final selection will not be based solely on the cost but on the range of services provided as well. For instance the bank might serve as the transfer agent or registrar for the firm's stock certificates.

The bank's ability to provide international banking connections is a service a growing firm may require. If the bank has branch offices overseas in areas where the firm has operations or exports outlets, the conduct of international operations is considerably easier. Of course you want to be sure that the cost of these international services is reasonable. The bank should also be able and willing to provide you with information on potential markets for your products and put you in touch with suppliers and potential customers. A well-connected international bank can provide information on the political and economic climate of foreign countries and their business customs. The bank should also be able to aid you in obtaining government and international agency backing such as Export-Import bank guarantees and shipping documentation.

The bank should offer data processing services to help in the preparation of your payroll and inventory control. It should be able to assist you in planning your employee pension fund. Your task is to decide what services you presently require and are likely to need in the immediate future and then to locate a bank which offers those particular services at a reasonable cost.

As important as the service consideration is the bank's willingness to lend to the firm and to be flexible in arranging for your loan needs. If the bank is flexible in its loan terms, you are more likely to be able to negotiate the loan most appropriate to your circumstances. This gives the firm the best environment under which to operate and to profit. A rigid bank, on the other hand, may unduly restrict your ability to operate and act as a detriment to your profits.

As financial officer, you want to be sure the bank can handle the size of the loan you require. Particularly among larger firms, the size of required loans is larger than many banks may be legally allowed to lend to any one company. For example, banking regulations prohibit loans to any one borrower for more than 10 percent of

---

[1] Some financial lending institutions are restricted in to whom and for what purpose they can lend. For example, the savings and loan associations specialize in mortgages and real estate financing and do not provide services such as checking accounts.

[2] J. B. Cohen and S. M. Robbins, *The Financial Manager,* Harper and Row, New York, 1966, pp. 423–425.

the bank's capital account, which consists of its stockholders' equity and any bond-holders' capital. If the bank is too small to handle the loans you need, it is time to find a larger bank.

Further, the willingness of the bank to lend to you during periods of tight money is extremely important. It is here in the pinch, when money is difficult to get from any source, particularly banks, that your bank can really come through for the firm. You have to check the bank's past record and see if it has stuck by its customers during tight-money periods in the past. If it let some of its customers fall by the wayside because it was unwilling to extend itself in the tight period, the bank is not for you. A desirable banking relationship runs on a two-way street and bears up in good and bad times.

It is imperative that all but the smallest firms have financial relationships with at least two different banks. If one bank lets you down in the credit crunch, the other might not. Banks are unevenly affected when the Federal Reserve System tightens the money supply. One bank may simply be unable to meet your short-term cash needs because of the crunch, while the other has no trouble in doing so. Having two banks serves to minimize the risk of being shut out during periods of tight money.

Still another important consideration in selecting a bank is the cost of the loan. Though it is not the only consideration, you would obviously like to have the least expensive loan possible. The interest rate should be low and the minimum required compensating balance should be small. We saw in Chapter 13 that as the compensating balance increases, the cost of the loan also increases. Since the financial officer's objective is to minimize the financing cost, you should look for a bank with as low a required compensating balance as possible.

Before making your selection you should examine the bank's management. It is important in dealing with a bank's loan officer to be able to communicate your problems and needs. Therefore, you have to be sure the loan officer has the technical knowledge of your field. If you are in the petroleum industry, you look for a bank which "talks the language" of the petroleum industry. One way of judging the bank's technical competence in any one area is by its reputation among your industry's financial officers.

You should also consider the bank's location. A conveniently located bank might offer communication advantages, although with today's long distance communication technology this is becoming a less important factor.

You should examine the bank's financial condition. Although most people take it for granted that a bank is secure and they will not lose their money, it is possible to suffer agonizing losses if your bank becomes insolvent. Even if the situation is only temporary, the inability to use the firm's deposits at the bank during that time may seriously hamper its operations. Unfortunately, the failure of banks is not as rare as we may think at first. Within recent years, large banks in Texas and California have failed, and the larger depositors in both instances suffered losses and delays. You should examine the bank's latest certified financial statements for such indications as the loan-to-deposit ratio, a sufficient reserve for bad loans, and a sufficient cushion of such liquid securities as United States Treasury securities to meet unforeseen withdrawals and demands on the bank's reserves. You want to make sure the loan-to-deposit ratio is not excessively high, exposing the bank to the undue risk of being illiquid and unable to meet withdrawals upon demand.

For the smaller companies with deposits under $40,000, you want to be sure that the bank is a member of the Federal Deposit Insurance Corporation (FDIC) so that in the event of the bank's failure the FDIC will, after some delay, reimburse you for your losses. Any amount over $40,000 in a single account is not insured. That is why it is so important for the financial officer to be sure that the bank is financially sound before making large deposits.

Another important indicator of the bank's financial condition and its willingness to lend at all times is the variability in the level of total deposits. A bank with a high variability is more likely to experience periods when it cannot meet your loan needs because it needs the funds itself to maintain its own liquidity. Banks with more stable deposit records are better suited to the firm's needs.

Approaching A Bank

When you approach a bank loan officer as a financial officer representing your firm, you must be able to negotiate. This requires that you appear competent and know what you are doing, although it is always safer to admit incomplete understanding of a particular point and ask for an explanation than to regret it later. You should always bear in mind that a bank is in business to lend; that is how it makes a profit. So a banker is always willing to talk to a prospective borrower.

If you are seeking a loan, you must approach the loan officer knowing such details as:

1. The loan purpose
2. The amount of the loan desired
3. A definite plan for repayment
4. Indications of your firm's creditworthiness, such as past records on short-term borrowings, a good record of paying your accounts payable, recent financial statements, and personal information on the reputation of the chief operating officers
5. A carefully drawn and conceived plan showing how the firm expects to perform in the future and attain a position which will allow it to repay the loan, such as a pro forma cash budget (Chapter 3) for the coming year
6. A list of collateral or endorsement guarantees the firm is willing to offer, if any

The financial officer who approaches the bank with such a portfolio of information would appear highly competent. In addition, the information would serve as a point of discussion between you and the loan officer and would certainly expedite the bank's deliberations, since it would not have to ask for additional information.

Remember that a banking relationship is a two-way channel of communication. A good banker stands ready to help and advise you as well as to loan you funds, provided you cooperate with the bank in providing a true picture of your operations. Usually the relationship builds over the years and the banker becomes a valuable contact. The banker is willing to help and advise you because your business is profitable to the bank, and as long as you remain alert to general financial conditions, you can always insure that the bank's interest costs and terms are the most reasonable you can expect and worth the services it is providing.

Interest Costs

Interest costs vary with the method used to figure them. Since the "true cost" may actually differ from the stated interest rate because of variations in methods of calculation, it is imperative that you, as the financial officer, always know how the bank is calculating the true interest cost on the loan.

Prime rate The *prime rate* is the interest rate charged the bank's best and most creditworthy customers, and it is the base from which the interest rates to less creditworthy customers are figured. When the prime rate rises or falls, the rate to other, less creditworthy customers also rises or falls, unless the bank has previously committed itself to a fixed interest rate. For example, if the prime rate were 10 percent, a less creditworthy customer might be charged 11 percent, and if the prime fell to 8½ percent, the less creditworthy customers would be charged only 9½ percent on new loans. The prime rate does *not* include the effect on the true interest rate of such compensating balances as may also be required.

The prime is very well publicized and closely followed as an indicator of bank credit. Changes in the prime are formally announced, and the financial officer can look up the prevailing prime rate in the financial section of most leading newspapers. Traditionally, except for very small banks, the prime is uniform throughout the banking system, although no regulation says it has to be. When one bank, particularly a leading money center in New York or Chicago, initiates a change in the prime, other banks usually follow suit quickly.

In recent years the prime rate, expressed as an annual percentage, has been derived by a formula designed to keep the prime in line with other short term-interest rates such as those on United States Treasury bills. In the past, the prime was administratively fixed by the banks and even now is occasionally fixed without regard to the exact formula or other short-term interest rates. To distinguish between the two methods of determining the prime rate, financial officers talk of the formula method as a *floating prime*.

Prime plus   Many bank loans, particularly those with a life longer than one year, are negotiated with an interest rate a few percentage points higher than the prevailing prime rate (*prime plus*) throughout the life of the loan. As the prime interest rate fluctuates, the interest rate on the loan also fluctuates, regardless of the originally negotiated rate. If the firm's interest rate is prime plus 2 percent, it will be 11 percent when the prime is 9 percent and only 9 percent if the prime drops to 7 percent. The two-percentage-point differential is continually maintained.

This can have a large effect on the interest cost to the firm and the firm's cost of capital. If, as financial officers, we had negotiated a $10,000,000 loan at prime plus 2 percent when the prime was 6 percent, the annual interest expense would be $800,000. But if the prime rose to 10 percent, as it has been known to do in a relatively short period of time, the annual interest expense would rise to $1,200,000—$400,000 more than before. That can greatly affect earnings per share; a firm with 1,000,000 shares outstanding would experience a drop of $.40 per share before taxes.

The true interest rate   As financial officers, we must be able to distinguish between a nominal interest rate such as the prime and the true, or "effective," interest rate which varies from the nominal rate because of the terms of the loan. We shall see shortly that a 9 percent nominal rate can be considerably higher depending on the conditions of the loan. Basically, we want to calculate the *true interest rate* as the interest payment in relation to the loan proceeds which we can actually *use* rather than the nominal interest rate, which calculates the interest payment in relation to the face amount of the loan. Banks have ways of retaining some of the face amount of the loan in their possession and prohibiting the firm from using that portion. Among these methods are the compensating balance and discounting. These procedures raise the true interest rate.

Simple interest   If the firm gets total use of the face amount of the loan, the annual true interest rate is equivalent to the nominal interest rate. The interest rate on loans of this type is called *simple interest* in the jargon of bankers. For example, if we borrowed $1,000 for one year and repaid that loan plus $90 interest at the end of that year, the true interest would be:

$$\frac{\$90}{\$1,000} = 9\%$$

The nominal interest would also be 9 percent, because the total proceeds went to the firm for the entire year.

This method of paying interest is also known as the add-on method, since the interest cost is added to the principal and the entire amount of the interest plus the principal is repaid.

Compensating balances   Frequently, in connection with a loan, the bank insists upon a *compensating balance,* which is nothing more than a commitment of the firm to maintain a specified percentage of the loan as idle cash in its checking account. The firm cannot use the funds (if it does the bank charges a substantial penalty), but the bank can loan out the idle balance. By varying the amount of the compensating balance with each new loan, the bank can effectively increase or decrease the true interest rate. During periods of high interest rates, banks tend to raise the required balance, and during periods of low interest rates, banks tend to lower the required balance. In fact, banks can raise and lower interest rates without ever formally changing the prime rate.

We can demonstrate the effect of the compensating balance on the firm's true interest rate using our $1,000 loan from the previous example. If instead of letting the firm use the entire proceeds, the bank insisted that it keep $100 in compensating balances, the usable part of the loan would be only $900, but the interest expense would still be $90, payable with the return of the principal at the end of the year. The true interest cost would then be:

$$\frac{\$90}{\$900} = 10\%$$

although the nominal interest rate would remain 9 percent. The very same loan has a higher true interest rate because of the required compensating balance.

Now if the firm normally keeps a $100 idle or compensating balance at the bank anyway in the regular course of business, there would be no increase in the interest rate above the nominal rate, since the firm already has the required $100 on deposit and therefore could use the entire $1,000 of the loan.

As financial officer you must remember that the extent and nature of the compensating balance can also be negotiated with some benefits to the firm. For example, the method of computing the compensating balance itself can be negotiated. There are two common methods of calculating the level of the balance that the firm has on deposit: the minimum required balance and the minimum average balance. The minimum required balance method is more severe than the other, since if the firm's deposit balance ever falls below the required balance during the period, it is charged and penalized by the bank. On the other hand, the minimum average required balance allows the firm's deposit to fall below the required balance at any point during the period, provided that on average over the entire period, the required balance is maintained. This allows the firm to occasionally drop below the required balance without penalty. As a financial officer, you would be well advised to negotiate a minimum average required balance method of calculating the deposit level once you have agreed with the bank on the specific level of the compensating balance.

Compensating time-deposit balances   Rather than keep your compensating balances in the form of noninterest-earning demand deposits, banks will sometimes let your firm put the required compensating balance into interest-bearing time deposits, such as certificates of deposit (CD). This still leaves the bank with a portion of the loan under its control and prohibited from your use, but at least you earn a little on what would otherwise be idle balances. The true interest rate is increased above the nominal interest rate, but not as much as before. Continuing with our $1,000, 9 percent nominal interest rate loan, for example, the true interest rate if the bank allowed you to put the $100 compensating balance in a 6 percent CD would be:

$$\frac{\$90 - .06(\$100)}{\$900} = 9.33\%$$

The 9.33 percent true interest rate is still above the nominal rate but below the 10 percent true rate when the compensating balance was kept in a checking account.

Discounted loans   Instead of adding the interest on to the repayment of the principal, the bank may discount the loan by taking the interest out in advance when the loan is made. The firm's usable proceeds are then reduced by the amount of the deducted interest, which in effect raises the true interest rate. For example, let us continue with our $1,000 one-year loan at a nominal interest rate of 9 percent. If the interest costs are deducted from the face amount of the loan, the usable proceeds would be $910, and the true interest rate would be:

$$\frac{\$90}{\$910} = 9.89\%$$

Notice that this discounting method reduces the loan proceeds by the amount of the interest, yet we still must repay the entire $1,000 at the end of the period.

Installment loans   Under the installment loan method of repaying the interest and principal, the borrower makes payment in equal installments so constructed that at the end of the period the interest and principal are entirely paid off. For example, a one-year installment loan would be repaid in twelve equal monthly installments. Our $1,000 one-year 9 percent nominal interest rate loan would be repaid in monthly installments of $90.83, where $83.33 is the monthly repayment of the principal ($1,000/12) and $7.50 is the monthly repayment of the interest ($90/12).

In essence, installment loans let the borrower use only approximately half of the one-year loan proceeds during the course of the year. During the first month, the borrower has use of the full amount, $1,000. After paying the first monthly installment at the end of the first month, the borrower has only $916.67 of the face amount of the loan to use. After paying the second monthly installment, the borrower is left with only $833.34. After the eleventh monthly installment, the borrower is left with only $166.66 of the proceeds, having already repaid the bank $833.34 of the principal. At the end of the twelfth month, the borrower has none of the proceeds left, having repaid the entire loan. On average over the year, the borrower has had the use of only $541.67, or approximately half the original loan amount. We can see from Table 16-1 that though at the beginning there was $1,000 available to use,

Table 16-1   Use of $1,000 Installment Loan Over Time

Beginning of month	End of month	Amount of loan available to borrower
1		$1,000.00
2	1	916.67
3	2	833.34
4	3	750.00
5	4	666.67
6	5	583.34
7	6	500.00
8	7	416.67
9	8	333.34
10	9	250.00
11	10	166.67
12	11	83.33
	12	0
		$6,500.00 TOTAL

Monthly average available to borrower:

$$\frac{\$6,500}{12} = \$541.67$$

during the coming months there was proportionately less to use each month. The true interest rate is then:

$$\frac{\$90}{\$541.67} = 16.62\%$$

Notice the true rate in this case is approximately double the nominal rate.[3]

General Characteristics of Bank Loans

In addition to the interest rate and cost, financial officers must understand the following general characteristics of bank loans in order to communicate and negotiate with bankers.

Maturity   The typical bank loan is for less than one year and may very likely be tied to the firm's inventory or accounts receivable cycle. Banks traditionally like to envision their loans being repaid within the short term and tied to a specific cashflow source, such as the liquidation of a seasonal bulge in inventory. Bank loans over longer than one year are considered to be intermediate financing, and we shall consider them in the next chapter.

Size   Banks cater to loans of all sizes from very small to very large, although the commercial loan department of any particular bank may have a lower limit on the size loans it will handle because small loans are costly to administer. Smaller borrowers may have to go to the personal loan department and pay a higher interest rate.

---

[3] A closer approximation is:

$$\text{True interest rate} = \frac{2(\text{Number of payments in year})(\text{Annual interest cost})}{(\text{Face amount of loan})(\text{Number of payments in one year} + 1)}$$

There are also upper limits on the amount of money any one bank can loan to a particular company. Under the prevailing guidelines, a single bank cannot lend more than 10 percent of its capital to any single borrower. Larger borrowers are forced to either borrow from the larger banks or deal with a bank with a sufficiently large correspondent network (working relationships with other banks) so that, acting in concert, the correspondent group can arrange a very large loan.

Security and collateral   Bank loans can be secured by such assets as accounts receivable or inventory or they can be unsecured, based simply on the firm's promise to repay. If the loan is unsecured, the bank might request that the promissory note be endorsed by a third party who promises to repay the bank if the firm defaults.

Repayment terms   The timing of the repayment can be a significant point in the negotiations between the firm and the banker. Obviously, the firm does not want to repay a short-term loan in equal monthly installments, for as we have seen, this increases the interest rate. On the other hand, the bank tries to avoid large lump-sum repayments because they increase the repayment burden and the associated risk of default.

Minimum balances   We have already seen how this loan requirement affects the true interest rate. It is a highly negotiable point, since the bank looks upon it as an additional profit opportunity, while the firm may already be keeping idle cash balances on deposit in the normal course of business. In that case, the financial officer might offer to continue to maintain that particular deposit level, pretending to be doing it to meet the minimum balance requirement of the loan, in exchange for a reduction in the interest rate or some different maturity.

TYPES OF SHORT-TERM BANK LOANS

What are the typical short-term loan arrangements that a financial officer can negotiate with a bank?

As financial officers, we should be aware that there are many types of loan arrangements that the firm can negotiate with a bank in addition to the specific terms such as interest rates and minimum balances. The more common types are single loans, the line of credit, and revolving credit.

Single Loans

As the name implies, the single loan arrangement is an individual loan negotiated by itself for a specific maturity and amount. This type of loan is used by firms with infrequent need for borrowing and whose relationship with the bank is more that of depositor than borrower. Of course even when the borrowing is infrequent, the financial officer still needs to negotiate the terms.

Line of Credit

The line of credit is a continuing borrowing relationship with the bank over an agreed-upon time. Under the terms of the typical line of credit, the bank agrees to loan the firm up to a maximum amount during a certain time period when the firm calls for the money ("takes down the credit"). After the original negotiation, the financial officer simply informs the bank that the firm wishes to "take down" so much of the line of credit at this time, signs a note to the effect that the firm has taken down that particular amount, and the bank automatically transfers funds to the firm's checking account. Although it is usually not a legally binding agreement between the firm and the bank, the line of credit is almost always honored by the bank and avoids the negotiation of another loan each time the firm needs funds.

The cost of a credit line to the firm is usually set at the original negotiation, although it is usually designed to fluctuate with the prime rate. Every time the firm takes down a portion of the line, it pays the agreed interest on that amount. Even if it does not take down any of the line, the firm typically agrees to keep a compensating balance, usually some proportion of the line, at the bank. This reimburses the bank for the guarantee that the funds will be available when the firm wants them.

The typical line of credit is unsecured and reserved for the more creditworthy borrowers. However, in some cases the bank might require endorsement or collateral before extending the line. The repayment of the line is typically handled in what is known as a period clean up. The firm is usually required to repay all outstanding take-downs during one 30-day period during each year. This, however, is negotiable. At the end of the originally negotiated time, the line ceases to exist, and the bank and the firm have to renegotiate another line if they so desire.

Revolving Credit

The revolving credit agreement is a legally binding commitment by the bank to loan a specific maximum amount over a specific period as required from time to time by the firm. The cost is usually in two parts. When the revolving credit is originally negotiated, the firm pays the bank a commitment fee. This, for example, might be 0.5 percent of the unused commitment, meaning that even if the firm never uses the credit, it still must pay the bank 0.5 percent of the total commitment each year the agreement is in force. When the firm takes down part of the commitment, it starts to pay interest at the agreed-upon rate on that amount and continues to pay the commitment fee rate on the part of the loan it did not take down. The maturity of the revolving credit agreement is usually such that the loan has to be renewed every few months during the commitment period. In a sense, the loan revolves or turns over periodically during the commitment period. The entire commitment period is often in excess of one year.

Revolving credit is commonly unsecured, and no inventory or accounts receivable are pledged. Frequently, the firm agrees to maintain a minimum level of working capital, insure the firm's merchandise, or incur no further debt as terms of the credit. These and other similar terms are required by the bank in an effort to insure the solvency and liquidity of the borrower and repayment of the loan.

The repayment terms of revolving credit are negotiable like the other terms, although the typical repayment is one lump sum at the end of the commitment period. Alert financial officers may have negotiated the renewal of commitment before the original period expired so that the firm would not have to repay the loan at that time. They might also have originally negotiated that the revolving credit could be converted into an intermediate-term loan at the firm's option. This added flexibility gives the firm an opportunity to lengthen the maturity of its debt and a bargaining alternative in its negotiations with other suppliers of funds.

EURODOLLAR LOANS

Eurodollars are that pool of United States dollars held in foreign countries, basically because they can draw a higher rate of interest overseas than they can in the United States. The original Eurodollars arose because foreign exporters to the United States acquired substantial sums of dollars in excess of their needs. Instead of cashing them in for their own national currency, they kept the dollars and loaned them out as dollar loans to whomever wanted to pay an attractive rate of interest. It turned out that many foreign branches of American banks as well as foreign national banks wanted to borrow the dollars. This led to the development of the Eurodollar market. Today it is a highly developed and structured market which operates to a large extent out of London and the Carribean. Not only foreigners but also Americans put dollars into these offshore Eurodollar time deposits in order to capture any prevailing higher interest rate. As we have seen, financial officers frequently use Eurodollar time deposits as temporary investments for excess cash.

By going to the banks that have borrowed these offshore Eurodollars through the creation of overseas dollar-denominated time deposits, the financial officer can arrange to borrow those dollars. Since most banks in the United States have foreign branches or correspondents, the financial officer simply negotiates with the international department of the firm's own bank for such a Eurodollar loan.

The cost of these Eurodollar loans varies with the supply and demand conditions which prevail in the Eurodollar market. Sometimes it is less expensive to borrow in the Eurodollar market than it is to borrow domestically. Sometimes government regulations require that any foreign capital expansion be financed with funds raised outside the United States. During periods when those regulations are in force, the financial officer must go to the Eurodollar market to raise dollars to finance the firm's foreign investments.

The maturity of the Eurodollar loan also varies extensively, although the majority of these loans are under one year and are for periods of multiples of three months, such as 90 days, 180 days, and so on.

The typical Eurodollar loan requires no minimum balance and no security. The true interest rate and the nominal interest rate are usually closer together than in domestic loans, and the financial officer must compare the domestic alternative on the basis of its true interest rate.[4]

COMMERCIAL PAPER

Commercial paper, or "paper" as it is sometimes called, is the unsecured promissory notes of the larger and most creditworthy firms in the country. Frequent sellers of paper are the finance companies of large manufacturers or retailers, such as General Motors Acceptance Corporation. Frequent buyers of paper are banks, insurance companies, pension funds, and other industrial firms seeking a short-term haven for temporary excess funds.

Commercial paper is categorized by the channels through which it is sold, by the seller's business, or by the quality of the issuer. If the paper is sold through a

---

[4] For a more detailed examination of the Eurodollar market, see Charles Ganoe, "The Eurodollar Market: A New Source of Financing," *Journal of Commercial Bank Lending,*" July 1968, 11–20; E. Zinn, "The International Money and Capital Market of the Euro-Currencies," *European Business,* April 1969; and J. F. Weston and B. Sorge, *International Financial Management,* Irwin, Homewood, Ill., 1972.

dealer, it is said to be *dealer-placed*. This means that the issuing firm has first sold it to a dealer who in turn resells it at a higher price to a client. The dealer usually takes a fee of $1/8$ of 1 percent of the total amount for handling the sale in this fashion. Alternatively, the issuer can sell the commercial paper directly to the buyer, saving the dealer's fee. This is known as *direct placement.*

When the issuer is a finance company rather than a manufacturer, the commercial paper is called *finance company paper* and traditionally sells at a slightly higher yield (lower price) than the paper of other issuers.

Finally, the paper may be classified as prime and other quality. Prime quality commercial paper is issued by the most creditworthy of all creditworthy customers, while slightly less quality paper is issued by only slightly less creditworthy customers. It is rare that a marginal company can even sell paper. However, when Penn Central collapsed, it had a relatively large amount of commercial paper outstanding, which, up to that point, had been rated as high quality. The holders of that paper lost their entire investment since commercial paper is unsecured and ranks low on the priority of creditors. The lesson for the financial officer is that the quality ratings are only general guides and should never be blindly relied upon or substituted for careful investigation.

The cost of commercial paper is traditionally $1/2$ of 1 percent below the prime rate, because whether it is sold directly or dealer placed, the bank's profit and costs are eliminated. This lower cost makes it attractive for the financial officer of a high quality firm to issue paper when in need of short-term funds.

The average size of any unit of commercial paper is usually over $100,000, although there have been some smaller issues of approximately $25,000, and it is not uncommon to find paper in $1,000,000 units.

The average maturity of commercial paper is three to six months, though issues of nine months and one year are sometimes offered. There is no minimum required balance, which again makes the true interest rate less expensive than the cost of the short-term bank loan.

Commercial paper issues are unsecured. In some instances, the issue is accompanied by a line of credit or a letter of credit arranged by the issuer to assure the buyers that in the event of repayment difficulty it can back up the paper with a loan arrangement at a bank. This is sometimes required of the lesser quality companies when they sell paper, and it increases the true interest rate.

The issuer repays the commercial paper at maturity, although in most instances the issuer can "rollover" the paper by replacing the maturing issue with a new issue. However, as financial officers we should be aware that there is no guarantee that the firm will be able to rollover the issue when it wants to. In the case of the Penn Central, the failure to rollover the commercial paper because of the then-prevailing credit crunch was the final, additional burden on the already overburdened financial structure which sent the railroad into bankruptcy.

As financial officers we should consider using commercial paper as a short-term source of funds, not only because it is less expensive than bank credit but also as a supplement to our usual bank borrowings. The judicious use of commercial paper can provide the firm with another source of funds when the banks cannot supply funds during periods of tight money or when the need exceeds the lending limits of the banks. This is particularly true for the prestigious company which would have no difficulty finding buyers for its paper. However we should always remember that commercial paper is used primarily to finance short-term needs such as working capital requirements and not to finance longer-term capital assets. Penn Central, at the end, was using commercial paper to finance the acquisition of locomotives. If the funding had been longer-term, Penn Central might have had enough breathing time to refinance; but with paper coming due every 90 days, it could not wait out the tight-money period and was forced into bankruptcy.

BUSINESS FINANCE COMPANY LOANS

There are business finance companies which specialize in providing loans to firms that banks, for one reason or another, will not lend. Such firms as C.I.T. Financial Corporation and Walter E. Heller and Company are examples of business finance companies. These companies typically deal with the more marginal firms and design loans especially for the particular situation in an effort to tailor the financing to the firm's needs and capabilities and to insure repayment. In return for their services and the loan, the business finance companies charge a higher rate of interest than the bank and may also receive fees for advisory and other services. The financial officer will generally go to these companies only when the firm's borrowing costs at its bank become too high. Business finance companies charge more than banks for their services, such as factoring.

SUMMARY

After having read Chapter 16, you should be able to answer these questions:

1. What do you, as the financial officer, look for in selecting a bank?

You should be sure the bank can provide the firm with the services it requires such as international marketing and banking information, stock registry and transfer, and loans which are sufficiently large enough to service the firm's funding needs. The bank should exhibit a willingness to loan funds to the firm by offering flexible terms and supporting firms in periods of tight money. The interest cost and service charges should be reasonable and competitive, the management should be competent, the location should be convenient, and the bank's financial condition should be strong.

2. As financial officers, how do we approach a bank to negotiate a loan?

It is advisable to approach a bank with an air of competence, although this does not mean we are smug or do not ask questions when we need clarification. Rather, we come prepared with a definite idea of the loan purpose, the amount desired, repayment plans, timely financial statements, concrete plans for the future of the firm and adequate collateral, if necessary.

We must also understand the various interest rates and how they are calculated. We saw that the true interest rate can vary substantially from the nominal interest rate, depending on the amount of the loan that the firm can actually put to use and on when the interest is paid.

3. What types of loans can you generally negotiate with a bank?

In addition to the general terms of the loan, the financial officer can negotiate single loans, lines of credit, or revolving credit commitments. The line of credit allows the financial officer to negotiate at one time for the firm's funding needs over a relatively longer future period than the single loan, which has to be negotiated each time. The revolving credit commitment also allows the financial officer to negotiate once for an entire future period's funding needs, but, unlike the line of credit, it is binding on the bank and more costly.

4. What other short-term sources of funds are available to the firm?

Financial officers can obtain Eurodollar loans as an alternative to domestic bank loans. Sometimes these are less expensive than the domestic loan, and sometimes the firm must use them to comply with government regulations on foreign investment.

Commercial paper is another alternative to the bank loan. It is typically less expensive and may be used to supplement short-term bank borrowings, but it has been traditionally reserved for the most creditworthy and larger firms. The marginal and less creditworthy firms have instead used business finance companies to supplement or replace bank credit, although their loans are more expensive.

QUESTIONS

16-1 Briefly identify some of the factors you might consider in selecting a bank for your firm.

16-2 Indicate the likely effect of the following occurrences on the prime interest rate charged by most banks:

Occurrence	Prime interest rate		
	Increases	Decreases	Unchanged
The Federal Reserve System raises the discount rate.			
Foreign demand for United States dollars increases.			
Congress passes legislation subsidizing the homeowner's mortgage cost.			
Congress passes an investment tax credit for all business.			
Congress incurs a large budgetary deficit.			
Congress requires all banks to join the Federal Reserve System.			

16-3 If a firm had negotiated a two-year loan from a bank on a prime rate +1 percent basis, what would happen to the firm's cost of capital and earnings per share if the prime rate rose? If the prime rate fell?

16-4 Explain the difference between the true interest rate and the nominal interest rate charged on a bank loan. Will they ever be the same?

16-5 Indicate how each of the following occurrences will affect the borrower's true interest rate:

Occurrence	Increases	Decreases	Unchanged
	True interest rate		

The minimum compensating balance is increased.

The minimum average compensating balance is increased.

Compensating balances are no longer allowed to be time deposits but must be demand deposits.

All loans are discounted.

All loans are repaid in equal monthly installments.

16-6 What is the difference between an "add-on" loan and a discounted loan?

16-7 What is the difference between dealer-placed commercial paper and direct-placement commercial paper?

16-8 On the average how would you rank the following sources of funds with respect to their costs to the borrower:

(a) Bank loans at the prime interest rate (simple add-on)
(b) Direct-placement commercial paper
(c) Eurodollars
(d) Dealer-placement commercial paper
(e) Loans from business finance companies

PROBLEMS

16-1 ANI Company has recently negotiated a prime rate plus 1 percent loan of $2,000,000 from a New York bank. Shortly after the loan was negotiated the prime rate at this New York bank rose from 9 percent to 10 percent. The loan is a simple add-on to be repaid in 1 year. ANI has 500,000 common shares outstanding.

(a) What was the effect on the interest cost to the firm when the prime rate increased?

(b) What is the effect of the increased prime rate on earnings per share?

16-2 Suppose a firm negotiated a prime rate plus 1.25 percent add-on loan of $500,000 on March 1, 1974, to be repaid in 4 months. The prime rate rose, however, from 8.75 percent to 11.75 percent in this period. The firm has 100,000 common shares outstanding.

(a) What is the effect of the increased prime rate on the interest cost of the loan?

    (b) What is the effect of the increased prime rate on the earnings per share of the firm?

16-3 Calculate the true interest rate to the borrower for each of the following loans:

    (a) A $1,000,000 loan for 1 year with a simple interest rate of 8 percent

    (b) The same loan as in item (a), but at least $50,000 has to be maintained in the borrower's demand account

    (c) The same loan as in item (a), but $50,000 of compensating balances has to be maintained in the borrower's time deposit account, which pays a 5 percent return

    (d) A $1,000,000 loan for 1 year discounted at a nominal interest rate of 8 percent

    (e) The same loan as in item (d), but $50,000 in compensating balances has to be maintained in the borrower's demand account

    (f) A $1,000,000 loan at an 8 percent nominal interest rate to be repaid in 4 equal installments of $270,000

BIBLIOGRAPHY

Agemian, Charles A. "Maintaining An Effective Bank Relationship." *Financial Executive,* 32 (January 1964), 24–28.

Baxter, Nevins D., and Harold T. Shapiro. "Compensating Balance Requirements: The Results of a Survey." *Journal of Finance,* XIX (September 1964), 483–496.

"Commercial Paper," *Money Market Instruments.* Federal Reserve Bank of Cleveland, Cleveland, Ohio, 1965, pp. 41–47.

Ganoe, Charles S. "The Eurodollar Market: A New Source of Financing," *Journal of Commercial Bank Lending,* 50 (July 1968), 11–20.

Gibson, W. E. "Compensating Balance Requirements." *National Banking Review,* 2 (March 1965), 298–311.

Jass, Robert L. "The Market for Commercial Paper." Ph.D. Dissertation, Stanford University, 1970.

Schadrack, Frederick C., Jr. "Demand and Supply in the Commercial Paper Market." *Journal of Finance,* XXV (September 1970), 837–852.

Selden, Richard T. *Trends & Cycles in the Commercial Paper Market.* National Bureau of Economic Research, New York, 1963.

Stewart, William C. "How Business Picks Banks." *Burroughs Clearing House,* XLIV (January 1960), 33–35, 80.

17

INTERMEDIATE-TERM SOURCES OF FUNDS

WHAT SOURCES OF INTERMEDIATE TERM FINANCING are available to the financial officer? As distinguished from short-term financing, which by custom tends to either liquidate or renew within the course of one year, intermediate-term financing usually matures in one to ten years, although it lacks the permanency of long-term funds considered in the next part of the text. We shall see that common intermediate-term financial sources are bank term loans, equipment financing loans, conditional sales contracts, insurance company loans and Small Business Administration loans.

When should the financial officer use intermediate-term financing instead of long- or short-term financing? Intermediate-term financing, particularly from the sources mentioned above, is a privately negotiated loan between the lender and the firm. This eliminates the public participation, which characterizes the sale of the security issue to many people. Private negotiation is frequently less expensive, not only because it might carry a lower interest rate, but also because it eliminates the necessity and cost of registration and documentation required by law for a public issue, as well as the flotation costs of a public issue.

Intermediate-term financing seems well suited to the financing of particular pieces of equipment and machinery because it coincides with the expected life of the machinery. Because it is privately negotiated, it can be tailored to the exact size and terms most suited to the firm's needs. It avoids the uncertainty of renewal or rollover associated with short-term sources, particularly when used to finance assets of intermediate life expectancy. On the other hand, intermediate-term financing is not well suited for funding the firm's working capital requirements or permanent financing needs.

TERM LOANS

Term loans are the financial officer's jargon for intermediate-term loans. The expression generally refers to fixed loan commitments from banks or other lending institutions for a period in excess of one year but usually less than ten years. The vast majority of terms are shorter than ten years, however; most mature in less than five.

Amortization and Interest

The repayment provisions of most term loans call upon the firm to amortize the principal over the life of the loan. That is, the firm is required to repay in install- ments. Although subject to negotiation, the typical amortization is equal quarterly, semiannual, or annual installments designed to have the loan entirely repaid by maturity. The lender hopes that this amortization will give the loan added protec- tion against default, because it is usually easier for a firm to repay gradually than to repay the entire amount at the end of the loan period. However, it is not un- common to find term loans with either a partial gradual repayment and a large por- tion of the original loan paid off at maturity in what is known as a *balloon* payment or the entire principal of the original loan paid off with one payment at maturity.

The equal annual amortization schedule would look like Table 17-1 for a 5-year, $8,200 term loan at a nominal interest rate of 7 percent. We can find the annual in- stallment which at 7 percent will repay the entire principal by maturity, as well as the interest on the unpaid balance, as follows:

$$P = \frac{L}{PV \text{ of } \$1 \text{ per year for } n \text{ years at } r\%} \tag{17-1}$$

where

P = the annual installment
L = the original loan size
n = the number of years to maturity
r = the nominal interest rate
PV = present value of an annuity factor

In our example:

$$P = \frac{\$8,200}{4.1000} \tag{17-2}$$
$$= \$2,000$$

As shown in Table 17-1, an annual $2,000 installment will totally amortize the loan at 7 percent interest at the end of 5 years. The 4.1000 factor in Equation 17-2 represents the present value of $1 each year for 5 years at 7 percent annual interest as read from Appendix D at the back of this book.

We can see from Table 17-1 that the $2,000 annual installment has paid off $8,200 in principal and $1,800 in interest over the 5-year life of the term loan.[1] Notice that while the installment size does not change, the portion allocated to interest declines each year, while the portion allocated to amortization of the principal increases each year. That is because the interest portion is calculated on the unpaid or remaining balance of the loan. Consequently column 3 of Table 17-1, which is calculated as the product of the 7 percent interest rate and the remaining loan balance at the begin- ning of that year, becomes smaller every year. What remains of the $2,000 payment

---

[1] We can compute the first four annual payments if there is a balloon repayment of $2,000 principal in year five as:

$$P = \frac{L - PV \text{ of the balloon at } r\%}{PV \text{ of } \$1 \text{ per year for } n \text{ years at } r\%}$$
$$= \frac{8,200 - 1,426}{4.100}$$
$$= \$1652.20$$

Table 17-1   Amortization Schedule

(1) End of year	(2) Annual installment	(3) Interest .07 × (5)	(4) Principal (2) − (3)	(5) Remaining balance
0	0	0	0	$8,200
1	2,000	574	1,426	6,774
2	2,000	474	1,566	5,248
3	2,000	367	1,633	3,615
4	2,000	253	1,747	1,868
5	2,000	132	1,868	0
		1,800	8,200	

after the interest is deducted is applied to the principal, shown in column 4 of Table 17-1. The exact amortization schedule depends on the creditworthiness of the borrower. If confident that the firm can repay in one lump sum at maturity, the lender will not insist upon an amortization schedule.

The interest rate charged on a term loan varies inversely with the creditworthiness of the borrower. The more creditworthy customers tend to receive the lower rates. Generally the interest rate is slightly higher than the prime rate because the bank is committing itself to a longer period and feels it must be reimbursed for that commitment. The term loan interest rate can either fluctuate with changes in the prime, as in the case of a prime plus loan (Chapter 16), or it can remain fixed at the originally negotiated interest rate over the entire life of the loan. If, as a borrower, you expect interest rates in general to decline, you try to negotiate a variable interest rate based on the prime rate. If you expect interest rates to rise, you try to negotiate a fixed interest rate based on the prevailing prime. Of course, if the bank has the same expectations as you about the interest rate, it will probably require a higher fixed rate than variable rate at the beginning to cover itself in anticipation of an increase in the prime interest rate.

Security Provisions

The security provisions of the term loan, which, as financial officers, we negotiate as well as the interest rate, are attempts by the bank to insure payment of the principal and interest. It is our job to see that those provisions are not overly restrictive and do not interfere with the firm's ability to operate or expand, while at the same time they are satisfactory to the lender and keep our interest rate low. The typical provisions obligate the firm to maintain a sufficient working capital position, honest and efficient management, and sufficient asset value which the lender can rely upon to satisfy the claim if the borrower defaults. While these provisions seem reasonable, their specific interpretation and implementation can be burdensome upon the operations of the firm. Since it is easier to negotiate the more restrictive provisions away at the beginning than to alter them later, the alert financial officer tries to anticipate those which might be troublesome and sees to it that they are not included in the original agreement.

The customary security provisions obligating the firm to maintain an adequate working capital position are varied, but let us enumerate the major ones. The firm is obligated to maintain a minimum level of net working capital. This curtails the firm's ability to use trade credit or short-term borrowing in its financing plans. The agreement might also limit the firm's ability to make cash withdrawals for such items as the payment of dividends or the redemption of its own stock. This might have the undesirable effect of discouraging purchases of the stock and increasing the cost of capital, but it maintains the equity cushion that the bank relies on in case of default. The firm is typically required to insure the inventory and the plant and equipment.

Among the provisions to maintain efficient management, the bank might insist upon the submission of current financial statements and operating data. This is to satisfy the bank that the firm is operating within expectations and can continue to meet the amortization schedule. The bank might also insist that the firm carry life insurance on its key officers, so that in the event of their death, the firm will be able to pay off the loan.

Among the provisions aimed at maintaining the firm's net asset base, the bank may require that the firm get the bank's approval before it can sell fixed assets. In some cases, the bank might even insist that the firm get approval before acquiring fixed assets *above* a certain dollar amount, either by buying the equipment outright or by leasing it. The provisions might restrict the firm's ability to use assets for collateral on other borrowings and its ability to borrow additional funds. As is obvious, if the financial officer is not careful, the security provisions of a term loan can be very onerous to the firm's management.

Other common security provisions include the acceleration clause. Under this provision if the firm defaults on any loan, whether it is this particular one or not, the entire loan is due immediately instead of as outlined in the amortization schedule. This provision is designed to protect the lender's priority position as a claimant in the event the borrower defaults. Without it, the bank would have to wait until the scheduled amortization payment was due before it could press its claim for that amount, and by that time the firm could be insolvent and unable to pay.

The term loan sometimes contains a penalty for early repayment of the loan ahead of the schedule. This is particularly true if the lender is an insurance company which likes to have its funds invested for long periods of time and if the loan is originally negotiated at a relatively high interest rate. The lender wants to discourage early repayment so that the loan continues to earn a higher than prevailing interest rate by making it too costly for the firm to pay off the loan and refinance at a lower rate. The security provisions may also specify the use of the loan proceeds or regulate the salaries of executives so that they cannot replace the prohibited dividend distributions with large salary increases.

This is only a partial list of possible security provisions, which are individually negotiated with each term loan agreement and can vary to fit the circumstances. The alert financial officer tries to keep the restrictive provisions to a minimum so as to give the firm maximum flexibility in dealing with the future events.

The term loan might also involve collateral. The customary collateral are such assets as stocks, bonds, machinery, and equipment. The size of the term loan can be tailored to the needs and repayment abilities of the firm.

COMMON SUPPLIERS OF TERM LOANS

After you have decided it may be an appropriate source of funds where do you look as a starting point in seeking a term loan?

Commercial banks and insurance companies are the major suppliers, but business finance companies also provide some term loans.

Commercial Banks

Commercial banks usually take the shorter-term loans. Some more conservative banks still refuse to make any term loans, although competitive pressures from other lenders are forcing most banks to make them. Some banks will only provide term loans to firms that are already their clients so as not to lose their business. As a financial officer, you should determine the bank's policy on term loans before establishing a banking relationship.

Insurance Companies

Life insurance companies in particular tend to undertake the longer-maturity term loans, in contrast to the banks which prefer the shorter-term loans. Sometimes the insurance company will take the longer portion of a term loan while the bank underwrites the shorter portion. For example, you might negotiate a 15-year term loan with the bank's part amortized in the first five years and the insurance company's part amortized in the last ten years.

The nominal interest rate on insurance company term loans tends to be higher than that on bank term loans, but the insurance company does not require compensating balances. The bank may. As the financial officer, you will have to determine the true interest rate before comparing the two interest costs. Conversely, insurance companies tend to penalize early repayment of the loan, while banks do not. Sometimes the penalty can be rather steep, such as one-half of one percent for each year remaining in the life of the loan at the time of prepayment. Security provisions are generally the same for the two types of lending institutions.

The insurance company is more likely to accept real estate as collateral than the bank, but it is also more likely to demand an equity participation in the form of stock options or warrants to purchase the common stock of the firm at a relatively low price as a condition of the loan. This might be very unattractive to the firm's management, especially if they are concerned about control.

Business Finance Companies

Business finance companies (Chapter 16) also engage in some term lending. These companies usually deal with the marginal borrowers and charge higher interest rates and require collateral. The security provisions that a financial officer dealing with these companies can anticipate are very similar to those required by banks and insurance companies.

EQUIPMENT FINANCING LOANS

When a term loan is used to purchase a particular and identifiable piece of equipment, it becomes an equipment financing loan. The distinguishing feature is that the machinery or equipment itself is pledged as collateral for the loan. Typically, these equipment financing loans are extended only to the purchase of highly marketable and resalable pieces of equipment and are used mainly by firms whose creditworthiness does not allow them to borrow on more general terms.

The size of the loan is less than the market value of the pledged equipment, for the excess of the market value over the loan is the lender's safety margin if the borrower defaults. The repayment of the loan is usually matched with the expected cash inflows generated by the machine over its expected life. This is designed to insure that the lender is repaid during the machine's most productive period. It also insures that the amount owed decreases as the machine's value diminishes with age, leaving the lender's safety margin intact. The maturity of the loan is also matched with the expected life of the equipment. For example, the typical maturity on equipment financing loans for the purchase of trucks is three years, while the typical equipment financing loan maturity for the purchase of railroad tank cars is ten to fifteen years.

The interest rate on this type of loan depends on the degree of marketability for the pledged equipment and the creditworthiness of the borrower. As the degree of marketability increases, the interest cost decreases. For example, railroad equipment loans generally have a lower interest rate because the equipment financed with such loans is highly resalable to other railroads in the event of default. As a consequence, and since the cars are so absolutely essential to the operations of the railroad, defaults are very rare.

The security provisions of the equipment financing loan are minimal compared to other term loans, except for the pledge of the specific asset, because the lender depends almost exclusively on being able to resell the equipment should the firm default.

Traditional suppliers of equipment financing loans have been the business finance company, commercial banks, and (less frequently) the insurance companies and the pension funds.

CONDITIONAL SALES CONTRACTS

Conditional sales contracts are agreements between the buyer and seller upon intermediate-term financing in the form of promissory notes for the purchase price of the equipment after the down payment. In these notes the firm gives the seller of the equipment the right to repossess the specific piece of equipment if the firm fails to make the promised payments. The title (evidence of ownership) remains with the seller, although the firm uses the equipment. The title or ownership passes to the firm once the final payment is made. For example, as financial officer you might negotiate the purchase of a milling machine on a conditional sales contract from the manufacturer of that machine. The firm takes possession of the machine and in return pays off the remaining balance plus some interest over the life of the equipment. The distinguishing feature of the conditional sales contract is that the title to the equipment remains in the hands of the seller, making repossession, if necessary, considerably easier.

The major collateral for the conditional sales contract is the title and ownership to the equipment with the right to repossess and sell it to satisfy the claim. The size of the contract is usually the amount of the purchase price remaining after the down payment, but this is negotiable. The amortization schedule is usually keyed to the expected cashflows over the expected life of the equipment and is so arranged that the entire note is paid off on or before the expected end of the equipment's life.

The interest rate charged by the holder of the sales contract depends largely on the marketability of the equipment itself, the creditworthiness of the firm, and the competitive climate in which the seller of the equipment is marketing the equipment. If there is a great amount of competition among suppliers, they might be willing to extend very attractive and low-cost terms in order to induce you to purchase from them. As a financial officer it is your responsibility to negotiate the best terms under the circumstances.

Unlike term loans, the conditional sales contract has no security provisions, since the holder of the note depends entirely on holding the title and the right to repossess.

The usual suppliers of this type of financing are the manufacturers of the equipment themselves. They can and frequently do endorse the contract over to a financial institution such as a bank or a business finance company, and the firm may find itself dealing with lending institutions after all.

SMALL BUSINESS ADMINISTRATION (SBA) LOANS

The SBA loan is either a government loan or a government-guaranteed loan from a local bank to a small business, generally defined as employing less than 250 people and controlling a relatively small volume of sales within its industry. Typically, the firm is unable to obtain more conventional financing on reasonable terms because of its size and the lack of an established financial track record.

SBA loans fall into three categories. *Direct loans* are obtained by applying directly to the SBA itself and are made from the agency to the firm. *Participation loans* are obtained from a local bank, but the SBA guarantees repayment of the principal and interest. *Minority enterprise loans* are designed to encourage minority businesses. The typical SBA loan is collateralized by a mortgage on the firm's plant and equipment, warehouse receipts, third-party guarantees, or accounts receivable assignment and a "good character reputation of the firm and its owners."

The loan size can range from $15,000 to $350,000, but the most common size is below $25,000. The average maturity is 5 years, although maturities range up to 10 years and loans for working capital average 6 years. The interest rate averages far less than the going interest rate on a similar loan without SBA guarantees, but it is about 1 percent higher than the prevailing United States Treasury bond rate. The security provisions are similar to those at any bank for a term loan.

SUMMARY

After having read Chapter 17, you should be able to answer these questions:

1. What are term loans?

Term loans are longer-term fixed commitments on the part of the lender, usually ranging up to five years for a commercial bank and longer for other lending institutions such as insurance companies. The typical term loan is amortized over the life of the loan so that at maturity the entire principal has been repaid, although there are balloon type term loans which let the firm repay a large portion of the loan at maturity.

The interest on a term loan is calculated on the unpaid remaining balance, and that portion of the installment not applied to interest is deducted from the remaining principal until the entire loan is repaid.

The security and other provisions of a term loan are negotiable. It is the financial officer's responsibility to insure that these provisions do not unduly restrict the firm's operations or expansion and to negotiate a low interest rate. The more common security provisions are restrictions on working capital and additional borrowings.

2. Who supplies term loans?

We saw that banks, insurance companies, and to a lesser extent business finance companies supply the majority of term loans.

3. What are equipment financing loans?

Equipment financing loans are essentially term loans taken for the purchase of and secured by the pledge of a specifically identified piece of equipment. In contrast to the bank or insurance company term loan, this type of term loan has minimal security provisions because the lender depends on the pledge of the asset to satisfy the claim should the firm default.

4. What is a conditional sales contract?

The conditional sales contract is a promissory note for the purchase price remaining after the down payment on a specific piece of equipment. Manufacturers of the equipment often use the conditional sales contract as part of their marketing program and depend upon retaining ownership of the equipment as their only source of security. If the firm defaults, the supplier can repossess the equipment and sell it to satisfy the claim.

5. What are Small Business Administration loans?

Small Business Administration (SBA) loans are government-backed or direct government loans to small or minority enterprises which would not customarily qualify for term loans at a reasonable cost from the more conventional suppliers.

QUESTIONS

17-1 What are some of the distinguishing characteristics of intermediate-term financing as opposed to short-term financing?

17-2 What does the word *amortize* mean with respect to term loans?

17-3 Enumerate some of the security provisions that banks often attach to intermediate-term business loans.

17-4 Why do you think insurance companies normally charge a higher nominal interest rate for intermediate-term loans than do commercial banks? How might this affect the borrower's decision about where to borrow?

17-5 What are the similarities and differences in equipment financing loans and conditional sales contracts?

17-6 Distinguish between direct, participation, and minority enterprise Small Business Administration (SBA) loans.

PROBLEMS

17-1 METCO Company has just negotiated a 4-year term loan with its local bank for $100,000 at a nominal interest rate of 8 percent on the remaining balance. The loan calls for equal installment repayments at the end of each year.

(a) Amortize the loan over the life of the loan.

(b) What is the total interest paid?

17-2 Amortize the same loan, but assume the loan calls for a $50,000 balloon payment at the end of the fourth year. Is the total interest charge different from that in Problem 17-1?

BIBLIOGRAPHY

Ferrara, William L. "Should Investment and Financing Decisions Be Separated?" *Accounting Review*, XLI (January 1966), 106–114.

Hayes, Douglas A. *Bank Lending Policies: Issues and Practices.* Bureau of Business Research, University of Michigan, Ann Arbor, Mich., 1964, Ch. 6.

Middleton, J. William. "Term Lending—Practical and Profitable." *Journal of Commercial Bank Lending*, 50 (August 1968), 31–43.

Moore, George S. "Term Loans and Interim Financing," in *Business Loans of American Commercial Banks*, ed. Benjamin Haggott Beckhart. Ronald, New York, 1959, pp. 208–282.

Robinson, Roland I. *The Management of Bank Funds.* McGraw-Hill, New York, 1962, Ch. 14.

Rogers, Dean E. "An Approach to Analyzing Cash Flow for Term Loan Purposes." *Bulletin of the Robert Morris Associates*, 48 (October 1965), 79–85.

Van Horne, James. "A Linear-Programming Approach to Evaluating Restrictions Under a Bond Indenture or Loan Agreement." *Journal of Financial and Quantitative Analysis*, I (June 1966), 68–83.

18
LEASING

INSTEAD OF BUYING PLANT OR EQUIPMENT, the firm sometimes has the option of leasing the assets. In effect, this is an alternative source of intermediate-term financing, since the lease is specifically tied to the expected life of the asset. What are the types of leases you, as financial officer, can consider? We shall see that these include operating leases, financial leases, and sale and leaseback arrangements. The alert financial officer should consider these leasing arrangements as alternatives to intermediate-term financing under the appropriate circumstances. You should consider such factors as what assets can typically be leased, who are the major suppliers of lease funds, and what are the basic provisions of the typical lease.

Once you have familiarized yourself with these factors, you must be able to answer the question: What are the advantages and the disadvantages of leasing? When the decision-makers to whom you are reporting ask for your evaluation of the alternative financing methods, you must be able to present your opinions, including those on leasing, in an intelligent and logical fashion.

How are leases treated by the accountants in the firm's financial statements? We shall see that the accountants accord special treatment to leases. They are treated as contingency liabilities not directly reported in the body of the balance sheet as debt or segregated as a separate expense in the income statement. This partially hidden view has led some financial officers to treat leasing as if it were not a debt, although security analysts and lenders have taken just the opposite view. The effect, as we shall see, has been to force the financial officer to give special consideration in the footnotes of the firm's financial statements to lease commitments and to recognize specifically the debt characteristics of leases in the firm's cost of capital and capital structure when using debt as a source of intermediate-term funds.

How does the presence of leases affect the firm's cost of capital? We shall see that investors tend to treat leases as imputed liabilities and accordingly require a greater rate of return as the firm's use of leases increases. As a rule of thumb, investors might capitalize the firm's leases and impute a higher debt/equity ratio and lower coverage ratios for the firm.

How do you, as the financial officer, evaluate the attractiveness of a lease? It is not sufficient to know that you can lease a particular asset instead of buying it or to know that you can negotiate different types of leases and lease terms. You must also analyze the choice of buying or leasing on some comparable basis. We shall see that

lease evaluation forces the financial officer to examine the different treatment accorded the various costs under each alternative, the ownership of the estimated salvage, the different tax treatments of each alternative, and the certainty of the
cashflows under each financing method. It is your responsibility to put these considerations together in one analytical framework upon which to compare the relative
attractiveness of buying and leasing and from which the appropriate decision can be
readily reported to the firm's decision-makers.

GENERAL CHARACTERISTICS OF LEASES

What types of leases can you consider when leasing is an alternative source of
funds? What basic provisions characterize the typical lease? What assets are commonly leased, and what are typical sources of leasing funds?

Types of Leases

Since the lease is a negotiated contract between the owner (lessor) of the property
allowing the firm (the lessee) the use of that property for a specific period of time for
a specific rental, its provisions can vary with the bargaining position and needs of
each party. However, the majority of leases fall into three general categories: the
financial lease, the operating lease, and the sale and leaseback arrangement.

The financial lease The typical financial lease resembles a term loan involving periodic, contractual payments over an intermediate period, usually equal to or shorter
than the expected life of the leased asset. Any remaining value to the asset at the
end of the lease belongs to the lessor and can be considered to be part of the lessor's
profit. The lessee (the firm) loses claim to the salvage value of the asset under the
lease arrangement (whereas the firm keeps the salvage value if it purchased the
asset).

Most financial leases are noncancelable, which means that the firm is obligated to
continue the contractual payments even if it abandons the asset and no longer has
any use for it. A noncancelable lease is in all respects as binding on the firm as the
interest payments it obligates itself to when it borrows. Failure to make the lease
payments is as damaging to the firm as not meeting its interest payments.

The distinguishing feature of the financial lease is that the firm (lessee) agrees to
maintain the asset even though ownership of the asset remains with the lessor.
Sometimes this is the only practical approach to maintenance of the asset, as in the
case of the diesel locomotive leased to the railroad. The leasing company is a specialist in finance and not in engine mechanics, while the railroad knows how to
repair the engine and probably has the facilities to do so.

Over the life of the lease, the total dollar amount of lease payments is going to
exceed the original purchase price because the lease payment must not only reimburse the lessor's original outlay but also return interest on the funds the lessor has
committed over the asset's life.

The operating lease The distinguishing features of the operating lease are that it is
usually cancelable by the lessee with proper notice and that the lessor usually maintains the asset. Most apartment leases are operating leases. The tenant can cancel
the lease under certain conditions and with a specified number of days notice, while

repairs to the apartment are usually handled by the landlord (lessor). The operating lease is also known as a maintenance lease.

The sale and leaseback This type of leasing arrangement arises when the owner of the asset, in our case the firm, sells it to another party who agrees to lease it back immediately after the sale. The sale and leaseback arrangement is most commonly used by the financial officer in real estate and buildings leasing. For example, hotels are frequently bought from the management company that runs them and then leased back to that same management company, who continues to run the hotel but no longer owns the building and/or land.

Net leases Any of the foregoing types of leases can be either net or gross leases. Under the terms of a net lease, the lessee bears such expenses associated with the asset as taxes, maintenance, and insurance. Under a gross lease, the lessor bears these expenses. However, since the lease is an individually negotiated contract, the financial officer can arrange for the firm to bear the maintenance costs but the lessor to bear the taxes and the insurance, or any other combination of terms. Most financial leases are written as net leases.

Basic Lease Provisions

The basic provisions of the typical lease include the period over which the asset is to be leased. This can range from a very short term such as one day for a car rental lease to several hundred years for a property lease. The common equipment lease, which is the type most likely to be encountered by the financial officer, usually lasts slightly less than the expected life of the leased asset. The lease also specifies the rental payments and the payment dates. The payment may be monthly, annually, or, since the lease is negotiated, at any interval that the parties agree upon.

The lease also has a provision which clearly assigns the responsibility for such associated costs as taxes and maintenance to one of the parties. Financial officers must read the lease carefully to insure that this provision appears in the lease and assigns the responsibility clearly. The typical lease has limited, if any, security provisions since the lessor retains title (ownership), and in the event of default can remove the asset or evict the lessee. To a great extent, the lessor depends on the creditworthiness of the lessee to insure payment. However, in instances where the lessor feels it appropriate, the lease can include security provisions much like those in a term loan. Sometimes the financial officer finds prohibitions in the lease against incurring additonal debt, paying dividends, or reacquiring common stock.

Leases may contain escalation clauses which let the lessor raise the periodic rental payments at some predetermined dates over the life of the lease or in response to increases in costs, particularly if it is a gross lease. The escalation clause is less typical of a net lease since the increased costs are borne by the lessee. However, in countries with high rates of inflation, it is not uncommon to find leases which allow the rental payment to rise as the cost-of-living index increases. The escalation clause has the effect of increasing the liability of the lessee.

Leases frequently contain options allowing the lessee to renew the lease or purchase the asset. However, the financial officer must be extremely careful when negotiating purchase options not to lose the tax deductibility of the lease payments. If the Internal Revenue Service interprets the option as a conversion of the lease to a conditional sales contract, the payments on which are not tax deductible, the firm cannot expense the lease payments. This can happen if the Internal Revenue Service feels the option purchase price is too small in relation to the total rental payments or that the periodic payments are too high in relation to the asset's value. Since the interpretation is subjective, the financial officer must obtain an IRS ruling prior to signing the lease to be certain that the lease is not interpreted as a conditional sales contract.

Commonly Leased Assets

Almost any asset can be leased. There are firms which specialize in leasing and are willing to lease almost any item that the firm needs. However, certain types of assets are traditionally leased. As the financial officer, you should be aware of these items so that you can evaluate the lease alternative as a matter of course for these assets. Among the most commonly leased assets are transportation equipment. Railroad cars, trucks, and airplanes are all readily leased. Real estate—particularly for plants, retail stores, and hotels—is a traditional lease item. Mineral rights to lands owned by the firm may be leased to another party or, if the firm is a natural resource company, leased from another firm or government. Computers are almost universally leased rather than purchased.

Sources of Leasing Funds

You should be aware of the types of financial institutions engaged in leasing so that you know who to contact when you feel leasing is a viable alternative. Commercial banks have in recent years developed large leasing subsidiaries. These bank subsidiaries tend to be general leasing firms able to lease almost any type of asset. There are leasing companies which engage in general leasing, and there are specialized leasing companies which engage in leasing only particular types of assets. Probably the greatest concentration of specialized leasing companies is in computers, but there are firms that specialize in trucks, restaurant equipment, and other particular assets.

Life insurance companies are another source of leasing funds. Those life insurers who do lease tend to be general lessors and will lease almost any item. However, in contrast to the leasing firms, they are likely to treat a lease as a term loan and demand security provisions which the leasing companies may not require. Pension funds are sometimes sources of lease funds, although not to the extent of other financial institutions, and they tend to concentrate in real estate leases. The Small Business Administration has a lease-guarantee program which allows small businesses to lease assets instead of purchasing them. The guarantee assures the lessor of the rental payments.

Sometimes the firm might have to provide lease insurance to the lessor as a provision of the lease. There are companies which specialize in insuring that the rental payments will be made. If the lessee defaults, the insurer pays off the lease. If your firm is a lessee, you might be called upon by the management to evaluate the attractiveness of purchasing such insurance.

ADVANTAGES AND DISADVANTAGES OF LEASING

As the financial officer, you are required to evaluate available leasing alternatives. This means you have to know the benefits and the disadvantages of leasing in order to determine if the leasing alternative is appropriate for the firm under the circumstances.

Advantages

The major advantage to leasing is the flexibility it gives the financial officer. The typical lease does not have the restrictive provisions of the term loan. The firm does not unduly restrict its ability to undertake an immediate change of plans or unscheduled action in order to grasp a sudden profit opportunity or adjust to a changing operating environment. The simple fact that the lessee may not require the prior approval of the lessor, whereas the term loan probably does, means a speedier reaction time.

The lease lends itself to piecemeal financing. The financial officer can fund small asset acquisitions with a lease when it is uneconomical to go to the capital markets with such a small offering, or because interest rates are temporarily too high. You can continue to lease until you have built up a sufficient need for more permanent capital or interest rates decline. Then you can go to the capital market with a security offering large enough to be economical or when interest rates are low.

The lease arrangement also lets the firm avoid the risk of rapid obsolescence. Since the firm does not own the asset, a deterioration in its value because of changing technology, for example, does not affect the firm's asset value. If the asset does not have any salvage value at the end of the lease, despite original expectations that it would, the lessor suffers the loss, not the firm.

Some firms look upon the lease as a method of evading budgetary constraints under a situation of capital rationing. If the firm has several projects it wants to undertake but is constrained because of limited funds, it can use leasing to extend the firm's asset acquisitions. This advantage may be illusionary, however, because the leasing funds are as much a part of the available funds as the other sources and should be evaluated along with these other sources. Further, leasing funds are as burdensome to the firm in almost all respects as additional term debt. The financial officer should not look upon leasing as an evasion of the budgetary constraints but simply as one alternative source of funds.

Lease payments are tax deductible as an operating expense, whereas ownership of the asset only lets the firm deduct depreciation as an operating expense. Since the payment is typically larger than the depreciation, the firm has a larger tax deduction if it leases. This is a special advantage to the sale and leaseback of older buildings, which the firm has almost completely depreciated. By selling it to new owners and leasing it back, the new owners get an opportunity to depreciate the building again at its new market value, which should lower the lease payments since it increases their cash inflows, while the firm can deduct the lease payments as an operating expense. This gives the firm further tax deductions after it has exhausted its ability to depreciate the asset while maintaining its use. In addition, the realized capital gain or loss from the sale of the building can be written off the firm's taxes, if it is a loss, or taxed at the lower long-term capital-gains tax rate, if it is a gain.

Leasing is sometimes used to evade loan restrictions. When loan provisions restrict the firm from additional borrowing, the firm might lease instead, using the technical excuse that leasing is not defined as additional debt. This interpretation is misleading since leasing is an imputed form of debt, and many lenders now explicitly restrict leasing as well as additional debt in the provisions of the loan.

The marginal firm may find that leasing is the only way it can finance the acquisition of assets. Since the title remains with the lessor, the risk is reduced, and the lessor may be willing to provide leasing when other lenders will not finance the firm.

As we shall shortly see, leases do not appear on the balance sheet as a liability as do other debt securities and loans. This may be important to some firms who want to "dress up" their balance sheet or mislead investors into thinking that the firm has lower fixed charges or less debt than it actually has.

Leases also afford the firm a small advantage if bankruptcy occurs. They are less burdensome to the firm at that time because the title is with the lessor. The asset cannot be seized by the firm's creditors. The firm can readily break the lease by simply returning the asset to the lessor with one to three years' payments, depending on the circumstances. This makes it considerably easier for the financial officer to reorganize the firm.

Disadvantages

The major disadvantage to the typical lease is that it is more costly than if the firm had purchased the asset. Over the life of the asset the firm can expect to have a larger total cash outlay associated with the lease than if it had purchased the asset. However, this does not mean that the lease is less attractive. It is possible that, considering the other uses to which the firm could put the purchase price of the leased asset, the time value of money, and the pattern of the net cash inflows, the leasing alternative could have a higher net present value than the purchase and would be the more attractive method of financing the project.

When the firm leases the asset it loses the depreciation and investment tax credit deductions as well as any salvage value which might remain at the end of the lease; these accrue to the lessor. In most instances, the lessor might lower the lease payments because of the cash inflows expected from these benefits, but the lessee never gets their full effect, as it would had it purchased the asset.

The noncancelable lease can inject a rigidity into the plans and operations of the firm. If the project should turn out to be unsatisfactory, the firm can abandon the operation, but it cannot abandon the lease payments. Unless it can buy out the lease or sublet to another party, who then assumes responsibility for the payments, the firm must continue the payments. For example, if the firm entered into a 20-year lease on a retail store, which after 2 years in operation proved unprofitable and had to be abandoned, the firm remains obligated to pay 18 more years of rent unless it can buy back the lease from the lessor or sublet.

ACCOUNTING TREATMENT

How does the accounting treatment of leases differ from that of loans and other debt instruments?

As financial officers, we must know what the differences are and how they affect the firm's financial statements and its decisions to undertake or reject projects.

The accounting profession does not treat the lease as a loan or debt security of the firm for the purposes of financial reporting, because it does not have the repayment-of-principal obligation associated with those securities. The lease is not reported on the balance sheet as a liability as are the other fixed-charges obligations of the firm. The asset the firm leases does not appear as an asset on the firm's balance sheet. The only reporting requirement is that the leases be treated as an integral part of the financial statements and be reported in the accompanying footnotes.

The footnote must contain certain information, which you must be sure is included in the firm's annual report.[1] The total rental expense must be reported in such a

[1] Accounting Principles Board Opinions, number 5 and number 31.

fashion that the reader of the footnote would know the minimum amount of rent under noncancelable leases that the firm had committed itself to in each of the next five years and each of the next three five-year periods, as well as a single amount for the minimum rent after that fifteen years. In addition, the leases have to be classified into categories reflecting the nature of the underlying asset, such as real estate and trucks. Any restrictive provisions of the lease, such as prohibitions on dividend payments or additional debt, must be reported.

The absence of the leases in the firm's balance sheet can be deceptive, particularly in ratio analysis. For example, the asset turnover ratio, the return to stockholders' equity, and the interest coverage ratios may appear deceptively high, while the debt/equity ratio may appear deceptively low. We can see this in Table 18-1 when we compare the effect on the balance sheet, income statement, and the above ratios of (1) leasing a $10,000 asset with an annual depreciation of $1,000 and no salvage value for an annual lease payment of $1,558 and (2) financing the purchase of the same asset with $10,000 in 9 percent bonds. While the lease and the purchase are essentially equivalent (see footnote 2), the financial statements and ratios differ.

We can see in Table 18-1 that because the leases are not included in the balance

Table 18-1   Purchase versus Lease

BALANCE SHEET

Assets	Buy	Lease
Current assets	$ 3,000	$ 3,000
Fixed assets	15,000	5,000
Total assets	18,000	8,000
Liabilities and stockholders' equity		
Current liabilities	1,000	1,000
Long-term debt (9%)	11,000	1,000
Total liabilities	12,000	2,000
Stockholders' equity	6,000	6,000
Total liabilities and stockholders' equity	$18,000	$ 8,000

INCOME STATEMENT

	Buy	Lease
Sales	$50,000	$50,000
Cost of goods sold	26,610	26,610
Selling and general administrative expense	20,000	20,000
Depreciation	1,100	100
Operating income	2,290	3,290
Interest on debt (9%)	990	90
Lease payments	—	1,558
Net before taxes	1,300	1,642
Income taxes (50%)	650	821
Net income after taxes	650	821

FINANCIAL RATIOS

	Buy	Lease
Asset turnover ratio (times)	2.8	6.25
Return on stockholders' equity	10.8%	13.6%
Return on total assets	3.6%	10.3%
Debt/equity	1.83	.16
Interest coverage	2.31	19.2

sheet, the firm's financial ratios appear deceptively better. The asset turnover ratio, the return on stockholders' equity, and the return on total assets, as well as the interest coverage, all appear higher than if the firm had purchased the asset. The debt/equity ratio appears deceptively lower. The real situation is disguised, and it is hard to tell the exact degree to which the ratios are distorted from the financial statements as they are presented. It is certain that the firm's financial risk is higher than it appears when the lease alternative is chosen. It is also certain that the firm's suppliers of funds are not deceived and that the use of lease debt is considered to increase the financial risk associated with providing funds. Consequently it raises the firm's cost of capital.

IMPLICATIONS FOR THE COST OF CAPITAL

How does the presence of leases affect the firm's cost of capital (k)?

Because of the sophisticated knowledge of investors and the disclosure requirements of footnotes in the financial statements, it is unlikely that investors in general will be misled into thinking that the firm's financial structure is better than it actually is merely because the firm leases instead of purchasing some of its assets. Rather, investors will adjust the financial statements and financial ratios to reflect the lease commitments as if they were loans or other debts which would have been reported in the body of the financial statements.

They will treat leases as an imputed liability to be added to the firm's outstanding debt, raising the firm's debt/equity ratio, increasing their perceived financial risk associated with the firm's securities, and raising their required rate of return and the firm's cost of capital. For example, if the firm's cost of debt, as measured by the yield to maturity on its bonds, were 9 percent, as in Table 18-1, investors might capitalize the $1,558 annual lease payments at 9 percent to derive an imputed liability of approximately $10,000.[2] Adding this $10,000 to both the liability and the asset side of the balance sheet, the investor would recompute the debt/equity ratio as 1.83 ($11,000/$6,000), which in Table 18-1 is the same as if we had purchased the asset. The 1.83 is considerably higher than the .16, which is the debt/equity ratio as computed from the unadjusted financial statements under the leasing alternative.

The impact on the cost of capital after investors have imputed the debt obligation associated with the lease is the same as if the firm had sold additional debt to finance the purchase of the asset and is reflected in a higher cost of capital.

LEASE EVALUATION

Once the financial officer knows what assets can generally be leased or purchased,[3] what types of leases exist, and how their basic provisions can be negotiated, how can the lease option versus the purchase option be evaluated to determine which is more attractive?

[2] This is the present value of the firm's lease payments, figured as the annual lease payment times the present value of $1 received annually at 9 percent, or $1,588 × 6.418 ≅ $10,000.00.

[3] Some have suggested that the decision is a lease-borrow analysis, or leasing versus borrowing to finance the asset purchase. It appears, however, that since the purchase may be made from funds generated by equity as well as by debt and that most financial theorists consider the overall cost of capital, which is a weighted average of the cost of the debt and the equity, to be the appropriate discount rate in a net present value analysis, the evaluation has to be of the more general lease-buy option.

The financial officer has to determine which method of financing moves the firm closer to its corporate objective. Since we have been customarily using maximization of share price as our objective, and since most financial theorists seem to agree that the maximization of the net present value (NPV) is an appropriate analysis for the financial officer to use in that case, we must determine which alternative has the greater net present value (see Chapter 5).[4] If we think of a machine with a 10-year life that can either be purchased for $10,000 or leased for 10 years at $1,558 a year, is it better to spend $10,000 now or $15,580 over the next 10 years?

Before we determine the net present value (NPV) of the product under each method of financing, we must notice that the net cashflows to the same project are different because of the financing methods. And we must notice that the cost of capital used as the discount rate in deriving the NPV also differs because of the financing method. Let us examine these two observations before settling on a particular method of evaluating the same project under the two financing methods.

Cashflows

When a project is financed through the sale of securities or a loan, the stream of benefits accruing to the project which must be discounted for time at the firm's cost of capital include:

1. The after-tax net income from operations of that project (NI)
2. The noncash expenditures, particularly depreciation (D), associated with the project
3. The after-tax cashflows generated from the sale of the asset at its salvage value
These variables are related as follows:

$$CF_{pi} = NI_i + D_i + S \tag{18-1}$$

where

$\quad CF_{pi}$ = the after-tax net cashflow in period i if the project is purchased
$\quad NI_i$ = after-tax net income from the project in period i
$\quad D_i$ = the depreciation (or noncash) expense for the project in period i
$\quad S$ = the expected after-tax salvage value

Conversely, when the same project is financed through a lease arrangement, the net cashflow which accrues to that project includes:

1. The after-tax net income of that project, as if it were owned (NI)
2. *Plus* any after-tax reduction in operating expenditures because the asset is leased rather than financed (which has the effect of increasing such after-tax cashflow $[A_i(1 - t)]$) as reduction in maintenance, insurance, taxes, etc., which the lessor pays
3. *Less* the after-tax noninterest portion of the lease payments $[L_i(1 - t)]$, which has the effect of lowering the after-tax net cashflows
The variables are related as follows.

$$CF_{1i} = NI_i + A_i(1 - t) - L_i(1 - t) \tag{18-2}$$

[4] This discussion is based on the approach suggested by R. W. Johnson and W. G. Lewellen, "Analysis of the Lease-or-Buy Decision," *Journal of Finance*, XXVII (September 1972), 815–824, as commented upon by William L. Sartoris and R. S. Paul, "Lease Evaluation—Another Capital Budgeting Decision," *Financial Management*, Summer 1973, 46–52.

where

CF_{li} = the after-tax net cashflow in period i if the project is leased

NI_i = the after-tax net income from the project in period i

$A_i(1-t)$ = the after-tax reductions in operating expenses during period i because the project is leased rather than purchased

$L_i(1-t)$ = the after-tax noninterest portion of the lease payment (the amortization of the principal)

t = the tax rate on the firm's ordinary income

Notice that when the asset is leased, the firm loses the depreciation and after-tax salvage value that accompany the purchase because the title (ownership) remains with the lessor. Also notice that in neither expression of the cashflow is the interest cost included, since this would be double counting, as we saw in Chapter 5. The interest cost is already imputed in the cost of capital as the discount factor in the NPV analysis. That means that the interest on the funds used to finance the purchase and the interest portion of the lease payment (as distinguished from that portion which serves to amortize the lessor's initial outlay) are both excluded from the cashflows.

The cashflow under the lease arrangement (CF_l) is reduced by the noninterest portion of the lease payment (L) after taxes because the lease payment is tax deductible. The increase in the cashflow under the leasing arrangement because of reduced operating expenses is also after taxes, because the firm must pay taxes on the additional dollars of income brought about by the reduction in expenses. If the firm retained the responsibility for all the operating expenses and experienced no reduction in them, the second term of Equation 18-2 would be zero, and the cashflow under the leasing alternative would be the net income less the after-tax noninterest portion of the lease payments.

The differences in the cashflows for the same project under the two financing methods are illustrated in Table 18-2. Notice that the cashflows under the lease arrangement decline as the noninterest portion of the lease increases over time.[5] Thus the cashflow under the lease is larger than the cashflow under the purchase at the beginning and smaller toward the end. Much of the advantage to this lease comes from the large annual cost reductions it allows the firm to make. Because of

---

[5] The noninterest portion of the lease payment is calculated on the same basis as the repayment of principal of a term loan (Chapter 17) as:

Year	Total lease payment	Interest (10%)	Noninterest portion	Remaining balance	After-tax L_i
1	$1,627	$1,000	$ 627	$9,373	$324
2	1,627	937	690	8,683	345
3	1,627	868	759	7,924	380
4	1,627	792	835	7,089	417
5	1,627	709	918	6,171	459
6	1,627	617	1,010	5,161	505
7	1,627	516	1,111	4,050	555
8	1,627	405	1,222	2,828	611
9	1,627	283	1,344	1,484	672
10	1,627	148	1,479	5*	740

(*Rounding error)

Table 18-2 Differences in Cashflows

Project description	
Original cost (C)	$10,000
Expected life (n)	10 years
Annual after-tax net income (NI)	$780
Ordinary income tax rate (t)	.50

If purchased:

Annual depreciation	$800
Expected after-tax salvage value	$2,000

If leased:

After-tax annual reduction in operating expenses	$320
Total annual after-tax income plus annual after-tax reduction in operating costs	$1,100

After-tax noninterest portion of the lease payment in each year (L)

$L_1 = \$324$	$L_6 = \$505$
$L_2 = 345$	$L_7 = 555$
$L_3 = 380$	$L_8 = 611$
$L_4 = 417$	$L_9 = 672$
$L_5 = 459$	$L_{10} = 740$

Year	Net cashflow (CF_{pi}) Purchased	Net cashflow (CF_{li}) Leased
1	$1,580	$776
2	1,580	755
3	1,580	720
4	1,580	683
5	1,580	641
6	1,580	595
7	1,580	545
8	1,580	489
9	1,580	428
10	3,580	360

differences in the timing and the sizes of the cashflows under each financing alternative, it is impossible to tell immediately which is preferred, if either, until a net present value analysis is performed. In order to do that, we must derive a cost of capital for leasing.

The Cost of Capital

As financial officers, we should recognize that the net cashflows to the lease arrangement (CF_l) are really two different streams. The inflow generated from the operations and the outflow required by the lease payment are two distinct parts of the cashflow. Therefore, the cost of capital used to discount the future net cashflows of each part must be different as well.[6] The net income after taxes (NI) plus the after-tax reduction in operating expenses incurred because of the lease $[A(1 - t)]$ can be discounted at the same cost of capital (k) as if the firm had purchased the asset. However, the after-tax noninterest portion of the lease payments (L) should be discounted at the default-free or pure interest rate (r) since these lease payments have such a high predictability and certainty of occurrence because of their contractual nature.

The after-tax weighted average cost of capital (k_0) and not the after-tax cost of debt (k_d) must be used to discount the net cashflows under the purchase option (CF_p), because funding for the purchase comes from mingled funds raised from all the firm's sources and cannot be associated with any one particular type of security offering. The same overall weighted average cost of capital has to be used to discount that part of the leasing net cashflows generated by the net income and cost reductions, because it lacks the contractual certainty of the lease payments.

Computing the NPV for Each Alternative

Since the same project has two different after-tax net cashflow streams because of the financing method, we must treat that project as if it were two separate, mutually exclusive projects. We can undertake it either as a leased asset or as a purchased asset, but we cannot undertake it as both. The financial officer's capital budget presentation to the board of directors would report the net present value of the leased project (NPV$_l$) and of the purchased project (NPV$_p$) and would rank them as mutually exclusive projects if both had net present values greater than zero. Of course, if the net present value for either was less than zero, that method of financing would be rejected. The same project under the other method of financing could still be undertaken if it had a net present value greater than zero.

To illustrate the capital budgeting procedure for leasing, let us evaluate the net present value under each financing method for the project described in Table 18-2. The net present value if purchased (NPV$_p$) would be:

$$\text{NPV}_p = \sum_{i=1}^{n} \frac{NI_i + D_i}{(1 + k_0)^i} + \frac{S_n}{(1 + k_0)^n} - C \qquad (18\text{-}3)$$

where

NPV_p = the net present value of the asset if purchased

NI_i = the after-tax net income in year i

n = the number of years in the asset's life

---

[6] We ignore any change in the weighted overall cost of capital associated with the increased use of debt or leasing for simplicity. However, the financial officer should recognize that since leasing is equivalent to additional debt, there would be an increase in the firm's cost of capital because the firm's financial risk has risen. Conversely, if the asset had been purchased with funds generated from a sale of equity or part-equity securities, the financial risk could decrease and lower the firm's cost of capital.

Further, the author does not necessarily agree with the two-stream premise, since all debt-obligation payments are relatively predictable and leasing is just another type of debt security for all practical purposes. In that case, the financial officer would use only the weighted overall cost of capital to the net present value of the project if leased. This problem is not resolved, and most financial theorists maintain that the default-free rate is appropriate for the noninterest portion of the lease payment.

D_i = the annual depreciation
S_n = the expected after-tax salvage value in period n
k_0 = the after-tax weighted average cost of capital
C = the original outlay for the project

If $k_0 = 9$ percent, then the NPV_p for the project in Table 18-2 would be:

$$NPV_p = \sum_{i=1}^{10} \frac{\$1,580}{(1.09)^i} + \frac{\$2,000}{(1.09)^{10}} - \$10,000$$

$$= \$967$$

The net present value for the project if leased (NPV_1) would be:

$$NPV_1 = \sum_{i=1}^{n} \frac{NI_i + A_i(1-t)}{(1+k_0)^i} - \sum_{i=1}^{n} \frac{L_i(1-t)}{(1+r)^i} \qquad (18\text{-}4)$$

where
NPV_1 = the net present value, if leased
NI_i = the annual after-tax income, if purchased
$A_i(1-t)$ = the annual after-tax reduction in operating expenses, if leased
t = the ordinary income tax rate
$L_i(1-t)$ = the after-tax noninterest portion of the lease payment
k_0 = the after-tax weighted average cost of capital
r = the default-free interest rate
n = the number of years in the asset's life

If $r = 7$ percent, then the net present value for this project, if leased, would be:

$$NPV_1 = \sum_{i=1}^{10} \frac{\$1,100}{(1.09)} - \frac{\$324}{(1.07)^1} - \frac{\$345}{(1.07)^2} - \frac{\$380}{(1.07)^3}$$

$$- \frac{\$417}{(1.07)^4} - \frac{\$459}{(1.07)^5} - \frac{\$505}{(1.07)^6} - \frac{\$555}{(1.07)^7}$$

$$- \frac{\$611}{(1.07)^8} - \frac{\$672}{(1.07)^9} - \frac{\$740}{(1.07)^{10}}$$

$$= \$4,382$$

Since the net present value under each financing method is greater than zero, both are acceptable projects, but it is obvious that the firm can only undertake the same project once. It can *either* lease or purchase the asset; it cannot do both. Since the net present value of the leasing alternative is greater than the purchase alternative, the firm would lease the project.[7]

---

[7] A direct comparison of the same project under each financing method could be obtained by subtracting Equation 18-4 from Equation 18-3, as follows, to get the difference in the net present value (ΔNPV), as done by Johnson and Lewellen, in "Analysis of the Lease-or-Buy Decision."

$$\Delta NPV = NPV_p - NPV_1$$

$$= \sum_{i=1}^{n} \frac{D_i + A_i(1-t)}{(1+k_0)^i} + \frac{S_n}{(1+k_0)^n} - C + \sum_{i=1}^{n} \frac{L_i(1-t)}{(1+r)^i}$$

If $\Delta NPV > 0$, purchase.
If $\Delta NPV < 0$, lease.

SUMMARY

After having read Chapter 18, you should be able to answer these questions:

1. What types of leases are available for the financial officer to consider?

There are three basic types of leases. All types are contracts between the firm (lessee) and the lessor allowing the firm to use the asset for a specified period in exchange for rent but leaving ownership with the lessor. The operating lease is generally distinguished from the financial lease because it leaves the responsibility for maintaining the equipment with the firm (lessee). The sale and leaseback arrangement involves the sale and immediate leasing of the property back to the seller. Any of the three basic types could be gross or net leases. In the net lease the lessee must bear maintenance costs, taxes, and other expenses.

2. What are the advantages and disadvantages of leasing?

The main advantage of leasing is its flexibility. Using the lease, the firm can finance on a piecemeal basis, avoid restrictive loan provisions, avoid the risk of obsolescence, stretch its fund-raising, deduct the lease payment from its taxes, and, perhaps, free cash for investment elsewhere. For the marginal firm that might be unable to raise funds at the bank or through security offerings, the lease may be the only alternative available.

The disadvantages are that the lease usually tends to be more expensive, the firm loses the depreciation and the salvage value, and, if the lease is noncancelable, the firm has locked itself into long-term payments even if the project is abandoned.

3. How are leases treated in the firm's financial statements?

Leases are not reported in the body of the financial statements, though they are reported in the footnotes accompanying the balance sheet. The balance sheet itself reflects neither the liability incurred nor the value of the asset leased. The lease payments are typically not segregated from other expenses in the income statement, although the annual lease commitment on the firm's noncancelable leases is reported in the footnotes.

We saw that this form of reporting can distort the financial ratios and make the firm appear in a healthier position than it actually is. The alert financial officer will realize that investors are typically not deceived and will impute a liability to the leases.

4. How do leases affect the firm's cost of capital?

Since the firm incurs fixed charges when it enters into a lease, the firm's financial risk rises just as if the firm had sold additional debt. This raises the firm's cost of capital.

5. As the financial officer, how do you evaluate the attractiveness of a project when there is a choice of leasing or purchasing it?

We must recognize that there are two distinct cashflow streams for a given project under the two financing methods. Under the purchase method the cashflow includes the after-tax net income, the depreciation, and the expected after-tax salvage value. Under the lease method, the cashflow consists of the after-tax net income plus the after-tax reductions in operating expenses associated with the lease less the after-tax noninterest portion of the lease payments.

We saw that as financial officers, we must also realize that the differences in the uncertainty of the cashflow between the two methods also forces us to use the weighted average overall cost of capital when deriving the net present value under the purchase method, while using the default-free cost of capital for the noninterest portion of the lease payments under the lease method. After computing the net present value of the project under each financing method, we can treat them as two separate, mutually exclusive projects in deciding which one to undertake.

QUESTIONS

18-1 From an accounting viewpoint how does a lease differ from debt obligations?

18-2 What effect will a lease obligation have on the following financial ratios of the lessee:
(a) Asset turnover ratio
(b) Return on total assets
(c) Return on stockholders' equity
(d) Debt/equity ratio
(e) Interest coverage ratio

18-3 What are the major similarities and differences between a financial lease and an operating lease?

18-4 Enumerate some of the advantages and disadvantages of leasing.

18-5 Why is the sale and leaseback method popular with firms owning older, fully depreciated assets that still have some usefulness?

18-6 What effect will a lease have on the lessee's cost of debt capital? Why?

18-7 Explain the similarities and differences in the cashflow streams resulting from leasing as opposed to purchasing an asset.

18-8 Explain when the following discount factors are used in "discounting" the cashflows resulting from leasing as opposed to purchasing an asset:
(a) After-tax cost of debt (k_d)
(b) Risk-free interest rate (r)
(c) Weighted average cost of capital (k_0)

PROBLEMS

18-1 Bolem is considering purchasing or leasing some additional computer hardware. The computer hardware may be purchased for $100,000 and depreciated at $20,000 per year for 5 years. The hardware is presumed to have no salvage value and will be financed by bonds sold at 10 percent. Alternatively, the lease payments are $26,380 per year for 5 years. Shown below are Bolem's existing balance sheet, income statement and selected financial ratios.
(a) Assuming that annual sales will increase by $400,000, cost of goods sold will increase by $250,000, and general administrative expenses will increase by $100,000, complete the following data for the purchase decision versus the lease decision.
(b) If the lease is treated as an imputed liability (debt), compute the adjusted balance sheet, income statement, and financial ratios.

	Current	Buy	Lease	Adjusted lease
Balance Sheet				
Assets				
Current assets	$ 200,000			
Fixed assets	800,000			
Total assets	1,000,000			
Liabilities and stockholder equity				
Current liabilities	100,000			
Long-term debt (10%)	200,000			
Total liabilities	300,000			
Stockholders' equity	700,000			
Total liabilities and stockholders' equity	1,000,000			
Income Statement				
Sales	4,000,000			
Cost of goods sold	2,500,000			
Selling and Administrative expenses	1,000,000			
Depreciation	100,000			
Operating income	400,000			
Interest on debt	20,000			
Lease payments	—			
Net income before taxes	380,000			
Income taxes (50%)	190,000			
Net income after taxes	190,000			
Financial Ratios				
Asset turnover ratio	4.0			
Return on stockholder equity	27.1%			
Return on total assets	19.0%			
Debt/equity	0.29			
Interest coverage	20.0			

18-2 Metco Company is trying to decide whether to purchase or lease a heavy-duty construction crane. If the crane is purchased at a cost of $100,000, incremental net income after taxes is expected to be $40,000 per year for the next 4 years. The after-tax salvage value at the end of the fourth year is expected to be $10,000. Alternatively, the crane may be leased for $30,192 per year for 4 years. In addition, leasing is estimated to result in an annual operating cost reduction of $10,000 due to reduced costs of maintenance and insurance. Metco has a 50 percent income tax and a weighted average cost of capital of 8 percent. The risk-free discount rate is 5 percent.
(a) What are the annual cashflows if the crane is purchased? Leased?
(b) Is the purchase or the lease more attractive from a NPV viewpoint?

BIBLIOGRAPHY

Beechy, Thomas H. "Quasi-Debt Analysis of Financial Leases." *Accounting Review,* XLIV (April 1969), 375–381.

Bower, Richard S., Frank C. Herringer, and J. Peter Williamson. "Lease Evaluation." *Accounting Review,* XLI (April 1966), 257–265.

Ferrara, William L. "Should Investment and Financing Decisions Be Separate?" *Accounting Review,* XLI (January 1966), 106–114.

Gant, Donald R. "A Critical Look at Lease Financing." *Controller* XXIX (June 1961).

Johnson, Robert W., and Wilber G. Lewellen. "Analysis of the Lease-or-Buy Decision." *Journal of Finance,* XXVII (September 1972), 815–824.

Law, Warren A., and M. Colyer Crum. *Equipment Leasing and Commercial Banks.* Association of Reserve City Bankers, Chicago, 1963.

McLean, James H. "Economic and Accounting Aspects of Lease Financing." *Financial Executive,* XXXI (December 1963), 18–23.

Mitchell, G. B. "After-Tax Cost of Leasing," *Accounting Review,* XLV (April 1970), 308–314.

Shillinglaw, Gordon. "Accounting for Leased Property by Capitalization." *N.A.A. Bulletin,* XXXIX (June 1958), 31–45.

Vatter, W. J. "Accounting for Leases." *Journal of Accounting Research,* 4 (Autumn 1966), 133–148.

six

LONG-TERM SOURCES OF FUNDS

LET US LOOK AT SOME OF THE MAJOR QUESTIONS which you, as a financial officer, must answer when advising your firm on raising long-term capital. As you read Part Six look for answers to the following questions:

1. How and with whom do I arrange to sell the firm's long-term securities?

2. What types of long-term securities can the firm sell?

3. Besides long-term debt, what other categories of long-term securities might the firm sell?

19

issuing and selling long-term securities

WITH WHOM DO YOU ARRANGE THE SALE of your firm's long-term securities? We shall see that the investment banker is the person to whom you will turn in this situation. Using his or her expertise and facilities, and willing to assume the risk of selling the securities in expectation of a profit, the investment banker offers the firm's securities to the capital market.

How does the investment banker facilitate the sale of the firm's securities? The investment banker can handle the offering in several ways. He or she can underwrite it in a negotiated bid, underwrite it in a competitive bid, offer it on a commission basis, or help in a private placement. When underwriting the offering, the investment banker usually has to go through a sequence of steps ranging from the initial negotiations to the formation of a selling group to the termination of the syndicate. As an alert financial officer, you should at least be familiar with the process so that you can judge the competence of the investment banker. If yours is found wanting, you should switch the firm's offerings to another investment banker.

What security regulations must you and your company comply with when selling long-term securities to the public? Although you will probably rely heavily on the advice of the firm's lawyers and the investment banker, you are ultimately responsible for seeing that the laws of offering securities are complied with. If they are violated, you personally (as well as the firm and the investment bankers) may be liable for rather large fines and, in certain cases, jail sentences. Obviously, you want to be familiar with the requirements of the law so as to avoid violations of any major points. We shall see that the federal government and some state governments require that you provide certain pertinent information to their agencies as a condition for the offering and for continuation of the firm's operations.

What alternative channels to the underwriter can the financial officer use in selling the firm's long-term securities? We shall see that private placements offer an alternative to the public offering. As the financial officer, you have to know who are the major suppliers of funds in the private-placement market so that you can contact them. You must also know the advantages and the disadvantages of a private placement so as to make an educated judgment as to its desirability under the firm's prevailing circumstances.

INVESTMENT BANKING

As financial officer, with whom do you arrange the sale of the firm's long-term securities?

The investment banker is the person you will most likely turn to when the firm is thinking of selling securities.

The Investment Banker

The investment banker is that person or firm which channels funds from those firms that want to invest to those that want to raise funds to finance their asset acquisitions. The investment banker brings the buyer and the seller of the security together for a fee or by purchasing the securities and reselling them, hopefully at a higher price. We can envision investment bankers as wholesalers of securities, typically buying in large quantities from the firm and reselling smaller quantities of the issue to many investors. They can usually do this with more ease than the firm can do it on its own, because they have taken the time to cultivate contacts among individual and institutional investors with whom they can readily place part of the offering. They have also gathered the facilities and specialized staff to handle this underwriting function. Since they do it almost every day, they can handle the process much more economically than the firm, which infrequently offers long-term securities. As we might expect, many brokerage houses are also underwriters. By handling many offerings of many firms, the investment banker achieves economies of scale and efficiencies in the selling of securities.

Primary versus Secondary Markets

The investment banking function operates mainly in the *primary market*, where the securities are offered for the first time to the public from the initial issuer. We might say the securities offered by the investment banker are previously unowned by any other investor. If we buy the securities from the investment banker, we would be the first buyers.

The first buyer who resells the security does so in the *secondary market*, where all sales subsequent to the initial sale occur. Some of the more famous secondary markets are organized exchanges such as the New York Stock Exchange and the London Stock Exchange. These organized secondary markets provide a physical location and other facilities for the purpose of bringing buyers and sellers together so that transactions can be made. All transactions on these organized exchanges are between owners subsequent to the initial purchase; none is by the underwriter or, in most instances, the firm itself. However, the secondary market is not always an organized exchange. It can be a transaction between two people in the same office or in a scattered network of secondary dealers, such as the Over-the-Counter market (OTC). OTC dealers stand ready to buy and sell the security after the initial offering, hopefully making a profit by buying the security at a lower price than the price at which they eventually sell it. Unlike the members of an organized exchange, they are not physically located in one trading area, but are scattered throughout the country and connected by telephone and the National Association of Securities Dealers' Automated Quotation computer telecommunications (NASDAQ), over which they convey their interest in buying or selling securities.

Regardless of the degree of organization, the various secondary markets all serve the same purpose. They increase the liquidity of a security and encourage the origi-

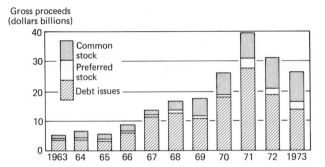

SOURCE: Securities and Exchange Commission *Annual Report*, 1973.

Figure 19-1 New Corporate Securities Effectively Registered

nal purchase from the investment banker when the firm offers a new issue. Listing the security on an organized exchange, as opposed to trading OTC, might also give the firm some prestige and convey an image of a more stable, lower-risk firm, because organized exchanges tend to trade only in the securities of the more established firms. For the firm to list its stock or bonds on an organized exchange may increase the security's liquidity and encourage ownership. This in turn will make it easier for the firm to offer further issues of securities in the primary market. As the financial officer, your main concern is with the primary market, for it is there that you will have to raise the funds.

Figure 19-1 illustrates that the amount and the composition of new issues has fluctuated. Debt seems to be the favored security, primarily because of its lower cost of capital and lower flotation costs. However, during years of high interest costs, such as 1971 and 1973, there is a larger proportion of common and preferred stock offered for sale.

Functions of the Investment Banker

The main function of the investment banker is to underwrite and sell the firm's securities. As an underwriter, the investment banker buys our securities from the firm, giving us the capital we wanted to raise—if, of course, we can agree on a mutually satisfactory price. He or she then tries to resell the security at a profit to such clients as financial institutions and individuals. In underwriting the issue, the investment banker assumes the risk of not being able to resell the security, either at all or at a loss. In the meantime, the firm has its required financing, regardless of the success of the banker's selling effort.

It is also the function of the investment banker to give advice and counsel to the financial officer. A competent investment banker should be able to advise you on prevailing conditions and market receptiveness to any particular type of security that the firm may want to offer. If, for example, the market is presently receptive to equity offerings such as common stock, the good investment banker will so inform you. There are different bond provisions which investors may demand in exchange for lower interest rates but which the firm may not want to agree to because they are overly restrictive. The investment banker can help you determine which provisions are necessary and which you can bargain away.

The investment banker should also advise you on the appropriate timing of any security offering. If the prevailing market interest rates are high but expected to recede, you should be advised of this prospect so that you may postpone the offering until interest rates drop. In the meantime the investment banker should be able to help you with short-term financing to carry you over until you make your security offering.

A competent investment banker would also be in constant touch with the firm to advise and help in its financing. Investment bankers should be invited to sit on the firm's board of directors so that they can be aware of the firm's financial needs and can use their contacts to help the firm raise funds even in periods when credit is not readily available. Sitting on the board, an investment banker knows what types of operations might be compatible with the firm's objectives and can be on the alert for suitable merger candidates. Of course, he or she is compensated if the suggested merger takes place. Since it is your responsibility to make the ultimate decision, you should be prepared to listen to and evaluate the arguments for promoting the merger. But remember that less reputable investment bankers may put the interest of their own firm above that of yours in order to generate fees.

The investment banker should also be able to report on conditions within the industry and might even manage your pension fund. The idea is for you, as the financial officer, to work closely with the investment banker but to remain objective. Hopefully, you will agree with good suggestions and reject bad ones.

Some firms use the prestige of the investment banker to sell their securities. When a relatively unknown firm's securities are underwritten by a reputable and known investment banker, the prestige of the banker may rub off on the issue. Clients have come to trust this professional's judgment and are prepared to buy the firm's securities almost on his or her word. As the financial officer of a less well known firm, it might pay you to seek out the most prestigious underwriter.

UNDERWRITING AND SELLING THE FIRM'S LONG-TERM SECURITIES

How does the investment banker facilitate the sale of the firm's securities?

You should know how the underwriting process works, if for no other reason than to judge the competence and reliability of the investment banker you have chosen. Let us review the typical sequence of a negotiated purchase underwriting, so we can familiarize ourselves with the basic procedure. In addition, let us briefly explore the other methods of selling securities and the costs of underwriting.

The Negotiated Underwriting Sequence

The typical underwriting sequence is negotiated between the firm and the investment banker. The firm decides it needs funds and directs the financial officer to initiate discussions with the investment banker. Sometimes the investment banker may initiate the discussions, or a third party known as a *finder* may bring the firm's financing needs to the attention of the investment banker. The finder receives a fee for this service, which the firm usually pays if the negotiations lead to an underwriting agreement.

The second step is usually a preunderwriting conference between the firm and the investment banker. At this conference they discuss such items as the approximate amount of funds to be raised, the receptiveness of the capital market to different types of long-term securities, the appropriate timing of such an issue, and the terms of the underwriting agreement between the investment banker and the firm. These terms include the approximate price the investment banker is willing to pay the firm and the *upset price,* below which the firm has the option of not proceeding with the offering.

Usually the approximate price the investment banker is willing to pay is a few dollars below the price of similar securities of other firms or of already outstanding similar securities of the firm, if any, prevailing shortly before the actual offering. For example, the agreement might call for the investment banker to pay $1.50 per share less than the closing price of the stock on the night before the offering. If the stock closed at $25 a share that night, the firm would receive $23.50 a share. If the price of those outstanding securities drops below the upset price after the preunderwriting conference, the firm may abrogate the agreement and look elsewhere for capital which is not as costly. Suppose the stock price drops from $25 to $19 between the time of the conference and shortly before the offering is to be made. If the upset price was set at the conference at $20 a share, the firm may cancel the sale because of the new low stock price.

Once agreement is reached formalizing the link between the issuer and the investment banker, the next step is the formation of the *underwriting syndicate* illustrated in Figure 19-2. This is a temporary association of several investment bankers, organized by the one who initiated the underwriting. The number of participants in the syndicate varies from one, when the initiating underwriter handles the whole issue, to several dozen if the amount to be raised is large. The initiating underwriter frequently becomes the manager of the syndicate and forms an agreement with the other underwriters in the syndicate which defines the responsibilities, liabilities, and fees of each and specifies the proportional amount of the issue each must purchase. The underwriters then formally sign an underwriting agreement with the issuer.

The purpose of forming the syndicate is to spread the risk. Each member hopes to make a profit on the spread between the price it pays the issuer and the price for which it resells the securities to the public less any commission paid the selling group members. If the selling price to the public is less than the price paid the issuer or is insufficient to cover the expenses, the members can split the loss equally among themselves. Or the manager, having agreed to limit the liability of the other members, can take the largest portion of the loss.

Once the formal agreement is signed, the firm must register (S-1 filing) the proposed offering with the proper authorities, such as the Securities and Exchange Commission and the state security board. This filing is accompanied by the issuance of a preliminary prospectus containing much of the information in the official registration. Through this preliminary prospectus (also known as a red her-

Figure 19-2 The Underwriting Sequence

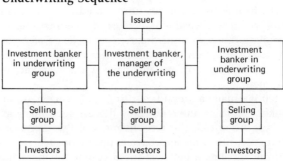

ring because of the required red-letter warning in the left-hand margin of the first page specifying that it is a preliminary and not a final prospectus), governmental authorities attempt to insure full disclosure of the facts, so that the investing public can make an informed decision. Included in the filing and the preliminary prospectus are a short history of the issuer, a statement of intended use of the proceeds raised by the offer, recent financial statements, a summary of the risks associated with the firm's operations, personnel profiles on the firm's management, the recent price range for the firm's already outstanding securities, a listing of the firm's assets, the proposed underwriters, a copy of the underwriting agreement, notice of any impending litigation in which the company is involved, and the accountants' certification of the financial statements.

The next step is the formation of the selling group. The underwriting group will contract with other members of the security industry to sell the securities that it has just agreed to purchase from the firm. This selling group might be looked upon as the retailers, while the underwriting group might be looked upon as the wholesalers of the security. The members of the selling group sell to the ultimate customer for a commission and may frequently return the unsold portion of their allocation to the underwriting manager, depending on the terms of the selling agreement. This agreement usually describes the issue, binds each seller not to undersell the *pegged price* set by the underwriters until the syndicate is dissolved, sets the duration of the selling group, and specifies that the seller loses the commission on any particular sale if the security is repurchased by the underwriting group from investors within a specified number of days. (This last provision encourages the sellers to find buyers who will hold on to the security long enough to give the syndicate a chance to sell out its own holdings at the underwriting price.) Members of the underwriting group can also be members of the selling group.

The next step is a *due diligence meeting* where the final underwriting price is set. This last-minute meeting of all the parties involved is designed to see that all pertinent information is included in the offering prospectus, as required by law. The meeting derives its name from the concept that everyone should diligently think of anything else that might possibly be pertinent. At this meeting the underwriters judge the prevailing market conditions and set the offering price accordingly. Immediately after the due diligence meeting, the final prospectus is printed and the offering made the next morning. Figure 19-3 is a representative final prospectus cover.

Only after the final prospectus has been printed can the selling group sell the securities. Up until then, they could only take indications of buyer interest. Hopefully the entire issue sells out quickly at the offering price. In some instances the issue may be oversubscribed, which means investors wanted to buy more than was offered. In other cases, the securities may linger in the inventory of the underwriting group because buyers cannot be found at the offering price. Under those circumstances, the syndicate will probably be terminated sooner than expected and the offering price abandoned in favor of a lower price which might attract investors to buy out the remaining inventory. If the price has to be lowered very much, the underwriter must bear the loss.

During the life of the selling syndicate, the managing underwriter tries to stabilize the market at the offering price so that the trading price in the secondary market does not fall below the offering price. Otherwise the syndicate will not attract enough buyers to clear out their holdings and will suffer a loss. This market stabilization is also called *price pegging*, keeping the secondary market price at or above the pegged offering price.

PROSPECTUS

GENERAL TELEPHONE COMPANY OF THE MIDWEST

150,000 Shares

Cumulative Preferred Stock, $10.50 Series (no par value)

Dividends payable February 1, May 1, August 1 and November 1

The New Preferred Stock will be redeemable at the option of the Company prior to May 1, 1980 at $110.50 per share; thereafter and prior to May 1, 1985 at $107.88 per share; thereafter and prior to May 1, 1990 at $105.25 per share; and on or after May 1, 1990 at $102.63 per share, plus accrued dividends. However, prior to May 1, 1985, no redemption may be made through certain refunding operations at an effective cost of money to the Company of less than 10.50% per annum. A sinking fund will retire 7,500 shares at $100 a share on each May 1, commencing May 1, 1980.

	Price to Public(1)	Underwriting Discounts and Commissions(2)	Proceeds to Company(1)(3)(4)
Per Share	$100.00	$1.25	$98.75
Total	$15,000,000	$187,500	$14,812,500

(1) Plus accrued dividends, if any, from the date of issuance.

(2) In the Purchase Agreement the Company has agreed to indemnify the Underwriters against certain liabilities, including liabilities under the Securities Act of 1933.

(3) After deducting underwriting commissions but before deduction of expenses payable by the Company estimated at $109,190.

(4) Up to $4,937,500 of proceeds from the sale of up to 50,000 shares may not be received until August 14, 1975 (see "Delayed Delivery Contracts" herein).

The New Preferred Stock is offered by the several Underwriters as, and if issued by the Company and accepted by the Underwriters and subject to their right to reject orders in whole or in part. It is expected that the New Preferred Stock will be ready for delivery on or about May 6, 1975. In addition, portions of the New Preferred Stock may be offered to certain institutional investors by the Company through the several Underwriters pursuant to delayed delivery contracts with the Company. See "Delayed Delivery Contracts" herein.

THESE SECURITIES HAVE NOT BEEN APPROVED OR DISAPPROVED BY THE SECURITIES AND EXCHANGE COMMISSION NOR HAS THE COMMISSION PASSED UPON THE ACCURACY OR ADEQUACY OF THIS PROSPECTUS. ANY REPRESENTATION TO THE CONTRARY IS A CRIMINAL OFFENSE.

PAINE, WEBBER, JACKSON & CURTIS
INCORPORATED

SALOMON BROTHERS

The date of this Prospectus is April 24, 1975

Figure 19-3 Representative Prospectus Cover

Finally the syndicate is terminated. Price stabilization operations cease. Any inventory is sold at the prevailing secondary market price. The groups break up and move on to the next underwriting. The next group may have the same or a different composition of members, customary working relationships are common among various cliques in the investment banking industry.

Other Methods of Selling Long-Term Securities

Alternatives to negotiated underwriting include competitive underwriting, commission sales, and direct sales.

Competitive underwriting   The competitive underwriting is similar in all respects to the negotiated underwriting except that the underwriting group bids against other underwriting groups for the initial purchase of the securities at a competitive public auction. The bids are usually solicited by public invitation of the issuer describing the securities to be offered for auction. The winning underwriting group sells the securities to the public in the same fashion as if the purchase had been privately negotiated.

Publicly regulated companies, such as electrical utilities and railroads, and governmental bodies must in most cases sell their securities in this fashion. The regulatory authorities feel it insures the lowest cost of capital for the issuer. The competitive underwriting does have the disadvantage of not promoting a permanent relationship with any one underwriting group, which may mean that during periods of restricted capital availability the firm may actually pay a higher rate because of the competitive bidding procedure. Further, as a financial officer for a publicly regulated company, you must still engage a financial adviser, usually an investment banker, to guide you in deciding what types of securities and terms to offer, judging the capital market conditions to achieve the best timing, and steering you through the legal requirements.

Commission-best efforts basis   Under the commission basis, the investment banker is a selling agent for the issuer and not an underwriter. The investment banker agrees to try his or her very best (best efforts) to sell the security in return for a commission on each share or bond sold. But there is no guarantee that the entire amount will be sold or that the firm will receive any particular amount of money.

This selling procedure is traditionally reserved for the riskier and less established issuers in which the underwriter does not have great confidence. Sometimes the offering is conditional upon the sale of a specific portion of the securities. The receipts from the amount sold are held in escrow until that portion is sold and are only then released to the company. The securities are likewise held in escrow and only then released to the buyers. If the specific portion is not reached, the offering is cancelled and the funds returned to the buyers.

Direct sale   In certain instances, the issuer may be able to sell the securities directly to the public, bypassing the underwriter entirely. This saves the firm the underwriting costs, but it does not avoid the legal requirements or the direct selling costs. Basically the same procedure is followed as if the securities were being underwritten, except that the firm is doing the underwriting itself. This procedure is rather rare, particularly among more established companies. However, beginning entrepreneurs sometimes sell their own securities to avoid the underwriting expense or because no underwriter will handle the issue, and American Telephone and Telegraph has used a direct sale procedure because it was less expensive.

Issuing Costs

The firm's costs associated with the issuing of long-term securities are comprised mainly of the underwriting commission, the expenses and fees borne by the firm, and, in some instances, noncash benefits to the underwriter. Taken all together, these are labelled the flotation costs.

The underwriting commission varies with the type of the issue, the size of the issue, the risk of the issue, and the uncertainty of the prevailing market environment. As a general rule, stocks have a higher commission than bonds, and the commission per share or per bond is smaller for the larger offerings. The commission increases as the risk to the underwriter increases and as the uncertainty of the market environment increases. If the firm is a small and relatively unestablished issuer, the underwriting risk is larger. Similarly, an uncertain market means that the underwriter's chance of loss is larger. To protect profits the underwriter will increase the commission under these circumstances.

The issuer must also bear the other expenses of the underwriting. These include the Securities and Exchange Commission filing fee, the legal fees, the accountant's fees, the printing of the prospectus, and the transfer agent's fees.

The issuer might also consent, as part of the underwriting agreement, to give the underwriter the right to purchase shares in the firm at a relatively low price for the next five or ten years as additional noncash compensation. While this does not cost the firm any money immediately, it does increase the potential number of shares outstanding and decreases the reported fully diluted earnings per share, which can lower the market price of the stock and raise the firm's cost of capital.

GOVERNMENT REGULATIONS

What security regulations must I comply with when selling the firm's long-term securities to the public?

Since ignorance of the law is no excuse and a mistake can be very costly, financial officers should be familiar with security regulations.

These regulations apply only to public sales and are supervised mainly by the federal Securities and Exchange Commission (SEC) under the Securities Act of 1934 as amended. If it deems it necessary, the SEC can stop the firm's public offering and can even bring criminal charges, where appropriate.

Basic Intent

The basic intent of the SEC regulations is to insure full disclosure so that potential investors can make an informed decision and to provide grounds for civil and criminal actions if the firm fails to do so. Misleading representations or the omission of material facts leaves the firm and the financial officer liable. That does not mean that the SEC approves or disapproves the offering or suggest any guarantee as to the value or price of the securities. Buyers can still lose money, but at least they had the pertinent information on which to base their decision.

Requirements

The SEC requires that the firm file a registration statement with the commission in which it provides the necessary information. Then there is a minimum twenty-day waiting period during which the SEC can ask for more information to amend or clarify the registration or can order the offering stopped. During that minimum period, which in many years has been considerably longer, the market environment might change and the firm can withdraw the offering with the consent of the SEC.

The SEC also requires that the prospectus accompany the distribution of the security. The prospectus, as we have discussed, contains the pertinent information from the registration filing. If misleading information appears, you, the firm, the legal counsel, the underwriters, and the accountants may all be liable for damages to the buyers and civil and criminal penalties.

There are exemptions from the federal securities laws which the financial officer of an exempt issuer should be aware of. Firms already under the regulatory authority of another federal agency such as the Interstate Commerce Commission (ICC) are exempt on the grounds of avoiding duplicate regulations. Banks and other financial institutions under the regulation of state or federal banking authorities are also exempt. Securities issued in reorganization under the authority of the bankruptcy court are exempt from SEC registration. The securities of nonprofit institutions, such as hospitals and churches, are exempt. Finally, if the issue is for less than $300,000 in any 12-month period, the firm may file a less rigorous registration statement under the "Reg A" rules. This is designed to accommodate smaller firms that cannot afford the cost of a full filing.

Some states also have laws governing public offerings within their jurisdictions. These are usually referred to as Blue Sky Laws after a comment by a judge who once declared in his decision on a security fraud case that the securities had as much value as a patch of blue sky (that was before smog). These laws may require a separate filing with the state securities board or coordination between the SEC filing and the state filing, in which case the state accepts the SEC clearance as its own.

Secondary Market Regulations

You should be aware of your legal responsibilities once the securities are traded in the secondary market, although you should also consult with the firm's lawyers on this point. Under the Securities Exchange Act of 1934, the SEC is empowered to regulate the trading of securities in the secondary market. This includes the regulation of insider trading, inside information, and required reporting procedures.

Insider trading   As a financial officer, you are considered to be an insider along with all the directors, other officers, and any investor who has a beneficial interest in more than 10 percent of the stock. As an insider you are required to file a statement of your holdings and report any transactions at the end of each month. Any profit you make in trading the stock within a period of less than six months must be returned to the firm, and you are not allowed to short sell the stock (sell borrowed stock in the anticipation of a price decline).

Disseminating information[1]   The SEC has extended your responsibility to the public investor beyond the necessity of full disclosure and the avoidance of misrepresentation. As the financial officer, you are required to see that all statements which might materially affect the firm's stock price are made to a public forum where wide dissemination is obtained, for example, a press conference. If this is not done, you are liable for stockholder action on the grounds that you misused privileged information, a form of tipping. This is particularly true when it comes to forecasting earnings, a most sensitive area of inside information. Despite the fact that you may have reasonably reliable projections of forthcoming profits, you should refrain from issuing such a statement except under the most appropriate circumstances.

Filing company data   The SEC requires that the firm file annual and quarterly reports on its financial condition and earnings—and monthly reports if necessary. The SEC 10-K form is used for annual reports, the 8-Q form for quarterly reports, and the 8-K form for monthly reports.

[1] A. R. Bromber, "The Law of Corporate Information," *Financial Analysts' Journal*, March–April 1969.

Trading regulations   In addition to regulating the firm and the insiders, the SEC also regulates the trading of the security itself in the secondary market. The basic intent is to prevent manipulations designed to defraud the investing public. Such nefarious practices as the pool and the wash sale are prohibited. In the pool, a group of manipulators would get together and behave as if something bad was happening to the firm, sending the stock price down. At that point they would buy the stock from panicked sellers and then make it look as if nothing bad was happening after all, selling the stock on the rebound as the panic stopped. In the wash sale, two parties would conspire to create the impression that there was a lot of interest in the stock by buying and selling the same shares back and forth to and from each other. Investors would be misled into thinking the sudden activity indicated some change in prospects for the firm and would rush in to buy or sell, whichever the case might be, creating a profit for the parties who contrived the wash sale. These activities are now illegal and they rarely occur.

PRIVATE PLACEMENTS

What alternatives to the public offering of the securities does the financial officer have?

The basic alternative is to bypass the public entirely and negotiate the private placement of the offering with one or a few investors.

Definition and Sources

The *private placement* is a security offering directly negotiated with one or more investors rather than the public. In private placement, the firm sits down at the same bargaining table with the ultimate buyers; in the public offering, the firm never meets the ultimate buyers.

The main source of private-placement funds is the insurance companies. Pension funds also engage in private placements. The firm does not necessarily avoid the services of the investment banker altogether, for in most instances, the financial officer looks to him or her for the initial introduction to the private-placement lender and for advice during the negotiations.

Advantages and Disadvantages

The advantages of the private placement are many, but they may not outweigh the disadvantages. It is up to you, as the financial officer, to evaluate each alternative and to decide between the two. The private placement is typically more convenient in that the firm usually gets the funds quicker than in the public offering. The smaller firm, which may not be able to go public, might find that the private placement is the only alternative open to it. The firm can tailor the securities to its exact needs because of the face-to-face negotiation, which it might not be able to do in the public offering. The issuer avoids the necessity, delay, and cost of registering with the SEC and the need for a public disclosure of what its management may consider confidential information. The private placement may allow the firm to draw down some of the funds from time to time rather than all at once as in the public offering, and this may assist the financial officer's effort to avoid the uncertainties of market fluctuations. Finally, though the interest cost of the typical private placement is higher than that of a public offering, the elimination of the underwriting commission and other expenses may offset that. It is up to the financial officer to make this determination.

The major disadvantages of the private placement (besides higher interest costs) are more restrictive provisions against such things as the raising of additional debt and the failure to maintain a specified level of working capital. Depending on the lending institutions, such provisions can be very restrictive, and the alert financial officer must try to bargain away the more burdensome ones. The private placement has a major disadvantage to the lending institution in that the issuer must register the securities with the SEC before reselling to a public buyer. To insure that the issue can be resold, many lenders insist that the firm commit itself to a future registration of the issue at the lender's option. This, in effect, voids the advantage of not having to register the offering in the first place and means that in the long run the firm has not avoided the costs and the undesired public disclosure.

SUMMARY

After having read Chapter 19, you should be able to answer these questions:

1. With whom does the financial officer arrange the sale of the firm's securities?

In the majority of cases, the financial officer arranges the sale with an investment banker, whose job it is to facilitate the sale of the firm's securities. Typically the firm builds up a working relationship with a particular investment banker who underwrites the firm's security offerings by purchasing the securities from the firm and then reselling them to the public. The investment banker may also give the firm advice and counsel on its financing and lend prestige to the firm's offerings.

2. How does the investment banker underwrite the firm's security offerings?

The investment banker negotiates the purchase of the offering directly with the firm. Then he or she and associates in the underwriting group form a syndicate in connection with a selling group to distribute the securities to the public after having met all legal requirements. Hopefully the underwriting group makes a profit by reselling the securities to the public at a higher price than they paid. There is no guarantee that they can do this, and the syndicate may suffer a loss.

We also saw that the firm can use competitive underwriting instead of the negotiated underwriting, and that publicly regulated firms are required to use the competitive procedure. If the investment bankers will not underwrite the issue, the firm can employ them on a commission basis agreement under which the investment banker agrees to make his or her best effort to sell the securities for a fee but does not purchase the securities from the firm. The firm can also bypass the investment banker entirely and sell the securities directly to the public, although it still has to comply with all the legal requirements.

3. What security regulations must the financial officer and the firm comply with when selling securities to the public?

The Securities and Exchange Commission (SEC) has responsibility for supervising the federal security laws. The basic intent of these laws is to insure full disclosure of material information and prevent misleading representations. We also saw that the firm must register any proposed public offering with the SEC and distribute to the public investor a prospectus containing the information in that registration filing. The SEC regulates insider trading and inside information and keeps periodic records on the firm's financial condition.

4. What channels other than the public offering can the firm use to sell its securities?

The firm can use the private placement procedures, which involve face-to-face negotiation with the ultimate purchaser of the security. The private placement offers the advantages of not requiring registration with the SEC or public disclosure, a speedier access to the funds, and a tailoring of the security provisions. On the other hand, private placements tend to have a higher interest cost and be more restrictive in their provisions.

QUESTIONS

19-1 Distinguish between primary and secondary security markets.

19-2 How is an investment banker similar to a commercial banker? Different?

19-3 What are some of the most important functions the financial officer should expect from the firm's investment banker?

19-4 The securities markets are replete with a myriad of unique terms and expressions. Explain briefly the meaning of the following:
(a) upset price
(b) red herring
(c) due diligence meeting
(d) Reg A
(e) Blue Sky Laws
(f) wash sale

19-5 What is an underwriting syndicate and what purpose does it serve?

19-6 Distinguish between underwriting syndicates and selling syndicates.

19-7 How do competitive underwriting and commission basis selling of securities differ from negotiated underwriting?

19-8 What are some of the flotation costs incurred by the firm issuing new securities?

19-9 As financial officer, what are some of the SEC regulations you must be aware of?

BIBLIOGRAPHY

Archer, Stephen H., and LeRoy G. Baerber. "Firm Size and the Cost of Equity Capital." *Journal of Finance,* XXI (March 1966), 69–84.

Block, Ernest. "Pricing a Corporate Bond Issue: A Look Behind the Scenes." *Essays in Money and Credit.* Federal Reserve Bank of New York, New York, 1964, pp. 72–76.

Brown, J. Michael. "Post-Offering Experience of Companies Going Public." *Journal of Business* (January 1970), 10–18.

Cohan, Avery B. *Private Placements and Public Offerings: Market Shares Since 1935.* School of Business Administration, University of North Carolina, Chapel Hill, N. C., 1961.

Evans, G. H., Jr. "The Theoretical Value of a Stock Right." *Journal of Finance,* X (March 1955), 55–61.

Friend, Irwin. "Broad Implications of the S. E. C. Special Study." *Journal of Finance,* XXI (May 1966), 324–332.

Miller, G. R. "Long-Term Business Financing From the Underwriter's Point of View." *Journal of Finance,* XVI (May 1961), 280–290.

Sears, Gerald A. "Public Offerings for Smaller Companies." *Harvard Business Review* (September–October 1968), 112–120.

Soldofsky, Robert M. "Classified Common Stock." *The Business Lawyer* (April 1968), 899–902.

––––––. "The Size and Maturity of Direct Placement Loans." *Journal of Finance,* XV (March 1960), 32–44.

Stoll, Hans R., and Antony J. Curley. "Small Business and the New Issues Market for Equities." *Journal of Financial and Quantitative Analysis,* V (September 1970), 309–322.

Sullivan, Brian. "An Introduction to 'Going Public.'" *Journal of Accountancy* (November 1965).

20

Long-term Debt

What types of long-term debt securities can you, as a financial officer, consider as a source of long-term capital? Among the more common are the bond and variations thereof, such as mortgage bonds, collateral bonds, debenture bonds, and others.

We shall see that not only does the type of debt vary, but each individual issue also has its own provisions and characteristics, because each is a separately negotiated contract between the borrower and the lender. However, there are general categories of contract provisions which seem to be included in one form or another in almost every issue. We will explore these so that you will be familiar with the general characteristics of the bonds you negotiate. But you must always remain alert to unusual provisions; they are as binding as the more common ones. We shall see that the general categories are the identification, the protective, and the repayment provisions.

After having explored the types and general provisions of long-term debt issues, we must evaluate the relative attractiveness of using long-term debt to raise capital. This means we have to consider the associated advantages and disadvantages. What are the advantages and disadvantages of long-term debt? As alert financial officers, we must be familiar with them.

Once the financial officer has decided to offer long-term debt securities, what does he or she have to know about bonds in order to tailor the offering to market conditions and investor needs? You should know bond terminology and be aware of how lenders see the firm's risk at this particular juncture in its history.

Finally, if the opportunity arises to refinance a portion of the firm's long-term debt with a less expensive issue because interest rates have dropped, how does the financial officer decide whether or not the refunding is worthwhile? We shall see that the analysis of bond refunding requires careful examination of the costs and savings associated with refunding.

TYPES OF LONG-TERM DEBT

What are the general types of long-term debt securities that the financial officer can consider as sources of long-term funds?

We shall see that almost all long-term debt takes the general form of bonds, but there are many variations on the basic bond which the financial officer can use in the appropriate situation as a negotiating tool to derive other advantages to the firm, such as lower interest costs.

Basic Bonds

The basic bond is a long-term, contractual I.O.U. by which the firm (borrower) agrees to pay the lender a specified amount of interest each year at specified dates within the year and then redeem the bond (return the original amount of the loan to the lender) at a specified future maturity date. For example, the American Telephone and Telegraph 6s 2000 are the long-term bonds of the American Telephone and Telegraph Company, paying 6 percent a year on the original loan of $1,000, or $30 every 6 months on February 1 and August 1 until the year 2000, at which time the American Telephone and Telegraph Company has promised to redeem the bond (return the original $1,000 loan).

In addition to the specified interest and maturity, each bond contract (indenture) contains certain provisions (covenants) designed to establish the bondholders' priority over the stockholders' claim on a portion of the firm's before-tax earnings and, in the case of liquidation, assets. Other provisions (protective covenants) are designed to safeguard the bondholders' claims by restricting the firm's ability to overextend itself.

Registered bonds The registered bond is the basic bond registered in the bondholder's name on the books of the corporation. Interest and return of principal are automatically mailed to the registered address.

Coupon (bearer) bonds The coupon or bearer bond is a basic bond, ownership of which is evidenced by possession rather than record. Interest is paid by the firm upon presentation of the appropriate coupon, which is attached to the bond. At the interest-payment date, the owner clips the correspondingly dated coupon from the body of the bond and presents it at the designated payment agent, usually a bank, in exchange for the interest.

Mortgage Bonds

The typical mortgage bond is the basic bond with a pledge to the mortgage bondholders (lien) of specific real property of the firm. In the event of the firm's liquidation, these bondholders should be able to acquire title to the pledged asset and sell it to satisfy their claims (the original loan amount plus any past-due interest). There is no guarantee that the liquidation sale will produce sufficient funds to satisfy totally their claims.

As a financial officer, you should note the wide variety of mortgage bonds that exist. During your negotiations for the sale of bonds, you can use the various types to bargain the firm into a lower cost of capital or a more flexible borrowing commitment.

First mortgage bonds The first mortgage bond is a senior mortgage bond with the first claim on the asset over all other bondholders who have a claim on the same asset. In the event of liquidation, the claims of these mortgage bondholders have to be satisfied first.

Second mortgage bonds The second mortgage bond is a junior mortgage with second claim on the specified asset in liquidation after the first mortgage bondholders' claims have been settled. Second mortgage bonds and even more junior claims are typically issued against the same asset when the first mortgage claim does not exceed the estimated value of the pledged asset. There is, again, no guarantee that there will be sufficient proceeds from any sale of assets to satisfy the first mortgage claims or the second and even more junior claims. Second mortgage bonds are generally considered less secure than first mortgage bonds.

Closed-end mortgage bonds Closed-end mortgage bonds restrict the firm's ability to issue more debt of equal priority on the same pledged assets. Until the mortgage issue governed by the closed-end clause is retired, the firm cannot issue additional debt of equal priority. Mortgage lenders favor this provision in the indenture because it means that once their claim is established it is not diluted or shared with others. Financial officers dislike this provision because it restricts their future financing options.

Open-end mortgage bonds In contrast to the closed-end provision, the open-end provision allows the firm to sell additional mortgage debt with the same priority of claim on the same pledged asset as the previously issued mortgage bonds. For example, if the firm already has a first mortgage bond on its electrical generating equipment, it can sell additional first mortgage bonds secured by a lien on the same equipment. However, the original bondholders usually have reserved the right to insist that additional assets of the same general nature, in excess of the additional amount of debt, be pledged to prevent the lien from becoming diluted. In our example, the electrical utility would most likely be required to increase the amount of generating equipment under the pledge in connection with the sale of the additional debt.

Limited open-end mortgage bonds The limited open-end mortgage bond falls between the closed-end and the open-end mortgage bond in that it allows the firm to issue additional mortgage bonds of the same priority against the same assets—but only up to a predetermined limit. At that limit the firm's ability to issue more debt of the same priority ceases, and the bonds become closed-end bonds.

General mortgage bonds Under the general or blanket mortgage bond, the firm pledges all or most of its real property as security instead of specific real property, buildings or land, as in the other types of mortgage bonds. General mortgage bondholders can look to all the firm's real property to satisfy their claims in the event of liquidation.

Debenture Bonds

Debenture bonds are unsecured long-term contractual promises to pay interest and return the original principal. They are based mainly on the creditworthiness of the firm. Unlike the mortgage bondholders, the debenture holders have no specific liens on the firm's assets to which they can turn in the event of liquidation. In the event of default, they become general creditors of the firm and have low claim priority.

Subordinated debenture bonds The subordinated debenture bond is the basic debenture bond with the lowest claim on earnings and assets of all the firm's bonds. As the name implies, the bond is subordinated to all others. It may even be subordinated to the firm's bank loans, if so specified in the indenture.

Convertible debenture bonds As we shall see in Chapter 22, these are unsecured bonds which allow the bondholder to convert into the common stock of the firm, at the holder's option.

Other Secured Bonds

In addition to the pledge of plant, property, and equipment as security in the mortgage bond, the firm can pledge other types of assets to secure other types of bonds.

Equipment trust certificates The equipment trust certificate is usually secured by the transportation equipment (rolling stock) of railroads and other transportation companies under either the Philadelphia (lease) plan or the direct obligation plan.
   Under the Philadelphia plan,[1] title to the equipment passes to a third party, usually a bank or trust company, which issues a certificate of interest in the property guaranteed by the railroad. The railroad pays the interest and redeems the principal to the bank who in turn passes it on to the equipment trust certificate owner. In the event of default, the bank, as owner, merely resumes possession and continues the interest payments as the certificate's issuer.
   Under the direct obligation plan, the railroad issues the certificate to pay for the equipment, instead of the bank or the trust company, although title still passes to the bank or trust company. In the direct obligation plan, the bank no longer guarantees the payment of interest or principal, but it administers the loan and reposesses the equipment in the event of default.
   The number of defaults among equipment trust certificates has been very small under either plan, even in the face of a relatively large number of railroad bankruptcies. The equipment is so easily repossessed and so essential for the railroad's continued operations that even when the line is not meeting its payments on other debt obligations, it continues to do so for these certificates.

Collateral trust bonds The collateral trust bond is secured by other property of the corporation than its real assets. Assets such as the stocks and bonds of other corporations and of the firm's subsidiaries are typical collateral. The firm places the pledged collateral in trust for the benefit of the lenders, although it typically retains the voting rights and receives any declared dividends. In the event the firm defaults on the loan, the securities in the trust are turned over to the lenders to satisfy their claims. Any type of tangible property can be pledged.

Other Unsecured Bonds

In addition to the debenture bond, the firm can issue other types of unsecured bonds, such as the income bond and the receiver's certificate, under certain circumstances.

[1] William H. Husband and J. C. Dockery, *Modern Corporation Finance*, Irwin, Homewood, Ill., 1972, p. 114.

Income bonds Not only is the income bond unsecured, but the firm is not committed to pay the interest unless it is earned. If during the period the firm does not earn a sufficient amount to cover the interest payment, it is omitted. In many cases, the omitted interest payment is never made up, while in some cases the missed payments accumulate and are paid when the firm earns enough to do so.

Income bonds have traditionally been reserved for those firms which have been reorganized after a bankruptcy or are too weak to withstand the financial burden of a fixed interest obligation, although any firm can offer them if it so chooses. From the firm's viewpoint, the income bond has the advantage that its interest payments, when paid, are tax-deductible expenses. If the firm had issued a preferred stock, which also allows it to omit dividend payments, the dividends would not be tax-deductible.

Receiver's certificates The receiver's certificate is issued by the bankruptcy court when it takes over the firm's operations in receivership. These certificates assume priority over all other existing claims and afford the receiver, who is operating the firm under the court's jurisdiction, a method of raising funds.

Bonds Carrying a Guarantee

Sometimes bonds are guaranteed as to payment by a third party other than the borrower. If the borrower should default, the lender hopes to collect from the third party.

Guaranteed bonds Guaranteed bonds are usually unsecured bonds whose interest and principal payments are guaranteed by the borrower's parent firm or a more creditworthy corporation. The bonds of the financing subsidiaries of many large corporations are guaranteed as to payment of interest and principal by the parent. The bonds of federal government agencies such as the Federal Home Loan Bank Board are guaranteed as to interest and principal by the United States Treasury. These bonds remain the obligation of the borrowing agency and usually have a higher interest rate than the direct obligations of the United States Treasury.

Assumed bonds When your firm takes over the debt of another firm and assumes responsibility for the payment of interest and principal, the assumed bond is created. This occurs frequently in mergers, where the acquiring firm assumes the responsibility for the debt of the firm acquired.

Joint bonds A joint bond carries the guarantee of two or more firms. This type of bond arises in situations where the issuing firm is a joint venture of two other firms, both of which guarantee the debt of the joint venture.

Industrial revenue bonds Industrial revenue bonds are issued by a local governmental authority for the purpose of providing land and/or buildings for the firm. The firm, in turn, guarantees the interest and principal of the bond by renting the buildings at a rate sufficient to cover these payments over the life of the bond.

The advantage of this type of financing is that the interest rate on governmental financing is cheaper than on the corporation's debt because the interest payment is tax-exempt to the lender. As a consequence, lenders are willing to accept a lower interest rate. In effect, this constitutes a cheaper source of funds to the firm in financing its plant. And it gives the local area which sold the industrial revenue bond an addition to its economic base and more employment.

Funded Debt

In addition to the variations in the basic bond created by the presence or lack of security provisions and guarantees, a bond can also be classified according to the repayment provisions, such as sinking funds and serial bonds. These repayment provisions, which are contained in the indenture, are designed to insure the repayment of principal by forcing the borrower to fund periodically over the life of the bond a portion of the total principal, so that by maturity sufficient funds have been put aside for the redemption of the issue. An example would be the Pittsburgh Plate Glass sinking fund debentures 3-1/2s 1986 which require periodic payments to a segregated escrow account in anticipation of the 1986 redemption. We shall cover the implications of sinking funds and serial bonds in more detail later in this chapter.

GENERAL PROVISIONS

Although we can readily see that there are a myriad of possible provisions which could be included in the bond indenture, since each bond is a separately negotiated contract between the borrower and the lender, we can summarize the more common provisions in general categories. In general, the provisions of the indenture are: (1) identification provisions, (2) protective provisions, and (3) repayment provisions.

As financial officers, we should never forget that these provisions do not substitute for a lack of creditworthiness in assuring the payment of interest and principal. Lenders will first examine our creditworthiness and then, if necessary, will negotiate the various protective and repayment provisions. As financial officers, we can negotiate a lower cost of capital and a more flexible contractual borrowing arrangement if the firm has a good credit rating to begin with. If the firm has a bad credit rating, incorporating protective and repayment provisions will not entirely make up for the lack of a good credit reputation.

These provisions are known as *covenants* and are contained in the *indenture*—the contractual agreement between the lender and the borrower. Since the enactment of the Trust Indenture Act of 1939, all bond issuers have had to qualify with the Securities and Exchange Commission and have had to appoint an independent third-party trustee to enforce the terms of the indenture. This trustee is usually a financial institution which has no relationship with either the lender or the borrower so that it can remain impartial in its duties, which include furnishing current reports to the bondholders on the borrower's compliance with the indenture.

Identification Provisions

Identification provisions serve to identify the borrower and the mechanical aspects of the bond. The borrower is explicitly named so that there is no mistake as to who is responsible for the interest and principal payments. The chosen trustee is named, and its duties are delineated. Authorization for issuing the bonds is documented, and the amount of the issue is set forth. Then the bond itself is described by type, maturity, and interest amount. The date and place of the interest and principal payments are stated, as well as the medium of payment, such as dollars, pounds, or marks. The certificate of registration with the Securities and Exchange Commission is attached, and, if the bond is registered, a registry agent is appointed. At the end of the indenture, we would find the signatures of the parties and witnesses, including that of a notary public.

Protective Provisions

The protective provisions are designed to enhance the security of the payment of interest and principal, particularly if the firm encounters operating or financial difficulties.

Security of principal The major security provision to protect the principal in case of default is the priority of its claim on specific assets. This is spelled out in the indenture through a detailed description of the pledged property and the priority of this particular bond's lien on that property. The indenture also requires that the borrower covenant that it has a legitimate title to the property and warrant that it is legally entitled to offer it as security. The firm usually covenants that it shall maintain the property, pay taxes, buy insurance, and otherwise make a diligent effort to preserve the collateral value of the pledged asset.

The security provisions usually restrict the firm from raising additional debt without the consent of the bondholders.

Provision is made for acceleration of maturity in the event that the borrower fails to meet the interest or principal payments or violates the covenants. This means that the bondholders have the right to declare the entire issue due immediately if the firm misses interest payments on this or any other debt. This serves to protect the lender's priority. The firm cannot continue to treat this particular bond as if nothing has happened while selling off its assets to satisfy other creditors' claims, eventually leaving nothing to satisfy this bond's claims when due.

The protective provisions also include any guarantees of interest and principal payments made on behalf of the firm by a third party. A debenture bond might contain a negative pledge clause making all unpledged assets "equal and ratable." This means that the firm is prohibited from pledging any unpledged assets after the debenture is issued. It makes all unpledged assets part of the general pool of assets that all unsecured creditors, including the debenture bondholders, can try to sell in satisfaction of their claims. The mortgage bond might contain an after-acquired provision extending the lien of this mortgage bond over property acquired after the original issue date.

Security of interest The major objective of the protective provisions designed to insure the timely payment of the interest is to keep the firm liquid with enough cash on hand to meet the interest obligation. To this end, the indenture usually contains provisions restricting the firm's ability to pay dividends. This may come in the form of restricting all dividends or the payment of dividends until a certain amount of retained earnings has been accumulated.

The firm might be required to maintain a minimum net working capital position to insure cash or readily convertible current assets in the firm's financial structure. The firm might also be required to attain certain levels of profitability or interest coverage ratios (Chapter 3).

As the financial officer, you should note that these restrictions may be very inhibiting to the firm's financing and operations. You may want to negotiate them away. Certainly if you must include them, you want to bargain for a lower interest rate in exchange. Our list is not exhaustive, and you must be prepared to negotiate on variations of these and other protective provisions lenders may require.

Repayment Provisions

The repayment provisions try to insure that the firm will be able to redeem the bond at maturity. Most, such as sinking funds, serial bonds, and staggered maturities, are designed to ease the burden of a lump-sum repayment at maturity and to spread the redemption effort over the life of the bond instead. Other repayment provisions, such as call premiums and deferred calls, specify the ability of the firm to repay the bond before maturity.

Sinking funds Sinking funds are the periodic payment of principal into an escrow account designed to retire most, if not the entire issue, by maturity. For example, if the firm had sold a $100 million bond to mature 50 years from now, the sinking fund might require that the firm place sufficient funds in an account used only to retire the bonds (escrow), so that $2 million of the bonds could be redeemed each year. This can be accomplished in either of two different ways, and the typical sinking fund allows the firm the option. The firm can deposit enough into the escrow account each year so that with the effect of compound interest (Chapter 4) there will be $100 million in the account at the end of 50 years. Or the firm can retire $2 million face value (the redemption value printed on the face of the bond, usually $1,000) during the year by buying the bond in the open market. The latter option is particularly attractive to the firm if the prevailing market price of the bond is less than the face value. For example, if the bond were selling at $900, the firm could redeem $2 million of debt for only $1.8 million. Sometimes, as a slight variation on the escrow account option, the firm is allowed to vary the amount deposited each year as earnings fluctuate. When earnings are high the deposit is high, and vice versa, although there is typically a minimum annual deposit regardless of the firm's earnings.

Serial bonds Serial bonds are a variation of the sinking fund repayment provision. Under the serial redemption plan, the firm is committed to redeem a certain portion of the issue each year until the entire issue is retired at maturity. The specific bonds to be redeemed are selected at random from a list of the serial numbers printed on each bond. As the bond's number is drawn, the bondholder is notified and that bond redeemed at the face value, usually $1,000, by the trustee. The selected bondholders must submit their bonds for redemption, even if they want to keep them.

Staggered maturities Staggered maturities are more frequently used by state and local governments when they raise funds. The bonds are sold in strips, which means that various segments of the original issue mature at different times, ranging from days to decades.

Call provisions and premiums The *call provision* gives the borrower the right to call the bond for redemption at a specified price, usually in excess of $1,000 (the original loan amount) before maturity. For example, the American Telephone and Telegraph Company 6s 2000 might be callable at $1,050 until 1980, at $1,025 until 1990, and at $1,010 until 2000, at which time they mature for $1,000.

The call provision gives the firm added flexibility in arranging its financing in future years. If there are inhibiting provisions in a particular bond or interest rates are lower, the bond can be redeemed. Lenders, on the other hand, do not necessarily want the firm to be able to call the bond for redemption at some future date when interest rates may be lower, since it means they have to replace the bond with a lower-yield one. So they demand the *call premium,* an excess over the face value, which can be constant at a predetermined amount over the entire life of the bond or decline as the years pass. In either case, investors hope that this call premium will deter the redemption of the bond during periods of lower interest rates. If not, it at least gives them extra compensation for surrendering the bond when they may not want to.

Deferred call privilege If a deferred call provision is negotiated into the indenture, the firm surrenders the right to call the bond for redemption at any time during the deferred call period, which has traditionally averaged five to ten years. This means that regardless of what happens to the general level of interest rates or how inconvenient the covenants of this particular bond become, the firm cannot call it. Investors usually insist upon a deferred call provision when interest rates are high in the hopes of preventing redemption if interest rates return to lower levels.

Financial officers can use the deferred call privilege to negotiate a lower rate of interest because investors are willing to give up a little of the relatively high yield in order to assure its continuation over the next few years. If financial officers feel that interest rates are going to remain high during the coming years, they may be most willing to exchange the deferred call privilege for a lower-than-prevailing interest rate at the time of the negotiations. On the other hand, if interest rates are likely to fall in the next few months, the financial officer may be willing to pay the prevailing higher interest rate in order to avoid the deferred call. He or she hopes to refund the bond with a lower-cost one within the next few months and does not want to lock the firm into a high-cost bond.

Balloon payment The balloon repayment provision allows the firm to repay the largest portion of the issue at maturity instead of gradually retiring the issue over its life. For example, if the sinking fund in the case of the $100 million, 50-year issue mentioned earlier retired only $50 million face value of the issue over the 50 years, the balloon payment would be $50 million.

ADVANTAGES AND DISADVANTAGES OF LONG-TERM DEBT

What are the advantages and disadvantages of long-term debt?

Advantages

A major advantage to long-term debt as a source of funds can be its lower after-tax cost of capital. Not only is debt traditionally less expensive than common stock, for example, but the interest payment is tax deductible, which, in effect, means the United States government is bearing a percentage of the cost.

Long-term debt is usually easier to sell, has lower flotation costs than stock, and, as we have seen in Chapter 10, can sometimes lower the overall cost of capital. In periods when the equity markets are unreceptive, the bond markets may still be a source of funds for the firm. And the use of bonds as a source of funds does not dilute present stockholders' control.

The permanency of long-term bonds over short-term sources facilitates long-range planning and consolidation of the firm's short-term indebtedness. This improves the firm's liquidity and working capital position. Even so, if the call provisions are skillfully negotiated, the firm retains a financial flexibility that resembles short-term financing.

Finally, the use of long-term debt opens the possibility of positive financial leverage and increased earnings per share.

Disadvantages

The principal disadvantage associated with the use of long-term debt is the increased financial risk. As we have seen in Chapter 10, investors require a higher rate of return, occasioning a higher cost of capital to the firm, as the proportion of debt in the capital structure increases.

Another major disadvantage is the larger cashflow requirements to meet the sinking fund. As the cash needed to amortize the debt increases, the financial burden and the chance of insolvency also increase. If the fixed charges increase to the point where the firm cannot generate sufficient funds to meet them, the firm is insolvent.

The third major disadvantage to the use of long-term debt is the restrictive nature of the indenture covenants. These can reduce the flexibility so necessary to the firm's financing program and impede its operations and expansion.

BOND FEATURES

In negotiating the long-term debt as a source of funds, the financial officer must be aware of the bond features and acquainted with market conditions and the lender's perceived risk of the firm. This means thoroughly understanding bond terminology, quality ratings, and the firm's financial position.

Bond Terminology

In tailoring the issue to the prevailing capital market conditions and lenders' requirements, the financial officer has to take the terms and characteristics of the typical bond into account. You must not only understand the terminology but also be prepared to bargain on many points. Let us review some of the more frequently used terms.

The *par value* or face value represents the redemption price at maturity as stated on the face of the bond. This is usually $1,000 per bond.

The *coupon rate* is the annual dollar interest expressed as a percentage of the par value. For example, if the annual interest cost were $90 per bond, the coupon rate would be 9 percent. This is the rate used to describe the bond, as in the ABC Corporation 9s 1999, for example. The 9s represent the coupon rate and distinguish it from the other bonds of the same company and maturity, if any. The actual yield may never equal the coupon rate; the coupon rate merely serves to identify the bond and the annual interest payment.

The *maturity* of the bond may vary, so it is a point of negotiation between the firm and the potential investors in the bond. Generally, the firm can tailor the maturity to its financing needs.

Denomination is the size of the par value. Most bonds are denominated in $1,000 units. However, to enhance appeal to smaller investors, bonds are sometimes issued in denominations of $100 and $500. To make the bonds more convenient and restrict them to larger investors, the bonds may be issued in $5,000, $10,000 and still larger denominations.

The *yield to maturity* is the actual annualized interest rate at the prevailing market price. It is this discount rate which equates the present value of the future interest payments and return of the par value to the current market price. For example, the yield to maturity of a 7s with 15 years to maturity when the prevailing market price is $769.40 is 10 percent.

The *current yield* is the annual interest payment in relation to the prevailing market price of the bond without considering the return of the principal. For example, the current yield on a 5s with 10 years to maturity when the market price is $500 is 10 percent ($50/$500). In using the current yield, we ignore the maturity and any differential between the prevailing price and the redemption price.

Market quotations on bonds are traditionally in *points*, not in dollars. Each point is worth $10, so that a bond quote of 90 translates to $900. Each point, in turn, is divided into 100 *basis points*. When you start bargaining with the investment banker on the price, you will probably be talking in points and basis points.

Deep discount bonds are bonds selling well below their par value. This occurs because as interest rates rise, already existing bonds sold during periods of lower interest rates must decline in price (see Chapter 4). This raises the yield on them to a competitive rate with the higher yields on newer issues.

The conditions of the capital market also influence the financial officer's bargaining strategy. If the market is presently tight and interest rates are high but expected to drop, the firm may have to pay the high rate unless it includes a high call premium or a deferred call provision to insure investors that they will not be deprived of the high yield when the rates drop. If rising rates of inflation are expected, the financial officer may be willing to pay a higher interest rate now.

Lenders' Risk

We have already seen in this chapter that investors try to limit their risk exposure by incorporating security provisions in the indenture. Each bond has a specified claim priority in the earnings and the assets. As the priority decreases, the interest rate increases because the lenders' risk increases. Thus, the mortgage bonds have a lower interest rate than the debenture bonds of the same company. We also find that bond quality varies among firms.

The rating agencies have attempted to summarize the quality of each bond in rating systems. As a new issue comes to the market for sale, the agency examines it and gives it a quality rating. As the quality rating drops, indicating a higher risk, the interest cost increases. Table 20-1 gives the rating system used in Standard and Poor's *Bond Guide*. As the financial officer, it is your job to design the bond and help manage the firm so that the rating agency gives the bond the highest quality rating possible. This may even require a visit to the agency to discuss the firm's present situation.

The Firm's Position

When your firm considers long-term debt as a source of funds, you must consider the following points. First, you want to lower the firm's over-all cost of capital as much as possible. Second, you want to be as certain as possible that the use of debt

Table 20-1   Standard and Poor's Risk Ratings

AAA	highest quality, possessing the "ultimate degree of protection"
AA	high grade obligation, differing only in a small degree from the AAA rating
A	upper medium grade, subject to adverse general economic conditions
BBB	medium grade, showing the beginnings of speculative elements
BB	lower medium grade, possessing minor investment characteristics
B	speculative, where interest payment cannot be assured under difficult economic conditions
CCC–CC	outright speculations
C	income bonds on which no interest is being paid
DDD–D	in default with the rating indicating the relative salvage value

financing will lead to positive financial leverage and raise earnings per share. Third, you want to check that the firm has sufficient earnings stability to service the debt, that is, to pay the interest and amortize the principal when required.

On the other side of the picture, you want to be sure you are using a sufficient amount of debt so that you are not passing up the opportunity for positive financial leverage or are relying so heavily on stock financing that you jeopardize control of the firm. You want to consider selling bonds when the firm's stock price is so depressed that equity capital is too expensive or the equity market is unreceptive at that moment. You want to consider selling bonds when you expect rapid inflation so that you can repay the loan in cheaper dollars in later years and when the firm needs to consolidate its short-term debt into a more manageable long-term structure which relieves some of the liquidity pressure. This is particularly true if you expect a credit crunch in which it will be very difficult, if not impossible, to refinance the short-term borrowings when they fall due.

BOND REFUNDING[2]

When should the financial officer refund presently outstanding long-term debt?

This depends on how much interest and other costs the firm saves by refunding in relation to how much expense it encounters in the refunding process. If the present value of the reduction in the annual net cash outflow (savings) exceeds the net cash outflow encountered in the refunding (costs), the firm should refund.

The bond refunding opportunity arises when the interest rates have dropped from the levels at which the original issue was sold and that original issue may be called for redemption, in effect replacing it with a new issue at a lower interest cost. During recent periods of lower interest rates which have succeeded periods of "unusually high" interest rates, numerous firms have refunded, replacing high-yield bonds with lower-yield ones.

[2] See Oswald D. Bowlin, "The Refunding Decision: Another Special Case in Capital Budgeting," *Journal of Finance*, XXI (March 1966), 55–68; and Eugene S. Merill, "A Guide to Bond Refunding," *Public Utility Fortnightly*, September 1962.

Refunding Cash Outflows[3]

Let us illustrate the initial cash outflows of the refunding and the cash flow savings by using a hypothetical bond. This bond is assumed to have 20 years to run on its original 30-year life and was originally issued at 10 percent. It is callable at $1,050, there are $40 million of the bond outstanding, and the tax rate for this firm is 50 percent. The firm finds it can now refund this bond with $40 million of an 8 percent, 20-year bond, selling at $1,000 each. The initial cash outflows to consider are (1) the after-tax cost of the call premium, (2) the after-tax flotation costs of the new issue, (3) the after-tax overlapping interest, and (4) the tax savings from the unamortized flotation costs of the old issue.

After-tax call premium costs   If the firm redeems the original issue, it incurs the call premium expense, which in this case is $50 per bond, or $2 million on 40,000 bonds. However, that is a tax-deductible expense, so the after-tax cash outflow is only $1,000,000 in our example.

After-tax flotation costs   In refunding the old issue, the firm must pay the costs incurred in selling the new bond. Such items as the underwriting commission, the registration fees, and the legal and accounting costs must be met, and if the refunding had not been undertaken they would never have arisen. In our example, let us assume that the flotation costs are $2 million. But, again, these are tax deductible expenses so that the after tax cash outflow is only $1,000,000.

After-tax overlapping interest   For a short time during the refunding, both the old and the new issue will be outstanding and the firm will be paying interest on both. This occurs because the firm must first sell the new debt to raise the money for the retirement of the old issue. There has to be a time lapse between the two events. If in our example the time lapse is 1 month, the firm would be paying an additional month's interest at 8 percent on the new bond, over and above the interest on the old bond. Since this additional interest would not have occurred had the refunding not been undertaken, it must be considered part of the refunding costs. In our example, the overlapping interest cash outflow would be:

$$\frac{.08}{12} \times \$40,000,000 = \$266,664$$

before taxes and $133,332 after taxes, since interest is a tax-deductible expense.

Tax savings from the amortization of the old issue's flotation costs and discounts   When the original issue which is now to be refunded was first sold, it, too, incurred flotation costs. These costs are amortized over the life of the issue, a proportionate amount expensed each year. When the issue is redeemed before maturity, the unamortized portion has to be entirely expensed as well. For example, if the origi-

---

[3] We are ignoring the unamortized discount for simplicity. This arises if the bond sold at less than the par value at the initial offering, say $980 for a $1,000 bond. The $20 must be amortized over the life of the bond; and if the bond is called early, the remaining unamortized amount of the discount must be expensed. For simplicity we also assumed that the original bond was refunded with a bond of equal maturity, but this does not have to be the case. If the new bond were of longer maturity, we would consider only the savings through the remaining life of the original bond.

nal issue cost $3,000,000, the unamortized portion of that cost remaining after 10 years would be $2 million, calculated as follows:

$$\frac{20}{30} = \$3,000,000 = \$2,000,000$$

These remaining flotation costs are a tax-deductible expense which may be written off against income in their entirety when the bond is refunded. The corporation thus has a noncash expense of $2,000,000 in this case (remember the cash outlay for the flotation costs of the old issue was encountered when that issue was originally sold). This is in effect a tax savings, because the write-off reduces taxable income and taxes paid by a multiple of the tax rate. In this case, the $2,000,000 write-off against income of the unamortized portion of the old issue's flotation costs leads to a $1,000,000 tax savings. The initial cash outlay connected with the refunding is, therefore, *reduced by $1,000,000.*

Discounts, which arise when a bond is initially sold at less than its par value (usually $1,000), are afforded the same tax treatment. They must be amortized over the life of the issue unless it is refunded before maturity. Then, the unamortized portion of the discount may be written off against income giving the corporation a tax savings, as in the case of the unamortized old issue's flotation costs.

Total after-tax initial cash outflow   The sum of all the after-tax cash outflows less tax savings would be:

Call premium	$1,000,000
Flotation costs, new issue	1,000,000
Overlapping interest	133,332
Total cash outlays, after taxes	
less tax savings	$2,133,332
Write-off of unamortized flotation costs, old issue	1,000,000
Total initial cash outflow, after taxes	$1,333,332

Refunding savings in annual cash outflows   We must weigh the after-tax reduction in the annual bond cash outflows against the after-tax initial cash outflow in order to determine if the refunding should be undertaken. The after-tax reductions in the annual cash outflows would be, in this example, the difference between the after-tax interest expense and the tax savings on the annual amortization of the flotation costs of the old issue and the new issue. We can determine this annual difference by first computing the annual cash outflow of the old issue, then of the new issue, and comparing the two.

The annual interest expense on the old issue is $4,000,000. After taxes, at the assumed rate of 50 percent, the *after-tax cost is $2,000,000.* The annual amortization costs associated with the flotation of the old issue are $100,000 before taxes and *$50,000 after taxes.* We can see this if we remember that the total flotation costs to be amortized over the 30-year life of the old issue were $3,000,000, or $100,000 a year. The annual net cash outflow associated with the old issue in this example is then:

After-tax interest expense	
less tax savings	$2,000,000
Annual amortization flotation costs	50,000
Annual net cash outflow, old issue	$1,950,000

The annual interest expense on the new issue is $3,200,000, which *after taxes is $1,600,000*. The annual amortization of flotation expense is $100,000 before taxes and $50,000 after taxes. We can see this as the $2,000,000 in flotation costs for the new issue are amortized in equal amounts over the 20-year life of the new issue.

The annual net cash outflow associated with the new issue in this example is:

After-tax interest expense	
less tax savings	$1,600,000
Annual amortization flotation costs	50,000
Annual net cash outflow, new issue	$1,550,000

The annual difference between the net cash outflows of the old issue and the new issue is:

Net cash outflows, old issue	$1,950,000
Net cash outflows, new issue	1,550,000
Annual savings	$ 400,000

By refunding the old issue, the firm can reduce its net cash outflows by $400,000 a year.

The Analysis

To determine if immediately incurring the refunding costs is justified by the annual savings over the next twenty years, we have to find the present discounted value for that stream of savings. Only then are the cost and the savings figures comparable. If the present value of the savings exceeds the costs, the firm should refund. If the present value of the savings is less than the costs incurred to generate those savings, we should not proceed with the refunding.

What is the appropriate discount rate to use in computing the present value of the savings?[4] The majority opinion seems to favor using the default-free (pure) interest rate (i) on the grounds that the future stream of savings is known with certainty once the refunding is completed. Therefore it resembles a riskless investment, and the majority argue that the discount rate should also be riskless.

Using the riskless discount rate at an assumed 7 percent, let us see if the financial officer should refund in our example. The present discounted value of the savings would be:

$$PV_s = \sum_{t=1}^{n} \frac{S_t}{(1+i)^t} \qquad (20\text{-}1)$$

where
PV_s = the present value of the annual savings
S_t = the annual savings
i = the default-free interest rate

[4] There is absolutely no agreement as to what discount rate should be used. The author believes that, despite the majority opinion, the appropriate rate is the weighted overall cost of capital (k_o) because the funds used to finance the refund come from the general funds of the firm and as such bear the overall cost of capital.

In our example:

$$PV_s = \sum_{t=1}^{20} \frac{\$400,000}{(1 + .07)^t}$$

$$= \$4,237,600$$

Since the present value of the reduction in the net cash outflows exceeds the total after-tax, initial refunding cash outflows, the firm should undertake the refunding.[5]

SUMMARY

After having read Chapter 20, you should be able to answer these questions:

1. What are the general types of long-term debt securities that the financial officer can consider as a source of long-term funds?

In addition to the basic bond, which is a long-term contractual agreement between the lenders and the firm, there are several variations. The bond can be a registered or a coupon (bearer) type. It can be secured as in the case of mortgage bonds or unsecured as in the case of debenture bonds. It can be guaranteed and it can be funded.

2. What are the typical provisions of the bond indenture?

The contractual agreement between the borrower and the lender is called the indenture, and it contains the provisions (covenants). Being an individually negotiated document, the indenture can contain almost any provision the parties agree to, but most of the provisions pertain to identification of the bond, protection for the interest and principal payments, and repayment.

3. What are the advantages and disadvantages of using long-term debt?

The major advantage is its lower after-tax cost of capital compared to other sources of funds. Under certain conditions, it may also be easier to sell than other long-term securities. Its use affords the firm a permanency of funding which facilitates long-range planning.

The major disadvantages are the increased financial risk, the larger debt-service burden, and the restrictive provisions of the indenture which may hamper the firm's progress toward its objectives.

4. What do financial officers have to know about bond features to negotiate with lenders?

They should be familiar with such bond terms as par value, coupon rate, yield to maturity, denomination, and current yield. They must understand prevailing capital market conditions and expectations for interest rates.

The financial officer should also be aware that lenders are very risk-conscious and demand higher interest rates as the quality of the bond decreases. There are rating agencies which attempt to summarize the quality of bonds for investors. The financial officer should be familiar with these and try to raise the rating of the firm's bonds and thereby get a lower interest rate and easier market access.

5. What factors should the financial officer consider in analyzing a potential bond refund?

He or she must consider the after-tax refunding costs such as call premium, flotation costs, and overlapping interest and the refunding savings over the remaining

---

[5] There remains the question of when the financial officer should time the refunding operation to maximize its benefits.

life of the refunded bond. Since the time dimension of the costs and the savings is different, the present value of the savings stream must be found before comparing the two. The appropriate discount rate appears to be the riskless rate. If the present value of the stream of savings is greater than the costs incurred, then the refunding should be undertaken; otherwise it should not be undertaken.

QUESTIONS

20-1 What are indentures and covenants as they relate to bonds?

20-2 What is the main difference between a registered bond and a coupon bond?

20-3 Explain the following excerpts from the listing of corporate bonds in a recent *Wall Street Journal:*

Bonds	Current Yield
LTV 5s 88	12.0%
TVA 9 1/4s 95	9.1
Tenneco 7s 93	10.0

20-4 Why is a first mortgage bond called a senior security and a second mortgage bond called a junior security?

20-5 Would a general mortgage bond or a debenture bond be the more senior security?

20-6 How is the income bond different from all other bonds?

20-7 Many communities offer industrial revenue bonds as an inducement for new industrial firms to locate in their communities. Why might this type of arrangement be attractive to a prospective firm?

20-8 Many indentures provide bond repayment provisions in the form of sinking funds and/or serial bonds. Distinguish between these two methods of bond repayment.

20-9 Under what conditions should a firm consider refunding a bond issue? What is the general criterion for the refunding decision?

20-10 What are the major costs associated with refunding a bond issue?

PROBLEMS

20-1 Select several advertisements from recent issues of the *Wall Street Journal* illustrating mortgage bonds, debentures (convertible and subordinated), income bonds, and industrial revenue bonds. Note the similarities and differences in the various types of bonds.

20-2 Suppose Firm A issues $10,000,000 of 8's with a maturity in 20 years. If the entire bond principal is to be retired in 20 years and the firm's opportunity return is 6 percent, what are the annual sinking fund payments required to retire the principal in 20 years? The first sinking fund payment is made a year after the bond is issued.

20-3 Suppose interest rates in general have declined recently and Bolcon Company wishes to analyze the feasibility of refunding part or all of its long-term debt. The firm has two types of long-term debt. Bonds A were issued 5 years ago and have 20 years remaining to maturity. There are $20,000,000 of Bonds A outstanding that pay a 10 percent annual interest payment. Bonds B were issued 10 years ago and have 20 years remaining to maturity. There are $10,000,000 of Bonds B outstanding that pay a 9 percent annual interest payment. Bonds A are callable at $1,020 and Bonds B are callable at $1,010. The firm can refund up to $30,000,000 of these bonds with an 8 percent 20-year bond selling at $1,000 per bond. The original flotation costs of Bonds A were $500,000 and $300,000 for Bonds B. The new flotation costs for refunding Bonds A are $650,000 and $400,000 for Bonds B. There are assumed to be 2 months during which the old and new issues will overlap. The firm's tax rate is 50 percent and the default-free interest rate is 5 percent. Is it feasible to refund Bonds A, Bonds B, or both?

BIBLIOGRAPHY

Bowlin, Oswald D. "The Refunding Decision: Another Special Case in Capital Budgeting." *Journal of Finance,* XXI (March 1966), 55–68.

Brown, Bowman. "Why Corporations Should Consider Income Bonds." *Financial Executive,* 35 (October 1967), 74–78.

Donaldson, Gordon. "New Framework for Corporate Debt Policy." *Harvard Business Review,* XL (March–April 1962), 123–136.

Everett, Edward. "Subordinate Debt—Nature and Enforcement." *Business Lawyer,* 20 (July 1965), 953–987.

Fisher, Lawrence. "Determinants of Risk Premiums on Corporate Bonds." *Journal of Political Economy,* LXVII (June 1959), 217–237.

Jen, Frank C., and James E. Wert. "The Deferred Call Provision and Corporate Bond Yields." *Journal of Financial and Quantitative Analysis,* III (June 1968), 157–169.

_____. "The Effect of Call Risk on Corporate Bond Yields." *Journal of Finance,* XXII (December 1967), 637–651.

_____. "The Value of the Deferred Call Privilege." *National Review,* 3 (March 1966), 369–378.

Johnson, Robert W. "Subordinated Debentures: Debt That Serves as Equity." *Journal of Finance,* X (March 1955), 1–16.

Pogue, Thomas F., and Robert M. Soldofsky. "What's in a Bond Rating." *Journal of Financial and Quantitative Analysis,* IV (June 1969), 201–228.

Pye, Gordon. "The Value of Call Deferment on a Bond: Some Empirical Results." *Journal of Finance,* XXII (December 1967), 623–636.

_____. "The Value of the Call Option on a Bond." *Journal of Political Economy,* LXXIV (April 1966), 200–205.

Spiller, Earl A., Jr. "Time-Adjusted Breakeven Rate for Refunding." *Financial Executive,* 31 (July 1963), 32–35.

Weingartner, H. Martin. "Optimal Timing of Bond Refunding." *Management Science,* 13 (March 1967), 511–524.

Winn, Willis J., and Aileigh Hess, Jr. "The Value of the Call Privilege." *Journal of Finance,* XIV (May 1959), 182–195.

21

PREFERRED AND COMMON STOCK

THE FINANCIAL OFFICER MUST EXAMINE all the long-term sources of funds before selecting which to tap. You will find that preferred stocks offer a middle ground between bonds and common stock because they possess some of the characteristics of each. Under certain circumstances, offering preferred stock may be a viable alternative. What major considerations in the use of preferred stock must you examine?

If neither long-term debt nor preferred stock seems appropriate, you can generally turn to common stock as a source of long-term funds. Under certain circumstances offering common stock is the most appropriate choice. What major considerations in the use of common stock must you examine?

Once you, as the financial officer, have decided that common stock is the most appropriate source of long-term funds, how can you arrange for its sale? We have already seen that most new issues are sold through an underwriter. In this chapter we explore the use of subscription rights as another method of selling new stock issues. We shall see that this method may also involve the services of an investment banker, but not to the extent of the underwriting procedure.

Once the stock has been sold, what other situations related to the stock may you be called upon to analyze? We shall see that even after the stock has been sold, the firm is still concerned with its value and may consider stock splits, reverse stock splits, listing, or repurchase. As the financial officer, you will be asked to determine the effect of such actions on the stock price and the firm's financing plans.

PREFERRED STOCK

What are the major issues that you must examine when considering preferred stock as a source of long-term funds? In order to compare the relative attractiveness of preferred stock versus long-term debt and common stock you must know its advantages and disadvantages. You should also know whom to contact in order to sell preferred stock. Only then can you use preferred stock wisely.

Definition

Preferred stock is part of the firm's capital stock. Ownership entitles holders to a claim on the corporation's after-tax earnings up to a specified amount and a claim on the firm's assets in case of liquidation up to a specified amount. The preferred claim's priority is above that of the common stock but below all debt obligations. For example, the Wheeling-Pittsburgh Steel $5 cumulative preferred stock entitles the holder to $5 in annual dividends before the common stock can receive any dividends. The cumulative designation means that if the firm omits the preferred dividend in any year, the omitted dividend remains a liability of the firm to the holder which must be paid before dividends on the common stock can be paid.

In many ways preferred stock resembles long-term debt. The annual promised dividend is typically fixed like the interest payment on a bond. In the Wheeling-Pittsburgh Steel $5 preferred, the dividend is fixed at $5 per year. Any after-tax earnings above this $5 belongs to the common stock. Because of this limited participation in the earnings of the firm, the preferred stock has no growth prospects—like the bond and in contrast to the common stock. Any growth in the firm's earnings above the fixed preferred dividend will benefit only the common stockholders and is reflected only in the common stock price. Like the bond, the preferred stock price tends to vary more with changes in interest rates than with growth in the firm's earnings.

Like the bond, the preferred stock typically does not carry voting rights in the election of directors if the dividend is paid, although some preferred stocks are explicitly entitled to voting rights. In most instances, however, the preferred assumes substantial voting power if its dividend is omitted for a specified number of quarters. Like the bond, it has a prior claim on the after-tax earnings of the firm to satisfy its dividend and on the assets of the firm in the event of liquidation to satisfy its principal. In terms of rank, it typically has the least priority of all claims except for the common stock.

On the other hand, the preferred stock resembles the common stock in many ways. The dividend on the preferred stock, like that on the common stock, may be omitted. In the case of most preferreds, the board of directors must declare the dividend before it can be paid, and they are not obliged to do so if, in their opinion, it is not in the firm's best interests. In some cases this means that the preferred stockholders never see that omitted dividend at all, while in other cases, such as the Wheeling-Pittsburgh Steel $5 cumulative preferred, the omitted dividends must be made up before the firm can resume dividends on the common stock.

Preferred stock resembles common stock in that it is part of the firm's equity capital (unlike the debt, which is part of the firm's liabilities). If we looked at a firm's balance sheet, we would find preferred stock listed below liabilities in the stockholders' equity accounts just above the common stock account. This positioning reflects a legal view of preferred stock as an equity security with a prior claim over common stock. Like other equity securities, but unlike debt securities, the preferred does not have the ability to press bankruptcy proceedings against the firm if its claims are not met.

Like common stock and unlike bonds, the preferred usually has no maturity date. After a specified waiting period, preferreds are typically redeemable at the firm's option for a specified price, although there are still a few perpetual preferred stocks which the firm has agreed never to redeem. For example, the Wheeling-Pittsburgh Steel $5 preferred is redeemable at $105 a share after 1975 at the option of the company.

Advantages and Disadvantages

The quasi-debt nature of the preferred stock gives the financial officer some unusual financing flexibility which may be advantageous to the firm under certain circumstances. Notice that the use of preferred stock allows the firm to avoid the rigidity of the bond's fixed-interest obligation. If the firm omits the preferred dividend, its image may be slightly tarnished but its financial integrity remains intact. This is particularly advantageous to firms with fluctuations in their earnings and cashflow. The firm also avoids the bond's fixed maturity or call date without losing the right to call the preferred stock. This latitude greatly enhances the financial officer's ability to time financing to periods of depressed interest rates and low capital costs.

The use of the preferred stock does not dilute the earnings per share to the common stock. In fact, if the return on the project financed by the sale of the preferred exceeds its capital cost, the firm experiences positive financial leverage and can actually increase the earnings per common share. For example, electric utilities have traditionally used preferred in this manner, since the cost of preferred capital has been less than the return on their assets allowed by the public utility commissions.

In those instances where the existing stockholders' control of the firm is a concern, the use of preferred allows the financial officer to expand the firm's equity base without jeopardizing control, since most preferred stocks do not have voting rights. The enlarged equity may, in turn, allow the firm to sell additional long-term debt, if it needs further capital. If it does not need capital at the time, the use of the preferred stock still increases the firm's borrowing capacity, which it may reserve for future needs.

The preferred is also particularly useful in merger and acquisition negotiations. The financial officer can use it as a bargaining tool in cases where the selling firm's stockholders emphasize income rather than capital appreciation. For example, many privately owned firms seek to merge when the founder wants to retire. At retirement the founder, as the major stockholder, may desire income; the preferred gives the desired emphasis on income. In other merger negotiations the financial officer may find the convertible preferred stock a more useful tool, since it allows the holder to have both dividend income now and participate later in any capital appreciation of the acquiring firm's common stock through the conversion option. The financial officer may find that the selling stockholders are more willing to settle for a lower acquisition price if a convertible preferred is offered.

Finally, the financial officer may find that the preferred is the only security the financial markets may be receptive to at certain times. When the capital markets are unreceptive to the firm's common stock or investors are more attracted to fixed-income securities, the preferred stock may be the only equity security for which the firm can find a buyer. As the financial officer, you should always keep preferred stocks in mind as an alternative source of funds.

Preferred stocks have, however, certain major disadvantages, which have led to their very sparse use since the end of World War II. The major disadvantage is the higher cost of preferred capital compared to debt capital. Since the bond's interest payments are a tax-deductible expense while the preferred's dividends are not, the cost of debt capital is considerably cheaper than that of preferred stock in most instances. At the same time the current dividend yield is considerably higher for the preferred stock than for the common stock in most cases. A growing firm which wishes to retain its earnings for reinvestment might choose to sell the common stock on which it does not have to declare any dividends for many years, preserving earnings. Thus, offering preferred stock may appear less attractive than either the common stock or bonds. This has been particularly true when debt capital is easily obtained.

Features of Preferred Stock

Just as in the case of bonds, the financial officer must be familiar with the features of preferred stock in order to effectively negotiate its sale and tailor the issue to the market's requirements.

Par value Par value typically represents the amount of the preferred's claim in liquidation. It is usually $100 per share. The dividend may be expressed as a percentage of the par value. For example, the Southern California Edison 7.58 percent cumulative preferred pays $7.58 per share in dividends each year.

The preferred may also be no par; in this case, the liquidation claim is stated in the rights of the preferred. When there is no par value, the annual dividend is traditionally stated in its dollar amount. Accordingly the Wheeling-Pittsburgh Steel $5 preferred pays $5 per share in dividends each year.

Protective provisions Like the bond, the preferred may contain protective provisions designed to insure payment of the dividend when due. Among the more common protective provisions are prohibition on the firm's sale of additional securities with a prior claim on earnings and assets, restrictions on the firm's ability to pay a dividend on common stock, and required levels of working capital. Traditionally, the preferred's protective provisions are not as inhibiting to the firm's future financing or expansion as are the bond's protective provisions, although these provisions are negotiable and may contain any mutually agreed upon terms.

Cumulative dividend Most preferred stocks allow for the accumulation of omitted dividends. If the board of directors decides not to declare the preferred dividend, it accumulates to the favor of the preferred holders and must be paid before dividends on the common stock. In the financial pages preferred stocks with this feature are designated by the abbreviation cum. or cm. as in "Wheeling-Pittsburgh Steel $5 cum. preferred."

The preferred stock may not contain a cumulative feature. In that case, the omission of the dividend means that the preferred holders are never paid that dividend and cannot press a claim for it.

Redemption Most preferred stocks are redeemable at the option of the firm after a certain elapsed time and usually for a premium over par value. The Southern California Edison preferreds are callable at the firm's option for $108 a share, an $8.00 premium. A few perpetual preferreds with no call date remain, and some preferreds have a sinking fund feature designed to retire the entire issue by some predetermined date.

Convertibility Some preferreds are convertible in that the holder has the right to convert the preferred into the associated common stock at a predetermined fixed price. As we shall see in Chapter 22, the value of the preferred can rise with an increase in the price of the associated common stock. Convertible preferreds in the financial pages are usually designated cv.

Voting rights Some preferreds carry voting rights identical to those of the common stock, and each preferred might be entitled to one vote, although there are preferreds with more than one vote per share. A preferred with this feature is abbreviated vtg. in the financial pages.

When the preferred dividend has been omitted for a specified number of quarters, the typical preferred acquires substantial voting power. In many instances, preferred stockholders may then have the right to elect a specified portion of the board of directors to look after their interests. In most cases, the portion is smaller than a majority, usually 25 percent to 35 percent of the board, though in some cases a majority of the board may pass to the preferred holders.

Participation A small number of preferred stocks may receive dividends over and above the stated amount under certain predetermined conditions. If the firm's after-tax earnings exceed a specified amount, for example, the preferred stock might receive a portion of the excess. Some of the participating preferreds are unrestricted as to their amount of participation so that as the firm's earnings continue to grow, the preferred's participation in those earnings also continues to grow. Other participating preferreds may have restricted or limited participation rights. If restricted, they typically must wait for the common stock to receive a dividend equal to the preferred's dividend. Then the preferred receives a fixed sum or percentage of any common stock cash dividend above that amount.

Buyers of Preferred Stock

Once you have decided to use preferred stock as a source of long-term capital, you must know to whom you are most likely to sell it. Traditionally, other corporations and particularly insurance companies have been the largest buyers of preferreds. Some are forced into the preferred market because they are legally restricted from purchasing common stocks, like many insurance companies. Others are attracted to the preferreds because of their relatively steady income. The vast majority, however, are buyers because the preferred dividend, unlike bond interest, carries an 85 percent exclusion from income taxes. Incorporated buyers do not pay income taxes on 85 percent of the preferred dividends they receive. In effect, a firm in the 50 percent tax bracket is paying only 7.5 percent on its preferred dividend income!

Unfortunately there are disadvantages to buying preferred stocks which should not be overlooked in the rush for the lower tax consideration. First, preferred stock prices fluctuate more in response to a given change in interest rates than do most bonds. This means that if preferred stockholders have to sell the preferred in a period of higher interest rates, they will suffer a loss. That is why insurance companies with their limited need for liquidity are the largest holders of preferreds. Further, preferreds usually have a small floating supply and low marketability, making them unattractive to any buyer who might want to sell in the future. Finally, the nonobligatory nature of the preferred dividend discourages many buyers, particularly when smaller, less seasoned, and less creditworthy firms try to sell preferreds. Since the buyer is relying on the firm's desire and ability to pay the dividend without any real recourse or method to force payment, only the most creditworthy firms find it relatively easy to sell preferreds.

COMMON STOCK

When you are considering raising long-term capital, you must examine all the alternatives to determine which source is the most appropriate. That means you have to consider common stock as well as bonds and preferreds. What are the major considerations you must take into account when examining common stock as a source of long-term funds?

Definition

Common stock is the residual ownership entitling the holder to a claim on the firm's earnings and assets after all prior claims have been satisfied. The common stockholders own and control the corporation, elect its board of directors, and receive the dividends declared out of residual earnings.

The common stockholders not only receive the benefits of a growing stream of earnings, which should increase the value of their ownership interest, but also bear the major portion of the risks, which in the extreme could be bankruptcy and the loss of their entire investment. Since common stockholders have the least priority in liquidation, they usually suffer the greatest losses. But because of the limited liability laws, the personal loss of any stockholder is limited to the purchase price of the shares.

Ownership of the stock is evidenced by the stock certificate, as illustrated in Figure 21-1. Stock certificates are typically registered, and all communications from the company to its stockholders, including dividend payments, are automatically forwarded to the address on record.

Features of Common Stock

As in the case of bonds and preferred stock, the common stock has certain unique features with which the financial officer must be familiar. You must consider these features before deciding to use common stock as a source of long-term capital.

Control   The common stockholders are the owners of the firm. Collectively they control it. As a class, they elect the board of directors and the independent auditors, who periodically examine the firm's financial condition and report to those stockholders who do not participate directly in the firm's operations. Common stockholders are the only ones who can amend the firm's charter and bylaws and authorize the sale of fixed assets, mergers, and new issues of common stock, preferred stock, and debt.

Stockholder rights Purchase of the stock entitles the owner to certain rights which may have a bearing on the financial officer's decision to finance with common stock. The owner can transfer the ownership to another party, in most instances. This means that voting power can readily pass into unfriendly hands who may oppose the present management or divert the present management's attention from attaining the firm's goals.

Ownership entitles stockholders to inspect the firm's books within reason. This means they can obtain a list of the stockholders, although sometimes the stockholder has to obtain a court order to that effect. Ownership also means that the stockholder has the right to share in the liquidation of the firm after prior claims have been satisfied and the right to receive the declared dividends.

Par value Par value is an arbitrarily fixed value attached to a share of stock. It is usually of little significance. It is used primarily in the accounts of the firm to establish the common stock account, although at one time it was the basis upon which

Figure 21-1   A Stock Certificate

stocks were taxed.[1] To avoid this type of taxation, many firms declared the stock to have a par value of either a few pennies or no par value at all. Instead, they adopted the stated value to be used in establishing the common stock account.

We can see how the par value establishes the common stock account on the firm's balance sheet in the following example. If the firm had one million $5-par-value common shares and sold them at $20 a share, $5 of the selling price would be allocated to the common stock account and the remaining $15 to the additional paid-in capital account, as follows:

Common stock ($5 per value) 1,000,000 shares	$ 5,000,000
Additional paid-in capital	$15,000,000
Total common stock and additional paid-in capital	$20,000,000

Maturity Unlike the bond, the common stock has no maturity. Its life is as long as the company exists. Since the standard anticipation is that the firm is an on-going concern with no planned date for extinction, the stock is assumed to have perpetual life.

Market value and risks Since common stocks are transferable, they have a market price at which the present owners and potential buyers are willing to transact. Theoretically, this prevailing market price reflects the value of the expected future benefits to the shareholder discounted to the present at an appropriate risk-adjusted discount rate. If the expected benefits or the appropriate discount rate changes, the prevailing price should also change, as we saw in Chapter 9. As the financial officer, you should watch the prevailing price of the security since it reflects your cost of equity capital. A higher stock price means a lower cost of equity capital and further progress toward the firm's goal of maximizing shareholder wealth.

Common stock, however, tends to have the widest price fluctuations of all the firm's securities, because it has the most uncertainty and the longest life. This means that the stock price will react to cross-currents in economic and capital market conditions and uncertainty in the firm's operating environment. The financial officer cannot hope to control all these factors but should, at least, stay alert to the ever-changing events and their impact on stock price. On the other hand, the stock price does *not* seem to be related to the firm's book value per common share or to its liquidation value in most instances.

Book value/liquidation value Book value is the common stockholders' equity per share, computed as the firm's assets minus its liabilities and preferred stockholders' equity. For example, suppose the stockholders' equity is:

Preferred stock ($100 par, 10,000 shares)	$ 1,000,000
Common stock ($5 par, 1,000,000 shares)	5,000,000
Additional paid-in capital	15,000,000
Retained earnings	10,000,000
Total stockholders' equity	$31,000,000

[1] Par value may be significant in bankruptcy. If the original investors, who first purchased the stock when the corporation was formed, paid the par value, the shares are "fully paid and non-assessable." Subsequent owners' losses are limited to the price they paid for the shares. These latter owners are not liable for the corporation's debt. However, if the original purchasers paid less than the par value, subsequent owners are liable for the firm's debts in bankruptcy up to the amount by which the original price was less than the par value.

Book value per share would be $30; that is, $\dfrac{\$5,000,000 + \$15,000,000 + \$10,000,000}{1,000,000}$.

The significance of book value in the market evaluation of the stock price is nebulous. As an historically based figure, it might not reflect the prevailing market price of the assets if they were sold.

The liquidation value reflects the prevailing market price of the assets if sold, including any goodwill or other intangible assets that may be of value, less liabilities and preferred stock. This is usually considerably less than the book value, particularly if the firm is being dissolved under financial duress.

Pre-emptive rights Under the corporation laws of certain states, pre-emptive rights insure present stockholders an opportunity to subscribe (purchase) any additional shares of common stock before they are offered for sale to others. The objective of the pre-emptive rights law is to preserve the proportional ownership of the present stockholders in the firm. We shall see later in this chapter that the subscription method is commonly used where pre-emptive rights are still part of the corporation's charter. The right exists in only a few states, and even in these it may be omitted from the firm's articles of incorporation at its option. Most firms find preemptive rights cumbersome and prefer to avoid them.

Authorized, issued and outstanding common stock The authorized number of shares is specified in the corporation's charter. The firm cannot exceed that number without amending the charter by a vote of the stockholders.

The issued shares represent the number of authorized shares actually sold. For example, the firm could authorize one million shares but sell any number less than that, keeping the rest for future issues. However, the firm could not sell more than one million shares without the stockholders' first authorizing additional shares.

The outstanding shares are the number of shares issued less any shares reacquired but not retired, known as treasury stock.

Treasury stock Treasury stock is stock reacquired but not cancelled. The firm can keep treasury stock on the books for a considerable length of time and use it for a variety of purposes such as mergers and employee stock options. But these shares are excluded from computation of the firm's earnings per share and other per-share figures, since they are owned by the firm.

Classified and restricted common stock Classified and restricted common stock are different types of common stock in the same company but with different rights. For example, the class A common stock may retain voting rights, while the class B common stock may have no voting rights but is entitled to preferential treatment in the declaration of dividends. The different classes have different rights. These classifications of common stock are generally discouraged for publicly held common stock by the organized stock exchanges, which may not allow a company with a classified common stock to be traded on that exchange, and by the Securities and Exchange Commission. They are not uncommon among privately held companies.

Restricted common stock contains provisions which restrict the typical rights of ownership. For example, the common stock may contain the right of first refusal, which prohibits the owner from selling the common stock to persons other than the present stockholders without first offering them the chance to buy it. Generally, these restrictive provisions are designed to keep control of the firm among the present stockholders.

Shares of beneficial interest Shares of beneficial interest (SBI) are a variation of common stock. The SBI represent stock deposited in a voting trust and give the holder a proportionate interest in the earnings and assets of the firm but no voting rights. For example, the Sutro Mortgage Investment Trust SBI entrust the voting rights to a separate board of trustees and not to the holders.

American depository receipts American Depository Receipts (ADR) are certificates issued by United States banks representing ownership of foreign shares deposited with these banks. For example, the Sony Corporation's ADRs are listed on the New York Stock Exchange. The objective of issuing ADR is to promote American ownership in foreign companies whose governments discourage foreign control. ADRs have no voting rights, and their value generally fluctuates with the value of the underlying shares of the foreign company.

Letter stock Letter stock is unregistered with the Securities and Exchange Commission and therefore cannot be sold to the public. This makes letter stock illiquid. Except for the restriction that it be sold to a private party, the stock is identical to publicly held shares. Although letter stock tends to sell at a lower price than the publicly traded stock, financial officers sometimes use it because it does not have to be registered with the Securities and Exchange Commission and may be sold quickly.

Voting rights Each common share is entitled to one vote in the election of the directors and other matters of concern to them. This vote may be cast in person at the appropriate stockholders' meetings or by *revokable proxy* (Figure 21-2). The proxy is a temporary assignment of the vote to an appointed trustee instructing the trustee how to vote the shares. The proxy is revokable at any time before the formal vote at the annual stockholders' meeting. This means that the stockholder can change his or her voting instructions on subsequently issued proxies or show up at the meeting to vote in person.

While the Securities and Exchange Commission regulates the content of the proxy itself, collecting and processing it is left up to the firm. The firm (or a contracted independent proxy firm) mails and processes the proxies, and the firm bears the cost.

The proxy is accompanied by a proxy statement which contains the pertinent information needed to cast an informed vote. The proxy statement includes the notice of the annual meeting and the voting procedures, such as who is eligible to vote. It also identifies the nominated board of directors and their relationship to the firm, including their stock ownership and their annual renumeration. Other matters of interest to the stockholders are also included for their vote, such as selection of the independent auditors, adoption of an employee's stock option plan, or authorization of additional securities.

Election of directors The election of directors may be conducted under the *cumulative* or the *direct majority* (straight voting) procedure. The cumulative procedure, required in certain states, is designed to distribute more evenly the stockholders' representation on the board of directors. The cumulative process entitles each stockholder to accumulate the voting power equal to the number of shares held times the number of directors to be elected. For example, stockholders who hold 100 shares will have 900 votes if 9 directors are to be elected. They can cast their 900 votes for any individual candidate or split the accumulated voting power among several candidates. By casting their accumulated voting power for any one can-

PROXY — ANDERSON, CLAYTON & CO.

The undersigned, a stockholder in Anderson, Clayton & Co., hereby constitutes and appoints Whitfield H. Marshall, Sydnor Oden, R. W. Sumners and W. W. Vann, and each of them, proxies and attorneys, each with power of substitution, for and in the name of the undersigned, to vote at the Annual Meeting of the Stockholders of Anderson, Clayton & Co., on October 28, 1974, and at any adjournment thereof, the shares of stock of the Company held of record by the undersigned on the record date for the meeting, for the election of directors and

For ☐
Against ☐ ratification of the appointment of Peat, Marwick, Mitchell & Co., as independent auditors,

and on such other matters as may properly come before said meeting, as fully and with like effect as the undersigned might or could do if personally present and voting thereat, hereby revoking all former proxies and ratifying and confirming all that said proxies and attorneys or any of them may lawfully do or cause to be done by virtue hereof.

(Please sign on reverse side)

This proxy is solicited by and on behalf of the management and will be voted as specified by the stockholder in the space provided on the reverse side for balloting. In the absence of such specification by the stockholder, this proxy will be voted in the election of directors and to ratify the appointment of Peat, Marwick, Mitchell & Co. as independent auditors.

Dated .... , 1974

(Signature)

Please sign exactly as name appears stenciled herein. When signing as attorney, executor, administrator, trustee or guardian, please give full title as such. If signer is a corporation, please sign in full corporate name by authorized officer and attach corporate seal.

Figure 21-2 A Typical Proxy

didate for election, a minority has a much better chance of representation on the board.

We can calculate the number of shares required to elect a specific number of directors via the cumulative voting procedure as follows:

$$N = \frac{D^* \times S}{T + 1} + 1 \qquad (21\text{-}1)$$

where

$N =$ the number of shares required to elect the desired number of directors
$D^* =$ the desired number of directors to be elected
$T =$ the total number of directors to be elected
$S =$ the total number of shares outstanding[2]

If, for example, we wanted to elect 1 director of a slate of 9 for a firm with 1 million shares outstanding, we would need:

$$N = \frac{1 \times 1,000,000}{9 + 1} + 1$$

$$= 100,001 \text{ shares.}$$

[2] It may be agreed to define S as the numer of shares voted. Control can then be assured with a smaller number of shares.

If we wanted to elect 2 directors, we would need:

$$N = \frac{2 \times 1,000,000}{9 + 1} + 1$$

$$= 200,001 \text{ shares.}$$

In the direct majority voting procedure, we would need 500,001 shares to insure the election of 1 or any number of directors. Under this procedure 500,001 shares would control the entire firm and could elect the entire slate of directors. In the cumulative procedure minority representation would still be possible even if 50 percent of the shares supported the majority. (In spite of these guidelines, less than 50 percent of the shares is usually sufficient for control of most larger corporations, however the election of directors is arranged.)

Sometimes firms stagger the election of their directors to make it more difficult for dissident blocks of shareholders to elect a majority to the board. Under the staggered procedure, only a portion of the board is elected each time, leaving the remaining members in power. If only 3 members of a 9-member board are elected every year, it takes 3 years for even a majority shareholder under the direct majority voting procedure to elect an entirely new board.

Advantages and Disadvantages

The advantages the financial officer should consider before selecting common stock as a source of long-term funds mainly involve its lack of fixed charges. Since the common stock does not obligate the firm to pay interest or redeem the issue at a maturity date, there is much less financial risk and pressure on the firm. In the extreme, a firm with nothing but common stock in its capital structure has very little chance of being forced into bankruptcy by its creditors. The greater use of common stock also improves the firm's credit rating.

On the other hand, the use of common stock is not without its disadvantages. First, common stock usually has a higher cost of capital than the other securities which can be used to raise long-term funds. It is more costly to sell because of the higher flotation costs connected with the underwriting. Liberal use of common stock can dilute the present stockholders' control as well as the earnings per share (via a proportionately greater increase in the number of shares than in the earnings attributable to the stock sale). A firm entirely financed with common stock has no opportunity to experience positive financial leverage, which could enhance the stock price. Generally, overemphasis on common stock as a source of long-term financing does not maximize shareholders' wealth, which may be the firm's objective.

SUBSCRIPTION RIGHTS

How do you go about selling the common stock, if you choose to use it as a source of long-term financing?

In addition to negotiated or competitive underwriting through the investment banker or a private placement, the financial officer can use subscription rights or specialized venture capital firms, if the firm is small.

Definition

We have already seen that if pre-emptive rights exist, the firm must first offer additional shares to the existing stockholders. This is usually accomplished through the use of subscription rights, although the subscription process may be used even where pre-emptive rights do not exist.

Subscription rights, or just rights for short, are given to the present stockholders on the basis of one right for each share owned. A specified number of rights temporarily entitles the stockholder to buy another share at a specified price, which is usually below the current market price, before a specified expiration date. Obviously, the rights have a value unto themselves since they entitle the holder to purchase shares below the current market price of the stock.

Offering and Selling Procedure

The typical offering and selling procedure is handled through an investment banker, who consults with the firm on arriving at a subscription price in relation to the current market price. A relatively low subscription price means that the firm is more likely to get the present stockholders to subscribe, but the firm has to sell a larger number of shares in order to raise the desired amount of funds. The lower subscription price also means that each right has a greater value.

The investment banker may act solely as an adviser, for a fee, or as an underwriter as well, guaranteeing that all shares will be subscribed even if he or she has to purchase the unsubscribed shares. This is known as a *standby agreement.* The underwriter collects a per-share fee for this standby arrangement.

Alternatively, the firm can bypass the services of the underwriter and conduct the subscription itself. This requires that the firm distribute the rights and solicit the shareholders to exercise them. Typically, self-underwriting requires a lower subscription price than if the services of the investment banker had been obtained.

Temporary Nature of Rights

Subscription rights have a limited period during which they must be exercised or the right becomes invalid. After the *expiration date,* the right is worthless.

The other important date in a subscription offering is the *ex-rights date,* when the stock first trades without the rights attached. Purchase of the stock prior to that date entitles the owner to receive the rights when they are distributed. Purchase of the stock after the ex-rights date does not entitle the stockholder to the rights. They belong to the prior owner. This is much like the ex-dividend date we observed in Chapter 11. For example, if the firm announces on January 1 that the rights will be distributed on March 1 to holders of record as of February 15, the ex-rights date would be 5 business days before, or February 10, if no holidays or weekends intervene. Prior to February 10, the stock is selling "rights on." At the ex-right date the stock price is lowered, reflecting the value of the rights that no longer belong to the stock.

Since the rights are temporary and become worthless after the expiration date, it is advisable to sell them if you do not intend to exercise them. Traditionally, the price of the rights is higher at the beginning of their life than toward their expiration because the opportunity for an increase in their price is limited to a shorter time and more rights owners are selling.

Value of Rights

The market value of the rights can be computed before and after they are detached from the stock. Before detachment the value of the right is:

$$R = \frac{M - S}{N + 1} \qquad (21\text{-}2)$$

where

R = the value of one right
M = the current market price of the stock
S = the subscription price
N = the number of rights required to subscribe to one share

For example, if $M = \$52$, $S = \$45$, and $N = 6$, the value of the right would be:

$$R = \frac{52 - 45}{6 + 1}$$

$$= \$1$$

Each right entitling the owner to purchase one-sixth of one share of stock at the rate of \$45 per share when the stock price is \$52 is worth \$1.

Since the right is worth \$1, while it remains attached to the stock, the value of the stock must be \$1 more. Once the stock goes ex-rights, the price will fall \$1 to \$51, and the investor who owned the stock on or before the ex-rights date will get the right.

We compute the value of the right after it is separated from the stock as follows:

$$R_x = \frac{M_x - S}{N} \qquad (21\text{-}3)$$

where

R_x = the value of the right by itself
M_x = the current market price of the stock, ex-rights
S = the subscription price
N = the number of rights required to buy one share

In our example, the value of the right after the ex-rights date would be:

$$R_x = \frac{\$51 - \$45}{6}$$

$$= \$1$$

Notice that the theoretical value of the right[3] has not changed, nor has the stock-

---

[3] We can see this as:

$$R = \frac{M - R - S}{N}$$

where net value of the one right (R) is subtracted from the market price of the stock (M) to separate the two. Then:

$$R = \frac{M - S}{N + 1}$$

But if R is already removed from M, as in the ex-rights situation, then:

$$R = \frac{M - S}{N}$$

holder gained or lost, because the sum of the value of the right and the stock price, ex-rights, is the same $52 as before. Of course, since the right is now traded as a separate security, its actual market price can deviate from the theoretical value because of supply and demand pressures.

Advantages and Disadvantages

When deciding whether or not to use a rights offering to sell additional shares of common stock, you must consider the advantages and disadvantages. The advantages include retention of the same proportionate ownership as before—if the rights are exercised. Particularly in firms where control is a concern, this consideration may be important. The rights offer typically has lower underwriter fees, although it also may have a lower subscription price than if offered through a negotiated underwriting. The rights offering might encourage stockholder loyalty, as stockholders come to believe you are thinking about their position. Under certain capital market conditions, the rights offering may make it easier to sell the common stock. This has to be decided in consultation with your investment banker. Finally, of course, the rights procedure gives the financial officer one more way to sell securities to raise long-term funds. An alert financial officer never disregards any method or dismisses it out of hand.

The major disadvantage of the rights offering is that the discount below the market price to entice stockholders to exercise the rights is usually considerably more than in the negotiated or competitive underwriting. This means the firm has to sell a greater number of shares to raise any specific amount of capital, and this might further lower earnings per share. The rights offering is also typically more costly than other methods because of the paperwork involved.

Small Business Investment Corporations

Still another alternative method for selling common stock is to deal directly and privately with specialized venture capital firms such as small business investment companies (SBIC). If the firm is relatively small, say under $5 million in assets, and has a riskier-than-average operating position, it may not be able to sell its common stock through the traditional channels. Instead, it might resort to an SBIC, which is specifically chartered by the federal government to provide capital for such firms. The cost is usually very high, and the SBIC may demand a controlling equity position as part of the price. As the financial officer of a firm in need of venture capital, you will have to weigh the need against the costs to decide the firm's appropriate course.

OTHER CONSIDERATIONS

In addition to the factors financial officers must consider in issuing additional shares of common stock, they also have to consider matters which affect the common stock after its issue. These include stock splits, reverse splits, listing on an organized stock exchange, and repurchasing the firm's own shares in the secondary market.

Stock Splits

A stock split is a proportionate increase in the number of shares through the distribution of additional shares to each present stockholder of record at a certain date. For example, if the firm's board of directors decided to split the stock 2 for 1, each present shareholder would then have two shares afterwards instead of one, a doubling of the number of shares held.

The effects of a stock split are (1) a decrease in the stock price on the date the stock is split and (2) a decrease in the par value and a proportional increase in the number of shares, leaving the common stock account on the firm's balance sheet unchanged. For example, if the stock price were $100 before the 2-for-1 split, the after-split stock price would be $50 and the firm's balance sheet would change as follows:

Before the 2-for-1 stock split

Common stock ($10 par, 1,000,000 shares)	$10,000,000
Additional paid-in capital	10,000,000
Retained earnings	10,000,000
Total stockholders' equity	$30,000,000

After the 2-for-1 stock split

Common stock ($5 par, 2,000,000 shares)	$10,000,000
Additional paid-in capital	10,000,000
Retained earnings	10,000,000
Total stockholders' equity	$30,000,000

The reason firms split their stock, despite the fact that it changes little in their financial condition, is to enhance the marketability of the shares. Firms hope to increase the number of shareholders, since some of the present stockholders sell the shares received in the split. The increased number of shares and shareholders may also qualify the firm for listing on an organized stock exchange where the shares may be more actively traded and, as a result, less subject to wide price fluctuations. The lower price may also attract new stockholders who would not otherwise purchase the stock. And some managements believe splitting the stock encourages higher stock prices and provides an image of a healthy, growing firm, particularly if an increase in the firm's dividend accompanies the split.[4]

Reverse Splits

The reverse split is the converse of the stock split. A reverse split proportionately decreases the number of shares outstanding. For example, in a 1-for-2 reverse split, the present owner of 100 shares would have only 50 shares after the split. In the process the par value of the stock would be doubled, but neither the common stock account nor the total stockholders' equity would change.

The reverse split is typically used by firms whose stock price is low and who want to increase it to a more "respectable trading range." The reverse split might even allow them to resume dividends because of the smaller number of shares outstanding.

---

[4] E. F. Fama et al., "The Adjustment of Stock Prices to New Information," *International Economic Review*, February 1969, 1–21. As we saw in Chapter 11 on dividend policy, a firm can achieve the effect of a stock split through a stock dividend.

Listing

Listing is the admission of the stock to trading on an organized stock exchange such as the New York Stock Exchange. To be listed the firm must meet certain listing standards, including a required number of shares and stockholders and a record of a specified number of consecutive years of profit.

The advantages of listing stem mainly from the wider publicity and public attention which accompanies the listing. Because the stock prices of firms listed on organized exchanges are more readily reported in the press and other places, the firm may come to the attention of an increased number of potential stockholders. The prestige of the exchange itself may lend an improved image of stability to the firm, which might be helpful in dealing with other firms. The purchase of the stock on margin (borrowed funds) is also easier for a listed stock. All in all, there is a feeling among many managements that listing may boost the price of the stock because of greater marketability of the shares and greater public recognition.

The disadvantages of listing stem mainly from the additional reporting requirements that may be a condition of listing. However, most of these requirements are becoming common even among unlisted firms.

Repurchase

Sometimes the firm may repurchase its own shares in the secondary market. As the financial officer, you have the option of either purchasing them without a formal announcement, using the services of a stockbroker, or purchasing them with what is known as a tender offer. The *tender offer* is a formal solicitation of the shares at a specified price before a specified expiration date (Figure 21-3).

As the financial officer, when and why should you consider repurchase of the firm's own stock? The most common reason seems to be that the firm considers its stock price "too low." During periods of depressed stock market prices, many firms consider their own stock to be a good investment. It may well be that compared to the other projects available to the firm, stock repurchase is an attractive undertaking.

Sometimes firms repurchase only the stock of smaller shareholders, perhaps twenty-five shares or less, because of the disproportionate administration expenses they cause. By eliminating the small stockholder, the firm can reduce its proxy solicitation expenses, for example, because it has fewer proxies to send out. Sometimes the firm repurchases its own shares in an effort to frustrate an attempt by another corporation to take control. In effect, the firm is outbidding the other corporation for control. Sometimes the firm repurchases its own shares to improve the firm's earnings per share, hoping this will increase the stock price. This strategy is dangerous, for investors may interpret the repurchase as signifying a lack of attractive projects for the firm to consider. Sometimes the firm repurchases its own shares to decrease the proportion of equity in the capital structure or to acquire treasury stock for future use in merger negotiations and employee option plans.

Under certain conditions the firm may use the repurchase of its own shares to lower the tax liability of its stockholders. When the stockholders are a small group of people in a relatively high income tax bracket, the firm may choose to repurchase its shares from them rather than pay a cash dividend. In this way the stockholders get the cash payment, but it is taxed at the lower long-term capital gains rates rather than at the higher ordinary income tax rates. In the meantime those stockholders who do not sell their shares back to the firm should be compensated by the rise in the stock price in response to the decreased number of shares and the higher

This announcement is neither an offer to purchase nor a solicitation of an offer to sell these securities. The offer is made only by the Offer to Purchase mailed to shareholders of Common Stock of Pier 1. Imports, Inc. and is not being made, nor will tenders be accepted from holders of shares of Common Stock in any jurisdiction in which the making or acceptance thereof would not be in compliance with the securities laws of such jurisdiction.

NOTICE OF OFFER TO PURCHASE
500,000 SHARES
OF COMMON STOCK OF
PIER 1. IMPORTS, INC.
AT $7^{50} PER SHARE

Pier 1. Imports, Inc. is offering to purchase 500,000 shares of its Common Stock at $7.50 per share net to the seller in cash, upon the terms and conditions set forth in the Offer to Purchase dated September 18, 1973 and the related Letter of Transmittal. The Offer to Purchase contains important information which should be read before tenders are made.

THE OFFER TO PURCHASE SHARES WILL EXPIRE AT 5:00 P.M. CENTRAL DAYLIGHT TIME, ON OCTOBER 3, 1973, UNLESS EXTENDED.

Payment for all shares duly tendered and purchased will be made as soon as practicable after the expiration of the Offer to Purchase. The Company reserves the right to return all stock tendered if the total number of shares tendered is less than 100,000 shares and if more than 500,000 are tendered, purchases will be prorated.

Offers to Purchase, Letters of Transmittal and the Company's 1973 Annual Report are available from the Company, Pier 1. Imports, Inc., 2520 W. Freeway, Forth Worth, TX.

Figure 21-3 A Share Repurchase Tender Offer

earnings per share. Of course, the tax authorities will question—and may disallow—such a practice if its only justification is tax avoidance.

SUMMARY

After having read Chapter 21, you should be able to answer these questions:

1. What are the major considerations you, as the financial officer, must examine in using preferred stock as a source of long-term funds?

Because of the quasi-debt nature of the preferred stock, you should consider how it fits into your financing strategy. It has the advantages of allowing the firm to omit the dividend and increase its financing flexibility, but it is also more costly, particularly since the preferred dividend is not tax-deductible as is bond interest.

We also saw that the common features of the preferred stock are a par value, protective provisions, and cumulative dividends. Other less common features include redemption, convertibility, voting rights, and participation.

2. What are the major considerations you, as the financial officer, must examine when using common stock as a source of long-term funds?

Since common stock represents the ownership and claim on the residual profits and assets of the firm, the alert financial officer must consider the effect on the control and profits of the firm when using common stock. Too liberal use of common stock may let control pass to another group of stockholders and could dilute the firm's earnings per share.

We saw that common stock has a par or stated value and no maturity date. It does, however, have a market value, a book value, and a liquidation value, although the last two may have little bearing on the first. We also saw that common stock can have pre-emptive rights and can be classified or restricted, although these are relatively rare among publicly held firms and are being discouraged by the regulatory authorities. We also saw variations on the common stock, such as the Share of Beneficial Interest and the American Depository Receipt.

The voting procedure for the election of directors can be cumulative or direct majority. In the former procedure, minority interests stand a much better chance of representation on the board if they pool their votes.

3. How can you, as the financial officer, sell the firm's common stock?

In addition to the underwriting procedures discussed in an earlier chapter, the firm can also use the subscription method. In this method the firm offers its present shareholders the right to subscribe to a limited number of additional shares at a price below the prevailing market price.

These rights, as a consequence, have a value. When the right is still attached to the stock, before the ex-rights date, its value is included in the share price. After the right is detached from the stock, the value of the right remains the same and the stock price is adjusted downward to reflect the detachment. If the right is not exercised before the expiration date, it becomes worthless.

The typical selling procedure for rights is for the firm to have an investment banker underwrite the offering, agreeing to purchase any unsubscribed shares, in exchange for a fee. This is known as a standby agreement.

4. What are some of the situations you may be asked about the firm's common stock after it has been sold?

These situations include stock splits, reverse splits, listing, and repurchase. All affect the stock price in the secondary market, yet all are under the control of the firm's management.

QUESTIONS

21-1 Enumerate some of the similarities between (a) preferred stock and long term debt, and (b) preferred and common stock.

21-2 From the firm's viewpoint, what are some of the major advantages and disadvantages of preferred stock?

21-3 What does the par value of preferred stock represent? The par value of common stock?

21-4 Suppose a firm has 500,000 shares of common stock outstanding, $10 par value, that was sold for $15 per share. Illustrate the common stock and additional paid-in-capital accounts below:

Common stock ($10 par value) 500,000 shares	$
Additional paid-in capital	$
Total common stock and additional paid-in capital	$

21-5 May a preferred stock be both cumulative and convertible?

21-6 Distinguish between authorized, issued, and outstanding common stock. Under what conditions will they be the same? Different?

21-7 From the firm's viewpoint, what are some of the major advantages and disadvantages of common stock?

21-8 Explain briefly the meaning of the following terms:
  (a) Subscription right   (c) Ex-right date
  (b) Standby agreement   (d) "rights on"

21-9 From the firm's viewpoint, what is the difference between a 2-for-1 common stock split and a 100 percent stock dividend? From the stockholders' viewpoint?

PROBLEMS

21-1 Calculate the book value of a firm with the following stockholder equity accounts:

Preferred stock ($100 par; 50,000 shares)	$ 5,000,000
Common stock ($10 par; 5,000,000 shares)	50,000,000
Additional paid-in capital	25,000,000
Retained earnings	20,000,000
Total stockholder equity	$100,000,000

21-2 A group of dissatisfied stockholders of Bolcon Company would like to obtain majority representation on the firm's board of directors, which has eleven members. Bolcon has 500,000 common shares outstanding.
  (a) If the board of directors are elected under the direct majority procedure, how many shares must the group control to elect its six board members?
  (b) If the board of directors are elected under the cumulative majority procedure, how many shares must the group control to elect its six board members?
  (c) Suppose four of the existing board members are in full agreement with the dissatisfied group of stockholders. Under the cumulative majority procedure how many shares must the group control to elect two new board members? (Assume the four existing board members are assured of reelection.)

21-3 Nast Company announced on June 6 that subscription rights would be distributed on August 15 to holders of record as of August 1. The subscription price of the new common stock is $30, and four rights are required to subscribe to one new share. On July 1, the market price of existing common is $35.
  (a) What is the ex-rights date?
  (b) What is the value of the subscription right on July 1?
  (c) What is the value of the subscription right after the ex-rights date?

21-4 Suppose the stockholders' equity accounts of a firm are currently as follows:

Preferred stock ($100 par; 20,000 shares)	$ 2,000,000
Common stock ($20 par; 1,000,000 shares)	20,000,000
Additional paid-in capital	20,000,000
Retained earnings	5,000,000
Total stockholders' equity	$47,000,000

(a) Illustrate the effects on the above accounts if the firm declares a 4-for-1 common stock split. The common stock price before the split is $40.

(b) If the firm announces a reverse stock split of 1-for-3, illustrate the effect on the above accounts. (Ignore Problem (a).)

(c) When might a firm consider it advantageous to declare a common stock split? A reverse split?

BIBLIOGRAPHY

Donaldson, Gordon. "Financial Goals: Management vs. Stockholders." *Harvard Business Review*, 41 (May–June 1963), 116–129.

———. "In Defense of Preferred Stock." *Harvard Business Review*, 40 (July–August 1972), 123–136.

Elsaid, Hussein H. "The Function of Preferred Stock in the Corporate Financial Plan." *Financial Analyst's Journal* (July–August 1969), 112–117.

Fisher, Donald E., and Glenn A. Wilt, Jr. "Nonconvertible Preferred Stock as a Financing Instrument, 1950–1965." *Journal of Finance*, XXIII (September 1968), 611–624.

Furst, Richard W. "Does Listing Increase the Market Price of Common Stocks?" *Journal of Business*, 43 (April 1970), 174–180.

Pinches, George E. "Financing With Convertible Preferred Stock, 1960–1967." *Journal of Finance*, XXV (March 1970), 53–63.

Sametz, Arnold W. "Trends in the Volume and Composition of Equity Financing." *Journal of Finance*, XIX (September 1964), 450–469.

Sprecher, C. Ronald. "A Note on Financing Mergers with Convertible Preferred Stock," *Journal of Finance*, XXVI (June 1971), 683–686.

Thompson, Howard E. "A Note on the Value of Rights in Estimating the Investor Capitalization Rate." *Journal of Finance*, XXVIII (March 1973), 157–160.

Williams, Charles M. *Cumulative Voting for Directors*. Graduate School of Business Administration, Harvard University, Boston, 1951.

22

CONVERTIBLE SECURITIES AND WARRANTS

CONVERTIBLE SECURITIES ARE A SPECIAL CASE in long-term financing because of their unusual nature. They allow the holder to convert the original, more senior security into the common stock of the firm. In evaluating convertible securities as a source of long-term funds, what major considerations must you, as the firm's financial officer, examine to be sure that their use is appropriate? We shall see that the financial officer must analyze the convertible security as both a bond and as a common stock. You must also consider the unique advantages and disadvantages of this special kind of security. It is an alternative source of long-term funds which the financial officer must use wisely. In fact, we shall see that because of these special features, the convertible security is a very useful tool in negotiating lower capital costs and more flexible indenture provisions.

The warrant is another special type of security sometimes used in raising long-term funds. As an adjunct to another security used to facilitate fund-raising, the warrant adds still another tool to the financial officer's negotiating kit. Before you can use the warrant effectively, however, what major considerations must you examine? Like all securities, the warrant has advantages and disadvantages which must be examined before you can be certain it is appropriate for any particular financing effort. And, as in the case of the convertible securities, the financial officer must know how to analyze the warrant, in order to determine if investors actually will be more attracted to the fund-raising effort because of its presence. It does the firm very little good to offer a warrant which does nothing for the sale of the security to which it is attached. It is your job, as the financial officer, to see that such an error does not occur and to insure that the use of the warrant in the firm's long-term financing plans is appropriate.

CONVERTIBLE SECURITIES

A convertible security is a bond or a preferred stock which, at the option of the holder, may be exchanged for the common stock of the company during a specific period at a predetermined price. Since convertible bonds are more numerous than convertible preferred stocks and since the principles of the analysis are the same for each, we will couch our discussion in terms of convertible bonds only.

The Ashland Oil and Refining convertible subordinated debenture 4¾s due 20 years from now are an example of the convertible bond. This convertible debenture has all the features of a regular subordinated debenture (see Chapter 20) with the additional provision that the holder has the option of exchanging the debenture bond for 20 shares of Ashland Oil and Refining common stock at $50 a share (the conversion price) until maturity. The holder does not have to convert and may continue to treat the debenture as a straight bond, collecting 4¾ percent interest on the face value every year until the bond is redeemed at par by Ashland Oil and Refining 20 years from now. Hence the convertible security combines features of the common stock and the straight bond and takes its value from both. Accordingly, as the financial officer, you must consider the impact of convertible debt financing on both the common stock *and* the long-term debt of the firm.

Analyzing the Convertible Bond

The convertible bond has three separate values which we, as financial officers, must analyze. These are (1) the conversion value, which reflects the worth of the bond as if it had been exchanged for the associated common stock, (2) the straight bond value as if the bond had no conversion option; and (3) the actual market price of the bond for which it is presently selling.

Conversion value The conversion value reflects the value of the bond as if it had already been exchanged for the associated common stock. Since the holder of the convertible security has the option of converting into the associated common stock at any time when the conversion privilege is in force, the security must be evaluated as if it were exchanged for the common.

Since the Ashland bond in our example allows the holder to convert into the common stock at $50 a share, each $1,000 par-value bond can be exchanged for 20 shares of the associated stock. This is computed by simply dividing the conversion price of $50 into the $1,000 par value of the bond:

$$N = \frac{\text{par}}{CP} \tag{22-1}$$
$$= \frac{\$1,000}{\$50}$$
$$= 20 \text{ shares}$$

where
  N = the number of shares into which the bond is convertible
  par = the par value of the bond
  CP = the conversion price

Owning the bond is equivalent to owning 20 shares of the common stock, since the bondholder can convert at any time.

The conversion value is, therefore, the number of shares into which the bond can be converted times the price per share:

$$CV = N \times P \tag{22-2}$$

where
  CV = the conversion value
  N = the number of shares into which the bond is convertible
  P = the prevailing price per common share

For example, if the prevailing price (P) were $60, the conversion value of the Ashland bond would be:

$$CV = 20 \times \$60$$
$$= \$1,200$$

Notice that the conversion value is above the par value. As the prevailing price of the associated common stock increases, the bond's conversion value also increases because the number of shares into which it is convertible (N) remains constant. Of course, the reverse is also true. When the prevailing price of the associated common stock decreases, the conversion value decreases. In our example, the conversion price rises and falls by a factor of 20: for each $1 fluctuation in the stock price, the bond's conversion value fluctuates $20.[1]

Bond value   The Ashland Oil and Refining convertible debenture bond also has a value independent of the conversion value, because it is still a bond with a promised stream of interest payments and a promised return of principal at maturity. Disregarding the conversion value for a moment, the bond would sell like any other bond without a conversion feature. As interest rates rose, the bond value would decline, and as interest rates fell, the bond value would rise. For example, if the Ashland 4¾s bond had no conversion feature, it would have a straight bond value of $761.64 $\left(\text{the present value of } \sum_{t=1}^{20} \frac{\$47.50}{(1.07)^t} + \frac{\$1000}{(1.07)^{20}}\right)$, when the prevailing required rate of return (yield to maturity) on bonds of this maturity and risk was 7 percent. If the required rate of return rose above 7 percent, its value as a straight bond would fall still further from the par value.

Market value   The market value is the prevailing price of the convertible bond as it actually exists in the bond market. It represents the price as of the last transaction between a buyer and a seller of the bond. The market price has to be at least as high as the higher of either the conversion value or the bond value. If the market price were below the conversion value, *arbitrageurs* (investors who look for discrepancies in prices between equivalent securities) would buy the bonds, exchange them for the associated common stock, and sell the stock for a profit, assuming transactions costs did not make the arbitrage unprofitable. The arbitrageurs would continue this process as long as it remained profitable; in so doing, they would force up the price of the bond by their buying pressure and force down the price of the stock by their selling pressure until the bond sold at its conversion value. We can see how this type of arbitrage would be profitable if, for example, the Ashland common stock were selling at $60 a share, but the market price of the bond was only $1,100. The arbitrageur would buy the bond for $1,100 and convert it into 20 shares of common stock for a conversion value of $1,200, collecting a $100 profit when the 20 shares sold at $60 each. Furthermore the whole process of buying the bond, converting it,

---

[1] Other features that may affect the conversion value are the antidilution provision and a variable conversion price. The antidilution provision insures that if the price of the common stock is caused to fall by an administrative action on the part of the firm, such as a stock split, stock dividend, or a rights offering, the conversion price will also be adjusted to insure that the conversion value is not adversely affected. For example, if the firm split its common stock 2 for 1 and the $50 market price became $25, the antidilution provision changes the conversion price from $50 to $25, and the number of shares into which the convertible bond can be exchanged would double. Some convertible bonds have variable conversion prices such that the conversion price usually rises over the life of the bond.

and selling the common stock takes only a few minutes, so as long as the arbitrage opportunity remains profitable, the arbitrageur will continue the process.

On the other hand, if the conversion value option were inoperative such that the price of the associated common stock is less than the conversion price, no arbitrage opportunity would exist. If the prevailing price of the common stock were $30 a share, no one would want to buy the bond with the right of converting at $50 a share. Why should the investor pay more for common stock than the prevailing price?

At a $30 common stock price, the bond's conversion value would be only $600 ($30 × 20 shares). Yet, assuming that the required rate of return from this bond without the conversion feature is 7 percent, we saw that as a straight bond it would still be worth $761.64—more than the conversion value. Obviously bond investors will not let the market price of the bond fall below $761.64 for any length of time, for they will snap it up as a bargain.

The higher of either the prevailing conversion value or the straight bond value will be the floor below which the market value cannot fall.[2] If the market price should temporarily slip below the conversion value, arbitrageurs would almost immediately force it back up. If the market price should temporarily slip below the straight bond value, bond investors will force it back up.

Typically, however, the market value of the convertible security is above both the straight bond value and the conversion value. Our Ashland Oil and Refining convertible bond sells at $1,250, $50 above the conversion value. This difference between the conversion value and the market price is known as the conversion premium. Even if the conversion option were inoperative, as for example when the stock price of Ashland common was $30, the market price would probably still be above the $761.64 straight bond value.

Conversion premium[3]   Investors are willing to pay a slight premium over either the conversion value or the straight bond value, whichever is larger. This willingness exists partly because ownership of the convertible bond is relatively less risky than direct ownership of the associated common stock. Even if the stock price falls well below the conversion price, making the conversion value very low, the market price of the bond will not sink as far, because the straight bond value will act as a floor to support the price. For example, if the market price of the Ashland Oil and Refining common stock sank from $50 to $30 a share, a 40 percent decline, the conversion value would fall from $1,000 to $600, but the market price of the bond would not fall any farther than the straight bond value. In our example, the market price would not sink below the straight bond value of $761.64. This would be a decline in the market price from $1,000 to $761.64, or only a 24 percent, compared to the 40 percent decline in the conversion value and the associated common stock. Investors are willing to pay a premium for that reduction in downside risk.

At the same time that investors get this bond value support which limits the downside risk, they also get an upside potential equal to that of the associated common stock when the stock price exceeds the conversion price. For example, if the stock price of Ashland Oil and Refining rose above the conversion price of $50 a share to $60, the conversion value would rise from $1,000 to $1,200, or 20 percent.

---

[2] Note that the straight bond floor can also fluctuate as the required interest rate on this bond rises and falls.

[3] E. F. Brigham, "An Analysis of Convertible Debentures: Theory and Some Empirical Evidence," *Journal of Finance*, XXI (March 1966), 35–54.

The market price of the convertible would also have to rise 20 percent, from $1,000 to $1,200, since arbitrageurs force the bond to sell at least as high as its conversion value. This upside potential, coupled with the limited downside risk, make investors willing to pay the conversion premium.

The convertible bond usually has a higher current income from the interest payment than from the equivalent investment in the associated common stock, making it more attractive for investors to hold the bond than the associated common stock while waiting for the anticipated price appreciation. For example, if the market price of the bond were $1,000, the owner of one bond would receive $47.50 in interest payments each year. The same $1,000 invested in the associated common stock at the prevailing price of $33.25 a share would purchase only 30 shares. At the prevailing annual dividend per share of $1.30, investors in the associated common would receive only $39 in dividends each year as compared to $47.50 in interest payments, for the same $1,000 investment.

Graphic presentation of the three values[4]   We can see the relationship between the conversion value, the bond value, and the market value in Figure 22-1. The market price lies above both the conversion value and the bond value by the amount of the conversion premium, as represented by the shaded area portion of the graph. When the bond value is greater than the conversion value, to the left of point *q* at the intersection of the bond value and the conversion value, the conversion premium lies above the bond value. This is representative of the straight bond floor support. To the right of point *q*, the conversion premium lies above the conversion value floor.

Notice that the conversion premium is not constant. It first increases and then decreases as the stock price rises. The rise in the conversion premium can be attributed to the increasing profit potential which accompanies the rising stock price. As the stock price approaches and exceeds the conversion price, the market price of the bond has to rise.

After a certain point, however, when the conversion value floor has lifted the market price well above the straight bond floor and the redemption price (usually close to $1,000), the conversion premium decreases. In terms of the Ashland Oil and Refining convertible debenture bond, the conversion premium shrinks as the stock price approaches and exceeds the $50 a share conversion price, as illustrated in Figure 22-1. This shrinkage occurs primarily because the downside risk protection from the straight bond value diminishes as the stock price rises. The market price and conversion value rise because of the increased stock price, and the bond floor falls farther and farther away from them. This means that if the stock price should recede, the market value of the bond can have a substantial downside movement before its fall is stopped by the straight bond value support level.

The dividend on the common stock may have increased since the bond was purchased, while the interest payment on the bond has remained contractually fixed. The annual dividend income may now actually exceed the annual interest income to investors, and they are no longer as willing to pay the conversion premium. The bond's advantage of offering a larger income while waiting for the expected price appreciation has vanished.

The fear of a forced call at a price lower than the prevailing market price also makes investors unwilling to pay a conversion premium, causing the observed decrease in that premium as the bond's market price exceeds the call price. If the

[4] *Ibid.*

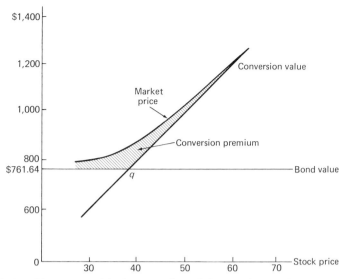

Figure 22-1   Relationship Among Market, Bond, and Conversion Values

bond, for example, is called at the firm's option at $1,000 when its market price is $1,200, the investor can either submit the bond for redemption and suffer a $200 loss or convert into the stock for the conversion value. If the conversion value is less than the market price of the bond, as it is if a conversion premium exists, the investor loses the difference, which *is* the conversion premium. Since the possibility of a call increases as the stock price rises, investors are no longer as willing to pay a conversion premium because of the increased fear of suffering a loss from a call. This is observed in Figure 22-1 as the narrowing of the call premium at the higher common stock prices.

The nearness of the call may be judged by the degree to which the conversion value exceeds the call price in conjunction with the firm's need for additional capital. When a firm with outstanding convertible bonds wishes to expand its equity base so that it can sell additional debt, it can call the convertible bond for redemption. If the conversion value is greater than the redemption price, bondholders are forced to convert into the common stock or suffer a loss. This forced conversion decreases the firm's debt and increases the firm's number of outstanding shares and equity. Of course, if the conversion value is less than the redemption price, the firm gains nothing by calling the convertible security because none of the investors will convert; instead, they will all submit their bonds for redemption. As the possibility of a forced conversion increases, investors become less willing to pay a conversion premium for fear of losing that amount in the redemption call.[5]

---

[5] The conversion premium may also be influenced because margin requirements (down payments) on convertible bonds are typically less than on common stock. The transactions costs of buying and selling the convertible bond are typically less than those on a common stock. The length of the conversion option remaining (a longer life encourages a higher premium) and the prohibition of financial institutions on buying the common stock but not the bond also influence the conversion premium. See R. L. Weil, Jr., J. E. Segall, and D. Green, Jr., "Premiums on Convertible Bonds," *Journal of Finance,* June 1968, 445–464.

Advantages and Disadvantages of Convertible Bonds[6]

The primary advantage of convertible bonds to you, the financial officer, is their use as an indirect source of equity financing. Because the convertible bond remains as debt on the firm's balance sheet until the firm forces its conversion, the time lag between sale of the security and realization of earnings from the project financed by that sale does not cause an unreasonable drop in the reported earnings per share.[7] Since there is frequently a period between the financing and the commencement of the project, you may find that convertible debt allows you to raise the necessary funds without selling additional shares, diluting the earnings per share and perhaps jeopardizing the dividend during the lag. You can use the convertible bond as a less expensive source of funds until the project comes on full steam and then force conversion into the common stock.

Convertible bonds can aid your financing effort. If the bond market or the stock market is unreceptive, for example, to new common stock or a straight bond, you might find that a bond with a convertible feature as a *sweetener* would be more warmly received. You might even be able to negotiate a lower interest rate and/or less restrictive indenture provisions by adding the conversion feature. And, by selling a convertible bond instead of stock, you open up an entirely new market for your securities, because financial institutions which may be prohibited by law from buying your stock can buy your convertible bonds.

The cost of capital for the convertible bond is also less than that of the firm's equity capital. This is partly due to the senior position of the convertible bond over the common stock, but mostly due, as we have seen, to the fact that interest payments on the convertible bond are tax-deductible.

Still other advantages to the convertible bond are the lower underwriters' fees on bonds and the higher conversion price received than that which prevails on the common stock at the time of offering. For example, if the common stock is temporarily depressed at say $30 a share, rather than sell the stock at that price, the firm can sell convertible bonds with a conversion price of $35 a share. In effect, when the stock price recovers and the firm forces conversion, the firm has sold the stock at $35 a share, or $5 more than it could have received for it at the time of the offering. Of course, if the stock price does not recover, the firm cannot force the conversion and there is no advantage to be gained.

Convertible bonds are not without their disadvantages, however. First, they are a source of potential dilution in the firm's earnings per share as the bonds are exchanged for common stock. For example, if $2 million of 9 percent convertible bonds were exchanged for 100,000 shares of stock, the effect on earnings per share of a hypothetical firm would be:

	Before conversion	After conversion
Earnings before interest and taxes	$2,000,000	$2,000,000
Interest	180,000	—
Earnings before taxes	1,820,000	2,000,000
Taxes (50%)	910,000	1,000,000
Earnings after taxes	910,000	1,000,000
Shares outstanding	500,000	600,000
Earnings per share	$1.82	$1.67

Notice that conversion has lowered the earnings per share because of the increased number of shares, but the fall has been cushioned by the decline in the interest cost which accompanied the conversion, since the firm no longer had to pay interest on those bonds. The exact impact on the price of the common stock is not clear, because at the time of the initial offering of the bonds investors will most likely have already treated the earnings per share as if the conversion had already occurred—and valued the common stock accordingly.

There is always the danger that the convertible bonds will "overhang" and interfere with future financing plans. If the price of the associated common stock does not rise sufficiently to allow the firm to force conversion, the convertible bond remains as a debt obligation until redeemed. Obviously this is not what the firm intended when it sold the convertible debt; it had every intention of forcing conversion. With this overhanging convertible bond, the financial officer can neither broaden the firm's equity base through forced conversion nor sell additional debt. A substantial amount of financial flexibility has been lost.

Negotiating with Convertible Bonds

Convertible bonds provide you with yet another tool in your negotiations with suppliers of long-term funds. You can bargain a lower interest rate or less restrictive covenants in exchange for adding the conversion option to the bond or lowering the conversion price if the option is already included in the proposed offering. With a lower conversion price, suppliers of long-term capital feel there is a greater chance for realizing part of their required return through price appreciation and are often willing to reduce the interest. For example, if the prevailing common stock price were $50 a share, the chance of profit through price appreciation is greater if the conversion price is $51 a share rather than $60 a share. In the former case, the associated stock price has to rise only $1 before the conversion feature is of value. Since lenders are willing to take their required return in either price appreciation or interest, they are likely to accept a lower interest rate at the lower conversion price.

If you, as the financial officer, can convince suppliers that the price potential for the stock is great and that they can make their return through capital appreciation instead of interest, they will settle for a lower interest cost. For example, if they are convinced that there will be an average 2 percent annual increase in the conversion value until the bond is called, they will be willing to accept a 2 percent lower annual interest rate, ignoring tax considerations, if you bargain correctly. It is up to you to bargain correctly.

WARRANTS

What are the major considerations that you, as the financial officer, must weigh when using warrants as part of your long-term financing strategy? How do you analyze warrants and what are the advantages and disadvantages attached to their

---

[6] J. B. Cohen and S. M. Robbins, *The Financial Manager*, Harper and Row, New York, 1966, pp. 598–599.

[7] The accounting treatment does, however, require that the earnings per share on a fully diluted basis be reported as if the convertible bonds had already been converted. The firm's primary earnings per share do not have to reflect this potential conversion unless the current yield at the time of issue was equal to or less than $66\frac{2}{3}$ percent of the then-prevailing prime rate. See Accounting Principles Board Opinion Number 15.

use? Once you have weighed all these considerations, where do the warrants fit into a firm's financial planning?

Definition

A *warrant* is an option to purchase a specific number of common shares at a specified, predetermined price before a given expiration date, if any. For example, the Greyhound Corporation warrants allow the owner the option to purchase one share of Greyhound common stock at $23.50 a share until May 14, 1980.

The *exercise price*, which in our example is $23.50, is typically fixed over the life of the warrant, though there are warrants with variable exercise prices. The North Central Airlines warrant, for instance, has an exercise price which, at the option of the firm, can be lowered from $5.50 to $4.50 a share. Other options have exercise prices which rise at predetermined future dates.

The warrant also specifies the number of shares which it entitles the owner to purchase. The Greyhound warrant entitles the owner to purchase one share, while other warrants may entitle the owner to purchase only a fraction of one share or several shares. The life of the warrant can vary from a few days as it approaches expiration to an indefinite life with no expiration date. For example, the TriContinental warrant entitles the owner to purchase 3.28 shares of the TriContinental common stock at $8.87 a share forever.

The warrant does not entitle the owner to participate in the declared cash dividends, but the typical warrant does participate in larger stock dividends and stock splits. This participation is formalized in the anti-dilution provision of the warrant. For example, if the associated common stock is split two shares for every share held (a 2-for-1 stock split), the number of shares which the warrant can buy is doubled and the exercise price is halved.

Most warrants come into existence as a sweetener to a stock or bond issue, much as the conversion feature sweetens the bond. The added attraction of possible profit as the price of the associated common stock rises allows you, the financial officer, to negotiate better terms. The warrant is then detached (sold separately) from the bond or the stock and assumes a value all its own, although in a few instances the warrant is not detachable from the bond, and the two must be sold together as one security.

Evaluating Warrants

Like the convertible bond, the warrant has a theoretical value and a market value (price). The two do not always have to agree, and in most instances the market price is above the theoretical price because of the associated premium. The market price, on the other hand, rarely if ever sinks below the theoretical value.

The theoretical value can be determined as follows:

$$V = (P - O)N \tag{22-3}$$

where
V = the warrant's theoretical value
P = the prevailing market price of the associated common stock
O = the exercise price
N = the number of shares that can be bought with one warrant

For example, if the prevailing market price of the associated common stock (P) is

$30, the exercise price ($O$) is $25, and the number of shares that could be purchased (N) is 1, then the theoretical value of that warrant would be:

$$V = (\$30 - \$25)1$$
$$= \$5.00$$

The market value, however, is typically higher than that theoretical value. The difference between the two is known as the *premium*. For example, if our warrant sold at $7.00 instead of the theoretical $5.00 just computed, the premium would be $2.00. The market price could be any premium above the theoretical value dictated by the supply and demand pressures among the warrant's buyers and sellers, but it could never fall below the theoretical value. If the market price did temporarily fall below the theoretical value, the same arbitrageurs who operated in the convertible bond market would buy the warrant, exercise it for the common shares, and sell the shares for a profit until the warrant's market price was at least above the theoretical value. For example, if our warrant sold at $4.00 each while the theoretical value was $5.00, arbitrageurs would buy the warrant for $4.00, purchase the stock for $25, and sell the stock for $30, making a profit of $1.00 for each warrant, excluding transactions costs. They would continue the process until the profit opportunity disappeared or until there were no more warrants to purchase.

The premium exists mainly because the warrants offer leverage to investors. A greater number of warrants can be purchased for the same dollar investment than in the associated common stock, yet the price appreciation potential of the warrant is proportionally more once the exercise price is exceeded. For example, in our illustrative case the market price of the associated common stock is $30 a share and the warrant's value is $5.00 each. A lump sum of $10,000 would buy either 333 common shares or 2,000 warrants. As the market price of the stock rises past the $25 exercise price, the theoretical value, which is the lowest price the warrant can sell for, rises dollar for dollar with the stock. If the stock rose to $31 a share, the warrant's value would rise to $6.00. The worth of the 333 common shares would now be $10,333, while the worth of the 2,000 warrants would now be $12,000. Obviously, the warrants' leverage has caused a more rapid increase in the investment. In this case, the stock value increased 3.3 percent while the warrant value increased 20 percent— about six times as much. Of course the downside risk is equally magnified. If the stock price had dropped $1 instead of rising $1, the 333 common shares would have declined only $333, but the warrant investment would have declined $2,000.

The premium, however, does not remain constant as the warrant's theoretical value changes. Figure 22-2 illustrates that the premium shrinks as the theoretical value increases. The reasons for this premium behavior are the diminution of the leverage and the forfeiture of the declared cash dividends by the warrant. As the warrant value rises the leverage factor disappears, and investors who were previously willing to pay the premium because of the leverage are no longer willing to do so. For example, if the stock price of our hypothetical example had risen to $100 a share from the previous $30 a share, the warrant's value would be:

$$V = (\$100 - \$25)1$$
$$= \$75$$

The same $10,000 lump-sum investment would now buy only 100 common shares or 133 warrants, a significantly smaller spread between the two and an almost total loss of leverage. Now a $1 price rise in the stock leads to a $100 jump in the value of the shares and only a slightly higher $133 jump in the value of the warrants. This is much different from before when the stock was selling at $30 a share, and a $1

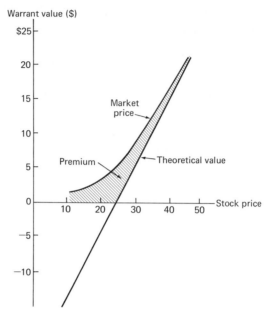

Figure 22-2   Relationship of The Warrant's Market Price to Its Theoretical Value

increase in the price jumped the warrant investment almost 7 times as much as the common stock investment.

The premium also shrinks as the theoretical value rises, because in most instances the cash dividends to higher priced stocks are relatively large in absolute dollar terms. This means that the warrant holder is forfeiting substantial dividend income without gaining much leverage. Investors begin to think twice and wonder if the dividend sacrifice is worth the relatively small amount of leverage they gain by buying the warrants. The answer is probably no, and they become less willing to pay a premium for the opportunity to forfeit the dividend.

While the premium shrinks as the theoretical value rises, the exact size of the premium for any given warrant at any corresponding point on the theoretical value line in Figure 22-2 depends on the remaining life of the warrant, the size of the forfeited dividend, the volatility of the associated common stock, and the prevailing interest rates. As the warrant's life increases, there is a greater probability that the associated common stock price may actually increase, forcing up the price of the warrant as well. It is just common sense that a warrant with only a few days before expiration does not stand the same chance of appreciating in price as does a warrant with years remaining before it expires.

We have already seen that as the size of the forfeited dividend increases, the premium shrinks. As the volatility of the associated common stock increases, the premium also increases. Increased volatility means that the associated stock price has a better chance of rising sometime during the life of the warrant, making the warrant more valuable. Investors are willing to pay a premium for this increased chance of price appreciation. Finally, the premium shrinks as interest rates rise, because the opportunity cost of holding a non-income-producing warrant when high yielding investments are available increases.

Advantages and Disadvantages

Before financial officers use warrants, they must weigh their advantages and disadvantages. The basic use of the warrant is as a sweetener to facilitate the sale of the firm's bonds and the financial officer's negotiations. When offered in conjunction with the sale of other securities, the warrant adds an attractive feature which may lead some otherwise uninterested parties to buy the bond. This is particularly true of those lenders who like an opportunity to participate in the equity position of the firm without buying the common stock.

There are other advantages. When the warrant is exercised, additional funds flow into the firm. In effect the firm has sold additional common stock, enlarged its equity base, and financed some of its expansion. The warrant also has a tax advantage to the firm. The warrant portion of the debt issue can be deducted from the debt principal and amortized over the life of the bond. This allows the firm a tax deduction of debt principal, something which cannot be accomplished with straight debt.

Finally, the firm can specify the par value of the bond to which the warrant was originally attached, as payment for the common stock when the warrant is exercised. The investor can present the bond with the warrant and receive the common stock. This has the effect of reducing the debt and increasing the equity. A growing firm may find this very helpful in its financing plans.

The warrant is not without disadvantages. If the warrant is exercised for cash, the debt to which it was originally attached remains a liability of the firm, unlike the convertible bond which disappears from the firm's liability when exchanged for the common stock. Warrants can cause dilution in the firm's reported earnings per share. Under the prevailing accounting rules, warrants must be considered as if they had been exercised in computing the firm's primary earnings per share. This can lead to lower reported earnings per share.

Negotiating with Warrants

Much like the convertible feature discussed earlier, the warrant can be used by the financial officer to negotiate a lower interest rate or less restrictive covenants. If you, as the financial officer, can convince the lenders that the stock price will rise above the exercise price, you can trade off either the inclusion of a warrant or a lower exercise price of an included warrant for better terms.

Sometimes the warrant is very helpful in merger negotiations. For example, when Loews acquired Lorillard, it used a warrant and cash instead of additional common stock in the exchange. The effect was to eliminate the dilution of earnings per share that usually occurs with a merger when common shares are exchanged. In fact, in this case the earnings per share of Loews actually rose because so few additional shares were issued. It also assured control of the combined firm to Loews, for the Lorillard holders received no new shares in the surviving corporation.

SUMMARY

After having read Chapter 22, you should be able to answer these questions:

1. What are the major considerations that you, as the financial officer, must weigh when using convertible securities as a source of long-term funds?

A convertible security really has three values which you have to consider. First, the conversion value reflects the value of the security as if it had already been exchanged for the associated common stock. Second, the straight bond value reflects the value as if the bond had been sold without the conversion feature. Third, the actual market price depends on supply and demand pressures for the security. The difference between the market price and the higher of either the conversion value or the straight bond value is known as the conversion premium.

The conversion premium exists because convertible securities offer the investor some downside risk protection without impairing his upside price appreciation potential. Yet the conversion premium shrinks as the dividend on the associated common stock increases. The downside risk protection diminishes, and the chance of a forced conversion increases.

2. What are the advantages and the disadvantages of using convertible bonds?

The advantages are: the indirect equity financing, facilitation of the bond sale, the tax deductibility of the interest payment, and lower underwriting commissions than common stock. The disadvantages of the convertible bond are its dilution of earnings per share and its possible overhang.

3. How can the financial officer use the special features of the convertible bond in negotiations with suppliers of long-term capital?

In exchange for including the conversion feature or lowering the conversion price, the financial officer can bargain a lower interest rate or less restrictive indenture terms.

4. What are the major considerations that a financial officer has to weigh when using warrants in long-term financing plans?

Like the convertible bond, the warrant has a theoretical value and a market price which do not have to agree. The difference between the two is known as the premium. Investors are willing to pay this premium because of the leverage inherent in most warrants. However, as the leverage factor starts to disappear with the increase in the theoretical value, investors are less willing to pay this premium and it, too, starts to disappear.

The size of the premium at any given theoretical value can vary among warrants with the size of the forfeited dividend, the volatility of the associated common stock, the level of interest rates, and the life of the warrant.

5. What are the advantages and the disadvantages of using warrants?

The advantages stem from facilitation of the bond or stock sale to which the warrants were attached, the tax deductibility of the warrant portion of the debt principal, and the additional funds generated when the warrant was exercised. Warrants sometimes offer advantages in negotiating mergers and better terms for bonds. The major disadvantage is retention of the bond as a liability of the firm when the warrant is exercised.

QUESTIONS

22-1 Briefly explain the differences between the conversion value, market value, and bond value of a convertible bond. Do the same for a convertible preferred.

22-2 Why must the market price of a convertible bond be at least equal to the higher of the conversion value or the straight bond value?

22-3 What is the conversion premium of a convertible bond? What are some of the main reasons such premiums exist?

22-4 Existing empirical evidence suggests that the conversion premium diminishes rapidly when the market price of the convertible bond exceeds the call price. What would account for this observation?

22-5 Consider Figure 22-1.

(a) What will happen to the bond value line if the general level of interest rates increases?

(b) What determines the slope of the conversion value line?

22-6 What are warrants and how are they principally used by the firm?

22-7 Briefly explain the difference between the theoretical value, market value, and premium of a warrant.

22-8 Why does the warrant premium decrease as the theoretical value of the warrant further exceeds the prevailing common stock price?

22-9 If Bolcon Company is anticipating a substantial capital budgeting increase in the near future, would you recommend convertibles or warrants?

PROBLEMS

22-1 Suppose a firm has outstanding $5,000,000 of convertible subordinated debentures that pay 6 percent interest per year, mature in 20 years, $1000 par value, and have a conversion price of $50. Convertibles of similar risk have a required yield of 8 percent.

(a) What is number of shares each debenture is convertible to?

(b) If the current price of the firm's common stock is $60, what is the conversion value of the debenture?

(c) What is the debenture's straight bond value?

(d) If the current value of the convertible is $1300, what is the conversion premium?

(e) If the market price per share of common declines to $45, what is the conversion value of the bond?

(f) If the market price per share of common declines to $35, what is the conversion value of the bond?

(g) What is the probable minimum market price of the bond?

22-2 A firm has just issued $20,000,000 of $1,000 par value, 6 percent convertible subordinated debentures with a conversion price of $40. If the current market price per share of existing equity is $45, what is the potential dilution of the firm's earnings per share?

Selected Income Statement Items Before Conversion

Earnings before interest and taxes	$40,000,000
Interest	1,200,000
Earnings before taxes	38,800,000
Taxes (50%)	19,400,000
Earnings after taxes	19,400,000
Shares outstanding	4,000,000
Earnings per share	$4.85

22-3 A subordinated debenture being issued by Bolcon Company has a warrant attached to each $1,000 bond specifying that 2 common shares may be purchased at a price of $35 during the next 3 years.

(a) If Bolcon common is currently at $38 per share, what is the theoretical value of the warrant?

(b) If Bolcon common is currently at $50 per share, what is the theoretical value of the warrant?

(c) At what common price would you expect the warrant premium to fall to zero?

(d) If the market price of the warrant fell to $4 when the common price was $38 per share, could the $4 market price be sustained?

BIBLIOGRAPHY

Brigham, Eugene F. "An Analysis of Convertible Debentures: Theory and Some Empirical Evidence." *Journal of Finance,* XXI (March 1966), 35–54.

Broman, Keith L. "The Use of Convertible Subordinated Debentures by Industrial Firms, 1949–1959." *Quarterly Review of Economics and Business,* 3 (Spring 1963), 65–75.

Miller, Jerry D. "Longevity of Stock Purchase Warrants." *Financial Analysts Journal,* 27 (November–December 1971), 78–85.

Melicher, Ronald W. "Financing With Convertible Preferred Stocks." *Journal of Finance,* XXIV (March 1971), 144–147.

Pilcher, C. James. *Raising Capital With Convertible Securities.* Bureau of Business Research, University of Michigan, Ann Arbor, Mich., 1955.

Poensgen, Otto H. "The Valuation of Convertible Bonds, Parts I and II." *Industrial Management Review,* 6 and 7 (Fall 1965 and Spring 1966), 77–92 and 83–98.

Samuelson, Paul A. "Rational Theory of Warrant Pricing." *Industrial Management Review,* 6 (Spring 1965), 13–31.

_____, and Robert C. Merton. "A Complete Model of Warrant Pricing That Maximizes Utility." *Industrial Management Review,* 10 (Winter 1969), 17–46.

Shelton, John P. "The Relation of the Price of a Warrant to the Price of Its Associated Stock." *Financial Analysts Journal,* 23 (May–June and July–August 1967), 143–151 and 88–99.

Soldofsky, Robert M. "Yield Risk Performance of Convertible Securities." *Financial Analysts Journal,* 27 (March–April 1971), 61–66.

Sprinkle, Case. "Warrant Prices as Indicators of Expectations." *Yale Economic Essays,* I (1961), 179–232.

Van Horne, James C. "Warrant Valuation in Relation to Volatility and Opportunity Costs." *Industrial Management Review,* 10 (Spring 1969), 19–32.

SEVEN

OTHER TOPICS
IN FINANCIAL MANAGEMENT

LET US LOOK AT SOME OF THE MAJOR QUESTIONS which you, as the financial officer, might be called upon to answer for your firm. As you read Part Seven look for the answers to the following questions:

1. What are the types of mergers and acquisitions that you might have to consider?

2. What are the reasons your firm might want to merge?

3. What is the accounting treatment of a merger and how does it affect the firm's financial statements?

4. How must you change the firm's working capital management in order to handle the firm's international operations?

5. What particular types of international working capital financial instruments might you consider?

6. How should you handle the firm's foreign exchange risk?

7. How do you adjust your firm's capital budgeting procedures for foreign investment?

8. How and where do you raise international funds?

9. What can you do to help your firm if it has failed to compete successfully?

23

MERGERS AND ACQUISITIONS

As YOUR FIRM'S FINANCIAL OFFICER, you are going to be deeply involved in the firm's merger activity. At the outset, you will be required to advise on the appropriate type of merger. What types of merger are there? We shall see that mergers are classified not only by their legal status but also by their impact on the firm's operating economies and resources.

Once you know the types of mergers available to the firm, for what reasons might you recommend that the firm merge? Among them are economies of scale, diversification, and acquisition of management talent. Regardless of the specific reason, the ultimate aim of any merger is to aid the firm in its effort to achieve its corporate goal. If that goal is to maximize the firm's share price, we must analyze the effect of the merger on the firm's expected stream of earnings and dividends as well as on its cost of equity capital (k_e).

Since the impact of the merger on the firm's earnings is such an important consideration, how does the accounting profession treat a merger and how does a merger affect the firm's financial statements? We shall see that there are two basic methods by which a merger can be reflected in the firm's financial statements: the pooling of interests method and the purchase method. We shall also see that the choice of the method, which is not solely at the option of the company, can make a large difference in the reported earnings per share. We shall examine the circumstances under which each method can be used and the effects of each.

As financial officer, you will certainly be involved in the merger negotiations, which are an art unto themselves. How are mergers negotiated? Talent is needed to analyze the situation and decide that merger is the appropriate method of expansion in the first place. Then once that has been decided, you must screen prospective merger candidates, negotiate with the other firm's management on such items as the exchange ratio, and finally consummate the merger, avoiding such obstacles as antitrust regulations and adverse tax rulings.

Even after the merger is completed, what do you do about dissident stockholders of the other firm who, though a minority, remain opposed? And what do you do about eliminating (spinning off) unwanted operations, if asked by the firm's decision makers.

TYPES OF MERGERS

How are mergers commonly classified?

Traditionally, they are classified either by their legal status or by their economic impact on the firm's operations.

Mergers Based on Legal Status

Statutory merger   A statutory merger occurs through a tax-free exchange of shares whereupon one company survives and the other disappears. The survivor assumes the other firm's assets and liabilities as well as any future liabilities which may arise. For example, if the Internal Revenue Service were to audit the books of the firm that disappeared for the years prior to the merger, the surviving firm would be responsible for any tax deficiencies.

Usually the statutory merger is voted on by the stockholders of both companies. Depending on the articles of incorporation and bylaws, the necessary vote for approval varies from a simple majority to a two-thirds majority of both firms. The exchange of shares used to effect the merger is usually tax-free because it is an exchange only and no cash price has been established. This allows the shareholders of the disappearing firm to postpone their tax liabilities until they sell the shares received in the exchange. The tax-free exchange status is not, however, a blanket interpretation by the IRS; it must be so ruled in each individual case.

Consolidation   The consolidation is another legal classification of merger. Under this arrangement, the two separate firms merge into a newly created corporation and both disappear. When the Pennsylvania Railroad and the New York Central Railroad consolidated into the PennCentral Railroad, the shareholders of each former company exchanged their shares for the shares of the new company. The former companies disappeared.

The newly created firm assumes the liabilities and the assets of both firms. The type of merger also requires the approval of the stockholders in most instances, and it is usually consummated by a tax-free exchange of shares.

Sale of assets   The sale of assets resembles a merger and, for the financial officer's purposes, may accomplish the same objective—expansion. Under this procedure one firm sells its assets to another and both survive. The seller usually keeps some or all of its liabilities, but receives cash, stock, or some other remuneration from the buyer to do with as it sees fit. Sometimes the seller distributes the proceeds of the sale to its stockholders and dissolves; sometimes it reinvests the proceeds in other operations. The option is the seller's.

In sales of large portions of the firm's assets, the bondholders and the stockholders frequently must vote their approval. The sale of assets is typically not a tax-free exchange.

Lease   Like the sale of assets, the lease accomplishes much the same objective as the merger without formally being a merger. Under this arrangement, the acquiring firm leases the operations of the other firm. For example, it is common among railroads for one to lease the property of another for its own use.

The lessee gains control of the leased line in return for a payment to the leased line. The leased line typically becomes a shell whose only income is the lease payments, and these are usually distributed to its stockholders as a dividend.

Holding Companies

While not a formal merger procedure, the holding company arrangement occurs when the firm acquires control of another firm(s) through the ownership of a controlling block of stock. For example, when the holding company can elect the majority of the board of directors, it controls the other company and can direct its operations to complement those of the holding company itself. The holding company need not own a majority of the other firm's shares—just enough to give it control.

Advantages   From the financial officer's viewpoint, the holding company arrangement has certain inherent advantages. First, the control and any subsequent separation may be accomplished with relative ease. No formal stockholder vote is required; it is merely a matter of purchasing enough shares on the open market. If the control is unsuccessful or must be dissolved for some reason, separation is accomplished just as easily by selling the controlling interest.

Second, the holding company may be able to gain control of the other firm with a limited investment, if there is no opposing block of stockholders. This means that the holding company has a very high leverage factor in the sense that it can control substantial assets with limited investment.

Third, since the controlled firms do not lose their identity, they can maintain their local image and get the advantages of being in their own locality, such as lower incorporation taxes and better public sympathy. This is particularly true of international operations where the holding company may not have a good image in a certain nation, while the controlled firm does. In the extreme, this could help prevent nationalization of the firm.

Fourth, the holding company may, in certain limited circumstances, be used to avoid the prohibitions and restrictions on expansion in some industries. In certain banking jurisdictions, banks are not allowed to have branches, yet by forming a bank holding company, several independent banks can be owned by the holding company and operated as a network in much the same manner as branches. In banking and other industries where regulations have prohibited the expansion of the firm outside its own specialized area of business, holding companies have allowed the firms to diversify outside their own areas by acquiring the stocks of other firms.

Disadvantages   The holding company is not without its disadvantages, and, in the United States at least, they seem to outweigh the advantages. There is the double taxation on the dividends from the controlled company to the holding company because each is a separate entity in the eyes of the tax authorities. (The parent pays taxes on only 15 percent of the dividends received from the other companies and can file a consolidated return if it owns more than 80 percent of the stock.) There are the additional costs of maintaining separate operations which might otherwise be consolidated at a savings. For example, the accounting departments might be merged if the two firms were operated as one.

The major disadvantage, at least in the United States, has been adverse regulations designed to discourage the formation of holding companies. Wherever possible the federal and state regulatory authorities have encouraged antitrust action against holding companies and have been relatively successful because of the ease with which holding companies can be broken up and the separate market shares of each company identified.

Ever since the Public Utility Holding Company Act of 1935 and the Federal

Reserve System regulation of bank holding companies, this concept has been discouraged despite efforts to revive the arrangement among banks during the late 1960s and early 1970s. Of course, this governmental control arose for good reason. During the 1920s and early 1930s, the holding company arrangement led to some disreputable abuses. There was, for example, unfair restraint of trade caused by "pyramiding," or the practice of gaining control of a firm for the purpose of choking off the holding company's competition, raising prices, and increasing profits because of the garnered monopoly power. Other instances occurred where the holding company unfairly "milked" the subsidiary for its own benefit and to the detriment of the controlled firm's stockholders. Today's regulations prevent abuses by discouraging holding companies in almost any form, an attitude which may represent an extreme opposite position.

Mergers Based on Economic Impact

Mergers are also classified by their economic impact on the firm's operations. This is probably the most appropriate way for a financial officer to look at mergers, because it deals directly with the firm's profitability and operating risks. The three economic classifications are horizontal, vertical, and conglomerate.

Horizontal   As its name implies, the horizontal merger expands the firm's operations in the same business at the same level. For example, if a retail food chain bought out another retail food chain, the merger would be classified as horizontal. This is true even if the merger between the two food chains diversified the operations of the survivor into different geographical areas. In general, mergers between two firms at the retail level, between two firms at the wholesale level, between two firms at the manufacturing level, or between two firms at the raw materials level in the same business are considered to be horizontal.

Vertical   Vertical mergers are characterized by expansion into different levels in the same business. A vertical merger would occur if the retail food chain were to acquire a wholesale grocery supplier or the steel manufacturer were to acquire a coke producer who supplies the raw materials needed in the manufacture of steel. Vertical mergers can occur up and down the entire chain of production. For example, a gasoline retailer could own its refinery operations and control its own crude oil resources.

Conglomerate   The conglomerate merger is an expansion of the firm into fields unrelated to the existing interests of the firm. For example, an automobile parts manufacturer might acquire a major producer of motion pictures. There is no increased concentration in any one field, as would occur in the horizontal merger, and no new control of raw material or outlets as would occur in the vertical merger. There *is* an increased concentration of total economic activity in all fields as various companies from different fields merge into one firm.

REASONS FOR MERGER

What are the reasons for merging? Many particular reasons may bring the firm to consider merger, and we shall discuss several of them. However, the ultimate reason for merging is to maximize the firm's share price, and we shall explore what you, as the financial officer, must analyze to determine the impact on your firm's share price.

Operating Economies of Scale

The firm might consider merging if it could obtain economies of scale which allow it to spread its fixed costs over a greater number of units produced. When two firms merge, the surviving firm needs only one accounting department instead of two, and it may be large enough to lease a computer economically. A wholesale drug firm might merge to acquire another product which its present sales force can sell without additional personnel or expense when they make their regular calls on customers.

The savings effected through the operating economies of scale are known as *synergistic effects*, although the word has been greatly abused in recent years. The idea behind synergism is that two combined can operate more efficiently and effectively than two separately.

Diversification

The firm might consider merger for the purpose of geographical or countercyclical diversification.

Geographical diversification is accomplished when, for example, the retail food chain headquartered and centered in the East merges with another retail food chain in the South. Together they cover broader economic area, such that if one area suffers population loss, the other area may grow, offsetting the decline.

Countercyclical diversification is designed to offset fluctuations in earnings caused by the general business cycle. The idea is to bring together two different areas or products which react in different ways to the general level of economic activity. For example, if Firm A's and Firm B's historical earning patterns fluctuated over time as shown in Table 23-1, we can see that a merger would be appropriate. The cyclically prone earnings of Firm A and the countercyclically prone earnings of Firm B would smooth out the effect of general economic conditions on the merged firm's earnings. We can represent this schematically as shown in Figure 23-1.

Smoothing out the earnings over the fluctuations in the business cycle tends to reduce the risk investors associate with the firm and could reduce the firm's cost of equity capital (k_e), not to mention the easier financial planning it affords the financial officer.

There is no guarantee that a merger will smooth out the cyclical pattern in the firm's earnings. The historical pattern does not have to repeat itself in the future, especially if the operating environment of either firm changes. The exceptionally smooth earnings suggested in Figure 23-1 are not likely to be found. Almost all firms respond in some degree to the business cycle, making it very difficult for any firm to find an exactly offsetting earnings pattern. A partial offset is much more likely.

Table 23-1 Earning Patterns Suggesting Countercyclical Diversification

Economic conditions	Normal	Expansion	Recession
Firm A earnings	$3,000,000	$5,000,000	$1,000,000
Firm B earnings	$3,000,000	$1,000,000	$5,000,000
A + B earnings	$6,000,000	$6,000,000	$6,000,000

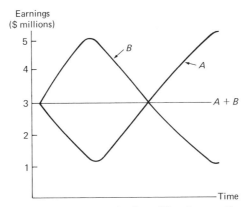

Figure 23-1   Effect of Countercyclical Diversification on Earnings

Growth

Firms frequently consider merging as a method of growing rapidly. Unfavorable capital market conditions which are unreceptive to the firm's securities may be frustrating the firm's expansion plans. As an alternative, the firm might exchange some of its securities for those of another firm and grow by merger.

The accompanying growth may have side effects on the firm's cost of capital. As the firm's size grows, particularly in the early stages of that growth, investors may be willing to look upon the firm as less risky because of its increased size. This might lower the firm's cost of capital.

Earnings Per Share

The firm might consider merger as a means of increasing its earnings per share. If the firm acquires another company which is profitable, the earnings of the two companies are combined. If this combination is coupled with circumstances such that the acquiring firm issues proportionately fewer shares per dollar of the acquired firm's earnings, the earnings per share of the merged firm are increased. Suppose Firm A and Firm B have the following financial data:

	Firm A	Firm B
Earnings	$1,000,000	$200,000
Number of shares	1,000,000	200,000
Earnings per share	$ 1.00	$ 1.00
Stock price	$20	$10
Price/earnings ratio	20×	10×

Because Firm A sells at $20 per share while Firm B sells at only $10 a share,[1] Firm A can exchange 100,000 of its shares for Firm B without reducing the market value of Firm B's stock.[2] This has the effect of increasing the earnings per share of A and B

---

[1] Firm A might sell at a higher price/earnings ratio for many reasons, such as better growth prospects or a more stable business environment.

[2] Typically, the acquiring firm must pay a premium above the prevailing market price of the stock of the acquired firm.

when they are combined:

	Firm A + B
Earnings	$1,200,000
Number of shares	1,100,000
Earnings per share	$1.09

While the effect is to raise earnings per share, the stock price may not increase. As the financial officer, you should be aware of this. Any increase in the share price depends on what investors are willing to pay for the higher earnings per share now that a portion of those earnings comes from the absorbed operations of Firm B. And Firm B by itself had sold for only ten times earnings per share, not the twenty times that Firm A sold for. Investors may reduce the price/earnings multiple to reflect this, keeping the price of the A + B stock unchanged despite the higher earnings per share, as we shall explore in some detail later in this chapter.

Taxes

Sometimes firms are motivated to merge because of tax considerations. This is true for privately held firms that may wish to merge with a public firm to avoid the onus of additional taxes on retained earnings. It is more common for publicly held corporations to merge for the purpose of acquiring tax-loss carryforwards. Under the appropriate circumstances, a profitable firm may acquire another firm with accumulated losses and apply those losses against its taxable income. This has the effect of lowering the profitable firm's tax liability.

Equity Base

A firm might consider merger in order to acquire an expanded equity base. If the firm has a relatively top-heavy capital structure with too much debt, it can quickly change that by merging with a firm that has little or no debt. This enlarges the acquiring firm's assets and equity base and reduces its debt/equity ratio. The firm can use the expanded equity base to borrow additional funds and hopefully achieve positive financial leverage. The firm with too little debt in its capital structure can reverse the procedure. It can increase its positive financial leverage by acquiring another firm with an exchange of its debt for the acquired firm's stock.

Management Talent

Sometimes a firm considers merging if it needs management talent. This is particularly true if the acquiring firm has a strong leader and little management depth. The acquisition of another firm without a leader but with a strong secondary management team would produce a strong management in depth. In certain situations, however, the merger is undertaken to bring a top manager into the firm.

Public Ownership

Sometimes a privately held firm will merge with a publicly held corporation in order to avoid the costs and negotiations of selling a privately held firm's stock to the public through an underwriting. This may be less expensive than the traditional underwriting, particularly in times when the stock market is unreceptive to new public issues. In some instances the management of the privately held concern assumes control, while in other cases the reverse is true.

Speed and Cost

Sometimes a firm is motivated to merge in order to obtain speedy entry into a field already controlled by established firms or very time-consuming to enter. Certain industries require years of groundwork before they become profitable. Rather than spend the time and money in building such groundwork, the acquiring firm may decide it is less costly and faster to merge with another company already in the field. As entry into the field becomes more restrictive for any reason, the firm is more likely to consider gaining entry through merger. And as the severity of head-on competition between the firm as a new entrant and the established firms in the field increases, the firm is more likely to use merger to gain entrance.

Eliminating Competition

Sometimes the firm considers merger as a method of eliminating the competition. If the firm can merge with another and increase its monopoly power, it can increase its profits. Of course merger for the sole purpose of diminishing competition is prohibited by the antitrust laws. As financial officer you should not undertake any merger for this purpose, because it is illegal.

Maximizing Share Price

Maximizing share price is the most important objective and the ultimate reason for merger. The financial officer must examine the effect on the share price as part of any analysis of possible merger. We saw in Chapter 9 that share price reflects the two major considerations of the investors' expected reward and the investors' risk-adjusted required rate of return.

Earnings per share   Investors judge the expected future reward by the earnings and dividend prospects of the firm. If the merger enhances those prospects, the firm's share price is likely to rise. However, the more typical immediate effect of the merger is a dilution in the surviving firm's earnings per share. Suppose firms with the following characteristics were to merge:

	Firm A	Firm B
Earnings	$2,000,000	$1,000,000
Number of shares	1,000,000	500,000
Share price	$20	$20
Earnings per share	$ 2	$ 2

There will probably be dilution in Firm A's earnings per share if it acquires Firm B, because Firm A will have to pay a higher price than $20 a share in order to buy all 500,000 shares of Firm B. Let us assume that Firm A gives 3 of its shares in exchange for every 2 of Firm B's shares, or the equivalent of $30 a share in Firm A stock. After the merger is consummated, the earnings per share of the combined firm would be as follows:

	Firm A + B
Earnings	$3,000,000
Number of shares	1,750,000
Earnings per share	$1.71

The earnings per share of the combined firms is less than that of either of the firms separately due to the immediate dilution of the share exchange.

At first it would seem that the share price of the combined firms would be depressed because of the lower earnings per share. But since potential investors look at the expected earnings per share as far ahead as they can to get an idea of the future stream of rewards they can anticipate, they will estimate what may occur *after* the immediate dilution. In most instances, since acquiring firms merge only when they anticipate that the combination will lead to higher earnings per share, rapid growth in earnings per share is envisioned after the immediate dilution.

Figure 23-2 illustrates that the combined firm's earnings per share are for a limited time below what they would otherwise have been for the surviving firm without the merger. This is caused by the immediate dilution of the share exchange. After point X on Figure 23-2, the merger firm's earnings per share surpass what the earnings per share would have been without the merger. This acceleration in the growth of the merged firm's earnings per share could be for any number of reasons —the tapping of a new market, economies of scale, and others we have discussed.

If investors anticipate this acceleration at the time of the merger, they will tend to overlook the immediate, lower earnings per share in expectation of future earnings per share *higher* than they had previously expected. Of course, if investors cannot envision rapid recovery from the immediate dilution, the share price will be depressed.

Investors' required rate of return Prospects for the earnings per share are only half the story. The merger also influences the investors' risk-adjusted required rate of return, which is affected by such characteristics as the firm's business risk, financial risk, and marketability risk. A merger directly influences these three risks, which, in turn change the investors' risk-adjusted required rate of return and the stock price. Hence the merger can lead to immediate higher earnings per share and the

Figure 23-2   Firm A's Expected Earnings Per Share With and Without Merger

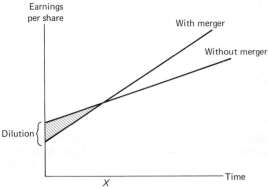

stock price can nevertheless be depressed, because of an increase in the required rate of return. (The general financial market risk factors of interest rates and inflation, which are also part of the risk-adjusted required rate of return, are not influenced by the merger since they are beyond the firm's control.)

A merger can affect the firm's business risk by changing its operating environment. A more stable operating environment due to the merger usually leads to a lower required rate of return, and vice versa. For example, the vertical merger of a bacon packer with a hog farmer would dampen the periodic profit squeezes caused by the combination of sticky retail bacon prices as a result of customer price resistance and the volatile prices of hogs in the wholesale market. The merger would give the bacon packer a more stable and certain wholesale supply, which would increase investor confidence in the firm's ability to meet its debt obligations and achieve the expected earnings per share.

A merger can affect the firm's financial risk by changing the proportion of debt to equity in the capital structure. For example, the acquisition of a firm burdened with debt by a debtless firm can produce a reasonable debt/equity ratio when the two are combined. The decreased debt/equity ratio would probably imply to investors that the firm would meet its debt obligations and stand an improved chance of achieving the expected earnings per share. This, in turn, would lower the cost of the firm's equity and debt capital and put upward pressure on the firm's share price.

A merger can affect the firm's marketability risk. In a typical merger situation, the number of outstanding shares for the surviving firm is increased, and the average daily trading volume in the shares rises. This lowers the marketability risk, for investors can now trade the shares with more ease and less price fluctuation. This, in turn, encourages investors to purchase the stock and puts upward pressure on the share price.

We can observe how the earnings prospects and the risk-adjusted required rate of return together influence the share price by thinking of the case of the conglomerates for a minute. As we saw earlier in this chapter, a firm can achieve higher earnings per share by exchanging its high-price/earnings-ratio stock for the stock of a lower-price/earnings-ratio firm. The same could be accomplished if the firm acquired another with debt instead of stock. In principle, the acquiring firm gets the earnings without proportionally increasing the number of outstanding shares, raising its earnings per share. The conglomerates did exactly this for a time. They created a growth image which was undeserved; and in the long run, their share prices dropped despite their higher earnings per share.

We can trace the depressed share prices of these conglomerates to many causes. Their diversification proved ineffective. When the economy entered a recession, their earnings per share fell, despite the diversification, because there was insufficient countercyclical response among the various divisions and subsidiaries to offset the slow economy. The synergism was not very large and the anticipated economies of scale did not materialize. The conglomerates used excessive amounts of debt to acquire other companies, which increased their financial risk and depressed their stock prices. Their excessive acquisition of lower-price/earnings-ratio firms eventually led investors to reconsider the high price/earnings ratio they were paying for the conglomerate and to look upon it more as a large grouping of low-price/earnings-ratio firms, which in itself should command a low price/earnings ratio (higher cost of equity capital). The tax laws were changed so that the tax-free exchange of debt for common stock was no longer easy. Finally, there was a change in the accounting rules which adversely affected the conglomerates' ability to consolidate the earnings of their acquisitions with their own reported earnings.

ACCOUNTING FOR MERGERS[3]

How are mergers accounted for in the financial statements? There are two different approaches, depending on the circumstances surrounding the merger: the purchase method and the pooling of interests method.

Pooling of Interests

The pooling of interests accounting approach may be used only under the following circumstances:

1. The companies to be merged were autonomous and independent firms for at least two years prior to the merger.

2. The merger is completed in a single transaction or within one year according to a fixed plan.

3. The shares offered by the acquiring firm are identical to those already outstanding.

4. The acquiring firm acquires at least 90 percent of the voting stock of the acquired firm.

5. There have been no changes in the equity interest of the voting stock in contemplation of the merger.

6. The acquired firm's shareholders will maintain a proportional equity interest in the combined firm.

7. The former accounting basis is retained.

8. No significant disposal of the acquired firm's assets is planned by the merged firm.

Balance sheet   The effect of a pooling of interests on the firm's balance sheet may be observed in Table 23-2. As we can see from that table, the basic concept behind the

Table 23-2   Balance Sheet Under the Pooling of Interests Accounting Method

	Firm A	Firm B	Firm A + B
Assets			
Current Assets	$100,000	$100,000	$200,000
Net fixed assets	200,000	200,000	400,000
Total assets	300,000	300,000	600,000
Liabilities and stockholders' equity			
Current liabilities	50,000	50,000	100,000
Long-term debt	60,000	60,000	120,000
Total liabilities	110,000	110,000	220,000
Stockholders' equity			
Common stock ($1 par 100,000 shares for the separate firm; $1 par 250,000 shares after pooling of interests)	100,000	100,000	250,000
Additional paid-in capital	60,000	60,000	70,000
Retained earnings	30,000	30,000	60,000
Total liabilities and stockholders' equity	$300,000	$300,000	$600,000

[3] See Accounting Principle Board Opinion #16, upon which this section is based.

Table 23-3 Income Statement Under the Pooling of Interests Accounting Method

	Firm A	Firm B	Firm A + B
Net earnings after taxes	$100,000	$150,000	$250,000
Number of shares	100,000	100,000	250,000
Earnings per share	$1.00	$1.50	$1.00

pooling is to simply combine the assets and the liabilities of the two firms into one. Using the historically based cost as recorded on the balance sheet of each firm, the assets of each are summed to determine the assets of the merged firm. The liabilities of each are summed to find the liabilities of the merged firm, and the stockholders' equity of each is combined to again find the stockholders' equity of the merged firm.

We have assumed for illustration that Firm A has exchanged 3 of its shares for every 2 shares of Firm B, creating 250,000 shares of outstanding stock for the merged firm. Notice that the total assets, the total liabilities, and the total liabilities and stockholders' equity merely reflect the summing of the firms' accounts. The only difference is that the merged firm has had to transfer $50,000 of additional paid-in capital to its common stock account to reflect the increased number of shares, for now instead of each firm having 100,000 shares outstanding, the merged firm has 250,000 shares outstanding.

Income statement   The effect of pooling of interests on the income statement is illustrated in Table 23-3, where we can readily observe that earnings for the merged firm are the sum of the earnings for the separate firms. The only distinguishing feature not revealed in the balance sheet is that the earnings for the entire year during which the merger took place are combined, even if the actual consummation did not occur at the beginning of the year. If the pooling of interests took place on December 31 of that year, the earnings for the entire year would be pooled, just as if the merger had occurred on the first day of that year.

Purchase

If pooling of interests is not undertaken, either by choice or because the merger did not qualify under the circumstances, the firm uses the purchase method. The two are never combined; it is either one or the other. While the pooling method treats the merger as a joining of two firms, the purchase method treats the merger more like an acquisition of the acquired firm by the surviving firm. The acquiring firm exchanges its securities or cash for the fair value of the acquired firm's assets. Table 23-4 illustrates the effect of the purchase method on the balance sheet.

Balance sheet   The distinguishing feature of the purchase method shows up as the payment the acquiring firm makes in excess of the recorded costs of the assets and the assumed liabilities of the acquired firm. The acquired assets are usually valued at their historical book value but may, at the option of the firms, be appraised for their fair market value. This excess payment over that fair value appears as *goodwill* on the balance sheet. Goodwill is an intangible asset representing, in theory, those intangible items such as customer relations which the firm has built up over the years of its existence. It must be amortized over a period not to exceed 40 years and is not a tax-deductible expense.

Table 23-4   Balance Sheet Under the Purchase Accounting Method

	Firm A	Firm B	Adjustments		Firm AB
			Credit	Debit	
Assets					
Current assets	$ 90,000	$ 5,000			$ 95,000
Net fixed assets	120,000	10,000			130,000
Goodwill	–	–		23,000	23,000
Total assets	210,000	15,000			248,000
Current liabilities	30,000	3,000			33,000
Long-term debt	20,000	5,000			25,000
Total liabilities	50,000	8,000			58,000
Stockholders' equity					
Common stock ($10 par)	40,000	3,000	3,000	10,000	50,000
Additional paid-in capital	20,000	3,000	3,000	20,000	40,000
Retained earnings	100,000	1,000	1,000		100,000
Total liabilities and stockholders' equity	210,000	15,000			248,000

We can readily observe the creation of $23,000 in goodwill in Table 23-4, where we assume that Firm A acquires Firm B for 1,000 of its own shares (par value $10) worth $30,000 at their prevailing market price.

Firm A has paid $30,000 in stock for Firm B's assets, which after deducting the liabilities assumed by Firm A had a book value of $7,000. We can see this as the difference between the total assets ($15,000) and the total liabilities ($8,000). The excess payment of $23,000 over the book value of the assets becomes the goodwill account. This additional $23,000, which appears as an intangible asset, has to be balanced somewhere in the stockholders' equity. We can see that the stockholders' equity of Firm B is eliminated with the merger; it becomes the credits to the adjustments. The additional 1,000 shares of Firm A issued in the exchange increase the common stock account of the merged firm by $10,000, reflecting 1,000 shares at a par value of $10 each, and the remaining $20,000 of the exchange's market value is included in the additional paid-in capital account. These adjustments exactly balance the additional asset, goodwill.

Income statement   The effect of the purchase method on the income statement differs from pooling because earnings are combined only from the date the merger is consummated, not from the beginning of the income statement period. Table 23-5 illustrates the income statement if the merger between Firm A and Firm B occurs at the beginning of the year.

Table 23-5   Income Statement Under the Purchase Accounting Method

	Firm A	Firm B	Firm AB
Net earnings before taxes	$20,000	$2,000	$22,000
Net earnings after taxes (50%)	10,000	1,000	11,000
Number of shares	4,000	3,000	5,000
Earnings per share	$2.50	$3.33	$2.20

If the merger were consummated half-way through the year, only one-half of Firm B's earnings would be consolidated with Firm A's yearly earnings. The total for Firm AB for the year in which the merger took place would then be $10,500, or $2.10 per share.

In the ensuing year, assuming the goodwill created in the merger were amortized at 2.5 percent a year for 40 years, earnings, if there were no growth, would be:

Net earnings before taxes	$22,000
Net earnings after taxes (50%)	11,000
Goodwill expense	575
Net earnings after taxes and goodwill	$10,425
Earnings per share	$2.09

Notice that the goodwill is not a tax-deductible expense and reduces net income after taxes on a dollar for dollar basis. It has no effect on total net cash inflow from operations. Also notice that since the firms have been merged for the entire year, the total earnings of Firm B are consolidated with Firm A.

Pooling versus Purchase

The major difference between the two accounting treatments of mergers is the goodwill. The effect of that goodwill is to increase the surviving firm's intangible assets and to decrease its reported earnings as the goodwill is amortized. Naturally firms prefer the pooling method because it enables them to report higher earnings per share. However, not all mergers qualify for the pooling treatment under the more stringent requirements enacted by the accounting profession after abuses when conglomerates and others used pooling as a method of simulating a growing earnings stream.

MERGER NEGOTIATIONS AND MECHANICS

How is the typical merger conducted?

The actual process involves many steps, which we have up to now called merger and acquisition. We shall now discuss them in four general categories: (1) search, (2) investigation, (3) negotiation, and (4) acquisition and integration.[4]

Search

The search for merger candidates begins as soon as the firm decides that merger is a likely way to solve existing problems or provide expansion. Once we have so decided, we must contact people who might know of possible merger candidates. Among the first persons we would normally contact would be our investment banker and our accountants. We can also turn to professional finders, lawyers, and management consultants who in their daily routine might become aware of firms willing to merge.

[4] J. B. Cohen and S. M. Robbins, *The Financial Manager*, Harper and Row, New York, 1966, pp. 818 ff.

Investigation

Once we have isolated a few likely candidates, we would start investigating their merits as merger partners. First we would examine their public records, even before contacting their management. This would include examinations of their financial statements and such credit checks as a Dun and Bradstreet report.

If we were still interested in exploring merger with the candidate after examining their public record, we would proceed to contact the firm's management and ask to examine their unpublished financial background material. We would want to see the latest audit of their inventory and books, their pro forma financial statements for the coming year(s), and their insurance policies. We would also check with their bank for a credit reference and evaluate their accounts receivable, fixed assets, pension fund obligations, inventory, and management, and we would obtain a list of their liabilities, patents, deferred income accounts, and contingency liabilities, particularly lawsuits.

Finally, if we remained interested in a merger, we would have to check the antitrust implications. This means we might have to go so far as to ask for a ruling from the Federal Trade Commission and examine previous court decisions and the prevailing antitrust attitude of the Department of Justice. It is likely that the government or competitors might bring antitrust action against the firm if the merger tends to substantially lessen competition in the area or if the sheer size of the merged firm concerns the Justice Department, as in the case of some large conglomerates. You might issue a public communication stating that the firms have made contact for the purpose of exploring a merger to protect the firm from accusations of misusing inside information by the Securities and Exchange Commission.

Negotiation

The actual face-to-face negotiations can occur anywhere, but the distinguishing feature of most is the amount of time they consume. Sometimes they go on for days on end. In the words of one famous negotiator, the secret is to eat a big meal so you can sit there and continue to negotiate while the other party becomes so hungry that he or she is willing to agree to anything just to get food. The moral, of course, is that if you are negotiating on behalf of your firm, do not do it in haste. Take your time and allow yourself the privilege of revision before the final signing.

Terms   One of the most important points you will be negotiating is the terms of the merger. They focus upon the *exchange ratio*—the number of shares or amount of cash that the acquiring company exchanges for the shares of the acquired company. A formalized mathematical model for determining the negotiating range of the exchanged ratio is presented in Appendix 23A.

The basic bargaining positions which determine the exchange ratio depend on the relative market values of the firms before merger negotiations began, although relative book values, dividends, and earnings also enter into the bargaining. Exchange ratio bargaining based on the relative market values must, at the lower limit, leave the stockholders of the acquired firm with exactly the same wealth or market value of stock in the acquiring company as they had in the acquired company. In other words, if the acquired company stock sold for $15 a share and the acquiring company's stock sold for $30 a share, the lower limit of the exchange ratio would be half a share of the acquiring company for each share of the acquired company. The upper limit is that point at which the acquiring company's stock price declines because of the merger: the exchange ratio is too high and investors foresee too much dilution or additional risk resulting from the merger. Somewhere between those two limits, the bargaining ability of the negotiators will settle the exact exchange ratio. If the acquiring firm's negotiator is better, the exchange ratio is at or near the lower limit, and vice versa.

Sometimes a negotiator will try to bargain on the basis of the firm's book values if convinced that using the historical cost of the firm's assets as a starting point for negotiations gives an advantage over the other party. However, this is rarely done today because of such difficulties as different depreciation methods and business risks. Sometimes the relative dividends between the two firms are used by one of the bargaining negotiators. If the dividend income is a particularly strong demand of one negotiator, a convertible preferred stock or bond might be an appropriate bargaining tool for the acquiring firm. Sometimes the relative earnings of the two firms are used as a starting point in setting the exchange ratio, but, as in the case of the book value, their failure to reflect future earnings prospects and the relative risks of the individual companies usually leads the negotiators back to the firms' relative market values as a starting point in bargaining the exchange ratio.

Other negotiated points   The negotiators have to come to agreement on other items besides the exchange ratio. For example, if the management of the acquired firm is to stay on, the acquiring firm might offer contingency payments based upon the acquired firm's earnings performance after it is merged. These contingency payments are designed to encourage the management of the acquired firm to work as hard as part of a larger firm as they did when they were the major stockholders of the acquired firm.

As a negotiator, before you sign the final agreement, you should always insist that your firm's commitment be contingent upon such items as clearance from the antitrust authorities and a favorable ruling finding the exchange of shares to be tax-free.

You might also negotiate restrictions on the resale of the stock or the commencement of a competing firm by the former stockholders of the acquired firm. You might offer these managers contracts as consultants or officers in the surviving firm. If you are a manager in the acquired firm, you might insist upon a consulting contract for yourself. You should also be certain that the firm has assigned all its trademarks, patents, and other particular assets in the final agreement. And you should make implementation of the agreement contingent upon the approval of your stockholders. Remember that it is always easier and less costly to negotiate before the final signing than to renegotiate after implementation of the agreement.

At this point you would probably issue an initialed *letter of intent* to acquire, which is a preliminary agreement, subject to further negotiation, audits, and appropriate approvals before the signing of a formal merger agreement.

Acquisition and Integration

After all the approvals and formalizing of the agreement, you must help in the physical acquisition. This involves your services in such mechanical aspects of the merger as notifying the transfer agent, listing the new shares on the stock exchange, filing the share exchange with the proper authorities, consolidating the payrolls, and other similar functions. More importantly, it involves your efforts in raising funds if the firm has to borrow to finance the acquisition, refinancing the capital structure, and making important contacts with bankers, lenders, and security analysts to acquaint them with the firm's new complexion and how it affects their position.

Guidelines for Expansion[5]

After the debacle of the conglomerate expansion-through-merger campaign of the 1960s, there emerged certain common sense guidelines which had been ignored. Before you lead your firm into any merger, you might review the following ten-point checklist to see if the proposed merger is right for your firm:

1. Expand in your own field of expertise.
2. Evaluate the potential of the market for the product before expanding.
3. Check for possible monopoly restrictions.
4. Evaluate your financial resources; especially determine the potential adverse effect on your working capital position if things do not go according to plan.
5. Check what your competitors are doing to ensure that you are not expanding into an already overcrowded field.
6. Do not expand just for the sake of size.
7. Coordinate the engineering and production activities.
8. If the merger requires a production change be sure that the tooling and machinery is immediately modified to accommodate the change.
9. Do not expand beyond the limits of your skills.
10. Be sure that the required skills are transferred from the acquired company.

The Tender Offer

If negotiations fail or the firm decides not to contact the other firm's management, we might use a tender offer. This bypasses the other firm's management and deals directly with its stockholders. The tender offer is designed to catch the other firm's management off guard and entice the stockholders to tender their shares, passing control of the company to us, before their firm's management can counter the offer. The strategy is to announce our willingness to acquire a large block of the other firm's stock at a higher-than-prevailing market price. Of course, the tender offer does not always have to be against the wishes of the other firm's management, although it typically is.

The terms of the typical tender offer specify not only the price we are willing to pay for the shares, but also the number of shares we are tendering for and the conditions of the offer. No tender is unconditional. Typical conditions are that the shares be tendered before a specific expiration date or the tender offer lapses unless extended and that our obligation to purchase the shares is void if fewer than the requested amount are tendered to us. For example, if we offer to purchase one million shares, we may condition the offer to allow us to refuse all the shares tendered if fewer than one million are received by us. If more than one million are received, we can accept the requested million shares either on a first-come-first-accepted basis or on a pro rata basis. Under the pro rata basis, we purchase a proportional number of shares from each person who tendered. For example, if we had requested one million shares but received two million, we would purchase 50 percent of every person's tender.

In addition to the tender price, the expiration date, and the conditions of the obligation to purchase those tendered shares, the offer also specifies such details as

[5] Thomas S. Dudick, "A Backward Look at Forward Planning," *Management Planning,* January–February 1972, 15–19.

Notice of Offer to Purchase

1,800,000 Shares of Common Stock of

VCA Corporation

For Cash At $13 Per Share Net

Offer Expires 5:00 P.M. New York Time on March 15, 1974
(unless extended as provided in the Offer to Purchase)

Thyssen-Bornemisza Group N.V., a Netherlands company with its headquarters situated at Amstelveen, The Netherlands ("TBG"), is offering to purchase up to 1,800,000 shares of Common Stock, $.25 par value (the "Shares"), of VCA Corporation ("VCA") at $13 per Share net to each selling stockholder, in cash, upon the terms and conditions set forth in the Offer to Purchase, dated February 21, 1974, and in the related Letter of Tender.

Payment for purchased Shares will be made as soon as practicable after the expiration date given above.

Copies of the Offer to Purchase and the Letter of Tender are being mailed to stockholders of VCA. If 1,175,000 or more Shares are tendered, and remain tendered, TBG will purchase all of such Shares properly tendered up to 1,800,000 and may extend the Offer. If fewer than 1,175,000 Shares are tendered, TBG reserves the right, at its option, to elect (a) to extend the Offer from time to time, during which extension all Shares previously tendered and not withdrawn will remain subject to the Offer and may be purchased by TBG, (b) to purchase all Shares validly tendered pursuant to the Offer and to extend the Offer, or (c) to terminate the Offer and purchase none or all of the Shares duly tendered. If more than 1,800,000 Shares are tendered and remain tendered on the initial expiration date, purchases will be made from all tendering stockholders *pro rata* according to the number of Shares tendered by each (with appropriate adjustments to avoid the purchase of fractional Shares). If this Offer is extended, Shares tendered during such extension may be purchased on a first-come, first-served basis.

Figure 23-3   A Tender Offer

the depository to whom the tendered shares are to be delivered and the brokerage fee that the firm will pay to those brokers whose customers tender. Figure 23-3 illustrates a tender offer announcement.

Fighting a Tender Offer

If your firm happens to be the target of a tender offer takeover, you will be asked to help fight the attempt if management decides it does not like the offer at the present price or does not want to merge at all. There are several tactics that the firm can use in its effort to thwart the tender takeover bid. These include legal action, competing tenders, and publicity campaigns.

The firm could immediately institute legal action to block the tender offer, although the grounds for such action are somewhat tenuous. The mere desire not to be taken over is insufficient by itself. The firm's legal counsel must look for violations of antitrust laws, foreign investment regulations if relevant, and federal government agency rules.

Another tactic is to solicit a competing tender offer at a higher price from a friendlier firm. The higher price is designed to attract the tender of the shares to this offer instead of the other one. Meanwhile the firm's present management has come to agreement with the friendly firm that management will stay on or be more generously compensated than if the first tender offer succeeds. You might also arrange to issue additional shares of stock or make other financing arrangements which would make it difficult for the takeover to gain control.

Finally, the firm could mount a publicity campaign to convince stockholders that they should not tender. This would include belittling the offer as too small or not in the long-term best interests of the firm. If the present management has compiled a good record and has maintained good stockholder relations, the chances of the tender succeeding can be diminished by a publicity campaign.

DISSENTING STOCKHOLDERS

How does the firm handle dissenting stockholders of the acquired firm who protest the merger terms?

Even after a majority of the acquired firm's stockholders has approved the merger and it is consummated, protesting stockholders can still demand satisfaction. If negotiations fail to placate them, a court hearing can be requested by the firm in which a "fair market value" is determined. This may be more or less than the value at the exchange ratio for the other share. The dissenters generally receive the determined value in cash.

Alternatively, the stockholders who do not exchange their shares may remain minority holders in the acquired company. A proportional share of the earnings and assets of the acquired company is segregated on the income statement and balance sheet of the merged firm to reflect their position.

SPIN-OFFS

The spin-off is the reverse of the merger. In the spin-off, the firm distributes the shares it owns in a subsidiary to the firm's present stockholders. For example, the Georgia-Pacific Company distributed the stock of its Louisiana-Pacific Company, which operated certain lumbering facilities of the Georgia-Pacific Company in certain geographical regions, to its stockholders. This created two separate and competing companies.

There are several reasons for spin-offs. The Louisiana-Pacific spin-off arose because the antitrust division of the Justice Department had won a judgment ordering Georgia-Pacific to divest itself of certain operations. Spin-offs can also arise because the firm wishes to dump a losing operation. The concept is to amputate the losing part, letting it assume as much of the firm's debt and other liabilities as possible in the process. This should help maximize the share price of the parent firm as its earnings prospects pick up and its cost of capital falls. Of course, there are limits to how much debt you can force the losing operation to assume. The stockholders of the newly created company and the bondholders who are to be switched may object and can force you to spin off a more viable firm with less debt and improved earnings prospects.

Sometimes, the spin-off is designed to increase the total value of the shares. The firm might find that the stock market has placed a much higher value on the stock of the new, independent company than it did when it was a smaller part of the parent firm. The total value of the parent company stock and the newly created company stock may be more than that of the parent company stock alone before the spin-off. For example, a United States firm with its major interests in an unstable area of the world would probably benefit from spinning off 20 percent of the stock in its United States subsidiary to create a public market for that stock. The United States subsidiary stock would probably command a higher price/earnings ratio because of its lower-risk operating environment than when it was hidden as part of a company looked upon as operating in unstable political areas. Yet the parent company can still consolidate its earnings with those of the 80 percent-owned United States company. The United States company might also be able to sell some of its own debt now at a lower cost of capital than the parent company because it has its own public image and stockholders.

SUMMARY

After having read Chapter 23, you should be able to answer these questions:

1. What methods of merging are available to the firm?

Mergers are classified either by their legal status or by their economic impact on the firm. As financial officers, we are mainly interested in the latter. The horizontal merger expands the firm's operations at the same level in the same industry. The vertical merger expands the firm's operations either backwards or forwards in the chain of production. The conglomerate merger expands the firm's operations into unrelated fields. We also saw that the firm could effect the same result as a merger through a holding company, a sale of assets, or leases.

2. What are the reasons for merging?

The ultimate reason is to enhance shareholder wealth: to raise share prices. This can result from a merger if investors either foresee an increase in the expected earnings or a decrease in the business, financial, or marketability risks of the firm because of the merger. Other reasons for merging include economies of scale, diversification, growth, increased reported earnings per share, tax savings, expanded equity bases, the acquisition of management talent, public ownership, and speed and lower cost of entry into a new market.

3. How does a merger affect the firm's financial statements?

The merger can be accounted for either under the purchase method or the pooling of interests method, depending on the circumstances. Under the pooling method the two firms are joined on their financial statements by adding the accounts together for the entire year. Under the purchase method, the balance sheet reflects the purchase price paid in excess of the book value of the acquired firm in the newly created goodwill account, which must be amortized over a maximum of 40 years without benefit of tax deduction from the firm's income statement.

4. What can the firm do about dissenting stockholders after a merger?

If negotiations fail, it can have a court determine a cash settlement price or it can, at the option of the dissenting stockholders, recognize them as a minority interest.

QUESTIONS

23-1 Distinguish between a consolidation and a statutory merger.

23-2 Identify some of the advantages and disadvantages of holding companies.

23-3 What is the difference between a horizontal and a vertical merger? Give an example of each.

23-4 Much empirical evidence suggests that many of the conglomerate mergers of the 1960s were characterized by the acquiring firms' PE ratios exceeding those of the acquired firms. In addition, many of the acquired firms had lower debt/equity ratios than the acquiring firms. What type of merger strategy does this suggest to you?

23-5 Most of the conglomerate mergers of the 1960s used the pooling of interests accounting approach as opposed to the purchase method. Why do you suppose the pooling of interests method was so popular?

23-6 Different analysts have suggested that the market value of assets, the book value of assets, and the liquidation value of assets should be the basis for establishing the minimum price or exchange ratio to be paid for another firm. Which seems the most reasonable to you?

23-7 If a firm wished to expand the equity portion of its capital structure, how might its objective be furthered through merger?

23-8 What is a tender offer and under what circumstances might it be appropriate?

PROBLEMS

23-1 Listed below are selected pre-merger data for acquiring Firm A and prospective acquirees, Firms B and C.

Pre-Merger Conditions

Firm	After-tax earnings	Common shares	Price per share	P/E
A	$5,000,000	1,000,000	$100	20.0
B	$1,000,000	500,000	$ 25	12.5
C	$1,000,000	500,000	$ 60	30.0

(a) What is the exchange ratio set according to the prevailing market values of the two firms if Firm A acquires Firm B by an exchange of common stock? If Firm A acquires Firm C?

(b) Assuming Firm A acquires Firm B at the above-calculated exchange ratio, what is the effect on Firm A's earnings per share?

(c) Assuming Firm A acquires Firm C at the above-calculated exchange ratio, what is the effect on Firm A's earnings per share?

(d) If Firm A wishes to set an exchange ratio such that its earnings per share is at least maintained, what exchange ratio should it set if it acquires Firm B? Is this a maximum or minimum exchange ratio?

(e) If Firm A wishes to set an exchange ratio such that its earnings per share is at least maintained, what exchange ratio should it set if it acquires Firm C?

(f) If the acquiring firm wishes to at least maintain its earnings per share during the initial accounting period of merger, and both participants wish to at least sustain their respective stockholder wealth (price per share or equivalent), what firm should be purchased, and what is the appropriate exchange ratio?

23-2 Firm A is considering acquiring Firm B by exchanging 3 shares of newly issued common for each share of Firm B's common. Firm A's common is currently selling at $20 per share, and Firm B's is selling at $60 per share. Shown below are the pre-merger financial statements of each firm:

Selected Income Statement Items	Firm A	Firm B
Net income after taxes	$4,000,000	$2,000,000
Number of common shares	500,000	500,000
Earnings per share	$8	$4

Balance Sheet		
Assets		
Current assets	$10,000,000	$10,000,000
Fixed assets	10,000,000	10,000,000
Total assets	20,000,000	20,000,000

Liabilities and stockholders' equity

Current liabilities	$5,000,000	$5,000,000
Long-term debt	3,000,000	3,000,000
Total liabilities	8,000,000	8,000,000
Common stock ($10 par)	5,000,000	5,000,000
Additional paid-in capital	6,000,000	6,000,000
Retained earnings	1,000,000	1,000,000
Total liabilities and stockholders' equity	20,000,000	20,000,000

(a) If the pooling of interests method is used in the accounting procedures, show the immediate post-merger financial statements for the combined firms.

(b) If the purchase method is used in the accounting procedures, show the immediate post-merger pro forma financial statements for the firm. Assume the merger occurs half-way through Firm A's accounting period. (Hint: Goodwill must be accounted for.)

(c) Explain some of the differences that result in the financial statements when the purchase method is used, as compared to the pooling of interests method.

(d) If the goodwill created by the merger is amortized at 2.5 percent a year for 40 years, and assuming no growth in earnings, calculate the firm's earnings after taxes and goodwill, and also its earnings per share for the year following the consummation of the merger.

23-3 Suppose Firm A is considering acquiring Firm B and their respective pre-merger data are as follows:

	After-tax earnings	Common shares	Earnings per share	Price per share	Price/ earnings ratio
Firm A	$10,000,000	1,000,000	$10	$300	30
Firm B	2,000,000	200,000	10	120	12

The merger is to be a common-for-common exchange, but the exact exchange ratio has not been finally negotiated. Neither participant expects any real synergy to result from the merger in the accounting period of consummation, but each firm would like to at least maintain its stockholders' wealth status (price per share or equivalent) in the initial period of merger.

(a) If the exchange ratio is set equal to the ratio of the market values of the acquired and acquiring firms, respectively, what price/earnings multiple is expected following consummation?

(b) Suppose a P/E multiple of 30 was expected by each firm following consummation. What is the maximum exchange ratio Firm A would offer? What is the minimum exchange ratio Firm B would accept?

(c) Can you think of any shortcomings of the Larson-Gonedes model for the exchange ratio? (See Appendix 23A.)

BIBLIOGRAPHY

Alberts, William W., and Joel E. Segall, eds. *The Corporate Merger,* University of Chicago Press, Chicago, 1966.

Ansoff, H. Igor, and J. Fred Weston. "Merger Objectives and Organization Structure." *Quarterly Review of Economics and Business,* II (August 1962), 49–58.

Austin, Douglas V. "A Defense of the Corporate Pirate." *Business Horizons* (Winter 1964), 51–58.

Bock, Betty. *Mergers and Markets.* National Industrial Conference Board, Inc., New York, 1962, 1964.

Cunitz, Jonathan A., "Valuing Potential Acquisitions," *Financial Executive,* XXXIX (April, 1971), 16–29.

Goudzwaard, Maurice B. "Conglomerate Mergers, Convertibles, and Cash Dividends." *Quarterly Review of Business and Economics* (Spring 1969), 53–62.

Hayes, Samuel L., III, and Russell A. Taussig. "Tactics in Cash Takeover Bids." *Harvard Business Review,* 45 (March–April 1967), 135–148.

Hogarty, Thomas F. "The Profitability of Corporate Mergers." *Journal of Business,* 43 (July 1970), 317–327.

Kraber, Richard W. "Acquisition Analysis: New Help From Your Computer." *Financial Executive* (March 1970), 10–15.

Larson, Kermit D., and Nicholas J. Gonedes. "Business Combinations: An Exchange Ratio Determination Model." *Accounting Review,* XLIV (October 1969), 720–728.

MacDougal, Gary E., and Fred V. Malek. "Master Plan For Merger Negotiations." *Harvard Business Review,* 48 (January–February 1970), 71–82.

Melicher, Ronald W. "Financing With Convertible Preferred Stock: Comment." *Journal of Finance,* XXVI (March 1971), 144–147.

Mueller, Dennis C. "A Theory of Conglomerate Mergers." *Quarterly Journal of Economics,* LXXXIII (November 1969), 643–659.

Pinches, George E. "A Reply to Financing With Convertible Preferred Stock: Comment." *Journal of Finance,* XXVI (March 1971), 150–151.

Ramanathan, K. V., and Alfred Rappaport. "Size, Growth Rates, and Merger Valuation." *Accounting Review,* XLVI (October 1971), 733–745.

Rockwell, Willard F., Jr. "How to Acquire a Company." *Harvard Business Review,* 46 (May–June, 1968), 121–132.

Shad, John S. R. "The Financial Realities of Mergers." *Harvard Business Review,* 47 (November–December 1969), 133–146.

Shick, Richard A. "The Analysis of Mergers and Acquisitions." *Journal of Finance,* XXVII (May 1972), 495–502.

Weston, J. Fred, and Sam Peltzman, eds. *Public Policy Toward Mergers.* Goodyear Publishing Co., Pacific Palisades, Calif., 1969.

Appendix 23A **Model for a Formal Exchange Ratio**

Larson and Gonedes[1] (LG) have developed a more formal model to determine the negotiating area between the upper and the lower boundaries of the exchange ratio. Based on the prevailing price/earnings ratios and the net after-tax income of each party, the LG model concludes that the upper boundary would be that which left the prevailing stock price of the acquiring company unchanged. The lower boundary (minimum exchange ratio) acceptable to the acquired company would be that which left their prevailing stock price unchanged.

If the prevailing stock price of Firm A, the acquiring company, is:

$$P_A = \frac{(P/E_A)Y_A}{N_A} \tag{23A-1}$$

where

P_A = the prevailing stock price of A
P/E_A = the prevailing price/earnings ratio for A
Y_A = the net after-tax income for A
N_A = the number of shares outstanding for A

and the prevailing stock price for Firm B, the acquired company, is:

$$P_B = \frac{(P/E_B)Y_B}{N_B} \tag{23A-2}$$

then the expected prevailing stock price after the merger is:

$$P_{AB} = \frac{P/E_{AB}(Y_A + Y_B)}{N_A + (ER)N_B} \tag{23A-3}$$

where

P_{AB} = the expected stock price after the merger
P/E_{AB} = the price/earnings ratio of the combined firm
$Y_A + Y_B$ = the earnings of the combined firm
(ER) = the exchange ratio
N_A, N_B = the number of outstanding shares for each firm prior to the merger

To keep the stock price of the merged firm from falling below the prevailing stock price of Firm A, P_A must equal P_{AB}, as in Equation 23A-4, which sets Equation 23A-1 equal to Equation 23A-3:

$$\frac{(P/E_A)Y_A}{N_A} = \frac{(P/E_{AB})(Y_A + Y_B)}{N_A + (ER)N_B} \tag{23A-4}$$

Solving for the exchange ratio gives:

$$(ER)_A = \frac{(P/E_{AB})(Y_A + Y_B) - (P/E_A)(Y_A)}{(P/E_A)(Y_A)(1/N_A)(N_B)} \tag{23A-5}$$

[1] K. D. Larson and N. J. Gonedes, "Business Combinations: An Exchange Ratio Determination Model," *Accounting Review*, XLIV (October 1969), 720–728; and Robert L. Conn, "Price/Earnings Differentials and Pure Conglomerate Mergers," unpublished manuscript.

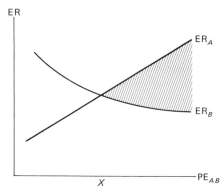

Figure 23A-1   The Upper and Lower Boundaries in Exchange Ratio Negotiations

where $(ER)_A$ is the maximum exchange ratio Firm A is willing to offer.

Similarly, P_B must equal P_{AB} so that the wealth of the acquired firm's stockholders remains at least unchanged. Setting Equation 23A-2 equal to Equation 23A-3 and solving for the exchange ratio gives:

$$(ER)_B = \frac{P/E_B(Y_B/N_B)(N_A)}{(P/E_{AB})(Y_A + Y_B) - (P/E_B)(Y_B)} \qquad (23A\text{-}6)$$

where $(ER)_B$ is the minimum exchange ratio acceptable to Firm B's stockholders.

We can graph the negotiating range between $(ER)_A$ and $(ER)_B$ for the different levels of P/E_{AB} as shown in Figure 23A-1. Notice that to the left of X there is no possible negotiation. Firm A is not willing to offer as much as Firm B needs just to stay even. To the right of X, the actual final exchange ratio agreed to by the parties occurs in the shaded area. If Firm A is the better bargainer, the actual exchange ratio will fall closer to the lower limit, $(ER)_B$; if Firm B is the better bargainer, the actual exchange ratio will fall closer to the upper boundary, $(ER)_A$.

24

MULTINATIONAL FINANCIAL MANAGEMENT

As THE FIRM EXPANDS, IT EVENTUALLY LOOKS toward the rapidly growing areas outside its home country, which we shall assume to be the United States. This is a natural progression as the firm sees foreign profit opportunities perhaps even more rewarding than those at home. In many respects profit is where the firm finds it and is not limited to any particular country. As the financial officer, you would invest in those countries which had the highest-ranking projects and finance in those countries with the least expensive capital. As the international barriers to trade and finance are removed, you must be more alert to foreign opportunities and take a global approach to the firm's investment and financing activities in order to maximize the corporate objective.

Once you have seen that international operations are a viable option, how do the particular characteristics of operating internationally affect the financial officer's method of managing working capital? We shall see that there are short-term credit instruments used almost exclusively in international finance with which you should now acquaint yourself. There are special government programs which the firm should use in its sales and overseas marketing efforts; these are designed to support our economic and political foreign policy. There are peculiarities of international accounts receivable which affect the firm's policy in this area, and there are obstacles to cash management and remittance of profits with which the financial officer must be acquainted.

Once the firm is engaged in foreign trade or overseas operations, it encounters foreign exchange risk, which can quickly turn the envisaged profit of an undertaking into a loss, unless the financial officer takes steps to counteract this potential threat to profits. How do you, as the financial officer, counter this unique risk to international operations? We shall see that the available methods include balancing your assets and liabilities in the foreign currency, forward hedging, and swaps.

Once the firm has decided to explore the possibility of investing overseas, how must the financial officer adjust the capital budgeting procedures and decision criteria to fit the international circumstances? We shall see that this entails an evaluation of the alternatives of exporting, licensing, and investing, as well as specific adjustments to the decision criteria, such as net present value and the internal rate of return, to account for the additional risks and differing circumstances of international projects.

627

Once the decision has been made to undertake overseas investments, where does the financial officer raise the capital? Specific sources include the government, quasi-government agencies such as the World Bank, foreign capital markets, and particular securities in those markets such as Eurodollar and composite currency loans.

All this overseas activity has to be reflected in the firm's financial statements. How are the financial statements affected? We shall see that generally accepted accounting principles dictate certain reporting procedures. The income statement is adversely affected by foreign exchange losses, while the balance sheet requires some interpretation in translating international operations into United States dollars.

INTERNATIONAL WORKING CAPITAL MANAGEMENT

How does operating internationally affect the financial officer's management of working capital?

The extension of credit to our international customers and their methods of payment vary from traditional domestic procedures. The international movement of working capital balances also requires special attention to such policy areas as transfer pricing, remittance, and taxes.

International Credit Instruments

In promoting international sales, the marketing force has to offer credit terms in competition with other exporters. The creation of this credit involves unique credit instruments which must be administered by the financial officer.

Bills of exchange   A bill of exchange is a draft (check) drawn to the favor of the exporter. For example, if a United States farm equipment manufacturer sold $3 million of tractors to an Irish importer, a draft for that amount is drawn to the order of the United States manufacturer. Usually arrangements are made so that the exporter draws the check against the Irish importer's established line of credit at a United States bank. The United States farm equipment manufacturer presents evidence that the machinery has been shipped, and the United States bank lets the exporter draw a draft against the line of credit. The check is typically a *time draft*, meaning that it cannot be cashed or deposited for credit to the exporter's bank account until the date specified on the draft. However, there are also sight drafts which may be cashed upon presentation.

The bill of exchange may be either "clean" or documentary. The clean bill of exchange does not have attached the documents of title, which identify the owner. The documentary bill of exchange, on the other hand, has the documents of title attached.

Bankers' acceptances   A banker's acceptance is a time draft for which a bank has guaranteed payment. The bank literally accepts the responsibility for payment, should the importer default, by turning the bill of exchange over and stamping "accepted by XYZ Bank" on the back. This acceptance may arise immediately upon creation if the importer has already arranged for the bank to act as a guarantor or when the exporter requests the action after receiving the draft. There is no compulsion for the bank to guarantee the payment if it feels the chance of default is too great.

Once accepted, the bill of exchange becomes a negotiable instrument with a high degree of marketability. Usually, the exporter will choose not to wait for the payment date on the time draft, but will instead sell what is now the banker's acceptance. The purchaser pays less than the amount on the face of the check. This discount from the face amount represents the profit to the purchaser, who can hold the time draft until the payment date, collecting the full face amount at that time. The discount reflects the prevailing annual rate of interest required by the purchaser. As the annual rate of interest increases, the discount has to widen, and vice versa. Since most time drafts are for periods of less than one year, the financial officer would have to annualize the rate of interest to determine the appropriate discount. For example, if the required annual interest rate were 10 percent, a 90-day $100,000 time draft would have to sell at $97,500 at the beginning of its life and at a progressively higher price as it approached the payment date, provided the required annual interest rate did not change.

Bills of lading Bills of lading are used in international trade in much the same way they are used in domestic trade. They accompany the documentary drafts as evidence of shipment. Typically the bills of lading are no more than a receipt by the transportation company showing that the exporter has shipped the goods. Sometimes they are negotiable such that the shipment can be redirected in transit to a party other than the one designated on the bill of lading. Sometimes they are non-negotiable, or straight, allowing shipment only to the designated party.

The bill of lading will also specify who is responsible for the goods in transit. If the shipment is designated F. O. B. (free on board) point of export, the transportation costs from that point forward are the responsibility of the importer, and title passes to the importer at the point of export. If the bill of lading is C. I. F. (cost, insurance, and freight) the title remains with the exporter until the import point, and the exporter bears the transportation costs.

Letters of credit A letter of credit represents credit extended to the importer by its bank, which in many cases allows the named exporter to draw upon it. For example, the Bank of Ireland may establish a letter of credit for the Irish tractor importer. The Bank of Ireland's correspondent bank in the United States would then be notified and would, in turn, inform the United States exporter that a letter of credit had been established upon which it could draw under the appropriate circumstances. The Irish importer naturally pays for this service, by a fee and/or interest on the amount used. Of course if the Irish importer's credit were not satisfactory, the Bank of Ireland would not establish the letter of credit in the first place.

The letter of credit may be irrevocable on the part of the lending bank, which means it stands behind the credit at all times until the loan lapses. Alternatively, the letter of credit can be revocable, allowing the bank to withdraw from the agreement at its option.[1]

The letter of credit reduces the risk of extending credit. With an irrevocable letter of credit, the financial officer can be sure that the money for the exported goods is there, for the bank guarantees it will extend the necessary funds to the importer. Without a letter of credit, the financial officer has to bill the importer as if it were a firm with an established credit record, which is less readily determined when dealing with foreign companies.

---

[1] J. F. Weston and B. W. Sorge, *International Financial Management*, Irwin, Homewood, Ill., 1972, Ch. 9.

Export-Import Assistance

The government and quasi-official agencies can help the firm export and import. The firm can use their facilities in its international marketing.

Bureau of International Commerce Through its Bureau of International Commerce, the Department of Commerce provides specific marketing services which the firm might use. It conducts foreign trade missions designed to acquaint other countries with the products of the United States. A typical trade mission might consist of agricultural producers from Texas meeting interested parties who have previously been contracted by the bureau. The bureau has a large intelligence network which can provide information on the potential of particular foreign markets for particular products as well as tariff and related information. The bureau arranges for the firm to exhibit at foreign trade shows, where potential foreign purchasers assemble. The government has commercial attachés within the consulates and embassies who relate information on the general business climate and on potential individual purchasers in certain countries. They also provide credit ratings and financial information on overseas distributors, agents, and the like.

Private sources In addition to the public sources of information and foreign trade help, there are private sources. Foreign branches of your bank can often act as overseas intelligence units for information on the general business climate and individual customers. These same foreign branches can also make the financial arrangements needed for international trade and issue such documents as letters of credit.

Foreign Credit Insurance Association The Foreign Credit Insurance Association (FCIA) insures the firm against the nonpayment of any credit extended to foreign purchasers. FCIA policies provide for payment in the event of default because of such commercial risks as the purchaser's insolvency and/or such political risks as blocked accounts—governmental regulations on removing money from the foreign country.

FCIA policy terms vary with the purchaser's country, the credit terms, and the security offered, such as a letter of credit. The insurance is more readily available for those countries which allow full convertibility between currencies and which have stable governments. The FCIA does not insure against foreign exchange losses caused by currency devaluations. Usually the exporter is required to self-insure 10 percent of the payment, meaning that in the event of default, the exporter bears 10 percent of the loss, while the FCIA reimburses the other 90 percent. The premium rates have averaged approximately 1.25 percent for 90-day coverage, although they change with the circumstances. As the financial officer, you could arrange for either blanket coverage of all the firm's foreign accounts receivable under a comprehensive policy or for individual coverage of selected accounts under separate insurance policies.

Cash Management

One of the major duties of international cash management is remitting foreign profits back to the parent company in the United States. As the financial officer, you will have to set a remittance policy which maximizes the firm's objectives and most satisfies its international cash needs. This involves consideration of transfer methods, the obstacles to remittance, and taxes.

Remittance policy The objective of remittance policy is to promote the safety and profitability of the firm's working capital balances. This entails moving those balances to where they are exposed to the least chance of nationalization or currency devaluations. In order to promote profitability, cash balances have to be moved where needed in undertaking the firm's most profitable projects, including tax considerations. The safety and profitability objectives are not always completely compatible, and the financial officer has to find the policy that best satisfies both. For example, the firm's most profitable undertaking may be in a highly unstable country, which means that the firm does not want to keep large cash balances on hand in that country. The financial officer may want to transfer the profits from that foreign subsidiary to the United States parent company.

The technical means of transfer vary. The most direct method is for the foreign subsidiary to declare a dividend out of profits payable directly to the parent company. After the declaration, payment is made by a wire or cable transfer from a foreign bank to the parent company's United States bank. This is merely a telegraph from the foreign bank authorizing its United States correspondent to credit the parent's bank account with the amount of the dividend, a simple bookkeeping entry which assures the safety of the cash balances.

The foreign government may, however, be hostile to the idea of this transfer of money; it would prefer to have the profits reinvested in the country. To discourage transfers, a withholding tax on dividend payments may be levied before transfer can take place, or the transfer of any money may be blocked. These techniques have conflicting effects for the foreign government's policy. In the short run, they tend to keep funds within the country. In the long run, they tend to discourage further investment in the country by international companies and to promote illegal networks for the clandestine transfer of funds.

If the foreign country has hostility to the firm's repatriation of profits, the financial officer may consider repatriation in other forms besides dividends. The parent company might loan the foreign subsidiary money instead of investing in its equity, because the interest on the loan is not considered profit and can be transferred more readily than dividends in most instances. Similarly royalties, licensing fees, technical service fees, and management fees are more readily transferable than profits.

The financial officer can frequently use *transfer pricing* as a tool for facilitating repatriation and avoiding taxes. Transfer pricing refers to the pricing of goods among the firm's subsidiaries in various countries. For example, if the firm's raw materials came from a subsidiary in country A, if its manufacturing subsidiary were in country B, and if its marketing subsidiary were in country C, the movement of goods along the chain of production and distribution requires that one subsidiary sell its production to another until the sale to the ultimate customer. Since it makes no difference to the company's total profit picture, which reflects all its subsidiaries, the transfer price ploy makes those particular subsidiaries where the profits tax is lowest have the highest profit, and vice versa. If country A had the highest profits tax, the firm would charge very low prices for raw materials sold to its manufacturing subsidiary in country B where the profit taxes were low. This means the firm shows little profit in the high-tax country and a large profit in the low-tax country. Of course governmental officials of country A prohibit flagrant distortions in transfer pricing, and they may even take it upon themselves to establish the export price of the raw materials.

Obstacles to remittance It is not always easy to remit funds. Foreign governments sometimes intentionally make the transfer difficult through the use of exchange controls or blocked accounts. Under the exchange control technique, all transfers out of the country must first be approved by the government. Those the government deems most necessary are granted the right to transfer and are given a relatively low exchange rate. The exchange rate is the rate at which the foreign currency can be converted into the currency of the country to which the funds are to be transferred, for example, pesos to dollars. If the foreign government deems the transfer less important to its objectives, it either rejects the right to transfer or gives a very high exchange rate, which makes it too expensive to transfer. For example, a low exchange rate of 5 pesos to buy $1 might be granted for the importation of industrial machinery, while a high exchange rate of 100 pesos to buy $1 might be granted for the dividend transfer. This naturally makes the dividend transfer less attractive than the importation of machinery, since it costs 20 times as much to buy the same transferable dollar.

If the foreign cash balances are entirely blocked, they cannot be transferred to another country at all. The cash must be spent in the foreign country or remain idle. In some instances, the financial officer can arrange for the sale of blocked account balances. After World War II, Walt Disney Productions had substantial blocked cash balances in Japan from its showings of *Cinderella* and other motion pictures. Since Disney had no need to invest in Japan, the money was essentially idle. On the other hand, the Salvation Army needed Japanese currency after World War II to establish missions in that country. Disney sold its blocked cash balances in Japan to the Salvation Army at a discount from the prevailing exchange rate. This gave the Salvation Army its needed Japanese currency at a discount and converted Disney's blocked accounts to dollars for use in the United States.

Lack of a foreign exchange market   The transfer of funds out of a foreign country may be difficult because of the lack of a foreign exchange market in which to convert the foreign currency into dollars. Even if the firm can physically transfer the foreign currency to the United States, the currency is useless unless converted into dollars because no one is willing to buy that particular foreign currency. The market for a particular currency may be so very small that the firm has to sell it at a very low price in order to entice someone to buy. This lower price upon conversion reduces the firm's profits, for it represents a cost of doing business to the parent firm, which measures its profits in dollars.

Exchange rate fluctuation   In any situation where the foreign currency has to be converted into the home currency, the firm runs the risk that the exchange or conversion rate will have dropped and the anticipated dollar profit will be reduced or wiped out. This applies to either a remittance from a foreign subsidiary or the receipt of foreign currency as payment for accounts receivable in the firm's export business. If the foreign currency is *devalued* (declines in value vis-a-vis the dollar) before the firm can convert, the firm receives fewer dollars when it finally converts. For example, if the firm had exported on 90-day credit farm equipment to Britain for one million British pounds (the British currency) when one pound was worth $2.50, it would expect to receive $2.5 million at that exchange rate. If the pound had fallen to $2 by the end of 90 days, when the British importer paid off that one million pounds, the United States exporter of the tractors would have only been able to convert that payment into $2 million, a loss of $500,000.

As you can see, loss from fluctuations in the exchange rate can be substantial. In this case it amounted to one-fifth of the $2.5 million sale. We shall see later in this chapter that financial officers are responsible for preventing such exchange rate losses and explore the techniques available to help them in this job.

Taxes The foreign country has the right to tax the profits of the foreign subsidiary and to enforce a withholding tax on the payment of dividends from that subsidiary. As a general rule, the profits of the firm are taxed where they are earned. In the United States, foreign profits are not taxed until remitted to the United States parent company. The United States firm can, however, apply the foreign taxes that it pays to other governments as a credit against its United States tax liability, although both these tax provisions have been questioned frequently and may be changed at any time. The effect of the present tax laws is to encourage foreign investment instead of exporting and to discourage the remittance of profits to the United States. In order to encourage remittance, the United States government established Domestic International Sales Corporations (DISC).[2] These are exporting arms of United States companies that qualify for lower tax rates. The DISC itself pays no taxes, and the parent company pays only 50 percent of its regular income tax rate on the qualified export-import profits of the DISC. In effect, the DISC attempts to make exporting from the United States as attractive as establishing overseas operations.

FOREIGN EXCHANGE RISK

How do you, as the financial officer, handle foreign exchange risk?

As we have seen, fluctuations in currency exchange rates impart a risk that expected profits from international sales can be eroded and that the dollar value of the foreign-denominated working capital balances and investments can be diminished. An alert financial officer protects the firm against these potential losses through adroit use of the foreign exchange market and other risk-offsetting techniques.

The Balance of Payments Setting

Prevailing exchange rates are the price your firm has to pay for United States currency (the dollar) when it converts its holdings of a foreign currency to dollars.[3] For example, the British pound exchange rate may be one pound (£) for $2.50, and the West German mark (DM) may be exchanged for $.38. In other words, it would cost $.38 to buy one mark. If the mark rose in value, it would cost more, 1 DM = $.40, for instance. If the mark fell in value, it would cost less, perhaps 1 DM = $.35.

Table 24-1 illustrates various exchange rates. Notice how many of them fluctuate substantially and could cause foreign exchange losses for the firm. The exchange rate is determined by the supply and demand for United States dollars in terms of the foreign currency. If the supply of marks offered on the foreign exchange markets around the world in exchange for United States dollars is greater than the demand for marks from people who want to convert dollars to marks, the price of the mark has to sink. In that case the mark might fall from 1 DM = $.40 to 1 DM = $.35. This makes the mark less costly in terms of United States dollars and

[2] For specific regulations covering the establishment and operations of a DISC, see the Department of Commerce booklet entitled *Domestic International Sales Corporations.*

[3] We can really convert into many currencies, but for convenience let us assume that the home currency is the United States dollar and that all foreign currencies are to be converted into the United States dollar.

Table 24-1 Foreign Exchange Rates in Cents per Unit of Foreign Currency April 1973

Period	Argentina (peso)	Australia (dollar)	Austria (schilling)	Belgium (franc)	Canada (dollar)	Ceylon (rupee)	Denmark (krone)	Finland (markka)	France (franc)
1968	.28473	111.25	3.8675	2.0026	92.801	16.678	13.362	23.761	20.191
1969	.28492	111.10	3.8654	1.9942	92.855	16.741	13.299	23.774	[1]19.302
1970	[2]26.589	111.36	3.8659	2.0139	[3]95.802	16.774	13.334	23.742	18.087
1971	22.502	113.61	[4]4.0009	2.0598	99.021	16.800	13.508	23.758	18.148
1972	19.960	119.23	4.3228	2.2716	100.937	16.057	14.384	24.022	19.825
1972—Mar		119.10	4.3342	2.2757	100.152	16.650	14.361	24.121	19.835
Apr		119.10	4.3236	2.2672	100.430	16.650	14.301	24.088	19.852
May		119.10	4.3277	2.2737	101.120	16.650	14.332	24.084	19.944
June		119.10	4.3421	2.2758	102.092	16.772	14.336	24.136	19.937
July		119.10	4.3674	2.2814	101.630	15.878	14.368	24.035	19.990
Aug		119.11	4.3470	2.2795	101.789	15.611	14.438	24.020	19.986
Sept		119.10	4.3354	2.2742	101.730	15.600	[5]14.388	24.015	19.977
Oct		119.07	4.3102	2.2640	101.756	15.605	14.453	23.562	19.906
Nov		119.09	4.3064	2.2685	101.279	15.026	14.510	24.022	19.839
Dec		[12]120.74	4.3172	2.2670	100.326	14.936	14.601	24.000	19.657
1973—Jan		127.16	4.3203	2.2665	100.071	14.904	14.536	23.986	19.671
Feb		135.46	4.8582	2.3981	100.440	15.407	15.386	24.728	20.987
Mar		141.29	4.8759	2.5378	100.333	15.774	16.275	25.628	22.191

Period	Germany (Deutsche mark)	India (rupee)	Ireland (pound)	Italy (lira)	Japan (yen)	Malaysia (dollar)	Mexico (peso)	Netherlands (guilder)
1968	25.048	13.269	239.35	.16042	.27735	32.591	8.0056	27.626
1969	[6]25.491	13.230	239.01	.15940	.27903	32.623	8.0056	27.592
1970	27.424	13.233	239.59	.15945	.27921	32.396	8.0056	27.651
1971	[7]28.768	13.338	244.42	.16174	.28779	32.989	8.0056	[7]28.650
1972	31.364	13.246	250.08	.17132	.32995	35.610	8.0000	31.153
1972—Mar	31.545	13.716	261.81	.17161	.33054	35.409	8.0000	31.384
Apr	31.468	13.735	261.02	.17138	.32943	35.406	8.0000	31.142
May	31.454	13.763	261.24	.17175	.32854	35.446	8.0000	31.124
June	31.560	13.754	[10]256.91	.17142	.33070	35.475	8.0000	31.296
July	31.634	13.072	244.47	.17208	.33219	35.918	8.0000	31.424
Aug	31.382	13.030	245.02	.17203	.33204	36.026	8.0000	31.158
Sept	31.318	13.016	244.10	.17199	.33209	36.110	8.0000	30.969
Oct	31.184	12.806	239.48	.17145	.33221	36.063	8.0000	30.869
Nov	31.215	12.540	235.05	.17109	.33224	36.124	8.0000	30.964
Dec	31.262	12.467	234.48	.17146	.33196	35.531	8.0000	30.962
1973—Jan	31.288	12.494	235.62	.17079	.33136	35.523	8.0000	31.084
Feb	33.273	12.910	242.75	[14].17421	.36041	37.679	8.0000	33.119
Mar	35.548	13.260	247.24	.17604	.38190	39.922	8.0000	34.334

allows the holders of any given amount of dollars to convert into a larger number of marks. At the time of this writing, most of the world's major currencies were on a floating exchange rate system which allows the forces of supply and demand to set the exchange rate, usually without government intervention.[4] Under the floating, or flexible, exchange rate system, the price of the mark, for example, varies from day to day in response to the supply and demand for marks. The mark could fall from 1 DM = $.40 to 1 DM = $.35, which would mean that 1 million DM could be converted

---

[4] During other periods, fixed exchange rate systems prevailed, with government intervening on the supply or the demand side to fix the exchange rate at a particular level instead of allowing it to fluctuate as it now does.

Period	New Zealand (dollar)	Norway (krone)	Portugal (escudo)	South Africa (rand)	Spain (peseta)	Sweden (krona)	Switz- erland (franc)	United King- dom (pound)
1968	111.37	14.000	3.4864	139.10	1.4272	19.349	23.169	239.35
1969	111.21	13.997	3.5013	138.90	1.4266	19.342	23.186	239.01
1970	111.48	13.992	3.4978	139.24	1.4280	19.282	23.199	239.59
1971	113.71	14.205	3.5456	140.29	1.4383	19.592	[8]24.325	244.42
1972	119.35	15.180	3.7023	129.43	1.5559	21.022	26.193	250.08
1972—Mar	119.29	15.161	3.6930	133.77	1.5369	20.956	25.974	261.81
Apr	119.36	15.151	3.6950	133.32	1.5487	20.907	25.920	261.02
May	119.41	15.214	3.7075	133.82	1.5492	21.032	25.903	261.24
June	119.13	15.303	3.7083	132.63	1.5509	21.101	26.320	[10]256.91
July	119.31	15.367	3.7178	125.26	1.5754	21.134	26.561	244.47
Aug	119.45	15.335	3.7211	125.28	1.5752	21.160	26.449	245.02
Sept	119.33	15.209	3.7221	125.26	1.5754	21.146	26.403	244.10
Oct	119.21	15.141	3.7080	[11]124.47	1.5750	21.078	26.332	239.48
Nov	119.45	15.144	3.7140	127.52	1.5753	21.076	26.346	235.05
Dec	119.53	15.187	3.7248	127.57	1.5753	21.080	26.526	234.48
1973—Jan	119.52	15.128	3.7280	127.55	1.5755	21.092	[13]26.820	235.62
Feb	126.87	16.038	3.8562	134.91	[14]1.6355	21.935	29.326	242.75
Mar	132.21	16.954	4.1005	141.43	1.7183	22.582	31.084	247.24

[1] Effective Aug. 10, 1969, the French franc was devalued from 4.94 to 5.55 francs per U.S. dollar.

[2] A new Argentine peso, equal to 100 old pesos, was introduced on Jan. 1, 1970. Since Apr. 6, 1971, the official exchange rate is set daily by the Government of Argentina. Average for Feb. 1–27, 1972.

[3] On June 1, 1970, the Canadian Government announced that, for the time being, Canada will not maintain the exchange rate of the Canadian dollar within the margins required by IMF rules.

[4] Effective May 9, 1971, the Austrian schilling was revalued to 24.75 per U.S. dollar.

[5] Danish krone—Sept. 26, 1972, n.a.; Sept. 27 and 28 rates nominal.

[6] Effective Oct, 26, 1969, the new par value of the German mark was set at 3.66 per U.S. dollar.

[7] Effective May 10, 1971, the German mark and Netherlands guilder have been floated.

[8] Effective May 10, 1971, the Swiss franc was revalued to 4.08 per U.S. dollar.

[9] Effective Oct. 20, 1971, the Spanish peseta was revalued to 68.455 per U.S. dollar.

[10] Effective June 23, 1972, the U.K. pound was floated.

[11] South Africa repegged the rand at 127.32 cents Oct. 25, 1972.

[12] Effective Dec. 23, 1972, the Australian dollar was revalued to 127.50 cents.

[13] Effective Jan. 23, 1973, the Swiss franc was floated.

[14] Effective Feb. 13, 1973, the Italian lira and Japanese yen have been floated.

NOTE.—Effective Aug. 16, 1971, the U.S. dollar convertibility to gold was suspended; as from that day foreign central banks did not have to support the dollar rate in order to keep it within IMF limits.

During December 1971, certain countries established central rates against the U.S. dollar in place of former IMF parities.

Averages of certified noon buying rates in New York for cable transfers. For description of rates and back data, see "International Finance," Section 15 of *Supplement to Banking and Monetary Statistics*, 1962.

SOURCE: *Federal Reserve Bulletin*, April 1973, p. A91.

into $350,000 instead of $400,000. We can see that if the firm were to receive marks 90 days from now and the price of the mark fell during that time, the firm would have suffered an exchange rate loss.

The financial officer must try to keep up with supply and demand factors to judge whether the United States dollar will be higher or lower in price when the firm wishes to convert its foreign currency holdings and expected foreign-denominated revenues.[5] What are the supply and demand factors that the financial officer should

[5] For a more complete discussion of the balance of payments in accounting see J. F. Weston and B. Sorge, *International Financial Management*, Irwin, Homewood, Ill., 1972; C. P. Kindleberger, *International Economics*, 5th ed., Irwin, Homewood, Ill., 1972; and Paul Enzig, *A Textbook on Foreign Exchange*, St. Martin's Press, New York, 1966.

watch in order to keep abreast of developments that affect foreign exchange rates?

We can isolate the general categories of supply and demand for the United States dollar so that you, as the alert financial officer, can examine them more closely when trying to prevent your firm from suffering exchange rate losses. These general categories are in the United States balance of payments (BOP), which reflects the inflows and outflows of dollars from the United States. As a general rule, outflows increase the foreign ownership of dollars and the supply of dollars offered in the foreign exchange markets. This forces down the price of the dollar. Conversely, an inflow of dollars into the United States creates a foreign demand for dollars to spend or invest in the United States and increases the price of dollars in terms of other currencies. If the inflow is greater on balance than the outflow, the price of the dollar tends to rise, and vice versa. Alert financial officers try to evaluate the foreseeable future and the extent of imbalance. If they foresee a larger net outflow, they take precautions against a lower dollar exchange rate and the increased chance of exchange rate losses.

The major categories of dollar outflows are as follows:

1. United States merchandise imports These are goods which the United States has purchased abroad and for which it must pay by converting dollars into a foreign currency. This increases the supply of dollars.

2. United States service imports These are foreign services which the United States purchases and in so doing creates a large supply of dollars in the foreign exchange market. This category includes such items as travel abroad by United States tourists.

3. United States government transfers and grants These are outflows connected with such items as United States foreign aid and military assistance. When the United States distributes foreign aid or maintains overseas military bases, for example, dollars spent are converted into other currencies, putting further downward pressure on the price of the dollar.

4. Long-term foreign investment When United States firms and individuals invest in long-term foreign securities or acquire other assets abroad, they create an outflow of dollars into the hands of the foreigners who sold these securities or assets. This increases the supply of dollars offered in the foreign exchange markets and puts downward pressure on the price of the dollar.

5. Short-term foreign investment When United States corporations or individuals purchase short-term securities of foreigners, such as United Kingdom (Great Britain) Treasury bills because the interest rate on them is more attractive than on similar United States Treasury bills, dollars pass into the hands of foreigners. This increases the supply and forces down the price of the dollar.

The offsetting inflows which the financial officer has to watch include:

1. United States merchandise exports These are goods which the United States has sold abroad and for which it will receive foreign currency in payment. This foreign currency will be converted into dollars, creating a demand for dollars in the foreign exchange market and putting upward pressure on the price of the dollar.

2. United States service exports These are services which the United States has sold to other countries, such as investment income from dividends and interest from foreign securities bought by the United States.

3. Long-term investment in the United States When foreigners invest in the United States by purchasing domestic securities or assets, they must convert their currencies into dollars before making the purchase. This creates a demand for dollars and puts upward pressure on the price of the dollar.

4. Short-term investment in the United States When foreigners are attracted to

the short-term securities of the United States, such as United States Treasury bills because of higher interest rates or more attractive capital gains opportunities, they, like the other foreigners who invest long-term, must first convert their currency into dollars. This creates a demand for the dollar in the foreign exchange market and puts upward pressure on the price of the dollar. This circumstance might have special significance in your financial planning. As the United States monetary authorities see a balance of payments deficit, they may try to offset it by raising interest rates in the United States to higher levels than those which prevail in other countries, in an attempt to attract short-term investment and support the price of the dollar in the foreign exchange market. This might make your cost of capital much more expensive.

The alert financial officer looks at the various categories as well as the overall balance and tries to gauge the chances of particularly large shifts in the balance and to take precautionary measures to combat any adverse effects of such shifts.

The Risk

Changes in the balance of payments can result in changes in the exchange rate and losses for the United States firm. A decline in the United States balance of payments could cause the dollar's exchange rate to decline. Even changes in the probabilities of shifts or revised expectations can change the exchange rate. For example, the Arab oil embargo of 1974 caused extensive currency realignments in anticipation of the impact higher oil prices would have on the balance of payments of various countries.

These balance of payments shifts and accompanying changes in the exchange rate can erode or wipe out the expected profit on international sales. For example, let us assume that the United States farm equipment exporter had sold £100,000 (pounds) worth of tractors to a British importer when the pound was worth $2.50: each pound could be converted into $2.50. If the United States exporter worked on a 10 percent profit margin, it would have had a $25,000 profit when the pound was worth $2.50:

Expected gross revenue (£1 = $2.50)	$250,000
Total expenses (90%)	225,000
Profit (10%)	25,000

However, if before the United States exporter received those funds the pound dropped to $2, the exporter would actually lose $25,000 at the time of converting the payment to dollars:

Revenues at conversion time (£1 = $2.00)	$200,000
Total expenses	225,000
Total loss	(25,000)

Notice that the loss occurred solely because of fluctuations in the exchange rate. It had nothing to do with the efficiency or solvency of either importer or exporter, and it is totally beyond their control. The drop from $2.50 to $2 in the value of the pound has changed an expected $25,000 profit into a realized $25,000 loss. Fortunately there are techniques which financial officers can use to protect the firm against such loss exposure. Many of these techniques involve the forward foreign exchange market.

The Forward Foreign Exchange Market

In addition to the immediate (spot) market for foreign exchange, forward markets have been developed in many currencies. These forward markets allow the financial officer to buy or sell (convert) from one currency to another in anticipation of future needs. For example, the United States farm equipment exporter could sell the pounds it expected to receive in 90 days from the British importer for dollars in the forward market. It would not have to wait until it received the £100,000, as it would if only the spot market existed. The United States exporter does not actually deliver the £100,000 when dealing in the forward market. It merely contracts with a buyer of those pounds to deliver £100,000 on a specified future date in return for the buyer's promise to purchase the pounds at that date for the presently negotiated contract price. Of course the spot price for immediate delivery of pounds and the forward price for future delivery do not have to be the same on any one day, for the two markets are separately negotiated, though the behavior of one tends to influence the other.

The financial officer can use the forward market to mitigate the chances of exchange rate loss. For example, if the 90-day forward market at the time our United States exporter sells the tractors to the British importer is £1 = $2.45, the exporter can immediately contract with a buyer in the forward market (usually a bank) for a price of $2.45 for 90-day delivery. The United States exporter is now certain of profit and no longer has to worry about fluctuations in exchange rates eroding it:

Revenue (1 90-day forward pound = $2.45)	$245,000
Total expenses	225,000
Total profit	20,000

Notice that the exporter knows in advance exactly what the profits are going to be, since both revenue and costs are now locked in terms of dollars. No matter how the British pound fluctuates in terms of the United States dollar, the exporter's profits remain $20,000. Notice, however, that the total profit has decreased $5,000 from our earlier example, in which the expected profit was $25,000 when the expected conversion price of the pound in the spot market was $2.50. The $.05 difference between the spot price ($2.50) and the forward price ($2.45) caused the decline in total profits of $5,000. The firm had to accept $2.45 a pound from the forward buyer at the time of export instead of the prevailing $2.50 spot price. This $5,000 may be looked upon by the financial officer as insurance costs against devaluation of the pound during the 90 days that the firm has to wait for the £100,000 payment. If the firm had not contracted for the forward sale at $2.45, it would have had to wait 90 days until payment was received before it could sell the pounds for dollars in the spot market. During that interval the price of the pound could have dropped, and the firm's profits would have eroded more than $5,000.

If the financial officer foresees a potential erosion in the firm's profits because of exchange rate fluctuations greater than the expense of using the forward market with its discounted pound price in terms of dollars, he or she should definitely contract for future delivery in the forward market. Some firms, not wishing to expose themselves to *any* exchange risk that can be avoided, automatically contract for forward delivery as soon as the sale is consummated. Other firms, more willing to risk the chance of exchange rate loss, may not use the forward market if they feel the discount is too large compared to the foreseen chance of loss. And it happens that sometimes the forward is at a premium to the spot price, and the firm's profits increase upon forward sale.

Where competitive circumstances allow, other firms who do not wish to expose themselves to exchange rate loss sell only in terms of the United States dollar. This avoids all exchange risk for the United States firm since it eliminates the necessity of converting foreign currencies to dollars. Of course, not all firms can negotiate international sales in terms of their own domestic currency.

The forward market, where it exists, also allows the financial officer an opportunity to use international money market instruments as part of the cash management program with limited foreign exchange rate risk. For example, if United Kingdom treasury bills are offering higher yields than comparable money market instruments in the United States, financial officers might put temporary excess working capital balances in the United Kingdom bills in order to get the higher interest rate. At the same time they would want to guard against the chance of a devaluation during the interval the firm was invested in those bills. A devaluation could mean that when the financial officers converted the United Kingdom treasury bill proceeds, which are denominated in British pounds, the dollar amount might be less than if they had invested in United States bills. However, the use of the forward market again allows financial officers to protect their short-term foreign investments against exchange rate risk. Suppose the following rates and relationships prevail:

90-day United States bill rate = 9%
90-day United Kingdom bill rate = 15%
Spot exchange rate £1 = $2.40
90-day forward exchange rate £1 = $2.37

By investing in the United Kingdom bill, the United States financial officer gets a 6 percent higher yield on an annual basis but runs the risk that, if during the 90-days of investment in the United Kingdom bill the pound is devaluated more than 6 percent on an annual basis, the firm actually earns less in dollars than if it had originally bought the lower-yield United States bills. However, if the firm had sold the pounds it expected to receive 90 days from now, when the United Kingdom bill matures, in the forward market at $2.37 upon purchasing the United Kingdom bills, it would have eliminated the exchange rate risk. Of course it would have had to buy the pounds needed to purchase the United Kingdom bills in the first place in the spot market at $2.40, which entails a guaranteed loss on the purchase in the spot market and simultaneous sale in the forward market of $.03 for 3 months or 5 percent on an annual basis. Thus, the 6 percent annual interest rate differential would be cut to only 1 percent in favor of the United Kingdom bills after the cost of exchange rate protection is considered. This is still 1 percent more than the United States bills at no additional risk, and the financial officer may still find it attractive to put temporary excess working capital balances in United Kingdom bills.

Hedging Assets and Liabilities

The financial officer is also required to protect the firm from losses in the translation of foreign-denominated working capital balances, assets, and liabilities into dollars. When the exchange rate changes, the assets and liabilities on the United States firm's financial statements have to be revalued. Since the foreign currency value of the foreign asset or liability remains the same, exchange rate fluctuations cause the dollar value of that asset or liability on the United States financial statements to change. For example, if the firm had 100,000 marks (DM) in cash at a German bank, the value of that cash balance on the United States firm's financial statements if 1 DM = $.40 would be $40,000, while the value of that same 100,000 DM if

1 DM = $.35 would be only $35,000. The firm's balance would show a lower asset figure. On the other hand, the firm's mark-denominated liabilities would have decreased in terms of dollars. The net effect on the financial statements depends on the relative quantities of foreign-denominated assets and liabilities.

Financial officers can use this relative balance to hedge against any devaluation in two ways. In those countries where the firm has a greater-asset-than-liabilities position, they can sell the currency of that country now, promising to deliver the actual currency later. If there is a devaluation of that currency in the meantime, the loss on the translation of the assets is offset by the gain on the sale of the currency. The gain from the currency arises because the financial officers are able to buy the currency they have already promised to deliver at a lower price than they agreed to deliver it for. The difference is the firm's profit, and the technique is known as going short in the exchange market. Usually, this technique is reserved only for those periods when the financial officer feels the devaluation is close at hand.

More typically, the financial officer will not attempt a forward market short sale to cover an impending devaluation of a foreign currency, but will try instead to match any foreign-denominated assets with liabilities of that currency. The effect of a devaluation would then be offset. This procedure is applied over the entire life of the foreign subsidiary as a matter of standard practice to forestall any devaluation effects. For example, if the firm had a German subsidiary, it might finance it with long-term debt denominated in marks. The firm could also match its revenues and its costs in the same currency to prevent devaluation causing an unfavorable distortion in earnings upon translation.

INTERNATIONAL CAPITAL BUDGETING

How must you, as the financial officer, adjust the firm's capital budgeting procedures to reflect the circumstances of international investment projects?

When evaluating international investment opportunities, the financial officer must examine such impacts on the project's attractiveness as different political, social, and economic environments which may be more or less risky than that prevailing in the United States. We shall see that the project's net cashflows and its associated cost of capital must be adjusted accordingly.

The Investment Environment

When operating in a foreign country, the firm experiences different political systems and climates. Each different system has a different impact on the profitability of the project. The financial officer must understand what political risks exist before committing the firm to the project in order to incorporate the proper degree of risk into the capital budgeting analysis. The firm's decision-makers should at least be made aware of the risks, even if they are hard to quantify. Among the more prevalent political risks of operating in foreign countries are nationalization, governmental instability, different and changing tax laws, and bureaucracy. While all countries have these risks in varying degrees, they are more serious in some than others.

In addition to the political risks, the financial officer must be aware of the social responsibilities that the firm encounters in different countries. For example, some countries have very rigid and costly employee benefits. In some instances, firing an employee is not allowed. Local customs and employee attitudes toward work, honesty, population, and religion must be considered.

Finally, the economic climates differ. Tariff barriers, local business customs, general economic activity, repatriation of earnings, foreign exchange rate stability, and the existence of a foreign exchange market, labor costs, and technological expertise must all be taken into account.

While all these factors are hard to quantify and vary greatly among countries, their impact on the success of the project must be assessed. Sometimes the judgment is more intuitive than statistical, but some conclusion must be reached before an appropriate analysis can be made.

Three Alternatives

Before discussing the particulars of capital budgeting as it applies to the international projects, let us consider the three basic alternatives the firm has when considering international expansion. These are export, license, and foreign subsidiaries. The firm can service the foreign market by *exporting* from its home country, and this is usually the first step in international expansion. It offers the advantages of not leaving the home environment, but it is usually very costly because of transportation charges. Another firm can easily take over the foreign market by establishing itself in the foreign country and selling at a lower price and, in some cases, by operating behind a protective tariff wall.

Alternatively, the firm can *license* another firm in the foreign market to produce and sell its products. This has the advantages of evading the tariff walls, having local problems handled locally, and perhaps smoothing over the political considerations of local production and local control. On the other hand, it may undermine the firm's technological advantage and jeopardize the quality and reputation of the firm's product.

Finally, the firm can establish a *foreign subsidiary* to produce and sell the product in the foreign country, when the social and political climate permits. The subsidiary can be 100 percent owned by the United States company or it can be a joint venture with local participation. The 100 percent ownership has the advantages of control and policy flexibility. The parent firm can dictate dividend remittance and transfer pricing policy without objection from local interests, if the law allows.

The joint venture with local participation, on the other hand, enhances the subsidiary's local political connections and its knowledge of local customs. Such knowledge may be very helpful in guiding the firm through the pitfalls of local operating conditions. The joint venture also allows the parent firm to share the risk by more readily obtaining local capital and by receiving tax advantages not otherwise available. The major disadvantages to the parent are a loss of control, particularly in situations where the voting power is shared and in decisions on remittance policy. It is up to the financial officer to weigh the advantages and the disadvantages carefully.

Capital Budgeting Analysis

With the three major international alternatives of export, license, or foreign subsidiary in mind, let us turn to specific adjustments in the capital budgeting evaluation procedure. International projects must be made comparable to domestic projects so that all may be ranked in descending order of attractiveness. In order to achieve this comparability, we must adjust the project's net cashflows as well as its cost of capital for those unique international risks.

The expected net cashflow to the foreign investment project must be viewed almost as if the parent firm were a stockholder in an outside corporation. Particularly in joint ventures, but even in 100 percent owned foreign subsidiaries, the parent firm resembles a stockholder, because the investment in the foreign subsidiary is in the securities of that subsidiary and not directly in assets. Capital budgeting analysis should reveal whether the purchase of the foreign subsidiary securities is worth the outlay, not, as in the case of the domestic capital budgeting, whether the purchase of a piece of productive machinery is worth the outlay. The local officers and decision-makers of the foreign subsidiary do their own capital budgeting and decide on individual projects locally, in most instances.[6] Accordingly, the pertinent cashflow to the parent in deciding to invest in the foreign subsidiary is the remittance it expects to receive in terms of United States dollars.

It is important to recognize that only the *remitted cashflow in terms of dollars* is appropriate. Any funds forced to remain in a country beyond the control of the parent are of little value to the parent and cannot be counted as part of the net cashflow. The first adjustment is to consider only the expected remitted cashflows.

Sometimes, however, the use of the funds in the foreign subsidiary enhances its value even if the funds are not remitted to the parent, just as when domestic earnings are properly reinvested. To account for that useful part of the net cashflow which remains in the foreign subsidiary, the financial officer might assume that the book value, including any increase in value because of the reinvestment, will be returned to the parent, if the foreign country allows, at the end of the planning horizon (an arbitrary number of years used for planning foreign investment). Instead of the book value, the financial officer could use a market value if one has been established, since the domestic stockholder might look upon an increase in the share price caused by growth in the firm's dividends and earnings as a future gain. The second adjustment is to calculate a book value of the parent's security holdings in the foreign subsidiary, which, if the security holdings are sold at some future date, could be remitted much like a salvage value.

Thirdly, since the earnings of the foreign subsidiary have to be converted into United States dollars, the financial officer has to adjust the expected remitted cashflows and remitted book value at the end of the planning horizon to their expected United States dollar equivalency, based upon expectations for exchanged rate fluctuations over the planning period.

For example, let us assume we are considering a 5-year, $100,000 investment in a Latin American subsidiary with the following expectations:

Original outlay	$100,000
Present exchange rate	$1.00 = 5 pesos
Expected annual net cashflow	200,000 pesos
Expected annual allowed remittance	50% of the net cashflow
Expected value of the exchange rate	10% less in years 3 and 5 because of devaluations
Estimated book value at the end of year 5	1,234,568 pesos

[6] In those cases where capital budgeting for the individual projects is centralized and the foreign subsidiary is treated more like a division of the domestic corporation without remittance worries, such as happens between a United States parent and its Canadian subsidiary, there is no need to adjust the capital budget procedures for remittance—only for expected exchange rate fluctuations. Then, the whole net cashflow to the project can be discounted as if it were a domestic project.

The appropriate net cashflow stream for the United States parent to consider in its decision is:

Year	0	1	2	3	4	5
	−$100,000	$20,000	$20,000	$18,000	$18,000	$16,200 + $200,000

Notice that the expected cashflows to the parent reflect the remittance in terms of dollars and are adjusted for the devaluation in years 3 and 5. The book value at the end of year 5 is expected to be remitted in full and has risen $2\frac{1}{2}$ times in pesos but only 2 times in terms of dollars.

The Cost of Capital

In addition to adjusting the net cashflows for the remittance and the devaluation considerations, the financial officer has to adjust the firm's cost of capital (k) for international projects. The required rate of return demanded by suppliers of capital when the firm uses the funds for international investment may differ from that required when they are used for United States domestic investment. For example, if the project is in a politically unstable country where a threat of nationalization exists, investors would demand a higher return, and the firm's cost of capital would increase. The financial officer cannot use the prevailing cost of capital for evaluations since international expansion will change it. On the other hand, if international expansion is undertaken in countries with political stability and the risk is the same as in the United States, the firm's cost of capital may not change.

Decision Criteria for International Capital Budgeting

We must adjust the net cashflows of the decision criteria (Chapter 5) for remittance restrictions and expected devaluations, and we must adjust the cost of capital (k) for any additional risk.

Internal rate of return Our adjusted international decision criterion for internal rate of return would be:

$$C = \sum_{t=1}^{n} \frac{\overline{CF}_{US}}{(1 + r_1)^t} + \frac{BV_{US}}{(1 + r_1)^n} \tag{24-1}$$

where
$\overline{CF}_{US}$ = the expected net after-tax dollar remittance to the United States parent, adjusted for devaluation expectations
BV_{US} = terminal value of the foreign subsidiary in United States dollars
r_1 = the internal rate of return
C = the original outlay in dollars
n = the number of years in the planning horizon

If $r_1 > k_1$ the project should be ranked among the acceptable projects which may be undertaken. The k_1 is the cost of capital adjusted for the international risk differential. In our example:

$$\$100{,}000 = \frac{\$20{,}000}{(1+r_1)^1} + \frac{\$20{,}000}{(1+r_1)^2} + \frac{\$18{,}000}{(1+r_1)^3} + \frac{\$18{,}000}{(1+r_1)^4} + \frac{\$216{,}200}{(1+r_1)^5}$$

$$r_1 \cong 30\%$$

If we assume $k_1 = 15$ percent, the firm should consider undertaking the project.[7]

Net present value Our adjusted international decision criterion for net present value would be:

$$NPV = \sum_{t=1}^{n} \frac{\overline{CF}_{US}}{(1+k_1)^t} + \frac{BV_{US}}{(1+k_1)^n} - C \tag{24-2}$$

where

NPV = net present value

C = original outlay in dollars

$\overline{CF}_{US}$ = expected net after-tax dollar remittance to the United States parent, adjusted for devaluation expectations

BV_{US} = expected book value at the end of the planning horizon in United States dollars

n = the number of years in the planning horizon

k_1 = risk adjusted cost of capital

If $NPV > 0$, the firm should rank the project among its acceptable possibilities. In our example, if $k_1 = 15$ percent:

$$NPV = \frac{\$20{,}000}{(1+.15)} + \frac{\$20{,}000}{(1+.15)^2} + \frac{\$18{,}000}{(1+.15)^3} + \frac{\$18{,}000}{(1+.15)^4} + \frac{\$216{,}200}{(1+.15)} - \$100{,}000$$

$$= \$62{,}111$$

Since the project's net present value is positive, the firm should consider undertaking it.

Payback On occasion, the prospects for future remittance after a given number of years are so uncertain that the firm chooses to ignore any possible remittance beyond that period in its international capital budgeting. It would be as if the book value or salvage in the previous methods were totally ignored, along with any other possible remittances after a specific cut-off date. Under these circumstances, the firm may use the payback decision criterion to determine the period necessary to recover its investment. This method is only appropriate in the most unstable countries and is frowned upon by most foreign governments who prefer that firms treat investments as long-term commitments. The payback decision criterion for international operations would be:

$$N = \frac{C}{\overline{CF}_{US}} \tag{24-3}$$

[7] We could also use a certainty-equivalent approach (see Appendix 7A) by reducing the expected cashflow from the foreign subsidiary to its certain equivalent and discounting by the risk-free rate.

where

$C =$ the original outlay

$\overline{CF}_{US} =$ the expected net after-tax dollar remittance to the United States parent, adjusted for devaluation expectations

$N =$ the payback period

If N is less than some predetermined number of years (N^*) during which the firm feels it is safe to operate in the country in question, the firm should accept the project. In our example, the recovery of the $100,000 would not occur until year 5.

OPIC

The Overseas Private Investment Corporation (OPIC) is a quasi-public insurance company which insures the firm's international capital projects against political risks, nationalization, and currency inconvertibility in certain countries. The typical OPIC policy runs from 3 to 20 years but does not insure against exchange risk and is not issued in all countries. The financial officer may find that previously unacceptable projects become acceptable when some of the risks can be insured.[8]

SOURCES OF INTERNATIONAL FUNDS

Once the firm has decided to undertake an international investment, where does the financial officer raise the capital?

Either by choice or by government regulations, financial officers have turned to international capital markets for funds. Let us look at some of the international securities used in those markets and at government-associated sources of funds for international investment. Of course private sources of funds also exist, and the parent firm can always finance internally by investing its own retained earnings in a foreign subsidiary.

Government Sources

The government and quasi-governmental authorities are sources of funds or payment guarantees for the financial officer.[9]

The World Bank The International Bank for Reconstruction and Development (World Bank) finances development projects through foreign exchange loans to governments and their agencies and provides guarantees of payment to private firms who undertake the project. Its International Finance Corporation affiliate makes higher-risk loans and takes equity positions in firms in developing areas. Its International Development Association makes low-interest, long-term loans ("soft loans") to developing nations. An international firm would bid on projects announced by the bank.

Regional development banks Various regions around the world have set up banks to provide development and trade loans to the nations of that region, usually with

[8] More detailed information on OPIC may be obtained by writing to OPIC, Washington, D. C.

[9] Weston and Sorge, *International Financial Management*, Ch. 8.

United States participation, such as in the Inter-American Development Banks. While these banks do not usually deal directly with the United States parent firm, they may finance projects in which the parent is involved or help associated firms within the region.

The Export-Import Bank Unlike the World Bank and regional development banks, the Export-Import (Ex-Im) Bank works directly with the firm. It is designed to encourage United States exports by financing their purchase. Sometimes this involves a direct loan to the foreign purchaser. Sometimes it is a guaranteed bank loan to the exporting firm at relatively low interest rates to help produce the export goods. Sometimes it is an advance to foreign financial institutions to help them finance foreign importers of United States exports. Working through a local commercial bank, the alert financial officer can arrange to take advantage of Ex-Im programs.

AID The Agency for International Development (AID) makes direct loans to other governments to purchase needed goods, hopefully from the United States. They also issue investment guarantees against currency inconvertibility, expropriation, war, and similar situations.

Foreign Development Authorities Many foreign countries have established development authorities to attract foreign investment. In some cases the development authority will not only arrange tax holidays which allow the firm to avoid taxation in that country but will also give the firm grants to train workers and construct plants, all of which lowers the firm's original outlay.

Sources Outside Government

Swaps The swap technique allows the financial officer to avoid the exchange rate and inconvertibility risks.[10] Under the swap arrangement, the firm and a foreign lender, usually the foreign central bank or a commercial bank, agree to trade the use of dollars for the use of the local currency for a given period, at the end of which the swap is reversed and the arrangement terminated. For example, the United States firm deposits United States dollars in a United States bank for the foreign bank's use for one year. In return the foreign bank loans the foreign subsidiary local currency for one year. The foreign bank gets the use of the dollars and charges the foreign subsidiary interest on the loan. At the end of that year, the foreign subsidiary repays the loan and interest in local currency, and the foreign bank returns the United States deposit to the parent company. Since the loan is borrowed and repaid in local currency by the foreign subsidiary, there is no exchange rate risk exposure. The United States dollars are never converted into any other currency by the parent, so there is no exchange rate risk exposure at the parent company level either.

The swap is costly. First, the foreign subsidiary pays interest on the foreign currency loan. Second, the swap usually requires that the parent company deposit a larger number of dollars for any given number of foreign currency units than it would have to if it converted to that foreign currency at the prevailing spot rate. For example, the foreign bank might require a United States deposit of $250,000 for a loan of one million pesos ($1 = 4 pesos) when the exchange rate was $1 = 5 pesos in the spot market—in effect a 20 percent premium. Third, the parent has lost the

---

[10] Weston and Sorge, *International Financial Management,* pp.105 ff.

opportunity to earn a return on the United States dollars it has deposited for the use of the foreign bank. But if the expected devaluation over the life of the loan is greater than the costs, it is less costly to use the swap than to have the parent company convert its dollars and run the risk of exchange rate fluctuations. If the financial officer anticipated that the foreign currency would be devalued 30 percent during the life of the loan, a swap costing less than 30 percent would be preferred.

Eurobonds The financial officer, in conjunction with an investment banker, may decide to offer the firm's securities in capital markets outside the United States. These bond or stock offerings may be denominated either in United States dollars, in which case the firm is attempting to borrow the excess dollars held by foreigners, or in foreign currency denominations. Recent issues besides the dollar-denominated bond have been in marks, Swiss francs, and Dutch guilders. The United States firm borrows the currency in that particular denomination and promises to pay interest and return the principal in that same denomination. If the dollar is devalued in relation to that other currency while the United States firm owes the money, its liability is increased in terms of dollars. Conversely, if the foreign currency is devalued in terms of the dollar, the firm's liability is reduced and the owner of the bond suffers a reduction in its value in terms of that foreign currency.

Composite currency loans To avoid the risk of exchange rate fluctuations associated with the Eurobonds, several firms have arranged to borrow loans comprised of several different currencies, sometimes called *eurco*. If one currency is devalued, the loss is offset by the gain in the other currencies. By diversifying over several currencies, the firm and the lender have reduced their exchange risk exposure. And of course the firm can borrow in eurco and convert to any currency it may need for investment purposes, though doing so reduces the diversification benefits.

Eurodollar loans The Eurodollar loan is a dollar-denominated loan from foreign holders of dollars. Usually the financial officer can arrange a Eurodollar loan through the local domestic bank, who contacts a foreign branch or a foreign correspondent bank holding dollars which it lends to the United States firm. The typical Eurodollar loan is for less than one year and most commonly for less than 90 days, although the maturity is negotiable.

Edge Act banks Edge Act banks are specially chartered subsidiaries of United States banks created for the express intent of financing international transactions. Under charters granted from the federal government, they are restricted solely to international transactions, although they may be located anywhere within the United States or around the world. Thus we would find the California-based Bank of America with Edge Act subsidiaries throughout the exporting centers of the United States.

The financial officer will generally find these Edge Act banks extremely skillful in handling export and import financing through government sources such as the Export-Import Bank and through private channels. They are also able to finance foreign investment needs.

Government Regulations

Governments take an unusually active interest in the capital outflows from their country because they are very conscious of the exchange rate and the impact it can have on domestic economic activity. Almost all countries for one reason or another strive for equilibrium in their balance of payments. If a country is in a deficit balance-of-payments posture (outflows exceed inflows), it may take restrictive measures against capital outflows in an attempt to restore balance. In the United States, for example, interest-equalization taxes have been applied to investments in foreign securities in order to discourage the outflow of capital during times of balance-of-payments deficits. Licensing and quasi-voluntary measures applied to the foreign investments of United States businesses have forced the international expansion of many firms to be financed in capital markets outside the United States. The financial officer must be aware of these regulations when making plans for financing international expansion.

ACCOUNTING CONSIDERATIONS

How do the financial statements reflect the firm's international operations?

Let us briefly explore how foreign operations, and particularly exchange rate fluctuations, affect the balance sheet and the income statement.[11]

Losses and Gains on Foreign Exchange

If the losses or the gains have been realized, the amount of the loss or the gain must be charged or credited to the income statement. If there has been a decline in the translation of the current or working capital assets, even if it has not been realized, the losses must be charged against income, but the unrealized gains are accumulated in a reserve account to offset any losses.

Balance Sheet

Current assets are translated at the prevailing rate of exchange. Fixed assets, on the other hand, are carried at the rate prevailing when acquired or constructed, unless shortly after that a substantial and permanent change in the exchange rate occurred.

Current liabilities are translated at the prevailing rate of exchange. Long-term liabilities are also translated at the rate prevailing now if they were issued shortly before a substantial and presumably permanent change in the exchange rate. For example, the Gulf Oil Company sold an issue of long-term debt denominated in marks shortly before the mark was revalued upward. The incurred loss in translation had to be charged to operations and resulted in a rather substantial reduction in reported profits. Under certain circumstances, however, the accounting profession still recognizes a translation of long-term liabilities at the rate which prevailed when they were first sold.

Income Statement

The parent's income statement allows foreign subsidiary profits to be translated at the average monthly rate over the accounting period, unless the change in the rate has been substantial. In that case, the new exchange rate is used in the translation.

---

[11] Accounting Research Bulletin No. 43, Ch. 12, and Financial Accounting Standards Board Statement No. 1.

Footnotes to the Financial Statements

The accounting profession requires that the firm disclose whether the current or the historical rate was used in the translation, the aggregate amount of the exchange adjustments originating in the period, the amount thereof reflected in the present income statement, and the amount thereof deferred. The footnotes must also disclose the amount the balance sheet would be affected if the long-term receivables and payables translated at the historic exchange rate were translated at the current exchange rate instead, and the amount of unrealized gains and losses.

Inflation

In some countries with severe inflation, the value of the assets may be increased on the financial statements to reflect the higher prices, but the exact procedures and rules vary among countries. Some of the countries which require or permit write-ups of assets also tax those write-ups as profit.

SUMMARY

After having read Chapter 24, you should be able to answer these questions:

1. How do international operations affect the firm's working capital management?

There are credit instruments unique to international trade, such as the bill of exchange, bankers' acceptances, letters of credit, and international bills of lading. We also saw that the financial officer can get assistance in promoting the firm's international sales and handling its credit operations from the Department of Commerce and the Foreign Credit Insurance Association.

In handling the firm's international cash management operations, the financial officer has to consider the firm's remittance policy and the methods of transferring funds across national boundaries. We saw that international cash management requires understanding transfer pricing among the firm's subsidiaries and such techniques as establishing Domestic International Sales Corporations for surmounting blocked accounts, exchange controls, and taxes.

2. How does the financial officer handle foreign exchange risk?

Fluctuations in the rate of exchange between currencies can cause the firm to suffer losses or realize gains beyond its control when converting foreign currency receipts into United States dollars. The exchange rate fluctuates with the supply and demand for the various currencies, and it is the financial officer's responsibility to keep track of potential shifts in the supply-demand relationship in the balance-of-payments context to avoid adverse effects on the firm's international profits.

We also saw that the financial officer can use the forward foreign exchange market to hedge the firm's expected foreign currency revenues and avoid the exchange risk. We saw that there is a cost to such hedging if the forward contract price is less than the spot market price. Still another hedging technique to avoid exchange rate fluctuations is for the firm to balance its foreign liabilities and assets so that any exchange rate change effect is neutralized.

3. How must the financial officer adjust the firm's capital budgeting procedures when evaluating international projects?

Procedures must be adjusted to consider only that portion of the expected cashflow which will be remitted to the parent firm, and the cashflow must be adjusted for any expected devaluations. The unremitted portion of the cashflow should be considered as accumulating to the end of the time horizon and then treated as salvage value in many instances.

The firm's cost of capital has to be adjusted to reflect the increased or decreased risk of raising funds for international investment projects. Then the internal rate of return or the net present value using these adjusted figures can be employed in an analogous fashion to the domestic decision criteria. The acceptable international projects should be ranked along with the acceptable domestic projects, and the most attractive should be undertaken first.

We also saw that due consideration has to be given to the investment environment, including the political, economic, and social risks of operating in a foreign land. If the firm does not want to commit itself entirely to the foreign venture, it can export, license, or use a joint venture approach instead.

4. Once the firm has decided to invest overseas, where can the financial officer raise the necessary funds?

Assistance can be obtained from government-associated programs, particularly the Export-Import Bank. Private sources include the firm's domestic earnings, swaps, Eurobonds, Eurodollar loans, and composite loans such as eurco.

5. How do international operations affect the firm's financial statements?

Realized and unrealized losses must be deducted from the firm's earnings during the period, while unrealized gains are held in reserve until offset by losses. We also saw that the different accounts on the balance sheet were subject to different translation rates of exchange. Some were translated at the historic rate, while others were translated at the current rate.

QUESTIONS

24-1 How is a bill of exchange similar to a banker's acceptance? How is it different?

24-2 What is the Foreign Credit Insurance Association (FCIA)?

24-3 Enumerate some of the methods used to remit foreign profits back to United States parent firms.

24-4 Suppose a Texas sugar manufacturer signs a contract with a Ceylon sugar cane cooperative to purchase 1,000 tons of unrefined sugar pulp for 1,000,000 rupees, payable in 90 days. (a) If the foreign exchange rate per rupee is currently $.1490 but changes to $.1550 in 90 days, is the Texas firm worse or better off? By how much?

24-5 When the United States dollar was devalued by 10 percent in 1971 and again by 8 percent in 1972, did foreign goods become more or less expensive to United States citizens? Did United States goods become more or less expensive to foreign consumers?

24-6 If all payments to United States citizens are exports and all payments to foreigners imports, identify each of the following international transactions as an export or import entry in the United States balance of payments:
(a) Japanese tourist visits Disneyland.
(b) General Motors buys Canadian Government bonds.

(c) ITT receives profit dividends from a Chilean subsidiary.

(d) A West German firm buys a dairy farm in Wisconsin.

(e) A United Kingdom ship transports American goods to Mexico.

(f) The United Humanitarians Association in the United States sends $50,000,000 to Sudan for disaster relief.

24-7 How can a United States firm use the forward foreign exchange market to reduce the exchange rate risk associated with international transactions?

24-8 Suppose Bolcon has a foreign subsidiary in West Germany. If the West German government devalues the West German currency by 8 percent, and also imposes a 30 percent foreign dividend tax, what will happen to the expected remittances to Bolcon?

24-9 If a United States firm is considering establishing a foreign subsidiary in Japan, what general adjustments would you suggest in the firm's evaluation of the proposal as compared to domestic capital expansions.

24-10 Explain the following assertion: "If the expected loss from devaluation over the life of a foreign loan exceeds the costs, it is less costly to use the swap than to borrow from a foreign bank."

PROBLEMS

24-1 Mogas is considering a 7-year petroleum investment in a North African country. Engineers have estimated that most of the crude petroleum could be extracted in 7 years, with an annual cashflow of 200,000,000 sudans (the unit of foreign exchange). The estimated book value of the subsidiary at the end of the seventh year is 100,000,000 sudans. At the present time it takes $.10 to purchase one sudan, but economists at the World Bank are predicting the sudan will be devaluated to $.05 per sudan 3 years from now. Also in 3 years the country is expected to impose a 70 percent tax on foreign dividends. The original cost outlay for the subsidiary is $50,000,000 and the firm's cost of capital is estimated to be 15 percent. Using the net present value (NPV) method, should the subsidiary be established? (Note: Ignore the effects the devaluation and dividend tax will have on the subsidiary's annual sales and costs in future periods.)

24-2 Bolcon wishes to purchase 1,000 calculators from a Japanese firm. The Japanese firm and Bolcon have agreed to a price of 350,000 yen, payable in 60 days. The exchange rate is $.38 per yen, but substantial fluctuations are common in the dollar-yen exchange rate market. Financial analysts expect the price per yen to vary between $.30 and $.40.

(a) What is the maximum (minimum) payment Bolcon will have to make (in dollars)?

(b) If the forward exchange rate is $.375, would you be interested in buying the required currency now? Assume the following probability distribution of possible exchange rates and associated probabilities of occurrence.

Possible exchange rates	Probability of occurrence
.30	.02
.31	.03
.32	.05
.33	.10
.34	.10
.35	.10
.36	.10
.37	.10
.38	.10
.39	.20
.40	.20

24-3 The annualized yield on 180-day United States Treasury Bills is currently 8 percent, while the yield on 180-day West German Bills is 13 percent. The spot exchange rate is $.35 per mark, and the 180-day forward exchange rate is $.32 per mark. Under what conditions is the West German Bill a better investment?

BIBLIOGRAPHY

Baker, James C., and Thomas H. Bates. *Financing International Business Operations.* Intext Educational Publishers, Scranton, Penn., 1971.

Bell, Geoffrey. "The International Monetary Crisis." *Financial Analyst's Journal,* 27 (July–August 1971), 19–21.

Hodgson, Ralphael W., and Heigo Uyterhoeven. "Analyzing Foreign Investment Opportunities," *Harvard Business Review* (March–April 1962).

Lillich, Richard B. *The Protection of Foreign Investment.* Syracuse University Press, (Syracuse, N. Y., 1965).

Nehrt, Lee Charles. *The Political Climate for Private Foreign Investment.* Praeger, New York, 1970.

Smith, Don T. "Financial Variables in International Business." *Harvard Business Review* (January–February 1966).

Zenoff, David B., and Jack Zwick. *International Finance Management,* Prentice-Hall, (Englewood Cliffs, N. J., 1969).

25

FAILURE AND REORGANIZATION

Sometimes a firm finds itself in financial difficulty despite the best efforts of its management. Part of the financial officer's responsibility, as a member of management, is to prevent this from occurring. You will not only have to be alert to impending financial difficulty but also know how to undertake remedial action. What are the common causes and symptoms of impending failure? What are the appropriate remedial actions to restore the firm to a more viable position?

Once the firm has started failing, how can an alert financial officer negotiate the firm out of that situation? Alternatives include voluntary reorganization and voluntary liquidation.

What legal recourse does the firm have to protect itself if voluntary arrangements cannot be negotiated or do not work? We shall see that it can seek the protection of the court in a bankruptcy proceeding under which it works out an immediate involuntary reorganization or liquidation.

CAUSES AND SYMPTOMS OF FAILURE

What are the common causes and symptoms of impending failure which an alert financial officer must recognize and respond to with remedial action?

Despite the best efforts of management, many firms fail each year, particularly among the smaller and more recently organized firms. When failure occurs, it is encumbent upon the management to renegotiate the firm into a more viable position if possible. If it is not possible for the firm to continue, then it is the management's responsibility to arrange and supervise liquidation. An orderly retreat has frequently preserved enough viable parts to provide a fresh and more successful second start, parts which would otherwise have been lost in a disorganized rout.

Definition of Failure

We can identify varying degrees of business failure. They range from very mild short falls in cashflow expectations, which leave the firm in a weaker-than-expected position but which do not threaten the firm's existence, to those which require the firm's liquidation and total demise. In this chapter we are concerned with the more serious forms of business failure that threaten the firm's existence.

The firm is technically insolvent when it does not have sufficient cash to meet its immediate payments. But *technical insolvency* does not mean immediate dissolution of the firm. The firm can operate for a long period of time as a recognized failure, particularly under bankruptcy court protection, as does the PennCentral.[1] During a period of technical insolvency, the firm can work itself into a solvent position, though a constant possibility of dissolution lurks in the background.

In the next degree of failure, a clear-cut choice emerges between returning shortly to a more viable operating status or being dissolved. This stage is typified by a legal declaration of *bankruptcy* wherein the firm formally declares itself in a state of financial duress and asks the bankruptcy court's protection from its creditors while attempting to rectify the situation. This second degree stage is usually associated with a negative net worth: the firm's liabilities exceed its assets.

The third and most severe stage of financial duress is *liquidation*. The firm admits its failure and its inability to reorganize. It is just a matter of time before the firm is dissolved.[2]

Common Causes of Failure

The causes of a particular business failure can be legion, but we can categorize the major ones in order to recognize them if we encounter any.

Undercapitalization Probably the most common cause of failure, particularly among the smaller and less established firms, is undercapitalization—a lack of funds to properly maintain the firm's operations. This situation arises either because of excessive debt in the capital structure or because of an initial shoe-string capitalization. Excessive use of debt, especially if it is short-term, usually leads to business failure if the firm is unable to refinance the maturing debt during tight money conditions or if it has an inadequate cashflow. Initial undercapitalization usually leads to business failure because of an inadequate cushion to handle unexpected delays in the early generation of revenues, larger-than-expected losses in the start-up period, or credit crunches when expansion money is not available. Just before the difficulty becomes obvious, the working capital balances are usually insufficient.

Poor management The second most common cause of business failure is poor management. This manifests itself in such areas as inexperience, neglect, fraud, and insufficient skills. Often a firm is organized around the talents of one or several people with expertise in only one area, and the business fails because the other areas of management are not properly looked after.

Inadequate marketing Another common cause of business failure is inadequate marketing of the product. The firm may choose the wrong selling price. If the price is too low, the firm may not be able to make a profit, even if it sells the product. If the price is too high, the firm may not be able to attract customers. Incorrect judgments on the general economic climate and changes in the industry's operating environ-

---

[1] For a description of the PennCentral bankruptcy see R. F. Murray, "The PennCentral Debacle: Lessons for the Financial Analyst," *Journal of Finance*, May 1971, 327–332.

[2] This is not be be confused with some liquidations which are not associated with failure, but which nevertheless dissolve the firm. While rare, these liquidations during solvency are usually associated with the firm's decision to sell its operating assets and distribute the proceeds to its stockholders.

ment have also led to failure. For example, the shift in government spending from aerospace to other areas left many aerospace firms in financial duress, while the gasoline crisis of 1974 left manufacturers of pleasure products powered by gas engines with excessively large inventories and few customers.

Production problems Firms have become financial casualties because of bad production efforts. Inefficient production methods, excessive costs, and poor quality control have caused business failures.

External factors Sometimes adverse external events have caused business failures. Firms have had to cease operations because of changes in government health and safety regulations, labor disputes, and even natural catastrophes such as floods. The very least a firm needs for a fighting chance to survive and prosper is expertise in financial management, marketing, and production, the three critical areas of business skills.

Symptoms of Failure

Certain statistics seem to foreshadow impending financial difficulty, and the financial officer should continually examine them for early signs of trouble.[3] Certain ratios have been shown to exhibit early warning characteristics when compared to industry norms or changes over time.

Cashflow/total debt Studies have shown that this ratio is significantly lower for failures than for viable firms. The ratio deteriorates rapidly as impending failure approaches.

Market price The median market stock price declines at an increasing rate as failure approaches, reflecting investors' decreasing confidence in the survival of the firm.

Working capital/total assets This ratio declines as failure approaches because it reflects the inadequacy of working capital.

---

[3] Wm. H. Beaver, "Financial Ratios as Predictors of Failure," *Empirical Research in Accounting Selected Studies; Journal of Accounting Research,* Autumn 1966, 71–111; and E. I. Altman, "Financial Ratios, Discriminant Analysis, and the Prediction of Corporate Bankruptcy," *Journal of Finance,* XXIII (September 1968), 589–609.

Altman's discriminant model (see Appendix 14A for a discussion of the discriminant technique) for smaller companies is:

$$Z = 1.21X_1 + 1.4X_2 + 3.3X_3 + .6X_4 + .999X_5$$

where
  X_1 = working capital/total assets
  X_2 = retained earnings/total assets
  X_3 = EBIT/total assets
  X_4 = market value of the equity/book value of the debt
  X_5 = sales/total assets

If Z > 2.99   no potential bankruptcy
If Z < 1.81   potential bankruptcy
If 1.81 < Z < 2.99   indeterminant

For Altman's railroad model see "Railroad Bankruptcy Propensity," *Journal of Finance,* May 1971, 333–346.

Retained earnings/total assets This ratio reflects the lack of an adequate cushion to withstand temporarily adverse conditions due to unexpected costs, delays, or credit crunches. The ratio declines as failure approaches.

Earnings before interest and taxes/total assets This ratio reflects the lack of an adequate cashflow in relation to the firm's debt obligations. A lower ratio indicates a lessened ability to meet those payments.

Market value of the equity/book value of the debt This ratio reflects the excessive use of debt as it drives down the stock price because of increased financial risk.

Sales/total assets This ratio reflects a lack of a market for the product, particularly a diminishing market which finds the firm with the assets to produce the product but no sales. It also reflects the size of the firm in terms of sales and its general ability, because of size, to survive longer than a smaller firm. As the ratio declines, the firm approaches failure.

VOLUNTARY ARRANGEMENTS FOR REORGANIZATION

How can the financial officer help negotiate the firm out of impending failure?

It might be strategically wise to approach the firm's creditors, explain the firm's predicament, and ask them to voluntarily lift some of their collection pressure so the firm may have a breathing spell in which to resolve its problems. These voluntary arrangements usually involve reorganization under extension or composition agreements.

Definition of Reorganization

Reorganization is usually a revision of the firm's financial structure, including short-term liabilities as well as long-term debt and stockholders' equity, in order to correct gradually the firm's immediate inability to meet its current payments. Such reorganization may be done voluntarily with the cooperation of the creditors under a mutually accepted plan.

Extension

The extension form of voluntary reorganization postpones the payment dates on at least a portion of the firm's short-term liabilities, including maturing long-term debt. In effect, it simply gives the firm more time to pay its creditors. Sometimes the extension is also called a "work-out," implying that the firm gains additional time in which to work out its problems.

The majority of the firm's creditors may consent to an extension in the hope that the firm can overcome its immediate payment problems and later meet the entire amount of its obligations. Financial officers stress in their attempts to get an extension that unless the extension is granted the firm may be forced into bankruptcy and be less likely to pay the creditors. Creditors generally agree to the extension if they feel there is a good chance of recovery.

The typical extension is arranged by the firm's bank, which acts as chief negotiator and spokesman for the creditors. Those smaller creditors who refuse to agree to the extension plan may be paid entirely, and the firm's debt may be consolidated with a few lenders. The creditors then assume a direct voice in the firm's management to protect their interests and to insure compliance with the plan.

Composition

In those cases where the creditors feel there is a significantly less chance of the firm's recovery, they may voluntarily agree to a composition plan. The creditors settle for a percentage of the amount owed them on the theory that something is better than nothing. It is as if the creditors are getting out with what they can salvage before the entire firm collapses.

Composition has the advantage of not dragging on like the extension. With one negotiated plan all the firm's major creditors' claims are settled, and the firm starts out with a less onerous financial structure. Small creditors who do not agree to the composition are usually paid in full to avoid the nuisance of their claims.

Creditor Committee

The creditor committee, representing the creditors, is established and brought together with the firm for the purposes of negotiating a plan by an adjustment bureau. The committee's function is to arrange and supervise the extension or the composition. The committee enforces the terms of the agreement, usually assumes a voice in management (perhaps even taking over control of the firm), seeks new capital if needed, settles the small nuisance claims, and generally takes all possible steps to correct the problem.

Recapitalization

During the process of reviving the firm, the committee might find it necessary to reorganize the firm's capital structure in an effort to lessen the debt burden. This is known as recapitalization. If additional funds are needed in the recovery effort, the committee might arrange for present lenders to subordinate their claims to the new financing. They might exchange the firm's debt for stock or income bonds, reducing the strain on the firm's cashflow. The committee might also get the preferred stockholders to waive the arrears on the preferred dividends.

REORGANIZATION UNDER BANKRUPTCY

What legal recourse does the firm have if voluntary arrangements cannot be made?

At that juncture the firm must file for bankruptcy and seek the protection of the courts. This involves legal counsel and action well beyond the scope of this text, but let us review the major features of reorganization under bankruptcy. In the next section we will review the major features of liquidation under bankruptcy.

The Federal Bankruptcy Act

The general procedures of the typical bankruptcy are set out in the Federal Bankruptcy Act.

Chapter XI Chapter XI of that act deals with the firm's reorganization or arrangement, which is a court-supervised extension or composition plan. The debtor firm files a detailed statement of the firm's financial condition and a proposed plan of reorganization covering such items as the terms of the extension or composition, recapitalization, and the expected duration of recovery.

After filing the Chapter XI petition, the bankruptcy court typically lets the present management continue to run the firm provided they obtain a surety bond to indemify creditors from further losses. If the firm's present management is, in the court's opinion, unable to continue properly, the court appoints a receiver to take possession of the property until a bankruptcy hearing is convened and a trustee appointed to manage the firm's affairs.

At that bankruptcy hearing, a presiding judge or referee decides which creditor claims are valid and modifies the firm's proposed reorganization plan, if advisable. This modified plan is submitted to the creditors for their approval. If a majority consents, the plan is enforced upon all the creditors by the court. This approved plan must generally (1) meet the general provisions of the bankruptcy act, (2) be fair, equitable, and feasible, (3) insure that the debtor firm has bargained in good faith, and (4) not be objected to by the Securities and Exchange Commission in the case of a publicly held firm. If one of these conditions is not met, the firm cannot reorganize under Chapter XI and must resort to the more stringent Chapter X bankruptcy regulations.

Chapter X Chapter X of the Federal Bankruptcy Act is typically reserved for large corporations and those with publicly held stock. The firm may voluntarily petition the court for a reorganization under this chapter. Alternatively, the indenture trustee for the firm's bonds or three or more creditors with claims totaling at least $75,000, may petition the court for an involuntary reorganization in an effort to protect the creditors' position.

For the court to consider a Chapter X proceeding, the petitioners must show that at least one of the following conditions applies:

1. The debtor has attempted to conceal assets from the creditors or has attempted to defraud them.

2. The debtor firm has given preferential treatment to one of the creditors.

3. The creditor's legal lien on the property, which arose as pledged collateral, has not been discharged. This occurs, for instance, when a landlord is not able to regain possession of property within a reasonable time.

4. The firm has assigned its assets to the general good of the creditors, in effect admitting that it wants to turn the firm over to the creditors' benefit.

5. The court has already appointed a receiver or a trustee in earlier proceedings.

6. The debtor has admitted in writing that it is bankrupt.

Upon receipt of the petition and a determination by the court that one of the conditions for Chapter X bankruptcy proceedings has been met, the court appoints a trustee to caretake the property pending reorganization or liquidation. A hearing is held on the plans for reorganization to determine that they are fair, equitable, and feasible. If the court approves the plan, the Securities and Exchange Commission does not object, and two-thirds of each class of claim consents, the plan binds all the creditors.

Section 77 of Chapter VIII This section of the bankruptcy act deals with railroad reorganization. The procedures are similar to other types of bankruptcy except that the Interstate Commerce Commission and the trustee are responsible for the reorganization plan. This section was amended by the Mahafee Act, which simplifies the procedure if 75 percent of each class of claim consents.

Reorganization Plans

Under the terms of the bankruptcy act, the reorganization plan must meet the criteria of fairness, equitability, and feasibility if it is to be approved by the court. The objective of the plan is to recapitalize the firm's financial structure so that fixed charges are reduced and can be adequately covered by expected operating cashflows after the reorganization. Once a new and less burdensome recapitalized financial structure has been established, the securities must be distributed to the claimants according to the priority of each claim. In general, the recapitalization plan must be designed to turn the company into a financially sound and viable firm.

The first step in establishing a recapitalized financial structure is the evaluation procedure. The person responsible, usually the trustee, will examine the present capital structure as illustrated in Table 25-1, ranking the debt in descending order of priority. (Table 25-1 reveals that this firm is in poor financial condition. Notice its high debt/equity ratio and its low fixed charge coverage.)

The trustee must determine how much debt can the firm reasonably support and how much is the firm worth. Estimating the future sales and earnings of the firm gives an indication of the firm's prospects. Capitalizing the expected future earnings at an appropriate rate establishes a fair value for the firm. For our firm in Table 25-1, the trustee might estimate the expected future annual earnings for the firm after reorganization at $2,500,000. These expected earnings might be capitalized at 10 percent to derive a fair value for the reorganized firm of $25,000,000:

Expected future annual earnings	$ 2,500,000
Appropriate capitalization rate	.10
Total fair value	$25,000,000

After determining the fair value, the trustee must next distribute the new securities in the amount of the capitalized value to the old securities holders according to the *rule of absolute priority*. Under that rule, the highest priority claim must be totally satisfied first before the next highest priority claim may be paid. In the illustration of Table 25-1, the first mortgage bonds of the firm represented in the table would have to be totally satisfied before payment could be made on the senior debentures. If the funds ran out before all securities were recapitalized, the lowest priority securities would suffer the most, as illustrated in Table 25-2. We can see that the $25,000,000 of securities under the trustee's recapitalization plan cannot satisfy the entire $50,000,000 of security claims outstanding at bankruptcy.

Table 25-1   Capital Structure at Bankruptcy in Descending Order of Priority

Issue	Amount	Annual fixed charges
First mortgage bonds 1995	$10,000,000	$1,000,000
Senior debentures 1985	20,000,000	2,500,000
Junior subordinated debentures 1990	5,000,000	500,000
Common stock	15,000,000	
	$50,000,000	$4,000,000

Annual cashflow	$2,000,000
Fixed charges earned	.5
Debt/equity ratio	2.33/1

Table 25-2   The Recapitalized Capital Structure

Issue	Amount	Fixed charge
Debentures 2010	$ 4,500,000	$ 250,000
Income bonds 2050	8,000,000	1,000,000
Preferred stock	2,500,000	250,000
Common stock	10,000,000	–
Total	$25,000,000	$1,500,000

Annual cashflow $4,500,000
Fixed charges earned = 3.0
Debt/equity ratio = 1/1

The trustee would distribute the new securities in Table 25-2 in exchange for the old securities in Table 25-1 in the following manner under the rule of absolute priority:

Old security	New security
$10,000,000 first mortgage bonds	$4,500,000 debentures and $5,500,000 income bonds
$20,000,000 senior debentures	$2,500,000 income bonds, $2,500,000 preferred stock, and $10,000,000 common stock
$ 5,000,000 junior subordinate debentures	Nothing
$15,000,000 common stock	Nothing

Notice that in this case the common stock and the lowest-priority debt receive nothing. The previous senior debenture holders become the new stockholders. Notice also how the recapitalization plan has lengthened the maturities of the debt as well as reduced the entire amount of the debt and the firm's fixed charges. The debt/equity ratio has been reduced from 2.33/1 to 1/1, and the fixed charges earned has been increased from .5 to 3. The presence of income bonds and preferred stock in place of the previous debt allows the firm more flexibility because the interest and dividends on those securities may be omitted without the threat of bankruptcy.

LIQUIDATION

If the sale of the company's assets, as a whole or by the piece, appears to be worth more than its value as an on-going concern, the firm and its creditors may voluntarily agree to liquidation. If the creditors cannot agree or no feasible and fair plan is adopted at the bankruptcy hearings, the court may order the liquidation. The former is a voluntary liquidation which may occur outside the courts, while the latter is a mandatory liquidation under bankruptcy. For our purposes, we define liquidation as the process of converting the firm's assets to cash and distributing that cash to the creditors according to the priority of their claims.

Voluntary Liquidation

The firm and its creditors may agree to a voluntary liquidation under an *assignment* arrangement. Under this procedure the firm assigns (transfers) its assets to an assignee for disposition on behalf of the creditors. This must occur with the consent of all the creditors; if a single creditor objects, the entire liquidation is thrown into the courts. The advantages of voluntary liquidation are that it is less costly and less publicized, and it allows the principals a fresh start free of the former debts.

Involuntary Liquidation

If the firm cannot agree to voluntary liquidation with its creditors, it can resort to enforced liquidation under the protection of the bankruptcy court. In an analogous fashion to the steps in reorganization, the firm or its creditors petition the court for bankruptcy and file a proposed plan of liquidation. The court appoints a receiver to preserve the assets until a hearing on the plan can be held and a trustee appointed by the creditors committee with the approval of the court to supervise the liquidation. At that hearing the proposed plan can be modified, and then, if approved by the judge, it is sent to the creditors for their consent. Upon their consent, the trustee will start to sell the assets and distribute the proceeds from those sales to the creditors according to their priority. Sometimes this sale and distribution may take time, and the trustee may actually operate parts of the firm in anticipation of their sale. At the completion of the liquidation, the debtor is discharged from bankruptcy and free to start anew without the burdens of the previous debts.

Priority of Claims

In either reorganization or liquidation, there is a priority of claims. We have already seen the priority of claims in the recapitalization of the capital structure, but there are prior operating-expense claims which must be satisfied. In order of priority, the general list includes:

1. Cost of operating the bankrupt firm, including trustee and receiver expenses as incurred debt
2. Accrued wages up to a specified limit for the three-month period before the bankruptcy petition
3. Federal and state taxes
4. Unpaid rents
5. Secured creditors
6. Unsecured creditors, including vendor accounts payable, debentures, and similar claims
7. Subordinated debentures and other subordinated claims of unsecured creditors
8. Preferred stock
9. Common stock

SUMMARY

After having read Chapter 25, you should be able to answer these questions:

1. What are the common causes and symptoms of impending failure?

The common causes of failure are undercapitalization, poor management, poor marketing, inefficient production and external factors such as government regulations. For firms to avoid failure, particularly newer firms, they must be efficient in the three basic areas: financing, marketing, and manufacturing.

2. How can a good financial officer negotiate the firm out of a failing situation?

A failing firm can reach voluntary agreements with its creditors to alleviate the situation. These include the extension and the composition plans. Usually under these voluntary agreements the creditors assume a direct voice in the firm's management and might even force the company to recapitalize.

Alternatively, the firm can file for involuntary reorganization under the Federal Bankruptcy Act. This can be done under Chapter XI of the act, which permits the firm's present management to continue, or under Chapter X, which generally turns the firm over to a third party trustee appointed by the court. In either case the firm would probably be recapitalized.

We saw that the typical recapitalization plan substitutes a less burdensome capital structure for the one prevailing at bankruptcy, within the principles of fairness, equity, and feasibility. The new capital structure reflects the trustee's evaluation of the future earning power of the firm. Under the rule of absolute priority, the recapitalization is distributed to satisfy the highest-priority claims first. Some of the claims may be left totally unsatisfied.

3. What legal recourse does the firm have if reorganization is not feasible?

The firm can enter into a voluntary agreement with its creditors to liquidate. Alternatively, it can petition the court for court-enforced liquidation.

QUESTIONS

25-1 What is meant by the term *business failure?* Identify several legal forms that such a failure may take.

25-2 Empirical evidence suggests that the incidence of business failure is greater during periods of high interest rates than when interest rates are low. What might account for this finding?

25-3 What financial ratios provide prior warning of business failure?

25-4 Distinguish between the extension and composition forms of voluntary reorganization.

25-5 Rank the following securities in terms of descending priority of claims in case of bankruptcy.
  (a) Preferred stock
  (b) Common stock
  (c) Income bonds 2002
  (d) First mortgage bonds 1985
  (e) Second mortgage bonds 1990
  (f) Convertible debentures 1998
  (g) Subordinated debentures 2010
  (h) Debentures 2008

25-6 Would you expect liquidations to be more common in regulated firms (banks, savings and loan associations, railroads) or in unregulated industrial firms?

25-7 In case of liquidation, do federal and state taxes have a higher or lower priority for payment than the securities listed in question 25-5?

25-8 Under what circumstances might merger seem more attractive than liquidation or reorganization from a common stockholder viewpoint?

PROBLEMS

25-1 Bolcon recently found itself in a distressed position financially and had to file for bankruptcy. The court has ordered recapitalization of the firm's capital structure to reduce the annual fixed charges and also reduce the debt/equity ratio. Bolcon's present capital structure is shown below:

First mortgage bonds, 8%, 2000	$ 50,000,000
Second mortgage bonds, 10%, 2010	50,000,000
Debentures, 12%, 1990	10,000,000
Subordinated debentures, 13%, 1995	10,000,000
Common stock	60,000,000
Total	$180,000,000

The estimated annual cashflow for the foreseeable future is $8,000,000 and the firm's weighted-average cost of capital is thought to be 8 percent.

(a) By how much do the firm's annual fixed charges exceed its estimated cashflow?

(b) If the court rules that the firm's recapitalized capital structure is limited to the discounted value of the firm's future expected cashflows, what is the maximum new capital that can be raised?

(c) Can you suggest a new capital structure that will meet the court's requirements? The owners of which of the firm's securities will be left out of the reorganized firm?

25-2 The following balance sheet is for NOGO Company:

Cash	$ 10,000,000	Notes payable	$ 20,000,000
Accounts receivable	40,000,000	Accounts payable	50,000,000
Inventories	40,000,000	Accrued taxes	20,000,000
Current assets	$ 90,000,000	Current liabilities	$ 90,000,000
Fixed assets, net	100,000,000	Long-term debt	100,000,000
Goodwill	30,000,000	Equity	30,000,000
Total assets	$220,000,000	Total liabilities	$220,000,000

(a) Does NOGO Company seem to be in any present or potential danger of insolvency? Why? What corrective actions might management take?

(b) Is bankruptcy a potential problem for the firm? Why? What corrective actions might management initiate?

(c) Can you suggest other financial data that would aid in determining the insolvency or bankruptcy potential, in addition to the above balance sheet?

BIBLIOGRAPHY

Altman, Edward I. "Corporate Bankruptcy Potential, Stockholder Returns and Share Valuation: Reply." *Journal of Finance,* XXVII (June 1972), 718–721.
———. "Equity Securities of Bankrupt Firms." *Financial Analysts Journal,* XXV (July–August 1969), 129–133.
———. "Financial Ratios, Discriminant Analysis, and the Prediction of Corporate Bankruptcy." *Journal of Finance,* XXIII (September 1968), 589–609.
Beaver, William H. "Financial Ratios as Predictors of Failure." *Empirical Research in Accounting: Selected Studies,* Supplement to *Journal of Accounting Research* (Autumn 1966), 71–111.
———. "Market Prices, Financial Ratios, and the Prediction of Failure." *Journal of Accounting Research,* VI (Autumn 1968), 179–192.

Deakin, Edward B. "A Discriminant Analysis of Predictors of Business Failure." *Journal of Accounting Research*, 10 (Spring 1972), 167–179.

Hanna, Mark. "Corporate Bankruptcy Potential, Stockholder Returns and Share Valuation: Comment." *Journal of Finance*, XXVII (June 1972), 711–717.

Murray, Roger F. "Lessons for Financial Analysts." *Journal of Finance*, XXVI (May 1971), 327–332.

Weston, J. Fred. "The Industrial Economics Background of the PennCentral Bankruptcy." *Journal of Finance*, XXVI (May 1971), 311–326.

Wilcox, Jarrod W. "A Simple Theory of Financial Ratios as Predictors of Failure." *Journal of Accounting Research*, 9 (Autumn 1971), 389–395.

Appendices

Appendix A Compound Sum of One Dollar

n	1%	2%	3%	4%	5%	6%	7%	8%	9%	10%	n
01	1.0100	1.0200	1.0300	1.0400	1.0500	1.0600	1.0700	1.0800	1.0900	1.1000	01
02	1.0201	1.0404	1.0609	1.0816	1.1025	1.1236	1.1449	1.1664	1.1881	1.2100	02
03	1.0303	1.0612	1.0927	1.1249	1.1576	1.1910	1.2250	1.2597	1.2950	1.3310	03
04	1.0406	1.0824	1.1255	1.1699	1.2155	1.2625	1.3108	1.3605	1.4116	1.4641	04
05	1.0510	1.1041	1.1593	1.2167	1.2763	1.3382	1.4026	1.4693	1.5386	1.6105	05
06	1.0615	1.1261	1.1941	1.2653	1.3401	1.4185	1.5007	1.5869	1.6771	1.7716	06
07	1.0721	1.1487	1.2299	1.3159	1.4071	1.5036	1.6058	1.7138	1.8280	1.9487	07
08	1.0829	1.1717	1.2668	1.3686	1.4775	1.5939	1.7182	1.8509	1.9926	2.1436	08
09	1.0937	1.1951	1.3048	1.4233	1.5513	1.6895	1.8385	1.9990	2.1719	2.3580	09
10	1.1046	1.2190	1.3439	1.4802	1.6289	1.7909	1.9672	2.1589	2.3674	2.5937	10
11	1.1157	1.2434	1.3842	1.5395	1.7103	1.8983	2.1049	2.3316	2.5804	2.8531	11
12	1.1268	1.2682	1.4258	1.6010	1.7959	2.0122	2.2522	2.5182	2.8127	3.1384	12
13	1.1381	1.2936	1.4685	1.6651	1.8857	2.1329	2.4098	2.7196	3.0658	3.4523	13
14	1.1495	1.3195	1.5126	1.7317	1.9799	2.2609	2.5785	2.9372	3.3417	3.7975	14
15	1.1610	1.3459	1.5580	1.8009	2.0789	2.3966	2.7590	3.1722	3.6425	4.1773	15
16	1.1726	1.3728	1.6047	1.8730	2.1829	2.5404	2.9522	3.4259	3.9703	4.5950	16
17	1.1843	1.4002	1.6529	1.9479	2.2920	2.6928	3.1588	3.7000	4.3276	5.0545	17
18	1.1962	1.4283	1.7024	2.0258	2.4066	2.8543	3.3799	3.9960	4.7171	5.5599	18
19	1.2081	1.4568	1.7535	2.1069	2.5270	3.0256	3.6165	4.3157	5.1417	6.1159	19
20	1.2202	1.4860	1.8061	2.1911	2.6533	3.2071	3.8697	4.6610	5.6044	6.7275	20
21	1.2324	1.5157	1.8603	2.2788	2.7860	3.3996	4.1406	5.0338	6.1088	7.4003	21
22	1.2447	1.5460	1.9161	2.3699	2.9253	3.6035	4.4304	5.4365	6.6586	8.1403	22
23	1.2572	1.5769	1.9736	2.4647	3.0715	3.8198	4.7405	5.8714	7.2579	8.9543	23
24	1.2697	1.6084	2.0328	2.5633	3.2251	4.0489	5.0724	6.3412	7.9111	9.8497	24
25	1.2824	1.6406	2.0937	2.6658	3.3864	4.2919	5.4274	6.8485	8.6231	10.835	25

n	20%	19%	18%	17%	16%	15%	14%	13%	12%	11%	n
01	1.2000	1.1900	1.1800	1.1700	1.1600	1.1500	1.1400	1.1300	1.1200	1.1100	01
02	1.4400	1.4161	1.3924	1.3689	1.3456	1.3225	1.2996	1.2769	1.2544	1.2321	02
03	1.7280	1.6852	1.6430	1.6016	1.5609	1.5209	1.4815	1.4429	1.4049	1.3676	03
04	2.0736	2.0053	1.9388	1.8739	1.8106	1.7490	1.6890	1.6305	1.5735	1.5181	04
05	2.4883	2.3864	2.2878	2.1925	2.1003	2.0114	1.9254	1.8424	1.7623	1.6851	05
06	2.9860	2.8398	2.6996	2.5652	2.4364	2.3131	2.1950	2.0820	1.9738	1.8704	06
07	3.5832	3.3793	3.1855	3.0012	2.8262	2.6600	2.5023	2.3526	2.2107	2.0762	07
08	4.2998	4.0214	3.7589	3.5115	3.2784	3.0590	2.8526	2.6584	2.4760	2.3045	08
09	5.1598	4.7855	4.4355	4.1084	3.8030	3.5179	3.2520	3.0040	2.7731	2.5580	09
10	6.1917	5.6947	5.2338	4.8068	4.4114	4.0456	3.7072	3.3946	3.1059	2.8394	10
11	7.4301	6.7767	6.1759	5.6240	5.1173	4.6524	4.2262	3.8359	3.4786	3.1518	11
12	8.9161	8.0642	7.2876	6.5801	5.9360	5.3503	4.8179	4.3345	3.8960	3.4985	12
13	10.699	9.5965	8.5994	7.6987	6.8858	6.1528	5.4924	4.8980	4.3635	3.8833	13
14	12.839	11.420	10.147	9.0075	7.9875	7.0757	6.2616	5.5348	4.8871	4.3104	14
15	15.407	13.590	11.974	10.539	9.2655	8.1371	7.1379	6.2543	5.4736	4.7846	15
16	18.488	16.172	14.129	12.330	10.748	9.3576	8.1373	7.0673	6.1304	5.3109	16
17	22.186	19.244	16.672	14.427	12.468	10.761	9.2765	7.9861	6.8660	5.8951	17
18	26.623	22.901	19.673	16.879	14.463	12.376	10.575	9.0243	7.6900	6.5436	18
19	31.948	27.252	23.214	19.748	16.777	14.232	12.056	10.107	8.6128	7.2633	19
20	38.338	32.429	27.393	23.106	19.461	16.367	13.744	11.523	9.6463	8.0623	20
21	46.005	38.591	32.324	27.034	22.575	18.822	15.668	13.021	10.804	8.9492	21
22	55.206	45.923	38.142	31.629	26.186	21.645	17.861	14.714	12.100	9.9336	22
23	66.247	54.649	45.008	37.006	30.376	24.892	20.362	16.627	13.552	11.026	23
24	79.497	65.032	53.109	43.297	35.236	28.625	23.212	18.788	15.179	12.239	24
25	95.396	77.388	62.669	50.658	40.874	32.919	26.462	21.231	17.000	13.586	25

n	30%	29%	28%	27%	26%	25%	24%	23%	22%	21%	n
01	1.3000	1.2900	1.2800	1.2700	1.2600	1.2500	1.2400	1.2300	1.2200	1.2100	01
02	1.6900	1.6641	1.6384	1.6129	1.5876	1.5625	1.5376	1.5129	1.4884	1.4641	02
03	2.1970	2.1467	2.0972	2.0484	2.0004	1.9531	1.9066	1.8609	1.8159	1.7716	03
04	2.8561	2.7692	2.6844	2.6015	2.5205	2.4414	2.3642	2.2889	2.2153	2.1436	04
05	3.7129	3.5723	3.4360	3.3038	3.1758	3.0518	2.9316	2.8153	2.7027	2.5937	05
06	4.8268	4.6083	4.3981	4.1959	4.0015	3.8147	3.6352	3.4628	3.2973	3.1384	06
07	6.2749	5.9447	5.6295	5.3288	5.0419	4.7684	4.5077	4.2593	4.0227	3.7975	07
08	8.1573	7.6686	7.2058	6.7675	6.3528	5.9605	5.5895	5.2389	4.9077	4.5950	08
09	10.605	9.8925	9.2234	8.5948	8.0045	7.4506	6.9310	6.4439	5.9874	5.5599	09
10	13.786	12.761	11.806	10.915	10.086	9.3132	8.5944	7.9260	7.3046	6.7275	10
11	17.922	16.462	15.112	13.863	12.708	11.642	10.657	9.7489	8.9117	8.1403	11
12	23.298	21.237	19.343	17.605	16.012	14.552	13.215	11.991	10.872	9.8497	12
13	30.288	27.395	24.759	22.359	20.175	18.190	16.386	14.749	13.264	11.918	13
14	39.374	35.339	31.691	28.396	25.421	22.737	20.319	18.141	16.182	14.421	14
15	51.186	45.588	40.565	36.063	32.030	28.422	25.196	22.314	19.742	17.449	15
16	66.542	58.898	51.923	45.799	40.358	35.527	31.243	27.446	24.086	21.114	16
17	86.504	75.862	66.461	58.165	50.851	44.409	38.741	33.759	29.384	25.548	17
18	112.46	97.862	85.071	73.870	64.072	55.511	48.039	41.523	35.849	30.913	18
19	146.19	126.24	108.89	93.815	80.731	69.389	59.568	51.074	43.736	37.404	19
20	190.05	162.85	139.38	119.15	101.72	86.736	73.864	62.821	53.358	45.259	20
21	247.07	210.08	178.41	151.31	128.17	108.42	91.592	77.269	65.096	54.764	21
22	321.18	271.00	228.36	192.17	161.49	135.53	113.57	95.041	79.418	66.264	22
23	417.54	349.59	292.30	244.05	203.48	169.41	140.83	116.90	96.889	80.180	23
24	542.80	450.98	374.14	309.95	256.39	211.76	174.63	143.79	118.21	97.017	24
25	705.64	581.76	478.91	393.63	323.05	264.70	216.54	176.86	144.21	117.39	25

n	40%	39%	38%	37%	36%	35%	34%	33%	32%	31%	n
01	1.4000	1.3900	1.3800	1.3700	1.3600	1.3500	1.3400	1.3300	1.3200	1.3100	01
02	1.9600	1.9321	1.9044	1.8769	1.8496	1.8225	1.7956	1.7689	1.7424	1.7161	02
03	2.7440	2.6856	2.6281	2.5714	2.5155	2.4604	2.4061	2.3526	2.3000	2.2481	03
04	3.8416	3.7330	3.6267	3.5228	3.4210	3.3215	3.2242	3.1291	3.0360	2.9450	04
05	5.3782	5.1889	5.0049	4.8262	4.6526	4.4840	4.3204	4.1616	4.0075	3.8580	05
06	7.5295	7.2126	6.9068	6.6119	6.3275	6.0534	5.7893	5.5349	5.2898	5.0540	06
07	10.541	10.025	9.5313	9.0592	8.6054	8.1722	7.7577	7.3614	6.9826	6.6206	07
08	14.758	13.935	13.153	12.410	11.703	11.032	10.395	9.7907	9.2170	8.6730	08
09	20.661	19.370	18.152	17.001	15.917	14.894	13.930	13.022	12.167	11.361	09
10	28.926	26.925	25.049	23.292	21.647	20.107	18.666	17.319	16.060	14.884	10
11	40.496	37.425	34.568	31.910	29.440	27.144	25.012	23.034	21.199	19.498	11
12	56.694	52.021	47.703	43.717	40.038	36.644	33.516	30.635	27.983	25.542	12
13	79.372	72.309	65.831	59.892	54.451	49.470	44.912	40.745	36.937	33.460	13
14	111.12	100.51	90.846	82.052	74.053	66.784	60.182	54.191	48.757	43.833	14
15	155.57	139.71	125.37	112.41	100.71	90.159	80.644	72.073	64.359	57.421	15
16	217.80	194.19	173.00	154.00	136.97	121.71	108.06	95.858	84.954	75.221	16
17	304.91	269.93	238.75	210.98	186.28	164.31	144.80	127.49	112.14	98.540	17
18	426.88	375.20	329.48	289.05	253.34	221.83	194.04	169.56	148.02	129.09	18
19	597.63	521.53	454.68	396.00	344.54	299.46	260.01	225.52	195.39	169.10	19
20	836.68	724.93	627.45	542.51	468.57	404.27	348.41	299.94	257.92	221.53	20
21	1171.4	1007.7	865.89	743.25	637.26	545.77	466.88	398.92	340.45	290.20	21
22	1639.9	1400.6	1194.9	1018.3	866.67	736.79	625.61	530.56	449.39	380.16	22
23	2295.9	1946.9	1649.0	1395.0	1178.7	994.67	838.32	705.65	593.20	498.01	23
24	3214.2	2706.1	2275.6	1911.1	1603.0	1342.8	1123.4	938.51	783.02	652.40	24
25	4499.9	3761.6	3140.3	2618.3	2180.1	1812.8	1505.3	1248.2	1033.6	854.64	25

Appendix B Present Value of One Dollar Due at the End of n Years

n	1%	2%	3%	4%	5%	6%	7%	8%	9%	10%	n
01	.99010	.98039	.97007	.96154	.95238	.94340	.93458	.92593	.91743	.90909	01
02	.98030	.96117	.94260	.92456	.90703	.89000	.87344	.85734	.84168	.82645	02
03	.97059	.94232	.91514	.88900	.86384	.83962	.81630	.79383	.77218	.75131	03
04	.96098	.92385	.88849	.85480	.82270	.79209	.76290	.73503	.70843	.68301	04
05	.95147	.90573	.86261	.82193	.78353	.74726	.71299	.68058	.64993	.62092	05
06	.94204	.88797	.83748	.79031	.74622	.70496	.66634	.63017	.59627	.56447	06
07	.93272	.87056	.81309	.75992	.71068	.66506	.62275	.58349	.54703	.51316	07
08	.92348	.85349	.78941	.73069	.67684	.62741	.58201	.54027	.50187	.46651	08
09	.91434	.83675	.76642	.70259	.64461	.59190	.54393	.50025	.46043	.42410	09
10	.90529	.82035	.74409	.67556	.61391	.55839	.50835	.46319	.42241	.38554	10
11	.89632	.80426	.72242	.64958	.58468	.52679	.47509	.42888	.38753	.35049	11
12	.88745	.78849	.70138	.62460	.55684	.49697	.44401	.39711	.35553	.31683	12
13	.87866	.77303	.68095	.60057	.53032	.46884	.41496	.36770	.32618	.28966	13
14	.86996	.75787	.66112	.57747	.50507	.44230	.38782	.34046	.29925	.26333	14
15	.86135	.74301	.64186	.55526	.48102	.41726	.36245	.31524	.27454	.23939	15
16	.85282	.72845	.62317	.53391	.45811	.39365	.33873	.29189	.25187	.21763	16
17	.84438	.71416	.60502	.51337	.43630	.37136	.31657	.27027	.23107	.19784	17
18	.83602	.70016	.58739	.49363	.41552	.35034	.29586	.25025	.21199	.17986	18
19	.82774	.68643	.57029	.47464	.39573	.33051	.27651	.23171	.19449	.16351	19
20	.81954	.67297	.55367	.45639	.37689	.31180	.25842	.21455	.17843	.14864	20
21	.81143	.65978	.53755	.43883	.35894	.29415	.24151	.19866	.16370	.13513	21
22	.80340	.64684	.52189	.42195	.34185	.27750	.22571	.18394	.15018	.12285	22
23	.79544	.63414	.50669	.40573	.32557	.26180	.21095	.17031	.13778	.11168	23
24	.78757	.62172	.49193	.39012	.31007	.24698	.19715	.15770	.12640	.10153	24
25	.77977	.60953	.47760	.37512	.29530	.23300	.18425	.14602	.11597	.09230	25

n	20%	19%	18%	17%	16%	15%	14%	13%	12%	11%	n
01	.83333	.84034	.84746	.85470	.86207	.86957	.87719	.88496	.89286	.90090	01
02	.69444	.70616	.71818	.73051	.74316	.75614	.76947	.78315	.79719	.81162	02
03	.57870	.59342	.60863	.62437	.64066	.65752	.67497	.69305	.71178	.73119	03
04	.48225	.49867	.51579	.53365	.55229	.57175	.59208	.61332	.63552	.65873	04
05	.40188	.41905	.43711	.45611	.47611	.49718	.51937	.54276	.56743	.59345	05
06	.33490	.35214	.37043	.38984	.41044	.43233	.45559	.48032	.50663	.53464	06
07	.27908	.29592	.31392	.33320	.35383	.37594	.39964	.42506	.45235	.48166	07
08	.23257	.24867	.26604	.28478	.30503	.32690	.35056	.37616	.40388	.43393	08
09	.19381	.20897	.22546	.24340	.26295	.28426	.30751	.33288	.36061	.39092	09
10	.16151	.17560	.19106	.20804	.22668	.24718	.26974	.29459	.32197	.35218	10
11	.13459	.14756	.16192	.17781	.19542	.21494	.23662	.26070	.28748	.31728	11
12	.11216	.12400	.13722	.15197	.16846	.18691	.20756	.23071	.25667	.28584	12
13	.09346	.10420	.11629	.12989	.14523	.16253	.18207	.20416	.22917	.25751	13
14	.07789	.08757	.09855	.11102	.12520	.14133	.15971	.18068	.20462	.23199	14
15	.06491	.07359	.08352	.09489	.10793	.12289	.14010	.15989	.18270	.20900	15
16	.05409	.06184	.07078	.08110	.09304	.10686	.12289	.14150	.16312	.18829	16
17	.04507	.05196	.05998	.06932	.08021	.90293	.10780	.12522	.14564	.16963	17
18	.03756	.04367	.05083	.05925	.06914	.08080	.09456	.11081	.13004	.15282	18
19	.03130	.03669	.04308	.05064	.05961	.07026	.08295	.09806	.11611	.13768	19
20	.02608	.03084	.03651	.04328	.05139	.06110	.07276	.08678	.10367	.12403	20
21	.02174	.02591	.03094	.03699	.04430	.05313	.06383	.07680	.09256	.11174	21
22	.01811	.02178	.02622	.03162	.03819	.04620	.05599	.06796	.08264	.10067	22
23	.01509	.01830	.02222	.02702	.03292	.04017	.04911	.06014	.07379	.09069	23
24	.01258	.01538	.01883	.02310	.02838	.03493	.04308	.05322	.06588	.08170	24
25	.01048	.01292	.01596	.01974	.02447	.03038	.03779	.04710	.05882	.07361	25

n	30%	29%	28%	27%	26%	25%	24%	23%	22%	21%	n
01	.76923	.77519	.78125	.78740	.79365	.80000	.80645	.81301	.81967	.82645	01
02	.59172	.60093	.61035	.62000	.62988	.64000	.65036	.66098	.67186	.68301	02
03	.45517	.46583	.47684	.48819	.49991	.51200	.52449	.53738	.55071	.56447	03
04	.35013	.36111	.37253	.38440	.39675	.40960	.42297	.43690	.45140	.46651	04
05	.26933	.27993	.29104	.30268	.31488	.32768	.34111	.35520	.37000	.38554	05
06	.20718	.21700	.22737	.23833	.24991	.26214	.27509	.28878	.30328	.31863	06
07	.15937	.16822	.17764	.18766	.19834	.20972	.22184	.23478	.24859	.26333	07
08	.12259	.13040	.13878	.14776	.15741	.16777	.17891	.19088	.20376	.21763	08
09	.09430	.10109	.10842	.11635	.12493	.13422	.14428	.15519	.16702	.17986	09
10	.07254	.07836	.08470	.09161	.09915	.10737	.11635	.12617	.13690	.14864	10
11	.05580	.06075	.06617	.07214	.07869	.08590	.09383	.10258	.11221	.12285	11
12	.04292	.04709	.05170	.05680	.06245	.06872	.07567	.08339	.09198	.10153	12
13	.03302	.03650	.04039	.04472	.04957	.05498	.06103	.06780	.07539	.08391	13
14	.02540	.02830	.03155	.03522	.03934	.04398	.04921	.05512	.06180	.06934	14
15	.01954	.02194	.02465	.02773	.03122	.03518	.03969	.04481	.05065	.05731	15
16	.01503	.01700	.01926	.02183	.02478	.02815	.03201	.03643	.04152	.04736	16
17	.01156	.01318	.01505	.01719	.01967	.02252	.02581	.02962	.03403	.03914	17
18	.00889	.01022	.01175	.01354	.01561	.01801	.02082	.02408	.02789	.03235	18
19	.00684	.00792	.00918	.01066	.01239	.01441	.01679	.01958	.02286	.02673	19
20	.00526	.00614	.00717	.00839	.00983	.01153	.01354	.01592	.01874	.02209	20
21	.00405	.00476	.00561	.00661	.00780	.00922	.01092	.01294	.01536	.01826	21
22	.00311	.00369	.00438	.00520	.00619	.00738	.00880	.01052	.01259	.01509	22
23	.00239	.00286	.00342	.00410	.00491	.00590	.00710	.00855	.01032	.01247	23
24	.00184	.00222	.00267	.00323	.00390	.00472	.00573	.00695	.00846	.01031	24
25	.00142	.00172	.00209	.00254	.00310	.00378	.00462	.00565	.00693	.00852	25

n	40%	39%	38%	37%	36%	35%	34%	33%	32%	31%	n
01	.71429	.71942	.72464	.72993	.73529	.74074	.74627	.75188	.75758	.76336	01
02	.51020	.51757	.52510	.53279	.54066	.54870	.55692	.56532	.57392	.58272	02
03	.36443	.37235	.38051	.38890	.39754	.40644	.41561	.42505	.43479	.44482	03
04	.26031	.26788	.27573	.28387	.29231	.30107	.31016	.31959	.32939	.33956	04
05	.18593	.19272	.19980	.20720	.21493	.22301	.23146	.24029	.24953	.25920	05
06	.13281	.13865	.14479	.15124	.15804	.16519	.17273	.18067	.18904	.19787	06
07	.09486	.09975	.10492	.11040	.11621	.12237	.12890	.13584	.14321	.15104	07
08	.06776	.07176	.07603	.08058	.08545	.09064	.09620	.10214	.10849	.11530	08
09	.04840	.05163	.05509	.05882	.06283	.06714	.07179	.07680	.08219	.08802	09
10	.03457	.03714	.03992	.04293	.04620	.04973	.05357	.05774	.06227	.06719	10
11	.02469	.02672	.02893	.03134	.03397	.03684	.03998	.04341	.04717	.05129	11
12	.01764	.01922	.02096	.02287	.02498	.02729	.02984	.03264	.03573	.03915	12
13	.01260	.01383	.01519	.01670	.01837	.02021	.02227	.02454	.02707	.02989	13
14	.00900	.00995	.01101	.01219	.01350	.01497	.01662	.01845	.02051	.02281	14
15	.00643	.00716	.00798	.00890	.00993	.01109	.01240	.01387	.01554	.01742	15
16	.00459	.00515	.00578	.00649	.00730	.00822	.00925	.01043	.01177	.01329	16
17	.00328	.00370	.00419	.00474	.00537	.00609	.00691	.00784	.00892	.01015	17
18	.00234	.00267	.00304	.00346	.00395	.00451	.00515	.00590	.00676	.00775	18
19	.00167	.00192	.00220	.00253	.00290	.00334	.00385	.00443	.00512	.00591	19
20	.00120	.00138	.00159	.00184	.00213	.00247	.00287	.00333	.00388	.00451	20
21	.00085	.00099	.00115	.00135	.00157	.00183	.00214	.00251	.00294	.00345	21
22	.00061	.00071	.00084	.00098	.00115	.00136	.00160	.00188	.00223	.00263	22
23	.00044	.00051	.00061	.00072	.00085	.00101	.00119	.00142	.00169	.00201	23
24	.00031	.00037	.00044	.00052	.00062	.00074	.00089	.00107	.00128	.00153	24
25	.00022	.00027	.00032	.00038	.00046	.00055	.00066	.00080	.00097	.00117	25

Appendix C Compound Sum of an Annuity Due of One Dollar

n	1%	2%	3%	4%	5%	6%	7%	8%	9%	10%
00	1.0000	1.0000	1.0000	1.0000	1.0000	1.0000	1.0000	1.0000	1.0000	1.0000
01	1.0100	1.0200	1.0300	1.0400	1.0500	1.0600	1.0700	1.0800	1.0900	1.1000
02	2.0301	2.0604	2.0909	2.1216	2.1525	2.1833	2.2143	2.2463	2.2778	2.3100
03	3.0604	3.1216	3.1836	3.2464	3.3101	3.3750	3.4400	3.5063	3.5733	3.6410
04	4.1810	4.2040	4.3091	4.4163	4.5256	4.6367	4.7180	4.8663	4.9844	5.1050
05	5.1520	5.3081	5.4684	5.6330	5.8020	5.9750	6.1529	6.3363	6.5233	6.7160
06	6.2135	6.4343	6.6625	6.8983	7.1420	7.3933	7.6543	7.9225	8.2000	8.4870
07	7.2857	7.5830	7.8923	8.2142	8.5491	8.8983	9.260	9.637	10.028	10.436
08	8.3685	8.7546	9.159	9.583	10.027	10.491	10.978	11.488	12.021	12.579
09	9.462	9.950	10.464	11.006	11.578	12.181	12.816	13.487	14.193	14.937
10	10.567	11.169	11.808	12.486	13.207	13.972	14.784	15.645	16.560	17.531
11	11.683	12.412	13.192	14.026	14.917	15.870	16.888	27.977	19.141	20.384
12	12.809	13.680	14.618	15.627	16.713	17.882	19.141	20.495	21.953	23.523
13	13.947	14.974	16.086	17.292	18.599	20.051	21.550	23.215	25.019	26.975
14	15.097	16.293	17.599	19.024	20.579	22.276	24.129	26.152	28.361	30.772
15	16.258	17.639	19.157	20.825	22.657	24.673	26.888	29.324	32.003	34.950
16	17.430	19.012	20.762	22.698	24.840	27.213	29.840	32.750	35.973	39.545
17	18.615	20.412	22.414	24.645	27.132	29.906	32.999	36.450	40.301	44.599
18	19.811	21.841	24.117	25.671	29.539	32.760	36.379	40.446	46.019	50.159
19	21.019	23.297	25.870	26.778	32.066	35.786	39.995	44.762	51.160	56.275
20	22.239	24.783	27.676	30.969	34.719	38.993	43.865	49.423	56.764	63.002
21	23.472	26.299	29.537	33.248	37.505	41.392	48.006	54.457	61.873	70.403
22	24.716	27.845	31.453	35.618	40.430	45.996	52.436	59.893	68.532	78.543
23	25.973	29.422	33.426	38.083	43.502	49.816	57.177	65.765	75.790	87.497
24	27.243	31.030	35.459	40.646	46.727	53.865	62.249	72.106	82.701	97.347

n	11%	12%	13%	14%	15%	16%	17%	18%	19%	20%
00	1.0000	1.0000	1.0000	1.0000	1.0000	1.0000	1.0000	1.0000	1.0000	1.0000
01	1.1100	1.1200	1.1300	1.1400	1.1500	1.1600	2.1700	2.1800	2.1900	2.2000
02	2.3418	2.3742	2.4069	2.4393	2.4723	2.5056	3.5388	3.5722	3.6063	3.6400
03	3.7100	3.7792	3.8500	3.9214	3.9933	4.0666	5.1406	5.2156	5.2896	5.3680
04	5.2282	5.3525	5.4800	5.6100	5.7423	5.8769	7.0147	7.1544	7.2968	7.4415
05	6.9127	7.1150	7.3231	7.5357	7.7540	7.9775	9.2071	9.4422	9.6832	9.9300
06	8.7836	9.089	9.405	9.730	10.067	10.414	11.772	12.142	12.523	12.916
07	10.859	11.300	11.757	12.233	12.723	13.240	14.774	15.327	15.902	16.499
08	13.164	13.776	14.415	15.085	15.786	16.518	18.285	19.086	19.924	20.799
09	15.722	16.549	17.420	18.337	19.304	20.321	22.393	23.521	24.709	25.959
10	18.562	19.655	20.815	22.044	23.349	24.733	27.200	28.755	30.404	32.150
11	21.714	23.133	24.650	26.271	28.002	29.850	32.824	34.931	37.180	39.580
12	25.212	27.029	28.985	31.089	33.352	35.786	39.404	42.219	45.245	48.497
13	29.095	31.393	33.883	36.581	39.505	42.672	47.103	50.818	54.842	59.196
14	33.405	36.280	39.418	42.842	46.581	50.659	56.112	60.965	66.263	72.035
15	38.190	41.753	45.672	49.981	54.717	59.925	66.647	72.939	79.853	87.440
16	43.501	47.883	52.739	58.118	64.073	70.675	78.984	87.067	96.021	105.93
17	49.396	54.750	60.725	67.393	74.840	83.144	93.406	103.74	115.27	128.12
18	55.939	62.440	69.054	77.971	87.213	97.606	110.28	123.41	138.17	154.74
19	63.203	71.053	79.946	90.029	101.31	114.38	130.04	146.63	165.94	186.69
20	71.265	80.700	91.469	103.77	117.81	133.84	153.20	174.02	197.85	225.03
21	80.214	91.500	104.49	119.44	136.63	156.41	180.17	206.34	236.44	271.03
22	90.145	103.60	119.21	137.30	158.28	182.60	211.80	244.49	282.36	326.24
23	101.17	117.16	135.83	157.66	183.17	212.98	248.81	289.49	337.01	392.49
24	113.42	132.33	154.62	180.87	211.79	248.21	292.11	342.61	402.04	471.98

n	21%	22%	23%	24%	25%	26%	27%	28%	29%	30%
00	1.0000	1.0000	1.0000	1.0000	1.0000	1.0000	1.0000	1.0000	1.0000	1.0000
01	1.2100	1.2200	1.2300	1.2400	1.2500	1.2600	1.2700	1.2800	1.2900	1.3000
02	2.6743	2.7086	2.7430	2.7778	2.8124	2.8477	2.8830	2.9186	2.9541	2.9900
03	4.4457	4.5241	4.6039	4.6842	4.7656	4.8481	4.9315	5.0157	5.1007	5.1870
04	6.5690	6.7395	6.8926	7.0483	7.2072	7.3685	7.5326	7.7000	7.8700	8.0430
05	9.183	9.442	9.708	9.980	10.259	10.544	10.837	11.136	11.442	11.756
06	12.321	12.740	13.171	13.615	14.074	14.546	15.033	15.534	16.051	16.583
07	16.119	16.762	17.430	18.123	18.842	19.588	20.361	21.163	21.995	22.858
08	20.714	21.670	22.669	23.712	24.802	25.940	27.129	28.369	28.664	31.017
09	26.274	27.657	29.113	30.643	32.253	33.946	35.722	37.592	39.555	41.620
10	33.001	34.962	37.039	39.238	41.568	44.031	47.641	49.399	52.317	55.407
11	41.141	43.873	46.787	49.985	53.208	56.738	60.500	64.510	68.783	73.327
12	50.990	54.745	58.739	63.110	67.760	72.750	78.107	83.853	90.017	96.627
13	62.910	68.009	73.526	79.496	85.948	92.927	100.47	108.61	117.41	126.91
14	77.329	84.191	91.670	99.820	108.69	118.35	128.86	140.30	152.75	166.29
15	94.781	103.94	113.98	125.01	137.11	150.38	164.92	180.87	198.65	217.47
16	115.90	128.02	141.43	156.25	172.64	190.73	210.72	232.79	257.14	284.01
17	141.44	157.40	175.19	195.00	217.04	241.58	268.89	299.25	333.01	370.53
18	158.07	193.25	215.71	243.03	272.56	305.66	342.76	384.32	430.86	482.97
19	209.76	236.99	267.79	302.60	341.94	386.38	436.59	443.21	557.10	629.17
20	255.02	290.35	330.60	376.47	428.68	488.12	555.70	632.61	719.97	819.23
21	309.78	355.45	407.87	468.04	537.12	616.27	707.04	811.00	930.03	1066.3
22	376.05	434.86	502.91	581.63	672.64	777.77	899.19	1039.4	1201.0	1387.5
23	456.22	531.77	619.83	722.46	842.04	981.27	1143.3	1367.4	1550.7	1805.0
24	553.24	649.95	763.61	897.08	1053.8	1237.7	1453.2	1705.8	2001.6	2347.8

n	31%	32%	33%	34%	35%	36%	37%	38%	39%	40%
00	1.0000	1.0000	1.0000	1.0000	1.0000	1.0000	1.0000	1.0000	1.0000	1.0000
01	1.3100	1.3200	1.3300	1.3400	1.3500	1.3600	1.3700	1.3800	1.3900	1.4000
02	3.0261	3.0625	3.0988	3.1356	3.1726	3.2097	3.2470	3.2845	3.3226	3.3600
03	5.2742	5.3625	5.4518	5.5418	5.6633	5.7250	5.8184	5.9124	6.0077	6.1040
04	8.2194	8.3984	8.5806	8.7659	8.9543	9.146	9.341	9.539	9.741	9.846
05	12.077	12.406	12.742	13.086	13.438	13.800	14.167	14.568	14.930	15.324
06	17.131	17.696	18.277	18.876	19.492	20.126	20.782	21.451	22.141	22.853
07	23.752	24.678	25.639	26.632	27.663	28.732	29.838	30.982	32.167	33.395
08	32.423	33.895	35.430	37.029	38.697	40.435	42.246	44.137	46.103	48.153
09	44.787	46.062	48.452	50.959	53.591	56.352	59.249	62.287	65.474	68.814
10	58.671	62.122	65.770	69.624	73.697	77.998	82.541	87.337	92.397	97.739
11	78.168	83.320	88.803	93.735	100.84	107.44	114.45	121.90	129.82	138.24
12	103.74	111.30	119.44	128.15	137.49	147.48	150.17	169.61	181.82	184.93
13	132.17	148.24	160.18	173.07	186.95	201.93	218.06	235.44	254.28	274.30
14	181.00	197.00	214.37	233.25	253.74	275.98	300.11	326.29	354.64	385.42
15	238.42	261.36	286.45	313.88	343.89	376.69	412.78	451.63	494.36	543.50
16	313.65	346.31	382.30	421.94	465.60	513.67	566.51	624.66	688.56	761.53
17	412.19	452.19	509.79	566.77	629.94	699.94	777.51	863.42	958.49	1066.2
18	541.26	606.47	679.36	760.79	851.74	953.28	1066.6	1192.9	1333.7	1493.1
19	710.39	801.88	904.88	1020.8	1151.2	1297.8	1462.5	1647.4	1855.2	2091.7
20	931.90	1059.8	1204.8	1369.2	1555.5	1766.4	2005.1	2275.0	2578.5	2927.5
21	1222.1	1400.2	1603.7	1836.1	2101.3	2405.6	2748.5	3140.8	3587.7	4098.8
22	1606.3	1849.6	2134.3	2461.7	2838.1	3270.4	3766.6	4335.8	4988.5	5738.8
23	2100.3	2442.8	2840.2	3300.2	3832.7	4449.0	5161.4	5984.8	6935.2	8034.5
24	2752.7	3225.9	3778.4	4423.4	5175.6	6052.1	7072.8	8260.3	9641.6	1124.0

Appendix D Present Value of One Dollar Per Year for n Years

n	1%	2%	3%	4%	5%	6%	7%	8%	9%	10%
01	.9901	.9804	.9709	.9615	.9524	.9434	.9346	.9259	.9174	.9091
02	1.9704	1.9416	1.9135	1.8861	1.8594	1.8334	1.8080	1.7833	1.7591	1.7355
03	2.9410	2.8839	2.8286	2.7751	2.7233	2.6730	2.6243	2.5771	2.5313	2.4868
04	3.9020	3.8077	3.7171	3.6299	3.5459	3.4651	3.3872	3.3121	3.2397	3.1699
05	4.8535	4.7134	4.5797	4.4518	4.3295	4.2123	4.1002	3.9927	3.8896	3.7908
06	5.7955	5.6014	5.1172	5.2421	5.0757	4.9173	4.7665	4.6229	4.4859	4.3553
07	6.7282	6.4720	6.2302	6.0020	5.7863	5.5824	5.3893	5.2064	5.0329	4.8684
08	7.6517	7.3254	7.0196	6.7327	6.4632	6.2098	5.9713	5.7466	5.5348	5.3349
09	8.5661	8.1622	7.7861	7.4353	7.1078	6.8017	0.5152	6.2469	5.9852	5.7590
10	9.4714	8.9825	8.7302	8.1109	7.7217	7.3601	7.0236	6.7101	6.4176	6.1446
11	10.3677	9.7868	9.2526	8.7604	8.3064	7.8868	7.4987	7.1389	6.8052	6.4951
12	11.2552	10.5753	9.9539	9.3850	8.8632	8.3838	7.9427	7.5361	7.1607	6.8137
13	12.1338	11.3483	10.6349	9.9856	9.3935	8.8527	8.3576	7.9038	7.4869	7.1034
14	13.0038	12.1062	11.2960	10.5631	9.8986	9.2950	8.7454	8.2442	7.7861	7.3667
15	13.8651	12.8492	11.9379	11.1183	10.3796	9.7122	9.1079	8.5595	8.0607	7.6061
16	14.7180	13.5777	12.5610	11.6522	10.8377	10.1059	9.4466	8.8514	8.3125	7.8237
17	15.5624	14.2918	13.1660	12.1656	11.2740	10.4772	9.7632	9.1216	8.5436	8.0215
18	16.3984	14.9920	13.7534	12.6592	11.6895	10.8276	10.0591	9.3719	8.7556	8.2014
19	17.2201	15.2684	14.3237	13.1339	12.0853	11.1581	10.3556	9.6036	8.9501	8.3649
20	18.0457	16.3514	14.8774	13.5903	12.4622	11.4699	10.5940	9.8181	9.1285	8.5136
21	18.8571	17.0111	15.4149	14.0291	12.8211	11.7640	10.8355	10.0168	9.2922	8.6487
22	19.6605	17.6581	15.9368	14.4511	13.1630	12.0416	11.0612	10.2007	9.4424	8.7715
23	20.4559	18.2921	16.4435	14.8568	13.4885	12.3033	11.2722	10.3710	9.5802	8.8832
24	21.2435	18.9139	16.9355	15.2469	13.7986	12.5503	11.4693	10.5287	9.7066	8.9847
25	22.0233	19.5234	17.4131	15.6220	14.9039	12.7833	11.6536	10.6748	9.8226	9.0770

n	20%	19%	18%	17%	16%	15%	14%	13%	12%	11%	n
01	.8333	.8403	.8475	.8547	.8621	.8696	.8772	.8850	.8929	.9009	01
02	1.5278	1.5465	1.5656	1.5852	1.6052	1.6257	1.6467	1.6681	1.6901	1.7125	02
03	2.1065	2.1399	2.1743	2.2096	2.2459	2.2832	2.3216	2.3612	2.4018	2.4437	03
04	2.5887	2.6386	2.6901	2.7432	2.7982	2.8550	2.9137	2.9745	3.0373	3.1024	04
05	2.9906	3.0576	3.1272	3.1993	3.2743	3.3522	3.4331	3.5172	3.6048	3.6959	05
06	3.3255	3.4098	3.4976	3.5892	3.6847	3.7845	3.8887	3.9976	4.1114	4.2305	06
07	3.6046	3.7057	3.8115	3.9224	4.0386	4.1604	4.2883	4.4226	4.5638	4.7122	07
08	3.8372	3.9544	4.0776	4.2072	4.3436	4.4873	4.6389	4.7988	4.9676	5.1461	08
09	4.0310	4.1633	4.3030	4.4506	4.6065	4.7716	4.9464	5.1317	5.3282	5.5370	09
10	4.1925	4.3389	4.4941	4.6586	4.8332	5.0188	5.2161	5.4262	5.6502	5.8892	10
11	4.3271	4.4865	4.6560	4.8364	5.0286	5.2337	5.4527	5.6869	5.9377	6.2065	11
12	4.4392	4.6105	4.7932	4.9884	5.1971	5.4206	5.6603	5.9176	6.1944	6.4924	12
13	4.5327	4.7147	4.9095	5.1183	5.3423	5.5831	5.8424	6.1218	6.4235	6.7499	13
14	4.6106	4.8023	5.0081	5.2293	5.4675	5.7245	6.0021	6.3025	6.6282	6.9819	14
15	4.6755	4.8759	5.0916	5.3242	5.5755	5.8474	6.1422	6.4624	6.8109	7.1909	15
16	4.7296	4.9377	5.1624	5.4053	5.6685	5.9542	6.2651	6.6039	6.9740	7.3792	16
17	4.7746	4.9897	5.2223	5.4746	5.7487	6.0472	6.3729	6.7291	7.1196	7.5488	17
18	4.8122	5.0333	5.2732	5.5339	5.8178	6.1280	6.4674	6.8399	7.2497	7.7016	18
19	4.8435	5.0700	5.3176	5.5845	5.8775	6.1982	6.5504	6.9380	7.3650	7.8393	19
20	4.8696	5.1009	5.3527	5.6278	5.9288	6.2593	6.6231	7.0248	7.4694	7.9633	20
21	4.8913	5.1268	5.3837	5.6648	5.9731	6.3125	6.6870	7.1016	7.5620	8.0751	21
22	4.9094	5.1486	5.4099	5.6964	6.0113	6.3587	6.7429	7.1695	7.6446	8.1757	22
23	4.9245	5.1668	5.4321	5.7234	6.0442	6.3988	6.7921	7.2297	7.7184	8.2664	23
24	4.9371	5.1822	5.4509	5.7465	6.0726	6.4338	6.8351	7.2829	7.7843	8.3481	24
25	4.9476	5.1951	5.4669	5.7662	6.0971	6.4641	6.8729	7.3300	7.8431	8.4217	25

n	30%	29%	28%	27%	26%	25%	24%	23%	22%	21%	n
01	.7692	.7752	.7813	.7874	.7937	.8000	.8065	.8130	.8197	.8264	01
02	1.3609	1.3761	1.3916	1.4074	1.4235	1.4400	1.4568	1.4740	1.4915	1.5095	02
03	1.8161	1.8420	1.8684	1.8956	1.9234	1.9520	1.9813	2.0114	2.0422	2.0739	03
04	2.1662	2.2031	2.2410	2.2800	2.3202	2.3616	2.4043	2.4483	2.4936	2.5404	04
05	2.4356	2.4830	2.5320	2.5827	2.6351	2.6893	2.7454	2.8035	2.8636	2.9260	05
06	2.6427	2.7000	2.7594	2.8210	2.8850	2.9514	3.0205	3.0923	3.1669	3.2446	06
07	2.8021	2.8682	2.9370	3.0087	3.0833	3.1611	3.2423	3.3270	3.4155	3.5079	07
08	2.9247	2.9986	3.0758	3.1564	3.2407	3.3289	3.4212	3.5179	3.6193	3.7256	08
09	3.0190	3.0997	3.1842	3.2728	3.3657	3.4631	3.5655	3.6731	3.7863	3.9054	09
10	3.0915	3.1781	3.2689	3.3644	3.4648	3.5705	3.6819	3.7993	3.9232	4.0541	10
11	3.1473	3.2388	3.3351	3.4365	3.5435	3.6564	3.7757	3.0918	4.0354	4.1769	11
12	3.1903	3.2850	3.3868	3.4933	3.6060	3.7251	3.8514	3.9852	4.1274	4.2785	12
13	3.2233	3.3224	3.4272	3.6381	3.6555	3.7601	3.9124	4.0530	4.2028	4.3624	13
14	3.2487	3.3507	3.4587	3.5733	3.6949	3.8241	3.9616	4.1082	4.2646	4.4317	14
15	3.2682	3.3726	3.4834	3.6010	3.7261	3.8593	4.0013	4.1530	4.3152	4.4890	15
16	3.2832	3.3896	3.5026	3.6228	3.7509	3.8874	4.0333	4.1894	4.3567	4.5364	16
17	3.2948	3.4028	3.5177	3.6400	3.7705	3.9099	4.0591	4.2890	4.3908	4.5755	17
18	3.3037	3.4130	3.5294	3.6536	3.7861	3.9279	4.0799	4.2431	4.4187	4.6079	18
19	3.3105	3.4210	3.5386	3.6642	3.7985	3.9424	4.0967	4.2627	4.4415	4.6345	19
20	3.3158	3.4271	3.5458	3.6726	3.8083	3.9539	4.1103	4.2786	4.4603	4.6567	20
21	3.3198	3.4319	3.5514	3.6792	3.8161	3.9631	4.1212	4.2916	4.4756	4.6750	21
22	3.3230	3.4356	3.5553	3.6844	3.8223	3.9705	4.1300	4.3021	4.4882	4.6900	22
23	3.3254	3.4384	3.5592	3.6885	3.8273	3.9764	3.1371	4.3106	4.4985	4.7025	23
24	3.3272	3.4406	3.5619	3.6981	3.8312	3.9811	4.1428	4.3176	4.5070	4.7128	24
25	3.3286	4.4423	3.5640	3.6943	3.8342	3.9849	4.1474	4.3232	4.5139	4.7213	25

n	40%	39%	38%	37%	36%	35%	34%	33%	32%	31%	n
01	.7143	.7194	.7246	.7299	.7353	.7407	.7463	.7519	.7576	.7634	01
02	1.2245	1.2370	1.2497	1.2627	1.2760	1.2894	1.3032	1.3172	1.3315	1.3461	02
03	1.5889	1.6093	1.6302	1.6516	1.6735	1.6959	1.7188	1.7423	1.7663	1.7009	03
04	1.8492	1.8772	1.9060	1.9355	1.9658	1.9969	2.0290	2.0618	2.0957	2.1305	04
05	1.9352	2.0699	2.1058	2.1427	2.1807	2.2200	2.2604	2.3021	2.3452	2.3897	05
06	2.1680	2.2086	2.2506	2.2939	2.3388	2.3852	2.4331	2.4828	2.5342	2.5875	06
07	2.2628	2.3083	2.3555	2.4043	2.4550	2.5075	2.5620	2.6187	2.6775	2.7386	07
08	2.3306	2.3801	2.4815	2.4849	2.5404	2.5982	2.6582	2.7208	2.7860	2.8539	08
09	2.3790	2.4317	2.4866	2.5437	2.6033	2.6653	2.7300	2.7976	2.8681	2.9419	09
10	2.4136	2.4689	2.5265	2.5867	2.6495	2.7150	2.7836	2.8553	2.9304	3.0091	10
11	2.4383	2.4956	2.5555	2.6180	2.6834	2.7519	2.8236	2.8987	2.9776	3.0604	11
12	2.4559	2.5148	2.5764	2.6409	2.7084	2.7792	2.8534	2.9314	3.0133	3.0995	12
13	2.4685	2.5286	2.5916	2.6576	2.7268	2.7994	2.8757	2.9559	3.0404	3.1294	13
14	2.4775	2.5386	2.6026	2.6698	2.7403	2.8144	2.8923	2.9744	3.0609	3.1522	14
15	2.4839	2.5437	2.6106	2.6787	2.7502	2.8255	2.9047	2.9883	3.0764	3.1696	15
16	2.4885	2.5509	2.6164	2.6852	2.7575	2.8337	2.9140	2.9987	3.0882	3.1829	16
17	2.4918	2.5546	2.6206	2.6899	2.7629	2.8398	2.9209	3.0065	3.0971	3.1931	17
18	2.4941	2.5573	2.6236	2.6934	2.7668	2.8443	2.9260	3.0124	3.1039	3.2005	18
19	2.4958	2.5592	2.6258	2.6959	2.7697	2.8476	2.9299	3.0169	3.1090	3.2067	19
20	2.4970	2.5606	2.6274	2.6977	2.7718	2.8501	2.9327	3.0202	3.1129	3.2112	20
21	2.4979	2.5616	2.6285	2.6991	2.7734	2.8519	2.9349	3.0227	3.1158	3.2147	21
22	2.4985	2.5623	2.6294	2.7000	2.7746	2.8533	2.9365	3.0246	3.1180	3.2173	22
23	2.4989	2.5628	2.6300	2.7009	2.7754	2.8543	2.9377	3.0270	3.1197	3.2193	23
24	2.4992	2.5632	2.6304	2.7013	2.7760	2.8550	2.9386	3.0271	3.1210	3.2209	24
25	2.4994	2.5634	2.6307	2.7017	2.7765	2.8556	2.9392	3.0279	3.1220	3.2220	25

Appendix E Sum of an Annuity of One Dollar

n	1%	2%	3%	4%	5%	6%	7%	8%	9%	10%	n
01	1.0000	1.0000	1.0000	1.0000	1.0000	1.0000	1.0000	1.0000	1.0000	1.0000	01
02	2.0100	2.0200	2.0300	2.0400	2.0500	2.0600	2.0700	2.0800	2.0900	2.1000	02
03	3.0301	3.0604	3.0909	3.1216	3.1525	3.1833	3.2143	3.2463	3.2778	3.3100	03
04	4.0604	4.1216	4.1836	4.2464	4.3101	4.3750	4.4400	4.5063	4.5733	4.6410	04
05	5.1010	5.2040	5.3091	5.4163	5.5256	5.6367	5.7180	5.8663	5.9844	6.1050	05
06	6.1520	6.3081	6.4684	6.6330	6.8020	6.9750	7.1529	7.3363	7.5233	7.7160	06
07	7.2135	7.4343	7.6625	7.8983	8.1420	8.3933	8.6543	8.9225	9.2000	9.4870	07
08	8.2857	8.5830	8.8923	9.2142	9.5491	9.8983	10.260	10.637	11.028	11.436	08
09	9.3685	9.7546	10.159	10.583	11.027	11.491	11.978	12.488	13.021	13.579	09
10	10.462	10.950	11.464	12.006	12.578	13.181	13.816	14.487	15.193	15.937	10
11	11.567	12.169	12.808	13.486	14.207	14.972	15.784	16.645	17.560	18.531	11
12	12.683	13.412	14.192	15.026	15.917	16.870	17.888	18.977	20.141	21.384	12
13	13.809	14.680	15.618	16.627	17.713	18.882	20.141	21.495	22.953	24.523	13
14	14.947	15.974	17.086	18.292	19.599	21.051	22.550	24.215	26.019	27.975	14
15	16.097	17.293	18.599	20.024	21.579	23.276	25.129	27.152	29.361	31.772	15
16	17.258	18.639	20.157	21.825	23.657	25.673	27.888	30.324	33.003	35.950	16
17	18.430	20.012	21.762	23.698	25.840	28.213	30.840	33.750	36.973	40.545	17
18	19.615	21.412	23.414	25.645	28.132	30.906	33.999	37.450	41.301	45.599	18
19	20.811	22.841	25.117	27.671	30.539	33.760	37.379	41.446	46.019	51.159	19
20	22.019	24.297	26.870	29.778	33.066	36.786	40.995	45.762	51.160	57.275	20
21	23.239	25.783	28.676	31.969	35.719	39.993	44.865	50.423	56.764	64.002	21
22	24.472	27.299	30.537	34.248	38.505	42.392	49.006	55.457	62.873	71.403	22
23	25.716	28.845	32.453	36.618	41.430	46.996	53.436	60.893	69.532	79.543	23
24	26.973	30.422	34.426	39.083	44.502	50.816	58.177	66.765	76.790	88.497	24
25	28.243	32.030	36.459	41.646	47.727	54.865	63.249	73.106	84.701	98.347	25

n	20%	19%	18%	17%	16%	15%	14%	13%	12%	11%	n
01	1.0000	1.0000	1.0000	1.0000	1.0000	1.0000	1.0000	1.0000	1.0000	1.0000	01
02	2.2000	2.1900	2.1800	2.1700	2.1600	2.1500	2.1400	2.1300	2.1200	2.1100	02
03	3.6400	3.6063	3.5722	3.5388	3.5056	3.4723	3.4393	3.4069	3.3742	3.3418	03
04	5.3680	5.2896	5.2156	5.1406	5.0666	4.9933	4.9214	4.8500	4.7792	4.7100	04
05	7.4415	7.2968	7.1544	7.0147	6.8769	6.7423	6.6100	6.4800	6.3525	6.2288	05
06	9.9300	9.6832	9.4422	9.2071	8.9775	8.7540	8.5357	8.3231	8.1150	7.9127	06
07	12.916	12.523	12.142	11.772	11.414	11.067	10.730	10.405	10.089	9.7836	07
08	16.499	15.902	15.327	14.774	14.240	13.723	13.233	12.757	12.300	11.859	08
09	20.799	19.924	19.086	18.285	17.518	16.786	16.085	15.415	14.776	14.164	09
10	25.959	24.709	23.521	22.393	21.321	20.304	19.337	18.420	17.549	16.722	10
11	32.150	30.404	28.755	27.200	25.733	24.349	23.044	21.815	20.655	19.562	11
12	39.580	37.180	34.931	32.824	30.850	29.002	27.271	25.650	24.133	22.714	12
13	48.497	45.245	42.219	39.404	36.786	34.352	32.089	29.985	28.029	26.212	13
14	59.196	54.842	50.818	47.103	43.672	40.505	37.581	34.883	32.393	30.095	14
15	72.035	66.263	60.965	56.112	51.659	47.581	43.842	40.418	37.280	34.405	15
16	87.440	79.853	72.939	66.647	60.925	55.717	50.981	46.672	42.753	39.190	16
17	105.93	96.021	87.067	78.984	71.675	65.073	59.118	53.739	48.883	44.501	17
18	128.12	115.27	103.74	93.406	84.144	75.840	68.393	61.725	55.750	50.696	18
19	154.74	138.17	123.41	110.28	98.606	88.213	78.971	70.054	63.440	56.939	19
20	186.69	165.94	146.63	130.04	115.38	102.31	91.029	80.946	72.053	64.203	20
21	225.03	197.85	174.02	153.20	134.84	118.81	104.77	92.469	81.709	72.265	21
22	271.03	236.44	206.34	180.17	157.41	137.63	120.44	105.49	92.500	81.214	22
23	326.24	282.36	244.49	211.80	183.60	159.28	138.30	120.21	104.60	91.145	23
24	392.49	337.01	289.49	248.81	213.98	184.17	158.66	136.83	118.16	102.17	24
25	471.98	402.04	342.61	292.11	249.21	212.79	181.87	155.62	133.33	114.42	25

n	30%	29%	28%	27%	26%	25%	24%	23%	22%	21%	n
01	1.0000	1.0000	1.0000	1.0000	1.0000	1.0000	1.0000	1.0000	1.0000	1.0000	01
02	2.3000	2.2900	2.2800	2.2700	2.2600	2.2500	2.200	2.2300	2.2200	2.2100	02
03	3.9900	3.9541	3.9186	3.8830	3.8477	3.8124	3.778	3.7430	3.7086	3.6743	03
04	6.1870	6.1007	6.0157	5.9315	5.8481	5.7656	5.6842	5.6039	5.5241	5.4457	04
05	9.0430	8.8700	8.7000	8.5326	8.3685	8.2072	8.0433	7.8926	7.7395	7.5690	05
06	12.756	12.442	12.136	11.837	11.544	11.259	10.980	10.708	10.442	10.183	06
07	17.583	17.051	16.534	16.033	15.546	15.074	14.615	14.171	13.740	13.321	07
08	23.858	22.995	22.163	21.361	20.588	19.842	19.133	18.430	17.762	17.119	08
09	32.017	30.664	29.369	28.129	26.940	25.802	24.712	23.669	22.670	21.714	09
10	42.620	40.555	38.592	36.722	34.946	33.253	31.693	30.113	28.657	27.274	10
11	56.407	53.317	50.399	48.641	45.031	42.568	40.288	38.039	35.962	34.001	11
12	74.327	69.783	65.510	61.500	57.738	54.208	50.985	47.787	44.873	42.141	12
13	97.627	91.017	84.853	79.107	73.750	68.760	64.110	59.739	55.745	51.990	13
14	127.91	118.41	109.61	101.47	93.927	86.948	80.496	74.526	69.009	63.910	14
15	167.29	153.75	141.30	129.86	119.35	109.69	100.82	92.670	85.191	78.329	15
16	218.47	199.65	181.87	165.92	151.38	138.11	126.01	114.98	104.94	95.781	16
17	285.01	258.14	233.79	211.72	191.73	173.64	157.25	142.43	129.02	116.90	17
18	371.53	334.01	300.25	269.89	242.58	218.04	196.00	176.19	158.40	142.44	18
19	483.97	431.86	385.32	343.76	306.66	273.56	244.03	216.71	194.25	159.07	19
20	630.17	558.10	494.21	437.59	387.38	342.94	303.60	268.79	237.99	210.76	20
21	820.23	720.97	633.61	556.70	489.12	429.68	377.47	331.60	291.35	256.02	21
22	1067.3	931.03	812.00	708.04	617.27	538.12	469.04	408.87	356.45	310.78	22
23	1388.5	1202.0	1040.4	900.19	778.77	673.64	582.63	503.91	435.86	377.05	23
24	1806.0	1551.7	1368.4	1144.3	982.27	843.04	723.46	620.83	532.77	457.22	24
25	2348.8	2002.6	1706.8	1454.2	1238.7	1054.8	898.08	764.64	650.95	554.24	25

n	40%	39%	38%	37%	36%	35%	34%	33%	32%	31%	n
01	1.0000	1.0000	1.0000	1.0000	1.0000	1.0000	1.0000	1.0000	1.0000	1.0000	01
02	2.4000	2.3900	2.3800	2.3700	2.3600	2.3500	2.3400	2.3300	2.3200	2.3100	02
03	4.3600	4.3226	4.2845	4.2470	4.2097	4.1725	4.1356	4.0988	4.0625	4.0261	03
04	7.1040	7.0077	6.9124	6.8184	6.7250	6.6633	6.5418	6.4518	6.3625	6.2742	04
05	10.846	10.741	10.539	10.341	10.146	9.9543	9.7659	9.5806	9.3984	9.2194	05
06	16.324	15.930	15.568	15.167	14.800	14.438	14.086	13.742	13.406	13.077	06
07	23.853	23.141	22.451	21.782	21.126	20.492	19.876	19.277	18.696	18.131	07
08	34.395	33.167	31.982	30.838	29.732	28.663	27.632	26.639	25.678	24.752	08
09	49.153	47.103	45.137	43.246	41.435	39.697	38.029	36.430	34.895	33.423	09
10	69.814	66.474	63.287	60.249	57.352	54.591	51.959	49.452	47.062	44.787	10
11	98.739	93.397	88.337	83.541	78.998	74.697	70.624	66.770	63.122	59.671	11
12	139.24	130.82	122.90	115.45	108.44	101.84	94.735	89.803	84.320	79.168	12
13	195.93	182.82	170.61	159.17	148.48	138.49	129.15	120.44	112.30	104.74	13
14	275.30	255.28	236.44	219.06	202.93	187.95	174.07	161.18	149.24	138.17	14
15	386.42	355.64	327.29	301.11	276.98	254.74	234.25	215.37	198.00	182.00	15
16	544.50	495.36	452.63	413.78	377.69	344.89	314.88	287.45	262.36	239.42	16
17	762.53	689.56	625.66	567.51	514.67	466.60	422.94	383.30	347.31	314.65	17
18	1067.2	959.49	864.42	778.51	700.94	630.94	567.77	510.79	453.19	413.19	18
19	1494.1	1334.7	1193.9	1067.6	954.28	852.74	761.79	680.36	607.47	542.26	19
20	2091.7	1856.2	1648.4	1463.5	1298.8	1152.2	1021.8	905.88	802.88	711.39	20
21	2928.5	2579.5	2276.0	2006.1	1767.4	1556.5	1370.2	1205.8	1060.8	932.90	21
22	4099.8	3588.7	3141.8	2749.5	2404.6	2102.3	1837.1	1604.7	1401.2	1223.1	22
23	5739.8	4989.5	4336.8	3767.6	3271.4	2839.1	2462.7	2135.3	1850.6	1603.3	23
24	8035.5	6936.2	5985.8	5162.4	4450.0	3833.7	3301.2	2841.2	2443.8	2101.3	24
25	1125.0	9642.6	8261.3	7073.8	6053.1	5176.6	4424.4	3779.4	3226.9	2753.7	25

Appendix F Values of the Standard Normal Distribution Function

$$\phi(z) = \int_{-\infty}^{z} \frac{1}{\sqrt{2\pi}} e^{-u^2/2}\, du = P(Z \leq z)$$

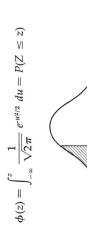

z	0	1	2	3	4	5	6	7	8	9
-3.	.0013	.0010	.0007	.0005	.0003	.0002	.0002	.0001	.0001	.0000
-2.9	.0019	.0018	.0017	.0017	.0016	.0016	.0015	.0015	.0014	.0014
-2.8	.0026	.0025	.0024	.0023	.0023	.0022	.0021	.0020	.0020	.0019
-2.7	.0035	.0034	.0033	.0032	.0031	.0030	.0029	.0028	.0027	.0026
-2.6	.0047	.0045	.0044	.0043	.0041	.0040	.0039	.0038	.0037	.0036
-2.5	.0062	.0060	.0059	.0057	.0055	.0054	.0052	.0051	.0049	.0048
-2.4	.0082	.0080	.0078	.0075	.0073	.0071	.0069	.0068	.0066	.0064
-2.3	.0107	.0104	.0102	.0099	.0096	.0094	.0091	.0089	.0087	.0084
-2.2	.0139	.0136	.0132	.0129	.0126	.0122	.0119	.0116	.0113	.0110
-2.1	.0179	.0174	.0170	.0166	.0162	.0158	.0154	.0150	.0146	.0143
-2.0	.0228	.0222	.0217	.0212	.0207	.0202	.0197	.0192	.0188	.0183
-1.9	.0287	.0281	.0274	.0268	.0262	.0256	.0250	.0244	.0238	.0233
-1.8	.0359	.0352	.0344	.0336	.0329	.0322	.0314	.0307	.0300	.0294
-1.7	.0446	.0436	.0427	.0418	.0409	.0401	.0392	.0384	.0375	.0367
-1.6	.0548	.0537	.0526	.0516	.0505	.0495	.0485	.0475	.0465	.0455
-1.5	.0668	.0655	.0643	.0630	.0618	.0606	.0594	.0582	.0570	.0559

z										
−1.4	.0808	.0793	.0778	.0764	.0749	.0735	.0722	.0708	.0694	.0681
−1.3	.0968	.0951	.0934	.0918	.0901	.0885	.0869	.0853	.0838	.0823
−1.2	.1151	.1131	.1112	.1093	.1075	.1056	.1038	.1020	.1003	.0985
−1.1	.1357	.1335	.1314	.1292	.1271	.1251	.1230	.1210	.1190	.1170
−1.0	.1587	.1562	.1539	.1515	.1492	.1469	.1446	.1423	.1401	.1379
−.9	.1841	.1814	.1788	.1762	.1736	.1711	.1685	.1660	.1635	.1611
−.8	.2119	.2090	.2061	.2033	.2005	.1977	.1949	.1922	.1894	.1867
−.7	.2420	.2389	.2358	.2327	.2297	.2266	.2236	.2206	.2177	.2148
−.6	.2743	.2709	.2676	.2643	.2611	.2578	.2546	.2514	.2483	.2451
−.5	.3085	.3050	.3015	.2981	.2946	.2912	.2877	.2843	.2810	.2776
−.4	.3446	.3409	.3372	.3336	.3300	.3264	.3228	.3192	.3156	.3121
−.3	.3821	.3783	.3745	.3707	.3669	.3632	.3594	.3557	.3520	.3483
−.2	.4207	.4168	.4129	.4090	.4052	.4013	.3974	.3936	.3897	.3859
−.1	.4602	.4562	.4522	.4483	.4443	.4404	.4364	.4325	.4286	.4247
−.0	.5000	.4960	.4920	.4880	.4840	.4801	.4761	.4721	.4681	.4641

SOURCE: *Introduction to Probability and Statistics*, second edition, by B. W. Lindgren and G. W. McElrath. Copyright © 1966 by B. W. Lindgren and G. W. McElrath. Reprinted with permission of The Macmillan Company.

Appendix G **Security Evaluation Models**

Although the determination of the cost of equity (k_e) as the rate of return required by potential stockholders of the company and as the discount rate that equates the expected future stream of benefits to the prevailing market price of the stock is far from being completely defined, there are still many useful interpretations as to what does determine the firm's stock and bond price. As a financial officer, you must be familiar with the typical models that explain security prices so that you know what potential investors in your firm's stocks and bonds examine in formulating their required rate of return. Then, if you, as the financial officer, can make these important factors conform to the specification investors desire, you can lower the firm's cost of equity capital.

What do financial theorists generally think are the major factors investors use to judge the return they require? We will examine several models that are commonly used to explain security price, in an effort to grasp what factors have seemed important in the past.

What exactly have financial empiricists observed as significant factors as well as the degree to which those factors affect the stock price? Can you, as financial officer, change the value of those factors to your firm's advantage, and can those factors serve as a guide to good financial management? We shall explore in this appendix various empirical models that attempt to tell us what the important considerations are.

SOME THEORETICAL SECURITY EVALUATION MODELS

What are the important considerations in security prices according to the theoretical models that can be categorized as dividend models, price/earnings ratio models, and behavioral models?

Dividend Models

We have already seen that the investment evaluation of the stock reflects the anticipated future stream of dividends discounted back to the present by a rate of return required by investors to compensate them for the surrendering of their capital and the associated risk. Since the stock certificate, which represents ownership, only entitles the holder to receive the dividends declared by the firm, its theoretical value can be expressed as:

$$P_0 = \sum_{t=1}^{\infty} \frac{\hat{D}_t}{(1 + k_e)^t} \qquad \text{(G-1)}$$

where

P_0 = the prevailing price
$\hat{D}_t$ = the anticipated dividend stream
k_e = the required rate of return

This can be adjusted slightly to derive the Bolten equilibrium model of stock price,[1] which is:

$$\Delta P_0 = \sum_{t=1}^{\infty} \frac{\Delta \hat{D}_t}{(1 + \Delta k_e)^t} \tag{G-2}$$

where

$\Delta k_e = \Delta r.i. + \Delta p + \Delta b + \Delta f_e + \Delta m$
Δ = signifies a change in investor attitude toward the variable of model G-1
$r.i.$ = real interest rate
p = purchasing power risk premium
b = business risk
f_e = financial risk to equity
m = marketability risk

Notice in the equilibrium model that stock price changes are explained by changes in the variables, so that the model, unlike the static model G-1, allows the financial officer to focus on changes in the cost of capital and stock price. It assumes that the present stock price is the equilibrium price and that the stock market has carefully and accurately digested into this price all the pertinent information on the firm that it has available or can reasonably forecast. Then, price changes, which may upset the financial officer's plans, are caused by new information coming into the market and upsetting previous expectations that were based on prior information. This model gives the financial officer more insight into the cost of equity and maximizing the firm's share price. To lower the cost of equity, the financial officer tries to lower any of the factors in k_e which can be changed. To maximize the share price, the officer can, in addition, raise investors' expectations of future dividends, most likely by raising their expectations of future earnings. To see how the firm's share price is going to change, the officer must anticipate or simulate changes in each of the factors that might change for reasons either within or beyond the financial officer's control.

The Gordon constant growth model,[2] which we saw was:

$$P_0 = \frac{D_0}{k_e - g} \tag{G-3}$$

where

P_0 = the prevailing price
D_0 = the prevailing dividend
k_e = the required rate of return
g = the constant growth rate in dividends

This theoretical model tells us that the important consideration in the cost of equity for the firm is growth. As the rate of growth increases, it continually offsets the cost

---

[1] Steven E. Bolten, *Security Analysis and Portfolio Management*, Holt, Rinehart and Winston, 1972.
[2] Myron J. Gordon, *The Investment, Financing and Valuation of the Corporation*, Richard D. Irwin, 1962.

of equity and maximizes share prices. To maximize share price under this model, the financial officer has to maximize growth.

The Malkiel model[3] states:

$$P = \frac{D(1+g)}{(1+k_e)} + \frac{D(1+g)^2}{(1+k_e)^2} + \cdots + \frac{\overline{M}_sE(1+g)^n}{(1+k_e)^n} \tag{G-4}$$

where

P = the prevailing price
D = the prevailing dividend
g = the anticipated growth rate
E = earnings per share
$\overline{M}_s$ = the standard price/earnings multiple expected to prevail in year n for a standard nongrowth stock

Model G-4 states that the stream of future benefits which investors anticipate is comprised of two parts: the growing dividend stream during the firm's growth phase and the price of the stock at the beginning of the nongrowth phase. That price is determined as of period n for the earnings per share which are expected to prevail then $-E(1+g)^n-$ times the price/earnings multiple of the standard nongrowth $(\overline{M}_s)$. The financial officer must then try to anticipate the duration of the growth phase and the standard nongrowth multiple. This model allows a little more flexibility because of its explicit consideration of the termination of the firm's growth phase.

The quadratic model can be used if the financial officer does not want to or feels unsure in stipulating the duration of growth as required by the Malkiel model. He can assume a smoother industrial life cycle during which earnings first grow rapidly, then level off to a standard growth, and then decline and represent this as the growth factor in expected dividends as in G-5:

$$P_0 = \sum_{t=1}^{\infty} \frac{D_0 \prod_{t=1}^{\infty} (1 + at^2 - bt + c)}{(1+k_e)^t} \tag{G-5}$$

where

P_0 = the prevailing market price
D_0 = the prevailing dividend
k_e = the cost of equity capital

$\prod_{t=1}^{\infty} (1 + at^2 - bt + c)$ = a quadratic representation of the growth cycle in anticipated dividends

Price/Earnings Models

In the price/earnings (P/E) models, the stock price is some multiple (m) of the firm's earnings, such that:

$$P = m(E) \tag{G-6}$$

[3] Burton G. Malkiel, "Equity Yield, Growth, and the Structure of Share Prices," *American Economic Review*, December, 1963.

where
> P = the prevailing price
> m = the multiple
> E = the earnings per share

In this model it is not exactly clear what determines the P/E, although we know it is easily observed in the stock market by simply dividing the observed price by the appropriate earnings per share. The P/E reflects what investors think the stock should sell at on the appropriate earnings per share and obviously reflects their interpretation of the risk adjusted time value of money discount rate used to find the present value of the future stream of dividends. However, since the P/E is only a shorthand notation, which can be derived from the present discounted future stream of dividends if there is no growth, it conceals the individual factors such as real interest rates, purchasing power risk premium, and business, financial, and marketability risks, so that the financial officer who relies strictly on the P/E ratio, or its reverse the E/P ratio, for an indication of the cost of equity will always be at a loss to explain or anticipate changes in the stock market environment. The financial officer will only have observed the change after the fact when it finally showed up in a change in the P/E ratio, which, since it is only a proxy for the other variables, changes last.

Financial officers who exclusively follow the P/E ratio also tend to emphasize increased earnings as the sole approach to maximizing share prices because they assume the multiple is constant, and, therefore, stock prices change only in response to changes in earnings per share. This is, as we have seen, a misleading and incomplete picture, for the stock price can also change when the general risk factors which comprise the cost of equity, i.e., the required rate of return, change. There is nothing more discouraging to security analysts than to see financial officers make a presentation to them in an effort to bolster interest in the stock and then maintain that they cannot understand why the firm's stock price has fallen even though the firm's earnings per share have risen; therefore, the stock market is irrational. It shows their ignorance of the financial markets and tells the security analysts whom they are trying to impress that they are unaware that financial leverage, changing operating environments, and general factors beyond their control also enter into the evaluation of their firm's stock.

Behavioral Models

Sometimes, investor's behavior towards a stock can influence its price.[4] Investors have often become accustomed to certain standards by which they judge the risk associated with the firm when deriving the required rate of return. That is, of course, in addition to the time value of money as reflected in the real interest rate and the purchasing power risk premium. For example, investors have come to expect current ratios of 2:1 in most industrial companies. If your firm deviates from that, investors will require a higher rate of return because of the increased uncertainty associated with something that is not the norm. In model G-7 the deviations from the industry standard increase the cost of equity as measured by the earnings yield:

$$E/P_j = a_n Y_n + b_i |X_{i_{STD}} - X_i| \tag{G-7}$$

[4] Steven E. Bolten, "A Behavioral Note on Security Evaluation," unpublished manuscript.

where
$$E/P_j = \text{the earnings yield for company } j$$
$$Y_n = \text{nonbehavioral variables}$$
$$X_{i_{STD}} = \text{the norm of behavioral variable } i$$
$$X_i = \text{the actual value of behavioral variable } i$$
$$|X_{i_{STD}} - X_i| = \text{the absolute deviation from the norm}$$

The results of model G-7 were:

$$\frac{E}{P_j} = .27824 \left|\frac{D}{E}\right| j + .04057|CR|j - .40114PM_j + .09506\sigma_j$$

$$- .73541PO_j - .10623PLT_j + .91498 \frac{E}{P\,MRKT} \tag{G-8}$$

where

$\left|\dfrac{D}{E}\right| j = $ the absolute deviation from the norm for firm j's debt/equity ratio

$|CR|j = $ the absolute deviation for firm j's current ratio

$PM_j = j$'s profit margins

$PO_j = j$'s payout ratio

$PLT_j = j$'s net plant

$\sigma_j = $ standard deviation in its prior 5 years earnings per share

$\dfrac{E}{P\,MRKT} = $ the average earnings yield for all stocks used to judge investors' required real interest rate and purchasing power risk premium.

Model G-8 says that the cost of equity capital for firm j, as measured by the firm's earnings yield, increases as the firm's financial leverage, as measured by the debt/equity ratio, and the firm's liquidity position deviate from the norm investor associated with a standard firm of standard risk. Also, as the firm's size, profit margins, and payout ratio increase, all indicating a less risky situation, the firm's cost of equity decrease. On the other hand, if the variability in the firm's earnings per share increases, the firm's cost of capital will also increase.

The financial officer can use this model to gain some insight into the effect a maverick course from the industry standard will have on the firm's cost of equity capital. If the financial officer chooses to deviate from the industry norms, he or she had better be able to more than compensate for the accompanying upward pressure on the cost of equity capital by such things as higher profit margins and greater stability in the firm's earnings per share.

SOME EMPIRICAL MODELS

Now that we have seen what some financial theorists believe are the important variables in the determination of stock prices, let us examine what financial empiricists have been able to observe as important variables in the determination of stock prices and see if the two agree.

The Whitbeck and Kisor Model (WK)

Whitbeck and Kisor[5] tested model G-9 to try to determine the normal P/E ratio that should exist:

$$\frac{P}{E_N} = a_0 + a_1(g) + a_2(PO) + a_3(\sigma)$$ (G-9)

where

$\frac{P}{E_N}$ = normalized P/E ratio based on earnings per share that would exist at the mid-point in the business cycle

g = the projected growth rate in earnings per share over the next 5 years

PO = the firm's payout ratio during the last 10 years

σ = the standard error of the estimate for the projected five-year growth rate

WK's results were:

$$\frac{P}{E_N} = 8.2 + 1.5(g) + 6.7(PO) - .2(\sigma)$$ (G-10)

so that, for example, IBM's with a projected growth rate of 17 percent, a 25 percent payout ratio and a standard error of 5 percent should have a P/E ratio of:

$$\frac{P}{E_N} = 8.2 + 1.5(.17) + 6.7(.25) - .2(.05)$$

$$= 34.4$$

WK interpreted this to imply that if the prevailing P/E were greater than 34.4 for IBM, the stock was overvalued; and if the prevailing P/E for IBM were less than 34.4, the stock was undervalued. To financial officers the WK model demonstrates that the growth rate, the payout ratio, and the variability in earnings per share are factors they should pay attention to in order to maximize their firms' share price and minimize their firms' cost of equity capital. If they wanted to sell a new issue of equity and were using the WK model, they would wait until the stock appeared overvalued and then sell the new issue.

The Benishay Model (BM)

The BM[6] tried to empirically establish a relationship between the firm's cost of equity capital, as measured by its earnings yield, and an array of possibly significant variables. The BM tested the following variables as influencing the firm's earnings yield:

X_1 = rate of growth of earnings over the prior 9 years

X_2 = the rate of growth in market value of the common equity over the prior 9 years

X_3 = the log of the average payout ratio for the prior 3 years

X_4 = the expected stability of the anticipated dividend stream measured as the mean value for the prior 9 years divided by the standard deviation of the earnings around a trend

---

[5] V. Whitbeck and M. Kisor, Jr., "A New Tool in Investment Decision Making," *Financial Analysts Journal*, May–June, 1963.

[6] H. Benishay, "Variability in Earnings-Price Ratios of Corporate Equities," *American Economic Review*, March, 1961.

X_5 = the expected stability of equity value, as measured by the mean value of the equity value for the prior 9 years divided by the standard deviation of the equity value around the trend

X_6 = the size of the firm and liquidity of the firm's shares as measured by the market value of the equity

X_7 = the firm's debt/equity ratio

Benishay tested the relationship between these variables and the earnings yield for the years 1955–1957 and found, using 1957 data only, that:

$$\frac{E}{P} = +.0014X_1 - .0076X_2 - .380X_3 - .079X_4 + .131X_5 \\ - .079X_6 - .00195X_7 \tag{G-11}$$

where variables X_2 and X_5 were statistically insignificant and only variables X_6, X_4 and X_1 were consistently statistically significant and not misleading for each year 1955–1957.

The Arditti Model (AM)

The AM[7] tested to see if the observed rate of return required by investors, as measured by dividends plus capital gains over the period under examination, were related to an array of possibly significant factors in the following regression:

$$R = a_0 + a_1X_1 + a_2X_2 + a_3X_3 + a_4X_4 + a_5X_5 \tag{G-12}$$

where

R = investors' required rate of return

X_1 = the variability in the required rate of return distribution

X_2 = the skewness in the distribution of the required rate of return

X_3 = the market correlation factor which measures the correlation between the return to the individual stock and the return to all stock in general

X_4 = the debt/equity ratio

X_5 = the payout ratio

Arditti had expected to find that the coefficients a_1, a_3, and a_4 were positively related and that a_2 was negatively related to the observed rate of return. The skewness variable supposedly decreased the required rate of return as it increased, reflecting increased chances that if the mean value was not realized it would be exceeded rather than undershot—an obviously more attractive situation to investors. Arditti's results, G-13, showed that for all firms in the Standard and Poor's Index:

$$R = .1375 - .0165(X_4) - .0179(X_5) + .2632(X_1) - .0279(X_3) \tag{G-13}$$

When Arditti repeated the tests for particular industries, he found for the retail industry, model G-14, and for the chemical industry, model G-15:

Retailing

$$R = .1787 - .0761X_4 - .1701X_5 + 1.1712X_1 - 1.0135X_2 + .0354X_3 \tag{G-14}$$

Chemicals

$$R = .2867 - .1198X_4 - .2208X_5 + .2602X_1 - .0865X_2 - .0747X_3 \tag{G-15}$$

[7] Frederick Arditti, "Risk and the Required Return on Equity," *Journal of Finance*, March, 1967.

Arditti's results tell the financial officer that variability in the distribution of expected returns increases the firm's cost of equity capital, while skewness in the same distribution reduces the firm's cost of equity capital.

The Nerlove Model (NM)

The NM,[8] like the other empirical analyses reviewed so far, tried to relate a series of possibly significant variables to the required rate of return (R) as observed in the stock market as the dividends and the capital gains accrued to the stockholder during the period under examination.

Nerlove's explanatory variables were:

$X_1 =$ the rate of growth in net sales
$X_2 =$ the rate of growth in earnings available for common stock
$X_3 =$ the mean retained earnings per \$1 of total assets for the period
$X_4 =$ the mean dividends per \$1 of total assets for the period
$X_5 =$ the mean reciprocal of the debt/equity ratio for the period
$X_6 =$ the mean inventory turnover for the period
$X_7 =$ the mean share turnover (a measure of the marketability)
$X_8 =$ mean gross plant per \$1 of total assets
$X_9 \ldots n =$ industry dummy variables to equalize business risk

Nerlove's results for the various periods tested were:

1950–1954 $R^2 = .425$

$$R = .076 + .196X_1 + .076X_2 + 2.105X_3 + .278X_4$$
$$- .046X_5 - .0017X_6 + .044X_7 + .010X_8$$

Insignificant variables: X_8

1955–1957 $R^2 = .515$

$$R = .064 + .326X_1 + .032X_2 + 2.075X_3 + .240X_4$$
$$- .020X_5 - .00056X_6 + .138X_7 - .060X_8$$

Insignificant variables: X_4, X_5, and X_6

1960–1964 $R^2 = .280$

$$R = .052 + .469X_1 + .015X_2 + 1.253X_3 + .226X_4$$
$$- .061X_5 + .0024X_6 - .021X_7 - .0034X_8$$

Insignificant variables: X_4, X_7, and X_8

1950–1964 $R^2 = .493$

$$R = .130 + .157X_1 + .0094X_2 + 2.022X_3 + 0.225X_4 - .066X_5$$
$$- .0003X_6 + .0035X_7 - .028X_8$$

Insignificant variables: X_6 and X_7

Notice that over the period, 1950–1964, and in the subperiods, the parameters and the significance of the variables changes. This tells financial officers that they must

[8] Marc Nerlove, "Factors Affecting Differences Among Rate of Return on Investment in Individual Common Stock," *Review of Economics and Statistics*, August, 1968.

be prepared for a shift in the financial market environment when considering the cost and the type of each security they may want to use.

Generally, Nerlove found that as the growth in sales and earnings increased the realized rate of return also increased. Similarly, the observed rate of return increased as the return per $1 of total assets increased and as the use of financial leverage increased. However, the required rate of return sank as the size of the firm increased. The other variables of share turnover and dividend payout appeared, to Nerlove, to vacillate, being significant in some periods and not significant in others.

The implications of the Nerlove model for the financial officer are far from clear. As with all the models that use the realized rate of return, the fact that the anticipated rate of return required by investors does not have to be realized throws the empirical results off. At the beginning of the period, the financial officer may face an entirely different cost of equity than is eventually realized and may find that different variables from those tested are the significant factors in the determination of the anticipated rate of return required by the financial markets.

The Gordon Empirical Model (GEM)

The GEM[9] (G-16) tries to empirically verify the constant growth model:

$$P_0 = \frac{D_0}{k_e - g} \tag{G-3}$$

such that:

$$\ln P_0 = \ln b_0 + b_1 \ln D + b_2 \ln (g_e) + b_3 \ln \sigma g_e + b_4 \ln \left(\frac{D}{E}\right)$$
$$+ b_5 \ln AL + b_6 \ln S \tag{G-16}$$

where
$\ln P_0 =$ the log of the prevailing price
$\ln D =$ the log of the prevailing dividend
$\ln g_e =$ the log of the growth in earnings
$\ln \sigma g_e =$ the log of the standard deviation in the growth in earnings
$\ln \dfrac{D}{E} =$ the log of the debt/equity ratio
$\ln AL =$ the log of the asset liquidity
$\ln S =$ the log of the firm's size

The GEM results for the period 1954–1958 for the food and machinery industries were:

Food $\qquad$ $R^2 = .925$

$$\ln P_0 = 2.521 + .803 \,(\ln D) + 10.090 \,(\ln g_e) - 5.078 \,(\ln \sigma g_e)$$
$$- .844 \left(\ln \frac{D}{E}\right) + .273 \,(\ln AL) + .090 \,(\ln S) \tag{G-17}$$

Machinery $\qquad$ $R^2 = .881$

$$\ln P_0 = 2.524 + .843 \,(\ln D) + 5.886 \,(\ln g_e) - 2.379 \,(\ln \sigma g_e)$$
$$- .095 \left(\ln \frac{D}{E}\right) + .038 \,(\ln AL) + .104\,(\ln S) \tag{G-18}$$

[9] Myron J. Gordon, *op. cit.*

Bower and Bower (BB)

The BB[10] model tried to relate various possibly significant factors to the firm's P/E ratio, such that:

$$\ln \frac{P}{E} = a + b_1 \ln(1 + g) + b_2 \ln PAY + b_3 MKT + b_4 \ln RHO$$
$$+ b_5 VAR + b_6 \ln FIR \qquad \text{(G-19)}$$

where

$\ln \dfrac{P}{E} =$ the log of the prevailing $\dfrac{P}{E}$ ratio

$(1 + g) = 1$ plus the growth rate

$PAY =$ the payout ratio

$MKT =$ a measure of marketability

$RHO =$ the correlation coefficient of the stock price with stock prices in general

$VAR =$ the variability in the firm's stock price

$FIR =$ the firm effect, as measured by the difference between the actual and the predicted P/E ratio for each year 1956–1964 divided by the standard error of the regression of P/E on b_1 through b_5

The BB model results for 1960–1964 were:

$$\ln P/E = .084\, g + .095\, PAY + .080\, MKT - .077\, RHO$$
$$+ .534\, VAR + .976\, FIR \qquad \text{(G-20)}$$

As with all the other empirical models, the results must be interpreted with care if they are to have meaning for the financial officer. In the BB model, for example, the cost of equity capital, as measured by the log of the P/E ratio decreases as the firm's growth rate, payout ratio, marketability, variability in its share price, and the firm effect increase, and the correlation with the market in general decreases. This might be opposite from what one might expect. Because of the ability to diversify, investors are more likely to pay a higher price for prevailing earnings, if they are indicative of the anticipated stream of future dividends, because of a lower correlation with the general price movements of the market. And, it hardly seems right that investors are willing to pay a higher price for prevailing earnings as the variability in the stock price increases.

The Stewart Behavioral Model

The Stewart model[11] attempts to explain stock price determination through the supply and demand for stock from the different sectors, which may be a help to the financial officers' timing. By looking at the behavior of the various demanders and suppliers, Stewart hoped to explain stock prices through the following set of supply/demand equations:

[10] Dorothy H. and Richard S. Bower, "Risk and the Valuation of Common Stock," *Journal of Political Economy,* May/June, 1969.

[11] S. S. Stewart, Jr., "A Behavioral Model for Predicting Stock Prices," *Journal of Business Research,* Fall, 1973.

$$q^s = f_2(p,Z) \tag{G-21}$$
$$q^d = f_1(p,X) \tag{G-22}$$
$$\sum_{i=1}^{n} q_i^d = \sum_{j=1}^{m} q_j^s \tag{G-23}$$

where

q^s = the supply of corporate securities in the primary market
p = the securities prices
Z = other factors influencing the supply of securities
X = other factors influencing the demand for securities

Equation G-23 says the total demand has to equal the total supply.

Stewart then specified the demanders of securities as households, pension funds, investment companies, life insurance companies, other insurance companies, and foreigners. He also specified what he considered to be the important other variables in the demand and the supply of securities, for 1952–1959, which were:

r_e = the quarterly rate of return on stocks
r_b = the quarterly rate of return on bonds
c = the cash holdings of each market participant
b = the bond holdings of each market participant
e = the equity holdings of each market participant
EPS = the earnings per share

He found that the equity holdings of households (H); the bond holdings of other insurance companies (OIC), and the cash holdings of foreign demanders (F) were the most significant factors in the determination of stock prices, such that:

$$P_{t+1} = -.000681(H) + .03355(OIC) - .050027(F) \tag{G-24}$$

As the specific holdings for each of these sectors changed, stock prices change according to equation G-24.

Appendix H **Special Situations in Inventory Management**

As the financial officer, you might be faced with two somewhat less typical situations while managing the firm's inventory. One, your supplier might offer discounts in the price of the item if you purchase a quantity above the EOQ when you order. Two, you might have to coordinate a production process with your warehouses when the two have different EOQ. How can you analyze these situations?

QUANTITY DISCOUNTS

Quantity discounts are sometimes given by your supplier if your firm purchases more than you would normally purchase at one time, i.e., in excess of your EOQ. This has the effect of lowering the price of the inventory and the number of times your firm orders in one period, while it increases the carrying costs of the inventory. It is your responsibility to weigh the increases against the decreases in the costs in order to determine if the quantity discounts should be taken.[1]

The typical quantity discount is couched in terms such that if your firm buys more than a specified number of units, it receives the discount on all the units ordered. For example, your supplier might offer a 5 percent price discount if you buy 1,000 or more units. That means if your firm buys 1,500 units it gets a 5 percent discount on all 1,500 units. Your firm can order any number of units in excess of 1,000 and still receive the discount. In order to analyze such a situation, the financial officer has to determine what would be the maximum order quantity that the firm could afford considering the discount offered. If the number of units to qualify for the discount is less than the maximum affordable, we should order that number.

We can compute the new maximum affordable order quantity under the offered discount as:

$$Q_d = \frac{2dD}{I} + (1-d)Q^* \tag{H-1}$$

where
Q_d = the maximum affordable order quantity under the discount offered
d = the quantity discount expressed as the percentage by which the the price is reduced
D = the demand
I = the carrying costs as a percentage of the dollar value of the order
Q^* = the EOQ without the quantity discount

---

[1] R. G. Brown, *Decision Rules for Inventory Management*, Holt, Rinehart and Winston, 1967, p. 199; and J. F. Crowther, "Rationale for Quantity Discounts," *Harvard Business Review*, March/April, 1964.

Obviously, when the quantity discount is zero, the order quantity without the discount (Q^*) equals the order quantity with the discount (Q_d). When you apply the discount, the two differ as in the following example. Let us assume, as we did in Chapter 13 that the annual demand (D) for the product was 3,000 units, each costing (S) $100, and that the firm incurred a carrying cost (I) of 25 percent of the inventory value and a ordering cost of $50 per order. The EOQ without any quantity discount would have been:

$$Q^* = \sqrt{\frac{2(3000)(50)}{.25(100)}}$$

$$n \cong 109 \text{ units}$$

Now, let us assume that our supplier offered a 5 percent quantity discount if the firm purchased 200 or more units, instead of its usual 109 units. Using expression H-1, we can determine if the offer is sufficiently attractive to increase our order to 200 units, at what amounts to a price of $95 each, instead of the previous $100 a piece.

$$Q_d = 2 \times .05 \times \frac{3,000}{.25} + (.95)(109)$$

$$= 1,303 \text{ units}$$

Since the maximum affordable order quantity is larger than 200 units, we should take advantage of the supplier's offer and order 200 units instead of 109 units.

COORDINATING DIFFERENT EOQ's

The situation sometimes rises that the manufacturing plant and its central warehouse have different inventory costs than do the regional warehouses which store the finished items for final sale to the customer, and the two have different EOQ's.[2] The plant and central warehouse, after considering its start up (ordering) costs and its carrying costs, might find that its EOQ is 1,000 units, while each regional warehouse might find that its EOQ is 100 units. If you instruct the plant to start up and produce only 100 units whenever a regional warehouse submits an order, the total inventory costs at the plant and central warehouse will be much higher than their least cost level which is at 1,000 units. It is up to you, as the financial officer, to find the minimum inventory costs when both the central and the regional inventory costs are combined.

The typical approach in this type of analysis is the trial and error method of varying the length of the inventory cycle and seeing which has the lowest total cost for both the central and the regional warehouses. We can see from Table H-1 that if we reorder less frequently by extending the length of the inventory cycle, the firm has lower set up costs at the plant and the central warehouse and lower total ordering costs at the regional warehouses but higher carrying costs at both locations. We must determine which inventory cycle has the lowest overall total cost.

Notice that the least cost inventory cycle, which is determined by dividing the economic order quantity into the number of days in the operating period, for the regional warehouses is 28 days, but that the least cost inventory cycle for the plant

[2] J. F. Magee, "Guide to Inventory Policy," *Harvard Business Review*, March/April, 1956.

Table H-1

	14	28	42
Length of cycle (days)	14	28	42
Annual regional inventory costs			
Safety stock ($10/unit)	100	70	130
Average inventory on hand ($10/unit)	550	1,100	1,650
In transit stock ($2.50/unit)	275	275	275
Total ordering costs ($50/order)	1,300	650	433
Total regional warehouse costs	2,225	2,095	2,488
Annual factory inventory costs			
Safety stock ($15/unit)	150	165	180
In production stock ($15/unit)	1,650	3,300	4,950
Annual ordering costs ($50/order)	1,200	600	450
Total factory costs	3,000	4,065	5,580
Total inventory costs	5,225	6,160	8,068

and the central warehouse is 14 days. The conflict is resolved by seeing that the least total inventory cost is incurred in the 14-day cycle because the reduction in the total factory inventory costs when the firm switches to a 14-day cycle from a 28-day cycle more than offsets the increase in the total regional inventory costs.

Appendix I **Timing the Bond Refunding Decision**

In Chapter 20, we saw how to analyze the bond refunding situation, but how does the financial officer attempt to time that refunding so as to maximize the interest cost savings? Obviously, that depends to a great extent on how much lower the interest cost on the new bond is than on the original bond. The savings in interest cost increases as the spread between the two interest rates increased. It is up to the financial officer to time the refunding so that the spread is maximized. Dynamic programming has been suggested as one method the financial officer might use in this attempt.[1]

THE DECISION TREE

We can use the decision tree technique as explored in Chapter 7 and as illustrated in Figure I-1 for the analysis. In that figure we can keep the original issue at any decision point, signified by K, and continue to pay the original interest, or we can refund at a lower interest rate, signified by R, and bear the call premium penalty and flotation costs. The idea is to determine which path has the least cost by working backwards to point 0.

On Figure I-1, we can see that at point 0, we can either keep (K) the original bond or refund it (R). At point 1, if we had already refunded the bond at point 0, we can keep the bond used in that refunding at point 0 or refund it again. At point 1 if we had kept the original bond at point 0, we can refund the original bond or keep it for at least one more year. In fact, at any decision point on Figure I-1, we have the choice of keeping or refunding the then outstanding bond, which may still be the original bond or a bond from a refunding in a prior year.

With this choice procedure in mind, let us trace the paths in Figure I-1. Path 1 reflects the keeping of the original bond for years 1 through 3 at the original interest costs with no savings in interest costs, because interest rates are not expected to drop.

Path 2 reflects that the old bond was kept in years 1 and 2 but was refunded at the beginning of year 3. The costs would be the original interest cost for the three years less the interest savings, effected in year 3 because of the refunding, plus the call premium and flotation costs.

Path 3 costs would be the original interest for the three years less the interest cost savings in years 2 and 3 plus the call premium and the flotation costs.

---

[1] See H. M. Weingarten, "Optimal Timing of Bond Refunding," *Management Science*, March, 1967; and E. Elton and M. Gruber, "Dynamic Programming Applications in Finance," *Journal of Finance*, May, 1971 on which this appendix is based.

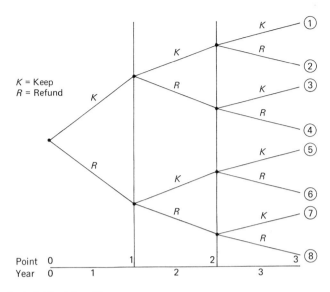

K = Keep
R = Refund

Point   0   1   2   3
Year   0   1   2   3

Figure I-1 Illustrated Decision Tree

Path 4 costs would be the original interest cost for the three years less the interest cost savings in year 2 from the first refunding and the still greater interest cost savings in year 3 from the second refunding plus the flotation costs and the call premium associated with each refunding.

Path 5 reflects the original interest cost for the three years less the interest costs savings during years 1 through 3 after the flotation costs and call premium associated with the refunding at point 0.

Path 6 costs are the original interest costs less the interest costs savings after flotation costs and call premium during years 1 and 2, effected in the point 0 refunding, and the interest costs savings during year 3 after the flotation costs and call premium associated with the refunding at the beginning of year 3.

Path 7 costs are the original interest costs less the interest costs savings after flotation costs and call premium during year 1 effected in the point 0 refunding and the interest cost savings after flotation costs and call premium during years 2 and 3 effected in the refunding at point 1.

Path 8 costs are the original interest costs less the interest costs savings after flotation costs and call premium during year 1, effected in the refunding at point 0, and the interest costs savings after flotation costs and call premium during year 2, effected by the refunding at point 1, and the interest costs savings after flotation costs and call premium during year 3, effected in the refunding at point 2.

The least cost at point 0 depends on the financial officer's expectation of interest rates points 1, 2, and 3. The officer would assign an expected interest rate to each point and compute the costs based on the expected interest rate to each point and compute the costs based on the expected interest costs savings along each path. The officer must discount the more distant savings to the present for the time value of money. Adding up the costs at each of the three points for each path, the officer could determine the least cost path. If any of the refunding paths had a lower cost than the none refunding path 1, the officer would choose the least cost refunding path.

MATHEMATICAL REPRESENTATION

In the mathematical representation of Figure I-1, the objective is to minimize the discounted present value of the expected costs as expressed in equation I-1:

Minimize

$$I - \left\{ k_{t,T} \sum_{R_i^*} [(R_i^*)_{t,T}][P(R_i^*)_{t,T}] + k_{t,T}[C_{T-t,M}] + k_{t,T}[F_{T-t}^*] \right\} \qquad \text{(I-1)}$$

where

I = original interest cost

$k_{t,T}$ = the appropriate discount rate each year from the initial period t through the end of the maturity period T

$P(R_i^*)_{t,T}$ = the probability distribution of the interest cost savings expected each year, t to T

$(R_i^*)_{t,T}$ = the distribution of the expected interest rates each year, t to T

$C_{T-t,M}$ = the call premium at time $T - t$ left on either the original bond or bond outstanding from a prior period refunding at each possible refunding point specified by M

F_{T-t}^* = expected flotation costs at each decision point

That option which minimizes expression I-1 should be undertaken.

Appendix J An Integrated Mathematical Model for Financial Management

Various attempts have been made at formulating a mathematical model which would incorporate all the aspects of what to invest in, how to finance it, and how to combine the two in order to maximize shareholder wealth. These models are efforts to demonstrate quantitatively the interactions of all aspects of the financial officer's responsibilities in working toward the corporate goal. Although none of these models has totally succeeded, it is informative to study at least one attempt so that you can see how a mathematical representation of the corporate objective can be constructed and used to pretest the financial decisions of the firm, thereby serving as a guide for the financial officer. As you work through the following model,[1] notice how it is constructed step by step to incorporate all the facets of the firm and how, by plugging in possible values for each of the important areas mathematically represented in the model, the financial officer might gain insight into the workings of the firm and the effect of decisions on the corporate objective.

We must start with the evaluation function, which expresses the determination of the firm's share price that we are trying to maximize. The traditional share price evaluation model is:

$$P_0 = \sum_{t=1}^{\infty} \frac{D_t}{(1 + k)^t} \tag{J-1}$$

where
    P_0 = the price of the share
    D_t = the dividends in period t
    k = the discount factor applied to the future dividends by the firm's stockholders
    Σ = sigma, the summation sign over $t = 1$ to infinity

Equation J-1 determines the present value of the future stream of dividends that the shareholders expect to receive, i.e., the present value discounting of an uneven stream.

However, we can define the dividend as:

$$D_t = C_t + X_t - F_t \tag{J-2}$$

where
    C_t = internally generated funds
    X_t = externally generated funds
    F_t = funds invested in the firm
    D_t = the dividends in period t

---

[1] This appendix draws heavily on D.E. Peterson, *A Quantitative Framework for Financial Management*, Irwin, 1969, and uses his notation. His model, in turn, draws on the Gordon and other predecessor models.

705

Substituting equation J-2 into J-1 gives us:

$$P_0 = \sum_{t=1}^{\infty} \frac{C_t - [F_t - X_t]}{(1+k)^t} \qquad \text{(J-3)}$$

Notice how the variables in the model have already capsulated all the major decisions management must make in order to maximize shareholder wealth. Equation J-3 incorporates considerations for profits, financing (raising funds both internally and externally), investment decisions (what to invest in), and the cost of funds (k).

Now, if there is a continuous growth stream,

$$P_0 = \frac{D_0}{k-g} \qquad \text{(J-4)}$$

as demonstrated in Appendix 4A.

The dividend can be expressed as a percentage of the firm's earnings, the payout ratio, as

$$D_0/Y_0$$

where

$$Y_0 = \text{firm's earnings}$$

and if $\lambda =$ the percentage of earnings retained, not paid out, then:

$$D_0 = (1-\lambda)Y_0 \qquad \text{(J-5)}$$

and we have incorporated the dividend policy decision, i.e., how much to pay out.

We can incorporate the financing decision in terms of the firm's debt/equity ratio, i.e., how much should it borrow in relation to the amount provided by the stockholders, as:

$$i = f(\psi) \qquad \text{(J-6)}$$

where
$\quad i =$ the cost of borrowing
$\quad \psi =$ the debt/equity ratio

As the proportion of debt increases, interest costs are expected to rise. Then, the return on additional retained earnings is

$$r_e = \frac{\lambda Y_0 r + \psi \lambda Y_0 r - \psi \lambda Y_0 i}{\lambda Y_0} \qquad \text{(J-7)}$$

where
$\quad r_e =$ the return on retained earnings added during that period
$\quad \lambda =$ the retention rate
$\quad Y_0 =$ income during the period
$\quad r =$ the return on all investment during the period
$\quad \psi =$ the debt/equity ratio
$\quad i =$ the interest paid on the firm's debt

If we divide equation J-7 by λY and factor out r, then:

$$r_e = r\left[1 + \psi - \left(\psi\frac{i}{r}\right)\right]$$

and

$$g = \lambda r\left[1 + \psi - \left(\psi\frac{i}{r}\right)\right] \qquad \text{(J-8)}$$

$$g = \lambda r_e \tag{J-9}$$

We can now express the growth rate (g) in J-4 in terms of the specific decisions facing the financial officer. Notice how the growth rate is a function of the dividend policy, the financing policy, and the investment policy as represented by the variables in equation J-9.

Finally, if

$$Y_0 = r_e \times \text{assets } (A)$$

then

$$P_0 = \frac{(1 - \lambda)Ar_e}{k - \lambda r \left[1 + \psi - \left(\psi \frac{i}{r}\right)\right]}$$

$$= \frac{(1 - \lambda)Ar \left[(1 + \psi) - \left(\psi \frac{i}{r}\right)\right]}{k - \lambda r \left[1 + \psi - \left(\psi \frac{i}{r}\right)\right]} \tag{J-10}$$

Notice how the model, as in equation J-10, shows the direct and interactive effects of dividend policy (λ), financing policy (ψ), investment opportunities (A), and asset selection (r) on the corporate objective (P_0). By experimenting with the model before committing the firm, the financial officer might be able to determine the maximizing course of action in all areas of responsibility. The officer could plug in a dividend policy and see its effects on P_0, could plug in different financial policies and see each's effect on P_0, and could do the same for investment opportunity and selection policy. Most importantly, the officer can see how the variables interact and derive the right combination of policies in all areas. Assuming the model is inherently correct and accurately reflects reality, it can be a very useful tool to you. However, remember, as a warning, that it is almost impossible to build a precise integrated model of the firm that is of manageable proportions. What we have here and to date elsewhere are useful and educational models that you can use within their limitations.

Art Credits

Author Index

Subject Index